D1481387

Schooling and Achievement
in American Society

STUDIES IN POPULATION

Under the Editorship of: H. H. WINSBOROUGH

Department of Sociology
University of Wisconsin
Madison, Wisconsin

Schooling and Achievement in American Society

Edited by
William H. Sewell
Robert M. Hauser
David L. Featherman

Department of Sociology
University of Wisconsin
Madison, Wisconsin

ACADEMIC PRESS   New York   San Francisco   London

A Subsidiary of Harcourt Brace Jovanovich, Publishers

ACADEMIC PRESS, INC.
111 Fifth Avenue, New York, New York 10003

United Kingdom Edition published by
ACADEMIC PRESS, INC. (LONDON) LTD.
24/28 Oval Road, London NW1

Library of Congress Cataloging in Publication Data
Main entry under title:

Schooling and achievement in American society.

(Studies in population)
Papers originally presented at meetings of an ACT
Research Institute seminar between Oct. 1971 and
May 1973.
        Bibliography: p.
        Includes index.
        1.   Education, Higher—United States—Addresses,
essays, lectures.   2.   College students' socio-
economic status—United States—Addresses, essays,
lectures.   I.   Sewell, William Hamilton, (date)
II.   Hauser, Robert Mason.   III.   Featherman, David
L.   IV.   Series.
LA227.3.S33   378.1'98'0973   75-16881
ISBN 0–12–637860–6

To Ralph W. Tyler

Contents

List of Figures

List of Tables

List of Contributors

Numbers in parentheses indicate the pages on which the authors' contributions begin.

Duane F. Alwin (309, 343),* Department of Sociology, Indiana University, Bloomington, Indiana

John W. Atkinson (29), Department of Psychology, The University of Michigan, Ann Arbor, Michigan

T. Michael Carter (133), Department of Sociology, University of Minnesota, Minneapolis, Minnesota

David L. Featherman (133), Department of Sociology, University of Wisconsin, Madison, Wisconsin

Kenneth A. Feldman (373), Department of Sociology, State University of New York, Stony Brook, New York

Robert M. Hauser (9, 309, 443), Department of Sociology, University of Wisconsin, Madison, Wisconsin

Alan C. Kerckhoff (443), Department of Sociology, Duke University, Durham, North Carolina

Willy Lens (29),† Department of Psychology (N.F.W.O.), University of Leuven (Louvain)

Henry M. Levin (267, 291), School of Education and Department of Economics, Stanford University, Stanford, California

P. M. O'Malley (29), Institute for Social Research, The University of Michigan, Ann Arbor, Michigan

Kenneth Manton (443), Department of Sociology, Duke University, Durham, North Carolina

William M. Mason (443), Population Studies Center, University of Michigan, Ann Arbor, Michigan

Sharon Sandomirsky Poss (443), Department of Sociology, Duke University, Durham, North Carolina

William H. Sewell (9, 309), Department of Sociology, University of Wisconsin, Madison, Wisconsin

William G. Spady (185), National Institute of Education, Washington, D. C.

* Present address: Laboratory of Socio-environmental Studies, National Institute of Mental Health, Bethesda, Maryland.
† Present address: Tiensestraat 102, B-3000 Leuven, Belgium.

Joe L. Spaeth (103, 161), Department of Sociology and Survey Research Laboratory, University of Illinois at Urbana–Champaign, Urbana, Illinois

John Weiler (373), Department of Sociology, University of California, Santa Barbara, California

David E. Wiley (225, 413),* Departments of Education and Behavioral Sciences, University of Chicago, Chicago, Illinois

Trevor Williams (61), Department of Sociology, Research School of Social Sciences, The Australian National University, Canberra

   * Present address: The ML-GROUP for Policy Studies in Education, CEMREL, Inc., The John Hancock Center, 875 North Michigan Avenue, Chicago, Illinois 60611.

Preface

The present book is an outgrowth of an interdisciplinary seminar on achievement processes, and consists of fifteen papers selected from approximately thirty discussion papers presented over its course. These were selected by the editors, after consultation with the associates of the ACT Research Institute, to reflect the varied styles and approaches of members and to represent the most important of the papers that were finished in time for inclusion in the volume. Several interesting manuscripts are still in process, and doubtless will appear later in journals and books; others never got far off the ground but were fun to talk about. The editors have tried wherever possible not to republish work that has appeared elsewhere, but this rule was broken in four instances in which the papers were either published in places where they were not readily available to the audience of this book or were needed to give an adequate coverage of the topics discussed in the seminar. The articles falling under this category are William H. Sewell and Robert M. Hauser, "Causes and Consequences of Higher Education: Models of the Status Attainment Process," orginally published in the *American Journal of Agricultural Economics* **54** (December 1972); Henry M. Levin, "Measuring Efficiency in Educational Production," originally published in *Public Finance Quarterly* **2** (January 1974); Henry M. Levin, "A New Model of School Effectiveness," published in U.S. Office of Education, *Do Teachers Make a Difference? : A Report on Recent Research on Pupil Achievement* (Washington, D.C.: U.S. Government Printing Office, 1970); and William G. Spady, "The Impact of School Resources on Students," originally published in Fred N. Kerlinger (Ed.), *Review of Research in Education* (Itasca, Ill.: F. E. Peacock Publishers, 1973). The associates thank the original publishers of each of these papers for permission to reprint them.

The fifteen chapters of this book are distributed into three substantive sections. Part I includes a series of chapters dealing in one way or another with achievement in the life cycle. (At this point, we shall indicate only briefly the subjects of these chapters; the content and the findings of the chapters will be discussed in more detail within the introductions to the three sections.) Chapter 1, by Sewell and Hauser, discusses the causes and consequences of higher education and interprets a structural equation model, based on longitudinal data from a large sample of Wisconsin youth, which traces the influences of family background on educational and socioeconomic achievements, particularly as these influences are mediated by social psychological variables. In Chapter 2, Atkinson and his associates deal with motivation and ability, stressing the interactive psychological forces that help to determine intellective performance and educational achievement. Chapter 3, by Williams, examines the sociological basis of intelligence by means of a structural equation model and tests this model on a small sample of Canadian families. In Chapter 4, Spaeth writes on cognitive complexity as a dimension that he believes to underlie the socioeconomic achievement process. In Chapter 5, Featherman and Carter examine discontinuities in schooling during the socioeconomic life cycle, using a sample of Michigan men, and show how these discontinuities are related to educational and occupational achievements. In Chapter 6, Spaeth, using data from a national sample of employed males, looks into the characteristics of work-setting and job as determinants of earnings and finds that they contribute a good deal more to the explanation of earnings than do family background variables.

Part II, "Institutional Effects," includes a series of papers that attempt to assess the unique effects of various features and climates of school and colleges on cognitive and socioeconomic achievements. Spady, in Chapter 7, looks into the very difficult question of the effects of school resources on students' intellectual and attitudinal development, reviewing and evaluating the deluge of studies that were stimulated by the Coleman report. In Chapter 8, Wiley argues that the quantity of schooling, in terms of the number of hours of classroom exposure, is far more important to how much a child learns in school than are the usual variables employed to measure school resources. His analysis is based on data selected from the Equality of Educational Opportunity study. In Chapter 9, Levin presents a highly tentative production-function model for measuring school effectiveness. He applies this model to a limited·

sample drawn from the Equality of Educational Opportunity study and interprets the model and discusses its possible policy implications. In Chapter 10, Levin continues and extends his efforts to apply econometric techniques to the measurement of efficiency in educational production, using a technique called "frontier functions," and suggests that the optional combination of inputs for maximized educational achievement relative to a given budget may vary considerably from school to school. Hauser and his co-workers in Chapter 11, using data from the Wisconsin longitudinal study, relate sex, social background, ability, and social psychological facets of high school experience to subsequent educational attainments and find that high school effects on educational aspirations and achievements are rather small and not systematically related to the social composition of schools. In Chapter 12, Alwin examines the closely related question of the effects of colleges on postcollegiate achievements, using the Wisconsin longitudinal data, and finds rather small but persistent effects of colleges on occupational and economic achievements that are not accounted for by the social backgrounds or personal characteristics of the students. Chapter 13, by Feldman and Weiler, examines the impact of college experience on several measured personality characteristics—particularly initial differences in the scores of the recruits to various major fields at the University of Michigan. Over the course of the college career, initial group differences tend to be accentuated, but this is only one of the several patterns of change and stability among groups.

Part III, "Methodological Issues," contains two chapters, both of which deal with specific methodological problems. Almost every chapter in the book contains extensive methodological discussions, and several modify or extend existing statistical techniques, but their principal focus is on substantive issues, not methodological developments. In Chapter 14, Wiley takes up the problem of measuring institutional effects when there are confounding variables and a limited number of cases or observations, as is frequently true in research involving schools, and he indicates how standardization techniques may be applied in these instances. In Chapter 15, Mason and his associates report on an important study of response error in students' reports of their parents' socioeconomic characteristics. Using a complex strategy for assessing the validity of student reports, they find that, by grade twelve, the quality of these responses is very high for both white and black youth but is less valid at the lower grades, especially for blacks.

The editors believe that this book contains a wealth of recent substantive findings on the effects of schooling on educational and socioeconomic achievement in American society. We wish it were possible for all of the analysis reported or suggested in this book to be undertaken in a national sample which would represent all schools and students in the United States. But, of course, no such sample exists. The national samples that are available are based on selected schools, or school grades, or age categories, and do not possess data of the type and quality necessary for the multifaceted analysis contained in the various chapters of this book. Neither we nor the chapter authors wish to imply that the findings reported in this book are generalizable to all of American society. Rather, the findings reported in the various chapters are illustrative of the complex process by which and through which schools influence achievements in our society. In some instances, the results are based on small and selected samples; in others, they rest on large and representative state and national samples. But, whatever the representativeness of their data, the authors have disclosed the details of their respective samples together with the methods of data collection and analysis. Other workers may wish to challenge their conclusions, either by reanalysis of the data, or by replication, or by formulating better designs, because only through such a process will current understandings of the effects of schooling be improved.

We wish to point out that this book, although it was not intended to be primarily a methodological contribution, contains a wealth of information on the application of modern multivariate statistical techniques to the analysis of various aspects of the complex process of educational and socioeconomic achievement. Ten of its chapters use structural equation models of varying complexity in the analysis of their data. Other multivariate techniques are used or discussed in each of the remaining chapters. We doubt that the careful reader can come away from this book without a greater knowledge and deeper appreciation of how quantatively oriented sociologists, psychologists, and economists approach the very complex problem of schooling and achievement. We believe that the techniques the associates have used are widely applicable to these and other complex problems; doubtless they can be applied equally well to data on other societies.

Acknowledgments

We editors and our fellow associates wish to acknowledge with gratitude the help of the ACT Research Institute Advisory Council, without whose support the seminar and this book would not have been possible. We wish also to thank Fred F. Harcleroad, past President of ACT, Oluf M. Davidsen, current President of ACT, and Leo A. Munday, Vice President of ACT for Research and Development, for encouragement and assistance in numerous ways. We are grateful for the excellent support we had throughout the life of this project, to Robert H. Fenske who, as Director of the ACT Research Institute, arranged all seminar meetings and provided intellectual, moral, and financial support for the seminar and the associates. In addition, he participated fully and usefully in all the meetings of the seminar. He made the task of the chairman of the seminar especially easy and greatly facilitated the work of all the associates.

We are especially indebted to Ralph W. Tyler, Chairman of the ACT Research Institute Advisory Council and Chairman of the Board of Trustees of ACT, for his encouragement over the years. Throughout his career as a professor at Ohio State University and the University of Chicago; Dean of the Social Sciences at Chicago; Director of the Center for Advanced Study in the Behavioral Sciences; President of the Social Science Research Council; and chairman of numerous boards and commissions, Ralph Tyler has advanced the social sciences and especially their application to education. We gratefully dedicate this book to him.

We wish also to acknowledge the cooperation and patience of the associates in the long editorial process that has been necessary in the production of this book. Through the entire process, our colleagues have been understanding and forgiving; we have enjoyed working with them.

We wish to thank Alice J. Thompson, Rebekah Heideman, Pat

Klitzke, and Judy Stout for manuscript typing and proofreading, and Carol Betts who typed the tables and prepared the bibliography. We are especially indebted to Christine Waldo who helped in innumerable ways with the editorial process.

Finally, we are indebted to the staff of Academic Press for cooperation and help throughout the publication process.

None of those whose assistance or support we have acknowledged bears any responsibility for any opinions or implications stated in this volume. The responsibility lies solely with the authors of these chapters.

William H. Sewell
Robert M. Hauser
David L. Featherman

Background of the Volume

In the fall of 1969, Fred F. Harcleroad, President of the American College Testing Program (now Professor of Education at the University of Arizona), announced the creation of a research institute to encourage significant and timely research in the field of education. An advisory council of leading national educational authorities, to assist in the planning and development of the institute, was appointed, consisting of Ralph W. Tyler, Chairman of the Council, Director Emeritus of the Center for Advanced Study in Behavioral Sciences, Stanford, California; Theodore M. Newcomb, Professor of Psychology, University of Michigan; William H. Sewell, Vilas Research Professor of Sociology, University of Wisconsin; and John M. Stalnaker, President Emeritus of the National Merit Scholarship Corporation. Later Jack C. Merwin, Dean of the College of Education and Professor of Educational Psychology, University of Minnesota, and John W. Atkinson, Professor of Psychology, University of Michigan, were added to the advisory council.

In 1970, the institute began its operation with a summer research program on schools, colleges, and universities as social systems, under the direction of Robert E. Herriott, then Professor of Sociology, Florida State University, and with a program of pre- and postdoctoral fellowships and internships at the headquarters of the American College Testing Program in Iowa City. In 1971, a third phase of the Institute's program was established to emphasize research on the transition of students from school to college and to occupational careers. To forward this work, William H. Sewell was asked to establish and chair an interdisciplinary seminar on achievement processes, whose activities would focus on the role of social background factors and of intervening social psychological and social structural variables in post-secondary educational and socioeconomic achievements. The seminar met periodically, about twice a year, over a period of two years, to discuss early drafts of papers, prepared in advance, by members of the seminar. Usually, the seminar considered not more than three papers a day and met for two and a half to three days.

The regular members of the seminar became Associates of the ACT Research Institute, which provided them with a small annual grant to be used to forward their own research. The meetings of the seminar usually were held away from the campuses of the associates and, on occasion, at the headquarters of ACT, so selected members of the research staff of ACT could participate. From time to time, a graduate student who was working with an associate would be invited to participate in the sessions. But, for the most part, participation was limited to the associates. The following were members of the seminar from the beginning: John W. Atkinson, psychologist, University of Michigan; David L. Featherman, sociologist, University of Wisconsin, Madison; Kenneth A. Feldman, sociologist, State University of New York, Stonybrook; Robert M. Hauser, sociologist, University of Wisconsin, Madison; Henry M. Levin, economist, Stanford University; William M. Mason, sociologist, Duke University (now at the University of Michigan); Theodore M. Newcomb, psychologist, University of Michigan; William H. Sewell, sociologist, University of Wisconsin, Madison; William G. Spady, sociologist, Ontario Institute for Studies in Education (now at the National Institute of Education); Joe L. Spaeth, sociologist, University of Illinois; and, David E. Wiley, educational psychologist, University of Chicago.

Others who participated on invitation were: Duane F. Alwin, a postdoctoral fellow, working with Hauser and Sewell at Wisconsin (now at Indiana University); T. Michael Carter, a graduate student working with Featherman at Wisconsin (now at the University of Minnesota); John Weiler, a graduate student working with Feldman at the State University of New York at Stony Brook (now at the University of California at Santa Barbara); and Trevor Williams, a graduate student working with Spady at Ontario Institute for Studies in Education (now at the National Institute of Education).

In addition, Robert H. Fenske, Director of the Research Institute (now Professor and Director of the Center for Higher Education at Arizona State University), was an active participant in all of the sessions.

The seminar held four meetings, with the first meeting on October 1–2, 1971, and the last meeting on May 24–26, 1973.

Approximately thirty discussion papers were prepared for the meetings of the seminar.

It would be impossible to portray adequately the nature or the excitement of the meetings. For the most part, the papers were in first draft form and in the hands of the discussants well before the time of the meetings. Usually, the author would summarize briefly his paper, and two persons with differing views were designated to lead an informal but critical discussion of the work. Often, these discussions became rather heated and would be continued over drinks and dinner after the session. Eventually, most of the papers were heavily revised as a result of the discussions. The associates are agreed that we all learned a great deal from each other and came away from the exchange with greater knowledge and respect for the interests and approaches of others. This volume is one of the results of that exchange.

William H. Sewell
Robert M. Hauser
David L. Featherman

Part 1 | ACHIEVEMENT IN THE LIFE CYCLE

Part 1 | ACHIEVEMENT IN THE LIFE CYCLE

Introductory Notes

Few contemporary researches into the relationship between schooling and achievement in American society have been as influential as the 1962 benchmark survey, "Occupational Changes in a Generation," and the resulting monograph on socioeconomic stratification, *The American Occupational Structure* (Blau and Duncan, 1967). Its scientific importance emanated from a restatement of social mobility research in terms of transitions of individuals among hierarchical roles over the entire course of the life cycle. Students of schools, social change, and mobility alike draw on O. D. Duncan's (1967) schema of the socioeconomic life cycle (reproduced as Figure 5.1 in Chapter V of this volume) as an apt representation of the linkage of schools and education to the socioeconomic and cultural resources of families, on the one hand, and to the socioeconomic and cultural stocks of the next generation, on the other. In our opening section, therefore, it is not surprising to find the influence of the pioneering empirical work of Peter Blau, Otis Dudley Duncan, and their colleagues on the achievements of men in American society and that the focus of the organization of the chapters is the socioeconomic life cycle.

In Chapter I, "Causes and Consequences of Higher Education: Models of the Status Attainment Process," William H. Sewell and Robert M. Hauser review one program of research of the last fifteen years that rivals and complements the scientific contributions of Duncan and Blau. In some respects, the longitudinal study of the process of status attainment among 1957 Wisconsin high school graduates is more complete than the national research of Blau and Duncan. Although the data are confined to a single Wisconsin cohort, Sewell and associates have differentiated, where necessary, the causal patterns associated with the status attainments of females from those of males. In addition, the longitudinal design of the Wisconsin studies, permits a more complete analysis of each stage of the socioeconomic life cycle.

Sewell and Hauser focus principally upon post-high school education to underscore the central role of schooling, both directly and indirectly, in socioeconomic achievement. For young adults, post-secondary education is the chief direct access to occupations of higher social standing and to the consumption and life styles commensurate with higher earnings. At the same time, the major link between the socioeconomic origins of young men and women and their intellectual resources, on the one hand, and the socioeconomic achievements in their early careers, on the other hand, is schooling. Consequently, Sewell and Hauser reaffirm the conclusions of Blau and Duncan that post-secondary education is the major mechanism for social mobility in American society, offering a springboard for talent to overcome the handicaps of social origins. At the same time, the process of achievement in American society is not free from discrimination; there is serious wastage of talent, especially among youth of lower socioeconomic origins, young women, and blacks.

Finally, Sewell and Hauser's chapter significantly extends previous analysis of achievement in America, at least with respect to the antecedents of educational attainment (i.e., level of schooling completed). Unlike Blau and Duncan, the Wisconsin group has collected an array of social, economic, as well as social psychological information about their sample, including intellectual ability, academic performance, social influences stemming from parents, peers, and teachers, and student aspirations for schooling and jobs. Together with standard measures of family socioeconomic status, these social psychological variables comprise a hypothetical causal model that explains 54% of the variance in years of schooling. In addition, this model enables the authors to speculate about the various roles of teachers and parents in responding to the social and cognitive characteristics of youth as they sponsor and encourage young adults' educational and (through schooling) later socioeconomic achievements and to comment on the likely origins of the distinct educational attainments of young people from different socioeconomic strata.

Chapter II, "Motivation and Ability: Interactive Psychological Determinants of Intellective Performance, Educational Achievement, and Each Other," by John W. Atkinson, Willy Lens, and P. M. O'Malley, is to the psychology of achievement what the foregoing work of Duncan, Sewell, and their co-workers is to the sociology of status attainments. This second chapter, an overview of some twenty-five years of programmatic research, describes Atkinson's latest revision of his theory of achievement motivation and offers a psychological or social psychological model of "intellective" (academic) performance and educational achievement.

Atkinson's model is embedded in his more general theory of action (Atkinson and Birch, 1970), which assumes a continuous stream of activity, or a constantly motivated individual (although not always to the same goal). The specification of this motivational theory within achievement settings and situations (e.g., schools, jobs) is found in recent work (Atkinson and Raynor, 1974). It illustrates how both an actor's personality (abilities, motives, knowledge, beliefs, conceptions) and the structure of the situation (real and imagined incentives, opportunities, and the nature of the task) shape observable behavior and performance. In the latter case, they may sometimes yield (academic) performances at variance with what one might expect on the basis of personality (ability) data per se (e.g., underachievement).

Specifically, Atkinson's chapter differentiates the causal antecedents of performance at immediate tasks, such as the level of performance on an academic or IQ test, from the antecedents of long-range cumulative achievement, such as GPA or years of schooling completed. In tracing the implications of his theory of action and achievement motivation for each of these domains of activity, Atkinson makes several observations of interest to educational practitioners and researchers alike. First, the theory allows for students to be "over-motivated" and to "underachieve," relative to their scholastic abilities. This situation arises when the nature of the task and the set of resultant motivational tendencies combine in a nonlinear function to yield "inefficient" performances. Atkinson admonishes educational researchers for adopting the "mental testing mentality" which assumes a linear relationship between IQ and performance. Second, research by Atkinson and associates implies that tests of ability are themselves performances and, as such, constitute tests of motivation as well. Moreover, one should expect and find a nontrivial positive correlation between ability and motivation in the general population. Finally, in the last section of his chapter, Atkinson draws out the implications of his model for the feedback of cumulative performances on motives, abilities, and other components of personality. By extension, Atkinson argues for social psychological models of achievement which are dynamic—permitting personality change in adults as well as young children—and which allow for nonlinearities and interactions among the component parts.

In Chapter III, "Abilities and Environments," Trevor Williams examines the biosocial genesis of intelligence (and, if we follow Atkinson, motivation) among families in a Canadian city. The author opens with a critique of conventional social deprivation models which attempt to account for socioeconomic variance in IQ scores and, at the same time, usually ignoring the important biosocial relationships between parental IQ and filial IQ— both the direct biogenetic one and the more indirect biosocial and sociocultural ones through parental socioeconomic status. Williams argues further that the major mechanism by which family socioeconomic status and, to some extent, parental intelligence and size of sibship shape the mental abilities of the child is primarily through the behavioral rather than the physical family environment. From the perspective of a social learning theory, Williams identifies the important elements of this environment as parental efforts to offer diverse stimuli (people, events, things) with which to interact, as reinforcement practices on cognitively relevant behaviors, and as parental expectations for appropriate cognitive performances. Finally, Williams echoes Atkinson in stating that the child is his or her own agent of cognitive growth, a capable and effective manipulator of the behavioral elements that are the family environment (e.g., the parental behaviors). Thus, Williams specifies a nonrecursive structural equation model to explore the credibility of a "triple-advantage" model—namely, that children from high-status backgrounds benefit genetically, enjoy richer family behavioral environments, and interact more effectively or competently with their behavioral environments, all toward higher levels of cognitive ability.

Although the findings from Williams' work are provisional, given the characteristics of his data, his analysis exemplifies modern social psychological research into achievement processes in which, as Atkinson and others suggest, one's theory is dynamic (i.e., with nonrecursive, feedback relationships). If Williams' findings were replicated, they would substantially challenge conventional wisdom about the favorableness of the behavioral environments, now characteristic of middle class families, for engendering intellectual competence.

What was implicit in the relevance of Atkinson and Williams for Sewell, Hauser, and Duncan becomes explicit in Joe L. Spaeth's "Cognitive Complexity: A Dimension Underlying the Socioeconomic Achievement Process," Chapter 4. Spaeth synthesizes a large body of social psychological research which he interprets within the framework of life cycle model of achievement. He maintains that most of the causal paths from social origins to schooling and from schooling to jobs and earnings in adulthood are manifestations of exposure to settings or environments that stimulate capacity for complex cognitive processing and content. The latter, in turn, are requisite for advancement through levels of schooling and into jobs, which themselves are ordered hierarchically according to complexity of tasks. Williams' research on the family behavioral environments of the various socioeconomic strata, as they shape different intellectual capacities, illustrates Spaeth's general framework as applied to family settings, treatments, and resultant capacities. Children of higher abilities tend to attend school longer, or to be exposed to school environments for longer durations. Spaeth argues that Wiley's research (see Chapter VIII) supports his own conclusion that longer exposure to schooling implies stimulation by increasingly complex curricula, which should intensify cognitive complexity. This feedback between ability and environment is in the nature of Atkinson's model for the interplay of cumulative achievement and personality (motives and abilities). While all of this transpires within schools, nontrivial between-school variation in exposure to education (cf. Wiley in

Chapter VIII) qua differential length of the school year and school day comprise an explanation for viable "school effects" on youths' IQ and educational achievements.

Since jobs vary in their cognitive requisites or "substantive complexity" (Kohn and Schooler, 1973), Spaeth is not surprised by a positive causal relationship between educational attainment and occupational prestige (which he sees as a surrogate for the substantive complexity of jobs), even though the substantive interpretation of that relationship is not unique. Others argue that cognitive complexity does not underlie this association, but, instead, it arises from certification preferences of employers. Spaeth outlines strategies for measuring exposure to educational complexity apart from certification level and for measuring exposure to job complexity which, like schools and families, can be construed as settings and stimuli for the enhancement of cognitive complexity. Finally, Spaeth completes the intergenerational cycle by recapitulating Kohn's seminal work on the relationship between parental socialization in occupational settings and the simultaneous socialization of offspring in the family socioeconomic environments created by these parents.

It should be clear that the intergenerational processes discussed by Spaeth and earlier contributors, are not as deterministic as proponents of a "vicious cycle" of stratification (poverty) suggest, but, in Chapter V, "Discontinuities in Schooling and the Socioeconomic Life Cycle" by David L. Featherman and T. Michael Carter, some of the causes of slippage in the process of achievement are discussed. Featherman and Carter focus on the transition from school to work, which for a substantial minority of the Michigan males in their sample is not an irreversible transition. Instead, it is marked by delays between high school and some form of post-secondary education, or it is laced with one or more interruptions in post-secondary schooling, owing to work, military service, ill health, and the like. However, both delays and interruptions appear uncorrelated with measures of family socioeconomic status, despite the fact that these discontinuities in schooling have direct influences on years of school ultimately completed and bear indirectly on the socioeconomic standing of jobs in the early career. In short, such discontinuities comprise contingencies in the life cycle that contribute to the variance of schooling in a cohort, irrespective of the causal association of family background and achievement. Featherman and Carter interpret the educational effects of these interruptions in terms of normative life cycle patterns of cohorts.

To a limited extent, Featherman and Carter have taken seriously Spaeth's suggestion to separate exposure to schooling (e.g., years of attendance) from certification (e.g., years of school completed) and both from complexity of curriculum (e.g., college versus nonregular post-secondary education). They find that men who attend college ultimately complete more schooling (i.e., higher certification) than those who matriculate in vocational, technical, and business programs, even among men who attend school for equal numbers of years. Those who complete more grades exchange their certification for higher status occupations in the early work career, and this return to certification is independent of duration of school attendance and the level of curricular complexity (i.e., whether college or non-college curriculum). Level of curriculum, however, also influences socioeconomic achievement in its own right: Those who attend college enjoy more prestigious occupations in the early career than do those who do not go to college, among men of equivalent socioeconomic origins, educability, duration of attendance, and years of education completed. In short, there is some apparent early career import to complexity of curriculum and also to educational achievement per se (i.e., a "certification" effect). Only the years of certification have a statistically significant effect on occupations later in the career, and none of the educational discontinuities bear any substantial relationship to achievements later in the life cycle.

The last chapter on achievement in the life cycle, Chapter VI, by Joe L. Spaeth, "Characteristics of the Work Setting and the Job as Determinants of Income," addresses the problematic specification of an earnings function that can account effectively for the variance in earnings. Most status attainment research of the kind reported in this volume is reasonably successful in elaborating models for educational and occupational achievement—statuses that appear responsive to the family background, educability, aspirational and motivational, and schooling variables discussed earlier. At best, these causal factors account for one-fifth of the variance in earnings at any point in the life cycle. Spaeth speculates on the reasons for less success in accounting for economic achievement than for educational and occupational statuses. Using data from a national sample of males collected by Kohn, Spaeth estimates an earnings function which incorporates job-related predictors, such as job experience, number of subordinates, and the substantive complexity of work. Even with this specification, which includes more proximate causal variables, only about one-fourth of the variance in earnings is explained. Spaeth then speculates that earnings, as an achievement variable, differs from both occupational status and education in that the former signifies both economic status attainment and task (job) performance. He suggests, following Mincer (1974), that future analyses decompose annual earnings into a multiplicative function of a rate of pay and the time per year spent at work. In Mincer's analysis, the addition of time spent in the employed labor force doubles the explanatory power of earnings specifications.

We think these papers on achievement in the life cycle demonstrate the kinds of productive mutual influences the ACT seminar has encouraged among the contributors to this volume. One instance of this influence emerges in the discussions about time—effects of exposure, duration of activity and cohort membership—that pervade chapters in this and other sections. It is not unreasonable to expect that this insight into the importance of time in the process of achievement may bring social scientists of different disciplinary perspectives into a still more unified framework.

I | Causes and Consequences of Higher Education: Models of the Status Attainment Process*

William H. Sewell
Robert M. Hauser
University of Wisconsin, Madison

Sociologists' interest in education dates back to the earliest days of the discipline. Auguste Comte, Herbert Spencer, Lester F. Ward, Emile Durkheim, Charles H. Cooley, Edward A. Ross—to mention only a few—were writing on the sociological aspects of education more than a half century ago. Although their interests were more in education as a basic institution for melioration and for passing on the social and cultural heritage from generation to generation, they were not unaware of some of the consequences of educational attainment for the individual and for society. The role of education in social stratification systems, however, was first spelled out in some detail by the late Pitirim A. Sorokin in his classic book, *Social Mobility* (1927). Sorokin correctly saw the school to be a major channel of vertical circulation and emphasized the extent to which the school served as a mechanism of social testing, selection, and distribution of individuals within different social strata, thus determining the properties of the

* Reprinted from *American Journal of Agricultural Economics*, Vol. 54, No. 5, December, 1972. The research reported herein was supported by grants from the National Institutes of Health, U.S. Public Health Service (M-6275), and the Social and Rehabilitation Service, Social Security Administration (CRD-314). Services of the Madison Academic Computing Center, were provided by grants from the Graduate School Research Committee.

9

different social classes. Much later, Talcott Parsons (1959) elaborated on Sorokin's theme in his well known article, "The School Class as a Social System: Some of Its Functions in American Society." Parsons stressed not only the selection and allocation functions of the school but also emphasized its role in the socialization of the child, particularly in inculcating societal values and norms, and its stress on achievement.

Since the publication of Sorokin's *Social Mobility*, few if any students of social stratification have failed to emphasize the role of education in social mobility. However, it is only in the past decade that empirical studies have begun to appear with the promise of elucidating both the mechanisms by which social origins influence educational attainment and the importance of educational attainment in the determination of one's place in the social hierarchy.

The reasons for this are many, but only three will be briefly mentioned. (1) In the past, students of stratification have been preoccupied with father-to-son occupational mobility. The principal means of measuring occupational mobility has been the mobility table, which shows a cross-classification of son's occupation by father's occupation. Although a great deal has been learned from studies using the mobility matrix, it is difficult to decompose the movement between statuses into its component parts. Consequently, such analysis has shed very little light on the process of vertical mobility or on the way in which mobility is helped or hindered by individual characteristics and experiences or by the events and conditions in society. (2) Past studies have suffered from a lack of appropriate data on large samples of persons—particularly data on social origins, ability, educational attainment, occupational careers, and earnings experience. (3) The multivariate statistical models that are required for the analysis of complex processes, such as those involved in status attainment, have only recently become known to students of social stratification.

Blau and Duncan, in their classic study, *The American Occupational Structure* (1967), and particularly Duncan (1966, 1969, 1970, 1971; Duncan, Featherman, and Duncan, 1972; Duncan and Hodge, 1963) in other writings, were the first to overcome these limitations. They suggested a new approach to the study of social mobility—viewing it as a process of status attainment that develops over the life cycle—and indicated techniques appropriate for its analysis. This approach differs from traditional social mobility analysis because it focuses on the degree to which the dependence of occupational status of the son (or some other achieved status) on his social origins (including his father's occupation) is explained or interpreted by experiences or characteristics of the son that intervene between origin and destination statuses. This is accomplished by arraying the relevant variables in a recursive structural model of the socioeconomic life cycle. Thus, the status attainment approach includes, and goes well beyond, the traditional interest in movement among occupations between generations.

Using data from a 1962 national sample survey of males 20 to 64 years old, Blau and Duncan proposed a causal model of status attainment beginning with educational and occupational status of the father, followed by son's education, son's first job, and son's occupation in 1962. They estimated the dependence relationships in this model through a series of recursive equations. This provided a quantitative assessment of the antecedent conditions of socioeconomic achievement and of the relative importance of social origins and educational attainment for such later socioeconomic achievements as first job and current occupation. In the basic model of Blau and Duncan, educational attainment accounts for nearly all of the effects of father's occupational status and father's education on son's occupational status in 1962. Holding constant social background statuses, education was more influential than the first job in determining later occupational status. Because educational attainment was largely independent of family background, it had a large independent influence on later achievements. These general results hold for the various age cohorts into which the sample was subdivided and indicate the crucial role that education plays in the occupational attainment process. While there are many other analyses reported in the Blau–Duncan (1967) study and in later extensions of it (Duncan, Featherman and Duncan, 1972), these may be less important contributions to stratification research than are the approach and methodology that lie behind the basic model.

The Wisconsin Data

During the same period that Blau and Duncan were at work on their project (beginning in 1959), Sewell and his associates at Wisconsin were engaged in a closely related study of social, economic, and psychological factors in educational and occupational aspirations and achievement. Work was begun in 1959 when Professor J. Kenneth Little (1958) turned over a set of data he had collected using questionnaire methods on public, parochial, and private high school seniors in Wisconsin in 1957. According to his best estimates, completed questionnaires were obtained from 95% of the high school seniors. Information was obtained on the post-high school educational and vocational plans of the seniors; educational, occupational, and economic backgrounds of their parents; perceived influence of their teachers, parents, and friends on their plans; their interest and action in applying for admission to college and for scholarships; their opinions about the value of going to college; and a number of related matters. Information regarding the seniors' scores on the Henmon–Nelson Test of Mental Maturity (Henmon and Nelson, 1954), administered annually to all high school juniors in Wisconsin, was obtained from the State Testing Service of the Student Counseling Center of the University of Wisconsin; in addition, information was obtained from the schools on the rank of each student in his high school class.

From the original questionnaires and punched cards, we selected a random sample consisting of approximately one-third of the total respondents; in addition, we coded all of the information on all students who scored in the top tenth of the intelligence distribution. After checking for the reliability of coding, some of the original survey data were recoded, and several new indexes were constructed from both the original data and information from various public sources. A series of studies of educational and occupational aspirations, based on the analysis of these data, clearly indicated the important influence of social origins on educational and occupational aspirations, even when the intelligence, community background, and various social psychological characteristics of the students were controlled (Sewell, 1964; Sewell and Armer, 1966a,b; Sewell and Haller, 1965; Sewell and Orenstein, 1965; Sewell and Shah, 1968a,b; Haller and Sewell, 1967; Portes, Haller, and Sewell, 1968).

In the late spring of 1964, seven years after the students were seniors in high school, a follow-up study was carried out for all students in the one-third sample. Information on the post-high school educational and occupational attainments, marital status, military service, and present residence of these young men and women was obtained from their parents by means of a mailed questionnaire or by telephone interview. After four waves of mailed questionnaires followed by telephone interviews to nonrespondents for whom telephone numbers could be obtained, responses were obtained for 87.2% of the sample. Various comparisons between known characteristics of the 1957 sample and the respondents to the 1964 follow-up study indicate no significant differences between the respondents and the original sample (Sewell and Hauser, 1975:15–42).

In the fall of 1965, with the cooperation of the Wisconsin Department of Revenue and following their strict arrangements to guarantee the privacy of individual records, information on parents' occupations, reported income, and number of exemptions claimed—as reported in their 1957–1960 state income tax returns—was obtained for the students who were in the sample. Information on the annual earnings of the male students for each of the years in covered employment since 1957 was obtained from the Social Security Administration, Washington, D.C., following an elaborate linkage procedure for protecting individual identity. These records have now been extended to cover earnings in subsequent years. In addition, information was collected from several published and unpublished sources regarding the characteristics of the institutions of higher learning attended by the seniors. Several articles using these data have been published, and several others are in process (Sewell and Shah, 1967, 1968a; Sewell, Haller, and Portes, 1969; Sewell, Haller, and Ohlendorf, 1970; Wegner and Sewell, 1970; Hauser, 1970b, 1972; Sewell, 1971; Gasson, Haller, and Sewell, 1972; Hauser, Sewell, and Lutterman, 1975; Sewell and Hauser, 1975). The next section of this chapter briefly summarizes some of these results as they bear on the question of the influence of social origins on educational attainment and on the crucial role of education in the status attainment process.

Socioeconomic Origins and Educational Attainment

Before proceeding to a discussion of the models we have developed to elucidate the status attainment process, it may be worthwhile first to describe briefly some of the results of our descriptive analysis of the effects of socioeconomic origins on educational attainment—which we take to be the *key* variable in the attainment process because it serves both as a status variable of considerable importance in its own right and as a major facilitator of achievement in the occupational, economic, and social spheres. Whatever measure of socioeconomic status we use—parental income, father's or mother's education, father's occupation, or any combination of them—we find enormous differences in the educational attainments of the socioeconomic groups. These differences are large regardless of how broadly or restrictively educational attainment is defined—whether it is defined as merely continuation in some kind of education beyond high school, college entry, college graduation, or professional and graduate study.

For example, when our sample is divided into quarters on a socioeconomic status index, we find that a student in the high socioeconomic status category has a 2.5 times greater chance of continuing his or her education beyond high school than one in the low socioeconomic status category. The high status student has approximately a 4 to 1 advantage in entering college, a 6 to 1 advantage in college graduation, and a 9 to 1 advantage in graduate or professional education. In the middle socioeconomic status categories, the rates are consistently between these extremes: the lower the socioeconomic status category, the lower the educational attainment. These socioeconomic status differences in educational attainment hold for both sexes, but the educational attainments of women are uniformly less than those of men at every socioeconomic level. However, the advantage of males is greatest in the lower socioeconomic levels and least in the highest socioeconomic status category.

When academic ability is controlled by dividing the sample into fourths according to the students' scores on the Henmon–Nelson Test, we still find that higher socioeconomic status students have substantially greater post-high school educational attainment than lower status students. Thus, among students in the top quarter in ability, a student from the lowest category of socioeconomic status is approximately half as likely to attend college or to graduate from college as a student from the high socioeconomic status category. The chances of a high ability student obtaining graduate or professional education, where one would presume ability considerations to be determinant, are approximately 3.5 times better if he comes from a family with high socioeconomic status than from a low socioeconomic status family. The pattern described for the high ability quarter is repeated for each ability quarter and for both sexes but is most marked for the lowest ability group, where a student from the high socioeconomic category enjoys a 4 to 1 advantage in attending college and a 9 to 1 advantage in graduating from college. These patterns hold equally well for both sexes.

One must also point out that some members of even the most socioeconomically disadvantaged groups make it through the system to the highest educational levels, and a few from the highest socioeconomic levels do not continue their education beyond high school. Nevertheless, the findings reported briefly earlier lead to the inevitable conclusion that at least in one area of status attainment—higher education or post-high school education, to be more precise—the members of this cohort found it difficult to escape the effects of their socioeconomic origins. The effects of socioeconomic background operate independently of ability and for both sexes at every stage of attainment in the higher education process. Those who overcome the handicap of status origin at one transition point find themselves again disadvantaged at the next transition point.

Models of Status Attainment

Beyond the measures of socioeconomic background and measured intelligence used in the preceding analysis, our data include measurements of the individual's performance in high school, perceptions of the influence of "significant others" (persons to whom the individual seems to be responsive in making judgments), post-high school educational plans, and occupational aspirations. This has made it possible to interpret the important social psychological processes which these variables reflect as potential mediators of the influence of socioeconomic origins on educational attainment. At the same time, we have examined their direct and indirect effects on other attainments, such as occupational status and earnings. Thus, we have been able to extend and elaborate the basic Blau–Duncan model of the status attainment process.[1]

---

[1] The differences between our two data sets probably have more to do with the differences in the details of our attainment models than to our differences in sociological orientation. The Wisconsin data differ from the Blau–Duncan data in the following major ways: Their data are for a sample of U.S. males aged 20 to 64, while ours are for a sample of Wisconsin high school seniors in 1957. Their data are cross-sectional; ours are longitudinal. Our data include measures of the individual social psychological variables aforementioned while theirs do not. The latter two factors make it possible for us to stress social psychological variables in our models, whereas Duncan and his associates, for the most part, have had to use information from other data sets when they wished to estimate the effects of social psychological variables in their models. The Blau–Duncan data do not include parental income or respondents' earnings over a period of years but do have first occupation and occupation later in the respondents' careers. Our data contain Social Security earnings for all respondents employed in covered occupations for the period 1957–1967, but this is, of course, early in the earnings career and may not fully reflect the effects of education. Our occupational attainment data are restricted to 1964, the year of the last follow-up. Featherman and Hauser (1975) are doing a replication and extension of the Blau–Duncan research in 1973, which will enable

Our first causal model was developed to explain the status attainments of the young men in our sample. In this model, we began by considering socioeconomic status (as measured by a weighted index composed of father's education, mother's education, parental income, and father's occupation) and academic ability as exogenous variables; then we introduced as intervening variables son's grades in high school, a significant others index (based on the son's perceptions of encouragement for high educational aspirations by parents, teachers, and peers) followed by son's educational and occupational aspirations, and finally as dependent variables we entered son's post-high school educational attainment and the socioeconomic level of son's occupation in 1964. We first tested this model on farm boys (Sewell, Haller, and Portes, 1969), then on boys from various rural and urban subsamples by community size, finally adopting a general model which seemed to work well for all residential groupings (Sewell, Haller, and Ohlendorf, 1970). With this model we succeeded in accounting for more than half of the variance in educational attainment and two-fifths of the variance in early occupational status. In addition, the model shows the fundamental role of educational attainment in determining occupational achievement; educational attainment has a large direct effect on occupational status, and it mediates most of the effects of variables preceding it (with the notable exception of level of occupational aspiration).

Hauser, reflecting on this model, suggested that information is needlessly lost by combining the individual components of socioeconomic status and significant others' influence into indexes and by arbitrarily dropping paths of relatively small magnitude. Consequently, as an initial demonstration of this, he further elaborated the model by disaggregating these indexes and retaining all possible paths (Hauser, 1972). This analysis was restricted to a model in which educational attainment was the final dependent variable. The reason for this choice was again our central concern with educational attainment at the time and our conviction that the social psychological variables would be of primary importance in explaining educational attainment.

Recently we extended our model to include occupational achievement and earnings.[2] The extended model is described by a path diagram in Figure

---

them not only to replicate the Blau–Duncan models approximately 10 years later but also to develop new models of the attainment process using additional social structural and social psychological variables.

[2] It is important to note that the sample to which this model was applied was necessarily restricted to the 1789 men who in 1964 were in the civilian labor force but not in school and for whom information on 1967 Social Security earnings and all of the other variables in the model was available. The greatest loss was, of course, due to the exclusion of those in college, many of whom were pursuing professional and post-graduate education. The principal effect of these limitations was probably to lower the means and variances of the variables in the model because such men tend to score high on these variables. This also means that the results reported in other papers (Hauser, 1972; Hauser, Sewell, and Lutterman, 1975; Sewell, 1971), although parallel to those reported here, are not strictly comparable.

1.1. The curved, two-headed arrows represent unanalyzed relationships, while the straight, unidirectional arrows represent direct paths of causal influence found to be statistically significant. The correlations, means, and standard deviations of the variables are shown in Table 1.1. In Table 1.2, we present the final equation for each dependent variable in the model. In the discussion which follows, we present only major findings, relying heavily on the interpretation of reduced-form coefficients and other arrangements of the data which have not been presented here.[3]

Educational Attainment

We may begin our analysis with a very simple model that includes only the four socioeconomic background variables and educational attainment. We find that mother's and father's education, father's occupation, and parental income taken together account for 15% of the total variance in years of post-high school educational attainment. Whether we examine linear or nonlinear effects, each of the four socioeconomic variables has an approximately equal effect on educational attainment and on all of the intervening variables in the model, suggesting that there may be little merit

[3] For further details about path analytic techniques and the interpretation of recursive models see Duncan (1971).

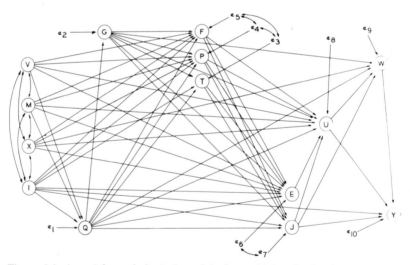

Figure 1.1 A social psychological model of post-high school achievement. Variables: *V* = father's education; *M* = mother's education; *X* = father's occupation; *I* = parental income; *Q* = mental ability; *G* = high school grades; *T* = teachers' encouragement; *P* = parental encouragement; *F* = friends' plans; *E* = college plans; *J* = occupational aspiration; *U* = educational attainment; *W* = occupational attainment; *Y* = earnings, 1967.

TABLE 1.1

Correlations Among Variables in a Model of Post-High School Achievement: Male Wisconsin High School Graduates of 1957 with Nonfarm Background

	V	M	X	I	Q	G	T	P	F	E	J	U	W	Y
V	–													
M	.520	–												
X	.439	.287	–											
I	.321	.247	.448	–										
Q	.246	.205	.181	.178	–									
G	.154	.140	.131	.121	.557	–								
T	.150	.140	.154	.173	.347	.415	–							
P	.248	.231	.261	.241	.345	.315	.437	–						
F	.237	.210	.219	.233	.288	.307	.339	.398	–					
E	.270	.257	.266	.275	.426	.450	.447	.522	.493	–				
J	.255	.227	.242	.238	.428	.460	.399	.477	.455	.755	–			
U	.306	.273	.290	.273	.446	.512	.406	.472	.474	.656	.580	–		
W	.252	.215	.268	.231	.376	.414	.331	.358	.360	.473	.476	.623	–	
Y	.082	.064	.083	.173	.163	.159	.113	.121	.091	.178	.190	.204	.211	–
Mean	10.31	10.51	33.63	650.0	100.7	96.01	.444	.608	.361	.386	49.38	13.30	43.23	757.4
Std. dev.	3.02	2.88	22.54	315.8	14.54	13.64	.497	.488	.480	.487	26.51	1.72	23.41	260.7

Variables are: V = father's education, M = mother's education, X = father's occupation, I = average parental income (10's), Q = mental ability, G = high school grades, T = teachers' encouragement, P = parental encouragement, F = friends' plans, E = college plans, J = occupational aspiration, U = educational attainment, W = occupational attainment, Y = earnings, 1967 (10's). Data pertain to 1,789 respondents with nonfarm background, employed in the civilian labor force in 1964 and not enrolled in school, who had nonzero earnings, 1965–67 and with all data present.

17

TABLE 1.2

Structural Coefficients of a Model of Post-High School Achievement: Male Wisconsin High School Graduates of 1957 with Nonfarm Background

A. Regression coefficients

					Predetermined Variables									
	V	M	X	I	Q	G	T	P	F	E	J	U	W	Constant
Q	.787	.475	—	.00472										84.49
G	—	—	—	—	.523									43.37
T	—	—	—	.000169	.00514	.0116								-1.298
P	.0081	.0147	.00249	.000153	.00619	.0059								-1.005
F	.0118	.0121	.00143	.000179	.00364	.0071								-1.097
E	.0030	.0088	.00085	.000100	.00346	.0060	.127	.242	.235					-1.043
J	—	—	—	.0058	.239	.398	4.42	12.29	12.12					-30.51
U	.030	.022	.0046	—	.0069	.0263	—	.313	.453	1.190	.0043			8.355
W	—	—	.0868	—	.0928	.1309	—	—	—	—	.1155	6.250		-70.41
Y	—	—	—	.0934	—	—	—	—	—	—	.7397	9.123	1.246	484.9

TABLE 1.2 (continued)

						Predetermined Variable								
	V	M	X	I	Q	G	T	P	F	E	J	U	W	R^2
B. Regression coefficients in standardized form														
Q	.164	.094	—	.102										.078
G	—	—	—	—	.557									.311
T	—	—	—	.108	.150	.318								.203
P	.050	.087	.115	.099	.184	.166								.202
F	.074	.072	.067	.118	.110	.201								.168
E	.019	.052	.040	.065	.103	.168	.130	.242	.232					.465
J	—	—	—	.069	.131	.205	.083	.226	.220					.408
U	.054	.037	.060	—	.058	.209	—	.089	.127	.336	.067			.540
W	—	—	—	—	.058	.076	—	—	—	—	.131	.458		.423
Y	—	—	—	.113	—	—	—	—	—	—	.075	.060	.112	.070

Variables are: V = father's education, M = mother's education, X = father's occupation, I = average parental income (10's), Q = mental ability, G = high school grades, T = teachers' encouragement, P = parental encouragement, F = friends' plans, E = college plans, J = occupational aspiration, U = educational attainment, W = occupational attainment, Y = earnings, 1967 (10's). Data pertain to 1,789 respondents with nonfarm background, employed in the civilian labor force in 1964 and not enrolled in school, who had nonzero earnings, 1965-67 with all data present.

19

in the efforts of some social scientists to interpret all social inequalities in terms of income differences.

The extent to which socioeconomic origins reduce the average educational achievement of members of the lower socioeconomic strata is impressive. For example, each year of father's or mother's education was worth .08 year of higher education for their son—after controlling for the effects of father's occupation and family income. Consequently, the sons of parents with only grade school education obtained on the average one and a quarter fewer years of higher education than the sons of parents who were college graduates, even if their fathers had similar jobs and their families had similar incomes.

A thousand-dollar difference in the annual income of the family also yielded .08 year of educational attainment, on the average. Thus a shift from the poverty level of $3000 (below which almost one-fifth of the families in the sample fell) to the median income at that time, $6000, increased the average years of education by a quarter of a year, when the effects of parental education and father's occupation were taken into account. A shift from $3000 to $10,000 in family income led to an increase of more than half an additional year in post-secondary schooling.

When academic ability is added to the model, the explained variance in educational attainment almost doubles, rising from 15 to 28%. The additional 13% represents a large component in the variance in the educational attainment of sons, which is completely independent of socioeconomic status. An important component, varying between 23 and 40%, of the effect of each socioeconomic variable is mediated by academic ability. At the same time, less than one-fifth of the association of ability with educational attainment may be attributed to its association with socioeconomic origins. Clearly, the effect of measured ability on schooling is not merely a reflection of one's socioeconomic status, the assumptions of some social scientists to the contrary.

In order to explain more fully the ways in which socioeconomic origins affect post-high school educational attainment, we further complicate our model by adding three sets of social psychological intervening variables: (a) high school performance, (b) significant others' influence, and (c) educational and occupational aspirations. On the basis of evidence from our previous research, we believe that these sets of variables intervene in the order indicated and help to mediate the effects of socioeconomic origins and academic ability on higher educational attainment. Taken as a group, these intervening variables account for a very large portion of the effects of each socioeconomic status variable on post-high school educational attainment. About 60% of the effect of mother's education on son's educational attainment, 70% of the effect of father's education, 55% of the effect of father's occupation, and all the effect of parental income are mediated by the other variables in the model. Their remaining effects represent the direct influence of resources and discrimination (or perhaps a critic might attribute them to our failure to include some relevant intervening variable).

Even with this model, which explains 54% of the variance in higher educational attainment, socioeconomic origins continue to directly influence one's chances for higher education.

The extent to which our model explains the effects of socioeconomic origins on eventual educational attainment is remarkable because all of our intervening variables pertain to the secondary school experiences of the men in our sample. Even for young men who successfully finish high school, the effects of social background on later educational attainment are largely explained by social psychological experiences during the high school years.

Again, with this complex model the interpretations for the total associations are generally similar for each of the socioeconomic status variables. Between 25 and 60% of the mediated effect of each background variable is due to the higher ability and grades of the advantaged, 30 to 50% is due to the higher expectations of their significant others, and the remaining 10 to 40% is due to their higher aspiration.[4]

Of course, the model interprets not only the several ways in which the socioeconomic variables influence higher education but also the effect of academic ability on higher educational attainment. Recall that of the total association between academic ability and higher educational attainment, only 18% is due to the mutual dependence of ability and schooling on socioeconomic background. The total effect of academic ability on post-high school educational attainment is large; for each 10-point increase in measured intelligence, the average student obtains nearly one-half year of post-secondary schooling. Of this total effect, 84% is mediated by the other intervening variables in our model (55% by high school performance, 18% by perceived expectations of others, and 11% by educational and occupational aspirations). Less than one-sixth of the influence of ability is unmediated by the variables in our model. This means that the influence of academic ability can be attributed only in a minor way to socioeconomic status considerations but rests quite solidly on its direct and pertinent influence on academic performance and its direct and indirect effects on significant others and on educational and occupational aspirations. In this connection, one should also stress that socioeconomic status has no effect on academic performance in high school independent of academic ability.

Next in the interpretation of this causal model, we examine the effects of perceived parental encouragement, teachers' encouragement, and friends' educational plans on post-high school educational attainment. We are struck by the evidence that parental encouragement and friends' plans depend heavily on the son's socioeconomic origin, while teachers' encour-

---

[4] In describing how the effects of each variable are mediated, we have consistently referred to the earliest variable in the chain as the mediating variable. Thus, when we say school performance mediates a percentage of the effect of background, this does not exclude the further mediation of those effects by subsequent intervening variables.

agement is more heavily dependent on the student's academic ability and performance. Indeed, teachers apparently do not engage in direct socioeconomic discrimination, as parents and peers seem to do, but rather depend mainly on judgments of the student's academic ability in school performance.

The influence of parents and peers on educational and occupational aspirations and on educational attainment is about equal and about twice that of teachers. Holding constant all other factors included in the model up to this point (the four socioeconomic origin variables—academic ability, school performance, parental encouragement, and friends' plans), we find that strong teachers' encouragement is worth an additional quarter of a year of higher education, whereas the net value of strong parental encouragement and of having friends who plan to go to college are six-tenths and three-quarters of a year, respectively. Shifts in educational plans and occupational aspirations account for about half the effects of parental encouragement and friends' plans, and they account for all of the effects of teachers' encouragement. Although all three significant others variables have important effects on students' educational attainment, we are led to conclude that teachers' expectations for students do not account for much of the effect of socioeconomic background on higher educational attainment. Far from reflecting overt or covert discrimination, on the whole, teachers' expectations appear to be based on students' ability and performance and, as such, make a fundamental though modest contribution to the equalization of educational opportunities.

Occupational Attainment

When we extend our model to include early occupational attainment (seven years after high school graduation) as measured by Duncan's Socioeconomic Index for Occupations (1961), we observe the central role that post-high school education plays in occupational attainment. Post-high school educational attainment alone adds 9% to the variance in occupational attainment explained by all of the other variables in the model. Almost three-quarters of the association between educational attainment and occupational status is attributable to the direct influence of educational attainment; the remaining quarter is due to the mutual dependence of schooling and jobs on causally prior variables.[5] Each year of education after high school is worth 6.25 points of status on the Duncan scale.

[5] Bowles (1972a) suggests that Duncan and others have underestimated the spurious component in the association of schooling with later social and economic achievements because of a failure to measure socioeconomic background reliably. In our research, we have found that no reasonable adjustment for unreliability in our socioeconomic background measures affects our results appreciably. Moreover, our estimates of "spurious" components of association between schooling and occupation or earnings are increased by our inclusion of socioeconomic variables that are mainly unrelated to socioeconomic background.

Except in the case of father's occupational status, all of the effects of the socioeconomic background variables on son's occupational attainment are mediated by intervening variables. For parental education and income, about 40% of the effect is mediated by academic ability and performance. The remaining effects are mediated by significant others' influences and aspirations. However, 57% of the effect of father's occupational status represents direct status inheritance which is unmediated by any of the intervening achievements in our model. (Since significant others' expectations and educational aspirations indirectly affect occupational achievement by way of educational attainment, so also do the effects of socioeconomic background, father's occupation excepted.)

Just as with educational attainment, more than 80% of the association of ability with occupational status represents its direct and indirect effects. A 10-point increase in measured ability leads to an average increase of 5 points in status on the Duncan scale. Of this total effect, half is attributable to the higher grades of more able students, 12% to higher perceived expectations of significant others, 7% to higher aspirations, and 12% to longer schooling; the remaining fifth is the direct effect of ability on the occupational achievement of men with similar levels of academic performance, significant others' expectations, aspirations, and educational attainment. The effect of academic performance on occupational status is as follows: A quarter is mediated by significant others' influence, about one-sixth by educational and occupational aspirations, one-third by educational attainment, and the remaining quarter represents a direct effect.

Net of prior variables, strong teachers' encouragement is worth 3.4 points on the Duncan scale, while high values on the parental and peer encouragement variables are worth 5.4 and 7.4 points, respectively. The effects of teachers' and parents' encouragement are due entirely to their effects on educational plans and occupational aspirations, as is one-third of the effect of friends' plans. The remaining influence of friends' plans is mediated by educational attainment, so none of the significant others' variables directly influences occupational achievement.

The effect of planning on college on occupational status is 6.7 points on the Duncan scale; all of it is attributable to the greater schooling obtained by those with college plans. An increase of 10 points of occupational aspiration on the Duncan scale is worth 1.5 points in occupational status, net of prior variables in the model. It is interesting that this total effect is virtually identical to the regression of son's occupational status on father's occupational status. Only a quarter of the effect of occupational aspiration on occupational status is mediated by educational attainment. The remainder represents an effect of aspiration on achievement that is completely independent of socioeconomic background, ability, high school performance, and educational attainment.

It is apparent from our analysis that the path to high occupational status is through higher education. Higher-status families appear to make most use of this route, perhaps by providing the genes and the stimulating environment that result in superior cognitive abilities and school perform-ance. Furthermore, their encouragement of high educational and occupa-tional aspirations leads to higher educational attainment and, ultimately, to higher levels of occupational achievement. In addition, but to a much lesser extent, higher-status families have also managed to provide further advan-tages to their sons through direct occupational inheritance, but our evidence shows that the social psychological influences, which result in higher educational attainment, are much more important than direct economic influences.

Earnings

When our model was finally extended to include Social Security earnings in 1967, 10 years after high school graduation, some expected and some surprising findings resulted. As expected, educational attainment and occupational attainment each play an important role in earnings. About half of the effect of educational attainment on earnings is due to the higher paying jobs held by men with more education, and half represents higher earnings within occupations. In the case of both educational and occupa-tional status, their effects on earnings represent just half of their correla-tion with earnings; the remaining half is attributable to the mutual dependence of earnings and of educational attainment or occupational status on prior variables. Net of all prior variables, one year of post-high school education is worth $178 in 1967 earnings, and 10 points on the Duncan scale is worth $125.

The most surprising finding is that average parental income during the four years following the son's graduation from high school has the largest effect on earnings of all of the variables in the model (Beta = .173). One thousand dollars in parental income is worth about $143 in son's earnings (note: earnings, not income) 10 years after graduation from high school. Neither the social psychological variables nor educational or occupational achievements explain the influence of parental income on son's earnings; these variables together mediate only one-third of the effect of parental income. Thus, after all intervening achievements are taken into account, $1000 in parental income is still worth $93 in son's earnings. Moreover, none of the other socioeconomic background variables affects earnings, once the influence of parental income has been taken into account. Statistical tests indicate that this income effect is not a consequence of large sampling errors due to multicollinearity among the socioeconomic background variables in the model (Hauser, Sewell, and Lutterman, 1975). Thus, there appears to be little doubt that the intergenerational effect of parental income cannot in any large measure be explained by the differing abilities, social psychological characteristics, educational attainments, or occupational achievements of the sons of wealthy or poor families.

Academic ability has an important effect on earnings, which is entirely mediated by later variables in the model. Only 16% of the correlation between ability and earnings is attributable to the mutual dependence of ability and earnings on socioeconomic background; the remaining 84% represents an increase in earnings of $244 for each 10 point increase in measured intelligence. Of this effect, 38% is attributable to the influence of ability on high school performance, 17% to its effect on occupational aspiration, and the remaining 45% is due to the higher educational attainments of the more able young men. The effects of high school performance are mediated in much the same fashion as those of ability.

Neither significant others' influence nor educational plans have a significant effect on 1967 earnings, but the son's occupational aspiration has a rather important effect on his earnings 10 years after high school graduation. A 10-point increase in occupational aspiration on the Duncan scale is worth $104 in 1967 earnings, net of all prior variables in the model. Of this effect, 11% is attributable to the greater educational attainment of those with higher aspirations, and an additional 18% is due to their higher-status occupations. The remaining 71% represents a direct effect of aspiration on earnings; net of intervening educational and occupational achievements, each 10 points in occupational aspiration (on the Duncan scale) is worth $75 in 1967 earnings.

Other social psychological and social background variables in the model have little or no direct effect on 1967 earnings. What effects they do have are mediated by educational and occupational attainments.

Conclusions

Our model has proved to be a rather powerful predictor of status attainment. It is especially effective in explaining educational achievement, accounting for 54% of the variance. It is a little less efficient in accounting for occupational attainment but still explains over 43% of its variance. It is much less effective in predicting earnings, where it accounts for only 7% of the variance in 1967 earnings.[6] Its better showing for educational and occupational attainment may be due, in large measure, to the fact that these attainments were probably more stable by the time they were measured than were earnings. Other evidence seems to indicate that earnings patterns had not stabilized by 1967, when the last data were available for this sample (Sewell and Hauser, 1975). The most likely explanation for this is the greater investment in on-the-job training among the more highly educated individuals with less labor force experience. We

---

[6] It should be noted that Solmon's (1973b) semi-log earnings equation explains about the same amount of variance in early income in the NBER–Thorndike sample, as ours does when expressed in that functional form.

will be following the earnings careers of our sample in the future, and we can test this hypothesis later.

The earlier variables in our model were also all selected for their relevance to educational and occupational attainment rather than to earnings. Important as these variables are, there are probably more pertinent and proximate influences on earnings that need to be considered in future models. For example, our occupational information is for 1964. We need information on more current jobs. Moreover, job-relevant information, such as years of experience on the job, on-the-job training, and additional formal schooling, would probably increase the efficacy of a model that sought to predict current earnings. Our primary interest has been to interpret the effects of socioeconomic background on educational and socioeconomic achievements, and we have not yet fully exploited some of the data we currently hold which might improve our ability to specify an earnings function. For example, we can also consider such factors as the extent and timing of military service, family formation, size of family, geographic mobility, characteristics of the labor market, and similar contingencies that doubtless have some effect on earnings experiences. We plan to restudy our sample during the next 18 months and will gather additional information on these and related matters.

To return to our model, we feel that it has been highly successful in the explication of the attainment process in the educational, occupational, and economic spheres—and this is what we as sociologists are concerned with. Our disaggregated model has clearly demonstrated the importance of socioeconomic origins for educational, occupational, and earnings attainments. It has illuminated the rather complex process by which the effects of socioeconomic background on educational, occupational, and economic attainments are mediated by various social psychological experiences. In addition to the various and sometimes quite indirect paths to status attainment, our model has also revealed that there is a modest amount of status inheritance that is completely independent of these social psychological processes and is not explained by other variables in the model. Most noteworthy of these are the rather sizable net effects of father's occupation in 1957 on son's occupation in 1964 and of average family income in 1957–1960 on son's earnings in 1967. This inheritance of the father's pertinent status characteristics by the son is indeed remarkable when we consider that the measurements of the son's status characteristics are from different sources and occur from seven to ten years later than the measurements of the father. It is even more remarkable that they persist when other socioeconomic, social psychological, and attainment variables in the model are controlled.

We expect that better models of the status attainment process will be developed in the future, and we hope to contribute to that development with the data from our longitudinal research program. We also are aware of the interests of social scientists in other consequences of education, such as for critical thinking, tolerance, humanitarianism, citizenship, responsibility, and other valued traits.[7] Perhaps we can develop models to explain these results, but we doubt that sociologists will be very excited about the task that some economists would like to assign to us: namely, the vexing business of obtaining the information that would enable economists to put a dollar value on them. Sympathetic as we are to the usefulness of being able to state everything in dollars, we honestly think economists may have about exhausted the pay dirt in this approach to educational benefits. We invite interested economists to join the small but hardy band of sociologists who seek to understand the process of educational attainment and its consequences for attainments in other spheres, even though we may never find a way to put a price on its benefits.

[7] The literature on the benefits of education has been reviewed in many places. The most comprehensive recent review is by Withey (1972). Withey's book is particularly useful because it stresses the consequences of higher education for economic behavior, political behavior, personality, and life styles.

Motivation and Ability: Interactive Psychological Determinants of Intellective Performance, Educational Achievement, and Each Other

John W. Atkinson   **Willy Lens**
The University of Michigan   University of Leuven

P. M. O'Malley
The University of Michigan

When behavioral science has matured, psychology will offer a generally useful and accepted theory of motivation to explain the actions of an individual. It will offer a similarly useful and accepted conception of the development of various motivational dispositions, particular abilities, beliefs, conceptions, and other personal attributes that influence socially significant actions. The construct validity of diagnostic tests of these various individual differences in personality will have been firmly established, and their predictive efficiency, as a result, greatly enhanced. Then sociology, concerned with the problem of achievement (i.e., how status attainment is influenced by one's origin in a social structure and other significant social influences along the way that enhance or constrain opportunity for education, and the instrumental role of the latter in social mobility), can look to psychology for some insights into the details and logic of the processes intervening between the antecedent and consequent of each link in its correlative chain. For example, one may anticipate a coherent and detailed answer to the question of why the socioeconomic status of one's family is so firmly related to the level of one's educational attainment. The picture of a living individual will come into sharp focus, one whose talents and character, that is, Personality (P), are the lawful products of heredity (H) and a formative social environment (E_F) that were certainly beyond that individual's own personal control, (i.e., $P = f(H, E_F)$).

The day-to-day actions of that individual and others with whom he or she is compared, underlying some correlation, will also come alive. They will always be seen as expressions of lawful interaction of different personalities with the particular challenges and opportunities, or threats and deprivations, that are defined by the immediate social environment in which the behavior occurs (i.e., $B = f(P, E)$). The particular activities initiated (when there are alternative possibilities), the time and effort expended doing one thing (instead of something else), the quality of the performance, and the cumulative effect of all this on the level of educational attainment and the occupational status ultimately achieved will then be coherently explained.

Now, as Paul once wrote in another context, "we see through a glass darkly." [1] Sociology is trying to identify the order and strength of the links in its correlative chain. Psychology is trying to formulate conceptions of motivation $(B = f(P, E))$ and of development $(P = f(H, E_F))$ that coherently capture the complexity of these two fundamental behavioral processes. How far along are we?

As a consequence of a 25-year program of research on achievement motivation, there is considerable progress to report in the understanding of human motivation and of the interaction of motivation and ability, both as the basic psychological determinants of intellective performance and cumulative achievement and also as determinants of one another. The view through the glass is becoming less murky.

The conception we present here is one that currently guides our program of empirical research on achievement motivation and action at Michigan. Its foundation consists of two pillars: a reconstruction of the theory of motivation in *The Dynamics of Action* (1970) with David Birch, and a report of the latest developments in theory and empirical work, specifically concerning achievement motivation in *Motivation and Achievement* (1974), with Joel O. Raynor and others. The conclusions in the latter work have already been extended in concurrent collaborative study by Atkinson and Lens on how "intelligence" and achievement-related motivation measured in sixth-, ninth-, and twelfth-grade boys is related to their subsequent cumulative academic achievement in high school and their ultimate educational attainment.[2]

A New Conception of Motivation and Action

As reconstructed in *The Dynamics of Action* (1970), the theory of motivation begins with the premise that the behavioral life of an individual

---

[1] 1 Cor. 13:12.

[2] An effort to determine the final level of educational attainment of these students, who were sixth graders in 1959–1962, is incomplete at this writing, as is the parallel study of girls initiated by Alice Yip.

is a stream of activity characterized by change from one activity to another. The new focus of theoretical interest is a change in activity, the cessation of one and initiation of another, rather than the mistakenly isolated simple goal-directed episode of the traditional paradigm of behavioral psychology. A change in activity can only occur if the relative strength of the inclinations (or motivational tendencies) of an individual to engage in one activity, as opposed to another, change. These changes in motivation must occur within the same interval of time that the observable change in activity occurs. So the actual causes of the strengthening or weakening of various inclinations must be identified with concurrent natural events.

The impact of the immediate environment, or stimulus situation of traditional psychology, is represented by the various psychological forces it produces, compelling an individual to engage or not to engage in different activities as a result of the prior life experience of that individual. If a certain kind of activity has been intrinsically satisfying or rewarding in this particular situation, there will be an *instigating force* for that activity. This will cause an increase (a change) in the strength of the individual's inclination to undertake that activity, an *action tendency*. If a certain kind of activity has been punished or frustrated in the past, there will be an *inhibitory force* and growth in the strength of disinclination or *negaction tendency* (i.e., a tendency *not* to do it). The anticipation of negative consequences, or inhibitory force, which functions to increase the strength of a negaction tendency (i.e., the disinclination to act), produces *resistance* to engaging in an activity. This opposes, blocks, and effectively dampens the resultant strength of the inclination to act. The *resultant action tendency* (strength of action tendency minus negaction tendency) competes with the resultant tendencies to engage in other activities. The strongest of them is expressed in the observable stream of behavior. This expression of a motivational tendency in behavior is what constitutes a *consummatory force*. The latter is responsible for a reduction in the strength of that inclination. Resistance to an action tendency is sufficient to produce a *force of resistance* that will reduce or dissipate the disinclination to act, the negaction tendency. This, in brief, describes the new conception of causal factors involved in the kind of rise, expression in behavior when dominant, and decline in strength of various inclinations as shown in Figure 2.1. It is a graph taken from a segment of one of the earliest computer simulations of what one could expect to happen if an individual were exposed to instigating and inhibitory forces of certain magnitudes for three incompatible activities in a given *constant* environment [Seltzer (1973), Seltzer and Sawusch (1974)].

A complete mathematical statement of the theory and discussion of the quantitative characteristics of other parameters, such as the consummatory value of particular activities, the way selectivity in attention favors the ongoing activity, and others, is fully presented in *The Dynamics of Action* (1970) and Birch (1972). A computer program for the whole theory has been included in the appendix of *Motivation and Achievement* (1974). In

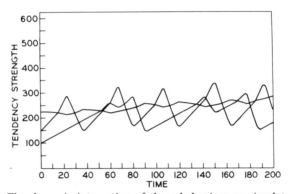

Figure 2.1 The dynamic interaction of three behaviors as simulated over time. Reprinted with permission of author and publisher from: Seltzer, Robert A. Simulation of the dynamics of action. *Psychological Reports,* 1973, **32,** 859–872, Fig. 2. The computer program is the theory of motivation developed in Atkinson and Birch (1970) to explain how strength of motivational tendencies change systematically over time to control the time spent engaging in various activities.

addition, we have already seen how the stream of conscious thought and its influence on overt action can be embraced by the same basic concepts (Birch, Atkinson, and Bongort, 1974). This means that systematic influences on action that are attributable to the content of conscious thought, now being emphasized by Heckhausen (1973) and Weiner (1972, 1974) in the new cognitive psychology of motivation, are compatible with the dynamics of action. The two approaches are not antagonistic, rather complementary.

The importance of this new conception of motivation for this discussion is that it constitutes a theory of operant behavior, of *actions* emitted by an individual even in a constant environment, not merely an account of reactions to the traditionally assumed constantly changing stimulus situation. It should be evident in Figure 2.1 that the individual can have an inclination to act in a certain way, carried over from the past and quite independent of the present stimulus situation, well before he is exposed to an appropriate instigating force for that activity in the present environment. Since the new theory accounts for actions emitted in the stream of activity, its basic principles account for various measurable aspects of molar time segments in the stream of activity, such as the number of times a particular activity is initiated, the total amount of time spent in that activity, and the derivative operant level (or rate) of a given activity (Birch, 1972). At the same time, its basic principle of a change in activity can also account for the quantitative characteristics of behavior that have long been the focus of interest within the short time segment, or episodic paradigm, of traditional behavioral psychology (viz., latency of response [time taken to initiate an activity], persistence of an activity, preference [or choice] among alternatives).

In our treatment of the effect of motivation on cumulative achievement, the principles of the dynamics of action tell us that the amount of time spent in a given activity (e.g., perseverance or persistence in studying and schoolwork) should depend upon the strength of motivational tendency for that activity relative to the number and strength of motivational tendencies for alternative incompatible activities as summarized graphically in Figure 2.2.

The Determinants of the Level of Intellective Performance Distinguished from the Determinants of Cumulative Achievement

The conceptual analysis of the role of ability and motivation as determinants of the level of intellective performance when a given task is being done (e.g., an intelligence test, studying math homework), and as the determinants of cumulative achievement (e.g., grade point average in a year of college, level of educational attainment), which depends upon both the level or quality of the ongoing activity *and* the time spent in that kind of activity, is spelled out in Figure 2.2.

Working backwards from the criterion of cumulative achievement, we confront first the simple assumption that achievement in the long run (e.g., productivity, grade point average based on appraisals of a lot of academic work over a long period of time, and so on) is the product of the level (or quality) of work, when it is being done, and the time spent in that activity.

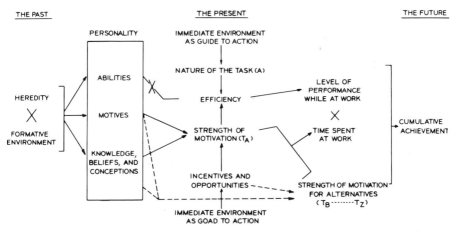

Figure 2.2 The dual role of motivation as a determinant of cumulative achievement. Time spent at work depends upon the strength of motivation for the critical task (T_A) relative to the number and strength of motivation for other activities $(T_B \ldots T_Z)$. Level of performance while at work is attributed to ability, the nature of the task, and the effect of strength of motivation (T_A) on efficiency of performance. (From Atkinson, 1974b, Figure 1, with permission.)

Obviously, the individual who is very strongly motivated for academic achievement will typically spend more time paying attention in class and more time doing homework and studying for exams, than one less motivated. The assumption of a linear relationship between strength of academic motivation and time spent in academic activity is given in Figure 2.3.

It is obvious that thus far we have assumed that the number and strength of inclinations for other competing, time-consuming activities are equal among individuals. It is equally obvious that having a great variety of outside interests, as compared to few, should produce a linear decrease in time spent in academic work, total available hours in a day being a constant of 24. We should expect, though definitive empirical evidence on the point is hard to find, that excessive motivation for nonacademic activities, *even when academic motivation is strong,* can as frequently be the cause of low cumulative academic achievement as a deficiency in motivation for academic work.

Moving back, now, another step in Figure 2.2 to the determinants of the level of intellective performance at a given time, we find the assumption that level of intellective performance (e.g., on a test of ability) depends upon the individual's true level of ability at that time and the efficiency of the performance. How efficiently or well does the individual execute the various kinds of mental operations required by the task? Here, once again, the strength of motivation being expressed in the performance of an activity plays a vitally important role, namely, as a determinant of the efficiency of that performance. From considerable evidence accumulated in recent years in the program of work on achievement motivation (Atkinson,

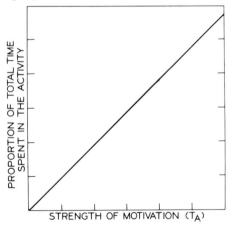

Figure 2.3 The effect of strength of motivation for some activity (T_A) on proportion of time spent in the activity. (From Atkinson, 1974b, with permission.) Computer simulations based on *The Dynamics of Action* show this to be a negatively accelerated function. The assumption of linearity is an approximation for simplicity in exposition.

1974a) we must now agree with others (e.g., Yerkes and Dodson, 1908; McClelland, 1951; Broadhurst, 1959; Eysenck, 1966; Vroom, 1964; Hebb, 1958) that the relationship is typically nonmonotonic and best described by an inverted U-shaped curve as shown in Figure 2.4.

This means, very simply, that the intellective test scores of three individuals, all of whom have exactly the same level of true ability (e.g., equal to 100), will be different. The true ability of the person who is less than optimally motivated will be underestimated by his test score. The true ability of the person who is more than optimally motivated, overmotivated given the requirements of the task, will similarly be underestimated. We shall, in a moment, show how this empirical generalization from current evidence about an inefficiency attributable to overmotivation, and hence decrement in intellective test performance, helps us to unravel the problem of "over-" and "under-" achievement as it has traditionally been defined (Thorndike, 1963), that is, in terms of the discrepancy between level of achievement, as predicted on the basis of intellective test performance, and actual level of achievement (e.g., GPA in college).

Before doing this, however, it is instructive to examine some implications of the assumption of nonmonotonicity regarding strength of motivation and level of performance that is mediated by the effect of motivation on efficiency of performance.

First, this enables us to define the true level of ability as the level of performance an individual is capable of achieving at a task when optimally motivated. It is the individual's maximum possible level of performance (at

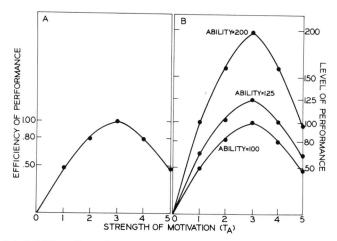

Figure 2.4 (A) The effect of strength of motivation on efficiency of performance, and (B) the effect of strength of motivation on level of performance when level of performance = ability × coefficient of efficiency. (From Atkinson, 1974b, with permission.) According to theory of achievement motivation, T_A is a summation of various components, such as to achieve success (T_S), to avoid failure (T_F), to obtain approval or some other extrinsic goal (T_{ext}).

the time) and would require conditions that produce the optimal level of motivation in him to be manifested in his test behavior.

Second, we may refer to the ratio of observed level of performance to the true level of ability as the *coefficient of efficiency*. It is the latter which we assume to be related to strength of motivation at the time of performance in a way that is often described by an inverted U-shaped curve.

Third, we might imagine the results of consistently running product-moment (linear) correlations between some measure of a single source of individual differences in motivation and the level of intellective performance if the total strength of motivation for the task is overdetermined; that is, a summation of a variety of components such as tendency to achieve success, tendency to avoid failure, and other extrinsic tendencies for social approval, money, and so on (as assumed, for example, in Atkinson and Feather's *Theory of Achievement Motivation* [1966] and Atkinson and Raynor's *Motivation and Achievement* [1974]). Ignoring the environmental conditions and assuming $B = f(P)$, rather than $B = f(P, E)$, is the traditional weakness of the correlational approach, which we identify with the mental test movement in psychology. (The presumption of constancy of state, linear relations, interval measurement, additivity, normally distributed error, and so on, all are required to justify factor analysis. In addition, the amazing capacity of the modern computer to spit forth both linear correlations and the factorial structure of a matrix of them has been too great a temptation to resist.)

If the correlation is sought between the strength of a particular motive and criterion performance under conditions that bring the range of individual differences in the intensity of motivation only to a relatively low level (Range 1–3 in Figure 2.4), then the product-moment correlation will be positive. If, however, the conditions or sample studied falls only in the moderate range of intensity of motivation (Range 2–4 in Figure 2.4), then the product-moment correlation will be zero. Finally, if the conditions and/or sample, or both in interaction, yield a range of intensities of motivation at the high end of the scale (Range 3–5 in Figure 2.4), then the product-moment correlation between strength of the motive and criterion performance will be negative. (Ability is here assumed to be equal among the individuals.)

This kind of inconsistency appears frequently in the psychological literature and is most puzzling to students of psychology who view the assumptions of traditional psychometrics as sacrosanct first principles from which should follow, by derivation, the orderliness of the behavioral world. In fact, the assumptions that justify the use of product-moment correlation constitute a very coherent theory of behavior, and inconsistency of results in most fields of science would normally constitute the empirical justification for abandoning some one or more theoretical assumptions and seeking new and hopefully more heuristic ones.

Those using the experimentally validated thematic apperceptive measure of strength of individual differences in achievement motive (see McClelland, Atkinson, Clark, and Lowell, 1953 and Atkinson, 1958) have had to face the wrong conclusion, continually drawn by investigators who, believing the premises of their psychometrics and knowing little or nothing about the process of motivation, have assumed that this kind of inconsistency necessarily implies that the measure of individual differences in motivation must be invalid. Perhaps the most formidable counterargument is the reconstruction of the theory of motivation and the current analysis of the role of motivation in achievement. Both are largely products of inferences based on systematic empirical study using the crude and controversial thematic apperceptive method of measuring motivation for 25 years.

Probably the most accurate portrayal of the relationship between strength of motivation and level of performance (mediated by the influence of motivation on efficiency) is one that would emphasize the dependence of the exact nature of the relationship upon the nature of the task: What mental operations are required of the subject? Figure 2.5 shows three hypothetical relationships distinguishing Tasks A, B, and C) see also Vroom, 1964:204). On Task A, the optimal level of motivation is very strong; on Task B, it is moderate; on Task C, it is fairly weak. If individuals differ in strength of motivation in a given test condition, obviously the same individual will not be equally efficient at all tasks, and his varying level of test performance relative to others will manifest this.

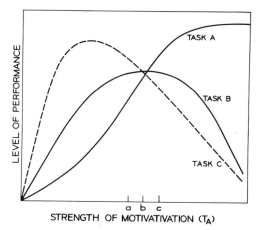

Figure 2.5 It is generally assumed that efficiency of performance depends on the nature of the task as well as on strength of motivation. A person (c) who has stronger motive than others (a, b) may, under certain conditions, perform better, worse, or the same as others on different tasks in the same situation (From Atkinson, 1974a, with permission).

Imagine the consternation of an investigator who had implicitly assumed that motivation was linearly related to level of performance no matter what the task (hence unquestioned use of product-moment correlation) and had unwittingly tested a group of subjects under environmental conditions that brought them all into the middle range of motivation (a, b, c, in Figure 2.5). On Task A, the correlation between strength of some component of motivation and level of performance will be positive, on Task B it will be zero, on Task C it will be negative. No measure of motivation that yields results like that could possibly be valid! It is believed by some. Again, the argument comes from those who do not recognize that the set of assumptions lying behind traditional methods of linear correlation and the conventional parametric statistical analysis of results is in itself a theory of behavior (and perhaps not the heuristic one we need for further development of behavioral science).

The Various Components of
Achievement-Related Motivation

It takes time to reach the empirical data when a problem has been studied long and intensively enough to move the conception of it well beyond that of traditional wisdom. But that, we must recall, is the paramount aim of basic science—to improve common sense, to provide new and more useful ways of thinking about the subject matter. Then prediction of consequences from antecedents is enhanced and new, more useful humane things can be done in applications of the new conception.

In Figure 2.2, the advance in conceptual analysis of achievement-related motivation published in *A Theory of Achievement Motivation* (1966) with Norman Feather and further elaborated in *Motivation and Achievement* (1974) with Joel Raynor, is succinctly summarized in the identification of the personality determinants of strength of motivation (T_A) as the relatively general and stable motivational dispositions of the individual (called motives) and the more easily learned and changeable knowledge, beliefs, and conceptions of the individual. In the case of achievement-related motivation, the latter includes the strength of an individual's expectation of success in an enterprise, that is, the subjective probability of success (P_s), and the presence or lack of a future orientation, that is, whether or not a person conceives of the immediate task as a step in a path leading on to more distant future goals. This latter elaboration of the theory of achievement motivation, the motivational implications of seeing a contingent relationship between success in some present activity and attainment of long-term goals, is the contribution of Joel O. Raynor (1969, 1974a,b) and his students. Ultimately it may be more important than the identification of the basic motives that are sources of motivation *because it is teachable.* Finally, Figure 2.2 identifies the incentives and opportunities (and also, by implication, the threats and deprivations) defined by the immediate environment as the major situational influence on strength of motivation. It has been assumed, and with substantial corroboration in empirical studies of achievement-oriented performance, risk preference or level of aspiration, and persistence, that the total strength of motivation to engage in a given activity (e.g., T_A in Figure 2.2) is an algebraic summation of separate positive tendencies, such as tendency to achieve success and tendency to gain social approval, and separate negative tendencies, such as tendency to avoid failure and tendency to avoid success, a factor that Matina Horner (1970, 1974) has found more prevalent in females and, therefore, an important key to understanding sex differences in achievement. The tendencies to avoid the possible negative consequences of academic activity are sources of resistance. They subtract from and, therefore, weaken the resultant motivation for an activity.

It will not take us too far astray from our theme merely to list some of the separate components of achievement-related motivation, in terms of which individuals differ, that have been identified as significant influences in empirical research: motive to achieve (as measured by thematic apperceptive n Achievement score (McClelland et al., 1953); motive to avoid failure (as measured by Test Anxiety [Mandler and Sarason, 1952]); subjective probability of success (P_s) as measured or inferred in a variety of ways (Atkinson and Feather, 1966); motive for social approval (as measured by thematic apperceptive n Affiliation score [Atkinson, 1958; Atkinson and O'Connor, 1966]); individual differences in *competence* (or ability) as a source of individual differences in *confidence* (O'Connor, Atkinson, and Horner, 1966; Moulton, 1974); motive to avoid success as indicated by evidence of fear of success in thematic apperception (Horner, 1970, 1974); and future orientation as measured by simply asking an individual to what extent a certain activity is instrumentally related to attainment of future goals (Raynor, 1969, 1974a; Atkinson and Raynor, 1974: Part II).

The way in which these (and still other unmentioned motivational variables) interact and combine to *over*determine the final strength of motivation for an achievement-oriented activity is coherently spelled out in the theory of achievement motivation. In this context, the main point of merely identifying and listing a number of the critically important components is to provide a realistic framework for judging how much of the variance in total strength of motivation one should expect to account for in terms of a measure of n Achievement, by itself, or Test Anxiety, by itself, or even a measure of Resultant Achievement Motivation (n Achievement-Test Anxiety), when the relative crudity, or early stage of development, of the measures currently being employed must also be taken into account. It is to be hoped that the conceptual analysis of the problem of achievement, to which we have been lead by empirical findings using admittedly crude tools, will become the strongest possible argument for the developmental research needed to improve the measurement of the various components of human motivation.

A Conceptual Analysis of Over-
and Underachievement

Table 2.1 (based on the logic of Figure 2.2) concretizes the conception of how *true ability* and *motivation* jointly influence level of intellective test performance (from which individual differences in ability alone are traditionally inferred) and cumulative achievement over a substantial period of time as recorded, for example, in the grade point average of a student in a year of work at college. We have hypothetical individuals at five levels of true ability ($A = 100$; $B = 80$; $C = 60$; $D = 40$; $E = 20$). We assume that *true ability* can change and that at any particular time it is the product of genetic and social background (i.e., $P = f(H, E_F)$). We also assume that our individuals also may differ in the total strength of motivation that is aroused and expressed in a *critical test situation* and in *normal academic work* from 5 (strongest) to 1 (weakest). We further assume that the strength of motivation is more intense (by one unit) for all individuals under the typical pressure situation of an intellective test than under the typical everyday conditions of normal work. To simplify matters, we restrict our sample to 20 subjects, each given a name which designates his *true level of ability* and *strength of motivation while taking a test*. Finally, we assume a symmetric inverted U-shaped function to describe the influence of motivation on efficiency of performance (see again Figure 2.4), a linear relationship between motivation and time spent in an activity (see again Figure 2.3), and, for simplicity, equivalence among the subjects in the number and strength of competing alternative interests.

Examining the left side of Table 2.1, one can see that the subjects have been ordered according to the level of their intellective test performance. Leading the list is A3, a person of great talent (true ability) but only moderate and thus optimal motivation at the time of the test, and way down in the middle of the second quartile on the test is A5, an equally talented but much too highly motivated person. His efficiency, attributable to that very strong motivation, is here estimated to be only .50.

Now consider the right side of Table 2.1. Note that *true ability* has not changed but the state of motivation is now assumed to be somewhat weaker in all subjects. The change in strength of motivation in normal work is paralleled by a change in efficiency and, thus, of the level of performance while at work. In the case of A3, who was optimally motivated for the critical test, the somewhat weaker motivation in normal work and correlated drop in efficiency (from 1.00 to .80) produces a comparable drop in the level of his performance. In contrast, A5, our other highly talented but very highly motivated subject profits by the somewhat lower level of motivation in normal work. His efficiency rises from .50 (on the test) to .80, and so also does the level or quality of his performance improve.

Now consider that time spent in work is proportional to the strength of motivation and that the cumulative achievement is the product of level (or quality) of performance while at work and time spent in work. The level of

TABLE 2.1

True Ability and Motivation as Determinants of the Level of Intellective Performance (e.g., on an Ability Test) and Cumulative Academic Achievement (e.g., Grade Average in College). A Hypothetical Numerical Illustration Emphasizing the Dual Role of Motivation Shown in Figure 2[a]

Name of Subject[b]	Ability Test Situation				Conditions of Normal Academic Work					
	True Ability	Motivation	Efficiency	Level of Test Performance	True Ability	Motivation[c]	Efficiency	Level of Performance	Time Spent in Work	Cumulative Achievement
A3	100	3	1.00	100	100	2	.80	80	2	160–
A4	100	4	.80	80	100	3	1.00	100	3	300[d]
A2	100	2	.80	80	100	1	.50	50	1	50–
B3	80	3	1.00	80	80	2	.80	64	2	128–
B4	80	4	.80	64	80	3	1.00	80	3	240
				–Q_1						
B2	80	2	.80	64	80	1	.50	40	1	40–
C3	60	3	1.00	60	60	2	.80	48	2	96
A5	100	5	.50	50	100	4	.80	80	4	320
C4	60	4	.80	48	60	3	1.00	60	3	180
C2	60	2	.80	48	60	1	.50	30	1	30–
				–Md						
B5	80	5	.50	40	80	4	.80	64	4	256
D3	40	3	1.00	40	40	2	.80	32	2	64
D4	40	4	.80	32	40	3	1.00	40	3	120
D2	40	2	.80	32	40	1	.50	20	1	20
C5	60	5	.50	30	60	4	.80	48	4	192
				–Q_3						
D5	40	5	.50	20	40	4	.80	32	4	128
E3	20	3	1.00	20	20	2	.80	16	2	32
E4	20	·2	.80	16	20	3	1.00	20	3	60
E2	20	2	.80	16	20	1	.50	10	1	10
E5	20	5	.50	10	20	4	.80	16	4	64

[a] From Atkinson, 1974 (b) with permission.

[b] Ss are named according to their true level of ability (A = 100, B = 80, C = 60, D = 40, E = 20) and their strength of motivation (T_A) in the ability test situation. See Figure 2.2 to identify determinants of T_A.

[c] It is assumed here that all Ss are less strongly motivated during normal work (–1) than in the test situation.

[d] The top quartile among the achievers are indicated by the underlined scores.

cumulative achievement (GPA in a year of college in our example) is shown in the extreme right hand column. The top quartile among the achievers are indicated by the underlined scores, and the biggest disappointments (predicting achievement from test performance) are indicated by a minus sign next to their achievement scores.

Who are the dramatic overachievers, those who do much better than expected in predictions based on linear correlation between test performance and criterion of achievement (which, in this case, was .37)? All of them, particularly A5 who heads the list, were more than optimally motivated during the critical test. Even C5, a person of modest talent, makes it into the top quartile on cumulative achievement as a consequence of greater efficiency in normal work and great perseverance or persistence (i.e., time spent in the activity).

Who are the biggest disappointments, the underachievers as traditionally defined? Leading the parade are the subjects of great or above average talent who were only moderately motivated, or slightly less than moderately motivated, for the big test. Under conditions of normal work, they show both a drop in efficiency and very little time spent at the task, which is symptomatic of their relative lack of motivation. Recall that, in this analysis, we have assumed that all subjects have the same number and strength of interests in other time consuming activities. We might expect superlative achievement from A3 if, but only if, he were very deficient in outside interests. Then his time spent at work might have equalled or exceeded that of A5, the top achiever in our example. Perhaps when Edison said "Genius is 1% inspiration and 99% perspiration," he had in mind the accomplishments that might be expected from someone with limited *true ability* but with a single-minded dedication to the task, a person of very limited outside (competing) interests.

Our most realistic computer simulations of the problem of predicting cumulative achievement (e.g., GPA in a year of college) from intellective test performance (e.g., college aptitude test given in high school) involve an N of 80 in which persons stronger in motive to achieve than to avoid failure were made to outnumber those more strongly anxious about failure by three to one (Sawusch, 1974). This estimate was based on results in much of the earlier work on achievement motivation in college student populations. The correlation between test score and achievement criterion then rose to .48. This happens because there are now some cases of substantially better cumulative achievement for persons considered disappointments in Table 2.1. For example, if subjects A2, B2, and C2 are weakly motivated at the time of taking a test *because of their stronger tendency to avoid failure than to achieve,* and this is a negative component and a source of anxiety that *depresses their resultant motivation,* then their motivation in normal work is paradoxically *stronger* (again assume by 1 unit) when the situational pressure is relaxed. Thus, they are more efficient in normal (non-anxiety producing) work and they spend proportionately more time *at* work. The levels of cumulative achievement become 300 (instead of 50),

240 (instead of 40), and 180 (instead of 30) for A2, B2, and C2 respectively. Even a person with very little talent, D2, would show a cumulative achievement of 120 instead of 20, if the reason for his motivational deficit while taking a test is a crippling, suppressive anxiety.

The socially significant implications of both these over- and undermotivational effects on efficiency of test performance which, by tradition, have been labeled "intelligence" or "ability" or "scholastic aptitude" are too obvious to require much more explicit discussion. It is argued elsewhere, in light of the simplistic interpretations of the meaning of differences in intellective performance levels we have habitually and vaguely referred to as "intelligence," that:

> The mental test movement for many years has implicitly made the claim, without adequate justification and certainly in the absence of knowledge, that level of motivation is either optimal for everyone being tested, or constant, or only negligibly different among all individuals at the time of performance.
>
> The evidence from our twenty-five years of research on effects of differences in achievement-oriented motivation challenges the habitual toleration of the simplicity of the mental tester's theoretical account of behavior. The stakes have become too high. It is apparent that we now have more and better theory of motivation than we ever have had of intelligence. Until proven otherwise, any measured difference in what has been called general intelligence, scholastic aptitude, verbal or mathematical ability, etc., which is always obtained from performance under achievement-oriented if not multiple incentive conditions, can be given a motivational interpretation with no less scientific justification than the traditional aptitudinal interpretation. (Atkinson, 1974b; 395)

When all of the conditions of the computer simulations based on Figure 2.2 were repeated, but random sampling from normal distributions of true ability, strength of motivation, and also number and strength of motivation for competing activities was included (and all explanatory variables except motivation for the task under two conditions were considered independent), the hypothetical linear correlation between diagnostic test score and cumulative achievement was .33, as shown in Table 2.2, taken from Sawusch (1974).

Obviously, one only gets out of computer the implications of what one has put into it, whether it is an explicitly stated theory about the motivational–behavioral process and conditions that influence the two measures between which one has determined the degree of linear correlation, or a more conventional data processing in terms of traditional psychometric assumptions (which actually do, though it is hardly ever explicitly recognized, constitute a theory of behavior). To demonstrate this point, Lens repeated the last simulation described with only a single change, and one that makes good theoretical sense. He assumed a linear correlation of .52 between true ability and the strength of motivation

TABLE 2.2

Product Moment Correlations Among Variables Described in Figure 2.1 Given the Relations Assumed in Figures 2.2 and 2.3 in a Computer Simulation by Sawusch (1974) [a]

	1	2	3	4	5	6	7	8
1. True Ability	1.00	-.02	-.02	.06	.86	.86	-.07	.50
2. Normal Motivation		1.00	.64	.08	-.18	.14	.69	.54
3. Test Motivation			1.00	-.04	-.18	.13	.51	.43
4. Alternative Motivation				1.00	.07	.11	-.57	-.38
5. Test Performance					1.00	.74	-.16	.33
6. Normal Performance						1.00	.07	.68
7. Time Spent							1.00	.74
8. Cumulative Achievement								1.00

[a] The hypothetical sample of subjects had characteristics derived in random sampling from normal distributions of ability (100 to 20), motivation for alternative activities (3 to 27), strength of test motivation (1 to 7) or (3 to 9) in the ratio of 1 to 3 to constitute an N = 80. It was assumed that strength of motivation under normal conditions increased 1 unit for the 1/4th of Ss whose test motivation was depressed because tendency to avoid failure was greater than tendency to achieve success in them. For all others, strength motivation is assumed weaker (by 1 unit) in normal academic work.

expressed in normal work.[3] The latter influences the amount of time spent in the activity, and differences in time spent should produce differences in growth of ability that are proportionate to the differences in cumulative achievement. The results of this simulation, with N again equal to 80, are shown in Table 2.3. Now the linear correlation between *test performance* and *cumulative achievement* becomes .45.

We have a satisfying sense of being on essentially the right track when we compare these various hypotheses derived from theory based on experimental research with the factual evidence reported by our major testing institutions. The expected degree of linear correlation between intellective test and cumulative achievement should fall somewhere in the range of .33 to .45 (assuming no error of measurement). The median of actually obtained correlations between verbal and mathematical aptitude scores and academic performance in freshman year of college ranges between .40 and .48, where there is substantial heterogeneity in the test scores of the colleges studied, and as low as .26 to .32 when there is less heterogeneity (Angoff, 1971; 129). The correlation of ACT scores with college grades has been found to range between .20 and .56 in similar studies (American College Testing Program, 1973, Vol. 1, p. 128).

Behavioral Science and Behavioral Technology

Our theoretically deduced linear correlation between *intellective test* and *cumulative achievement,* depending on various assumptions, defines a theoretical expectation assuming perfectly reliable measurement of the several variables. Theory about the motivational–behavioral process and the use of the computer to determine what should be expected given a theory and specified complex conditions is the *behavioral science* side of the problem. The development and refinement of adequate tools and empirical techniques is the *behavioral technology* side of the problem. The two issues are invariably confounded in educational research when one starts talking about what percentage of the total variance of the criterion is "accounted for" or "explained by" certain variables. It is quite conceivable that, at a given stage in the development of a science, variations in the less important of two influences on a criterion may be measured with much greater exactitude than variations of the more important influence.

Just to make the point—the confounding of the theoretical question and the *state of methodology* in every empirical correlation—consider again the theoretically expected correlations of .45 between test performance and cumulative achievement versus .53 between normal strength of motivation

---

[3] This correlation of .52 is intended to approximate that of .54 between normal motivation and cumulative achievement in Table 2.2. It is assumed that the cumulative growth in ability closely corresponds to the visible and evaluated evidence of cumulative achievement.

TABLE 2.3

Product Moment Correlations Among Variables in a Computer Simulation by Willy Lens[a]

	1	2	3	4	5	6	7	8
1. True Ability	1.00	.52[b]	.48	.06	.74	.87	.31	.70
2. Normal Motivation		1.00	.68	-.05	.26	.30	.67	.53
3. Test Motivation			1.00	-.14	.13	.45	.54	.57
4. Alternative Motivation				1.00	.02	.01	-.67	-.50
5. Test Performance					1.00	.62	.18	.45
6. Normal Performance						1.00	.24	.74
7. Time Spent							1.00	.78
8. Cumulative Achievement								1.00

[a]Following the same conditions and procedures as in Table 2.2 except now it is assumed that true level of ability is correlated .52 with the normal strength of motivation because of the cumulative effect of the latter's influence on time spent in academic activity.

[b]Assumed relationship.

and cumulative achievement in Table 2.3. Now make some realistic assumptions about the reliability of measurement in the field of ability testing (intellective performance) and achievement (grade point average) versus the field of motivation. The systematic study of intelligence has a more than 70-year history, the study of motivation only about 25 years. Let us then assume that the reliability of measurement is .90 for both the intellective test and the criterion, GPA, but is only about .50 for the measure of individual differences in motivation. If Table 2.3 were correct theoretically, and these estimates of different stages of technology are realistic, one would expect actually obtained intellective test scores to correlate .40 with GPA and current measures of motivation to correlate .35 with GPA, a reversal in order of magnitude attributable entirely to differences in the state of the art, or technology, of measurement.

Unless the distinction we make is appreciated, there is a tendency to identify the state of the science, itself, with the state of its technology. It is a common fallacy and may influence the appraisal of the meaning and importance of findings, such as those of P. M. O'Malley (1972, 1973) in secondary analysis of data collected by Bachman, Kahn, Mednick, Davidson, and Johnston (1967) in the *Youth in Transition* study by the Survey Research Center at Michigan. As shown in Tables 2.4 and 2.5 from O'Malley's preliminary report, a representative sample of high school sophomores who differed in resultant achievement motivation, as inferred from their standing above or below the median on thematic apperceptive *n* Achievement and Test Anxiety in 1966, also differed significantly in the percentage who went on to some form of post-high school education in 1970.[4] More variance in the criterion of educational achievement is obviously "accounted for" by an index of socioeconomic status that embraces all the influences in the formative environment (both true ability and motivation are products of it) as well as concurrent financial condition. Less is related to the Quick Test of intellective performance in which true ability (in part determined by motivational effects on time spent) and current motivational effects are confounded, as we have seen. Least is "accounted for" by the currently available tools for measuring only the strength of motivation;[5] these tools have not changed since their initial validation a quarter of a century ago. O'Malley's (1972, 1973) study has also confirmed earlier research on the relationship of achievement motivation and socioeconomic status (see Rosen, Crockett, and Nunn, 1969; Veroff, Atkinson, Feld, and Gurin, 1960) and, more immediately pertinent, has shown that the Quick Test of "intelligence" and motivation are also

[4] This includes all those in colleges, universities, theological, technical, vocational, agricultural, and business schools, junior and community colleges, military academies, preparatory schools.

[5] The reader interested in the further loss in reliability of measurement using thematic apperception in a national sample study is referred to Veroff *et al.*, 1960.

TABLE 2.4

*Percentage of a Representative Sample of Male Sophomores in
Public High Schools in the United States in 1966 Who Went on to
Some Form of Post-High School Education*[a]

n Achievement-Test Anxiety	N	% in Post-High School Education
High - Low	362	54.7
High - High[b]	408	50.0
Low - Low[b]	453	53.9
Low - High	518	40.3
$F = 8.318, p < .01$		

[a]From O'Malley, P. M. (1972) based on secondary analysis of
data from the study by Bachman, *et al* (1967) of *Youth in Transition* at Survey Research Center, Institute for Social Research,
with his permission.

[b]There is no *a priori* basis for ordering these two groups
according to the inferred strength of Resultant Achievement
Motivation and so the convention of earlier work is followed
(Atkinson and Feather, 1966; Atkinson and Raynor, 1974).

positively related, as suggested by the simulation analysis reported in Table
2.3.

Most important of all the findings in O'Malley's secondary analysis of the
Youth in Transition data is solid evidence of the joint motivational impact
of achievement-related motives and Raynor's *future orientation* (Raynor,
1969, 1974a,b). The latter was measured in this study by simply asking
students, "How important do you think your high school grades are in
making your plans work out?" Students who responded, "Very important,"
are classified high in perceived instrumentality of education in Table 2.6.
The expected behavioral evidence of intensification of motivation, deduced
from Raynor's elaboration of the theory of achievement motivation, which
embraces distant as well as immediate expected consequences of an
activity, is quite obvious in Table 2.6. Among the most highly motivated
students, 58.6% continue their education past high school. Among the least
highly motivated students, only 27.1% do.

TABLE 2.5

*Analysis of Variance of Post-High School Education Including
n Achievement-Test Anxiety, a Quick Test of Intelligence
(Trichotomy), and Socioeconomic Status (Trichotomy)*[a]

Source	df	MS	F	% Variance Explained[c]	
n Ach-TA	3	1.81	8.53[b]	SES alone	14.9%
SES	2	25.13	118.36[b]	QT alone	9.2%
QT	2	5.13	24.17[b]	n Ach-TA alone	1.8%
SES × n Ach-TA	6	0.29	1.36	QT plus SES	17.6%
QT × n Ach-TA	6	0.19	0.89	QT plus SES plus n Ach-TA	17.8%
QT × SES	4	0.27	1.28		
QT × SES × n Ach-TA	12	0.11	0.53		
Error	1655	0.21			

[a]Based on O'Malley, 1972 with permission.

[b]$p < .01$

[c]The analysis of variance is nonorthogonal. The figures for percent variance explained are for additive models.

Academic Achievement in High School Related to "Intelligence" and Motivation as Measured in Sixth- and Ninth-Grade Boys

Guided by the analysis of the motivational determinants of intellective performance and cumulative achievement presented in Figure 2.2, Lens began to study the educational attainments of boys whose "intelligence" and achievement-related motivation had been measured during 1959–1962 as part of an earlier study of the motivational effects of ability grouping (Atkinson and O'Connor, 1963; and O'Connor, Atkinson and Horner, 1966). Some of the students who were sixth graders in 1959 have now had enough time to achieve a Ph.D., if so moved. This earlier sample contained 142 sixth-grade boys and 75 ninth-grade boys in a moderate sized, midwestern, university city for whom the complete high school transcript, including

TABLE 2.6

Percentage of a Representative Sample of Male Sophomores in Public High Schools in the United States in 1966 Who Went on to Some Form of Post-High School Education[a]

n Achievement-Test Anxiety	Perceived Instrumentality of Education			
	N	Low	N	High
High - Low	77	40.3%	285	58.6%
High - High[b]	133	34.0	307	55.0
Low - Low[b]	100	48.9	318	56.3
Low - High	144	27.1	370	45.1

[a]From O'Malley, P. M. (1973) based on secondary analysis of data from the study by Bachman, *et al* (1967) of *Youth in Transition*, with his permission.

[b]There is no *a priori* basis for ordering these two groups according to the inferred strength of Resultant Achievement Motivation and so the convention of earlier work is followed (Atkinson and Feather, 1966; Atkinson and Raynor, 1974).

overall grade point average, was available. The details of procedure and results, including also those for 76 other twelfth-grade boys is presented elsewhere (Lens and Atkinson, 1973).[6]

As the work progressed, we began to distinguish two cumulative effects of individual differences in motivation and to become much more strongly aware than previously of the interdependency of motivation and ability. We present Figure 2.6, an elaboration of Figure 2.2, as a more comprehensive conception to guide research on both motivational and developmental problems. Figure 2.6 distinguishes the observable cumulative effect of the product of a certain level of performance and time spent in the activity on the world, or environment, called achievement, and what must be some of the positively correlated cumulative effects on the self. The latter include *a*

---

[6] Since motivation was not measured until late in the spring of the year for the twelfth graders, and, therefore, *after* rather than *before* most of the achievements that enter into the criterion, there arises a legitimate question of comparability of conditions in the three classes. The results and issues involved in their interpretation are included in the full report. A parallel study of girls is in progress.

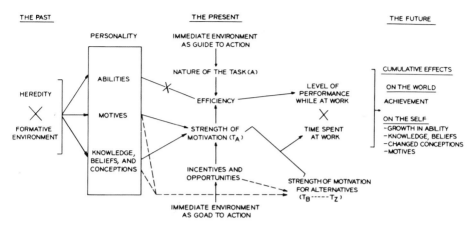

Figure 2.6 An elaboration of Figure 2.2 showing the role of motivation as a determinant of intellective performance and two distinguishable cumulative effects: achievement and growth in ability. (Based on Lens and Atkinson, 1973, with permission.) Here is assumed that the level of performance and time spent in a given activity (both influenced by motivation) provide the occasion for learning, a growth in ability, and other changes in personality.

growth in true ability, an increase and/or change in knowledge, beliefs, and conceptions, and perhaps even some change in those relatively general motives, which we have long tended to view as the enduring aspects of the basic personality structure acquired early in childhood (see, e.g., McClelland, 1951, 1958). In particular, it became obvious that even if *true ability* and the typical *strength of motivation* for a particular kind of activity were originally independent (as presumed in our earliest computer simulations of achievement), the influence of motivation on time spent in the activity should ultimately produce a positive correlation between these two factors, as assumed earlier in Table 2.3. This says no more, as an hypothesis about development of ability, than "Practice makes perfect!" There is some point to paying attention in class, to reading the homework assignments, to studying for exams, and so on. Whatever the genetic potential, the person who is highly motivated to engage in academic work (for whatever combination of reasons) should, in time, develop a higher level of true ability than one who is comparable in genetic potential but less highly motivated to spend time in the critical educational activities.

If the differential grades assigned by high school teachers sensitively reflect real observed differences in academic achievement that are attributable in part to the time spent in academic work, they should, at the same time, be indicative of the cumulative effect of this time spent on the self—the cumulative level of ability. Achievement and self-actualization are two sides of the same coin.

Once we have seen that ability or talent can be the egg produced by motivation, the chicken, the other possible interaction comes to mind, not only as equally plausible but perhaps even more basic since it would occur very early in life! Genetic differences in potential ability may influence the development of achievement-related motivation (see Feld, 1967; Veroff, 1965; C. P. Smith, 1969: Chapter 9, pp. 220–247) when a child is reared in a society that values achievement highly, and this value is repeatedly mediated by positive reactions of parents, peers, and teachers to early manifestations of talent (success) and by negative reactions to early instances of incompetence (failure). The earliest manifestations of differential competence must be largely the consequence of genetic differences in ability or potential to develop ability with practice (when, but only when, opportunity to practice is equal). In addition to early social reinforcements and disappointments that function as punishments, we are inclined to agree with Woodworth (1918) and White (1959), among others, who have argued that ability produces its own motivation *where there is opportunity for an individual to discover and exercise it.* This would be mediated by the intrinsic satisfaction accompanying any competent exercise of skill (e.g., standing up for the first time, walking across the room the first time) and the intrinsic annoyance and emotional outburst that typically accompanies frustration, the inability to do something when one has tried. These, along with the social reinforcements and punishments representing the societal imprint during early childhood, can become the foundation of what we have called an achievement motive (the spur to achieve) and a motive to avoid failure (the source of anxiety and resistance).

Thus, we arrive, by two different lines of argument, at the conclusion that, in time, the ability to do something and the strength of inclination to do it should be positively related. It is not a new idea. Kagan and Moss (1962:151), after intensive analysis of the longitudinal data at Fels Institute asserted: "For certain populations, the IQ can serve as an index of achievement concern."

To acknowledge that ability and motivation are both antecedent and consequence of each other is not to say that they represent a single variable or that they are functionally equivalent in their effects. Rather, it leads to the kind of computer simulation undertaken by Lens and reported in Table 2.3, which combined the hypothesis of a linear relationship of .52 between normal strength of motivation and ability with the hypothesis of an inverted U-shaped relationship between strength of motivation and efficiency of performance. This means that our general theoretical expectation in the study of the effects of strength of motivation on level of intellective performance (e.g., an intelligence test) should correspond neither to Graph A of Figure 2.7, nor to Graph B, but rather more to Graph C. If individual differences in motivation are relatively stable, then the effects of differences in time spent (practice) on ability should be cumulative and, therefore, more apparent later than earlier in the life of an individual.

Only among the most intensely motivated persons may evidence of a performance decrement attributable to overmotivation typically be evident. That is where we have been finding it in experiments with college students

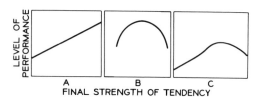

Figure 2.7 A positive but nonmonotonic function (Graph C) should typically describe the effect of strength of motivation on intellective performance after considerable opportunity for learning (if motivation influences efficiency of performance as presumed [Graph B] and growth of ability as now presumed [Graph A]) because of its positive effect on time spent in activity that affords the opportunity for learning. Linear correlations between level of intellective performance and strength of motivation are, therefore, not truly descriptive of the nature of the relationship.

that take advantage of both experimental manipulation of situational incentives for achievement and approval combined with the use of measures of individual differences in strength of three critical motives—to achieve, to gain social approval, to avoid failure. This yields a greater range of differences in strength of motivation than is possible in results to be reported here (Atkinson, 1974a).

Simply the effort to find a relationship between motivation, measured in sixth graders, and academic performance in high school implies assumptions: (*a*) that the crudely measured individual differences in motivation are, like the more adequately measured individual differences in intellective performance (called intelligence), relatively stable over a substantial period of time, and (*b*) that motivation does have the kinds of effects on efficiency of performance, time spent, and growth in ability that we have proposed.

Atkinson and O'Connor (1963: 22–29) present evidence of the relative stability of *n* Achievement, Test Anxiety, and resultant achievement motivation (*n* Achievement-Test Anxiety) from ninth to twelfth grade among boys using the conventional measures of motivation on the two occasions. The positive results, showing effects of resultant achievement motivation of sixth-grade boys on grade point average in three years of high school, are shown in Table 2.7 and of ninth-grade boys in Table 2.8. Both tend to lend additional support to the presumption that individual differences in both motivational and aptitudinal aspects of personality may be relatively stable over time.

As these tables are examined, we remind the reader once again to distinguish between the basic science question and the technological question, as the magnitude of differences in high school GPA attributable to earlier measured motivation and earlier measured intellective performance (California Test of Mental Maturity) are compared.[7]

---

[7] It was possible to divide the larger sample of sixth graders (N = 142) into quartiles on both variables and to show statistically significant overall effects for both motivation and intellective test score on high school achievement in the analysis of variance (Lens and Atkinson, 1973). We confine our present discussion to highest and lowest thirds to allow comparison of sixth- and ninth-grade samples.

TABLE 2.7

High School G.P.A. as a Function of Resultant Achievement Motivation and California Test of Mental Maturity Score in Sixth Grade (N = 142 Boys)

California Test of Mental Maturity		Resultant Achievement Motivation				High-Low Difference
		Low	Medium	High	Total	
High	N	12	15	19	46	t = 2.02
	S.D.	.45	.66	.51	.57	p < .03[a]
	$\bar{X}$	2.92	3.25	3.30	3.18	df = 29
Medium	N	16	19	15	50	t = -0.14
	S.D.	.56	.66	.55	.60	p < .55
	$\bar{X}$	2.70	2.74	2.68	2.71	df = 29
Low	N	19	14	13	46	t = 0.80
	S.D.	.50	.55	.51	.53	p < .25
	$\bar{X}$	2.39	2.28	2.54	2.40	df = 30
Total	N	47	48	47	142	t = 2.11
	S.D.	.55	.73	.63	.65	p < .025
	$\bar{X}$	2.63	2.77	2.89	2.76	df = 92

[a] All probabilities based on one tail t tests of predicted differences (from Lens and Atkinson, 1973).

TABLE 2.8

High School G.P.A. as a Function of Resultant Achievement Motivation and California Test of Mental Maturity Score in Ninth Grade (N = 75 Boys)

California Test of Mental Maturity		Resultant Achievement Motivation				High-Low Difference
		Low	Medium	High	Total	
High	N	3	9	12	24	t = 1.99
	S.D.	.43	.53	.49	.55	p < .05[a]
	X̄	2.72	3.40	3.38	3.30	df = 13
Medium	N	7	7	12	26	t = 2.70
	S.D.	.58	.38	.37	.51	p < .01
	X̄	2.38	2.67	3.00	2.74	df = 17
Low	N	15	9	1	25	t = -0.54
	S.D.	.50	.22	.00	.42	p < .70
	X̄	2.04	2.09	1.75	2.04	df = 14
Total	N	25	25	25	75	t = 5.69
	S.D.	.57	.69	.55	.71	p < .0005
	X̄	2.21	2.72	3.13	2.69	df = 48

[a] All probabilities based on one tail t tests of predicted differences (from Lens and Atkinson, 1973).

In both sixth and ninth graders, a trichotomous classification of students on each variable produces evidence (in the cell frequencies) of a positive relationship between strength of motivation and intellective performance. It is stronger and more obviously statistically significant ($p < .001$) in the ninth graders, as would be expected if the motivationally determined differences in time spent (paying attention in class, studying, preparing papers, and so on), which we assume to cause a growth in ability, are cumulative.

In the sixth-grade sample (Table 2.7), the expected effect of differences in motivation measured in sixth grade on GPA in high school is statistically significant only among the highest third on the earlier measure of intellective performance. In the ninth-grade sample (Table 2.8), the expected effect is statistically significant for both the highest and middle third on intellective performance. Viewing the sixth- and ninth-grade samples as independent tests of essentially the same hypothesis, we come to a single conclusion concerning the positive effect of motivation on cumulative achievement at each level of "intelligence" by calculating the combined probability of the observed differences as prescribed by Winer (1971, p. 49) for this purpose. The results are given in Table 2.9.

Among those in the low third on the so-called test of mental maturity the combined p is less than .50, and so there is no basis for inferring that individual differences in motivation in sixth and ninth grades are related to cumulative achievement in high school. For the middle third on the test of "intelligence," the combined p is less than .05, and for the highest third on the test of intelligence, the combined p is less than .02.

The trend of these results, showing the effect of differences in strength of motivation on subsequent academic achievement first, and most obviously, among the most able third of students, is consistent with the presumption in Figure 2.6 that *level of intellective performance* (mainly attributable to ability according to Tables 2.2 and 2.3) and *time spent* (mainly attributable to motivation) combine multiplicatively to determine cumulative achievement. Given a relatively crude measure of gross differences in motivation (and the small size of the samples), a certain critical amount of ability is required to show any demonstrable effect of differential motivation. Three years later, given time for differential growth in ability to occur (as reflected in the obvious positive relationship between motivation and intellective performance among the ninth graders), those in the middle third have, apparently, also now achieved that critical amount of ability. There is no evidence of any motivational effect on academic achievement among the lowest third in relative ability.

There are still other theoretical bases for expecting the differential effects of individual differences in motivation to be least evident among the least able students. Those acquainted with the details of the early theory of achievement motivation (Atkinson and Feather, 1966) know that, according to its assumptions, the largest motivational effects should occur where

TABLE 2.9

Combined Probability of Independent, Observed Differences in High School Grade Point Average Attributable to Earlier, Extreme Differences in Resultant Achievement Motivation[a]

Among highest third in intellective performance

6th grade: 3.30 - 2.92 df = 29, t = 2.02, p < .03, U_i = 3.507

9th grade: 3.38 - 2.72 df = 13, t = 1.99, p < .05, U_i = 2.996

6th + 9th grades: χ^2 = 13.01, df = 4, p < .02

Among middle third in intellective performance

6th grade: 2.68 - 2.70 df = 29, t = -.14, p < .55, U_i = 0.598

9th grade: 3.00 - 2.38 df = 17, t = 2.70, p < .01, U_i = 4.606

6th + 9th grades: χ^2 = 10.41, df = 4, p < .05

Among lowest third in intellective performance

6th grade: 2.54 - 2.39 df = 30, t = .80, p < .25, U_i = 1.386

9th grade: 1.75 - 2.04 df = 14, t = -.54, p < .70, U_i = 0.357

6th + 9th grades: χ^2 = 3.49, df = 4, p < .50

---

[a]Following justification by Winer (1971, p. 49). ($\chi^2 = 2\Sigma U_i$, where $U_i = -\ln P_i$ (df = 2k)). From Lens and Atkinson (1973).

subjective probability of success is intermediate, the middle third on the measure of intelligence. This has been reported by Gjesme (1971) among students in Norway. Those also acquainted with Raynor's (1969, 1974a) elaboration of the theory, which also takes into account the intensifying motivational effects of seeing the present activity as instrumental to attainment of future goals, know that, *among those who do view schoolwork as instrumental to future goals, the effect of individual differences in strength of motives to achieve and to avoid failure should be most pronounced among those with a very high subjective probability of success,* the highest third on "intelligence," *and least evident where the subjective probability of success is low,* the lowest third on "intelligence" (see Raynor, 1974a:134–136).

Both the earlier and the more recently elaborated theory agree that observed effects of individual differences in strength of motives should be small when probability of success is low, the lowest third on "intelligence." In addition, our results show no significant effect in that subgroup. Since we had no evidence of which students did and which did not see schoolwork as having important implications for them, we were unable to divide the subjects on that basis. The overall pattern of results implies, however, that Raynor's *future orientation* is fairly common among the students of this midwestern city, for the motivational effect is most consistently present among those who would have the highest subjective probability of success. Closer analysis suggests that only the brightest sixth graders see the relevance of schoolwork to their futures. By ninth grade, they are joined by those who are moderately bright. The last to discover this, and thus to profit or lose by its accentuation of their characteristic achievement-related motivation, are the least bright students.[8]

The relationship between intellective performance in sixth and ninth grades and GPA in high school is about twice as large as the GPA differences attributable to the measure of individual differences in motivation. We have presented two arguments explaining why this should typically be the case in contemporary educational research. First, we have argued theoretically that the intellective performance, typically called a test of ability or intelligence, represents a confounding of true ability (influenced in part by the role of motivation as a determinant of time spent in an activity and hence cumulative growth of ability) and the effect of motivation on efficiency of performance at the time of the test. Second, we have urged the reader to distinguish between the *basic science question,* the one that deals in ideal terms with the nature of the underlying processes, and what should be expected if we had perfectly reliable measurement from the *technological question,* how advanced and refined (i.e., reliable) is measurement (or techniques of control) today of intellective performance, cumulative achievement (when GPA is its index), and motivation. We have argued that the two basic questions are confounded in every empirical result and have suggested, as is commonly believed, that our technology regarding human motivation lags way behind our technology regarding intellective performance. It is, of course, our hope that the theoretical advance based on motivational research using crude tools is an unavoidably persuasive argument for theory-guided developmental research in the technology of motivation, namely, measurement of individual differences and control of environmental factors having motivational impact.

The Unification of Psychology

Now that the psychology of human motivation has something coherent to say about the determinative role of motivation and its interactions with

---

[8] Lens and Atkinson (1973) report a significant positive relationship between strength of resultant motivation to achieve (taken in May of twelfth grade) and GPA in high school among those in the lowest third on the California Test of Mental Maturity administered in ninth grade.

ability, it can provide a guide for the unification of the two traditionally isolated disciplines of scientific psychology (Cronbach, 1957). It forces us to recognize that the level of intellective performance is not merely a matter of ability, that all of the assumptions of traditional psychometrics (e.g., the constancy required to allow repeated measurements to achieve an estimate of reliability of measurement; the idea of exact replication of conditions; the logic of the normal curve of distribution) constitute a theory of behavior, not some special set of rubrics to govern all psychological inquiry. The approach of traditional psychometrics, like any other theory in science, must be judged ultimately in terms of its heuristic value. Now it must confront alternative theory in its own bailiwick—intellective performance and achievement—and it must confront the computer's capacity to deal with the implications of theoretical assumptions (guesses) about very complex but *systematic* behavioral processes that previously had to be assigned to that hodgepodge conceived as normally distributed error variance. It must confront the computer's capacity to deal with systematic changes in the motivational state and in the stream of behavior of an individual, through which the relatively constant attributes of personality are expressed.

Continued conceptual and experimental analysis of the achievement-oriented performance we are so used to calling a test of ability, with equal emphasis on the role of individual differences in personality dispositions and refinement of diagnostic tests of them, and on the impact of the immediate environment and the interaction between the two, as implied in $B = f(P, E)$, holds the promise of a unified psychology embracing both "personality" and "process."

Immediate Next Steps

We have both adequate diagnostic tests of individual differences in motivation and the possibility of realistic control of environmental conditions to study the effect of intensity of motivation on efficiency of performance as a function of the nature and requirements of the task empirically and definitively. This could conceivably result in a method of inferring the strength of an individual's motivation from the pattern or profile of his levels of performance on different types of intellective tasks. (Consider again the implications of Figure 2.5.)

The whole problem of assessing the determinative role of motivation for other time-consuming activities has been much neglected in the effort to study the effects of motivation on academic achievement. Time, like money, cannot be spent twice. The study of this problem should include not only positive interests in other time-consuming activities but also motivational factors (e.g., the effects of frustration, previous failure, deprivation) that are the source of time spent in covert activities that are incompatible with productive work (e.g., fantasy, continued self-appraisal and analysis, and so on).

Among the components of achievement-related motivation that have been identified and whose effects have been studied, the future orientation identified by Raynor (1969, 1974a,b), as a basis for his elaboration of the theory of achievement motivation, seems most promising for immediate applications. It is easily diagnosed and can, we think, be explicitly taught.

III | Abilities and Environments[*]

Trevor Williams
National Institute of Education

This investigation is concerned with the development and estimation of models explaining children's intellectual variability. Specifically, attention is directed to:

1. the role of parental status attainments and family environments in the transmission of intellectual advantage–disadvantage across generations;
2. the possibility that children's abilities affect the nature of the environment to which they are exposed; and
3. the dimensionality of family environment as a prerequisite to (1) and (2).

In order to quantify the arguments of (1) and (2) respectively, an attempt is made to develop models with the same basic configuration as Figures 3.1 and 3.2.

[*] The opinions expressed in this publication do not necessarily reflect the position, policy, or endorsement of the National Institute of Education.

An earlier version of this paper was presented at the annual meetings of the American Sociological Association, 1973.

61

Background

Ability Models

For the most part, attempts to explain intellectual variability among children fall into two broad categories: (*1*) "behavioral genetics" models utilizing naturally occurring controls over heredity and/or environment to estimate the proportions of phenotypic variability (variability in IQ scores) attributable to genetic variability (see, for example, Vandenberg, 1971); and (*2*) "social science" models that conform to what Eckland (1971:66) calls "the standard deprivation model of social class and intelligence," and that link parental status attainments, family environments, and children's abilities in obvious ways (see, for example, Bernstein, 1961; Whiteman and Deutsch, 1968). The latter category of models is the specific concern of this investigation, and Figure 3.3 outlines the basic relationships involved.

These "standard deprivation models" appear to be subject to a serious

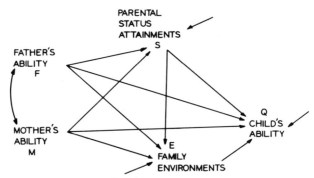

Figure 3.1 Inheritance of abilities: Attainments and environments as intervening variables.

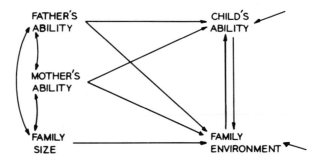

Figure 3.2 Inheritance of abilities: Mutual influence of family environment and child's ability.

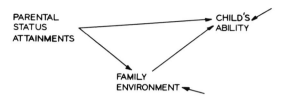

Figure 3.3 The "standard deprivation model of social class and intelligence." [From B. K. Eckland, "Social class structure and the genetic basis of intelligence," in R. Cancro (Ed.), *Intelligence: Genetic and environmental influences* (New York: Grune and Stratton, 1971), p. 66. Reprinted by permission of Grune and Stratton, Inc.]

specification error. ("When one has mistakenly either omitted or included variables in an equation assumed to capture the true causal structure to Y, or when the functional form chosen to represent the variables is incorrect, we say one has made a specification error [Bohrnstedt and Carter, 1971:128].") The error in question is the former and stems from the omission of parental abilities as antecedents to all variables in these models. (Errors of the second type are also a possibility—e.g., the failure to consider multiplicative and/or higher order terms—but are not a major concern of this investigation.)

Evidence from two sources supports this contention. First, there is a substantial behavioral genetics literature pointing to the direct effect of parental abilities on children's abilities via the biological mechanisms of inheritance. See, for example, Jensen's review (Jensen, 1969). Second, the literature on social stratification clearly implicates parental abilities as important causes of (parental) social and economic attainments. The work of Duncan, Featherman, and Duncan (1972) is a case in point. Less has been said about the effects of parental abilities on the nature of the family environment provided within the home, but what evidence there is suggests that the relationship is substantial. Burks (1928:286) reports parental ability–family environment correlations in the .6 to .7 range.

In terms of our understanding of those social processes contributing to children's intellectual variability, the consequences of this specification error are twofold. First, models linking family SES, family environments, and children's abilities, but failing to include (control for) parental abilities as antecedent variables, probably overestimate the importance of between-family differences in SES and family environments as causes of the variation in children's cognitive abilities (cf. the classic spurious correlation argument: Lazarsfeld, 1955; Blalock 1964:83). Second, such models ignore (a) the fact that intellectual advantage–disadvantage is transmitted from one generation to the next (Erlenmeyer–Kimling and Jarvik, 1963); and (b) the possibility that this occurs, at least in part, as a function of the variability in parental status attainments and family environments that accompanies parental intellectual variability. In other words, it seems likely that the parental ability–SES–family environment–child's ability linkages (apart from the direct parent–child ability effect) serve as an important social mechanism by which ability differences in one generation are passed on to the next. It follows that an explication of these linkages would provide a more comprehensive explanation of the reasons for children's intellectual variability.

The major concern of this investigation is the inheritance of ability via the latter set of biosocial (Heise, 1973:xiii) mechanisms, that is, the way in which intellectual advantage–disadvantage in the parental generation is transmitted to children via parental attainments and family environments. In terms of the relationships shown in Figure 3.1, these mechanisms are contained within the pattern of indirect effects of F and M on Q via S and E.

Heredity–Environment Covariance

Such concerns amount to an examination of some of the mechanisms contributing to the covariance of heredity and environment. Basically, the covariance argument is that more intelligent parents provide their children with "better" genes for intelligence—hence, greater intellectual potential—and "better" environments for the development of this potential, with the result that these children are doubly advantaged (Jensen, 1969:38; Jencks, Smith, Acland, Bane, Cohen, Gintis, Heyns, and Michelson, 1972:69). The second aspect of this double advantage (or double disadvantage)—the way in which parental abilities contribute to environments and thus to children's abilities—is at issue here.

There is, however, more to the covariance argument than this. It is conceivable that doubly advantaged children have a greater capability to affect the environment to their own cognitive advantage than do doubly disadvantaged children (Jensen, 1969:38). As a result, children of intellectually advantaged parents may have a *triple advantage:* "better" genes, "better" environments, and "better" control over the environments to which they are exposed. In this investigation, models are developed to test the latter proposition by allowing children's abilities and family environments to be simultaneously determined. Such a situation is shown in Figure 3.2, where the child's ability affects, and is affected by, the family environment.

The Nature of Family Environments

Over and above these issues, it seems that models of this sort suffer from an additional handicap. Our understanding of the specific mechanisms by which family environments affect children's cognitive development is rather limited. Shulman (1970:374) comments on this point: "Social scientists are dramatically impotent in their ability to characterize environments." He also points to the need to move away from unidimensional deprived–enriched conceptions of environments toward a multidimensional view: "characterizing the *educationally-relevant* facets of environments should be one of the major goals of educational research." [1]

Attempts to characterize the nature of family environments in terms of their effects on intellectual development fall into three broad categories.

1. *Gross indicators of environmental quality.* Such attempts amount to characterizing family environments as advantaged–disadvantaged or enriched–deprived according to the social, economic, ethnic, and other statuses of parents. Unidimensional models of this sort are of limited value for an understanding of the nature of family environment influence.

2. *Specific structural and process characteristics.* Studies linking specific aspects of family structure and/or process to children's abilities abound in the child development literature. On the whole, this accumulation of data lacks a unifying theoretical structure, and, as early as 1960, Hoffman and Lippitt (1960:978) noted the need for a conceptualization of "more genotypic psychological variables which capture the more general and underlying meanings of child-rearing practices."

3. *Broad dimensions of environmental influence.* Most systematic attempts to develop models and measures of the "genotypic" dimensions of these environments have followed a single tradition established by Dave (1963) and Wolf (1964). These models of family environments have been widely accepted (Dyer, 1967; Mosychuk, 1969; Weiss, 1969; Marjoribanks, 1972b; Linnan and Airasian, 1974). They postulate a multidimensional model in which the genotypic variables are "environmental presses" for specific categories of behavior, such as "language," "independence," "achievement," and the like. However, a recent examination of these "press" models and their data bases by Williams (1974) suggests that they are without much theoretical or empirical support. In fact, there are firm indications that a social learning theory model—involving stimulus, reinforcement, and expectation components—is more consistent with the data provided by these investigators.

The family environment model adopted for the present investigation is based on Williams' (1974) arguments and is organized around the basic concepts of social learning theory. Thus, the postulated major dimensions of family environments are as follows:

a. the stimuli parents provide by specifically structuring opportunities for the child to interact with a wide variety of people and things in his environment;

b. the reinforcement practices parents use to modify the child's performance on intellectually-relevant (i.e., school-related) behaviors; and

---

[1] Shulman, Lee S., "Reconstruction of educational research." *Review of Educational Research*, June 1970, Vol. 40, No. 3, pp. 374, 375. Copyright 1970, American Educational Research Association, Washington, D.C.

c. the expectations they hold out for appropriate performance on these behaviors.

Bijou (1971) argues for a similar model of these environments.

Data

Sample

The basic parameters of the sample were determined prior to this investigation. Measures of parental status attainments, family environment, and child's IQ, obtained by Mosychuk (1969) from a group of 100 families (original data set) were made available as the basis for the present investigation. This data set was extended by contacting the same families again and obtaining parental IQ measures (extended data set).

The original data set was based on a group of 100 families living in a major city in western Canada (population about 500,000). In designing the sampling frame, demographic data on income, education, and occupation were used to identify two areas in the city, one with predominantly low SES households, the other containing largely high SES households. Families with male children in grade four (approximately 10 years old) were contacted randomly until 50 from each area agreed to participate in the investigation.

The second contact with these families produced the extended data set. Of the original 100 families, 91 were contacted, 5 rejected further involvement at the outset, and another 14 were lost during the 9-month data collection period. IQ data on both parents were obtained for 55 of the remaining 72 families, for the mother only in a further 12, and for the father only in 2 households. Three sets of parent IQ data were unacceptable, leaving a total of 69 families in the extended data set with IQ measures on at least one parent.

The issue of sample representation was unimportant for Mosychuk's purposes but is a matter of concern for the present investigation. The accuracy of inferences about the postulated biosocial population processes contributing to intellectual variability among children depends heavily on the precision of the population sample. Attempts were made to evaluate, where possible, this sampling precision with respect to the major variables at issue, with the exception of family environment for which population data are unavailable.

An examination of the distribution of parental occupations in the sample allows some inferences about sampling on SES. The occupational distribution for households in the original data set is weighted toward professional and managerial occupations on the one hand and toward craftsman and unskilled occupations on the other. Occupations in the middle SES range (clerical, sales, service, transportation, primary industries) are underrepresented as a function of the sampling procedure used. When SES scores are assigned to occupations (Blishen, 1967), the resulting distribution of sample scores is rectangular. Comparisons with census data for the city in question show significant distributional differences when the full range of occupational categories is used. Comparisons based on a gross blue collar–white collar dichotomy, however, shows no significant differences and indicate a fairly adequate sampling of the major occupational groups, if not of the range of occupations.

The IQ distributions for fathers, mothers, and children in the sample all show degrees of negative skew but none deviate significantly from normality. Each distribution, however, shows a mean score some four-fifths to one standard deviation above the population mean of 100.

Clearly there are problems with the sample that make population inferences quite tentative. At least three characteristics of the sample make such inferences problematic. The first and most serious of these derives from the rectangular SES distribution. Because of this peculiar distribution, SES variance in the sample has been inflated to approximately twice that of the population (Blishen, 1967:53). The effects of this abnormality are discussed at a later point, where they present problems in the data analysis.

The second sample characteristic concerns the IQ distributions. While the shape of these distributions has not been seriously affected by the sampling procedures, the means have. All three distributions—fathers, mothers, children—have means well above their expected values, pointing to a sampling of the upper part of the IQ distribution in the population.

A third problematic characteristic of the sample is its size. For the most part, the nature of the population processes shown in the various models will be inferred from partial regression coefficients. With the present sample size of 100 or less, the standard errors of these coefficients will be quite large and their quantitative meaning less certain as a consequence. All three sampling issues serve to make the interpretations of the findings both qualitative and tentative.

Measurement

Ability measures were the WISC and WAIS (Wechsler, 1949, 1955) for children and parents respectively. Parental status attainments were obtained from mother's reports of parental education and occupation and from parent reports on income for the previous year. Family environment data took the form of a detailed interview with the mother in each family in which some 200 separate ratings of reported parental behaviors were made. The family environment instrument was similar to those cited earlier and grouped these 200 ratings into 59 separate behavioral indices. See Mosychuk (1969) for details.

Preliminary Analyses: The Structure of Variables

In these analyses, the raw data on parent and child ability, and the environment data are reduced to theoretically more meaningful and parsimonious dimensions. The principal technique is factor analysis.

Family Environment

The environmental model developed in this investigation is multidimensional. The dimensions hypothesized are dictated by the argument that family environments can be seen more profitably from a social learning theory perspective with major dimensions involving expectations, stimuli, and reinforcements as the broad categories of behaviors that vary between families.

The 59 family environment indices developed by Mosychuk (1969) provided the means to test these arguments. Most of these indices are aggregate measures, the mean of several items each rated on a 7-point scale. For example, see item 12 and the appropriate rating scales in the appendix. After an examination of all 59 indices, 14 were disaggregated into their constituent sub-items (58 in all) because of apparent heterogeneity in content. Item 12 in the appendix provides an example of this heterogeneity. It contains both stimulus and expectation components among the 5 sub-items. This procedure produced a total of 103 apparently homogeneous family environment items.

In order to deal with these effectively in a factor analysis, their number was reduced by some preliminary aggregations of items considered to measure the same aspect of parental behavior. Following these aggregations, a number of factor analyses were undertaken to clean up the correlation matrix by eliminating obviously irrelevant variables. These two actions served to reduce the number of family environment variables to 26. The makeup of these variables is specified in Table 3.2 and detailed in the appendix, which reproduces the pertinent items from Mosychuk's family environment measure, along with the rating scales used to score each item. The correlations among these 26 items are shown in Table 3.1.

A principal factor solution of this matrix was rotated obliquely and the resultant factor pattern is shown in Table 3.2.

The four factors extracted were interpreted as follows:

1. *Factor I* is a *stimulus* factor reflecting the extent to which parents specifically structure opportunities for the child to interact with people and things in his environment.
2. *Factor II* is a *parental dominance* factor dealing with the relative dominance of one or the other parent in child-rearing. The signs of the loadings indicate a "father involvement" interpretation of the factor as it stands. This factor reflects Mosychuk's (1969) extension of traditional "environmental press" models to include the parental

TABLE 3.1

Correlation Matrix for the Twenty-six Family Environment Variables[a]

	2	3	4	5	6	7	8	9	10	11	12	13	14	15	16	17	18	19	20	21	22	23	24	25	26	Mean	St. Dev.
1	.12	.34	.37	-.10	-.01	-.14	.23	.34	.47	.20	-.07	-.04	.11	.38	.08	-.07	-.10	.04	.32	.28	.22	.27	-.07	.31	-.18	6.98	2.63
2		.10	.29	-.13	-.02	.12	.16	.24	.23	.07	.02	-.02	-.01	.21	-.10	-.20	.13	-.08	.14	.33	.07	.13	-.02	-.03	.34	59.84	15.83
3			.32	.05	-.23	-.14	.17	.09	.28	.34	.04	-.08	.02	.22	.14	.03	-.24	-.10	.33	.28	.15	.29	-.04	.24	-.00	62.65	28.42
4				-.13	-.02	-.13	.40	.14	.41	.16	-.15	-.17	-.04	.26	.01	-.09	-.15	-.21	.27	.38	.25	.19	-.09	.20	.02	43.19	12.59
5					.28	.06	-.35	-.12	-.09	.08	.38	.36	.36	-.16	.15	-.08	.01	.01	.02	-.11	-.02	-.10	.02	.11	-.08	8.48	3.69
6						-.03	-.12	.04	-.05	-.06	.14	.29	.34	-.01	.03	.06	-.02	-.06	.19	.31	.15	-.06	-.02	.11	-.08	17.05	3.79
7							-.22	-.07	-.16	.08	.05	.08	-.04	-.17	.13	.33	.35	-.07	.08	.29	.14	.05	.14	-.09	-.08	41.53	20.17
8								.26	.32	.07	-.29	-.44	-.20	-.35	-.05	-.13	-.13	.22	-.08	-.26	-.03	.15	.49	-.13	.22	3.91	1.47
9									.23	.03	-.37	-.24	-.04	.23	.18	-.12	-.05	.04	-.01	.22	.05	-.06	-.02	.11	-.11	5.15	.91
10										.19	-.16	-.26	.10	.33	.26	-.05	-.05	.05	.31	.38	.37	.07	-.15	-.08	.01	3.34	1.13
11											.05	.02	.21	.12	.03	.04	-.16	-.13	.06	.21	.08	.09	.11	.09	.12	4.22	1.32
12												.50	.24	-.12	.05	.03	.09	.01	.08	.01	-.06	.00	.06	-.08	-.21	2.40	1.42
13													.38	-.31	-.24	-.10	-.09	.04	-.08	-.26	-.03	-.15	.11	.09	-.11	3.79	1.23
14														-.12	.10	.06	.05	.03	.05	-.10	.14	.05	-.03	.31	-.19	4.82	1.06
15															.33	.06	-.02	-.06	.19	.31	.29	.15	-.03	.18	.06	3.55	1.55
16																.20	-.08	-.11	-.05	-.03	.14	.05	.14	.14	.11	3.79	1.02
17																	.24	.17	-.02	-.14	-.10	.14	.14	.14	.11	4.57	1.05
18																		.28	-.01	-.05	-.20	-.21	.45	-.08	.11	4.23	.79
19																			-.06	-.15	.06	.30	.21	-.15	.01	3.75	1.23
20																				.07	.27	.21	.01	.16	-.08	4.99	1.16
21																					.18	.26	-.13	.18	.07	3.98	1.08
22																						.25	-.01	.37	-.03	4.22	1.28
23																							-.10	.25	-.14	4.12	1.10
24																								-.17	.03	3.47	2.00
25																									-.03	40.64	13.10
26																										4.62	1.17

[a] See Table 3.2 for a description of each variable.

TABLE 3.2

Family Environment: Pattern Matrix From Oblique Rotation[a] Of Principal Factor Solution

Item[c]	Rotated Factor Loadings				h^2
	I	II	III	IV	
1. Concrete evidence that parents are concerned with the child's education (3 + 4)	.62	.05	.05	.02	.41
2. Parental encouragement for the child to engage in school-related activities (12c + 12d + 13 + 14c + 51a + 55d + 56d + 56e + 58(axb) + 59b)	.14	-.18	.06	.94	.87
3. Availability of school-related learning materials in the home (12a + 15a + 15b + 51((d + e) × c))	.54	.04	-.00	-.03	.30
4. Degree of child's exposure to learning material outside school (14a + 14b + 15f + 15g + 16 + 17 + 55a + 55b + 56a)	.48	.14	.13	.18	.36
5. Female dominance in child-rearing: I (26(a + b))	.06	-.57	-.09	-.04	.35
6. Female dominance in child-rearing: II (29(a + c + d))	-.01	-.38	.11	.02	.14
7. Use of physical punishment: I (46((a + b) × c))	-.07	-.11	-.66	.25	.53
8. Father's interest in child's school activities (8)	.28	.51	.10	.04	.40
9. Family interaction: I (19)	.17	.23	.10	.23	.19
10. Family interaction: II (20)	.64	.14	.01	.13	.49
11. Child's interaction with non-parent adults (23)	.40	-.11	-.10	.04	.16
12. Degree of father/child contact: I (24)[b]	.00	-.56	-.04	.03	.31
13. Degree of father/child contact: II (25)[b]	-.08	-.76	.03	.04	.58
14. Female dominance in child-rearing: III (28)	.28	-.59	.05	-.04	.41
15. Family interaction: III (31)	.43	.27	-.01	.09	.30
16. Parental concern over nature of child's interaction with environment (42)	.30	-.11	-.24	-.12	.15

TABLE 3.2 (continued)

Item[c]	Rotated Factor Loadings				h^2
	I	II	III	IV	
17. Use of physical punishment: II (44)	.07	.23	-.66	-.20	.47
18. Rigidity of rules for behavior: I (45)	-.17	-.02	-.37	.19	.22
19. Rigidity of rules for behavior: II (48)	-.04	.01	-.35	-.01	.12
20. Child's hobby activities (49)	.41	-.02	-.01	.02	.17
21. Parent/child interaction in hobby activities (50)	.39	.14	.10	.29	.33
22. Child's interaction with environment through outdoor activities (52)	.49	-.03	.01	-.03	.24
23. Provisions for exploration/independence at early age (53)	.38	.03	.21	-.03	.22
24. Child's fear of physical punishment (47b)	.04	-.04	-.69	-.01	.48
25. Rating of mother's language quality	.52	-.14	.10	-.11	.31
26. Variety in methods of encouragement to complete tasks (59c)	-.03	.11	-.19	.35	.19

Factor Correlations

I	.08	.17	.06
II		.09	.26
III			.02

[a] Direct oblimin with delta = 0 (Harman, 1967:334).

[b] Reversed scoring: high contact scored as 1,
low contact scored as 7.

[c] Item makeup shown in parentheses and keyed to Appendix.

71

dominance variables Vernon (1965) thought were important. See also Marjoribanks (1972b).

3. *Factor III* is a *reinforcement* dimension pertaining (for these data) to the use of physical versus nonphysical punishment by parents.

4. *Factor IV* is a parental *expectation* dimension concerned with the expectations and encouragement provided for the child's academic performance.

The factors emerging from these data support the social learning theory model proposed earlier and, in addition, reflect the peculiarities of this particular data set. The support comes from Factors I, III, and IV. The peculiarities are the emergence of a parental dominance factor, the limitation of the reinforcement factor to the use of physical or nonphysical punishment, and the relative weakness of the expectations factor. None of this is very surprising given that this environment measure was developed by Mosychuk from a different theoretical framework. Note, however, that the relatively small sample size raises some questions about the stability of these factor structures for the population. To some extent, these questions are answered and support is provided in Williams (1974) where a similar factor analysis of data from a different—and larger—sample of Australian families produced the same general configuration of factors.

Parent and Child Abilities

In each instance, these abilities were measured on the respective Wechsler intelligence scales. Conventional treatment of the data provides 11 sub-test scores for the WAIS and 12 for the WISC, along with aggregates of these as "verbal" and "performance" IQ and a grand aggregate "total" IQ.

The treatment of these data in the present investigation differs from this and is guided by existing notions about the hierarchical structure of intelligence (see Cattell, 1971); that is, the Wechsler sub-test scores are seen as indicators of more fundamental underlying abilities (primary mental abilities), which themselves are indicators of a still more fundamental general intelligence. Clearly, this is a second-order factor model, and the data here are treated accordingly.

Table 3.3 contains the correlations among the Wechsler scale sub-tests for both parents and children.

With the exception of the "mazes" sub-test in the WISC, the Wechsler child and adult scales appear to have 11 comparable sub-tests. Separate principal factor solutions of these 11 sub-test correlation matrices were obtained and the first two factors rotated obliquely. The resultant pattern matrices are shown in Table 3.4.

The factors look similar in both groups and approximate those generally found (Cohen, 1959; Wechsler, 1958; Guertin, Ladd, Frank, Rabin, and Heister, 1966). Factor I is the *verbal comprehension* factor, which always

TABLE 3.3

WISC and WAIS Sub-test Correlations: Children[a] and Parents[b]

Wechsler Scale Sub-tests	Information	Comprehension	Arithmetic	Similarities	Digit Span	Vocabulary	Coding	Picture Completion	Block Design	Picture Arrangement	Object Assembly	Mazes[c]	Mean	St. Dev.
Information		.55	.52	.56	.39	.52	.22	.39	.35	.16	.30	.16	11.30	2.66
Comprehension	.74		.31	.44	.25	.63	.28	.40	.36	.17	.16	.15	12.22	3.14
Arithmetic	.49	.39		.41	.23	.27	.08	.22	.28	.08	.14	.05	11.54	2.22
Similarities	.66	.64	.45		.17	.66	.23	.32	.36	.23	.41	.00	12.86	3.31
Digit Span	.41	.33	.36	.45		.25	.11	.24	.26	.11	.10	.03	9.96	2.32
Vocabulary	.82	.79	.45	.75	.47		.28	.42	.38	.23	.29	.03	12.58	3.22
Digit Symbol	.34	.39	.23	.42	.34	.40		.30	.26	.21	.34	.28	11.55	2.54
Picture Completion	.64	.60	.39	.54	.25	.60	.21		.38	.16	.21	.11	11.90	2.96
Block Design	.49	.46	.41	.42	.43	.51	.29	.48		.18	.44	.21	11.80	2.83
Picture Arrangement	.48	.43	.27	.43	.22	.50	.28	.58	.45		.20	.01	11.20	2.67
Object Assembly	.40	.42	.22	.37	.11	.32	.13	.41	.34	.42		.22	11.81	3.16
Mean	11.50	13.07	12.06	11.94	10.05	11.62	9.46	10.19	11.12	9.56	10.40	11.56		
St. Dev.	2.72	3.29	2.99	3.01	2.89	3.10	2.46	2.56	2.45	2.41	2.76	2.71		

[a]Children above the diagonal.

[b]Parents below the diagonal.

[c]Mazes sub-test omitted from analysis.

emerges, and Factor II is the common *nonverbal* ("perceptual organization") dimension of the Wechsler scales.

Rotations to congruence were attempted to evaluate the *apparent* similarity of these factorial structures (Evans, 1970). Rotating the WISC and WAIS structures in this way showed them to be exceedingly congruent

TABLE 3.4

Intellectual Abilities: Pattern Matrices from Oblique Rotations of Parent and Child Principal Factor Solutions

Wechsler Scale Sub-tests	I		II		h^2	
	Parents	Child	Parents	Child	Parents	Child
Information	-.64	-.84	-.33	-.03	.76	.68
Comprehension	-.56	-.64	-.34	.10	.67	.48
Arithmetic	-.46	-.60	-.13	-.11	.30	.30
Similarities	-.67	-.53	-.20	.28	.64	.52
Digit Span	-.64	-.42	.17	-.02	.31	.16
Vocabulary	-.74	-.58	-.22	.26	.78	.57
Digit Symbol	-.48	.01	.02	.53	.22	.27
Picture Completion	-.16	-.35	-.70	.27	.65	.30
Block Design	-.34	-.23	-.35	.46	.38	.38
Picture Arrangement	-.05	-.04	-.67	.32	.49	.12
Object Assembly	.04	.08	-.60	.70	.34	.43

Factor Correlations

Parents

		I	II
Child	I		.59
	II	-.55	

in their overall structure, implying that they measure the same underlying ability dimensions in both parents and children.

The two abilities in parents and children were considered to be first-level abilities and potential indicators of a more general underlying ability whose structure will be developed later. Measures of these first-level abilities were estimated as factor scores as outlined in Harman (1967, p. 350).

Estimation of Model Parameters

Here variables with the structures derived in the preceding section are incorporated into the conceptual frameworks shown in Figures 3.1 and 3.2. Using the correlations among these variables, model parameters are estimated via the methods of path analysis. (Path analysis is a generalization of multiple linear regression procedures to systems of causally related variables. Blalock, 1971, provides basic references.)

Models of the type proposed in this investigation necessitate an attempt to correct the obtained correlations for attenuation due to measurement error. Established ability measures of the sort used here are among the most valid and reliable measures of human behavior that exist. They are contrasted with family environment measures whose validity and reliability are almost certainly of a lower order. Hence, as a function of these differences in measurement precision, ability–ability correlations are most likely nearer their "true" values than any correlation involving an environment dimension. Thus, in assigning meaning to parameters derived from uncorrected correlations, one runs the risk of attributing substance to effects—and differences in effects—that may result from differential measurement error. In the case of these models, this could mean placing family environments at an explanatory disadvantage when environment measures are used with parental abilities to predict children's abilities.

Corrections for attenuation were undertaken by estimating the correlations among unmeasured variables from the correlations among their (multiple) indicators (Hauser and Goldberger, 1971; Werts, Jöreskog, and Linn, 1973). In the case of ability measures, the two first-level abilities were taken as indicators of an unmeasured general cognitive ability in fathers, mothers, and children. Each of the four family environment dimensions was treated as an unmeasured variable with three indicators, the three family environment items with the highest loading on each factor. Parental occupational, educational, and economic attainments only had single indicators, and corrections for attenuation were attempted by using a slightly different procedure that will be explained later.

The basic data for these procedures are the correlations among the 2 first-level abilities (factor scores) in fathers, mothers, and children, the 12 family environment items (3 for each of the 4 factors), and the 4 parental attainment measures, along with family size which is used in the reciprocal

TABLE 3.5

Correlation Matrix: Parental Status Attainments, Family Size, Parent and Child Abilities, and Family Environment Indicators

	S_1	S_2	S_3	S_4	N	F_1	F_2	M_1	M_2	Q_1	Q_2	E_1	E_2	E_3	E_5	E_7	E_{10}	E_{13}	E_{14}	E_{17}	E_{21}	E_{24}	E_{26}
S_1		.82	.68	.61	-.30	.57	.39	.59	.46	.40	.42	.57	.09	.26	-.22	-.24	.41	-.12	.15	-.26	.27	-.35	-.05
S_2	100		.71	.55	-.22	.68	.34	.53	.50	.39	.41	.52	.16	.20	-.21	-.26	.36	-.11	.09	-.23	.29	-.27	-.11
S_3	100	100		.58	-.28	.70	.40	.52	.29	.34	.29	.52	.20	.30	-.18	-.24	.40	-.08	.11	-.23	.30	-.37	.05
S_4	58	58	58		-.22	.45	.39	.36	.34	.25	.34	.25	.27	.09	-.03	-.29	.28	-.05	.23	-.38	.31	-.27	-.00
N	100	100	100	58		.03	-.07	-.15	-.05	-.19	-.24	-.42	-.11	-.40	.08	.20	-.27	-.09	-.12	.20	-.24	.28	.13
F_1	57	57	57	58	57		.63	.49	.43	.32	.26	.21	.22	-.04	-.11	-.14	-.01	-.06	-.08	-.08	-.11	.19	.22
F_2	57	57	57	58	57	57		.41	.39	.33	.36	.22	.05	.12	-.08	-.13	.31	.37	.31	-.05	.16	-.21	.20
M_1	67	67	67	58	67	57	57		.72	.36	.20	.38	.08	.18	-.08	-.00	.30	.30	.36	-.11	-.11	-.14	.14
M_2	67	67	67	58	67	57	57	67		.07	.04	.42	.03	-.08	-.16	.11	.04	.04	-.04	.33	-.04	.49	.01
Q_1	100	100	100	58	100	57	57	67	67		.66	.42	.08	.18	-.16	.11	.44	-.17	-.08	-.09	.16	-.10	-.01
Q_2	100	100	100	58	100	57	57	67	67	100		.42	.12	.18	-.14	-.06	.42	-.04	-.07	-.20	.28	-.12	.06
E_1	91	91	91	53	91	52	52	61	61	91	91		-.05	-.08	-.16	.14	.47	.08	.02	.03	.28	.21	-.18
E_2	91	91	91	53	91	52	52	61	61	91	91	91		.34	.05	-.14	.23	-.08	-.01	.03	.33	-.04	.34
E_3	91	91	91	53	91	52	52	61	61	91	91	91	91		-.00	.06	.28	-.36	.02	-.08	.28	-.04	-.00
E_5	91	91	91	53	91	52	52	61	61	91	91	91	91	91		-.14	.09	.09	-.08	-.08	-.11	.21	-.08
E_7	91	91	91	53	91	52	52	61	61	91	91	91	91	91	91		-.16	.08	.36	.33	.28	.49	.22
E_{10}	91	91	91	53	91	52	52	61	61	91	91	91	91	91	91	91		-.16	-.04	-.05	.33	-.00	.13
E_{13}	91	91	91	53	91	52	52	61	61	91	91	91	91	91	91	91	91		.38	-.10	-.26	-.14	-.11
E_{14}	91	91	91	53	91	52	52	61	61	91	91	91	91	91	91	91	91	91		-.08	-.10	-.08	-.19
E_{17}	91	91	91	53	91	52	52	61	61	91	91	91	91	91	91	91	91	91	91		-.14	-.13	.07
E_{21}	91	91	91	53	91	52	52	61	61	91	91	91	91	91	91	91	91	91	91	91		.45	.11
E_{24}	91	91	91	53	91	52	52	61	61	91	91	91	91	91	91	91	91	91	91	91	91		.03
E_{26}	91	91	91	53	91	52	52	61	61	91	91	91	91	91	91	91	91	91	91	91	91	91	

TABLE 3.5 (continued)

NOTES: Correlation coefficients appear above the diagonal; figures appearing below the diagonal indicate the case base for each correlation coefficient. Correlation coefficients underlined are not significantly different from zero at the .05 level of confidence (two-tail test).

Key to the symbols used: S_1 = father's occupational prestige; S_2 = father's education; S_3 = mother's education; S_4 = family income; N = family size; F_1, M_1, Q_1 = verbal factor in fathers, mothers and children respectively; F_2, M_2, Q_2 = non-verbal factor in fathers, mothers and children respectively; E_1 to E_{26} = indicators of family environment dimensions shown in Table 3.2.

effects model (Figure 3.2). Table 3.5 contains these correlations and the case base for each.

"Double-Advantage" Models

Estimation of the "true" correlations among the unmeasured variables was undertaken as follows. (See Jöreskog, 1970, for the mathematical basis of the procedures used and Jöreskog, Gruvaeus, and van Thillo, 1970, for the computer program.) A factor model was specified in which the indicators of each unmeasured variable loaded on that variable (factor) and on no other variable. F_1 and F_2 loaded on F (father's ability), M_1 and M_2 loaded on M (mother's ability), Q_1 and Q_2 loaded on Q (child's ability), E_1, E_3, and E_{10} defined E_1 (the stimulus dimension of family environments), E_5, E_{13}, and E_{14} defined E_2 (the parental dominance dimension), E_7, E_{17}, and E_{24}, loaded on E_3 (reinforcement), and E_2, E_{12}, and E_{26}, loaded on E_4 (expectations).

Each of the parental attainment indicators, the S_i, defined a single factor. To allow for measurement error in this instance, the loading of each S_i on its respective factor was constrained to an estimate of the validity of the indicator (i.e., the correlation of the indicator with the factor). These estimates were obtained as the square root of the reliability coefficients reported by Siegel and Hodge (1968:37) for U.S. census data. This factor model is shown in Table 3.6.

Maximum-likelihood estimates of the correlations among these factors are taken as estimates of the true correlations among the ability, environment, and attainment variables, the F, M, Q, E_i, and S_i.

The "true" correlations estimated in this way pose two problems for subsequent model estimation procedures. First, the four parental SES measures—father's occupation, father's education, mother's education, and family income—are highly correlated with correlations ranging from .61 to .91. Because of this excessive collinearity among the SES components, attempts to estimate their separate effects (as partial regression coefficients) on family environments and children's abilities are rendered meaningless. Second, the "true" correlations of the four SES components with the parental ability measures are correspondingly high, ranging from .4 to greater than .7. As a result, meaningful estimates of the effects of parental abilities and parental status attainments on family environments and children's abilities are impossible within the one model. An alternative approach—specifying a single SES variable with the four components as indicators—does little to alter this situation as the SES–parental ability correlations obtained in this way are still exceedingly high at .7 and .9 for mothers and fathers respectively.

The source of the problem seems to be the peculiar SES distribution in the sample. Its rectangular nature results in a sizeable portion of the sample lying in the "tails" and, thereby, exerting a disproportionate effect on the various SES and SES–ability covariance terms (assuming the true

TABLE 3.6
*Hypothesized Oblique Factor Model: Father, Mother, and Child
Abilities, Family Environment Dimensions, Parental Status
Attainments*

Indicators	Factors										
	F	M	Q	E_1	E_2	E_3	E_4	S_1	S_2	S_3	S_4
F_1	f_1	0	0	0	0	0	0	0	0	0	0
F_2	f_2	0	0	0	0	0	0	0	0	0	0
M_1	0	m_1	0	0	0	0	0	0	0	0	0
M_2	0	m_2	0	0	0	0	0	0	0	0	0
Q_1	0	0	q_1	0	0	0	0	0	0	0	0
Q_2	0	0	q_2	0	0	0	0	0	0	0	0
E_1	0	0	0	e_1	0	0	0	0	0	0	0
E_2	0	0	0	0	0	0	e_2	0	0	0	0
E_3	0	0	0	e_3	0	0	0	0	0	0	0
E_5	0	0	0	0	e_5	0	0	0	0	0	0
E_7	0	0	0	0	0	e_7	0	0	0	0	0
E_{10}	0	0	0	e_{10}	0	0	0	0	0	0	0
E_{13}	0	0	0	0	e_{13}	0	0	0	0	0	0
E_{14}	0	0	0	0	e_{14}	0	0	0	0	0	0
E_{17}	0	0	0	0	0	e_{17}	0	0	0	0	0
E_{21}	0	0	0	0	0	0	e_{21}	0	0	0	0
E_{24}	0	0	0	0	0	e_{24}	0	0	0	0	0
E_{26}	0	0	0	0	0	0	e_{26}	0	0	0	0
S_1	0	0	0	0	0	0	0	.93	0	0	0
S_2	0	0	0	0	0	0	0	0	.97	0	0
S_3	0	0	0	0	0	0	0	0	0	.97	0
S_4	0	0	0	0	0	0	0	0	0	0	.94

NOTE: The f_i, m_i, q_i, and e_i represent factor loadings to be
estimated, while the zeros indicate hypothesized zero loadings.
S_i loadings constrained to validity coefficients shown.

NOTE: See Table 3.5 for definition of symbols.

relationship is bivariate normal). Scattergrams for these relationships show
narrow, elongated distributions, suggesting that disproportionate numbers
in the tails of the SES distribution may have inflated the correlations in
questions by "stretching out" the true bivariate normal form of the

relationships. In any event, the correlations among the SES components, and the SES–parental ability correlations exceed those usually found (see Jencks *et al.,* 1972:337), and pose multicollinearity problems for model estimation that are next to insurmountable (Farrar and Glauber, 1967).

Since there is no obvious transformation function to deal with the SES distribution difficulties, the decision was made to delete the SES variables from the model. Clearly, the elimination of this important intervening variable reduces the potential knowledge gain of the investigation. It does, however, leave the major argument intact: If one assumes that most SES effects on ability are mediated by family environments, then the major heredity–environment covariation linkages are still present and subject to quantification. Thus, the investigation is reduced to models linking parent and child abilities directly and indirectly via family environments: in other words, Figures 3.1 and 3.2 with the parental status attainments deleted. In this form, the models represent something of a replication—the only one (Vandenberg, 1971:189)—of the Burks (1928) study, which has achieved some prominence as the only attempt to look at the nature–nurture issue using direct measures of family environments.

Table 3.7 presents the hypothetical factor structure specified for the ability–environment–ability model that is now central to the investigation, together with the results of this structure's quantification using the correlational data of Table 3.5.

The factor correlations were used subsequently to estimate the parameters of the model shown in Figure 3.4 via standard path analytic methods. (In the interests of simplicity, the factor structure of each unmeasured variable is not shown in the figure. One can see this quite easily though, using the information contained in Table 3.7. For example, the factor loading of F_1 on F can be taken as the path coefficient p_{F_1F}, the effect of F, the unmeasured variable, on its indicator F_1. The relationships of the remaining indicators to their factors are analogous to this.)

The interpretation of the environment dimensions in this model differs somewhat from that of the dimensions shown in Table 3.2. All factor loadings for the E_i in Table 3.7 are positive (see Table 3.2), with the result that E_1 is interpreted as a stimulus dimension as before. E_2 now measures the extent of father's *noninvolvement* in child-rearing (i.e., mother dominance in child-rearing), E_3 now indicates the degree to which reinforcement tends to be in the form of physical punishment, and E_4 indicates high expectations on the part of parents, as it did in Table 3.2.

A detailed discussion of this model follows in the next section of this paper, but two matters arising from the model deserve comment at this point. First, the overall influence of father's ability on that of the child appears to be mostly direct (compare r_{QF} with p_{QF}), while that of mother's ability appears to be mostly indirect. Second, two aspects of family environment influence run counter to expectation. Physical punishment appears as a mildly beneficial means of reinforcement ($p_{QE_3} = .16$), and

TABLE 3.7

Maximum-Likelihood Estimates of Factor Loadings and Factor Correlations for Ability-Environment-Ability Model: Separate Parental Abilities

| Indicators | Factors | | | | | | | Residual |
	F	M	Q	E_1	E_2	E_3	E_4	
F_1	.75	0	0	0	0	0	0	.66
F_2	.84	0	0	0	0	0	0	.54
M_1	0	1.00	0	0	0	0	0	.00
M_2	0	.72	0	0	0	0	0	.70
Q_1	0	0	.80	0	0	0	0	.60
Q_2	0	0	.83	0	0	0	0	.56
E_1	0	0	0	.63	0	0	0	.78
E_2	0	0	0	0	0	0	.59	.81
E_3	0	0	0	.38	0	0	0	.92
E_5	0	0	0	0	.37	0	0	.93
E_7	0	0	0	0	0	.57	0	.83
E_{10}	0	0	0	.78	0	0	0	.63
E_{13}	0	0	0	0	.99	0	0	.12
E_{14}	0	0	0	0	.39	0	0	.92
E_{17}	0	0	0	0	0	.52	0	.85
E_{21}	0	0	0	0	0	0	.58	.82
E_{24}	0	0	0	0	0	.88	0	.48
E_{26}	0	0	0	0	0	0	.34	.94
Factor Correlations								
F		.54	.43	.44	-.05	-.40	.62	
M			.42	.42	.38	-.20	.20	
Q				.70	-.21	-.14	.24	
E_1					-.25	-.20	.59	
E_2						.10	-.25	
E_3							-.11	

NOTE: See Table 5 for symbol definitions.

high parental expectations appear to inhibit cognitive performance (p_{QE_4} = −.51), other things being equal.

In behavioral genetics models that examine the inheritance of intelligence, one estimate of heritability is the regression of offspring IQ on mid-parent IQ. Eckland (1971:68), for example, adopts this formulation in his "simplified polygenic model of social class and intelligence." Something similar is possible in the present investigation by defining a single parental ability (P) with four indicators (F_1, F_2, M_1, M_2) the two first-level abilities of father and mother respectively. The estimation of this factor model is shown in Table 3.8.

The factor correlations estimated under these conditions were used to calculate the parameters of Figure 3.5, the analogue of Figure 4 but with a single *parental* ability rather than separate abilities for each parent. This model is discussed later in the chapter.

"Triple-Advantage Models

Both of the preceding models deal with the part of the covariance argument that states that intellectually advantaged parents provide better environments for the development of their (genetically advantaged) children, with respect to intelligence. The two following models consider the third aspect of the covariance argument, namely, that children doubly advantaged (disadvantaged) in this way have, in fact, a *triple* advantage (disadvantage) as a function of their varying capability to influence the environment to their own cognitive benefit.

In these models, only one aspect of family environments—the stimulus dimension, the opportunities that parents provide for interaction with people and things in the environment—is considered. In the model proposed, this environment dimension affects, and is affected by, the child's ability in a mutual influence relationship (see Figure 3.2), and both

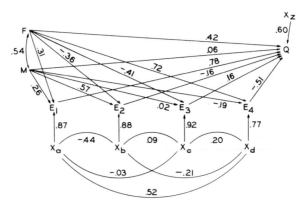

Figure 3.4 Causal model linking parent and child abilities across generations directly and indirectly via family environments: Separate parental abilities.

TABLE 3.8

Maximum-Likelihood Estimates of Factor Loadings and Factor Correlations for Ability-Environment-Ability Model: Single Parental Ability

| Indicators | Factors | | | | | | Residual |
	P	Q	E_1	E_2	E_3	E_4	
F_1	.56	0	0	0	0	0	.83
F_2	.51	0	0	0	0	0	.86
M_1	.92	0	0	0	0	,0	.39
M_2	.76	0	0	0	0	0	.65
Q_1	0	.79	0	0	0	0	.61
Q_2	0	.84	0	0	0	0	.55
E_1	0	0	.64	0	0	0	.77
E_2	0	0	0	0	0	.42	.91
E_3	0	0	.40	0	0	0	.92
E_5	0	0	0	.36	0	0	.93
E_7	0	0	0	0	.60	0	.80
E_{10}	0	0	.76	0	0	0	.65
E_{13}	0	0	0	1.0	0	0	.00
E_{14}	0	0	0	.38	0	0	.92
E_{17}	0	0	0	0	.57	0	.82
E_{21}	0	0	0	0	0	.77	.64
E_{24}	0	0	0	0	.81	0	.59
E_{26}	0	0	0	0	0	.20	.98

Factor Correlations

	P	Q	E_1	E_2	E_3	E_4	
P		.44	.41	.36	-.30	.28	
Q			.70	-.21	-.13	.27	
E_1				-.25	-.22	.63	
E_2					.09	-.30	
E_3						-.17	

NOTE: See Table 3.5 for definition of symbols.

variables are affected by parental abilities. Family size (N) is also included as an instrumental variable (Fisher, 1971), assumed to affect E_1 but not Q, the child's ability, directly. This assumption and the assumption that the disturbance terms for E_1 and Q are uncorrelated are necessary to render the system just-identified and, hence, capable of providing unique parameter estimates.

Table 3.9 presents the results of quantifying a hypothetical factor model incorporating F, M, Q, E_1, and N. Note that family size is a single indicator construct and that, for the purposes of this investigation, the measure was assumed perfectly valid with its factor loading constrained to 1.0.

Parameters for the model shown in Figure 3.6 were estimated from the factor correlations of Table 3.9 by the method of two-stage least squares (Duncan, Haller, and Portes, 1968). A quick look at the model indicates that it supports the argument that children's abilities affect the environment to which they are exposed. The model also points out the often documented negative effect of family size on ability, albeit an indirect effect here.

Table 3.10 and Figure 3.7 are the analogues of Table 3.9 and Figure 3.6, with the exception that father's and mother's ability are combined into a single parental ability as in the recursive models estimated above (Figures 3.4 and 3.5).

Discussion

The format of this discussion follows that of the preceding analyses. First, the way in which arguments about the structure of the ability and environment variables are supported by the data is considered. Second, the meaning of the estimated models for the heredity–environment covariance argument—the idea of a triple advantage or disadvantage—is examined. (Recall, however, that the peculiarities of the sampling framework and the

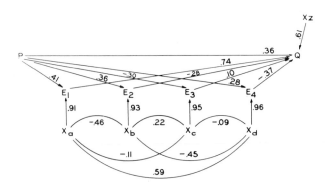

Figure 3.5 Causal model linking parent and child abilities across generations directly and indirectly via family environments: Single parental ability.

limited size of the sample make interpretations of the meaning of the findings qualitative at best.)

The Structure of Variables

1. *Ability.* Two clear and comparable ability dimensions appear to account for much of the covariation among the Wechsler scale sub-tests in

TABLE 3.9

Maximum—Likelihood Estimates of Factor Loadings and Factor Correlations for "Reciprocal Effects" Model: Separate Parental Abilities

Indicators	Factors					Residual
	F	M	Q	E_1	N	
F_1	.87	0	0	0	0	.50
F_2	.73	0	0	0	0	.68
M_1	0	1.00	0	0	0	.00
M_2	0	.72	0	0	0	.70
Q_1	0	0	.80	0	0	.60
Q_2	0	0	.83	0	0	.56
E_1	0	0	0	.73	0	.69
E_3	0	0	0	.45	0	.89
E_{10}	0	0	0	.65	0	.76
N	0	0	0	0	1.00[a]	.00
Factor Correlations						
F		.56	.42	.38	-.00	
M			.42	.44	-.15	
Q				.70	-.26	
E_1					-.56	

NOTE: See Table 3.5 for definition of symbols.

[a]Constrained to this value.

adults and children. The first of these is a verbal dimension identified by the predominantly verbal sub-tests (vocabulary, information, and so on), and the second is a nonverbal dimension on which such nonverbal tests as "block design" and "object assembly" load. This dimension is variously named "performance," "nonverbal," "space and visual motor organization," "perceptual organization," and sometimes "g." The term "nonverbal" ability is used here. (Other dimensions, sometimes derived as Factors III and IV in the Wechsler scales and identified respectively by the *digit span* and *digit symbol* sub-tests, were considered in this investigation. However, because these two factors have consistently presented problems in interpretation when found, and because they are not always found (Cohen, 1959), they were abandoned for the purposes of this investigation.)

An evaluation of the apparent similarity of both of these two-factor solutions—by rotating them to maximally congruent structures—indicated that they were, in fact, comparable dimensions in parents and children. The point of this, of course, was to ensure that the subsequent analyses were examining the transmission of the *same* abilities across generations and not, for example, the effect of verbal abilities in parents on nonverbal abilities in children.

The theoretical considerations that guided these analyses supported a hierarchical structure of intellectual abilities in which the two first-level

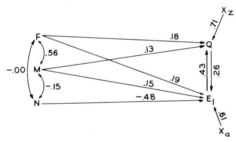

Figure 3.6 Causal model allowing for reciprocal influence between child's ability and one dimension of family environment: Separate parental abilities.

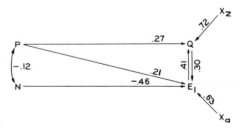

Figure 3.7 Causal model allowing for reciprocal influence between child's ability and one dimension of family environment: Single parental ability.

abilities identified in parents and children—verbal and nonverbal—explained the covariation among the respective Wechsler scale sub-tests. Subsequently, a higher order general ability (an unmeasured variable) was postulated as a cause of the covariation among these two abilities, its indicators.

2. *Family Environment.* Three major dimensions to family environments

TABLE 3.10

Maximum-likelihood Estimates of Factor Loadings and Factor Correlations for "Reciprocal Effects" Model: Single "Parental" Ability

| Indicators | Factors | | | | Residual |
	P	Q	E_1	N	
F_1	.62	0	0	0	.79
F_2	.55	0	0	0	.83
M_1	.88	0	0	0	.48
M_2	.77	0	0	0	.64
Q_1	0	.78	0	0	.62
Q_2	0	.84	0	0	.54
E_1	0	0	.74	0	.68
E_3	0	0	.46	0	.89
E_{10}	0	0	.64	0	.77
N	0	0	0	1.00^a	.00
	Factor Correlations				
P		.44	.40	-.12	
Q			.70	-.26	
E_1				-.56	

NOTE: See Table 3.5 for definition of symbols.

[a]Constrained to this value.

were postulated, with social learning theory as the overall theoretical orientation to these environments. These dimensions were supported by the data and suggested the following interpretation.

(a) A *stimulus* dimension (E_1), defined by items measuring the extent to which parents specifically structured opportunities for their child to interact with things and people in his environment. The quality and quantity of the learning experiences provided (for example, items 3, 4, 20, and 22 in Table 3.2) together with the quantity and the quality of exposure to adult models (for example, items 10, 11, 15, and 25 in Table 3.2) proved to be major components of this dimension.

(b) A dimension (E_2) concerned with *parental dominance* in child-rearing. This dimension was not postulated initially but emerges here, in addition to the three expected social learning theory dimensions, as a function of Mosychuk's (1969) extension of the more traditional Dave Wolf measures to include parental dominance items.

(c) The *reinforcement* dimension (E_3) is somewhat limited since it refers only to the overall nature of the sanctions used by parents along a scale ranging from nonphysical to physical punishment. Although this is a "social learning theory" dimension, its specific nature in this investigation is defined by the Mosychuk (1969) data. Obviously, much of the complexity that surrounds notions of the role of reinforcement in social learning theory is absent here.

(d) The *expectations* dimension (E_4) is the weakest of the four dimensions having a really substantial loading only on item 2 in Table 3.2, the "parental encouragement" item. Again this is partly the result of forcing data gathered to satisfy one conceptual framework to fit another.

The support for some of the family environment dimensions is relatively weak, and the limited sample size raises questions about the stability of the factors within the population. However, as noted earlier, similar analyses on another larger data set also produced clear stimulus, reinforcement, and expectation factors and, therefore, offer some independent support of these results.

Estimation of the Models

The focus of the models was on two aspects of the covariance argument, the parental abilities–environment–child's abilities linkages, following the notion of a double advantage (disadvantage), and the reciprocal influence of child abilities and environment, extending this notion to that of a triple advantage (disadvantage). The models are discussed in this order. All interpretations should be regarded as tentative and qualitative for reasons already noted. No meaning should be attributed to minor differences between path coefficients or to minor path coefficients. Because of the limited sample size, the standard errors of these coefficients tend to be large, and even apparently respectable path coefficients may not be significantly different from zero.

Double Advantage (Disadvantage)   The models provide evidence of the two links in this argument: first, that family environments affect children's abilities; second, that parental abilities contribute to this environmental variability and, hence, indirectly to children's intellectual variability.

Of the four dimensions to family environments, the stimulus and expectations dimensions exert the greatest influence on children's abilities. The effect due to the stimulus dimension ($p_{QE_1} = .78$ in Figure 3.4 and .74 in Figure 3.5) is considerable, a one standard-deviation change in E_1 (the metric of E_1 is unknown) resulting in a change of some 12 points in child's ability, assuming the common 15 point standard deviation for IQ. On the other hand, the substantial negative effect of the expectations dimension ($p_{QE_4} = -.51$ in Figure 3.4 and $-.37$ in Figure 3.5) means that the higher the expectations that parents hold for their child's cognitive performance, the lower that performance. The effects of the other two dimensions are relatively minor. Female dominance in child-rearing has a minor negative effect on boy's abilities ($p_{QE_2} = -.16$ in Figure 3.4 and $-.28$ in Figure 3.5), and the use of physical punishment (versus psychological) has a minor positive effect ($p_{QE_3} = .16$ in Figure 3.4 and .10 in Figure 3.5). The latter is, to some extent, at odds with the middle-class child-rearing model that sees love oriented techniques of discipline (i.e., involving withdrawal of love) as a more appropriate means of punishment.

A further point should be noted. There is substantial covariation between E_1 and E_4 ($r_{E_1E_4} = .59$ in Table 3.7) suggesting that families tend to be either high or low on both of these dimensions together. Assuming that middle-class families tend to be high on both and working-class families tend to be low on both, then one would have to conclude that the middle-class child-rearing model is not without liabilities with respect to promoting children's cognitive development. It seems that high expectations on the part of parents actually may inhibit children's cognitive performance. There are explanations of this sort of phenomenon, explanations based on notions of test anxiety (see for example, Bronfenbrenner, 1961; Smith, 1969:232). Given what is known about the antecedents of achievement motivation (Rosen and D'Andrade, 1959), moreover, it seems as if the environments most conducive to development of the motivation to achieve are not necessarily those best suited to the development of the abilities necessary for success (and vice versa). Again, recall that these interpretations must remain tentative and, to some extent, suspect as they do not coincide completely with our limited knowledge of these processes or with conventional wisdom about the characteristics and influence of "good" family environments.

The simplest model of parental influence on family environments is that of Figure 3.5 where a single parental ability is used. Families characterized by high ability parents provide plentiful stimuli in the form of opportunities for their children to interact with the environment ($p_{E_1P} = .41$), are high on female dominance in child-rearing ($p_{E_2P} = .36$), use nonphysical sanctions ($p_{E_3P} = -.30$), and hold out high expectations for their children's performances ($p_{E_4P} = .28$): all in all, the middle-class model.

Figure 3.4 presents the analogous model with separate parental abilities. High ability fathers appear to provide opportunities for their sons to interact with the environment ($p_{E_1F} = .31$), are involved in child-rearing ($p_{E_2F} = -.36$), tend to nonphysical means of sanctioning ($p_{E_3F} = -.41$), and hold out high expectations for their son's performance ($p_{E_4F} = .72$). High ability mothers, it appears, provide opportunities for environmental interaction ($p_{E_1M} = .26$) and tend to play an active role in child-rearing ($p_{E_2M} = .57$), but they differ little from low ability mothers in the use of physical punishment as a sanction ($p_{E_3M} = .02$) or in the expectations they hold for their child's performance ($p_{E_4M} = -.19$).

What appears to be happening, as far as the covariance argument is concerned, is that parental abilities exert substantial effects on these dimensions of the family environment, and at least two of these, in turn, exert substantial effects on children's abilities. However, the matter is complicated by the fact that these quite sizeable indirect effects tend to be opposing effects whose aggregate influence is relatively minor. For example, in Figure 3.5 the indirect effect of P on Q via E_1 amounts to .31 ($p_{E_1P} \cdot p_{QE_1}$); however, when the other indirect effects are taken into account, the total effect of P on Q via the E_i amounts to .08, some 18 percent of the total effect of .44 (r_{PQ}). This also appears to be true for the separate parental ability model shown in Figure 3.4, where each parental ability has patterns of opposing indirect effects on the child's ability via the four environment dimensions. To the extent that these figures come close to population values and do not merely reflect sampling peculiarities, the overall result is to make the total indirect effects relatively small in each case, although they are greater for mothers than fathers, as one might expect given the social definition of mothers as child-rearers and creators of family environments.

Triple Advantage (Disadvantage)   Figures 3.6 and 3.7 provide evidence in support of this last aspect of the covariance argument. In each model, the child's ability exerts a respectable influence upon the stimuli that his parents provide for him in the form of opportunities to interact with people and things in his environment ($p_{E_1Q} = .26$ or .30 respectively). Note, however, that the major direction of influence is from the environment to the child's ability and is greater than .4 in each case.

The remaining effects hold few surprises. In Figure 3.6, father's and mother's ability have roughly equal effects on the child's intellectual abilities and on the stimulus dimension of the environment. Family size exerts a sizeable negative effect on this same environment dimension as expected. The configuration of effects in Figure 3.7, where a single parental ability is used, follows the same pattern as in Figure 3.6.

To the extent to which one can take these somewhat fallible data to be a reasonable reflection of what is happening, it seems that the "middle-class child-rearing model" may be only marginally better than the "working-class model" because of the patterns of opposing effects involved. Nevertheless, some of the effects in question are quite substantial and point to the possibility of producing maximal intellectual development in children by manipulating the environment appropriately. The environment best suited to intellectual development, it seems, is one containing things and people of quality and in quantity. The frequently documented importance of appropriate adult models and a wide variety of learning situations is documented again here in the substantial effects of the stimulus dimension of family environments. Cognitive development, under these conditions, appears to be most enhanced by the relative absence of normative pressure for achievement (the expectations dimension) and, to some extent, by the use of physical punishment rather than love-oriented sanctioning techniques. However, because of fallible data and findings at odds with conventional wisdom, this picture of family environment influence is more an indication of what might be than a measure of what is. In this sense, these findings are more propositions awaiting an adequate test than they are social facts.

Summary

Models developed to examine the biosocial mechanisms involved in the covariance of heredity and environment provided general support for the existence of a triple advantage (disadvantage). It seems that children of intellectually advantaged parents are themselves advantaged in terms of genetic endowment (some part of the direct parent–child ability effect), the family environment in which they develop, and the degree of control they have over this environment.

Although there appear to be substantial indirect effects of parental abilities on children's abilities via the dimensions of family environment examined here, the existence of opposing effects leads to a relatively minor overall indirect influence. By far the greatest part of the parent–child ability correlation is explained by direct effects unmediated by family environments. The interpretation of these direct parent–child effects must remain equivocal as they represent the effects of biological inheritance and unmeasured environmental influences in some unknown mix.

Evidence from the two models that allow for a reciprocal influence between the stimulus dimension of family environments and the child's ability suggests that children also have a capability to influence the environment themselves, in terms of their own intellectual ability. In other words, "doubly advantaged" children have the additional advantage of being able to influence the environment to their own cognitive benefit and are, thus, "triply advantaged."

Appendix

Of Mosychuk's original 59 family environment items, 32 are reproduced as they appear in Mosychuk (1969). The seven point rating scales associated with these are also included. These 36 interview items constitute the data base for the 26 items shown in Tables 3.1 and 3.2.

Mothers of the children involved provided answers to these questions in a two-hour interview. Their responses were rated subsequently on a seven point scale, the dimensions of which are specified separately for each item. Items 12, 14, 15, 26, 29, 33, 46, 47, 51, 54, 55, 56, 58, and 59 were disaggregated. For the other items shown, aggregate scores produced by Mosychuk were used.

Interview Items

3. a. Have you made any plans to finance your boy's schooling beyond high school?
    b. Have you made any other plans about his higher education? What are they?
4. Is your boy taking training in activities such as music, dancing, art, swimming, or anything else outside the regular school program?
8. a. Does your husband ask your boy questions about school?
    b. What kinds of questions does he ask the boy?
    c. How many times has your husband asked him in the last two weeks?
12. a. Which magazines and newspapers do you subscribe or buy regularly?
    b. Which ones does the boy read?
    c. Which ones do you encourage him to read?
    d. What kinds of *books* do you encourage him to read?
    e. What were his last books from the public or school library about?
13. Do you encourage or request your boy to write letters or thank-you notes (for presents) and invitations (for parties)?
    If yes, what were some specific instances in the last year?
14. a. How many hours of T.V. does your boy watch per day (week day)?
    b. What are his favorite programs?
    c. Which particular T.V. programs did you recommend for your boy in the last month?
    d. Which ones do you not like him to watch?
    e. Why?
15. Do you have a dictionary or any reference books at home?
    a. Which dictionary?
    b. Reference books?
    c. Did you use the dictionary during the last month? If you did, how many times?
    d. Did you use the reference books during the last month? How many times?
    e. How many times has your husband used the dictionary in the last month?
    f. How many times a month does your child use the dictionary?
    g. How often does the boy use the reference books?

16. a. Does your child have a public library card?
    b. How often did he go to the library during the last two months?
    c. During an average two months?
17. Does your boy bring reading books home from school? How many did he bring during the last two weeks?
19. a. Is the whole family present for the entire evening meal?
       If not, what is the situation?
       How long has it been this way?
       What was the situation before?
    b. How do the meals go?
       Are they quiet or noisy?
       Could you elaborate a little?
    c. Does everyone have a chance to talk at the table?
    d. Is the radio or T.V. on during the evening meal?
       Which?
20. a. What events or activities do you have on weekdays or week-ends where the whole family takes part?
       In summer?
       In winter?
       Both?
    b. Do you have any word games or do you play any games (matches) which involve new words or considerable reading, speaking or spelling?
       What are they?
    c. Does your boy take part in any public speaking competitions, concerts (recitations), or plays (drama)?
       If yes, could you name some specific instances?
    d. Do you *as a family* attend concerts, plays or movies?
       If you do how many times have you attended in the last year?
23. a. Does your boy enjoy talking to and discussing things with adults other than his parents?
    b. What opportunities are available for him to talk to other adults?
    c. Do you encourage him to talk and discuss things with other adults?
       In what particular way do you encourage him?
24. a. At what time does your husband go to work?
       What time does he come home?
       Is this his schedule for every day of the week?
    b. Does he have a part-time job in addition to his regular job?
       If yes, how many hours a week does part-time job take?
25. a. How much time did your husband spend with the children after supper during the last week (average per day)?
    b. What is the average amount throughout the year?
    c. How much time did your husband spend with the boy during the last two week-ends?
  d. e. During an average two weeks? What did they do?
    f. What are some of your husband's activities during week-ends which take a large portion of his time and do not include the boy?
    g. Do you sense that the boy would like to do things with your husband more than he presently does?
26. a. Do you feel that, to a certain extent, the situation at home may be one where you "handle the kids" while the husband attends to the other affairs?

b. If not, then who usually has the final word with respect to the children's privileges and activities?

c. Do you feel that you would like your husband to be more involved in bringing up the children?
In what ways?

28. a. Who usually suggests that the children take out-of-school classes or activities?

b. Who makes the arrangements for these?

c. Does your husband listen to or watch the boy practice some of these activities (piano, hockey)?
Which activities?

d. Who watches or listens to him more, you or your husband?

29. a. If your child has some problems with respect to school, who usually settles the matter, you or your husband?

b. Why not; / you / or / your husband /?

c. Who arranges appointments and goes to talk with the child's teacher or the principal?

d. If your child has some problems with respect to the neighbors or other children who usually settles the matter, you or your husband?

e. Why not: / you / or / your husband /?

31. a. How often in the last two months did you have family "get-togethers" with your friends or relatives which included the children?

b. How often during any average two month period during the year?

c. Do you together as a family go to watch or take part in any sports?

42. a. What are some specific tasks that he wishes to do but you feel that he would not do well enough because he is too young?

b. What are some tasks that he should be doing well but he still doesn't?

c. Do you let him try them regardless or do you usually do them for him?

44. a. Does your boy "talk back" to you or your husband?

b. If not, why do you think that he doesn't?

c. What do you or your husband do if your child does "talk back" to you?

d. What do you do if your child interrupts your conversation with other adults?

45. a. What specific rules did you and do you have for your boy with respect to:
    (i)   bedtime,
    (ii)   mealtime,
    (iii) T.V.,
    (iv)   church,
    (v)   visiting?

b. How much say does he have in setting these rules?

c. Are the rules always enforced?

d. Would you say that these rules are generally for bringing out adult behavior in your child?

e. What other purposes do you have for setting the rules?

46. a. What do you do when the rules that you set are not obeyed?

b. If your boy repeatedly does not do some tasks or chores well how do you punish him?

c. When was the last time your boy had physical punishment?

47. a. Do you feel that your child really worries when he has done something wrong?

b. Why does he worry?

48. Do you or your husband "give in" to requests by your child which are contrary to your rules?
49. a. What were some of your boy's hobbies or keen interests in the last three years?
    b. What is his present hobby (ies)?
    c. How much time has he spent on it in the last two weeks?
    d. How much time during an average two week period?
50. a. What are your husband's hobbies or specific leisure activities?
    b. In what projects or sports do your husband and boy participate together? (includes e.g. building fence, painting).
    c. Is your boy interested in any of *your* hobbies or leisure activities? Which ones?
51. a. Would you say that during the boy's preschool years you bought toys for him "too soon", that is, before he really knew what to do with them?
    b. If yes, how did you feel if he didn't "take to them" at that time?
    c. Did you get him toys at any time of the year or just for special occasions?
    d. What types of gifts did he get for Christmas or birthdays when he was about 4–5 years old?
    e. What did he get for the last two birthdays and Christmases?
52. a. In the last year how many times has your boy gone fishing, hunting or on tours?
    b. How often has he gone hiking or camping in the last year?
    c. How many days did he spend on such activities during the year?
    d. Does your boy play any sports regularly? If yes, which?
53. a. Can you recall how old your boy was when he was allowed to use certain specific appliances such as the vacuum cleaner or record player? Other appliances?
    b. Which of your husband's tools or machines is he permitted to use?
    c. Which tools or appliances is he not permitted to use?
55. a. Does your boy do puzzles (crossword, jigsaw, word, drawing, arithmetic) in the daily paper, in books or in magazines? What are some that he does?
    b. Does he usually complete the ones that he starts?
    c. Do you think that the puzzles should always be completed?
    d. Do you or your husband take any interest in such puzzles? If yes, in what way?
56. a. What specific projects (models, collections, new games) has your boy undertaken on his own in the last one or two years?
    b. Which has he completed?
    c. Has he dropped any before completion?
    d. What do you do about his unfinished projects?
    e. Do you encourage him to start new projects? How?
    f. How do you show your pleasure in projects that the boy completes well?
58. a. Do you assign regular chores or tasks for the boy?
    b. After assigning them which chores is he expected to do regularly on his own without being reminded continually (e.g. clean room, brush teeth)?
    c. Does he?

(Interview items continued on p. 101.)

Rating Scales

	1	2	3	4	5	6	7
3a	None		Indep. wealthy		savings		Insur. plan (yes)
b	None	Yes	discussions				visits to aspired jobs.
4	None		sports, cubs				music, lang. art, dancing
8a,b	no questions		general questions				general and specific questions
c	none			2			5
*12a	Better H&G	Pop. M., W. Cath, Life, True, McCalls, Edmon. J., MacL., L.H.J.			Chatel.,	Nat. Geog.	Rd. Dig, Time
b	none		looks thru' some		looks thru' many		reads some
c	do not encourage			let him read what he wishes			encourage specific
d	do not encourage			let him read what he wishes			encourage specific
c	no knowledge		very general description				quite specific description
13	none		few thank you notes	many-t-y-n		few letters	many letters
14a	less than ½		¾		1		1½ hrs.
b	more than 4		3		2		
c	comics, gunfighters, crime, sports, sci. fiction, family, nature, educ. documentaries						
d	none			sports		comics, Disney	Nat. Geog.
e	no restrict.		horror			crime,	war
	nightmares		bad ideas			learn nothing	
15a	no dictionary		small pocket atlas			Oxford or Webster	
b	no books					encyclop.	encycl. & other series
c	none				1	2	4
d	none		1			3	4
e	none				1	1	5
f	none					6	10
g	none		1			7	10
16a	no						yes
b	none			4			8
c	none			2			4
17	none			1	3		5

	1	2	3	4	5	6	7
19a	no						always
b	rigid rules, no talk		part of time				meaningful interaction of whole family
c	no		disorder noise				yes
d	yes always						
20a	none	frequently			occas. T.V.		low radio, no
b	none	few indoor(non-group)		bought games	numerous indoor-outdoor	(4–5)	(both sum. & winter) bought & self-organized
c	none		simple routine (occas. class report, cubs)				school concert extra-ordinary (special group)
d	none						
23a	no		1	sometimes	3		5
b	no opport. or situat.				some		yes
c	no encourage — approve & allow discussion — request — organize and design situations					variety (visitors, relat, cubs, church)	
24	father home when child home		$\frac{1}{3}$ away		$\frac{1}{2}$ away	$\frac{2}{3}$ away	father always away when child home or awake
25a	3		2		1		none
b	2		1		$\frac{1}{2}$		none
c	16		8		4		none
d	16		8		4		none
e	interaction activities						T.V.
f	none						numerous (job, golf, social)
g	no						
26a	no			at times	at times		yes
b	not more involved				both		yes
c	father				more time with children		mother
28a	father			both or children	both	as a male model	mother
b	father						mother
c	yes						no
d	father				both same		mother

	1	2	3	4	5	6	7
29a	father			both			mother
a	mother doesn't want to			not avail.			father doesn't want to
b	father			both			mother
c	father			both			mother
d	mother doesn't want to			not avail.			father doesn't want to
31a	none		2		4		8
b	none		2		4		8
c	no		yes (one)				yes more than one
42a	no tasks			one task			variety of tasks
b	no tasks			one task			variety of tasks
c	let him do					do for him	
8. 44a	yes			sometimes		no conseq.	
b	knows he shouldn't —	respects parent decisions —		always obeys — afraid of punish.			
c	ignore	explain	gets angry scold	cut privileges phys. punish.			
d	explain, allow to interrupt — never interrupts — ask to keep quiet and wait until finished — get angry, punish						
45a	few rules					many rigid, specific rules	
b	considerable			very little		none	
c	seldom			usually		yes	
d	no	expected child behav.	no responsibility	obedience		yes	absolute
e	child's welfare —	charact. formation	responsib., order in house —	mother convenience		respect for obedience parents —	
46a	tell again — explain — ground —			anger, shout, threaten —	phys. punish.		
b	make do again — explain — ground —			anger, shout, threaten —	phys. punish.		
c	never			can't remember			recently (6 mos.)
47a	no						yes
b	guilty conscience bothers — afraid of scolding, grounding — afraid phys. punish.						
48	often			occasionally			never

	1	2	3	4	5	6	7
49a	low phys. and kinaesth. (rdg. T.V.)						phys. and kinaesth. rich (sports, building)
b	rdg., T.V.						sports, building, collections
c	none	1		2	5		10 hrs.
d	10 hrs	5		2	1		none
50a	none sleep T.V.		rdg.	sports	chores	repairs	crafts
b	none T.V.			cooking	sports	crafts	crafts
c	none			occasionally			
51a	no						yes
b	anxious						not anxious
c	special occasions	kept them for later				let him use regardless	anytime
d	money	clothes	books	pictures	trucks	blocks	
e	money	clothes	books	pictures	trucks	blocks	
52a	none	1	2	5	10	construction	25
b	none		1	3	7	construction	10
c	none		1	3	7		10
d	none			one summer or winter			more than one summer & winter
53a	9 yrs	8	7	6	5		4 yrs
b	none	hammer		screwdriver	saw	axe	mower
c	5 articles			2 articles			none
55a	none	class reqmt.	jigsaws	crossw.	journal	crossw. J. & Spec.	books
b	no		usually				yes
c	no		not always				yes
d	none		occas. self			occas. self & child	freq. self & children
56a	none		1		2	4 things	all
b	none						
c	yes		some				no
d	throw away	ask him		buy him things		nothing, put away, ask to finish, wait and have him do later, provide	a variety of opport. to choose from
e	no way			buy him things			
f	verbal comment			reward (privil., monet.)			buy him more projects display

	1	2	3	4	5	6	7
58a	no						yes
b	none	2	very few		3	4	5
c	always requires reminding			sometimes			never
d	no mention,			expected, weekly allow., parent checks, reward,			praise (verbal other)
59a	no			for good honest effort			yes
b	many		whatever boy wants				few & complete
c	no particular definite methods						use numerous techniques

d. If he attends to and completes the tasks or chores without having to be reminded repeatedly what rewards, praise or payments does he get?
59. a. Do you or your husband praise or reward your boy *only* if he *completes* the tasks, chores or projects?
   b. Do you prefer that your boy attempt many projects or, that he just attempt a few but completes them?
   c. What methods or techniques do you and your husband use to ensure that tasks are completed well by the boy?

Acknowledgments

The assistance of Harry Mosychuk and the support of Memorial University of Newfoundland is gratefully acknowledged.

IV | Cognitive Complexity: A Dimension Underlying the Socioeconomic Achievement Process

Joe L. Spaeth
University of Illinois, Urbana–Champaign

By now, the basic relations among measured variables in the socioeconomic achievement process are reasonably well understood. In fact, knowledge of that process has developed sufficiently to warrant beginning a search for general dimensions that may underlie it. This chapter attempts a conceptual extension of the model of the achievement process proposed by Blau and Duncan (1967) and elaborated by others (Alexander and Eckland, 1973; Duncan, Featherman, and Duncan, 1972; Hauser, 1971, 1972; Sewell, Haller, and Ohlendorf, 1970; Sewell, Haller, and Portes, 1969; Sewell and Hauser, 1975; Spaeth, 1968, 1970).

This extension will be carried out by showing that variables in the Blau–Duncan "basic model" correspond to environmental settings that vary in their cognitive complexity. In brief, it will be shown that occupational prestige is an indicator of the cognitive complexity of an occupation, that duration of schooling is a measure of exposure to educational environments of increasing complexity, and that parental SES is an indicator of the complexity of a child's cognitive environment.

This chapter also shows that the variables in the socioeconomic achievement process are components of a theory dealing with the development of the competency to cope with cognitively complex phenomena. In order to locate the achievement process in a broader framework, a general framework for this theory will be developed. Complete development of such a theory is, however, well beyond the scope of this endeavor, which will concentrate on the explication of variables in the achievement process.

Since sociologists have tended to slight the role of cognitive variables, it will be emphasized here, in the contention that this role is an important one in the achievement process. Obviously, such variables are not sufficient by themselves to account for the working of that process. In fact, it is impossible to develop a theory of the role of cognition without reference to other processes such as conation. Therefore, noncognitive variables will be discussed where appropriate later.

This chapter opens with a section that gives a general conceptual framework for the development of competencies. In the next section, measured variables in the achievement process are shown to be indicators of certain of the concepts. Then a series of three sections shows how measured variables in the achievement process can be reconceptualized in terms of cognitive complexity. This theme is developed through consideration of the process by which the family helps to inculcate competencies corresponding to intelligence and through discussion of years of schooling and occupational prestige as dependent variables. The next section proposes detailed measures of the degree of exposure to educational and occupational environments based on the idea that duration of schooling and occupational prestige represent measures of exposure to complex environments. Several propositions are derived to demonstrate how the new measures could contribute to an interpretation of the linkages between educational and occupational status and between occupational status and earnings. Then a section is devoted to the role of competency and complexity in the intergenerational transmission and intragenerational acquisition of status. The chapter concludes with a short summary.

Competency, Socioeconomic Achievement, and the Life Cycle

The idea of progression through the life cycle is a major component of current research on the achievement process, for the stages of the life cycle provide the ordering principle that warrants a recursive model of that process. Clearly, each of the crucial variables or sets of variables in the Blau–Duncan basic model corresponds to a stage of the life cycle—parental SES corresponds to infancy, childhood, and adolescence; duration of schooling to late adolescence or early adulthood; and occupational status to adulthood. The theoretical framework presented here contends that a task of each stage of the life cycle is the development of cognitive competencies, from intelligence in childhood and adolescence to academic knowledge and skills in adolescence and young adulthood to job-related competencies in adulthood. Table 4.1 relates the competencies that are relevant to each life cycle stage to the aspects of the environment that help produce them. Panel

Relationship of Setting, Treatment, and Competency to Life Cycle Stages

Life-Cycle Stage	Setting	Treatment	Competency
		A. Concepts	
I. Infancy and childhood	Home	Parental tutoring	General cognitive skills
II. Childhood, adolescence, and young adulthood	School	Instruction	Academic knowledge and skills
III. Adulthood	Work	On-the-job training/work experience	Specific job knowledge and skills
		B. Indicators	
I. Infancy and childhood	Parental SES	Measured parental tutelage	IQ tests
II. Childhood, adolescence, and young adulthood	Years of schooling	Effective hours per school year (Wiley, 1973)	Standardized achievement and admissions tests
III. Adulthood	Occupational status/job complexity	Duration of labor force and job experience	Tests under development (Educational Testing Service, 1973, 1974)

A summarizes these relationships at the conceptual level, as Panel B does at the level of measured variables.

The correspondence between life cycle stages and settings is loose: The influence of the home clearly extends beyond childhood into adulthood, and the transition from school to work is far from irreversible. Yet the life cycle stages are straightforward compared to the processes that take place within each stage. In this scheme, a "task" of each stage of the life cycle is the development of appropriate cognitive competencies, which are summarized in the last column of the table. In order for such developments to occur, persons must be exposed to environmental settings and to treatments. Competencies, treatments, and settings will be highly variable within a given cohort. Some persons will be exposed to simple environments and may receive negative treatment. As a consequence, their competencies will be slight. Others, exposed to highly complex settings and effective treatments, will have much higher levels of competency.

Competencies

As the cognitive outcome of each stage of the life cycle, competencies will be dealt with first. The general skills associated with the first stage of the life cycle include some fluency in the use and understanding of language and the ability to do simple computations, and they extend to the capacity to deal with various forms of abstractions. As is indicated in Panel B, such competencies can be measured by standardized intelligence tests.

As a result of schooling, people continue to develop these skills. In addition, they begin to acquire knowledge that may be useful in the world of work. The greater the duration of the schooling, the more knowledge is acquired and the more relevant it is likely to be to work. In the last years of college and in graduate or professional school, students gain increasingly specialized knowledge. Much of it is not detailed enough to stand alone as preparation for the performance of professional duties, but it is a fund of knowledge corresponding to "what everyone knows" in one's field.

Job knowledge and skills are even more highly specialized simply because someone holding a particular job needs to know how to do quite specific things. Only on-the-job training and experience can provide the skills and knowledge needed to meet the day-to-day contingencies of a particular job. Obviously not all jobs require vast stores of knowledge or highly developed skills, cognitive or otherwise. However, those that do have such requirements tend to be accorded high occupational prestige. Thus, many definitions of professions stress the application of a body of knowledge to the problems of clients. It has been widely held that the "post-industrial state" requires large numbers of experts for its functioning and that their expertise is based on the results of systematic scientific research learned in the course of formal training. According to this view, the higher the economic development of a modern society, the more its occupational roles must be staffed by knowledgeable experts (Bell, 1967

1968; Galbraith, 1967; Kahn and Wiener, 1967). Similarly, competent performance of occupational roles is considered a key element in modernization (Inkeles, 1966a,b; Stinchcombe, 1973).

An important point regarding the competencies mentioned in Table 4.1 is the progression from quite general skills and knowledge in the first stage of the life cycle to the very specific skills and detailed knowledge required for adequate performance of specific jobs. Educational and occupational status are nonspecific compared to the competencies required for successful on-the-job performance.

The specificity of occupational competencies for one profession is exemplified in Willingham's (1974) analysis of criteria for successful graduate education. Recipients of Ph.Ds may become practitioners, teachers, scholar–scientists, or some combination of the three. On-the-job criteria of success as a scholar–scientist include publication, citation, awards, eminence, and inventions. Practitioners may attain professional leadership, certification, advancement, and income; teachers may receive institutional recognition, student and alumni nominations for excellence in teaching, favorable judgments of colleagues, and recognition as faculty leaders. Each of the three lists is clearly incomplete, and the items included are very general even though they apply to entrants to a limited number of professions. Each of the criteria involves a complex mixture of skills. For example, publishing and being cited include at least the following competencies: appropriate problem selection, research design, data analysis, and presentation of results. The last competency alone is highly field-specific, as is clear, for example, in the differences between the formats of articles in psychology and sociology journals. Thus, competency of performance in jobs accorded high occupational prestige is a highly complex and specific matter.

Settings and Treatments

At any level of generality, competencies are developed in environmental settings by treatments. A setting refers to the variety of stimuli in a person's surroundings—the greater the variety, the more complex the setting. Settings provide the framework within which treatments may take place. The treatments themselves involve the intervention by an actor or set of actors in the development of another actor. When a mother sets out to teach her child to do something, from tying its shoes to reading, she is providing a treatment. So is a teacher who is trying to communicate the rudiments of arithmetic to an elementary school class. The intensity of treatment can be much greater in the mother–child situation than in the classroom situation because the mother can react specifically to one child's problems by providing detailed feedback, giving further instructions, and otherwise tailoring her approach to that child's specific successes and failures.

Treatments may be intentional or unintentional, positive or negative, carried out on a one-to-one or a many-to-one basis: Ego is treated by the actions of alter(s). The development of a child's intelligence in the family gives us a framework within which to exemplify some of these aspects of treatments. As we shall see in greater detail later, it is possible to measure aspects of parental treatments that seem to have important effects on the development of intelligence. Thus, each item in the following list has been shown to be correlated with parental SES, the child's performance on intelligence or achievement tests, or both: talking and playing with the child when it is very young (Friedlander, 1970; Lewis and Goldberg, 1969); including the child in dinner table conversations (Milner, 1951); providing explicit instructions and positive feedback (Hess, 1970; Hess and Shipman, 1965); and using "formal" as opposed to "public" language (Bernstein, 1961). In addition, the intentional provision of varied stimuli, the rewarding of acceptable linguistic and other performances, the correct use of language by the mother, and attention given by the mother to the language usage of the child have been shown to be highly related to the child's scores on intelligence and achievement tests (Dave, 1963; Marjoribanks, 1972a, b; Williams, 1973, and Chapter III in this volume; Wolf, 1964). These lists of treatments could be expanded, but the major point is that the effects of parental treatments on a child's IQ have been measured and shown to be important.

Parents can teach children a variety of cognitive skills, such as language usage, by tutoring them, correcting them, and encouraging them. At the same time, ordinary parent–child and parent–parent interaction provides the child with a set of models and subtle cues, such as the actual language usage of the parents, overtly and tacitly expressed intellectual and cognitive values, and expectations regarding the interests that the child will develop and the degree of independence with which he or she will pursue them. Thus, "an individual raised in a complex, multifaceted environment . . . is likely to be intolerant of external constraints, to be able to cope intellectually with complex and ambiguous situations, and to have a strong concern with and awareness of his inner life" (Schooler, 1972: 299).

From one point of view, what happens in the family is paradigmatic of treatments in schools and on the job, but from another it is not. Homes vary in the extent to which various pressures—some direct, others quite subtle—reinforce and enhance children's cognitive skills and interests, but the home has advantages as a setting that are not shared by schools or work settings. First, the kinds of treatments given by parents are applied during the ages when a child's intelligence is developing most rapidly (Bloom, 1964). Second, compared to schools and jobs, the family is a total institution. If parents are agreed on the kind of development that they want to foster and if they are able to foster it, they will face little competition from outsiders, at least until the child enters school. By contrast, teachers must face problems presented by the sheer number of students with whom they must deal simultaneously. Furthermore, students typically are exposed to several teachers who may not agree on the merits of their students' performances and the extent to which they should be rewarded or punished. The students' peers may also counteract the effects of the teacher by enforcing norms regarding the restriction of output and by other means. A similar situation can occur on the job, where workers are likely to receive different messages from superiors, peers, and subordinates. The problem is not that treatments are lacking in schools or on the job but that some of them will be contradictory.

It is important to note that one outcome of successful parental cognitive tutelage is that children develop not only the capacity for dealing with cognitive problems but an interest in doing so. Thus, the successful solution of problems becomes its own reward, and persons who have learned to seek and find such rewards are likely to develop interests in the intrinsic aspects of tasks. This orientation can presumably be reinforced or extinguished by exposure to rewards or punishments associated with tasks in schools or on the job, but it is likely that successful performance will lead to further successful performance. An orientation to intrinsic aspects of tasks and a tendency to seek out challenging tasks is likely to be useful at later stages of a career. For as persons move from home through school to work, they will discover that they are increasingly expected to provide their own treatments. These may take the form of persevering in difficult tasks, seeking help when it is needed, and generally applying old learning to new situations.

Little will be said here about treatments in schools and on the job. One can consider standard classroom instruction as a rather general treatment, but it is clearly not directed to individual students and therefore cannot be considered to be as intensive as parental tutelage. For the most part, the same is true of work experience and perhaps of on-the-job training. The latter is generally intended as an introduction to a particular job. The former exemplifies a phenomenon increasingly characteristic of late stages in the life cycle: Individuals are expected to provide their own treatments. In fact, it may be that concepts and indicators discussed as treatments should be considered as settings instead.

Measures of educational and occupational treatment, such as effective hours per school year (Wiley, Chapter VIII of this volume) and duration of labor force experience, are clearly measures of exposure and not of the content or intensity of treatment. Measures of contact or intensity would be difficult to construct, and as causes of specific competencies, they are not directly relevant to the socioeconomic achievement process.

Treatments oriented toward increasing the individual's competency in coping with complex phenomena tend to be successful. The success varies with the intensity of the treatment and the extent to which a particular treatment is univocal, that is, free from competition with other treatments.

As noted above, treatments take place within settings, but settings can be considered apart from treatments and have independent effects of their own. The central characteristic of a given setting is the variety and complexity of the stimuli that it offers. As children mature, the settings to which they are exposed increase in complexity. Correspondingly, developmental tasks increase in complexity with maturation. In response to their child's development, parents increase the complexity of stimuli to which the child is exposed and raise the level of competency that they judge to be adequate. The curriculum has the same effect on school children, and it exposes them to areas in which the parents' tutorial expertise may be slight.

The reason for distinguishing settings from treatments is to allow for both active and passive aspects of the environment. In the home, the passive aspect corresponds to the presence of a variety of physical objects related to cognitive performance. The longitudinal surveys of high school students that ask about possessions in the home give some indication of the kinds of physical objects that may be important: magazines, dictionaries, encyclopedias, other books, records, record players, works of art, the possession of a library card, even radios and televisions. Indices based on some of these items have found their way into generalized measures of socioeconomic background, and generally speaking, such measures correlate more highly with IQ than do a combination of "face sheet" items alone.

Effects of environmental settings have been observed in animals as well as humans. Recent psychological research shows that rats reared in groups with a daily change of toys show physiological changes compared to normally reared laboratory rats (Wallace, 1974). (The presumed functions of each increase will be given in parentheses.) Compared to normally reared rats, "enriched" rats had a heavier cerebral cortex (intellectual functioning and information processing), larger neural cell bodies and a higher RNA–DNA ratio (higher metabolic activity), more glial cells (transportation of materials between capillaries and nerve cells, insulation of axions, removal of dead neural tissue), increases in the size of the medial area of the hippocampus (long-term memory), larger synaptic junctions (cell-to-cell transmission of information), more branching of neural cells (greater connection between nerve cells), and less aggressive and emotional behavior (emotionality is a barrier to learning in rats). In short, whether these changes actually lead to an increase in learning ability, they do lead to "superior ability to adapt to novel environments" (Wallace, 1974: 1035). Although the physiological changes may be most marked early in the life cycle, they have been demonstrated in "elderly" rats, and they have been shown to be reversible. Reduction of complexity leads to reversal of the physiological effects.

In the human life cycle, complexity of schooling as a cognitive setting corresponds to the standard graded curriculum. Thus, the longer a person has been attending school, the greater the complexity to which he has been exposed.

The basic element that makes settings effective is exposure. Sometimes the length of exposure is crucial, as it is with schooling, in part because duration of exposure is highly correlated with degree of complexity. Sometimes the degree of complexity is the most significant aspect of the setting, as it is with work. The research of Kohn and Schooler has demonstrated the rather pervasive effects of a man's occupation on his own social and psychological functioning as well as on that of his family (Kohn, 1969; Kohn and Schooler, 1973; Schooler, 1972). A relevant aspect of this research is the direct assessment of occupations according to their substantive complexity. In terms of working with ideas, this complexity ranges from synthesis and analysis to reading instructions. A scale measuring the complexity of work with ideas, with people, and with things correlates .80 with the prestige of the man's occupation (Spaeth, Chapter VI of this volume).

The theoretical scheme underlying Table 4.1 is considerably broader than that encompassed by the measured variables most pertinent to current analyses of the process of socioeconomic achievement. Only the first row and the first column of the table are required to describe that process. Included in it are the inculcation of intelligence by the parental family in the first row and the movement through settings characterized by their cognitive complexity in the first column. Excluded are field- and job-specific competencies and the treatments that presumably enhance them.

One purpose of this discussion was to show that socioeconomic achieve-ment fits sensibly into a larger conceptual scheme. An attempt to broaden the conception of the achievement process to include academic and work-related competencies would require a shift from concerns with status to concerns with specific academic or on-the-job competencies. The perspective on statuses as settings manifesting varying degrees of cognitive complexity is a fruitful one in its own right, and the development of this perspective is a major concern of the remainder of this chapter.

Statuses as Indicators of the Complexity of Settings

The first step in this development will be a discussion of relevant indicators in Panel B of Table 4.1. Then the concepts developed earlier will be applied to dependent variables in the achievement process in order to show that this perspective can account for some of the findings of research on the achievement process. Finally, the same variables will be treated as independent variables that will be operationalized in terms of complexity in order to show that this theoretical orientation can also predict new findings.

The entries in the first column of Panel B merely refer to the basic model of Blau and Duncan (1967) and require little elaboration. The first row refers to the inculation of IQ in the home. The relationships among parental SES, parental tutelage, and a child's IQ have received considerable attention in the psychological literature. The arrows joining the cells in the first row of Panel B may be construed as a literal path-analytic picture of the process involved. The effects of complexity of the home environment, as measured by parental SES, on a child's cognitive skills, as measured by scores on IQ tests, are totally mediated by parental tutoring, as measured by a variety of actual indices of the tutelage and exposure to stimuli provided by parents for a child. These matters will be covered in greater detail later, but a brief discussion of the variables involved in the process is necessary here.

Parental SES has been measured by as many as four variables, all of which are based on standard survey "face sheet" items. Father's occupation is expressed in units of the Duncan SEI, NORC prestige scores, or Hollingshead occupation codes. Father's and mother's education are most often given in years of schooling or educational stages completed. The fourth variable is parental family income, which is an indicator of the material resources available to the family.

Variables of this kind are at best indicative of environmental settings. Greater parental affluence may produce a richer and more varied set of possessions and thereby a more complex set of stimuli available to a child. Parental education may lead to greater knowledge and skills on the part of the parents and therefore to a more complex environment for the child. The complexity of the father's occupation may have effects on the way in which children are reared (Kohn, 1969) and on the father's own IQ (Kohn and Schooler, 1973).

As indicated in Table 4.1, IQ is viewed as a competency. At least it indicates the ability to respond quickly and accurately to questions about the relations among abstract symbols, such as words and numbers. The known effects of IQ on education, occupation, and income indicate that such a capacity is of some utility for a person's attainments.

The link between intelligence and parental socioeconomic status—parental tutoring—refers specifically to the behavior of parents as actors explicitly concerned with their children's cognitive development. As currently measured, this variable combines indicators of variation in settings, such as the presence of books and encyclopedias, with treatments, such as the explicit intention of parents to make exposure to diverse experiences as cognitively stimulating as possible and the provision of opportunities for improvement of language usage. Findings bearing on transmission of the effects of parental SES on IQ by parental tutelage will be discussed in greater detail later.

More than cognitive complexity is needed to explain the linkage between parental status and a child's educational attainment. Implicit in the notion of parents as active socializing agents is the assumption that they have certain resources to aid them in their task. These resources include skills in handling interpersonal relations and in dealing with ideas and knowledge not only of academic matters but of the real world and the way in which it operates. In addition, family wealth influences the ease of furnishing instructive or enjoyable material objects for young children or prolonged schooling for older ones. These matters will be taken up again later. Suffice it to say that no claim is made here that the complexity of the parental home is an adequate mechanism for explaining the effects of parental SES on children's educational or occupational achievements. Appropriate statuses have direct effects on later attainments, and the values that children learn in and outside the home affect their choices among educational and occupational alternatives.

Nevertheless, the perspective that sees complexity as a salient dimension of status is important for educational and occupational status. As far as educational status is concerned, the complexity of the educational stimuli to which students are exposed is directly transmitted by the curriculum and is manifested in a wide variety of fields, even at the elementary and secondary levels. English ranges from reading readiness to creative writing, mathematics from counting to calculus, science from show-and-tell to physics and chemistry, and foreign languages from materials little more advanced than Dick and Jane stories to literary classics like the *Aeneid*. Complexity of subject matter becomes even greater at the college level. The relationship between years of schooling and exposure to curricular complexity is quite close.

Duration of schooling in years is a valid indicator of educational attainment because it connotes exposure to settings that differ in complexity, and this complexity is rather well measured by years of school completed. Assumptions about the importance of educational quality are shaky because most schools do not provide the kinds of treatments that might lead to results associated with differences in the quality of tutelage.

The last stage of the socioeconomic life cycle corresponds to the working career. A major element in the consideration of occupations as environmental settings that vary in complexity is the degree of correspondence between measured prestige and an independent measure of job complexity. A close correspondence has been demonstrated in the data of Kohn and his colleagues (Kohn, 1969; Kohn and Schooler, 1973). The correlation between the substantive complexity and prestige of occupations is .80 (Spaeth, Chapter VI of this volume).

The reader will note that earnings have not been included in Table 4.1. Earnings result partly from competent performance of job duties, but they are also a function of earlier statuses, labor force experience, and amount of labor force participation (Duncan *et al.*, 1972; Mincer, 1974; Spaeth, Chapter VI of this volume). In any event, earnings are too general a variable to be a good indicator of competency. Part of a later section of this chapter will be devoted to a decomposition of job experience suggested by a reconceptualization of occupational prestige as occupational complexity.

The remainder of this chapter will concentrate on further ramifications of the three basic statuses: parental SES, educational attainment, and occupation. Topics to be included will be an analysis of the process characterizing life cycle Stage I—the determination of IQ by parental SES operating through parental cognitive socialization. The validity of years of schooling as a measure of educational attainment, the meaning of size of sibship as a determinant of IQ and its implications for the possibility of effective educational treatment, and the very close relationship between occupational status and job complexity will also be discussed. In addition, consideration of statuses as settings varying in their complexity suggests new ways of measuring such exposure. Some new measures will be proposed and their implications discussed.

Parental SES and IQ

One purpose of this section is to demonstrate, as well as is possible with faulty data, that the cognitive socialization which parents provide for a child totally mediates the effects of parental SES on IQ. Another purpose is to show that at least one other determinant of IQ, number of siblings, can be subsumed under the general theory.

To mediate the effects of parental SES, a home-environment variable must correlate in the high .50s or .60s with IQ, correlations high enough by conventional standards to evoke interest in the measurement of such a variable.

The following are the basic facts bearing on the mediation hypothesis. Of 18 estimates of the correlation between parental SES and children's IQ derived from 8 data sets, the mean is .31.[1] Studies directly measuring the effects of the child's cognitive environment have found correlations between that variable and the child's IQ ranging from the high .50s to the low .70s (Dave, 1963; Marjoribanks, 1972a,b; Walberg and Marjoribanks, 1974; Williams, 1973, and Chapter III in this volume; Wolf, 1964). On the whole, these same studies found correlations somewhat under .50 between parental SES and environment. As crude estimates, the following correlations will serve: SES–IQ, .3; SES–environment, .5; and environment–IQ, .65. Solving the appropriate equations yields an estimate of the direct effect of parental SES of − .03. It seems reasonable to conclude that the effects of parental SES are indeed mediated by the child's cognitive environment.

With the exception of the British Plowden Committee data (Walberg and Marjoribanks, 1974), these results are based on small, geographically restricted samples. The fact that the important environment–IQ correlation has been replicated in several places and with somewhat different measurement procedures supports the view that a correlation of approximately .65

[1] The data sets include the following: two studies measuring the direct effects of home environment (Dave, 1963; Wolf, 1964); a survey of veterans carried out by NORC and CPS (Griliches and Mason, 1972); Project Talent (Spaeth and Greeley, 1970); a longitudinal survey of 1957 Wisconsin high school graduates followed up in 1964 (Hauser, 1972; Sewell et al., 1969, Sewell et al., 1970; Sewell and Hauser, 1975); a longitudinal survey of a national sample of 1955 high school sophomores (Alexander and Eckland, 1973); the Youth in Transition survey (Bachman, 1970; Bachman, Kahn, Mednick, Davidson, and Johnston, 1967); and a survey of psychological aspects of occupations (Kohn, 1969; Kohn and Schooler, 1973). Among other researches drawing on one or more of these data sets are O. D. Duncan (1968a), Jencks et al. (1972), and Spaeth (Chapter VI of this volume).

between IQ and environment is probably about right. Furthermore, the near zero value of a direct parental SES–IQ effect seems robust in the face of plausible manipulations of certain of the correlations involved. Based on several data sets, including large, diverse, and sometimes nationally representative samples, the estimate of about .3 for the parental SES–IQ correlation is probably reasonably accurate. Using the rather low value of .6 for the environment–IQ correlation makes the direct effect of parental SES zero. As the parental SES–environment correlation is increased above .5, the estimate of the direct effects of parental SES becomes even more negative than before. Although refined measurements from a single national sample would be desirable, it seems justifiable to conclude provisionally that measured cognitive environment transmits all the effects of parental SES on a child's IQ.

One reason why direct measures of a child's cognitive environment are such effective predictors of IQ is that they include assessments of the degree of intensive educational treatment provided by parents for their children. For purposes of comparison, a brief historical excursion will indicate the types of results to be expected when treatments are not assessed. Fraser (1959) summarizes 18 early studies of the relationship between environment and IQ, all based on small, local samples and carried out in 1939 or earlier. Among measures limited to or chiefly relying on mere "face sheet" indicators of parental SES, the correlation between "environment" and IQ was .33, closely similar to the more recent values reported above. Correlations utilizing assessments of the physical characteristics of the home (such as those contained in the Chapin Scale) reached a mean of .50. We may conclude that these early studies incorporated rather good measures of settings but rather ineffective measures of treatments, and we must examine the kinds of environmental measures that seem to produce higher correlations than those produced by measures of physical settings.

At least two common characteristics mark recent efforts to measure home environment directly: (1) the collection of data on child-rearing practices from the mother or both parents, a procedure also followed in the early psychological investigations of settings: (2) the use of quite detailed questioning of the parents on their behavior vis-à-vis a specific child. Included in this line of questioning is an attempt to assess the explicit intention of fostering cognitive growth in the child.

It is worth detailing one such procedure for measuring a child's cognitive environment, for it exemplifies the kinds of data that apparently need to be collected. In response to Bloom's (1964) review of longitudinal research on stability and change in certain human characteristics, Wolf (1964) and Dave (1963) carried out research attempting to measure the child's cognitive environment directly. The sample in Wolf's research was 60 mothers of fifth-grade children enrolled in the schools of a community on the western edge of Cook County, Illinois. Data were collected from these mothers on their practices in the rearing of a specific child. Scores on the Henman–Nelson IQ test were the dependent variable and were collected from school records independently of the rating of the child's home environment. The correlation between a global summed measure of home environment and IQ was .69.

Wolf's measures of cognitive environment clearly emphasize conscious parental efforts to enhance children's learning, as is shown by inclusion of scales rating dimensions such as the mother's efforts to stimulate language usage, correct inadequate usage, provide a variety of stimuli in and out of the home, provide learning materials, and encourage their use by the child. The conative dimension, in the form of ratings of parental desires and plans to encourage advanced schooling for the child, is also included. The emphasis is on "conscious efforts," "well developed and consistently executed plans," "exploitation of a variety of situations," "conscious effort to exploit the opportunities for learning," and so on. When one remembers that these assessments were made relative to a mother's socialization of a particular child, the inclusion of a heavy treatment component becomes manifest (Wolf, 1964:117–141). Of course, this does not deny the importance of more subtle forms of socialization, though it does raise the possibility that the reported presence of overt and intentional treatments is very highly correlated with the kinds of subtle and extensive pressures that also contribute to the development of intelligence. There is no reason to expect the direct effects of parental SES to be negative, as they would be if more accurate measurement were to increase the environment–IQ correlation.

Unfortunately, the actual measurement procedures used by Wolf and Dave raise at least as many problems as they help to solve. Ratings were the result of the researchers' judgments formed by evaluating answers to sets of open-ended questions. Information from one question was often applied to the ratings for more than one scale. This redundancy makes an empirical determination of the structure of the home environment extremely difficult. A task for future research is to develop much more rigorous measurement techniques and to integrate the newly derived measures into models of the determination of IQ based on large, representative, national samples. In addition, an attempt should be made to separate the measurement of settings from that of treatments by including independent measures of the extent to which varied physical and interpersonal stimuli are available and the extent to which indirect as well as direct parental efforts to enhance the child's cognitive development are undertaken.

The information we now have indicates that parental treatment of young children aimed at fostering their cognitive growth can be measured with some degree of reliability. This perspective leads to a consideration of other kinds of early influences on IQ that could be subsumed under the general principle of environmental complexity adduced earlier. One candidate virtually suggests itself: number of siblings; evidence on this variable is contained in the Plowden data (Walberg and Marjoribanks, 1974).

The negative relationships between number of siblings and IQ, educational attainment, occupation, and income are well known. The explanation of the handicap of relatively numerous brothers and sisters has long been thought to reflect a dilution of parental resources, and two kinds of resources have been singled out in particular: money and time. A family with three children presumably has two-thirds as much money to spend on the children's cognitive development as one with two children, other things being equal. At the same time, each additional child creates a decrement in the proportion of time that parents can spend with each child. The implication of limitations of parental time for effectiveness of parental treatment should be obvious.

Given the importance of parental treatment for cognitive development, an exercise designed to elucidate the notion of the restriction of parental resources imposed by a large family may be of some heuristic interest. For the sake of simplicity, assume that two parents constitute one "full-time-equivalent" tutor (cognitive socializing agent) for their children, that no economies of scale are possible and each additional child's demands thus compete with those of every other child, and that parents allocate time equally between their children. Under these conditions, one child will have one FTE tutor, two will have .5, and ten will have .1. The proportionality assumption dictates that available time will decrease by an order of magnitude for every order of magnitude increase in number of children.

Stated explicitly, these assumptions are clearly only approximations, but with regard to the scarce resource of parental time, they point out that the greatest proportional deficit will occur in relatively small families.

On the above assumptions, the role of cognitive environment in mediating the effects of sibsize has been assessed in the Plowden data. Just as the positive effects of parental SES are totally mediated by home environment, so are the negative effects of number of siblings (Walberg and Marjoribanks, 1974): the more numerous the children, the less parental tutoring available and the lower the children's IQ.

In summary, this section has shown that there is empirical evidence to support the proposition that ordinary measures of parental SES are indicators of a familial cognitive environment that influences a child's IQ. The effects of that environment, when it is directly measured, are strong enough to mediate the effects of parental SES on a child's IQ. Similarly, measured cognitive environment mediates the negative effects of sibsize on IQ.

Since all the effects of parental SES on IQ are indirect, it follows that this variable is irrelevant to an explanation of the linkage between home environment and IQ. Therefore, some other variable must account for this rather high correlation, and this variable will be only modestly related to parental SES.

The notion of parental behavior as tutelage leads directly to one such variable—the intelligence of the parents. Though skill as cognitive socializing agents has not been directly measured, the strength of the association between measured environment and IQ implies that parents' reports of their efforts must be rather closely related to their abilities. Thus, the model underlying the earlier discussion is misspecified because parental abilities have been omitted.

The extent of the specification error is unclear. One need not completely agree with the heritability estimates of Jensen (1969, 1973) to acknowledge that a major portion of IQ is inherited. Thus, some part of the zero-order correlation between parental SES and IQ is surely spurious, with the extent of the spuriousness a function of the heritability of IQ. Nevertheless, parental treatment still mediates the remaining effects of parental SES.[2]

Although at least one data set containing measures of parental IQ and child's cognitive environment exists, it is a sample from Edmonton, Alberta, and suffers from multicollinearity artifically induced by exaggeration of range (Williams, 1973, and Chapter III of this volume). Apparently the sample is biased by selection from the extremes of the occupational distribution. Thus, a determination of the relative effects of parental IQ and SES is impossible. Nonetheless, there are rather strong direct effects of home environment net of parental IQ in the Edmonton sample.

Educational Attainment as a Dependent Variable

The kinds of topics to be included in a discussion of education as a dependent variable are somewhat different from those treated already. These topics include the organizational problems of providing univocal treatments in schools, the logical difficulty in considering educational quality as an attribute of schools, evidence for the concept of exposure to settings as an indicator of educational effectiveness, and an explicit treatment of years of schooling as a theoretically relevant variable.

As a preliminary to analysis of the difficulty of schools in providing intensive educational treatments for their students, let us review the assumptions made with regard to the specification of the relationship between sibsize and IQ. There we assumed that two parents were the equivalent of one FTE tutor, that each additional child caused a proportional decrement in available parental time, and that attending to one child was incompatible with attending to another. The effectiveness of parents as cognitive socializing agents was thus specified as inversely proportional to the number of children in the family. Parental effectiveness would thus receive a score of 1 in a 1-child family, .2 in a 5-child family, .05 in a 20-child family, and .03 in 30-child family. Obviously, effectiveness scores for families of 20 or more children were chosen as illustrations because such sizes correspond to class size in many schools.

---

[2] In recent papers, Goldberger (1974a,b) concludes that Jensen's estimates of heritability are probably too high (see also Kamin, 1974). These estimates apparently rest on inadequate specifications of heritability models and on nonrepresentative "samples."

A school class cannot be run on the principle of allocating 3 to 5% of a teacher's time to each student individually, and the textbook–lecture–problem-discussion approach has thus become a standard substitute for direct tutelage. Students are exposed to the same subject matter, which is treated in a standard way and adjusted to a particular teacher's instructional idiosyncrasies. For the most part, treatment of individual students is perforce replaced by exposure of the class as a whole to certain stimuli, and most students spend a majority of their class time passively receiving stimuli in the form of information about subject matter.

This does not exclude the possibility of effective treatments in schools, but it does argue that drastic changes in the social organization of the classroom may be required. Dramatic improvements in student performance have been produced by a technique known as mastery learning (Block, 1971; Bloom, 1971a,b). This technique, which has been successfully applied at diverse educational levels, apparently requires the teacher to be capable of identifying learning outcomes, developing performance criteria, organizing instructional sequences, performing diagnostic evaluation, and providing timely feedback and correction (Spady, 1974). Clearly schools and classrooms require marked changes in their social organization before such a technique could be used on a widespread basis.

In the normal course of events, however, every school will contain a mixture of students and teachers arbitrarily exposed to each other. In certain classes, the effects of certain teachers will benefit certain students, but the students experiencing a treatment in one class may experience nothing of the kind in another class. Students can even receive negative treatment through failure to perform at the level of standards learned elsewhere. Thus, it is understandable that all efforts to assess the effects of school "quality" with indicators such as per pupil expenditure or proportion of the faculty with advanced degrees have found very feeble school "effects" at best.[3]

One should not assume, however, that schooling is ineffective. Exposure to schooling has demonstrable results, but these would be much stronger if specific treatments could be applied to particular students. Still, it is a platitude to say that students would know less algebra, French, English, and so on, if they had not taken classes in these subjects. This platitude often seems to be forgotten in polemics about the ineffectiveness of schooling. As Wiley (Chapter VIII of this volume) points out, the question, "Does schooling have an effect?" is inadequate. He adds:

[3] If parental SES is a surrogate for an environmental complexity variable that may operate at a rather early age, the specification of school effects models removing the effects of student input characteristics before assessing school characteristics is justified. It should be noted, incidentally, that many estimates in which school effects are found to be minor omit prior measures of student ability entirely. Inclusion of such measures could only further reduce the apparent effects of school characteristics. For a further discussion of this point, see Hauser (1971).

> A new mythology of schooling is snowing us. Based on a combination of poor detective work and no clues, it tries to convince us of what is manifestly not true: Schooling has no effect.

The argument presented here is simply that for most students schooling will represent little net treatment. The brighter students learn more, partly because they are motivated to do so and partly because their earlier socialization has prepared them to do so. Viewed in this light, the conclusion that quality of schooling is no different from quantity of schooling gains considerable plausibility. Further evidence is furnished by an analysis of *Equality of Educational Opportunity* data (Coleman, Campbell, Hobson, McPartland, Mood, Weinfeld, and York, 1966) carried out by Wiley (see Chapter VIII of this volume). For Detroit schools in the OEO data set, a variable, effective hours per school year, was constructed by forming the product of the average proportion of students attending a certain school per day, the number of hours in the school day, and the number of days in the school year. At the school level of analysis, effective hours per school year had substantial effects on tested verbal ability, reading, and mathematics. These effects were net of student input characteristics. The greater the exposure to schooling, the higher tested student performance was. The contrast between the effects of a duration-of-exposure variable and the usual objective indicators of school quality is thus quite marked.

The general principle that complex environments lead to higher later attainments has thus far found two instantiations with regard to educational attainment—the substantial effects of educational attainment on occupational status and the effects of duration of exposure to schooling on tested academic performance. Other such effects found in the literature on the causes and effects of educational attainment may also be subsumed under the same principle.

Several data sets include high school students' reports of the curricular track to which they were assigned (see Alexander and Eckland, 1973; Bachman, 1970; Bachman, Kahn, Mednick, Davidson, and Johnston, 1967; Spaeth and Greeley, 1970). Net of parental SES and a student's IQ, placement in a college preparatory track has substantial positive effects on students' educational plans and attainment. Parental SES and one's own IQ are rather strong predictors of track assignment, and the effects of educational plans and attainment on later variables are rather well documented. It requires no great leap of the imagination to hypothesize that curricular track corresponds to curricular complexity. Non-college tracks largely provide training for occupations of relatively low social standing. These occupations are less complex than higher-status occupations, and training for them presumably represents a lower level of complexity than that of the standard college preparatory curriculum. Thus, assignment to a college preparatory curriculum reflects exposure to a more complex setting than does assignment to a non-college track.

In summary, these research findings indicate that years of schooling as a variable might be usefully adjusted by inclusion of data that provide greater detail on exposure to complex settings, but they do not support the notion that there is a measurable dimension of educational quality independent of duration of exposure.

Thus, the results on tracking and duration of schooling can be considered as instantiations of the principle that exposure to complex environments leads to higher attainments. Such results support the theory adduced here, but they do not provide conclusive evidence in its favor. First, the possibility always exists that other variables could make this interpretation a spurious one. Second, no new findings have been predicted by the theory; established ones have simply been shown to be consistent with it. A later section will contain hypotheses based on the duration of exposure to educational and occupational complexity.

Occupational Status as a Dependent Variable

The link between educational attainment and current occupational status has been the subject of relatively little empirical investigation; the mechanisms relating the two variables have rarely been tested. Yet the importance of schooling for occupational attainment is manifest. Given the lack of research evidence on the transmission mechanism, we shall discuss some evidence on the similarity between occupational status and job complexity, and then briefly describe a measurement procedure that might help to bridge this gap.

As mentioned above, the measurement of job complexity by Kohn and Schooler (1973) rests on detailed information, including data on ratings of the complexity of a man's work in general and ratings of the complexity of a man's work with data or ideas, with people, and with things. In addition, the amount of time spent on each type of activity is included in the overall measure of substantive complexity, based on a factor analysis of these seven items. The scale of complexity of work with data ranges from "synthesizing," which includes discovering new knowledge, to "reading instructions." Working with people ranges from "mentoring," which refers to dealing with individuals in terms of their total personalities, to "serving" or "receiving instructions." Working with things ranges from "setting up" a machine to "handling," which refers to the bodily shifting of objects from one place to another. Overall complexity ranges from activities that are "routine and take no thought" to "the setting up of a complex system of analysis or synthesis."

The results of Kohn's factor analysis show that working with data and people had rather high positive loadings, that working with things had a low loading, and that the time spent working with things had a negative loading. These findings are consistent with the relatively low degree of complexity involved in setting up a machine in comparison with synthesizing or mentoring and with the substantial correlation of substantive complexity with occupational status (Melvin L. Kohn, personal communication).

The eight values (excluding zero) of the work-with-data ratings indicate the rather close relationship of this scale to curricular complexity in the schools. Starting with the reading of instructions, which is out of order as far as curriculum is concerned, the scale progresses from comparing to copying, computing, compiling, analyzing, coordinating, and synthesizing. The definition of synthesizing suggests an intellectual task at the level of theory construction or the production of a scholarly work. Clearly, the first four or five skills are learned in grade school, and the last three or four are learned in high school, college, or graduate or professional school (or on the job).

This argument is enough to make the substantial correlation of .6 between educational attainment and occupational prestige not surprising. Note that this correlation represents the relationship between exposure to two settings. The greater the exposure to curricular complexity, the greater the complexity of the occupational setting will be.

Education and Occupation as Independent Variables

Explaining the linkage between schooling and work is a particularly vexing problem for a variety of reasons. For one thing, very little empirical evidence exists on the mechanisms that might link educational and occupational achievement. In addition, it would be difficult to operationalize the devices most widely held to account for the transition. Interpretation of the linkage is often expressed in terms of the functions of the educational system for occupational selection and certification and not in terms of potentially measurable characteristics of individuals. This section attempts to explore possible ways of operationalizing such interpretations. In doing so, the notion of exposure to complexity will be used to develop more detailed measures of educational and occupational status than those currently in use.

The functions of schooling include the inculcation of cognitive competencies and skills; socialization in norms, values, and behavior appropriate to occupations and other adult social settings; custody and control of the young; certification; and selection (Spady, 1974). All but the custodial function are directly pertinent to the transition between school and work.

Information on certain of the linkages among these functions can be inferred from analyses of data of the kind provided by individual respondents in surveys dealing with the achievement process. To do so requires certain assumptions about the operation of the processes described earlier. Thus, research on career choice has indicated that much of the selection function is carried out through self-selection.[4] If so, one aspect of the relationship between selection and cognitive and conative socialization may be explained as follows. As a result of pressures from parents, students come to have certain expectations about the amount of education they would like to receive and their chances of receiving it. Those students who do well in school either continue to hold high expectations or come to hold them. Those who do poorly either continue to hold low expectations or lower their expectations. As a result, some students stay in school, leaving open to themselves careers in high-status occupations, while others drop out. The same mechanism helps to account for the successful transition from one level of schooling to another or the cessation of education at conventional stopping points. In the United States, at least, few students are formally denied the opportunity to continue their education, but many decide not to continue. To the extent that the process of selection is truly one of self-selection, this aspect of the functioning of the educational system can be tapped by responses to questions on educational and occupational plans. Currently available findings indicate that such plans are important both in transmitting the effects of social origins and in their own right (Alexander and Eckland, 1973; Hauser, 1972; Sewell *et al.*, 1969; Sewell *et al.*, 1970; Spaeth, 1968, 1970; Spaeth and Greeley, 1970).

Some of the other functions of the educational system are at least as difficult to operationalize; certification is a case in point. This issue is discussed in Jencks, Smith, Acland, Bane, Cohen, Gintis, Heyns, and Michelson (1972). The authors posit three explanations of the linkage between education and occupation: differential occupational preferences by education, differences in cognitive or noncognitive skills by education, and the rationing of access to high-status jobs by employers' use of "arbitrary educational requirements." Their discussion of the sketchy data bearing on this matter concludes that there may be some truth to each of these interpretations. As has already been noted, the existing evidence on the role of expectations indicates that they are quite important, both for educational and occupational choice.

Direct evidence on the role of credentials either does not exist or is negative. If one adopted the stringent definition of Jencks *et al.*, one would have to measure the intentions and behavior of employers in order to make certain that their use of a candidate's educational credentials was arbitrary. An empirically testable but equally stringent definition indicates that the effects of credentials are nil. Coefficients estimated for the OCG data set indicate that it makes no difference whether schooling measured in years or as the completion of educational stages is correlated with occupational status. A multiple classification analysis (MCA), which takes educational

---

[4] To my knowledge, the relevant information has not been codified as a research finding, but my impression is that investigators in this area generally conclude that self-selection is an important aspect of the process.

stages completed into account, "explained" 35.5% of the variance in occupational attainment (Blau and Duncan, 1967:133). Years of schooling "explained" 36.7% (Duncan et al., 1972:263).[5] Thus, possession of a piece of paper certifying completion of high school or graduation from college had no effect on occupational attainment beyond that associated with completion of the appropriate year of schooling.

It should be pointed out that any argument citing a low correlation between educational attainment or low test scores and job *performance* is invalid evidence of the ineffectiveness of cognitive variables as determinants of occupational status. Since educational attainment provides entry to an occupation and since the incumbent of an occupation is accorded the prestige of that occupation on the day that he enters it, such a low correlation is clearly a matter of false partialling (Gordon, 1968). That is, analyses of job performance must take into account the process by which job incumbents gained entry to their positions. It is all too common for analyses of persons in particular occupations to view the process as if entering an occupation were not the culmination of years of socialization, training, and selection. This oversight leads to the interpretation of correlations observed within occupations as if they were zero-order correlations pertaining to broader populations.[6]

An advance in our understanding of the education–occupation linkage might be possible if exposure to educational complexity could be operationalized independently of years of schooling. The analytical task would then be to estimate the direct effect of years of schooling on occupational status net of parental SES, filial IQ, occupational and educational plans, and the influence of significant others (measured prior to the completion of schooling). In addition, it would be necessary to estimate the extent to which exposure to educational complexity, post-schooling plans, significant others' influence, and certification transmit the influence of education on occupation.

To operationalize exposure to educational complexity would be a difficult task requiring considerable time and resources, especially since a measure of this variable must be operationally independent of student academic performance. One way of doing so would be to rate the educational stimuli to which students are exposed. A first attempt might include rating the difficulty of textbooks by readability criteria; another might be to rate assignments in terms of their substantive complexity as tasks on the scale

---

[5] The reason why the variable, years of schooling, explained more of the variation than did the MCA categories (which would be impossible if the calculations had been carried out on the same respondents) is that the Blau–Duncan MCA included a category for missing data.

[6] The failure to distinguish between occupational status and on-the-job performance has been used to justify the idea that grades have no effect on occupational achievement (Hoyt, 1965) and that schooling is irrelevant to occupational achievement (Berg, 1970).

used by Kohn and Schooler (1973). Syllabi might be rated according to similar criteria. The basic unit of analysis would be the course, and each course would be rated according to criteria of the kind just mentioned. With a complexity rating for each course, students could be scored according to the number of "complexity hours" to which they had been exposed. Presumably a measure of this kind would be more highly related to occupational status than would years of schooling. If so, the direct path from education to occupation would be reduced.[7]

The substantial degree of progress implicit in the successful construction and validation of a measure of educational complexity is only a first step in addressing the issue of the effects of certification. Given a reasonably substantial reduction in the years-of-schooling–occupation path as a result of complexity hours, two interpretations are possible: (1) The remaining direct path represents the effects of the arbitrary demand for credentials by employers or other screening agencies. This interpretation might or might not be plausible, but it would be logically insupportable since it would amount to giving a name to our ignorance as represented by the remaining direct path. (2) Exposure to educational complexity *is* what is certified. Again, further investigation would be necessary to establish this conclusion, but acceptance of this interpretation would be tantamount to denying that a part of the certification is arbitrary.

Neither of these two interpretations supports the idea that the educational system merely serves to perpetuate parental socioeconomic status (see Bowles and Gintis, 1972–1973). The phenomena considered here are independent of parental socioeconomic status since the direct effects of duration of schooling on occupation are net of parental SES. Educational attainment does transmit much of the influence of parental status on occupational achievement, but it does so to the extent that it has an influence independent of parental SES, not to the extent that its influence is spurious.

The idea of measuring complexity hours is a reasonably straightforward outgrowth of Wiley's findings on effective hours per school year and the interpretation of duration of schooling offered earlier. The difficulty with this concept lies in finding a practicable method of operationalizing it.

No such difficulty exists with regard to the development of a measure of exposure to occupational complexity. Conventional measures of occupational status are cross-sectional, but there is no reason why they cannot reflect duration of exposure as amount of schooling does for education. The

[7] The variable, complexity hours, would be partially validated if it had a reasonably large correlation with allocation to curricular track. A substantial correlation with track might also indicate the utility of attempting to develop a measure of exposure to educational complexity for cross-national research on socioeconomic achievement. Such a measure could permit valid cross-national comparisons of exposure to educational complexity, a variable that might then be used in place of conventional but noncomparable measures of educational attainment.

educational career is hierarchical and irreversible: n + 1 years of schooling denotes greater exposure to greater complexity than does n years (B. Duncan, 1968). Intragenerational occupational mobility, on the other hand, may be either upward or downward, but the principle of counting time units of exposure is still applicable. One method of creating a measure of occupational complexity relies on the virtual identity of occupational status and occupational complexity. Experience in a certain occupation at a certain prestige level represents exposure to a certain amount of complexity. Presumably the duration of this exposure is at least roughly related to the degree of "practice" gained in dealing with problems of a certain degree of complexity. Thus, a variable measuring amount of exposure to occupational complexity can be considered as a form of human capital investment. As such, it should yield returns in earnings.

Operationalizing such a variable would require some care, but it would certainly be feasible. It would require a detailed job history with information on the length of time each job was held. Complexity could be measured either directly or as occupational status. The unit of analysis might be "complexity months," the sum of the complexity of each job weighted by the number of months it had been held. The work history would allow the investigator to distinguish between the individual's past occupational experience, measured in complexity units, and the complexity or status of the current job in order to avoid confounding the two and to permit an unequivocal test of the effects of history on current status. Since complexity months would presumably be a cogent measure of work experience, it could be treated as a determinant of current occupational status as well as of earnings.

A certain amount of care is required in specifying the form of the function expected for complexity months. Since returns to total experience begin to decrease at some point in the working career (Mincer, 1974), one might expect a similar decrease for complexity months. Thus, an adequate test of the hypothesis that experience in coping with complex occupations leads to returns in the form of earnings could require the specification of curvilinear relations.

Although job complexity and occupational status can be considered as virtual equivalents, complexity has an interpretative advantage, at least in human capital models. Amount of exposure to complex occupational tasks should yield earnings returns, if for no other reason than the practice mentioned above. Occupational status has no such obvious interpretation.

Whether the proposed revision of socioeconomic achievement variables will contribute to a larger coefficient of determination than the standard measures is an open question, although they probably will. For example, relevant job experience has effects on earnings net of total experience (Spaeth, Chapter VI of this volume).

The proposal for the two new measures suggests that the conception of the achievement process proposed here may be a fruitful one. The next section attempts to show that a coherent picture of the status transmission and achievement processes is provided by considering exposure to complex settings and the capacity for coping with complexity as economic goods.

Completing the Cycle: The Intergenerational
Transfer of Status

Thus far, our attention has centered on the socioeconomic benefits resulting from exposure to complexity throughout the life cycle. In effect, this chapter has aged a cohort of children into adulthood. The cohort has undergone schooling and become established in occupational careers. Members of this cohort have also become parents and, thereby, socializing agents for a new generation of children. Moreover, the process by which socioeconomic rewards are accrued is also one by which certain resources useful to parents are allocated. This section will briefly discuss the nature of these resources, their genesis in the socioeconomic career, and their influence on the achievements of the new generation.

For the inculcation of the cognitive competencies conducive to achievement, the following parental characteristics may be considered as resources: general intellectual skills, information and knowledge, value orientations, and material resources such as wealth.

Just as certain cognitive competencies are useful in the achievement process, they are useful in socializing the young. For example, parents cannot teach what they do not understand. The ability to cope with complexity clearly has hereditary roots, and it develops most substantially in the early years of the life cycle. Even so, this ability can develop further at later stages through schooling and, perhaps, work experience (Kohn and Schooler, 1973). An aspect of this ability, knowledge or information, presumably continues to be acquired well into adulthood in response to a variety of experiences, though education is perhaps the preeminent determinant. Thus, education is a more important determinant of knowledge about jobs than is job experience or occupational status (Evers, 1972).

The parental family is also clearly an important source of values, but again experience throughout the life cycle is important. It is possible for persons to learn that successfully solving complex problems is intrinsically gratifying in a variety of settings including the home, school, and the job, just as they can acquire the skills helpful in coping with complex problems at any stage of the life cycle. Of course, persons may learn that failure to learn is unrewarding at any time and may thereby be persuaded to lower their aspirations.

Parental competence, interest, knowledge, and material resources combine to enhance a child's learning. The manner in which these variables combine is itself highly complex. The following examples are illustrative of this complexity but are by no means an exhaustive account of the process. Competency helps produce knowledge and information, which in turn enhance competency. Competency repeatedly demonstrated to self and others tends to increase interest. This plus material resources increases the probability that positive treatments will be attempted and that they will be effective in promoting a child's learning. At some point, the child also starts on its own cycle in which successful learning leads to further attempts to learn or unsuccessful learning leads to the cessation of such attempts.

The parents' material resources doubtless have effects independent of their facilitation of the child's learning. A degree of discretionary income tends to minimize pressure for early entry into the labor force. Money can always be used to purchase books and other learning materials and, if the child goes to college, to pay tuition, fees, and other expenses.

Similarly, parental knowlege and information is directly useful. Parents know the appropriate sources of help if it is needed, and they will encourage the child to seek such help. Knowing the ropes enables parents to help children make informed decisions. For example, educated parents know that there is a college for their child even if it is not very bright. They also tend to know more than less educated parents do about the occupational world.

In summary, the parents' exposure to complex environmental settings increases their ability to cope with complexity. This aids the cognitive socialization of their children by increasing parental skills and adding to the parental stock of knowledge and other resources.

The foregoing has briefly discussed the way in which advantages accumulated throughout the course of the socioeconomic life cycle can be applied to the intergenerational transfer of status. According to the view advanced here, status is transferred through transmission of the capacity to cope with cognitive complexity. This capacity is, in effect, an intergenerational medium of exchange. By focusing attention on *what* is transmitted, complexity gains considerable interpretive advantages compared to the statuses themselves.

Basically, socioeconomic status is not transferred by simple legal inheritance. Such a transfer is impossible with regard to educational achievement because the receipt of n years of schooling means that the child itself must go to school for n years. Though it is possible for a son literally to inherit his father's occupation, such transmission takes place for fewer than 10% of the sons in the population (Blau and Duncan, 1967:142).[8] Thus, statuses are not literally transferred from one generation to the next. Among the "commodities" that are transmitted are the capacity for dealing with cognitive complexity and the opportunity for exposure to complex settings.

At this point, it is necessary to caution the reader in two respects. First, the rhetoric of argumentation often makes social processes seem more deterministic than they really are. The intergenerational transmission of

---

[8] Blau and Duncan estimate an occupational inheritance rate of 10%, but they point out that this rate is based on status scores. Since father and son can have identical status scores and be in different occupations, the actual inheritance rate is less than 10%.

status is a probability process in which a series of contingencies influences the outcome. These include parental intelligence and tutelage, other parental resources, and the earlier achievements of the child. None of these contingencies completely determines the outcome, nor does the entire set. In other words, this is not an argument for a benign circle analogous to the vicious circle criticized by Blau and Duncan (1967:199–205).

As is true of all recursive causal processes among moderately intercorrelated variables, the socioeconomic achievement process automatically provides compensatory opportunities. Parental SES provides a very real head start for socioeconomic achievement, but parental skills heighten the capacity for coping with complexity independently of SES. Aspirations and expectations are also manifestations of parental SES, but they have effects of their own. Similarly, the fact that education transmits the effects of SES and IQ means that it has effects independent of occupation and earnings. Thus, parents in high-SES families inculcating cognitive competencies in their children did not necessarily come from high-SES backgrounds themselves. Their own competencies have quite likely been developed by socialization and selection unrelated to their own parents' socioeconomic status.

Second, the reader should remember that this chapter is concerned with developing the ramifications of only *one* dimension underlying the status achievement process—cognitive complexity. Even in the course of developing this argument, it was necessary to refer to other than cognitive matters. Other dimensions are clearly important, and the achievement process will not be well understood until they have been examined.

Summary

The major task of this chapter was a reconceptualization of measured variables in the socioeconomic achievement process. Parental SES, duration of schooling, and occupational prestige can be considered as manifestations of environmental complexity. A general proposition emerging from such consideration is the following: The more cognitively complex a person's earlier environments are, the higher the person's subsequent socioeconomic status will be. Thus, cognitive complexity is one dimension underlying the status achievement process. This chapter has developed some of the implications of this dimension for a theory of the achievement process.

Socioeconomic achievement takes place in stages that correspond to the life cycle, and it encompasses movement from the family of orientation through schools to work. A developmental task of each stage is the attainment of competency in coping with cognitive complexity. An outcome of socialization in the home is development of a general competency corresponding to intelligence. More specific competencies are developed in the course of schooling: the longer the duration of schooling, the greater the cognitive complexity to which persons are exposed and the more specific the knowledge and skills they learn. Job competencies are even more specific and must be learned through on-the-job training or in the course of actual work experience. Jobs vary in complexity of task performed, and this variation corresponds to variation in occupational prestige.

Statuses relevant to socioeconomic achievement can be considered as indicators of the complexity of settings to which persons are exposed. In the family of orientation, children may not only be exposed to complex stimuli, but parents may also manipulate those stimuli, serve as role and competency models, and bring about treatments that increase (or decrease) the competency of their children in coping with cognitive complexity. Parental tutelage transmits the nonspurious effects of parental SES on a child's intelligence. It also accounts for the negative effects of sibsize.

Exposure to schooling measured in years represents the duration of exposure to settings and generalized treatments of increasing cognitive complexity because the graded curriculum of schools is a systematic scheme calculated to bring about such exposure. The effects of schooling are a result of this exposure. The quality of schools has had little demonstrable effect on student academic performance because variations in the resources of schools do not correspond to variations in complexity of curriculum. In contrast to the negligible effects of school quality, variations in exposure to schooling, such as effective hours per school year, have marked effects on student academic performance on the school level of analysis (Wiley, Chapter VIII of this volume).

The correlation between occupational prestige and job complexity is .8, and the correlation between occupational prestige and years of schooling is about .6. Explanation of the latter relationship, as represented by a direct path of about .5, is generally couched in terms of the functions of education. Such macro-analysis is difficult to translate into the measurable micro-variables characteristic of analyses of the achievement process. In conjunction with certain assumptions about the operation of noncognitive variables, consideration of statuses as measures of exposure to complexity permits incorporation of macro-functions in analyses of micro-data. One such assumption is that much of education's function in selecting and screening persons for later roles is carried out through self-selection. If so, measures of occupational and educational aspirations and expectations may serve as surrogates for the selection function in equations dealing with occupational achievement. On the grounds that exposure to cognitive complexity is a valid interpretation of the effects of schooling, a more detailed measure of educational complexity was proposed: amount of complexity in each course taken weighted by the number of hours of exposure.

In an equation in which parental SES, the person's early IQ, and past educational and occupational expectations are entered along with years of schooling, the independent effects of complexity hours and current expectations were hypothesized to be nonnegligible. The extent to which the former reduces the direct effect of years of schooling was interpreted as evidence for the importance of exposure to cognitive complexity and an indication of the extent to which educational certification was nonarbitrary. The size of the direct path from years of schooling net of complexity hours and other variables could be interpreted as a measure of the arbitrariness of educational certification. This interpretation, however, assumes that the only source of our ignorance regarding the remaining direct effects of years of schooling is arbitrary certification. However plausible it may be, this assumption is not logically warranted.

Education based duration-of-exposure measures of complexity suggest the application of similar measures to occupations. It would be a simple matter to code occupational histories for the complexity of each job and the length of exposure (in months) to each job, especially if occupational prestige were to be treated as a surrogate for complexity.

Such a procedure would permit a decomposition of the effects of labor force experience on earnings. If prior experience were kept separate from current occupation, it would be possible to test the following propositions: Net of years of schooling and earlier variables, prior occupational complexity will have a nonnegligible direct effect on current occupational status; net of occupational status and earlier variables, complexity months will have a direct effect on earnings.

Cognitive complexity yields a reconceptualization of the achievement process by providing an inter- and intragenerational medium of exchange. As parents in families of procreation, the children of the preceding generation's families of orientation undertake the socialization of the young. The parents are equipped with the knowledge, skills, and other resources acquired from their families of orientation, from schooling, and from participation in the labor force. An important subset of such resources is experience and training in dealing with cognitive complexity, which the parents will pass on to their children and which the children will acquire through exposure to educational and occupational complexity.

Thus, this chapter has shown that it is possible to view the status achievement process as corresponding to the movement between environmental settings that vary in their cognitive complexity. This approach yields not only a dimension underlying the achievement process but proposals for constructing new measures of intervening variables in that process. One should remember, however, that cognitive complexity is only one dimension of a process that is clearly multidimensional, and its importance must be tested empirically.

Acknowledgments

I am grateful for criticism to C. Arnold Anderson, Otis Dudley Duncan, Bruce K. Eckland, Marcus Felson, Kenneth C. Land, Melvin L. Kohn, and especially David L. Featherman, whose rigorously perceptive comments were very helpful. Needless to say, the faults remaining are solely mine.

V | Discontinuities in Schooling and the Socioeconomic Life Cycle*

David L. Featherman
University of Wisconsin, Madison

T. Michael Carter
University of Minnesota

To the demographer, time is critically important. Time, or age–time relationships, constitute the very core of the concept of a population (Ryder, 1964). For the individual, date of birth is the benchmark against which personal growth and maturation are evaluated; age has normative significance as a criterion for gauging the appropriateness and value of behaviors vis-à-vis the social group. Date of birth also serves to link one to the social group or that part of it—the (birth) cohort—that experiences the same events at the same historical time (Ryder, 1965:845). This linkage to the cohort bears upon the individual, for it moulds behavior to historical circumstances and to the aggregate, structural circumstances of the member's (birth) cohort. Therefore, behaviors indexed by an individual's age manifest patterns appropriate to a certain stage in the life cycle as these behavioral norms have been temporized by history.[1]

* This research was funded by grants from the American College Testing Program, the National Science Foundation (GS-29031, A. O. Haller, Principal Investigator), and institutional support from the Graduate School, the Institute for Research on Poverty, and the College of Agricultural and Life Sciences, University of Wisconsin, Madison. The chapter grew out of work undertaken by associates of the Research Institute of the American College Testing Program, Iowa City, Iowa.
[1] For an appreciation of the impact of cohort and historical (period) forces within the contemporary scene, see Moynihan (1973).

Age is a variable with two analytical edges: It can be used to cut a population (sample) into birth cohorts, and it can be employed to dissect the passage of historical time for a given birth cohort into sequences of relatively homogeneous social experiences, or into stages of the life cycle. From the comparison of birth cohorts—intercohort analysis—the demographer ascertains social change, subject to the ability to hold constant the effects of maturation (age). From the comparison of behaviors or experiences of individuals at different ages, or stages of the life cycle—intracohort analysis—the demographer discovers the course of maturation and defines the nature of the life cycle, subject to the ability to control for history (time period).

In this chapter, we trace the experience of a birth cohort of males as its members leave high school, complete their schooling in colleges and other institutions, and/or assume their post-educational occupations. Our intracohort analysis aims to identify plausible causal antecedents and consequences of discontinuities in schooling—age–grade retardation and temporary dropouts both prior to post-high school education and subsequent to college or business-vocational-technical school matriculation—in the context of the cohort's socioeconomic life cycle (O. D. Duncan, 1967).

Figure 5.1 illustrates the sequence of major social statuses over the course of a person's life cycle. Students of social inequality and stratification often refer to this sequence of relationships in the socioeconomic life cycle as "the process of achievement," or "the status attainment process." Such labels, which emphasize the achieved nature of educational, occupational, and economic statuses, are accurate insofar as socioeconomic inequalities among families (e.g., heads' occupational prestige levels, heads' education, family incomes) are not highly associated with the socioeconomic statuses of their offspring (e.g., sons' schooling, occupational statuses, earnings). In industrial societies, such as the United States, Great Britain, Australia, and Canada, for which there are data, the product-moment correlations between paternal and filial socioeconomic statuses are in the range .2 to .4, indicating that only 4–16% of the social inequalities of

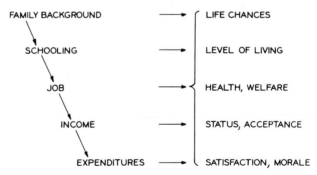

Figure 5.1 The socioeconomic life cycle: schematic representation [from O. D. Duncan, 1967:87].

the sons' generation stem from socioeconomic inequalities among their parents.

Moreover, the relationships among the sons' major status dimensions—occupational prestige, education, and earnings—are far less than deterministic. The highest correlation, between educational and occupational levels, $r = .6$ in the United States, denotes that only about one-third of occupational prestige inequalities among men are associated with their education inequalities. Achievement, or lack of it, in one dimension of social standing does not guarantee achievement (or preclude it) in another, although in all industrial societies one tends to find significant positive relationships between the statuses over the life cycle.

While the socioeconomic life cycle is largely organized around the principle of achievement, and substantial opportunity for between-generation and career mobility appears to characterize the stratification system in the United States, there are notable handicaps preventing perfect mobility. First, the modest dependence of sons' schooling upon their families' socioeconomic circumstances, the sizes of their sibships, their regions of residence during child-rearing and other factors is well documented in the national study of the process of achievement in 1962 by Peter M. Blau and Otis Dudley Duncan (1967). Furthermore, the Blau–Duncan study revealed small but significant direct effects of paternal occupational status on sons' occupations, even among sons of equivalent schooling. Clearly, not all men born into all families face the same chances of success, but the degree to which family background shapes the course of achievement and defines the level of attainment is not great.

All persons are exposed to the risks of birth into families where the head is poorly educated, underemployed, or reproductively prolific. Yet the socioeconomic statuses ascribed to an individual by such accidents do not accumulate over the life cycle, since the handicap of a father with low human capital does not ordinarily imply a similar fate for the offspring. However, persons born into black families face handicaps of racial discrimination: A black man must be better educated than his white counterpart to reap the same economic return for the same work. Inasmuch as the average black male is born into a family where the head's socioeconomic statuses are lower than those of the average white male, the black suffers the double handicap of racial discrimination in the form of generally poorer returns to human capital—a handicap that does accumulate over his life cycle—and of lesser socioeconomic resources for achievement within his family of orientation.

For the male population as a whole, the inequalities of socioeconomic status among families, whether evaluated as large or small, are not by and large transmitted between generations; opportunities for (upward) social mobility between generations and socioeconomic achievement in one's own career are generally available. Yet racial inequality of opportunity in the United States attentuates upward mobility for blacks, relative to whites, and handicaps their abilities to convert their own human capital into achievements on a par with whites. Whether similar inequality of opportunity based on sex pervades the American process of achievement is a matter of some speculation, but little data are available to assess these suppositions (see N. Carter, 1972; Suter and Miller, 1973).

We extend this discussion of inequality of status, of the stratification of inequalities (i.e., the extent to which inequalities of one generation persist into the next, which indexes the degree of opportunity for achievement), and of inequality of opportunity to cover the topic of this chapter: inequality of achievement, stemming from life cycle discontinuities.

Beverly Duncan (Duncan, Featherman, and Duncan, 1972:224) proposes insightfully that the timing of some events in the life cycle can be as critical for the individual as the events themselves. In using the term "discontinuities," we refer to the timing of those events within the experience of a birth cohort that differentiates the otherwise homogeneous histories of its individual members.[2] Discontinuities of interest for this chapter are those affecting components of the socioeconomic life cycle, either by facilitating or handicapping cohort members as they proceed through school, enter the labor market, and compete for wages and salaries.

One important discontinuity for a substantial minority of any cohort involves interruption in the course of schooling.

> Evidence is accumulating that the transition from student to worker is not an irreversible change in status which can be dated with precision. The transition seems rather to occur over a period of some years during which young men mix work experience with formal training, often interrupting both to fulfil a military obligation (B. Duncan, 1967:29).

Through an ingenious analysis of information on age at first full-time job and years of completed schooling in the national survey, "Occupational Changes in a Generation (OCG)," Beverly Duncan estimated that "as many as a tenth of the high-school graduates, a third of those with some college training, and a quarter of the college graduates did interrupt their schooling at some point" with labor force activity, and "a sixth of the teenage boys who left school may have returned for additional training" (B. Duncan, 1965b:131).

In a national sample of men aged 30–39 in 1968, Ornstein (1971:366) finds a greater frequency of interruption than is estimated by Duncan.[3] For white

---

[2] We distinguish discontinuities from career contingencies. The latter include marriage, divorce, childspacing (see Duncan, Featherman, and Duncan, 1972:Chapter 8), while the former focus upon the timing of such events within the life cycle. Both, however, can differentiate the experiences of the birth cohort, as at any one time some members of the cohort are married while others are not; some who are married were married before completing education while others were married later.

[3] If Beverly Duncan (1965a) is correct in reporting a positive relationship between the unemployment rate and school enrollment rates, discrepancies in dropping out and returning will appear in studies conducted in different years and market conditions.

men entering the labor force (for at least a period of 17 months), having just completed high school, 34.0% returned to school within a period of 8 years; for those with some college, 28.9% returned; for those with a college diploma, 16.5% continued after lengthy labor force attachment. Overall (including those with less than a high school certificate), the "dropouts who went back" within 8 years after entry into the labor force comprised 26.8% of the white men; the figure for blacks was 11.6%.

Finally, women as well as men experience discontinuity in schooling. Davis (1973) estimates that over one-fifth of the ever-married women in the United States in 1970 continued their educations after marriage. For women who first married less recently, the majority continued schooling after 10 or more years of marriage; women more recently married apparently returned to or continued schooling after shorter post-nuptial discontinuities.

The timing of education within the life cycle of an individual (and within those of different birth cohorts, cf. B. Duncan, 1968:626–634) is variable, thereby differentiating the otherwise homogeneous history of the cohort. Not only are there interruptions in education once underway, but age at school entry also varies, especially across geographical regions. Coupled with pervasive patterns of migration, these two discontinuities yield yet a third—age–grade retardation or acceleration of the school-age migrant child, as measured against the prevailing norms of the receiving community (B. Duncan, 1968:631). While documentation of the prevalence of these discontinuities accumulates, we know little of their causal antecedents and their impact on socioeconomic achievements.

In the OCG data for white men of nonfarm background (i.e., paternal occupations were nonfarm), Beverly Duncan concluded that "elements of the family's structure and status which are conducive to high educational attainment also are conducive to continuity in schooling" (Duncan et al., 1972:219). Early job takers (i.e., OCG men identified as having temporarily interrupted schooling with civilian labor force activity) were disproportionately drawn from larger families in which the head was less well educated and was employed in a lower-status occupation. Moreover, special Census tabulations for 1960 revealed a positive association between the educational level of family head and a younger age of school entry for the child (B. Duncan, 1968:631–634). Among college graduates in the OCG survey, early job takers were selectively recruited from lower-status families and from large sibships wherein the older brothers attained less schooling than in the families of later job takers. Early job takers in turn married at younger ages and obtained first full-time civilian jobs of lower socioeconomic rank than did other college graduates. The socioeconomic status of current (1962) occupations for early job takers, however, was only slightly below that for other graduates, an average difference of a tenth of a standard deviation (roughly a two-point difference on a scale from 1–100). For these men, temporary schooling interruptions were correlated with less than average intergenerational mobility to first jobs, but disproportionate upward career mobility to current job. On balance, however, educational discontinuity was moderately associated with diminished occupational status attainments. In all, educational discontinuities of this type add to the dispersion of occupational achievements, increasing the socioeconomic inequality within a birth cohort over its career.

To further explore the causal nexus involving temporary interruptions in schooling, we have collected panel data from a cohort born between July 1, 1939 and June 30, 1940; some 88% of the cohort was still in school at age 17. The sample of 17-year-old men was drawn from all high schools in Lenawee County, Michigan in 1957; documentation on the population and sample coverage appears elsewhere (Otto, 1973). A second interview, conducted largely by telephone in 1972, contacted 82.3% of the 430 eligible men from the original panel (N = 442) and yielded 340 usable cases with two-wave data, a response rate of 79.1% and covering 76.9% of wave one cases.

Our interest focuses upon three measures of discontinuity in schooling. The first, age–grade retardation at age 17, was indexed by assuming the cohort enrollment norm to be grades 11 or 12. If a young man was enrolled at age 17 in grades 8 through 10, he was considered retarded for our purposes, and on a dichotomy was scored "1" rather than "0." Some 9.4% of the working sample was retarded. A second discontinuity entailed a temporary interval of 6 months or more between date of exit from high school and entrance into any post-secondary education, either in colleges or as business, vocational, technical or apprenticeship training in nonregular schools. If such a delay in post-high school education occurred, and it did for 20.2% of the working sample, the respondent was scored "1" on a dichotomy. Finally, the third discontinuity identified an interruption of 6 months or more during the course of post–high school education. For the 22.3% experiencing such an interruption, a score of unity was registered on this dichotomy.

Table 5.1 gives a cross-classification of the three discontinuities by the two types of post-high school training: 41.% had no schooling beyond age 17, 8% had both college and some nonregular training, 34% had at least some college but no other schooling, and 17% had nonregular schooling but did not enter college. About 9% of our sample was age–grade retarded at age 17, and some 40% encountered either a delay prior to post-secondary education (19%) or an interruption (21%) once it was underway. Of the sample, 17 (5%) had both a delay and an interruption; this is 12% of those with both a delay and an interruption. There are few cases of age–grade retardation with either post-secondary schooling or further discontinuities beyond high school.

To interpret the impact of these discontinuities within the socioeconomic life cycle, we incorporate the three variables into a hypothetical model of the process of achievement. Figure 5.2 orders the variables of interest according to their assumed causal priorities, based upon the growing volume of research on the status attainment process (Blau and Duncan,

TABLE 5.1

Distribution of Educational Discontinuities by Type of Post-High School Education

| | AGRTD | | | | AGRTD | | | | |
| | DPHS | | No DPHS | | DPHS | | No DPHS | | |
	PHSI	No PHSI	PHSI	No PHSI	PHSI	No PHSI	PHSI	No PHSI	Total
COLLEGE	1	0	1	1	8	11	39	55	116
COLL & NREG	0	0	0	0	3	2	15	7	27
NON-REG	0	4	0	1	5	32	1	14	57
No PHS ED	0	0	0	24	0	0	0	116	140
Total	1	4	1	26	16	45	55	192	340

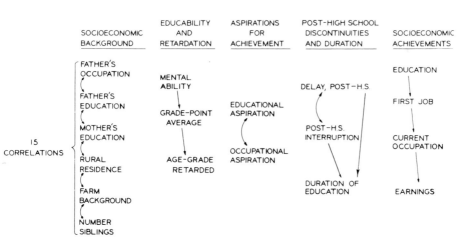

Figure 5.2 Causal scheme ordering events within the socioeconomic life cycle. Curved lines denote correlation, no causal priorities assumed; straight arrows denote causal ordering within a block of variables; otherwise, the causal specification is fully recursive between and within blocks.

139

1967; Sewell, Haller, and Portes, 1969; Sewell and Hauser, Chapter 1 of this volume; Duncan *et al.*, 1972). There are five major blocks of variables: socioeconomic background; educability and retardation; aspirations for achievement; post-high school discontinuities and duration of education; and socioeconomic achievements. Within each block, curved lines denote correlations and no causal priorities; straight arrows denote assumed causal priorities within the block; both within and between blocks we assume relationships are fully recursive for heuristic purposes.

Socioeconomic Background

In Table A-1 of the appendix, we find correlations among the predetermined status variables within the ranges expected from previous research (e.g., Sewell *et al.*, 1969; Sewell and Hauser, Chapter 1 of this volume). Father's occupational status, in units of Duncan's (1961) socioeconomic status index (SEI), and father's and mother's educations, in units of regular schooling,[4] are all positively correlated. We consciously avoid creating an overall index of family socioeconomic level, allowing each potential component to affect the later blocks of variables in its individual manner, and we have included maternal education in view of some considerable speculation that, despite substantial assortative mating on education, maternal education uniquely shapes the educability and attainments of offspring (see Ellis and Lane, 1963; Carter, Picou, Curry, and Tracy, 1972). Each of these status indicators is negatively correlated with the number of R's siblings, rural residence, and farm background, which in turn are positively correlated with each other. Rural residence (scored "1" in a 0,1 dichotomy) characterizes 64% of the sample, who lived in places with populations below 2500 in 1957. Farm background (scored "1" in a 0,1 dichotomy) indexes the 19% of boys whose father's occupations in 1957 were in farming (e.g., farmers, farm managers, farm foremen or laborers). In view of the percentages rural and farm, the lack of perfect correlation between these two characteristics ($r = .35$), and the variances in the background status indicators (see Table A-1), we argue that the sample is sufficiently heterogeneous to justify our inquiry. Since the origin of these 15 correlations in block one is not problematic to our anlysis, we proceed to block 2 variables.

Educability and Retardation

Within this block of variables we hypothesize that MA, mental ability (raw score on the Cattell Culture-Free test administered at wave one), will

---

[4] Paternal and maternal educations were coded in units of completed formal schooling: 0 = less than eight grade; 1 = 8 grades; 2 = 9–11 grades; 3 = 12 grades; 4 = some college; 5 = college degree or more.

affect positively the grade point average at age 17 (Sewell *et al.*, 1969) and both MA and GPA will exert separate and negative influences on the probability of being in school and age–grade retarded (AGRTD). Moreover, we expect rural boys (Haller, 1968), boys with lower-status parents (Sewell *et al.*, 1969), and boys with more siblings (Duncan *et al.*, 1972) to have lower mental ability. The parental status variables should affect GPA only through their correlation with MA (Sewell *et al.*, 1969), the only hypothesized direct effect on GPA arising from MA. Finally, we expect no direct effects on AGRTD, except from MA and GPA.

In Table 5.2, we find general confirmation of our expectations. Ordinary least squares regressions, both standardized and unstandardized, appear in the table; coefficients whose absolute values exceed twice their standard errors are asterisked as statistically significant. Higher mental ability is indicative of young men from smaller families in which maternal education is higher; paternal status characteristics and the rural, farm variables are not as significant, although they tend to operate in the directions predicted. Boys with mothers whose educations differ in degree such as by high school versus some college are separated by three-quarters of a point on the scale of mental ability, while those growing up in a two- versus three-child sibship, for example, are separated by one-quarter of an MA point. Since the MA scale is not normed, we would not make much of the unstandardized coefficients.

Apparently, mother's education does play a significant and different role from father's educational and occupational statuses, but this difference is more apparent than real. When we test for the difference between mother's education and the average of father's education and occupation as influences on son's intellectual ability,[5] we find no statistical difference. Clearly, mother is *not* more important than father, as indexed by these socioeconomic variables, although the consequences (in either standardized or metric units) of unit changes in maternal education, net of *both* paternal statuses, are larger than when either paternal educational or occupational statuses are altered, net of the other paternal status and maternal education.

Farmers' sons and rural boys are not substantially handicapped in mental ability, when differentials in maternal education, fertility, and parental SES are controlled.

While mental ability emerges as the most dominant causal antecedent of GPA, both mother's education and paternal occupational status affect GPA directly. Some 61% of the causal effect of maternal education is direct,

---

[5] A series of individual degrees of freedom tests were performed testing the hypothesis that the effect of mother's education was equal to the average effect of father's occupational SEI and father's education—that is, (2) (βMOED) = (1) (βFAED) + (1) (βFAOCC). This test was performed for each equation in our model, and we could not reject the hypothesis of equality in *any* case. For a thorough discussion on this test, the reader is referred to Li (1964: 110–116).

TABLE 5.2

Multiple Regressions of Educability and School Retardation Variables on Causally Prior Factors

Dependent Variables	Independent Variables								R²	α
	FAOCC	FAED	MOED	RURAL	FARM	SIBS	MA	GPA		

Path coefficients[a] (standardized regression coefficients)

Dependent Variables	FAOCC	FAED	MOED	RURAL	FARM	SIBS	MA	GPA
1. MA	.051 (.069)	.054 (.066)	.185[b] (.063)	-.110 (.058)	-.061 (.061)	-.110[b] (.053)		
2. GPA	.159[b] (.068)	.049 (.066)	.201[b] (.063)	-.046 (.057)	.049 (.061)	-.036 (.053)		
3. GPA	.138[b] (.062)	.026 (.060)	.123[b] (.058)	.001 (.052)	.075 (.055)	.011 (.049)	.425[b] (.050)	
4. AGRTD	-.093 (.071)	-.037 (.069)	-.141[b] (.065)	.000 (.060)	-.025 (.063)	.029 (.055)		
5. AGRTD	-.083 (.070)	-.026 (.068)	-.104 (.065)	-.022 (.059)	-.037 (.062)	.007 (.055)	-.199[b] (.056)	
6. AGRTD	-.051 (.069)	-.020 (.067)	-.076 (.064)	-.021 (.058)	-.020 (.061)	.010 (.054)	-.101 (.061)	-.231[b] (.061)

Regression coefficients

Dependent Variables	FAOCC	FAED	MOED	RURAL	FARM	SIBS	MA	GPA	R²	α
1. MA	.012	.209	.736[b]	-1.19	-.798	-.231[b]			.120	45.50
2. GPA	.006[b]	.030	.129[b]	-.080	.104	-.012			.121	- 1.84
3. GPA	.005[b]	.016	.079[b]	.002	.159	.004	.069[b]		.280	- 4.96
4. AGRTD	-.001	-.008	-.031[b]	.000	-.018	.003			.050	.821
5. AGRTD	-.001	-.006	-.023	-.013	-.027	.001	-.011[b]		.085	1.33
6. AGRTD	-.001	-.004	-.017	-.013	-.014	.001	-.006	-.080[b]	.124	.456

[a] Standard errors in parentheses.

[b] Indicates absolute size of coefficient equals or exceeds twice its standard error.

while roughly 39% influences GPA through MA. The effective role of mothers in nurturing the educability of their sons is manifest, although again maternal education is *not* more efficacious than the average of the two paternal socioeconomic statuses. Paternal socioeconomic status also affects GPA directly; approximately 87% of the causation is direct, inasmuch as the role of socioeconomic factors in moulding MA is minor in these data. This set of relationships involving socioeconomic factors was not anticipated, as Hauser (1972) finds virtually no socioeconomic variance in GPA once MA is controlled. (We hasten to add that Hauser's analysis is based on a different specification for the effects of status components on academic performance and uses different methods.) Clearly the bulk of the variance explained in GPA by our model stems from ability, 58% of $R^2 = .28$, and boys with fathers differing by 10 socioeconomic index (SEI) points have GPAs separated by .5 points (GPA scaled on the traditional 4-point system).

From the reduced-form equations, first, for the socioeconomic background regressors on AGRTD, and second for block one plus MA as a regressor on AGRTD, we observe that maternal education affects son's schooling retardation through his mental ability. In turn, the MA component of AGRTD is largely incorporated within the boy's academic performance, or GPA. Thus, we observe no direct effects of any block one regressors on AGRTD, as predicted. While nearly half of the explained variance ($R^2 = .12$) in AGRTD arises from the negative, direct effects of academic performance, the hypothesized direct effect of MA is not significant. Age–grade retardation in high school, for this cohort, is a reflection of poor academic performance. The overwhelming bulk of variance in this discontinuity is, however, unresponsive to the factors included in our model.

Achievement Aspirations

In turning to block three variables, educational and occupational aspirations, we hypothesize that school retardation among 17-year-old enrollees will imply lower goals for education and occupational status, ceteris paribus. Our measure of occupational aspiration is the Haller and Miller OAS scale (Haller and Miller, 1971); educational aspiration (EASP) is indexed by units of college planned.[6] We expect positive effects for parental socioeconomic characteristics to attenuate under controls for mental ability and GPA. Likewise, the negative effects of rural rearing and farm background are expected to diminish when educability is controlled. No net effect of siblings is predicted, and no effect of MA net of GPA is anticipated.

---

[6] Educational aspirations were given in post-secondary college years planned by the 17-year-old boys: 0 = none; 1 = 2 or fewer years; 2 = 3 or 4 years; 3 = 5 or 6 years; 4 = 7 or more years.

If our results are to parallel Sewell's Wisconsin data (Sewell, Haller, and Ohlendorf, 1970), we would expect GPA and parental status variables to be the prime causal antecedents of these two (correlated and not causally related) aspiration variables.

Taking first the regression results in Table 5.3 for educational aspirations, we find (in the reduced-form equations) again the positive force of maternal education in raising son's aspirations. However, her impact is no greater statistically (see Footnote 5) than the average of father's education and his occupational socioeconomic level, which is reflected positively in son's educational goals. Aside from the status characteristics of father's job, whether the father farms or not does not seem crucial. However, whereas we had expected farmers' sons to have lower educational goals, the net effect (although not quite significant by our standard) is positive. Rural residence during rearing is associated with lower educational aspirations. Taken together, the socioeconomic factors (all of block one) account for 22% of the variance in EASP.

Adding mental ability to the equations for EASP adds 3% to R^2, and adding GPA raises R^2 by another 15%. Of the two educability variables, GPA is the more important and by itself it accounts for one-third of R^2. While boys with greater MA and better grades set higher aspirations, the two educability factors substantially reduce most effects of parental characteristics on sons' EASP. About half of the causal effects of paternal occupational status and maternal education is not directly related to EASP but is channeled through MA and GPA. However, mother's education retains a positive net impact on son's aspirations. Educability factors do not affect the significant decrement in EASP stemming from rural residence.

Finally, age–grade retardation has no significant net negative effect on educational aspirations, and, therefore, its inclusion in the set of regressors does not affect the previous discussion of socioeconomic background and educability effects.[7] In addition, the expectation of no direct effect of MA on EASP was not confirmed, although about one-third of MA's causal effect is indirect through GPA. Grade point average, mental ability, rural residence, and maternal education are the major factors that bear directly on EASP.

Maternal education and, to a lesser extent, paternal education are the only statistically important family factors to shape occupational aspirations. While rural rearing and paternal occupational level were effective in shaping EASP, apparently they are not critical for all achievement aspirations. Both MA and GPA, when added to the reduced-form equations, increment R^2 by .11, but GPA carries about half of the effect of mental ability to OAS. Since maternal education is much a part of a son's MA and GPA, it is not surprising to observe the 50% diminution of causal effect on

---

[7] While the regression coefficient for AGRTD is not significant by our criterion, its impact on EASP is about the same (in metric terms) as having a mother with some high school rather than a high school diploma.

Multiple Regressions of Achievement Aspirations on Causally Prior Factors

Path coefficients[a] (standardized regression coefficients)

Dependent Variables	FAOCC	FAED	MOED	RURAL	FARM	SIBS	MA	GPA	AGRTD	R^2	α
1. EASP	.161^b (.064)	.111 (.063)	.227^b (.059)	-.166^b (.054)	.089 (.057)	-.041 (.050)				.221	-8.69
2. EASP	.146^b (.061)	.094 (.059)	.172^b (.057)	-.133^b (.052)	.107^b (.054)	-.008 (.048)	.300^b (.049)			.300	-11.9
3. EASP	.084 (.055)	.083 (.053)	.116^b (.051)	-.133^b (.046)	.073 (.048)	-.013 (.043)	.108^b (.048)	.451^b (.048)		.446	-1.41
4. EASP	.082 (.055)	.082 (.053)	.113^b (.051)	-.134^b (.046)	.073 (.048)	-.013 (.043)	.104^b (.048)	.441^b (.049)	-.040 (.044)	.447	-1.08
5. OAS	.090 (.066)	.162^b (.064)	.218^b (.060)	-.088 (.055)	-.055 (.058)	.051 (.051)				.192	86.3
6. OAS	.072 (.061)	.143^b (.059)	.153^b (.057)	-.049 (.052)	-.034 (.054)	-.013 (.048)	.352^b (.049)			.301	47.0
7. OAS	.019 (.057)	.133^b (.055)	.106^b (.053)	-.050 (.048)	-.062 (.050)	-.017 (.044)	.187^b (.050)	.386^b (.050)		.408	17.0
8. OAS	.015 (.057)	.131^b (.055)	.100 (.053)	-.051 (.047)	-.064 (.050)	-.016 (.044)	.180^b (.050)	.369^b (.051)	-.073 (.045)	.413	11.8

Regression coefficients

Dependent Variables	FAOCC	FAED	MOED	RURAL	FARM	SIBS	MA	GPA	AGRTD
1. EASP	.009^b	.101	.251^b	-.428^b	.278^b	-.021			
2. EASP	.008^b	.087	.163^b	-.343^b	.335^b	-.004	.071^b		
3. EASP	.005	.076	.110^b	-.344^b	.230	-.007	.026^b	.665^b	
4. EASP	.005	.075	.107^b	-.346^b	.227	-.006	.025^b	.651^b	-.171
5. OAS	.053	1.53^b	2.14^b	-2.35	-1.78	-.266			
6. OAS	.042	1.35^b	1.50^b	-1.32	-1.09	-.066	.865^b		
7. OAS	.011	1.26^b	1.04^b	-1.33	-2.02	-.088	.461^b	5.88^b	
8. OAS	.009	1.24^b	.983	-1.37	-2.07	-.085	.443^b	5.63^b	-3.20

[a] Standard errors in parentheses.

[b] Indicates absolute size of coefficient equals or exceeds twice its standard error.

OAS under controls for educability factors, and, therefore, its positive effect is not altered greatly when controlling block two components. Age–grade retardation displays a statistically nonsignificant negative effect on OAS. Being age–grade retarded implies an average decrement on the OAS of 3.20 points, net of other factors. This is roughly equivalent to a decrement suffered by having a father with some high school education versus one with a college degree or graduate schooling.

We would conclude from Table 5.3 that AGRTD is not a major factor in the socioeconomic attainments of our sample, at least not as mirrored in achievement aspirations. In addition, educational and occupational aspirations appear to respond to somewhat different sets of causal antecedents, although the role of maternal education is as important to both EASP and OAS as to educability.[8]

Post-High School Discontinuities and Duration of Education

Next we consider the two post-high school discontinuities—delay in post-high school training (DPHS) and post-high school interruption (PHSI);[9] the pertinent regressions appear in Table 5.4. On the basis of the analysis of OCG men reported by B. Duncan, we would expect the socioeconomic factors in block one to affect negatively each discontinuity and the sibling variable to have a positive effect. Aside from these anticipations, we have no predictions. In Row 1 of Table 5.4, we find no statistically significant effects on DPHS from any socioeconomic factor (the $R^2 = .015$ is not statistically different from zero), although the predicted direction is observed for FAOCC whose *beta* coefficient is just below the significance criterion. In fact, none of the causal factors prior to the delay variable predicts this discontinuity; $R^2 = .03$ in Row 2. Of course, one cannot have a delay unless one continues some form of schooling beyond age 17. When we introduce two dummy variables for whether or not a man entered college or undertook some other, nonregular schooling, these dummies explain about 26% of the variance in DPHS (row 3 of Table 5.4).

An interruption in schooling, after post-high school education is underway, has little to do with socioeconomic background, despite the fact that

---

[8] It is premature to argue too strongly for the inclusion of maternal education in models of status attainment applied to more general populations than ours. If we extracted from Sewell's Wisconsin sample of high school seniors those reared in counties like Lenawee County, Michigan, perhaps we would replicate our findings. Quite possibly, maternal education is more important for boys in more rural samples than for those in state- and nation-wide samples. We are exploring the possibilities of such an interaction. See also Footnote 5.

[9] The average length of DPHS was 5.8 years; mean length of PHSI was 3.45 years.

TABLE 5.4

Multiple Regressions of Post-High School Education Discontinuities and Duration of School Attendance on Causally Prior Factors

Path coefficients[a] (standardized regression coefficients)

Dependent Variables	FAOCC	FAED	MOED	RURAL	FARM	SIBS	MA	GPA	AGRTD	EASP	OAS	NREG	COLTN	PHSI	DPHS	R^2	α
1. DPHS	-.120 (.072)	.044 (.070)	-.032 (.067)	.000 (.061)	.011 (.064)	.005 (.057)										.015	-.109
2. DPHS	-.106 (.074)	.055 (.071)	-.014 (.069)	-.016 (.062)	.020 (.065)	.004 (.057)	.023 (.066)	-.024 (.074)	-.066 (.058)	-.097 (.084)	-.022 (.082)					.028	-.436
3. DPHS	-.092 (.063)	-.076 (.061)	-.052 (.059)	-.026 (.053)	.045 (.056)	.007 (.049)	.018 (.056)	-.085 (.064)	-.026 (.050)	-.069 (.079)	-.055 (.071)	.525[b] (.048)	.150[b] (.070)			.292	.252
4. PHSI	.119 (.070)	.036 (.068)	.195[b] (.064)	-.063 (.059)	.055 (.062)	.062 (.054)										.085	-1.91
5. PHSI	.077 (.068)	.020 (.065)	.132[b] (.063)	-.043 (.057)	.048 (.060)	.079 (.053)	.078 (.060)	.257[b] (.061)	.021 (.054)							.160	-.354
6. PHSI	.053 (.066)	-.011 (.064)	.095 (.062)	-.003 (.056)	.031 (.059)	.083 (.051)	.038 (.059)	.113 (.067)	.037 (.053)	.278[b] (.076)	.059 (.073)					.214	-1.47
7. PHSI	.038 (.061)	-.004 (.059)	.082 (.057)	-.006 (.051)	.009 (.054)	.082 (.047)	.013 (.055)	.029 (.062)	.031 (.049)	.086 (.077)	-.035 (.069)	.167[b] (.047)	.418[b] (.068)			.336	-.129
8. DURED	-.109 (.065)	.021 (.063)	.056 (.061)	-.020 (.055)	.032 (.058)	.012 (.051)	-.005 (.058)	.196[b] (.066)	-.040 (.052)	.226[b] (.075)	.112 (.072)					.234	-13.7
9. DURED	-.083 (.046)	-.001 (.044)	.022 (.043)	-.011 (.038)	.010 (.040)	-.025 (.051)	-.032 (.041)	.159[b] (.046)	-.025 (.036)	.153[b] (.053)	.097 (.051)			.427[b] (.038)	.469[b] (.034)	.630	-.731
10. DURED	-.098[b] (.039)	.019 (.037)	.010 (.036)	-.020 (.032)	-.022 (.034)	-.012 (.030)	-.044 (.034)	.088[b] (.039)	-.021 (.031)	.044 (.049)	.020 (.043)	.306[b] (.035)	.412[b] (.046)	.285[b] (.035)	.310[b] (.034)	.738	.263

Regression coefficients

Dependent Variables	FAOCC	FAED	MOED	RURAL	FARM	SIBS	MA	GPA	AGRTD	EASP	OAS	NREG	COLTN	PHSI	DPHS
1. DPHS	-.002	.013	-.010	.000	.012	.001									
2. DPHS	-.002	.016	-.004	-.013	.020	.001	.002	-.012	-.091	-.031	-.001				
3. DPHS	-.002	.023	-.016	-.022	-.046	.001	.001	-.040	-.036	-.022	-.002	.484[b]	.121[b]		
4. PHSI	.002	.011	.062[b]	-.055	.058	.010									
5. PHSI	.001	.006	.042[b]	-.037	.050	.013	.006	.127[b]	.030						
6. PHSI	.001	-.003	.030	-.002	.033	.014	.003	.056	.052	.093[b]	-.001				
7. PHSI	.001	-.001	.026	-.005	.009	.014	.001	.014	.044	.029	-.001	.160[b]	.405[b]		
8. DURED	-.022	.068	.190	-.182	.363	.022	-.004	1.03[b]	-.609	.809[b]	.039				
9. DURED	-.017	-.002	.074	-.102	.110	-.045	-.027	.840[b]	-.378	.548[b]	.033			4.55[b]	5.19[b]
10. DURED	-.020[b]	.063	.034	-.186	-.246	-.022	-.037	.463[b]	-.320	.155	.007	3.12[b]	3.70[b]	3.04[b]	3.43[b]

[a] Standard errors in parentheses.

[b] Indicates absolute size of coefficient equals or exceeds twice its standard error.

PHSI, like DPHS, is confounded with educational achievement. Only 8.5% of the variance in PHSI is explained by block one regressors ($R^2 = .085$ is statistically different from zero), with the positive effect of maternal education being the only significant coefficient. The confounding with educational achievement makes the significant effects of GPA and then of EASP (in Rows 5 and 6) difficult to interpret. We take the regressions in Row 7 to be diagnostic: Given that an individual goes beyond high school, factors such as socioeconomic background, educability, age–grade retardation, and achievement aspirations tell us little of his probability of doing so without an interruption. We note in passing that a young man entering college is somewhat more likely to encounter reasons for dropping out temporarily than his counterpart undertaking nonregular schooling, ceteris paribus.

In the last panel of Table 5.4 (Rows 8–10), we examine the duration of education. Our variable, DURED, is the total number of calendar years between age at high school exit and age of exit from the highest grade; the mean of DURED is 3.9 years, $\pm$ 4.45 years. Later, we will employ DURED to estimate efficiency of schooling; for the present we seek to discover what permits or limits the extension of education over lengthy periods. Clearly, DURED is confounded with educational attainment,[10] and that fact obscures the meaning of regressions in Rows 8 and 9 of Table 5.4. We do not

[10] While we prefer to specify our model, as in Figure 5.2 and Table 5.4, we did estimate the "time accounting" function for DURED (as the dependent variable) in which EDTOT (years of school completed) is a component (an independent variable), along with DPHS and PHSI (schooling delays and interruptions) and prior factors in blocks one through three. Unstandardized estimates for this equation are as follows (see Table 5.4 for definition of variables and notation):

$$
\begin{aligned}
\text{DURED} = &-8.32 - .019\text{*FAOCC} - .009 \text{ FAED} - .002 \text{ MOED} \\
&+ .197 \text{ RURAL} - .547 \text{ FARM} + .040 \text{ SIBS} - .038 \text{ MA} \\
&+ .004 \text{ GPA} - .034 \text{ AGRTD} - .006 \text{ EASP} - .011 \text{ OAS} \\
&+ 2.52\text{*PHSI} + 3.50\text{*DPHS} + 2.95\text{*NREG} + 2.18\text{*COLTN} \\
&+ .807\text{*EDTOT} \qquad R^2 = .801.
\end{aligned}
$$

A delay accounts for 3.5 years and an interruption for 2.5 years of schooling duration, while an additional year of school accreditation (attendance) accounts for about 9.7 months of (net) duration. Whether one experiences discontinuities or not, enrollment in either regular or nonregular post-secondary schools accounts for some two to three years. Note that those who enrolled in nonregular programs extended their (net) schooling over about nine more months than did college matriculants, within each grade of school completed (i.e., net of school discontinuities and completed years of education). Later we observe some greater inefficiency (i.e., fewer educational credentials) for nonregular attendance than for regular school attendance, given equivalent durations of attendance; this result is consistent with that observation.

However, we prefer the specification in Table 5.4, where EDTOT is a result of DURED and other factors. We will justify this choice later.

show the results for equations with block one only and with blocks one and two regressors. Of block one, only MOED affects (positively) DURED directly ($R^2 = .06$), but this direct effect disappears under controls for (primarily) GPA, and group two regressors raise R^2 to .18. Age–grade retardation has no direct effect on duration; one might have anticipated otherwise, although we observed earlier the slight causal influence of GPA on AGRTD. An additional 5% of explained variance stems from the aspiration variables (Row 8), largely EASP, and the introduction of aspirations diminishes the still significant direct effect of GPA by 58%.

The two discontinuities, DPHS and PHSI, expectedly affect DURED positively. *Beta* coefficients for these discontinuities are the largest in Row 9, and the two factors increment R^2 by .40, but they also attenuate the still substantial direct effect of educational aspirations.

To offset partially the confounding of DURED by years of school completed, we introduce two dummy variables, NREG and COLTN, to index who has had some form of post-secondary education; COLTN, or college training, includes two- or four-year institutions leading to an academic degree; NREG includes nonregular schooling, such as vocational, technical, business, and apprenticeship programs. (Note that the coefficients for NREG and COLTN *essentially* are deviations from the omitted category, "no post-secondary education.")[11] These two variables account for an additional 12% of variance in DURED, but their addition allows us to interpret the antecedents of DURED more clearly. Extension of schooling over lengthy periods naturally reflects periods of nonattendance, such as DPHS and PHSI; each of these discontinuities extends age at last grade attended (net of other factors) by about three years (see regression coefficients in Row 10 of Table 5.4). Moreover, enrollment in post-secondary schools also protracts the age at the last year attended, by three to four years, net other factors. By controlling for periods of enrollment and intervals of delay and interruption, those who are older at completion of schooling are those with better grades in high school and with lower-status families. Perhaps in interpreting the latter results, we can say that those who take longer to finish up are those whose family resources (e.g., FAOCC) do not permit continuous schooling but whose educability (e.g., GPA) permits them to continue on to the next grade with encouragement that educational goals can be achieved ultimately. Such an interpretation is consistent with Beverly Duncan's analysis of the social characteristics of OCG men who presumably interrupted their educations with periods of labor force activity. (Our "dropouts" do not necessarily take jobs, nor can

[11] The categories NREG and COLTN are *not* mutually exclusive (see Table 5.1) as we have defined them, although their correlation $r = -0.12$ indicates that so few men undertook both types of post-secondary education that they *essentially* are orthogonal. Were NREG and COLTN mutually exclusive, then the third and omitted category would be those not having post-high school training of any kind.

we decompose DURED into labor force and other activities completely exhaustive of intervening time.)

Socioeconomic Achievements

The last block of variables consists of the socioeconomic achievements, including education, occupational status, and earnings. Education (EDTOT) is in years of school completed at the second interview, with periods of nonregular attendance converted into equivalent units of regular, academic schooling. Occupational status, as was father's occupation, is scored in units of Duncan's SEI scale, and income is R's total salaries and wages in 1971.

From earlier research on the status attainment process (cited previously), we expect educability to be a major impetus to higher education, mainly GPA and aspirations, especially EASP. We hypothesize that maternal and paternal education will not affect EDTOT directly but only through GPA and aspirations. A small, positive socioeconomic effect from FAOCC is expected. We argue that farm origins and rural residence ought not affect EDTOT directly, after controls for siblings (Featherman, 1971a) and aspirations and educability (Haller, 1968) are imposed. Our three discontinuity variables are hypothesized to affect EDTOT negatively, controlling for DURED and the other variables.

We return to the concept of a cohort and the structure of the life cycle as the rationale for the last expectation. We argue that experiences of delayed post-secondary schooling and temporary dropouts from post-secondary education handicap the individual in attaining additional training. In many ways, the curricular assumptions of higher education incorporate expanding knowledge at lower levels. As high schools, for example, begin teaching subjects heretofore taught to college freshmen, the curricula for college students is altered to assume greater sophistication. In addition, if apparent intercohort rises in educability (GPA) and education signal real qualitative improvements, then the average against which the relative ranking of students is measured alters the conditions for acceptable student performance over time. These and other observations about intercohort changes in education imply that those who temporarily delay or drop out of school permanently drop out of their cohort. The school dropout who comes back competes against a younger cohort, a higher average GPA, and more knowledgable peers. Insofar as age–grade norms are clear, the former dropout is older than that norm and at a different stage of the life cycle, perhaps preventing social integration into a supportive, academic peer network. Post-secondary discontinuities differentiate the birth cohort into quasi-populations (Ryder, 1964:453), increase educational inequality within that cohort, and handicap, educationally, cohort members who experience them.

The first regression in Table 5.5 holds few surprises for those familiar

TABLE 5.5

Multiple Regressions of Educational Achievement on Causally Prior Factors

Dependent Variables	FAOCC	FAED	MOED	RURAL	FARM	SIBS	MA	GPA	AGRTD	EASP	OAS	PIISI	DPHS	NREG	COLIN	DUPED	R^2	α
						Path coefficients[a] (standardized regression coefficients)												
1. EDTOT	.126[b] (.064)	.127[b] (.062)	.213[b] (.059)	-.176[b] (.054)	.098 (.057)	-.103[b] (.050)												
2. EDTOT	.040 (.053)	.097 (.051)	.093 (.049)	-.143[b] (.045)	.079 (.047)	-.075 (.041)	.095[b] (.047)	.475[b] (.048)	-.051 (.042)									
3. EDTOT	.013 (.048)	.046 (.046)	.039 (.045)	-.093[b] (.040)	.070 (.042)	-.067 (.037)	.028 (.043)	.269[b] (.048)	-.024 (.038)	.304[b] (.055)	.197[b] (.053)							
4. EDTOT	.003 (.046)	.048 (.044)	.019 (.043)	-.092 (.039)	.063 (.041)	-.085 (.036)	.019 (.041)	.245 (.046)	-.031 (.036)	.246 (.054)	.185 (.051)	.213 (.038)	.012 (.035)					
5. EDTOT	.043 (.038)	.040 (.036)	.019 (.035)	-.083[b] (.031)	-.072[b] (.033)	-.072[b] (.029)	.026 (.033)	.149[b] (.038)	-.031 (.030)	.078 (.047)	.106[b] (.042)	-.044 (.037)	-.181[b] (.037)	-.127[b] (.037)	.161[b] (.050)	.583[b] (.054)		
						Regression coefficients												
1. EDTOT	.014[b]	.229[b]	.397[b]	-.892[b]	.605	-.102[b]											.228	-7.32
2. EDTOT	.004	.174	.173	-.728[b]	.490	-.074	.044[b]	1.38[b]	-.424								.484	9.47
3. EDTOT	.001	.083	.072	-.470[b]	.413	-.067	.013	.779[b]	-.202	.597[b]	.037[b]						.591	-6.29
4. EDTOT	.000	.086	.035	-.467[b]	.389[b]	-.084[b]	.009	.710[b]	-.261	.483[b]	.035[b]	1.25[b]	.071				.628	9.79
5. EDTOT	.005	.072	.035	-.420[b]	.445[b]	-.071[b]	.012	.432[b]	-.259	.154	.020[b]	-.257	-1.10[b]	-.714[b]	.793[b]	.296[b]	.758	8.68

Independent Variables

[a] Standard errors in parentheses.

[b] Indicates absolute size of coefficient equals or exceeds twice its standard error.

with the literature relating socioeconomic background to educational achievement. FAOCC, FAED, and MOED all make separate, positive contributions to EDTOT, while rural residence and number of siblings have negative effects. Farm background, while failing the criterion for significance, is associated with higher net educational attainments, a finding not expected beforehand. The collection of block one regressors accounts for 23% of the variance in EDTOT. Of block two variables, both GPA and MA positively affect education, with about two-thirds of the causal effect of MA working through GPA (reduced-form equation not shown). Age-grade retardation has no significant, negative effect, although one was expected. Not only is an additional 25% of variance in EDTOT explained by educability, but also the educability variables diminish all of the previously significant effects of background, save for RURAL.

While our hypothesized indirect effects for socioeconomic factors are largely supported, there are some exceptions. In Table 5.5 Row 3 regressions, aspirations are entered as regressors, and, as expected, each has a significant positive coefficient; the *beta* value for EASP is larger than for OAS. The significant negative coefficient (in Row 2) for RURAL is attenuated by a third in Row 3, but two-thirds of the causal effect is direct; further statistical controls hardly affect the size of this coefficient. Moreover, in Row 4 regressions, which enter the post-secondary education discontinuities, the negative coefficient for SIBS exceeds twice its standard error. Size of sibship persists as a negative direct effect, even in the full model regressions (Row 5).

We have predicted negative effects for DPHS and PHSI, but in the reduced form, Row 4, the estimates are positive. Rather than interpret these regressions, we estimate the equations for Row 5, in which the two dummy variables for type of post-secondary training, COLTN and NREG, and DURED are included. We control for DURED to separate the effects of differential attendance patterns for those enrolling in NREG versus COLTN from the certification effects of these types of schooling, thereby securing an estimate of efficiency of schooling (i.e., educational (cum certification) returns to regular (COLTN) versus nonregular (NREG) school matriculation for persons attending school [DURED, net of DPHS and PHSI] for equivalent numbers of years). The major differences between Rows 4 and 5 involve PHSI and DPHS, for each has a negative value, albeit only DPHS's value is significant. In metric units (unstandardized regressions), a delay prior to post-secondary education costs about a year of formal training relative to those not experiencing either a delay or an interruption after exit from high school.

Net of PHSI and DPHS, DURED indexes something like years of school enrollment. The large positive coefficient for DURED indicates that this is a major factor in explaining inequality in education: the longer one attends school, the more schooling qua certification one receives, ceteris paribus. For each year of attendance, one obtains roughly a third year more of certification credits (see raw regression coefficients). Those attending school for the same periods but undertaking different kinds of post-secondary schooling experience differing achievements. College attenders achieve about $1\frac{1}{2}$ years more educational certification than those enrolled in nonregular schools for equal periods of time.

Finally, an expected positive effect of aspirations is observed, although only from OAS and not EASP; the causal effect of the latter is indirect, largely through COLTN. GPA at age 17 affects EDTOT directly, despite the fact that 45% of its causal effect operates through aspirations and an additional 25% is reflected in the discontinuity, attendance duration, and training type variables. Lastly, there remain minor direct effects of RURAL, SIBS, and FARM, which run counter to the expectation of exclusively indirect effects of these background variables.

We conclude that educational discontinuities, especially post-high school delays, do in fact handicap members of a birth cohort who experience them and create additional educational inequalities among the cohort, but age–grade retardation does not alter educational inequalities in any direct way beyond age 17. We attribute the handicap of the "delayers" to disjunctions in the socioeconomic life cycle stemming from an individual's having dropped out of his cohort as it passed on through school and having experienced a competitive handicap, upon return, among a younger cohort. The fact that in our data "delayers" and "interrupters" are not systematically selected from lower socioeconomic strata largely rules out this factor as an explanation for the educational handicap of delayers.

An unanticipated finding was the educational cost (i.e., less efficiency of schooling) of post-secondary attendance at nonregular schools. While part of these results may be artifactual,[12] there is support for the observation that attendance of equal duration in nonregular institutions versus colleges yields fewer certification benefits. This interpretation holds for men of similar socioeconomic origins, degrees of educability, career aspirations, and patterns of schooling discontinuities.

We continue within block five variables in our causal diagram (Figure 5.2) and analyze the impacts of the schooling discontinuities on occupational and economic statuses in early adulthood, that is, until R reaches the age of 32. In view of the apparent reporting errors in the OCG information for R's first full-time civilian job subsequent to all schooling (B. Duncan, 1965b: Chapter 5), our interview schedule was designed to elicit first job detail from only those who could have had such jobs (e.g., those not currently enrolled) and after obtaining dates for last school exit and year of first full-time civilian job.

Educational achievement should be the most substantial determinant of first job socioeconomic status, while parents' education and socioeconomic status should affect son's early career status through educability and aspirations (Sewell and Hauser, Chapter 1 of this volume). Grades influence

[12] We translated two years of NREG attendance and course completion as the equivalent of one year of formal school (academic) credit.

TABLE 5.6

Multiple Regressions of Occupational and Economic Achievements on Causally Prior Factors

Dependent Variables	FAOCC	FAED	MOED	RURAL	FARM	SIBS	MA	GPA	AGRTD	EASP	OAS	PHSI	DPHS	NREG	COLIN	DURED	EDTOT	FJOB	OCC	R^2	α
							Path coefficients[a] (standardized regression coefficients)														
FJOB	.050 (.047)	.053 (.045)	-.096[b] (.043)	-.101[b] (.039)	-.048 (.042)	-.017 (.036)	.040 (.042)	.125[b] (.049)	-.011 (.037)	.014 (.059)	.056 (.053)	-.013 (.046)	.049 (.047)	.037 (.047)	.169[b] (.063)	.058 (.077)	.414[b] (.070)			.623	3.92
OCC	.043 (.048)	-.069 (.046)	.008 (.045)	-.015 (.041)	-.010 (.043)	.034 (.037)	-.027 (.043)	.077 (.051)	-.027 (.038)	.012 (.060)	.145[b] (.054)	-.037 (.047)	.041 (.049)	-.003 (.049)	.043 (.065)	-.095 (.079)	.219[b] (.075)	.490[b] (.057)		.607	9.08
INC	.084 (.073)	.085 (.070)	.037 (.068)	.074 (.062)	.023 (.064)	-.068 (.056)	-.013 (.064)	-.080 (.077)	-.102 (.057)	.088 (.091)	-.027 (.083)	-.086 (.072)	-.064 (.073)	.093 (.073)	-.007 (.099)	.033 (.119)	.050 (.115)	.076 (.096)	.062 (.084)	.105	-28.40
LNINC	.078 (.072)	.044 (.069)	.095 (.066)	.099 (.061)	.032 (.063)	-.057 (.055)	.003 (.063)	-.118 (.075)	-.111[b] (.056)	-.002 (.089)	-.015 (.081)	-.075 (.070)	-.097 (.072)	.016 (.072)	.031 (.097)	.138 (.117)	-.043 (.113)	.099 (.094)	.176[b] (.083)	.135	7.75
							Regression coefficients														
FJOB	.060	1.04	-1.94[b]	-5.57[b]	-3.19	-.186	.202	3.91[b]	-.968	.292	.116	-.828	3.25	2.22	9.00[b]	.346	4.48[b]				
OCC	.049	-1.28	.155	-.771	-.660	.343	-.128	2.31	-2.28	.232	.284[b]	-2.26	2.58	-.201	2.20	-.539	2.26[b]	.467[b]			
INC[c]	.267	4.36	1.95	10.80	3.98	-1.93	-.169	-6.60	-24.40	4.96	-.149	-14.50	-11.10	14.90	-.992	.522	1.42	.202	.172		
LNINC	.002	.016	.035	.099	.039	-.011	.000	-.067	-.184[b]	-.001	-.001	-.087	-.116	.017	.031	.015	-.009	.002	.003[b]		

[a] Standard errors in parentheses.

[b] Indicates absolute size of coefficient equals or exceeds twice its standard error.

[c] Income in 100-dollar units, for convenience of presentation.

educational level, but no direct effect on first job is anticipated. On the other hand, we expect a positive direct effect of occupational aspirations on first job attainments, net of educability, education, and socioeconomic background (Sewell *et al.*, 1970). Finally, we hypothesize a net positive effect of DURED, controlling for the discontinuity variables, educational achievement, and prior factors. We reason that DURED is a measure of age at first job (under the statistical controls described above), as well as an indicator of the temporal duration of schooling. Men who take longer to earn a college degree (e.g., five-year engineering courses) often enter first jobs of higher social status. Moreover, it is plausible that maturity, with typical entry jobs in the post-education labor market, can be the basis for positive discrimination.

Table 5.6, Row 1, contains the regressions pertinent to these conjectures and hypotheses. Indeed, educational attainment is the dominant antecedent of first job status; for each grade of additional schooling, first job SEI increases 4.5 points. Occupational aspirations fail to affect first job directly, as it appears that these causal effects operate through the encouragement of post-secondary education. However, boys with better grades at age 17 obtain more prestigious jobs upon finishing school; some 28% of the causal effect of GPA is direct upon FJOB, and for each increase of 1 point of GPA, FJOB level rises nearly 4 SEI points. The impacts of FAOCC, FAED and MOED are indeed indirect as expected, although the collinearity of MOED with other regressors (probably) forces what was a nonsignificant causal effect (not shown) to emerge as a small negative one. Rural background, however, extracts a cost of some 5.6 SEI points from rural boys as they enter first jobs. While this characteristic does affect FJOB directly, about half of its causal influence is indirect.

None of the discontinuity factors precludes entry into first jobs appropriate to educational preparation. Those who take longer to finish schooling (and who are older) do not benefit significantly from this factor alone; our expectation is unsupported, despite the positive sign on the coefficient for DURED. One unexpected finding is the rather large net effect of college attendance. For men of equal schooling and attendance duration, the one who holds a college degree (or has obtained post-secondary education in college versus some nonregular school) takes a higher-status first job. In other words, if two men, otherwise matched, with one year of post-secondary education (certification credits equal one year) enter the labor market in the same year, the one who has attended college for one year's credit will obtain a first job about 9 SEI points higher in status than the other, who attended vocational school for the equivalent of one year's academic credit. We interpret this result in light of the previous findings of the effect of nonregular school attendance on educational achievement. Apparently, otherwise able young men who choose to go on to nonregular post-secondary schools rather than colleges suffer a career cost, both in terms of fewer certification years of schooling for equal attendance years and in the form of a lower-status entry point into the full-time labor force.

The second socioeconomic status, occupational level in 1972, should reflect no direct influences of socioeconomic background, inasmuch as all these block one factors will only affect levels of aspiration and education. In fact, extant knowledge of socioeconomic careers (Featherman, 1971b, 1973; Kelley, 1973a) suggests that only first job and education will exert significant, positive influences on OCC. Since prior research has omitted timing variables, we amend these expectations to include a small, negative coefficient for the impact of DURED, controlling for the discontinuities and prior variables. As in the regressions for FJOB, DURED indexes something akin to age at entry into the full-time labor force after completion of *all* schooling. Therefore, in the regressions (Row 2) of Table 5.6, DURED is interpreted as the inverse of labor force tenure: Longer DURED implies shorter tenure; similarly, shorter tenure limits occupational achievement.

Table 5.6 (Row 2) replicates prior findings on the primary import of education and first job in shaping the course of occupational achievement over the early career. An additional year of schooling is about equal in force to an increment in first job status of 5 SEI points, both yielding a rise of roughly 2.3 SEI points in OCC. Education channels nearly all of the causal influence of socioeconomic background and educability into OCC. However, OAS does affect OCC directly, over and above the 46% of its causal effect which operates through education, type of post-secondary schooling, and educational discontinuities. Apparently OAS has predictive value for net achievement in middle career, which it does not have for early attainments (e.g., FJOB).[13] Finally, our expectation for a net negative influence of DURED is not confirmed, although the statistically nonsignificant coefficient points in the predicted direction.

Lastly, we examine the causal influences on earnings. Previous status attainment research has not produced equations capable of explaining income; we do not break with tradition. In Row 3 regressions of Table 5.6 we explain 10.5% of the variance in earnings (INC), and, in Row 4 we account for 13.5% of logged earnings (LNINC). We had anticipated positive coefficients for both OCC and EDTOT (Featherman, 1971b, 1973; Kelley, 1973a). Moreover, we extrapolated from Cutright's (1972) interpretation of a net negative effect of military service on earnings to a negative effect for DURED, controlling for discontinuities, educational level, and prior factors. If, as Cutright suggested, military service removes the inductee from the civilian labor force for the duration of service, then veterans suffer the handicap of lower tenure and commensurately lower earnings than nonveterans within equivalent occupations.

For neither INC nor LNINC are there any causal effects for socioeco-

---

[13] An occasional critic of Duncan-style stratification research takes issue with the "redundance" of first job in the equation for current job. Here, OAS operates quite differently with respect to each occupation, noting the qualitative difference in status attainments at different points in the socioeconomic career.

nomic background factors (reduced-form coefficient not shown in Table 5.6). While educability generally does not influence earnings, age–grade retardation does have a net negative effect, for reasons not altogether clear. From Row three, we see that being age–grade retarded at age 17 costs a man $2440 in earnings at age 31–32, net of all other factors, including education and occupational achievements. In fact, education has no direct impact on earnings (the reduced-form coefficients, while not shown, are also nonsignificant), and OCC has a small positive effect on LNINC but not on INC. Our prediction concerning DURED was wrong; the coefficient is nonsignificant and *positive,* not negative.

We can only speculate on our nonfindings and surprises concerning income. The cost of age–grade retardation, lagged in effect (the only significant effect for AGRTD in our tables) until mid-career, could represent behavioral disabilities (e.g., lack of punctuality, absenteeism) that negatively influence teachers as well as employers; whatever the case, AGRTD is not a manifestation of educability, as this is tapped by MA and GPA. DURED has no apparent effect on earnings, but whether this implies the same for tenure is unclear from our analysis. Both of the schooling discontinuities, DPHS and PHSI, like AGRTD, have negative influences on INC and LNINC, although their coefficients are not significant by our strict criterion. Note, however, that each discontinuity costs (net) over a thousand dollars in earnings (Row 3 regressions). Perhaps tenure per se is not as important as continuity in schooling; perhaps those who go through without interruption (and without retardation) are those with personalities most highly valued by employers. For example, they may be more punctual, better planners, more efficient, more persistent, more compliant, and less distracted; these traits may well be related to efficient progress through school and to lower "training costs" on the job, but maybe they are not. Surely our nonfindings encourage further work, but we would argue strongly for the inclusion of timing or discontinuity variables in future research on the socioeconomic life cycle.

In this chapter, we have identified three discontinuities in schooling that influence other events in the socioeconomic life cycle. These discontinuities arise virtually independently of the socioeconomic origins and other family characteristics of young men. Especially in the instances of delays and interruptions in post-secondary education, experiences of discontinuity of schooling are random shocks in the life cycle, and whether or not one proceeds through school continuously appears to be a matter of "luck." That is, whatever causes discontinuities apparently is not measured well by variables in our causal model.

Despite our inability to account for retardation, delays, and interruption in schooling, we observe in these discontinuities events in the structure of the life cycle that increase inequality of achievement (i.e., enlarge, primarily, the variation in education in the cohort but also affect occupational status and income as well) without altering opportunity for achievement (i.e., the stratification correlation between fathers' and sons' occupations) in the population.[14] Discontinuities in schooling handicap a man who experiences them because the socioeconomic life cycle in the United States is organized to process cohorts; the school, the economy, and society gain a certain operational efficiency from the relatively homogeneous experiences within the cohort. Apparently, all societies recognize a series of life stages which constitute the life cycle, although cultural variations in the number of such stages and the degrees of continuity of behavior (e.g., role discontinuities and conflicts) across them do occur (Benedict, 1938). Every culture, however, organizes its institutions of socialization according to its conception of the life cycle. In our own industrial society, there are sociologically rational connections between schools and the labor market; it would be surprising not to observe socioeconomic costs imposed on those who violate implicit age-specific behavioral norms which underlie the structure of education and which govern the transition from school to work.[15]

[14] Take the following two structural equations:

$$Y = b_{YX}X + b_{YU}U + b_{Y_u}u$$
$$U = b_{UX}X + b_{U_x}x$$

where X = father's occupation, U = son's education, and Y = son's occupation. According to the basic theorem of path analysis (Duncan, 1966), we can write the stratification correlation as follows:

$$r_{YX} = p_{YX} + p_{YU}r_{UX}$$

This can be rewritten in terms of path regressions and ratios of standard deviations:

$$r_{YX} = b_{YX \cdot U}\ \frac{S_X}{S_Y}\ + b_{YU \cdot X}\ \frac{S_U}{S_Y}\ b_{UX}\ \frac{S_X}{S_U}$$

$$= b_{YX \cdot U}\ \frac{S_X}{S_Y}\ + b_{YU \cdot x}b_{UX}\ \frac{S_X}{S_Y}$$

$$= \frac{S_X}{S_Y}\ b_{YX \cdot U} + b_{YU \cdot x}b_{UX}.$$

Increasing the variance in education (S_U^2) *does not alter the degree of opportunity for achievement,* r_{YX}, *ceteris paribus. If* r_{UX} *increased, of course* r_{YX} *would also, ceteris paribus. However, in our data, educational discontinuities are virtually uncorrelated with family factors, so that they do not enter into the relationship between* X *and* U, *while they do affect* S_U.

[15] Cutright's (1972) analysis of earnings profiles for veterans and nonveterans illustrates these costs, as does our own. We plan to extend our inquiry of life cycle discontinuities to include females as well as males. Clearly a substantial minority of women interrupt or delay their schooling owing to marriage and childbearing (Davis, 1973). We can only speculate whether or not the discontinuities in the life cycle affect women as they affect men.

TABLE A-1

Correlation Matrix From Lenawee County, Michigan Data on Respondents Interviewed During Follow-up: Spring, 1972 (N = 340)[a]

Variables	INC	LNINC	OCC	FJOB	EDTOT	DURED	COLTN	NREG	DPHS	PHSI	OAS	EASP	AGRTD	GPA	FAOCC	FAED	MOED	MA	RURAL	FARM	SIBS
Income	--																				
Ln Income	86	--																			
Occupational SEI	18	26	--																		
First Job SEI	20	25	74	--																	
Total Education	20	24	66	74	--																
Duration of Education	13	17	41	54	64	--															
College Training	15	21	58	66	75	58	--														
Non-Regular Schooling	06	03	-05	02	-03	44	44	--													
Delay in Post-High School Education	-02	-03	-02	04	-05	46	58	-12	--												
Post-High School Interruption	06	10	32	41	50	59	54	10	04	--											
Occupational Aspiration	16	19	57	56	63	38	62	-08	-09	35	--										
Educational Aspiration	19	19	55	59	69	43	71	-12	-12	43	70	--									
Age-Grade Retardation	-17	-19	-25	-25	-28	-19	-20	-06	-02	-12	-28	-26	--								
High School Grade Point Average	13	14	54	57	63	40	56	-01	-08	35	35	60	-32	--							
Father's Occupational SEI	16	16	31	34	30	07	29	-12	-12	19	30	32	-15	25	--						
Father's Education	20	19	24	31	35	17	29	-05	-03	20	35	35	-16	25	46	--					
Mother's Education	18	21	24	25	37	22	31	02	-05	25	35	37	-20	30	32	55	--				
Mental Ability	10	12	36	41	43	24	41	-04	-04	24	46	41	-24	48	23	22	26	--			
Rural Residence	-02	-01	-26	-31	-25	-08	-20	11	05	-11	-20	-25	05	-13	-39	-18	-12	-19	--		
Farm Background	01	01	-11	-12	-00	06	-05	15	06	00	-11	-02	00	-02	-42	-00	08	-11	35	--	
Size of Sibship	-14	-13	-13	-18	-22	-06	-14	01	03	-02	-16	-16	09	-13	-21	-20	-21	-19	11	04	--
x̄'s	12890.	9.35	47.1	39.6	13.7	3.95	.426	.255	.202	.223	36.9	1.17	.094	2.09	32.7	2.27	2.60	21.0	.638	.195	3.76
S.D.'s	6994.	.483	25.2	26.4	2.45	4.45	.495	.437	.402	.417	12.9	1.24	.292	.843	22.1	1.36	1.31	5.23	.481	.397	2.48

[a] Decimals omitted in correlation matrix.

A spin-off from our major inquiry was the discovery that college and nonregular post-secondary education (e.g., vocational, technical, business, apprenticeship training) are not functionally equivalent in the process of achievement. For young men intellectually and financially able to undertake post-secondary schooling, college offers more certification (credit) for equal periods of attendance than do nonregular schools, and having attended college versus vocational school, for example, enables the young man to begin full-time labor force attachment in jobs of higher social standing. Whether the benefit of college attendance (or the nonbenefit of nonregular schooling) signals nonintellectual returns to education in the form of personality traits and interpersonal styles that are marketable upon labor force entry, or whether these returns to college attendance (net years of school completed) represent other factors, such as employer discriminations in favor of collegians, cannot be ascertained from our data. However, in closing we will repeat another's interpretation of these findings.[16] Our data lend no support to policies which would divert scholarships from colleges and college attenders and share these scarce resources with vocational, technical institutes and their matriculants. Insofar as the rationale for public support of the education of able individuals depends on the quality of the labor force and personal mobility, our data support two- and four-year colleges (universities) as more effective at these tasks. Of course, our work was not designed to explore these issues, and our observations remain most tentative.

[16] We thank Bill Sewell for this observation.

VI | Characteristics of the Work Setting and the Job as Determinants of Income

Joe L. Spaeth
University of Illinois, Urbana–Champaign

One of the more tantalizing outcomes of recent research on the attainment process has been the limited extent to which the variation in income has been explained. Although publicity attendant on the release of *Inequality* (Jencks, Smith, Acland, Bane, Cohen, Gintis, Heyns, and Michelson, 1972) has made this finding something of a *cause célèbre*, the fact itself was already rather well known (Duncan, Featherman, and Duncan, 1972; Bowles, 1972a).

Among nonblack males in the experienced civilian labor force in March, 1962, only 17% of the variance in income is explained by the following predictors: father's educational and occupational status, number of siblings in the family of origin, educational attainment, and occupational status (O. D. Duncan, 1968b; Duncan et al., 1972:264). By contrast, the first four of these variables explained 39% of the variation in occupational attainment. With the number-of-siblings variable omitted, a measure of adult IQ added, and correlations corrected for attenuation, the data in Jencks et al. (1972) show that 22% of the variance in income is explained, compared with 45% of the variance in occupational status. Comparable equations estimated by Bowles (1972a) show that 25% of the variance in income and 60% of the variance in occupation are explained.[1]

---

[1] The Bowles estimates are almost certainly too high, since they are based on rather shaky corrections for attenuation. These corrections have apparently pro-

From evidence of this kind, Jencks concludes that a large amount of "luck" is an integral part of the process by which income is allocated to persons in American society—that a substantial amount of true chance is involved in the process.

It is, of course, logically impossible to prove such a contention because chance is an unknown component of the residual term in any regression equation. There is no way to separate the effects of chance from those of variables or forms of functions of which we are currently unaware.

Virtually all treatments of the income problem in recent sociological literature rely on a basic model introduced by Blau and Duncan (1967) and developed by Duncan *et al.* (1972). With one exception, the independent variables in that model are statuses: the educational and occupational status of a man's father and his own educational and occupational status. To these is added the number of siblings in the parental family; the effects of sibsize are largely indirect in the determination of occupation and income. The most common extension of this model introduces intellectual ability as measured by the Armed Forces Qualification Test (AFQT). This variable is taken to be a result of the parental statuses and a cause of the person's attainments. These independent variables account for about twice as much variance in occupational attainment as in income.

It is not hard to think of variables other than those in the basic model that might be determinants of income. Among them are such demographic variables as region and size of place, on the grounds that opportunities for success are greater outside the south and in larger places. Both effects have been shown to exist, although both are rather small (Mueller, 1973).

Another well-known set of determinants is work experience. Income is positively associated with length of time in the labor force and with the amount of "relevant" job experience.

Characteristics of the employer are also likely to be associated with income—the larger the firm, the higher the income, for example. A variable related to size of firm but conceptually related to a different dimension is span of control—the number of employees supervised by the person. Working for a sizable firm is virtually a necessary condition for having a large span of control, but the implications of this variable for the responsibility of the work may be substantively more important. Another variable related to job responsibility is the complexity of the work done—the more complex the work, the higher the income; the more responsible the job, the higher the pay.

------

duced some artificial multicollinearity, as may be seen by the fact that the standardized coefficient showing the direct effect of education on income is $-.21$ when occupational status is entered in the equation.

Research Related to Characteristics
of the Work

The literature contains few references to studies of the relationship between job characteristics and income that are based on large and representative samples. Apparently the only study of this kind was one designed by Melvin Kohn and his colleagues at the National Institute of Mental Health (Kohn, 1969). This study was intended to throw light on the effects of job characteristics on the psychological functioning of job holders.

Kohn's data contain a particularly complete set of information on the job characteristics of a national sample of employed males. The questionnaire was designed by Kohn and administered in 1964 by the National Opinion Research Center (NORC) to a sample of 3101 employed males. The questionnaire included the background and ability measures needed to estimate the parameters of the basic model of the attainment process.

The remainder of this chapter will be divided into four parts. The first will discuss in some detail the variables actually measured by Kohn and his colleagues and made available for the present analysis.[2] The second will be a detailed comparison of coefficients calculated from the Kohn data set with estimates from "Ability and Achievement" (O. D. Duncan, 1968a) and *Inequality* (Jencks et al., 1972). The third will consist of certain extensions of the basic model made possible by the Kohn data set. Finally, the fourth part will discuss certain implications of the results presented here and refer to results of other theoretical approaches to this problem.

The Kohn Data

Univariate statistics for the Kohn data set are shown in Table 6.1. Most of the measures, including those on ability and attainments, are not strictly comparable with the standard IQ tests and measures of attainment used in the researches connected with the basic model. Thus, comparison across samples must be in terms of standardized regression coefficients only. Fortunately, the availability of estimates from other research will allow a rather accurate assessment of the behavior of the coefficients in the Kohn data set.

As noted above, the Kohn data set does not permit a completely literal replication of the other studies. Father's education is measured in conventional survey categories, not in years of schooling. The measure ranges from a low of 1 for some or no grade school to a high of 7 for education beyond the bachelor's degree. Father's and own occupation are coded

[2] I am grateful to Melvin L. Kohn for providing the computations from his data set on which this paper is based.

TABLE 6.1

Means and Standard Deviations for Variables in 1964 Survey of 3,101 Employed Males (Kohn Data Set)

Variable	Mean	S. D.
Father's education	2.40	1.60
Father's occupation	4.70	1.50
Size of family of origin	4.93	2.91
IQ_1	50.03	9.99
IQ_2	49.95	10.15
Educational attainment	4.03	2.05
Status of current occupation	4.41	1.64
Size of community	2.36	1.05
Labor force experience	23.37	12.65
Relevant job experience	167.76	136.68
Size of firm	3.64	2.63
Number of subordinates	2.10	1.61
Substantive complexity of job	50.08	9.99
Job income	67.03	51.98

according to the Hollingshead categories, with 1 high and 7 low. Where appropriate, signs have been changed so that the higher values of variables will be treated as having high scores in the data. Size of family of origin refers to the number of children in that family, *including the respondent.* Its value is therefore larger than the conventional number-of-siblings measure, but its behavior should be the same. IQ_1 is the result of a factor analysis of several measures of intellectual functioning and refers to a "perceptual" dimension of "intellectual flexibility." IQ_2 is the "ideational" component derived from the factor analysis mentioned above and can be expected to behave much like a measure of verbal IQ (Kohn and Schooler, 1973). Both sets of scores have been standardized to means of 50 and standard deviations of 10.

Kohn's measure of educational attainment, which is an adaptation of the usual survey question on educational stages that incorporates "credit" for additional nonformal schooling, ranges from 1 to 9. Size of community is a 4-point scale, with larger categories at the high end; it ranges from 1 for metropolitan areas of 2 million or more to 4 for nonmetropolitan counties with no city of at least 10,000 people (Kohn, 1969:242). Labor force experience is the number of years that the respondent has been in the labor force since he first worked full time for at least six months. Relevant job experience is the number of *months* of experience in the person's current job or in jobs that could be considered as "stepping stones" to it. Size of firm and number of subordinates are both conventional measures, with larger intervals at the high end. The first ranges from 1 for 1000 or more employees to 9 for 1 employee; the second from 6 for more than 24 subordinates to 1 for no subordinates.

Substantive complexity of the job is "based on detailed questioning of each respondent about his work with things, with data or ideas, and with people" (Kohn and Schooler, 1973:104). The index is based on seven ratings: appraisals of the complexity of a man's work with data, with things, and with people; an appraisal of the overall complexity of a man's work; and his own estimates of the time he spends working in each type of activity. The single index of substantive complexity is based on a factor analysis of the seven ratings. The index is standardized to have a mean of 50 and a standard deviation of 10. Job income is simply the dollar amount earned from the respondent's *job* in hundreds of dollars. Since job characteristics are part of the analysis, job income is the dependent variable.

The Process of Income Attainment

Given our interest in whether characteristics of occupations and their settings influence income, the extent to which the Kohn estimates of effects in the basic model are consistent with others is an important matter. Furthermore, analysis of this problem gives us an opportunity that has been quite rare in sociology, that of examining the extent to which independent research produces replications of important findings.[3] To that end, we shall compare estimates of standardized regression coefficients from three sources: *Class and Conformity* (Kohn, 1969), "Ability and Achievement" (O. D. Duncan, 1968a), and *Inequality* (Jencks et al., 1972).

The Duncan and Kohn data sets are completely independent of one another. The data were collected at different times, 1962 and 1964,

---

[3] Jencks et al. (1972) also compare their findings with those of Duncan. In addition to the analysis reported in the text, coefficients of determination from the Kohn data set were compared with those calculated from data reported in Duncan et al. (1972) for four age cohorts and from Griliches and Mason (1972) for a young cohort. In every category of comparison but one, the Kohn coefficients approximated the median of the others.

respectively, and by different agencies, CPS and NORC. The CPS sample was of "men in the United States civilian noninstitutional population between the ages of 20 and 64 in March, 1962," but published analyses pertain to men in the experienced civilian labor force (Duncan *et al.*, 1972:32). The NORC sample was "chosen to be representative of all men employed in civilian occupations in the United States" (Kohn, 1969:9).

Furthermore, the measures of certain variables were quite different. The Duncan study used the Duncan SES scale to measure the occupational status of fathers and sons; the Kohn study used the Hollingshead 7-point scale. Duncan estimated correlations with IQ on CPS–NORC veterans data (Griliches and Mason, 1972) and used the AFQT. The estimates of IQ in the Kohn data set are peculiar to that study. IQ_2, the verbal factor, will generally be used here. Even the measurement of the education variables is slightly different; Duncan uses years of schooling, and Kohn uses a standard set of survey categories for father's education and an adaptation thereof for son's education.

The Jencks estimates are based on roughly the same sources as those in Duncan. The difference between the two sets of results must largely stem from the facts that correlations in the former are corrected for attenuation, whereas those in the latter are not, and that the Duncan analysis is limited to the 25–34 age cohort.

Given that two of the estimates to be analyzed are based on common data sources, it is somewhat anomalous that estimates from these sources are as inconsistent with each other as one of them is with the independent source. That is, the Kohn and Jencks estimates are often in closer agreement than the Jencks and Duncan estimates.

Thus, in Table 6.2, the reduced-form estimates of the effects of father's education (V) and occupation (X) on income are extremely close for Kohn and Jencks. In the first panel of Table 6.2, father's occupation is by far the stronger of the two regressors in these two data sets, with father's education having quite minor effects. The Duncan data, on the other hand, indicate that the two variables are about equal in their effects, with father's occupation slightly stronger.

When intelligence (Q) is added to the equations, the direct effect of father's education virtually disappears in the first two data sets but remains modest in the third. Father's occupation retains substantial direct effects in Kohn and Jencks and modest ones in Duncan. Estimates of the effects of intelligence, on the other hand, are closer for the second and third data sets, both of which are perceptibly higher than the estimates for the first set. Perhaps this discrepancy arises because the more traditional measure of IQ taps the relevant aspects of the determination of income more adequately than the ad hoc measure developed by Kohn and his associates. Nonetheless, the ordering of the three predictors is the same in all data sets.

Estimates of the effect of educational attainment (U) are higher for the Kohn and Duncan data sets than for the Jencks data set. Coefficients for the first two are about .2, for the third .16. The direct effect of IQ is still highest

TABLE 6.2

Regression Coefficients in Standard Form Showing the Influence on Income of Variables in the Basic Model (Kohn, Jencks, and Duncan Data Sets)

Data Set	Standardized Coefficients					
	V	X	Q	U	W	R^2
Kohn	.061	.237	--	--	--	.075
Jencks	.051	.254	--	--	--	.084
Duncan	.128	.147	--	--	--	.057
Kohn	.028	.197	.203	--	--	.112
Jencks	-.003	.181	.281	--	--	.149
Duncan	.081	.095	.260	--	--	.117
Kohn	-.010	.161	.120	.198	--	.137
Jencks	-.016	.148	.190	.159	--	.161
Duncan	.042	.050	.154	.221	--	.144
Kohn	.002	.105	.086	.026	.329	.199
Jencks	-.016	.095	.158	-.008	.331	.222
Duncan	.031	.019	.127	.089	.258	.181

NOTE: Variables are V = father's education, X = father's occupation, Q = adult IQ, U = educational attainment, W = status of current occupation.

in the Jencks estimates and lowest in the Kohn ones, but the Duncan estimate now virtually splits the difference between the other two. The direct effects of father's education and father's occupation are quite slight in the Duncan data set, whereas the direct effects of father's occupation are moderate and those of father's education negligible in the Kohn and Jencks data sets.

Own occupational status (W) is stronger in the first two sets of estimates than in the third. Moreover, this variable interprets virtually all the effects of educational attainment. In the Duncan data, the effect of occupational attainment is weaker, and the direct effect of educational attainment is not negligible. The direct effects of IQ are lowest in the Kohn data, higher in Duncan, and highest in Jencks. Father's occupation retains a direct effect in the first two data sets but not in the third. If one assumes that this direct effect is genuine, one might speculate that father's occupation is serving as a surrogate for parental family income. Results for the Wisconsin panel of high school seniors show that family income retains a direct effect on own income, whereas father's education, mother's education, and father's occupation do not (Hauser, Sewell, and Lutterman, 1975).

As a way of summarizing the results of these comparisons, let us average the values for coefficients of the three intervening variables. This yields an estimate of .25 for the total effects of IQ, .155 when those effects are mediated by education, and .12 when they are mediated by education and occupation. The total effect of education is estimated to be .19 and drops to .06 when the effects of occupational status are taken into account. Finally, the effect of occupational status is estimated to be .31.

All three sets of estimates agree that the effects of father's education are indirect, at least after educational attainment is introduced. Two of the three agree that father's occupation has a direct effect, though this variable may represent the impact of parental income. All three are in rough agreement that about one-half of the effects of IQ are direct, with the other half indirect mostly through educational attainment. All three agree that the effects of occupational status are substantial, although two give higher estimates than the third. Coefficients of determination are roughly consistent, especially between the Kohn and Duncan data sets. The fact that the Jencks data produce a slightly higher final R^2 may be attributed to correction for attenuation of correlations. None of them contradicts the conclusion of Jencks et al. (1972) that the great majority of the variation in income still remains to be explained after the effects of the variables in the basic model have been taken into account. The variance in income remaining in groups homogeneous on father's education, father's occupation, IQ, education, and occupational status is nearly 80% of the total.

Extensions of the Basic Model

As indicated earlier, several kinds of variables from the Kohn data set will be added to the basic model in an attempt to assess their importance as

determinants of income.[4] These include demographic characteristics, such
as size of place, two measures of labor force experience (total experience
and relevant experience), organizational characteristics (size of firm and
number of subordinates), and the substantive complexity of the job itself.

As a first step, we shall present a regression equation relating all the
regressors just named to job income. This will serve to summarize the
influence of a rather large number of variables and allow for the elimination
of several of the weaker ones. The equation, with coefficients in standard
form, is as follows:[5]

$$\hat{I} = .012V + .088X + .013N + .051Q_1 + .084Q_2 + .033U + .199W$$
$$+ .118P + .034L + .103E + .030S + .174R + .033C.$$

R^2 is .266.

The size of the coefficient of determination indicates that this equation
accounts for substantially more of the variance in income than does the
basic model alone. The increment in R^2 is .067, which represents a third
again as much variance as is explained by the basic model. It took six
additional predictors to bring about this increment, although three of them
are quite small and can be ignored.

A brief summary of these results will allow us to set the stage for
reestimating the model with some of the unimportant regressors eliminated. In the first place, the effects of father's education are still all indirect,
which can hardly come as much of a surprise. A substantial part of the
direct effect of father's occupation remains, despite the addition of the six
new regressors. The perceptual component of IQ has rather weak direct
effects, with the effects of the ideational component being somewhat
stronger. The direct effects of educational attainment remain small, and the
direct effects of occupational status remain rather large, although the latter
are considerably smaller than in the appropriate basic model equation. The
impact of three of the new regressors is quite trivial. The .034 value for
labor force experience is a reduction from the appropriate reduced-form
value of .119. This reduction is brought about entirely by the introduction of
relevant job experience. In other words, experience in the labor force is
conducive to greater earnings only if that experience is in a job that is
relevant to one's current job. The small coefficient for size of firm is not
primarily owing to collinearity with number of supervisees. Even before the
latter variable is entered, the coefficient for size is quite small (.062). The

---

[4] For expository convenience, the basic model will henceforth be taken to include a
measure of IQ.

[5] Variables are I = job income, V = father's education, X = father's occupation,
N = family size, Q_1 = perceptual intelligence, Q_2 = ideational intelligence, U = educational attainment, W = status of current occupation, P = size of community, L =
labor force experience, E = relevant job experience, S = size of firm, R = number of
subordinates, C = substantive complexity of job.

standardized coefficient of .033 for substantive complexity seems quite low, especially since this variable correlates with income to the extent of .418. In raw score form, the complete equation for the determination of income becomes

$$\hat{I} = .397V + 3.030X + .230N + .263Q_1 + .430Q_2 + .839U + 6.314W \\ + 5.834P + .140L + .039E + .590S + 5.619R + .173C - 80.827.$$

"Several years" of father's education are worth about $40, compared to more than twice that much for son's education. Neither coefficient is statistically significant. The two-to-one ratio also holds for son's and father's occupation, with one Hollingshead unit of the former being worth about $630 and one of the latter about $300. Both coefficients are significant. Sibsize has a small positive coefficient that is not statistically significant. Perceptual IQ scores seem to be worth about $43, compared to $26 for ideational IQ. A "unit" of size of place is worth nearly $600, a significant result but not one that is readily interpretable. A year of labor force experience is worth $14 (NS), compared to $47 (.0393 × 12) for relevant experience. Thus, relevant experience is worth over three times as much as total experience. In arbitrary units, size of firm has a value of about $60 (NS). Number of subordinates is worth $560 in arbitrary units, a value that is highly significant. A unit of substantive complexity has a value of about $17 (NS).

Three sets of two variables each refer to similar concepts: perceptual and ideational IQ, years in the labor force and months of relevant job experience, and occupational status plus substantive complexity of the work. The correlation between the two measures of IQ is .002, that between perceptual IQ and income is .089, and that between ideational IQ and income is .267. Clearly, only the latter is an important influence on income, and the former is superfluous, as indicated by its addition of .001 to the coefficient of determination in a reduced-form equation that included parental status and both measures of filial IQ.

As one would expect, total labor force experience and relevant experience are highly collinear, as indicated by their correlation of .723. In the appropriate reduced form, the two variables together contribute an increment of 1.7% to R^2, of which only .5% is independently contributed by years of work. Entered in separate equations, a year of labor force experience is worth about $50, compared to about $65 for relevant experience.

Somewhat surprisingly, occupational prestige and job complexity are more highly correlated (.796) than the two experience variables. Thus, the coefficient for complexity is virtually nil under the specification adopted here. When the two variables are treated as a block and entered after educational attainment, the standardized coefficient for status is .215 and that for complexity is .179. Raw score coefficients are 6.823 and .929, respectively. The redundancy of complexity is such that in combination with job status, it explains only 1.1% more of the variance than does status alone. In fact, the two variables are virtually perfect surrogates for each other. In analyses not reported here, standardized coefficients for father's education and occupation and son's education as predictors of each variable and for each variable as a predictor of income are at least as closely comparable as analogous coefficients for occupational prestige in the different data sets discussed earlier. To all intents and purposes, occupational prestige and substantive complexity of the work are the same thing.

Findings based on an equation omitting sibsize, perceptual IQ, total labor force experience, size of firm, and substantive complexity are given in Tables 6.3A and 6.3B. Although these tables present all possible reduced forms on one ordering of the variables, we shall ignore those pertaining only to the basic model. In addition, the relationships among the new regressors make attempts to trace out patterns of indirect effects among them fruitless, so we shall concentrate primarily on the value of coefficients as they appear in the appropriate reduced form. As was noted earlier, working in a larger rather than a smaller community makes a modest contribution to the determination of income, as the standardized coefficient of .14 shows. About the same contribution is made by relevant work experience, .13. It is worth repeating that, modest though this effect may be, relevant job experience makes the relationship between total labor force experience and income disappear. This finding throws some light on a practice that is not uncommon in literature on the determination of income. Age is often treated as a surrogate for labor force experience, since data on the former variable are more widely available than those on the latter. If present findings on relevant job experience are valid, age is a surrogate once removed, since it represents a particular kind of experience in the labor force.

On the assumption that the number of employees supervised represents at least one form of responsibility, its effects on income, as indicated by a beta of .19, may not be particularly surprising. These effects are, in fact, only slightly less than those of education and IQ, and not much less than those of father's occupation.

Taking metric coefficients from appropriate reduced forms in Table 6.3B, we may note that several years of father's education are worth about $20, a Hollingshead unit of father's occupation over $80, and a unit of ideational IQ about $100. Several years of schooling are worth about $500, as compared to over $1000 for a unit of Hollingshead status. A unit of size of place is worth nearly $700, a year's relevant job experience is worth about $60 ($.051 \times 12$), and supervisory responsibility about $370.

Evidence of indirect effects will be discussed in terms of standardized coefficients. As was mentioned earlier, in the set of variables introduced after those in the basic model, none of the later ones serves to interpret the

TABLE 6.3

Coefficients Showing the Influence on Job Income of Variables in the Basic Model Plus Demographic, Structural, and Job Characteristics (Kohn Data Set)

A. Standardized Coefficients

V	X	Q	U	W	P	E	S	R^2
.061	.237	--	--	--	--	--	--	.075
.028	.197	.203	--	--	--	--	--	.112
-.010	.161	.120	.198	--	--	--	--	.137
.002	.105	.086	.026	.329	--	--	--	.199
-.010	.108	.084	.001	.331	.140	--	--	.218
.010	.093	.086	.045	.275	.140	.133	--	.233
.010	.090	.077	.046	.213	.129	.115	.187	.262

TABLE 6.3 (continued)

				B.	Regression Coefficents			
V	X	Q	U	W	P	E	S	Constant
1.995	8.184	--	--	--	--	--	--	23.810
.895	6.811	1.041	--	--	--	--	--	-19.104
-.321	5.562	.614	5.014	--	--	--	--	-9.200
.070	3.627	.439	.670	10.418	--	--	--	-20.791
-.321	3.751	.428	.034	10.436	6.928	--	--	-33.733
.331	3.230	.441	1.188	8.712	6.913	.051	--	-39.058
.316	3.120	.394	1.950	6.757	6.353	.044	6.040	-40.775

NOTE: Variables are V = father's education, X = father's occupation, Q = ideational IQ, U = educational attainment, W = status of current occupation, P = size of community, E = relevant job experience, and S = number of subordinates.

173

effects of an earlier one. The greatest proportional reduction in coefficients is the 13% decline in the value of the beta for relevant experience, from .133 to .115 (Table 6.3A).

As for the variables in the basic model, coefficients for most of the early ones are reduced only slightly. The coefficient for educational attainment increases from zero to .045 when relevant job experience is introduced. By turning our earlier argument around and treating experience as a surrogate for age, we are able to formulate a sensible explanation for this finding. Since age and income are positively associated, as are education and income, whereas age and education are negatively associated, age is functioning as a suppressor for the effects of education. Since this is precisely the outcome to be expected from theory and since it has been found in the OCG data (Hauser, personal communication), there is no cause for surprise here. It was impossible to estimate the actual suppressor effects of experience since estimates for the appropriate equation were not available.

The coefficient for occupational status is gradually reduced as new regressors are entered. The largest drop occurs from .275 to .213 when number of subordinates is introduced. This finding is simply based on the tendency of supervisory jobs to be of higher status than nonsupervisory ones.

One final piece of evidence needs to be examined: the zero-order correlations of four regressors with income. Two of the correlations are rather low: The correlation between size of community and income is .20 and that between amount of relevant job experience and income is .18. The other two correlations are appreciable; between number of subordinates and income, it is .35, and between substantive complexity and income, it is .42.

Since appropriate reduced-form coefficients for the first two variables are .14 and .13, respectively, it is apparent that they are not strongly related to the variables preceding them, in particular those in the basic model. On the other hand, the effect of number of subordinates is materially lower than the corresponding zero-order correlation. Collinearity with earlier variables must therefore be rather great, and, as we have already mentioned, a major share of this collinearity may well be in relation to occupational status.

Summary and Conclusions

The results reported here can be summarized as follows:

1. The effects of socioeconomic background and achievement on income are rather modest. The set of such variables explains about 20% of the variation in job income. The findings reported here are in agreement with those of other investigators.
2. Demographic characteristics of the employment setting and the

structure of the job itself make modest contributions to the explanation of income.

3. The entire set of regressors reported here accounts for 26% of the variance in job income.

These findings raise two distinct questions:

1. Why do status background, attainment, and job characteristics explain a smaller proportion of the variance in income than the first two sets of variables explain in occupational status?
2. Is the proportion of unexplained variance likely to remain large, even if other regressors are taken into account?

As a partial answer to the first question, I have argued elsewhere (Spaeth, Chapter IV in this volume) that income is a different kind of variable from educational attainment and occupational prestige. The last two variables represent settings that vary in complexity, and the transition from the educational to the occupational realm represents passage from one kind of setting to another. Job income, on the other hand, is in part a reward for job performance. From this point of view, the determinants of income most often investigated by sociologists are qualifications for the entry into occupations and work roles and not measures of the adequacy of actual job performance. In an analogous manner, characteristics of the work, such as number of subordinates, are measures of duties, not of the performance of those duties. To the extent that income is a result of successful job performance, the relative failure of settings and qualifications as predictors may not be very surprising.

Apparently, income is by no means a unitary concept. Hauser and Sewell (personal communications) have suggested that variables of the kind treated in this chapter are determinants of a man's hourly wage rate, which is only one component of his income. Such a rate must be multiplied by the number of hours worked per year to produce annual earnings.[6]

Support for this point of view comes from recent developments in human capital economics (Mincer, 1974). This theory holds that there are two basic determinants of income—educational achievement and labor force experience. Both of these variables are viewed as investments producing returns in the form of income. Mincer's findings are not entirely comparable to those discussed earlier, but several points of comparison do exist. Thus, years of schooling explain 6.7% of the variance in the natural logarithm of income in Mincer's data and 10.3% of the variance in dollar income in Kohn's. Education and relevant job experience together explain 24.6% of the variation in the Kohn data. A more complicated function combining the linear effects of education with a linear and a squared term for total labor force experience (current age minus age at leaving school) explains 28.5% of the variance in log income in the Mincer data. A squared

---

[6] Wage rate and labor force participation are virtually independent: $r = -.118$ (Morgan, Dickinson, Dickinson, Benus, and Duncan, 1974).

term for education plus a multiplicative term for the interaction between education and experience adds 2.4% to the coefficient of determination (Mincer, 1974:92). The most important difference between the curvilinear specifications and the linear one is apparently the correction for curvilinearity in the effects of experience, which allows the returns to experience to decrease as age increases. Nonetheless, the improvement in the coefficient of determination is not dramatic.

When the natural logarithm of number of weeks worked during the year is added to the linear education and curvilinear experience terms, the coefficient of determination jumps from .285 to .525, a dramatic improvement indeed. Thus, a major component in the determination of income is the amount of time spent in the labor force during a given year.

This component has effects that are independent of education and labor force experience. Given the difference between Mincer's R^2 of .525 and the .266 of the specification employed in this chapter, we may infer that the effects of amount of time employed during a year will be independent of those of parental socioeconomic background and a man's own occupational status, plus a variety of characteristics of the work itself.

We may thus draw three tentative conclusions: (1) The combination of parental SES, own education, occupation, labor force experience, and other job characteristics can be expected to explain no more than a third of the variation in a man's wage rate; (2) the addition of amount of time employed during the year will explain about another fifth of the variation in income; (3) the explanation of employment patterns becomes an important problem in its own right.

Part 2 | INSTITUTIONAL EFFECTS

Introductory Notes

There is probably no single topic in the field of education that has fostered more heated debate than the effects of schools on the cognitive and moral development, sociopolitical attitudes, educational and occupational aspirations, and academic and socioeconomic achievements of their students. In the past 10 years, since the publication of the Coleman report, which revealed surprisingly small effects of school resources on students' academic performance, literally hundreds of books, monographs, and papers have appeared focusing on institutional effects. Some of these studies have attempted to reanalyze the data from the Coleman survey, using different analytical techniques and strategies and have either affirmed or modified the report's conclusions.

In Chapter VII of this volume, we have reprinted William G. Spady's careful review of this literature, "The Impact of School Resources on Students." Spady poses the basic question as follows: "Do measurable differences in the characteristics of schools lead to measurable differences in student outcomes?" Not surprisingly, he finds that methodologically adequate research on this topic is scarce. The difficulties in devising and executing appropriate strategies to isolate and accurately assess the effects of individual psychological characteristics, social background, and school characteristics on the outcomes of schooling have not been adequately dealt with in most of the research to date. Spady discusses these methodological problems in some detail, especially in relation to the Coleman report but also as they influence the findings of other studies. He concludes that the answer to his question is still somewhat cloudy. Clearly, there are statistically significant effects of school resources on student attitudes and achievements that are independent of the student's measured academic ability and family background. These effects tend to be smaller than might have been anticipated. Likewise, the socioeconomic and ethnic–racial composition of schools seem to have small but consistent effects on student outcome variables that are independent of individual characteristics and the family backgrounds of the students. Although the evidence indicates that family background and student characteristics are more important than school characteristics in determining educational outcomes, he believes that the effects of school may have been underestimated or even masked, especially in the studies using regression techniques, because of failure to take into account possible interaction, threshold, accentuation, and curvilinear trends in the data.

In Chapter VIII, "Another Hour, Another Day: Quantity of Schooling, A Potent Path for Policy," David E. Wiley presents two conceptions of school effects. Substantively, he argues that in any adequate assessment of schooling the primary input variable must be the quantity of schooling received by the student. Methodologically, he proposes a statistical model for a complex set of variables defined in a hierarchy, such as pupils and schools, which allows for efficient use of information at both levels and is very precise in the estimation of the effects of the variables. Using data for Detroit from the Equality of Educational Opportunity Survey, he applies the concept of quantity of schooling (based on average daily attendance, numbers of hours in the school day, and number of days in the school year), in his statistical model to estimate the effects of schools on reading comprehension, mathematical achievement, and verbal ability. By using quantity of schooling in his equations, his results show great increases in the effects of schools on these achievements as compared to models that do not take into account this particular aspect of schooling.

In Chapter IX, "A New Model of School Effectiveness," Henry M. Levin suggests that studies of the educational output process are analogous to econometric efforts at estimating production processes in industry. He points out that most studies of educational production-function have used standardized achievement scores as the sole output of the process, despite the fact that schools are expected to have other effects in addition to academic achievement. These include skills, attitudes, and (as economists say) "social externalities," such as better citizenship. Ideally, the estimation of the educational production process should be based on total educational output, and failure to do so has led to a high probability of bias in the estimates of the production coefficients. Levin proposes a simultaneous equation model and makes a tentative test of this model using data from the Equal Opportunity Survey on sixth-grade students in a large eastern city. He tentatively concludes that students from larger families probably have lower verbal scores on achievement tests because of poorer attitudes, rather than because of the link from family size and other background factors to achievement. His results also suggest that the higher verbal scores of females are attributable to a higher sense of efficacy rather than to any direct sex-achievement effect. A reduced-form equation shows all of the system's indirect influences of students' attitudes and aspirations, parents' attitudes, and the characteristics of schools on verbal scores, as well as the direct effects of each of these variables through the verbal score equation. The possible policy implications of these tentative findings are also discussed.

In Chapter X, "Measuring Efficiency in Educational Production," Levin continues his econometric approach but now explores the production set for educational achievement (scores on standardized tests) in "efficient" and "inefficient" schools. The inefficient or average production relationship is obtained by estimating a reduced-form equation for all schools in a sample drawn from a large eastern city. The efficient set is obtained by using a linear programming approach to yield coefficients for those schools that show the largest student achievement output relative to their resource inputs. A comparison of the two sets of technical coefficients suggests that the relative marginal products are probably different. Because of these differences, the optimal combination of inputs for producing educational achievement will vary between efficient and inefficient schools and may even vary from school to school. The result suggests that the use of such production-function estimates in an attempt to improve efficiency in the educational sector may have far less utility than its advocates have implied.

In Chapter XI, "High School Effects on Achievement," Robert M. Hauser, William H. Sewell, and Duane F. Alwin present the most recent findings from the Wisconsin longitudinal study on the effects of high schools on the educational aspirations and attainments of their students. An earlier paper by Sewell and Armer (1966a,b), which found very small net effects of neighborhood context on the educational aspirations of Milwaukee high school seniors, had led to a continuing controversy about the importance of school and contextual effects. The principal charges were that the regression model they used tended to mask the true contextual effects and that there were important statistical interactions that they did not take into account sufficiently in their analysis. Using a structural equation model of educational attainment, Hauser and his associates undertook an exhaustive search for first-order interaction effects of high schools on the aspirations and achievements of students in Milwaukee high schools. In 31 tests, they found only one statistically significant interaction effect. Moreover, their analysis of additive effects of schools supported the original findings of Sewell and Armer. They then did an intensive analysis of variations in educational aspirations and achievements within and between 424 high schools in Wisconsin. Again most of the variability in aspirations and achievement occurs within rather than between schools. The analysis of within-school models of achievement confirmed earlier findings of the

Wisconsin research regarding the effects of socioeconomic background and ability and the importance of significant others and of aspirations as intervening variables in the achievement process. The analysis also elaborated differences between the sexes in the educational achievement process and found interesting differences in the mechanisms by which academic performance and academic placement effect educational aspiration and achievement. The discovery that net school effects and contextual effects of student body composition account for no more than 1 or 2% of the variance in the population, above and beyond the effects of individual social, psychological, and academic factors, lead them to conclude that future research on the educational achievement process could profitably turn to issues other than school-to-school variations in educational aspirations and achievements.

In Chapter XII, "Socioeconomic Background, Colleges and Post-Collegiate Achievements," Duane F. Alwin assesses the unique effects of colleges on educational and occupational achievements and on earnings in the early career of the Wisconsin sample of males who attended college. Using a recursive structural equation model, he shows the extent to which colleges transmit the effects of precollegiate experiences, particularly socioeconomic background and social psychological factors that operate in the high school years, to later achievements. He finds that the several categories of colleges vary with respect to the post-collegiate achievements of their students, but that these gross differences in achievement represent only 5–8% of the variance in the outcomes studied. The analysis then turns to the effect of differential selection and recruitment into college. After a complex analysis that involves adjustments for selection and recruitment variables, the initial gross differences between colleges are reduced by about one-half. After taking out selection–recruitment effects, colleges explain only about 2–5% of the variance in educational, occupational, and earnings attainments during the early careers of the young men studied. The analysis also indicates that colleges do not act as major mediators of the effects of the precollegiate variables on the post-collegiate achievements studied.

In Chapter XIII, "Changes in Initial Differences Among Major-Field Groups: An Exploration of the 'Accentuation Effect'," Kenneth A. Feldman and John Weiler review a number of studies that have claimed that the various subenvironments within colleges, such as students pursuing a particular academic major, not only differ from each other but often differentially mediate any overall pressures from the general college environment. Thus, certain subenvironments may reinforce the total college influence while others may contradict or even challenge it. Using data from a study of University of Michigan students who were seniors in 1966 or 1967 and with comparable information on them as freshman, the scores of students in selected academic majors on a series of personality variables are compared. They find evidence that initial differences in scores of the various academic major groups tend to become greater over the course of the college career. However, this is only one of several patterns of change and stability between and among groups. For example, the personality characteristics that are most accentuated are different for males and females: Initial group differences for females on Complexity and Religious Liberalism were most accentuated while for males the greatest accentuation was on Theoretical Orientation. Moreover, accentuation of group differences is greater for females than males. For some personality attributes, there were no major-field differences, either at entrance or graduation from the university. In other instances, initial major-field differences diminished over time. All of these findings are elaborated and compared with the results of past studies of the accentuation effect.

We believe that the studies of institutional effects reported in this section constitute the most sophisticated attempts yet to determine the effects of schools and colleges on their students. The vexing problem of disentangling the effects of selection and recruitment from those of the institution, college, school, classroom, or subgroup was approached by the various authors through several different statistical models, depending on the specific problem and the training of the analysts. All were aware of the pitfalls involved in attempts to allocate and assess the separate and joint effects of selection and socialization in the educational process. We expect that the statistical techniques for assessing effects in complex social processes will be improved in the future, and we hope that the efforts reported in this section will help to stimulate that development.

VII | The Impact of School Resources on Students[*]

William G. Spady
National Institute of Education

At the heart of the controversies surrounding public education is the strongly held belief that schools should have a "positive impact" on their clientele. To most people, this premise implies that all schools should provide adequate training not only in basic literacy and computational skills but also in more advanced subject areas that are regarded as essential in technologically sophisticated societies. The impact of schooling on the young, however, is not limited to cognitive development. School experience is structured so that children also acquire values and attitudes that facilitate their integration into the competitive occupational and political worlds of adults (Dreeben, 1968). The school's emphasis on formal achievement, interpersonal competition, and certification strongly suggests how it may aid in the formation of values and attitudes and act to select students for the occupational, economic, and prestige structures of the society. Its impact as an institution on the life chances of the young is undeniable (Blau and Duncan, 1967; Kamens, 1971; Sewell, Haller, and Ohlendorf, 1970).

* This chapter appeared as Chapter 5 in Fred N. Kerlinger, Ed., *Review of Research in Education* (Itasca, Illinois: F. E. Peacock Publishers, Inc. 1973), pp. 135–177. Charles E. Bidwell, University of Chicago, was the editorial consultant for the chapter.

The opinions expressed in this publication do not necessarily reflect the position, policy, or endorsement of the National Institute of Education.

Critics suggest that schools teach conformity, inhibit individualism, creativity, and independent thinking, foster mediocrity, and discriminate against non-Anglo, non-middle-class students. This implies that the impact of schools depends on the quantity and quality of resources, staff, programs, and facilities that are made available to students from certain regions, localities, neighborhoods, ethnic groups, or social class backgrounds. The issue is: *Do measurable differences in the characteristics of schools lead to measurable differences in student outcomes?*

Do schools have an impact on their clientele? Methodologically adequate research evidence is scarce. North American schools do not provide ideal natural settings for manipulating organizational features, such as the distribution and utilization of various resources, the structure and student-body composition of schools and classrooms, the selection of students into schools and programs, the methods of instruction, evaluation, and promotion, or the operational goals of school programs. Although substantial heterogeneity in the organizational features of schools and school systems exists, it is such as to make conformity to rigorous research requirements difficult, especially the isolation of the effects of variables.

The selection of students and teachers with specified characteristics into schools with certain physical and instructional facilities and a variety of structural options occurs most often by choice, not by design. The choice is generally that of parents, school administrators, and teachers—not researchers. The result is a segregation of students into schools according to their socioeconomic status (SES) and race (usually reflected in local residential patterns), with parallel differentials of staff, curricular, and physical resources. The correlations among some of these resource measures are quite high. This "multicollinearity" (R. A. Gordon, 1968) poses difficult problems in the analysis and interpretation of data. Many of the major research studies to be cited in this chapter are plagued by this problem, and their findings are difficult to assess.

The research to be reviewed suffers from a second anomaly: the questionable documentation of "impact." Impact implies "effect," and "effect" implies "cause." This is tantamount to suggesting that because a statistical relationship between a school resource (such as library volumes) and some student performance criterion exists, that specific school resource *directly influences* students' performance. Most such assumptions are questionable and need to be documented by more rigorous methods and evidence.

Complex problems of interpretation arise out of the cross-sectional, ex post facto (nonexperimental) nature of the research cited. Most studies are based on research designs that fail to provide evidence of two essential conditions: The presumed outcome or effect under examination occurs as an unambiguous consequence rather than an antecedent of the school attribute specified, and variables or social mechanisms other than the condition in question are not present or responsible for the outcome. The latter point refers both to providing adequate controls for potentially confounding variables, such as size of school library in studies of the teacher composition of schools, and to specifying the mechanisms whereby the attribute in question influences the outcome. Astin (1970a,b) analyzes these related methodological problems in considerable detail.

There is a third problem: the crude and deceptive measures of supposedly relevant resource variables. The resources tapped in the majority of studies are selected on an ad hoc basis, are tangible or structural, are crudely and even unreliably measured, stress quantity or mere presence over quality or mode and degree of utilization, and are recognized proxies for presumably more important process variables that remain unmeasured. A statistical relationship between school resource A and student outcome B, for example, may provide few clues as to *why* the relationship exists, often because the mechanisms linking the two remain unspecified.

A fourth problem is that the bulk of the research dealing with school resource variables is limited and conservative in focus. Although cognitive development is one of the universally accepted aims of public schooling, the nearly monolithic focus on standardized achievement measures in research betrays a lack of imagination within the educational research community. There are, of course, studies that also investigate variability in student educational goals and plans, but the validity and reliability of these variables are also problematic. One must generally look beyond this literature to studies on classroom interaction, ability grouping, and research on the college experience to find more broadly defined evidence on the differential impacts of schooling on students. This suggests that kinds of impact may exist that have been ignored by researchers, both within and outside the cognitive domain.

The two areas this chapter will consider can be defined by the nature of the independent variables dealt with. The first involves differences in the distribution and availability of educational resources among schools, including school plant and instructional facilities, staff characteristics, expenditure levels, and programs and services. The basic question of most studies in this category, in an input–output research approach, is whether student achievement is associated with formal school resources.

The second area focuses on variability in the allocation of student body resources among schools. Although these resources mainly reflect student background characteristics, such as race and family SES, there also has been some research on the normative climates of schools. The major concern is whether a student's achievement and attitudes are related to the characteristics of his fellow students, irrespective of his own background attributes.

Educational Resource Allocation among Schools

Although input–output research is not new in education, the milestone in the field, *Equality of Educational Opportunity (EEO)* by Coleman, Campbell, Hobson, McPartland, Mood, Weinfeld, and York (1966), is comparatively recent. No other study of its kind, including the equally formidable Project TALENT survey by Flanagan, Davis, Dailey, Shaycoft, Orr, Goldberg, and Neyman (1964), has generated so much discussion, controversy, and reexamination of methodologies and data. Detailed commentary on the original *EEO* findings and on the numerous reanalyses of its data is not possible here. The most pertinent criticisms of the original study will be presented as a means of illustrating the methodological limitations of nearly all work of this kind, followed by a synthesis of the most credible findings that have emerged to date. Only a few of the many specific issues pertaining to *EEO*, most notably those raised by Bowles (1969), Bowles and Levin (1968a,b), Hanushek (1970), Johnson (1972), Levin (Chapter 9 of this volume), Michelson (1970), and virtually all of the contributors to the Mosteller and Moynihan (1972) volume, will be considered.

Major Methodological Problems

As Hanushek and Kain (1972) argue, much of the criticism of the *EEO* survey stems from the ambiguity of its original mandate to document inequality of educational opportunity. This could have been achieved by demonstrating inequalities either in the distribution of school resources (inputs) or in student achievements (outputs). The survey attempts to do both and, thereby, implies a third approach: an examination of the educational production process which translates inputs into outputs. Understanding of this process requires detailed information on the ability of the student, his past level of achievement, his motivation to learn, his nonschool environment, such as family and community status and values, his current school resource inputs, such as facilities, programs, staff characteristics, expenditures, and student body characteristics, and his current achievement (Armor, 1972; Hanushek, 1970; Levin, Chapter 9 of this volume).

By using some prior level of achievement as a benchmark against which to measure current achievement, this model specifies the amount of achievement *gain* that occurs when the student is exposed to a given set of school resources. It assumes that past exposure to school resources will be reflected in earlier achievements and that the benefits of current resource allocations will be fairly immediate.

The major drawbacks with most input–output studies from this perspective, including *EEO*, is that they lack data on student ability, motivation, and previous achievement and can use only crude measures of nonschool environments, current school resource inputs, and current achievement. This means that important variables, such as ability and motivation, are excluded from the statistical models used to explain student outcomes, although they may be reflected to an unknown degree by variables that are present, such as SES and race. There are several reasons why relations between school resources and student achievement are difficult to interpret.

1. It is not clear to what extent present student performance is a reflection of past performance, exposure to past resources, or exposure to current resources. For example, a student's achievement at the end of grade six can be affected not only by the instruction he received during that grade, but also by his prior experience and achievement, perhaps at a different school. Failing to take past experience and achievement into account falsely implies that current achievement is solely affected by current resource allocations.

2. In most studies of this kind, including *EEO*, the unit of analysis is neither the student nor the classroom, but the school or school district. This means that the achievement of individual students is not related to their documented exposure to resources of a given kind within a school, but rather the combined achievement of all of the students in a school (or district) is associated with gross differences in the aggregate distribution of resources across schools or districts. It must be assumed both that all students in a given school are exposed to each resource to the same degree, even though there is no way of knowing how or how often the exposure takes place, and that schools with similar resources utilize them in similar ways and amounts.

3. It is by no means clear that the variables measured actually tap those resources that do make a difference in student outcomes. There are two aspects of this problem: the qualitative rather than quantitative aspects of the variables in question, and their inclusion or omission in research studies. Most of the studies reported here show that *some* measure of instructional expenditure is associated with standardized student achievement. But why? What are these expenditures purchasing that has not been measured more explicitly? We have little way of knowing if it is "better" trained teachers, "better" textbooks, "better" instructional aids and supplies, or "better" administrators, because quantitative indicators of these factors are often missing and the attributes for which such indicators would serve as proxies remain unmeasured.

4. The omission of student intelligence and motivation is another difficulty. Although both are difficult to measure, their omission from an educational production function means that the analysis will necessarily provide an inaccurate, incomplete, and even misleading explanation of student achievement. Because effects of ability and motivation are partially reflected in family background factors, analyses in which independent measures of student ability and motivation are missing inflate the estimated impact of family SES on student achievement. It may be that intelligence and motivation are important conditional factors affecting the school's capacity to translate its human and material resources into student performance.

5. The inflation of family SES effects is also at the center of another

source of interpretive difficulty: What is to be done with achievement variance that family background and school resources share in common? The typical input–output study attempts to determine whether differences in school resources are associated with student achievement when other important variables are also taken into account. Major methodological and interpretive errors may result from falsely ascribing to school resources those effects that are actually due to other variables. Because family socioeconomic characteristics and school resource allocations are associated, much of the variability in student achievement cannot be exclusively or "uniquely" ascribed to either one.

The methodology of the initial *EEO* survey has been severely attacked by nearly all of the critics cited here. Coleman and his colleagues relied heavily on multiple regression analysis, in which all of the joint SES–school resource variance was inappropriately assumed to be SES based. School resources were assumed to account only for that proportion of the variance in student achievement that could not *initially* be accounted for by family background variables. This is commonly referred to as the "unique effect" of school resources. In subsequent computations of this effect, however, a substantial proportion of the explained variance continued to be shared jointly by SES and school resources, although a large proportion of it cannot be legitimately attributed to either family background or to school resources exclusively. Both Michelson (1970) and M. Smith (1972) argue that the selection of neighborhoods with "better schools" by higher-status parents and the selection of students into different ability groups, tracks, and even schools on the basis of their previous performance and SES both help to create a strong statistical bias against attributing an appreciable effect on student outcomes to school resources. This bias occurs especially when, as in *EEO*, such effects are calculated only on aggregated data. Paradoxically, however, Smith also shows that technical errors in the original *EEO* analysis actually overestimated the contribution of school resource variables to student verbal achievement.

Before turning to the available data, an additional methodological issue needs to be reviewed. Nearly all of the major input–output studies considered here have used some variation of linear multiple regression analysis. Although this is one of the more powerful multivariate techniques available, it is no panacea, particularly when research is nonexperimental. Multiple regression makes assumptions regarding the linear and ratio properties of the variables with which it deals. Although variables can be recoded in a variety of ways before being analyzed, the mathematical building blocks of the method typically used are Pearson product-moment correlation coefficients, which express the linear relations between variables and treat deviations from pure linearity as aberrations. They reflect the widely accepted but somewhat simplistic notion that increasing one variable will consistently lead to increases in the other, with no upper or lower bounds to the range of either one. When a product-moment correlation is high, the relationship being described is basically linear. The resulting regression coefficient can usually be interpreted unambiguously, unless the intercorrelations among a number of independent variables are all high (i.e., multicollinearity exists). A low product-moment correlation, however, may be low because the relation is nonlinear.

The conventional use of linear multiple regression analysis reflects only the linear and additive relations among variables. It leaves unexamined the curvilinear, interaction, and threshold effects that may actually exist in a data set, all of which may have important bearing on both educational theory and policies. Any modification of standard regression analysis that allows a researcher to specify which variables, or which levels of given variables, account for the largest variations in a given output measure is inherently more useful in research of this kind, as long as the direction of relation is specified. When regression output consists of raw or standardized regression coefficients, some interpretive problems are automatically circumvented because the sign of the coefficient indicates the direction of the effect. In partitioning variance, however, when entire clusters of variables are entered or removed from a regression equation at the same time, there is almost no way of knowing the direction of the effect represented by some specific amount of explained variance, which variables within the cluster account for it, and whether the variables in a cluster behave consistently with respect to direction. This problem is further compounded when any or all of the independent variables are criterion scaled (recoded to maximize their association with the dependent variable) or used as dummy variables, as in the case of the extensive but ambiguous reanalysis of the *EEO* data by Mayeske, Wisler, Beaton, Weinfeld, Cohen, Okada, Proshek, and Tabler (1969). These strategies allow the explainable variance in a regression model to be maximized, but often at the expense of knowing precisely what the numbers indicate.

The Equality of Educational Opportunity Data

In comparing several reanalyses of the original *EEO* data, which came from different geographical, racial, and grade-level subsamples, several points seem clear.

1. *The methodological limitations and interpretive ambiguities within the data are least severe for the elementary school sample.* In high schools, students were differentially assigned or tracked on the basis of previous achievement. Most ninth graders were exposed to the reported school resources only a few weeks before their achievement was measured, and unknown numbers dropped out of school before the twelfth grade. These factors distort the "true" relationship between school resources and student achievement. Most of the detailed reanalyses concentrate on the least problematic elementary group, the sixth graders. Major exceptions are the work of Bowles and Levin (1968a,b) and Cohen, Pettigrew, and

Riley (1972). Detailed criticisms of the third-, ninth-, and twelfth-grade data can be found in Armor (1972), Hanushek and Kain (1972), Jencks (1972), Levin (Chapter 9 of this volume), and especially M. Smith (1972).

2. The Mayeske *et al.* analysis of the entire data set suggest that: *The variability in student achievement that is explained jointly by family, school, and pupil attitude factors increases from the sixth through the twelfth grade.* The further a student goes in school, the more difficult it is to disentangle the statistical associations between his background characteristics, the resource inputs of his school, the attitudes he has toward his education, and his performance on standardized achievement tests. This difficulty occurs despite the biasing effect of differential attrition in the later years of high school. If the backgrounds, attitudes, and achievements of the students who dropped out of school before the twelfth grade were known, the pattern would probably be even stronger than it is. A similar but weaker pattern appears in Smith's reanalysis, using students from northern schools only. Because of the severe multicollinearity, selection, and attrition effects in the ninth- and twelfth-grade samples, sixth-grade findings are emphasized in this chapter.

3. *The between school variance in student achievement accounted for by school resource measures is much higher for the total national sample than for various regional and racial subsamples.* When Mayeske *et al.* estimate that 35.5% of the variance in sixth-grade composite achievement occurs across all schools, Smith's estimates are only 12.8 and 11.9% for northern whites and blacks, respectively. The reason is lucidly illustrated in several of Armor's (1972) tables. There are extensive differences in the mean characteristics of United States schools, the achievements of their pupils across regions and urban boundaries, and the racial composition of their student bodies; the largest differences occur across rather than within regions. For example, the mean unadjusted per-pupil expenditure for teachers' salaries in metropolitan Mid-Atlantic schools with mainly white students is $284, compared with only $163 for nonmetropolitan teachers in predominantly black schools in the South. This is a difference of nearly two standard deviations, yet within regions the largest urban-race mean differences are rarely this large. Actually, the sixth-grade verbal achievement differences between these two polar groups approach three standard deviations, with the differences mainly due to race rather than urban–rural location. These within region achievement figures, however, are uncontrolled for family background factors, which would reduce the differences appreciably if they were controlled.

Since nearly all of the *EEO* reanalyses use data from specific regions, urban areas, and racial groups, a great deal of this larger variability is lost. The major exceptions are Mayeske *et al.* and Armor (1972). This means that while most variability in student achievement occurs within schools, the limited school effects in the *EEO* data must be viewed in perspective, since they refer mainly to subpopulations of students whose schools and teachers may differ less from each other in terms of the variables measured than they do from their counterparts in other regions or localities. Particularly in metropolitan areas of the North, variability among school resource allocations is likely to be much lower than variability in student body SES characteristics. Districtwide teacher recruitment standards, salary schedules, and expenditures are more likely to be uniform than are the separate neighborhoods from which the schools draw their students.

4. Although race and SES are often confounded in both the original *EEO* analysis and several of the reanalyses, it appears that *the relationship between school resources and sixth-grade verbal achievement is stronger among blacks than whites.* (The major exception is Michelson's [1970] work, in which the statistical methods and regression model used are more sophisticated than most others. His sample, however, was limited to one eastern metropolitan area.) Hanushek (1970), for example, used a small number of teacher resource variables in a regression equation that included family size and SES, urban residence, student attitudes, and school racial composition to demonstrate that teachers' verbal ability and years of experience are more consistent and positive predictors of student achievement among northern blacks than whites. Smith (1972) used a more comprehensive group of variables in his regression equations but also found that teacher characteristics account for larger unique proportions of achievement variance among blacks. In what appear to be equally comprehensive regression equations, Armor (1972) showed that these black–white differences hold true not only within northern metropolitan areas but in the South as well. The verbal achievement of southern blacks appears to vary more consistently with the characteristics of their schools and teachers than that of any other group in the *EEO* sample.

Given that blacks are far more likely than whites to come from low SES backgrounds, the Mayeske *et al.* findings seem to provide further confirmation of this supposition. When the total *EEO* sample is broken into two SES levels and the relations between resources and achievement analyzed for each, the unique "effect" of background on achievement is higher among high SES students, but the joint school and background effects are much higher among lower SES students. This may suggest that higher SES students achieve more because of differences in the level of assistance and stimulation they receive at home, whereas lower SES students must depend mainly on the school for help.

To some extent the findings presented by Guthrie, Kleindorfer, Levin, and Stout (1971) run counter to this general pattern, but the analytic strategy used in assessing the statistical significance of school resource effects is altogether different. They divided a sample of 5,284 Michigan sixth graders into SES deciles and examined the relationship between each given school resource and verbal achievement one at a time within each decile. An unknown number of resources that appear to be "important" when considered in isolation might not be statistically significant if analyzed simultaneously. This seems particularly likely within groups of related variables, such as teacher attitudes toward their school and work, adequacy of school plant facilities, and size and density of the student body. Nonetheless, there is a pattern within their data that the authors failed to note: There are more significant correlations between school resources and student achievement within the high SES deciles than the low ones, especially among the school facilities variables. Although it is tempting to conclude from this that resources may not be as important for low SES black students as for higher SES whites, the absence of data on the size of the correlations in question, the geographically restricted sample, and the limited mode of data analysis weaken support for such a proposition.

Overall, then, the most rigorous reanalyses of the *EEO* data suggest that the achievement of lower SES and black students varies more consistently with the measured characteristics of their schools and teachers than does the achievement of higher-status whites. These findings seem to favor a compensatory, as distinct from a facilitative, model of school resource allocation. The compensatory model assumes that the school is providing formal learning opportunities to students whose out-of-school environment typically lacks intellectual stimulation and incentives to achieve, while the facilitative model applies more often to students from middle-class backgrounds whose preschool socialization and out-of-school environment are congruent with the academic goals of the school. In the compensatory model, achievement differentials should vary consistently with resource allocations, since the school is the presumed major locus of intellectual development for the child. In the facilitative model, school resource differentials interact with the student's family and community resource advantages and, to a greater or lesser extent, complement outside opportunities. This suggests that per-unit investments in school resources may have greater efficiency when nonschool resources are absent or weak. Depriving those already deprived will be more consistently deleterious to standardized achievement than will shortchanging those whose out-of-school environments can compensate for educational inadequacies. This holds true despite the questionable success of most compensatory education programs (Averch, Carroll, Donaldson, Kiesling, & Pincus, 1972).

5. Taking this interpretation too literally may prove to be dangerous, since these *EEO* data also point up a fifth major trend: *Blacks and whites respond differentially to specific school resources not only in consistency or magnitude of "effects" but also in direction.* While there are too many differences to discuss in detail and general patterns are difficult to identify, two important points should be made. First, in comparatively few schools are there sizable proportions of both black and white students. The characteristic pattern is racially imbalanced, both in students and in staff (according to Mayeske *et al.*, the two are correlated .85 among sixth graders). Second, the correlation between school racial composition and mean teacher's vocabulary score is .55 for the total sixth-grade sample, indicating that black students are also generally exposed to teachers with more limited verbal (and perhaps conceptual and teaching) abilities. These two substantial correlations are paralleled by a strong association between

pupil race and the proportion of whites in teacher's undergraduate institution (.82). There is a moderate correlation with teacher's preference for high-ability students (.36), but not by the level of teacher's formal training, salary, or experience. Thus, teachers of black students may not appear to differ appreciably from those of whites on many formal resource measures, but they do differ in their actual abilities and attitudes toward their students. This is especially important in view of the weak associations between teacher verbal ability and sex, age, training, experience, salary, credits beyond highest degree, and localism of career. When school systems allocate more money for experienced and highly trained teachers, they are not, it seems, purchasing higher ability in the process.

The paradox in these patterns is best illustrated in Armor's (1972) data, in which black–white differences can be compared by region. Among northern blacks in majority black schools, the correlations between school means for several different measures of teacher and school resources and mean sixth-grade achievement are virtually zero. The same is true for northern whites in majority white schools, with the exceptions of teachers' verbal ability in metropolitan areas (.25) and salaries in nonmetropolitan localities (.16). In the South, however, these correlations are higher for both races, ranging from .21 to .46 for verbal ability and .21 to .53 for teacher salaries.

With these correlations in mind, Armor's regression results are not surprising. Considering only the metropolitan data, with various family SES indicators and the proportion of black students in the school controlled, the achievement of northern blacks in majority black schools is negatively associated with teachers' verbal ability, background characteristics, and school facilities and positively associated only with salary levels. Among their white counterparts in mostly white schools, verbal ability is positive, but teacher background and school facilities are again negative. Among southern blacks, the strongest positive factor is teachers' salaries, followed by verbal score. The beta weight for facilities is also negative. Among southern whites, verbal ability is the strongest positive resource, while teacher background and school facilities, again, are both negative.

Although findings by Levin (Chapter 9 of this volume) and Michelson (1970), based on a single metropolitan area, do not agree with Armor's data, the latter reveal a pattern for whites in white schools that is similar across regions: Teachers' verbal scores and salaries appear to have positive "effects" on student achievement. With these two factors taken into account, teacher background characteristics and school facilites emerge as negative factors. One way of viewing this discrepancy is that school systems that give priority to formal teacher credentials and plant and program facilities may be handicapping their students' achievement as compared with those that concentrate on more able and better paid staff. The wisest resource allocations may be those that purchase able (as distinct from experienced) teachers rather than formal credentials, curricular materials, or modern facilities. This strategy of placing priority on human rather than material resources also reaps positive results among blacks in the South but not in the North. The main discrepancy is the negative verbal score effect; otherwise, the findings resemble those for whites.

The anomaly can be explained by taking into account some of the correlates of teacher verbal score, plus some small trends in Smith's data. Northern blacks in predominantly black schools achieve more if the educational background characteristics and verbal ability of their teachers are comparatively low. Given the correlations above, this means that the teachers of successful blacks are more likely to be black, young, and inexperienced, with a preference for working with low-ability students. The key factor may lie not in their credentials or ability per se, but in their commitment to and effectiveness in working with lower-ability blacks and their inherent advantage in providing a role model with which students can identify. Unfortunately, these key variables were not adequately measured in the EEO study nor in the other school resource studies discussed later. In addition, adequate attention has not been given to the potentially misleading inferences that can be drawn from partitioning variance without regard to the direction or inconsistency of effects. This is particularly important in view of the negative associations examined.

Other School Resource Studies

In addition to the EEO survey, nearly 20 other substantial studies have examined the relationship between school resources and student achievements. Most of these studies have been summarized by Guthrie *et al.* (1971) or Averch *et al.* (1972), but careful examination of the originals indicates that these reviews are, in places, too general and somewhat misleading. Only those findings that are methodologically adequate and substantively pertinent to the issues raised by the EEO data will be discussed here. Of the 12 studies cited, 9 deal directly with financial expenditures as well as other variables and present somewhat inconsistent results. The remaining three studies raise important questions about the importance of teacher experience and formal training.

Mollenkopf and Melville's (1956) national study of aptitude and achievement among 9000 ninth graders in 100 United States schools and 8357 twelfth graders in 106 schools is plagued by many of the measurement problems mentioned earlier, especially selective response bias. Of the 1877 schools in the original sample, only 506 principals both replied to the initial mailed questionnaire and agreed to administer the student achievement tests. The authors' concern for the adequacy of the data supplied on the availability of various school resources, community educational opportunities, and the SES characteristics of students in the school is, therefore, well taken. With SES and student body indicators controlled, they found mean student achievement to be most consistently associated with small class sizes and low pupil–teacher ratios, library and supply expenditures per student, and number of special staff in the school. Contrary to many of the *EEO* findings, the data show that achievement is highest when expenditure levels are high enough to justify "extras," such as nonteaching specialists, good libraries, and large numbers of teachers.

Two similar variables, special staff per 1000 students and per-pupil expenditures, were also reported by Goodman (1959), who measured the achievement on the Iowa Tests of Educational Development of 70,000 seventh and eleventh graders from 102 districts in New York State. With SES controlled, the strongest school resource associated with mean seventh graders' composite achievement score was the percentage of teachers in the *district* (not a given school) with over five years of training. The partial correlation was .37. Per-pupil expenditures and special staff followed in order of importance when analyzed singly, but the exceptionally high correlation between teacher training and school expenditures makes it likely that only one of these (probably training) would have emerged as significant had all three been analyzed simultaneously. Since school systems reward formal training and experience financially, it may be that expenditure levels are largely a proxy for these two variables.

In Kiesling's (1967) reanalysis of the same data, per-pupil expenditures emerged as a particularly salient variable in urban school districts with enrollments of at least 2000 students, large proportions of whom were disadvantaged. This further supports the interpretation of the school's compensatory function, but per-pupil expenditure was of little consequence in smaller, primarily rural, districts both in this study and in Kiesling's 1969 study of fourth- to sixth-grade achievement gains in 97 New York State districts. Indeed, the latter study did not reveal any beneficial resource effects in rural districts and, contrary to Kiesling's 1967 findings and Armor's *EEO* data, showed mainly negative associations between achievement and per-pupil expenditures in urban districts.

Discrepancies in findings between large and small school districts also emerged in the work of Benson, Schmelzle, Gustafson, and Lange (1965), in their examination of the association between school expenditures, SES indicators, and standardized pupil reading and mathematics achievement in 249 California school districts. In a regression analysis containing several SES and school expenditure measures, the net relationship between instructional expenditures per average daily attendance and mean reading achievement was positive and statistically significant. Within districts under 2000 pupils, the most important resource measures were the percentage of teachers in the lowest salary quartile (negative effect) and mean teachers' salaries. In districts with 2000 to 4500 pupils, the two strongest resource measures were percentage of teachers in the highest salary quartile and mean administrators' salaries, but both relations were weaker than those in small districts. In the largest districts, however, the data were more ambiguous and contradictory. The strongest measure was the teacher–administrator ratio, which seems to suggest that greater economies in administrative operation can somehow enhance student achievement. Teacher salaries, however, were negatively related to student achievement in these districts, a fact that parallels Kiesling's anomalous 1969 finding and undermines the overall thrust of the study. Although the authors contend that higher expenditures enable districts to attract more highly qualified (talented and effective) teachers, they have no direct measures of these variables. In addition, their findings with respect to district size generally oppose Kiesling's 1967 work.

The findings of Thomas (1963) and Burkhead, Fox, and Holland (1967) appear to support one trend in the Benson et al. data. Both studies used Project TALENT data to examine the relations between a variety of resource measures and the overall academic achievement of high school students in communities ranging in size from 2500 to 25,000. With various indicators of district SES taken into account, the most important single school resource in Thomas' study was the median salaries of the beginning male teachers. Although the Burkhead analysis contains many familiar multicollinearity problems, this same variable emerges as a significant predictor of mean twelfth-grade reading scores, but it was not as important as median teacher experience or the age of school building (which was negative).

Studies by Bowles (1969) and by Averch and Kiesling (1970), also based on Project TALENT data, examined the relationship between student achievement and school expenditures. Among Bowles' black male twelfth graders, the proportion of teachers with graduate training, the size of science and mathematics classes (small), and expenditures per student on nonteaching inputs were all independently related to achievement. Averch and Kiesling show that high teacher salaries and small class sizes were associated with the achievement of ninth graders, holding SES and student educational expectations constant. Unfortunately, however, their analysis lacked data on teacher experience and advanced training. The consistent feature in both studies was the presumed benefit of small class size, with some indicator of the value of financial expenditures.

Because Katzman (1968) analyzed a variety of school output measures within one large urban system (Boston), expenditure differentials were unavailable. His dependent variables included median sixth-grade reading achievement, several measures of school attendance, and the percentages who took and passed the entrance examination to Boston Latin School. With an index of cultural advantage held constant, he found reading achievement to be negatively associated with "overcrowding" in the classroom, the percentage of teachers in a school with less than 10 years of experience, and teacher turnover rate. Overall, students in large districts scored higher. Although Katzman's data reinforce the findings of Mollenkopf and Melville, as well as those of Bowles and Averch and Kiesling, on the deleterious consequences of overcrowded classrooms, they are not consistent with Goodman's and Bowles's data on the importance of formal teacher credentials and advanced training, since these variables were not statistically significant in Katzman's results.

Perhaps the resolution of this particular dilemma lies in the rigorously derived results of Hanushek (1970). In what appears to be the most methodologically adequate study of this kind, Hanushek examined the individual year-to-year reading achievement gains of 2445 third graders in a large California system, based on the characteristics of their own second- and third-grade teachers. With these stringent conditions applied, the original sample was reduced by more than half. The analysis was carried out for three separate subsamples: whites whose fathers were nonmanual workers, whites with fathers holding manual jobs, and Mexican-Americans with fathers holding manual jobs. In all three cases, formal teacher credentials, such as degrees and experience, had no significant bearing on reading gains. Consistent with the earlier *EEO* summary, the strongest positive relations occurred among the white *manual* (lower SES) group: the verbal ability and the most recent educational experiences of both second- and third-grade teachers seemed to pay off. Positive although weaker relations emerged for the children of white nonmanual (higher SES) workers, with teachers' most recent educational experience and years of experience with students of this SES being most important. In the Mexican-American data, however, no teacher resource variable was significant. This finding is quite different from that obtained with blacks in the *EEO* study.

Integration and Implications of Findings

Despite the apparent overlap and contradictions among variables in the studies cited, some comprehensible patterns appear once certain methodological and substantive disparities are reconciled. The main issue, of course, is the variety of indicators of school resources used and their meaning from study to study.

We have examined eight studies that used direct measures of financial expenditures. Of these, seven showed positive independent associations between expenditure levels and student achievement. Only the Kiesling (1969) New York State study and the Benson *et al.* data on large California districts contain any negative findings. Significantly, both anomalies occurred within large urban centers in which heavy concentrations of low SES and minority group students are hidden in the overall aggregation of district figures.

If taken literally, these two studies provide an argument against my compensatory interpretation of resource effectiveness: Resource expenditures are apparently not having a strong positive effect among these urban minorities. Such a judgment is premature on two grounds. First, the aggregation of both school and family SES data is so extensive in large districts that it is not at all clear which students in each district are responding in which direction to which resources. Second, given that expenditures may reflect differential living costs from city to city, it is not clear to what extent the figures used reflect relative costs and real purchasing power. Thus, the prevalent assumption supported by nearly all of the data examined is that higher teacher salaries are purchasing higher formal qualifications, which means training and experience. There is no evidence that either salaries or qualifications are associated with teachers' demonstrated ability, race, or attitude toward clientele that may be of particular importance to minority groups or lower SES students.

The remaining studies are less problematic in that they indicate ways in which expenditures may be paying off. One way involves the numbers of teaching and specialized staff available to students. The work of Goodman, Bowles, Katzman, and Mollenkopf and Melville shows that numbers of specialized staff, class sizes, or teacher–pupil ratios will have some independdnt bearing on aggregate student achievement. Either such school systems are so affluent that they can afford extra teachers and staff, or they are no more affluent than other systems but choose to concentrate on obtaining as many staff members as possible, perhaps at the expense of salary levels or supplies, libraries, and other instructional facilities. In conjunction with the Smith and Armor *EEO* findings, these data support the principle of concentrating expenditures on personnel rather than on tangible facilities.

Facilities themselves do pay off, however, as findings by Mollenkopf and Melville, Bowles (1969, 1970), Burkhead *et al.*, and Guthrie *et al.* suggest. There are at least three possible explanations. First, extensive expenditures beyond basic staffing needs are luxuries that few schools can afford. If they can afford them, the payoff may be positive, but probably only if the quality of staff is itself adequate and the resources are used adequately. Second, since both the Mollenkopf and Melville and the Bowles studies are restricted to high school students and since the Guthrie *et al.* results suffer from insufficient controls, these positive findings can be selection effects. That is, students with high elementary school achievements may be selected into specialized college preparatory high schools that have superior library and laboratory facilities, and high school achievement may merely reflect advantages upon entrance. Third, both of these interpretations can apply: These selective high schools may be more effective because they have better staff as well as better facilities to offer to students with superior achievements.

Unfortunately, the findings documenting the relationship between formal level of teacher training and student achievement are also open to multiple interpretation. In some ways, Goodman's analysis is pivotal, since it suggests that if salary levels and training were analyzed simultaneously the latter would emerge as the major variable. Since the two are correlated, only one is likely to emerge as significant in a regression analysis. In fact, under the right statistical conditions (see Gordon, 1968), one variable could emerge in a regression analysis as positive and the other as negative, though fairly weak. This is precisely what occurs in Armor's *EEO* data, except that both salaries and verbal ability are generally positive, and teacher background and school facilities are negative.

One must, therefore, ask whether teacher salaries are statistically significant in these other studies only because measures of teacher training are not used. The answer in most cases is no, with Benson et al. being the most conspicuous exception. Otherwise, most other studies include some measure of formal teacher training in the analysis or use salary figures for beginning teachers only. Since beginning salaries reflect previous training, it is safe to conclude that in most of these studies, salary levels and training levels are rough proxies of each other.

Why, then, is the verdict on formal teacher qualifications mixed? Aside from purely statistical considerations, the best answer seems to lie with the Hanushek data. Neither semester hours of graduate work nor years of experience is independently related to gains in student achievement. What is important is the recency of the teacher's latest educational experience. Involvement in periodically upgrading one's own education, rather than either collecting a terminal graduate degree or receiving no advanced training at all, seems to be one key to effectiveness. Overall, it appears that both school systems and researchers have been sensitive to the wrong aspects of teacher qualifications. They have been too conscious of measuring formal course credits and degree attainments rather than the teacher's ongoing engagement in expertise-enhancing activities, which now appears to be essential in advanced training.

This also applies to the teacher-experience variable, except that its interpretability may be even more ambiguous. It is assumed that a teacher becomes more skilled the longer he engages in teaching activities. As in all activities, however, sustaining interest and enthusiasm and improving performance beyond a given plateau are difficult. Beyond a given point, age and experience will quite likely inhibit capacity to learn and grow on the job. Thus, one would expect the most effective teachers to be those with a few but not too many years of experience. Only one study reported here handled teacher experience in such a nonlinear fashion: Armor's reanalysis of the *EEO* data. Even his transformation defines the "ideal" years (5 through 29) in gross terms. Treating teacher experience as a simple linear phenomenon is a conspicuous weakness in this line of inquiry.

Since experience and salary levels correlate substantially, and since salaries constitute a high proportion of overall expenditures, experience is consistently reflected in these figures as well. In those studies that use beginning teachers' salaries rather than overall salaries, some of the correlation is reduced, but there are no studies that report simultaneous experience and expenditure effects as significant and positive. There are three data sets in which a linear measure of experience is independently associated with student achievements: Katzman's Boston data, Burkhead's Project TALENT data and Chicago data (not discussed earlier). Note that two of these three studies were done in large urban systems. If Becker's (1952) research on teacher career patterns in the Chicago system is any indication of the causal processes that may be operating, it is possible that the relationship between student achievement and teacher experience is reciprocal, if not actually the reverse of what is implied in these studies. As teachers accumulate seniority, they transfer to schools in "good" neighborhoods with high achieving students, leaving the inner-city areas to the neophytes. The association between experience and achievement at least partially reflects this staff selection bias. Therefore, teacher experience must be regarded as an inadequately studied variable whose effect on student achievement remains obscure.

Until this point, I have tried to account for the resource variables that can be purchased by school expenditures, without making specific comments about the methodological and substantive problems inherent in the variables. Since we have already seen that expenditures for staff resources seem to be generally more important than those for supplies and facilities, two obvious questions remain. Does a given expenditure level have the same purchasing power across school districts? And, is the association between expenditure levels and student achievement linear? To the extent that the answer to either question is negative, the meaning of the research findings becomes more elusive.

The likely answer to the first question is that the actual purchasing power of educational dollars varies with the general cost of living in different regions and metropolitan areas of the country. While expenditures for instructional materials and supplies are fixed-cost items and may be standardized nationally, differentials in salaries, insurance, construction, and plant operation and maintenance costs are not. Therefore, unadjusted expenditure data across regions and localities may inflate the true nature of school system purchasing power (see Armor, 1972), but within region differentials should not. The effect of this on the association between expenditures and student achievement is impossible to assess without adequate data.

On the second question, the most revealing evidence is presented by Ribich (1968) in a series of detailed tabular analyses. Based on an index of nine separate family socioeconomic indicators, he isolates the lowest SES quintile of Project TALENT ninth graders who subsequently completed twelfth grade. His major independent variable is per-pupil expenditures within districts. For the sample taken as a whole, increased expenditures are definitely associated with higher academic aptitude, up to a level of $400. Beyond that point, there is little association. There is also a marked increase in student nonacademic technical knowledge until expenditure levels reach the $500 level; then a similar ceiling is reached. Clearly the relationships are generally positive but nonlinear. For these low SES students, at least, there is a definite threshold level beyond which increased expenditures have no visible payoff. Within regions, even these nonlinear patterns begin to break down, especially in cities under 250,000.

Since expenditures reflect salaries and salaries reflect formal teacher qualifications and experience, these figures may be suggesting that the benefits of teacher experience begin to taper off. Furthermore, these patterns attenuate when region and city size are controlled, and they may simply reflect regional and urbanization expenditure differences (similar to

Armor's data). This may mean that even low SES students from northern and western metropolitan areas achieve more not only because their communities spend more on schools, but also because the out-of-school learning opportunities in those areas are more extensive, complex, and stimulating than in smaller towns and the South. These data may also suggest that beyond a certain point schools cannot effectively utilize all of the available nonhuman resources. Having sufficient affluence to obtain expensive laboratory, audiovisual, and computerized instructional equipment may not benefit student achievement if these resources are not utilized effectively.

Since these SES measures account only for the background characteristics of the individual student and not his school characteristics, an unknown proportion attend highly financed schools containing many middle-class peers. Ribich argued that such students may be benefiting not from the abundance of formal school resources available but from the higher academic aspirations of their classmates and the more positive atmosphere for learning they generate, and that community environments affect achievement independently of their demographic and social characteristics. One community will spend less on its schools than another with identical SES composition for two reasons: an inadequate industrial tax base and a generally lower regard for the value of formal education. The latter attitude, he believes, will permeate the operation of the school system so that school and community expectations reinforce each other. This attitude, rather than the expenditures that reflect it, may be an important variable in student achievement.

These two factors raise issues pertinent to the potential importance of student-body resources in the achievement processes of the school that have not been apparent in the global data analyses reviewed thus far. Most studies assume that the only relevant human resources in the educational production process are those of the individual student and his parents, teachers, and administrators. This approach basically ignores the potential influence that the characteristics and attitudes of the student's peers may have on his academic ambition and achievement. It also assumes that given personal resource increments can be translated into given output units consistently across a variety of social contexts. By contrast, the student-body resource approach assumes that the educational outcomes of a student who is, for example, middle class (or female or intelligent) may depend on both the proportion of students in his school or classroom who are also middle class (or female or intelligent) and the nature of the outcome being measured. It is to such issues that we now turn.

The Allocation of Student Resources among Schools

An Interpretive Framework

Within the past 15 years, sociologists have begun to look more closely at both the distinctive characteristics of student collectivities and the possible consequences of membership in particular groups for the attitudes and behavior of their members. The underlying concern of much of this work is identification of the social processes that account for variability in the achievement or aspirations of similar individuals in distinctively different groups. For example, the positive relationship between student SES and aspirations for education beyond high school is widely documented but not all middle-class students attend schools with similar student-body characteristics. One school may have mostly middle-class students; another may have only a small proportion. The question at issue here is whether the aspiration levels of otherwise similar students are the same in the two school contexts. If they are not, then presumably some kind of intraschool influence process is taking place that is reflected in between school outcome differences (i.e., "contextual effects"). These theoretical ideas have been developed more fully by Blau (1960), Davis, Spaeth, and Huson (1961), and Turner (1964).

Although contextual effects may empirically conform to a variety of patterns, they are generally interpreted along two theoretical lines: reference group and interpersonal influence (Bidwell, 1972; Drew and Astin, 1972). According to reference group theory (Kemper, 1968), the individual adjusts his beliefs and behavior to the norms, performance standards, and rewards that are most salient within his membership group (or group to which he aspires to belong). The major operational assumption within this theoretical framework is that certain individuals or collectivities (commonly referred to as "significant others") are sufficiently important to the individual for him to attempt to meet their expectations.

Three major reference group processes or explanatory mechanisms can account for the apparent contextual effects in the literature on student achievement and aspirations to be reviewed. *Normative group influences* involve a rather diffuse set of mechanisms in which the individual responds to the dominant norms, values, standards, and rewards in his social milieu. Coleman (1961), Gordon (1957), and Waller (1932) have described the distinctive normative patterns that characterize the student culture of schools. These sets of collective orientations may stimulate or thwart individual students' interest in academic endeavor, thus serving as resources in the educational process.

The peer group may affect educational outcomes by providing *role models* whose behavior defines standards for what can be accomplished and how it is to be done. Within Kemper's analytic framework, the role model demonstrates both that a given activity or behavior is possible and how it may be accomplished. This is distinct from the normative group function of establishing whether or not the behavior should be done. Having many particularly bright or talented students in a school, for example, may make high achievement standards more visible and apparently realistic.

A third possible reference group process that may account for contextual effects is the *comparison group mechanism*, which is typically used to explain findings in which aspiration levels decrease as contextual achievement resources increase. Davis (1966) argues, for example, that college students evaluate their chances for future success in graduate school on the basis of their relative standing or performance within their most immediate reference group: their own department. Since able students are less likely to distinguish themselves academically in competition with large numbers of other able students (as in high SES school contexts), their comparative evaluation of their future achievement potential may be lower than that of able students in less demanding institutions.

In all three of these reference group processes, contextual effects are assumed to depend on the responses of students to visible trends in the behavior and values of "generalized others." The interpersonal influence paradigm, however, assumes that whatever influence is transmitted from significant others to the student is mediated directly by his association or friendship with them. It is, in effect, an attempt to specify the direct link between diffuse normative group and role model mechanisms and the individual. The achievement or aspirations of students may be higher in "high SES contexts" not merely because of exposure to dominant norms and particular kinds of role models, but because of the direct influence that may be exercised by the students they choose as friends.

In the discussion that follows, three dimensions of student body resources are used: racial composition, socioeconomic composition, and "normative climate." The apparent impact of each resource variable on both the achievement and the educational aspirations of students will be examined.

Racial Composition and Student Achievement

Documenting the effect of racial composition on achievement requires data that distinguish the racial characteristics of particular students from the racial characteristics of the schools they attend. This condition is basically met in the studies discussed.

Mayeske *et al.* (1969), in their analysis of the *EEO* data, show that the correlation between school SES composition and school racial composition is .67 for sixth graders, .68 for ninth graders, and .59 for twelfth graders. For ninth graders nearly half of the variance in school racial composition is also SES variability. Both are correlated with mean student achievement, .82 or better. The need for SES controls when examining racial context effects is obvious.

Unfortunately, Armor's (1972) reanalysis of the *EEO* data deals only with the verbal achievement of whites in schools over 50% white and blacks in schools over 50% black. It does not meet the rigorous design conditions necessary to judge how the achievement of blacks is affected by being in a minority black school or the achievement of whites by being in a minority white school, and its findings must be interpreted with this major drawback in mind.

Taking into account school resources, community and family resources, region, and locality, it appears that the verbal achievement of sixth-grade whites in majority white schools is unaffected by the proportion (up to 50%) of blacks in the school. The one exception is in the rural South, where achievement levels decreased slightly as the proportion of black pupils increased. Among blacks in mainly black schools, there was no contextual effect in the North but positive net relations in the South. With other controls held constant, it appears that southern blacks achieve more if they are in totally segregated schools. Armor's other data suggest that in southern metropolitan areas (where this relationship is strongest), the zero-order correlations between percentage black and community SES and school resource measures may be positive since they were all positively correlated with school achievement (.41 or greater). The blacks in totally segregated southern schools may have enjoyed somewhat better SES conditions at home and better resources at school than those in mainly black schools.

More statistically adequate findings for northern ninth-grade blacks are presented by Cohen et al. (1972). Verbal achievement was regressed on six individual background variables and five student environment measures (percentage of families owning encyclopedias, transfers in and out of the school, percentage average daily attendance, percentage in the college curriculum, and average hours spent on homework). They obtained a beta weight of $-.212$ for school percentage black. Unfortunately, the causal process in these data is not clear; ninth-grade achievement was measured a few weeks after most of these students entered high school. Thus, the percentage of blacks in the high school (as well as the other school environment measures) may have been an artifact of selection processes that differed from those in the individual elementary schools from which they came and in which their achievements were largely shaped. This reservation is less valid, however, in high schools with a large majority of one race or the other. Perhaps the most satisfying finding Cohen et al. present is the beta weight of .094 when northern sixth-grade black verbal achievement is regressed on school percentage white, with school SES and school quality measures held constant. Here the small but positive "integration effect" is more credible.

Roughly similar integration effects emerge in the analysis by St. John and Smith (1969) of the mathematics and reading achievement of 1388 black Pittsburgh ninth graders. They attempted to avoid some of the serious methodological limitations of the *EEO* ninth-grade data by collecting information on the educational history of each student, including patterns of racial exposure experienced, such as the average percentage of black students in the school from first through ninth grades. With student IQ and sex controlled, both present school percentage black and average school percentage black had, in separate analyses, fairly consistent negative associations with mathematics achievement for both sexes. The reading achievement associations were also negative among the women, but close to zero among the men. When specific longitudinal racial patterns were taken into account along with IQ and sex, the highest achievers in arithmetic were almost always those whose elementary experience had been exclusively in predominantly white schools. The exceptions were the high-IQ boys whose experiences had become consistently more racially integrated over time, further supporting the main trend in the data. The lowest achievers were those who had spent all or nearly all of their elementary schooling in majority black schools. Although many of these findings were weak, they lend support to the Cohen *et al.* data.

McPartland (1969) provided data that further clarify the nature of the impact of racial composition on school achievement by analyzing both classroom and school contexts simultaneously. He examined the association between the verbal achievement of 5075 *EEO* ninth graders from the New England and Mid-Alantic states and the percentage of whites in their classes the previous year, controlling for family SES, the percentage white in their current school, and another potentially confounding variable, student's program of study (i.e., academic track). While this particular combination of variables solves some major methodological problems, it creates others. Given that ninth-grade achievement was measured so early in the year, it is reasonable to use a measure of eighth-grade classroom racial composition, since the achievement measured was largely obtained during the elementary years. However, to compare this measure with current school racial composition clouds, rather than clarifies, the issue.

Nonetheless, using Coleman's (1964) "effect parameters," the net classroom racial composition association index (analogous to a standardized regression coefficient) is .20. When achievement and percentage white in the *school* are associated, controlling for SES and percentage white in previous year's classroom, the result is virtually zero. Further analyses suggest that the benefits of having been in integrated classrooms were greatest for those in the "general" academic high school program (.47). Of greater interest, however, is that this relation increases rather consistently with the percentage of whites in the school. The more whites there are in the school, the more the blacks appear to benefit from having been in classes with mainly whites. This may mean that only in high schools where there are many whites is the probability high that a black will have had a large proportion of whites in most of his elementary classes as well. When it does occur, his achievement is higher. When blacks are kept in basically segregated classrooms within such high school districts, their achievement suffers.

Further analyses of the verbal achievement of these black Northeast metropolitan ninth graders by McPartland and York (1967) help clarify the pattern. These findings were not reported in detail by the authors but were gleaned by dissecting and summarizing cross-tabular material. With parents' education and the socioeconomic composition of the current school held constant (McPartland and York, Table 4.3), the verbal achievements of these blacks increased rather consistently with the percentage of whites in their eighth-grade classes. Of even greater interest, however, are two trends in these differences. First, the higher the SES of the student, the greater is the effect of classroom racial composition on his achievement. Blacks with better educated parents respond more to the racial mix of their classes (i.e., benefit more from direct academic contact with whites) than do lower SES blacks. Second, the higher the status of the whites involved, the greater the overall benefit to blacks of being in predominantly white classrooms.

Further support for the positive classroom contextual effects in the *EEO* data for ninth-grade blacks was provided by Cohen *et al.* With parents' education, curricular assignment, and English track taken into account, the beta weight for eighth-grade classroom racial composition and ninth-grade verbal achievement was .112. It was subsequently reduced to .088 when the mean verbal achievement of all ninth-grade blacks was also entered into the regression equation. When the schools are divided into two groups based on the percentage of blacks in the current school, however, a strong interaction effect is apparent. In schools with fewer than 60% blacks, the beta weight increases to .165, but it decreases to $-.020$ in predominantly black schools.

Although the school categories here are cruder than those used by McPartland (1969), and assumptions must be made about the similarities in racial composition between high schools and their feeder schools, the basic findings are similar. Apparently, classroom racial composition affects blacks positively, when a sufficient critical mass of middle-class whites is present in the school. Otherwise, they do slightly better when completely segregated. In fact, part of this small positive segregation effect may reflect the virtually forced attendance of higher-status blacks in all black ghetto schools simply because of residence. Their superior achievement may help to pull school averages up.

When the interracial friendships of blacks are also added to this pattern of findings, the specificity of the influence processes that may account for achievement differences becomes even clearer. Again holding parents' education and school SES composition constant (McPartland and York, Table 6.9), the data show that the achievement benefits of having white classmates are definitely higher for those blacks with close white friends than for those with only black friends. A threshold effect appears to reinforce this finding. The achievement differences due to classroom racial composition are greatest as one moves from the "about half whites" to the "more than half whites" category. This spurt in achievement is also somewhat higher for those blacks with white friends, particularly in schools with a large proportion of high SES students.

Although the data for black twelfth graders lack the interracial friendship variable, it provides an example of family SES, school SES, classroom racial composition, and average teacher vocabulary score held constant simultaneously (McPartland and York, Table 7.18). As in the ninth-grade findings, there was still a positive classroom racial effect within all possible comparison groups, and the major threshold level appeared to be the majority white condition, especially in higher SES context schools.

Given this trend, the Armor (1972) findings may not be as anomalous as they originally appeared. The absence of a positive integration effect in his data may simply be due to arbitrarily excluding from analysis blacks in majority white schools. Otherwise, his finding that an "all black" context is slightly better than a "mainly black" one parallels that of Cohen *et al.*

The preceding data suggest that the distribution of students both among and within schools on the basis of race is consistently associated with achievement differences among blacks. As an educational resource, racial composition operates independently of family SES, school SES, and academic grouping, but not in a purely linear or additive fashion. The achievements of blacks are stimulated under particular racial and socioeconomic conditions: There must be many white students in both the school and the classroom; these whites should be middle class; and having such whites as close friends is a definite asset. Higher SES blacks generally gain more under these conditions.

Together these findings support the normative group, role model, and interpersonal influence paradigms. A large proportion of more academically oriented white middle-class students in a school appears to create a climate that supports academic achievement and provides numerous academic role models. Choosing such role models as friends further facilitates achievement, but these interpersonal contacts do not account for all of the variability in achievement due to racial composition. Either more diffuse normative group processes continue to operate simultaneously, or teachers are more effective in majority white schools and classrooms that are presumably less disruptive and more manageable enabling students to spend more time "learning."

The findings reviewed thus far, although consistent, pertain only to the short-run academic benefits of attending racially integrated schools. Crain (1970, 1971) provides evidence gathered from 1600 adult blacks in northern metropolitan areas that suggests that the educational, intellectual, attitudinal, occupational, and economic benefits of having attended an integrated elementary or high school are apparent beyond the school experience itself. Most of these advantages seem to hold with family background experiences, such as region of birth, time of migration to the North, and family SES, thus implying that racial integration both increases the formal achievement levels of blacks and stimulates aspirations for future success.

Racial Composition and Educational Aspirations

The best evidence available indicates that the influence processes that govern the acquisition of college goals are more complex than those that account for formal achievement. St. John and Smith (1969) show, for example, that with sex and IQ controlled, the college aspirations of blacks who have been in predominantly black schools throughout their careers are higher than those who have shared at least part of their educational experience with a majority of whites. These effects are concentrated among the high-IQ boys and, to a lesser extent, the low-IQ girls. This suggests that a comparative reference group process is operating among the high-ability boys who, in integrated schools, are ostensibly able to compete for top grades but may not be receiving them due to tougher competition from classmates. They see themselves as less capable of being high achievers than their white peers; this is subsequently reflected in their lower aspirations. Able blacks in predominantly black schools, on the other hand, are more likely to find themselves near the top of the class and apparently adjust their college attainment chances accordingly. They may lack a realistic perspective on how their objective achievement level compares with that of other ninth graders in other schools, however, and their aspirations may appear inflated or unrealistic (Katz, 1964; Veroff and Peele, 1969).

Evidence from the EEO survey also supports this position, particularly Armor's (1967) findings prepared for the United States Commission on Civil Rights, although some relevant findings are not reported in the text but are hidden in cross-tabulations. Armor examined the educational plans of Northeast metropolitan ninth-grade blacks and whites, holding constant student SES and verbal ability, the social class composition of the school, and the percentage black in the school. Among blacks, there is a tendency for both boys and girls to have higher aspirations in predominantly black schools, with the pattern being most consistent among the girls (Armor, Tables 9 and 12). The data suggest, however, that there is curvilinearity in these relations among both sexes. When the categories "1–20% black" and "21–50% black" are compared, in 6 out of 8 comparisons for each sex the percentage with college plans is at least as high if not higher in the former category. Thus, blacks in "nearly all white" schools actually have as high if not higher aspirations than comparable blacks in "majority white schools. The trend occurs because of the comparatively high aspiration rates of blacks in "65–100% black" schools. It is in these mainly black contexts that aspiration levels conform to the comparison group paradigm and appear unrealistically high.

Among whites of both sexes (Armor, Tables 15 and 16), college plans are also generally higher when there are more blacks in the school. The effects are stronger for boys than for girls, with the most important distinction occurring between all white schools and those with 1–20% blacks, but there is either a threshold level or a reversal in these data for the white boys as well: going from a majority white (under 50% black) to a mainly black context (over 65% black) either freezes or attenuates aspirations.

Basically, Armor's data describe an interaction between the normative and comparative reference group processes that is somewhat different for each race. For blacks, the comparison group process seems to be particularly strong in predominantly black school contexts, but, for whites, normative or role model processes reverse this tendency in nearly all white schools. For whites, the comparison group process also seems to be operating, but reversal takes place at the opposite end of the context spectrum. When the proportion of blacks in a school exceeds two-thirds, the visibility of effective academic norms and role models apparently diminished sufficiently to arrest further comparison group increases for whites. White boys, in particular, seem to require at least a minimal critical mass of effective role models in order to stimulate or reinforce achievement goals.

The McPartland and York data provide further specification of the influence mechanisms at work for black *EEO* metropolitan Northeast ninth graders. Holding parents' education, school SES, and interracial friendships constant (McPartland and York, Table 6.10), the "racial effect" on college plans is again curvilinear. For blacks with *no* close white friends, college plans are highest in completely segregated schools. They diminish as the percentage of white classmates increases, until the threshold between half and mostly white is reached. Then, in most cases, there is a sharp increase in aspirations, which usually matches the level of segregated blacks. This group conforms to the Armor pattern.

Blacks with close white friends, however, conform to the interpersonal influence model in most comparison groups. Their aspirations, like their achievement, increase rather steadily as the proportion of white classmates increases, especially among those with better educated parents. The aspirations and achievements of peers with no white friends are less congruent, except for a similar positive response to majority white contexts. This suggests that the key to realistic aspiration levels for blacks is a predominantly white school environment with some white friends.

Although the McPartland and York twelfth-grade analysis lacks a measure of interracial friendships, the findings are similar (McPartland and York, Table 3.2). The overall racial composition effect on college plans is stronger among higher SES blacks, and a curvilinear trend is present in several comparison groups, particularly among those with low SES parents. Under nearly all individual and contextual SES conditions, the largest positive increase in college plans occurs as the proportion of white students in the classroom passes the 50% level. This increase is especially high for higher SES blacks. The only groups whose aspirations are higher in completely segregated schools than in majority white schools are those from lower SES backgrounds. Since the work of Rhodes, Reiss, and Duncan (1965) indicates that most close friendship ties occur between students with similar SES backgrounds, the failure of these students to conform to a pattern of interpersonal influence mechanisms may well indicate that there are comparatively few cross-status interracial friendships in predominantly black schools.

In view of this possibility, a key point noted earlier should be repeated: The racial composition and SES composition of most schools are correlated substantially, and discussions of racial composition imply SES composition and vice versa. Even in those studies in which these two variables were differentiated, it is difficult to avoid making assumptions about the SES characteristics of the whites who presumably account for positive achievement and aspiration effects. Since SES appears to be such an important variable in these analyses, it is imperative that we consider briefly the available data on the distribution of student SES resources among schools and its association with student achievement and college aspirations.

Socioeconomic Composition and Student Achievement

The extent to which the socioeconomic characteristics of school student-bodies affect student outcomes independently of other resource variables has been the subject of considerable controversy in studies of student achievement and aspirations. There is, however, at least a reasonable degree of consensus on four points: (1) The methodological problems in accounting for contextual effects accurately are considerable but not insoluble (Astin, 1970a,b; Hauser, 1971; Johnson, 1972; Tannenbaum and Bachman, 1964). (2) The variability in either outcome measure between schools is usually much lower than that within them (Duncan, Featherman and Duncan, 1972; Hauser, 1971; Johnson, 1972; Sewell and Armer, 1966a; M. Smith, 1972). (3) Virtually the same authors agree that only a part of this between-school variance can actually be explained by SES composition itself. (4) Most of the effects that do occur are not linear and additive (Armor, 1967; Boyle, 1966b; Meyer, 1970; McPartland and York, 1967; Nelson, 1972; Spady, 1970), although this pertains mainly to aspirations rather than cognitive achievement.

Hauser's (1969, 1970a,b, 1971) skepticism on contextual effects must be kept in mind. He believes that the proportions of between school variance typically reported are too low to be of substantive significance, particularly since SES composition represents only a fraction of that fraction, which may be associated with other school resource variables as well. Hauser feels that the mechanisms that presumably underlie these effects, such as school climate and interpersonal influence processes, are rarely operationalized and examined in the same analysis, and he believes there is inadequate evidence to support the common assumption that SES composition is the unambiguous cause of other intraschool mechanisms.

The findings on the relationship between the SES composition of the school and standardized achievement can be found in McPartland and York and Hauser's (1971) secondary analysis of mathematics and reading achievement among 16,893 white public high school students in the Nashville metropolitan area in 1957.

With family SES and classroom social composition controlled, the McPartland and York data for ninth-grade blacks show a substantial independent association between the SES composition of the school and verbal achievement (McPartland and York, Table 4.3). This association is strongest among those exceptional blacks whose parents have had at least some college and those with mostly white classmates. Overall, SES appears to be about as strong as the classroom racial effect noted earlier, suggesting that there are both differential sensitivity and accentuation effects in these data. Students who benefit most from a high SES school context are those whose family resources are high and those in classrooms with mainly white students.

It also appears that more substantial differences occur at a dividing line that differentiates schools in which the parents are typically at least high school graduates from those in which they are not. Students in all black classes benefit more than any other group. Since Tannenbaum and Bachman (1964) and Johnson (1972) argue that the likelihood of showing spurious contextual effects decreases with the number of contextual levels analyzed, these data (based on an analysis of four contextual levels) are quite credible.

When interracial friendships are also taken into account (with family and school SES categories collapsed into dichotomies), the SES context effect retains most of its strength, again especially among higher SES students and in majority white classrooms (McPartland and York, Table 6.9). The one anomaly is that SES context affects blacks with no white friends more than those with interracial friendships. It may be that having white middle-class friends directly mediates the otherwise beneficial effect of being in a higher SES school, thus supporting Hauser's view to some extent.

The twelfth-grade findings (McPartland and York, Table 4.1) are consistent with the aforementioned set of trends, save one. The SES context effect is stronger in all black classrooms than in predominantly white ones; otherwise, the higher the SES of the student, the stronger the SES context effect on his achievement. The independent effect of SES context on twelfth-grade black achievement, however, does not appear to be as strong as the independent effect of classroom racial composition. Thus, the racial composition of a high school may be a more important educational resource for achievement than its SES composition.

Hauser (1971) provides data on the proportions of between-school variance in mathematics and reading achievement for each sex and grade. For white high school boys, these range from 16 to 29% for mathematics and 11 to 17% for reading. For girls the ranges are similar: 15 to 28% for mathematics and 10 to 21% for reading. Only about 30% of these amounts can actually be traced to a combined SES–IQ compositional effect, thus accounting for Hauser's skepticism on the independent effect of SES.

Part of the discrepancy between his data and the McPartland and York patterns may be due to the race of the students involved: Blacks may be more sensitive to differences in student resource allocations than whites. The methods of analysis are also different, with the detailed tabular approach facilitating the discovery of threshold, curvilinear, and accentuation effects, and Hauser's analysis including a measure of student IQ, which the *EEO* analysis did not.

Socioeconomic Composition and Educational
Aspirations

When the focus shifts from the explanation of achievement to the analysis of college aspirations, problems of inconsistency among studies become acute. There are a number of studies reporting a general positive association between SES context and aspirations, in which normative group or role model processes are assumed to operate in a relatively consistent fashion but remain unmeasured (Armor, 1967; Boyle, 1966b; McDill and Coleman, 1963; Michael, 1961; Ramsøy, 1961; Sewell and Armer, 1966a; Turner, 1964; Wilson, 1959). There are also studies that either attempt explicitly to attribute differences in aspirations to interpersonal influence mechanisms or argue that these mechanisms can account for most between-school differences (Campbell and Alexander, 1965; Duncan *et al.*, 1972; Duncan, Haller, and Portes, 1968; Hauser, 1971; Krauss, 1964; Woelfel and Haller, 1971). Both these groups attempt to account for positive contextual effects. A third group suggests that there are complex interactions between normative and comparative reference group processes. These are underscored by the appearance of curvilinear patterns and/or suppressor effects in the data that often remain obscured in standard linear regression analysis (Adams, 1970; Armor, 1967; Johnson, 1972; McPartland and York, 1967; Meyer, 1970; Nelson, 1972).

Most of the literature pertinent to the first group of studies is reviewed by Boyle (1966b), including his own analysis of a sample of Canadian girls. These studies of mainly white students tend to show that the SES composition of the school is associated with educational goals largely because of differences between students in the highest-status schools and those in other schools. The payoff comes when the threshold between mixed status and solidly middle-class and upper middle-class communities is passed. Since such communities or neighborhoods are usually found only in metropolitan areas, context effects seldom emerge in studies of rural and small town schools.

Sewell and Armer's (1966a) analysis of "neighborhood" SES effects on the college plans of a sample of Wisconsin public high school seniors in 1957 also supports this trend, although the authors failed to note it. The data were first analyzed in a set of cross-tabulations in which family SES, student IQ, and neighborhood SES (regarded by most sociologists as a reasonable proxy for school SES) were trichotomized, yielding a 27-cell contingency table for each sex. Sewell and Armer did not, however, determine the net effect of each of these three variables. Instead, they used a regression analysis to assess only the unique effect of neighborhood context on college plans after SES and IQ were taken into account. Potential joint effects with SES and IQ were ignored, and, judging by its low unique contribution, the authors concluded that neighborhood context had little bearing on college plans. The challenges of this interpretation by Boyle (1966a), Michael (1966), and Turner (1966) focused mainly on the issues of causal ordering of the variables in the regression model and the failure to examine either the unique effects of SES and IQ or the joint effects of the variables.

Spady (1970), by reanalyzing the cross-tabular data using the Weighted Net Percentage Difference technique, showed more complex relations among the Sewell and Armer variables. The independent effect of neighborhood context on college plans is substantial for both sexes, and the magnitude of this effect increases with the SES of the student's family. For girls, almost all of the effect is due to the difference between high- and middle-status neighborhood contexts closely resembling the pattern in Boyle's data for Canadian girls. Boys respond more moderately and consistently to high-status contexts, but their response to middle- versus low-status contexts is variable, decreasing as family status decreases. This means that high-status boys are affected about equally by high- and middle-level contexts, but low SES boys have higher aspirations than their status peers only if they are in a high- rather than middle-context school.

With verbal ability, father's education, and school racial composition held constant, the Armor (1967) findings for ninth-grade whites also show that the SES composition effect is fairly substantial for both sexes. Among boys, the effect is strongest for those high on both family SES and verbal ability, and for girls it is also strong for those with high SES backgrounds regardless of verbal ability and those with low SES and high verbal ability. For the girls, these effects also increase with the proportion of whites in the school.

Taken together, these studies portray a consistent picture of the interaction, threshold, and accentuation effects that appear to operate for white students. The higher a student's socioeconomic and intellectual resources, the more he (but especially she) responds positively to the presence of higher-status students in the school. Girls seem to require a large critical mass of high-aspiring (white) peers to stimulate and reinforce aspirations for education beyond high school. The only point at issue is whether these patterns are best explained by a normative reference group process or by direct interpersonal influence mechanisms.

Of the studies cited earlier, the most pertinent to this issue is that of Campbell and Alexander (1965), who showed that the relationship between the SES context of the school and educational aspirations could be reduced to almost zero by controlling for the SES of the student's school friends. Their data suggest that the advantage of being in a higher-status school lies in the greater likelihood of meeting and making friends with higher-status, high-aspiring students. There is no lack of evidence to document the congruence in college aspirations of high school students and their close friends (Duncan et al., 1968; Krauss, 1964; Woelfel and Haller, 1971). The Sewell and Armer and Boyle data imply, however, that more than acquaintance or friendship is involved, at least among the girls; for being in a middle-status school, where there is presumably a certain proportion of such girls, has virtually no advantage over being in a low-status school (where middle-status students may be largely absent) for girls from any SES category. Their aspirations increase only when there is a *concentration* of higher-status girls in a school.

Evidence also exists suggesting that these positive influence processes do not entirely account for between-school variability in educational aspirations. For example, the Armor (1967) findings for ninth-grade blacks reveal (Armor, Table 9) that school SES composition has its largest "effects" among higher-status boys with higher verbal ability (the now familiar accentuation effect). For both boys and girls, however, the effect is generally most consistent and substantial within predominantly black schools. The normative group or interpersonal influence processes operate most strongly for black boys whose verbal ability and higher SES dispose them toward college. For other students, these processes appear to operate jointly with a comparison group process: Given that more high-aspiring role models are present in a higher SES school, blacks are more likely to respond if they are not overwhelmed by competitive academic standards.

Further specification of the complex interactions among the explanatory mechanisms for blacks is provided in the McPartland and York data (McPartland and York, Table 6.10). The SES composition of the school appears to affect mainly higher SES students, particularly those with white friends. This suggests that direct interpersonal contacts with middle-class whites not only has its own positive effect on aspiration levels but makes the higher-status black student more susceptible to normative group influences. The problem is that these effects are essentially curvilinear; they are high both in majority white classrooms and in minority black classrooms. This finding, coupled with a similar finding for twelfth-grade blacks (McPartland and York, Table 3.2), suggests that a comparison group process is also operating here.

The nature of the process can be discerned by integrating the findings presented by Adams (1970), Johnson (1972), Meyer (1970), and Nelson (1972), each of whom used data from large national or regional samples of high school students. (There are similar results in the Hauser [1971] findings for boys, but he considers the trends too weak to support a definitive interpretation.) The relationship between the socioeconomic composition of the school and educational aspirations appears to be mediated by two mechanisms: the aptitude or academic rank of the student within his own school and his self-concept of ability. The higher the SES context (and academic competition) of the school, the lower a given student's academic or ability ranking and consequent sense of competence will be. If one or the other of these two variables is not taken explicitly into account, the relation of school SES to aspirations will be artificially depressed.

Thus, students in high SES schools do not appear to have much higher aspirations than comparable students in low SES schools because their relative performance and sense of competence will not be as high. This partially offsets the positive effect of having more academically oriented classmates. When students are further equated on either of these two variables, however, the relation of SES context to aspirations definitely increases. Given that two students have similar SES backgrounds *and* school grades, the one in the high SES school is more likely to have higher aspirations. As in several studies reported earlier, the Nelson data also show that this relation is strongest for students with higher socioeconomic backgrounds.

These findings support the notion that comparative reference group processes that affect students' desires for a college education do operate within schools. Because these processes tend to depress the relation of school SES context to goals when grades are not accounted for (as in most of the studies cited here), one can only conjecture how much stronger these otherwise positive relations would be if student performance or self-concept of ability had been taken into account. It is possible, however, to test the validity of the normative group paradigm that has been used to explain many of these positive contextual effects, since there are studies in which school climate has been explicitly measured.

School Climates and Student Outcomes

Work by Mitchell (1967) represents an attempt to measure school climate and its relation to college plans. He administered Stern's High School Characteristics Index (HSCI) and Activities Index to all 2933 seniors in 11 high schools in the Rochester area, 9 of them in the city itself. Of the 30 "press" or "climate" scales in the HSCI, Mitchell used the achievement press scale as an indicator of "intellectual climate." Comparison of the three highest and three lowest schools on this scale showed large differences in the general level of involvement and participation of students in activities and courses. More important, with the IQ and SES of students controlled, achievement press had a strong positive association with educational aspirations and was positively correlated with the mean SES of schools: the more high SES students in a school, the greater the likelihood of a pattern of expectations and behavior of students reflecting involvement and active pursuit of academic goals. This strengthens the assumptions made earlier on the relation of student SES to the normative character of the schools. Since Mitchell lacked an independent measure of school SES composition, however, it is impossible to judge whether or not climate and SES are proxies for each other.

Perhaps the most ambitious attempt to operationalize the concept of school climate independently of SES composition is that of McDill, Rigsby, and Meyers (1969). Their data are based on a sample of 20,345 students and 1029 teachers in 20 public coeducational high schools from 7 geographical areas and 8 states, selected to reflect variability in demographic, socioeconomic, and community characteristics. The school climate measures consisted of 39 aggregate characteristics of prevalent attitudes and behaviors in each school, based on both student and teacher reports. These items were factor analyzed and orthogonally rotated, using the varimax method. Six interpretable factors, accounting for 82% of the variance, were extracted. The first, Academic Emulation, had a substantial net association with both standardized mathematics achievement and college plans, controlling for student's SES, IQ, and academic values. Each of the other climate dimensions—Student Perception of Intellectualism–Estheticism, Cohesive and Egalitarian Estheticism, Scientism, Humanistic Excellence, and Academically Oriented Status System—yielded similar (though less impressive) results.

In addition, the authors attempted to trace the correlates of school "climate" scores, mathematics achievement, and college plans among certain organizational attributes of the school. Their examination of the relations between a variety of community cultural facilities and resources and climate scores yielded little. They showed that per-pupil expenditures and teacher salaries have virtually no association with either achievement or aspirations, but four curricular facilities were associated with these variables: accelerated curriculum for superior students, advanced placement credit courses, an accelerated graduation policy, and percentage of teachers with more than a B.A. degree. The relations were sharply reduced when student SES and IQ were controlled, and, for the three curriculum measures, the effects generally disappeared when climate scores were also added. The only school resource that seemed consistently to have some positive relation to achievement and college plans, with both student characteristics and climate dimensions controlled, was the percentage of teachers with more than a B.A. degree. Within this system of variables, the climate effects remained strong.

In view of the positive association between these climate measures on both outcome variables, with family SES, student IQ, and teacher educational levels held constant, it appears that the positive student orientations toward learning generated by a significant proportion of students in a school are more than reflections of ability, typical SES indicators, and teacher quality. What they do reflect, according to McDill *et al.* (1969), is the interest that parents (as perceived by teachers) show in the educational policies of the school and the academic progress of their children. With a parental involvement index included in the analysis, the effects of the climate measures on achievement and aspirations all but disappeared. This led the authors to conclude that active parental concern about the quality of their children's education was the major source of variability in school climates leading to significant differences in student outcomes, even with other important resource variables held constant.

Conclusions and Implications

The McDill *et al.* study is unique for four reasons: (*1*) Both school resource and school context variables were used in the same analysis. (*2*)

These variables were used to examine both formal achievement and college plans. (3) Both sets of variables were also analyzed with a measure for parental concern. (4) There was an independent measure of student intelligence. Its major drawbacks were the absence of separate analyses for student race or sex and the size of the sample—only 20 schools. Nonetheless, its findings indicate that the normative structure of the school is an important resource in both the educational achievement and aspirations processes, after other curriculum, staff, and student resources are taken into account.

This supports both Ribich's (1968) interpretation of the linkage between formal resource allocations and student achievement and his contention (also supported by Hauser's findings) that SES measures, such as parental education, occupation, and income, are partial but inadequate proxies for the value parents place on their children's education. These parental attitudes are associated with student achievement independently of more objective SES factors and school resource measures in both the McDill *et al.* study and in Levin's (Chapter 9 of this volume) reanalysis of the *EEO* data for sixth-grade northern whites. In addition, it seems likely that they may underlie many of the normative climate effects on both achievement and college plans discussed in the literature on racial and SES composition effects.

The "value climate" of the family partially reflects its socioeconomic status and is carried to school by the child, who, in his interaction with other students, reflects at least some of these attitudes and is also presumably influenced by those of his peers. The higher the proportion of students in the school with positive attitudes toward academic achievement and future success, the greater the salience of these values in shaping the dominant character of the peer value system. This is consistent with sociological interpretations of the separate peer culture of the school as early as Waller's (1932). Many of the studies reviewed have suggested that the higher the ability or SES of the student, the more both his achievements and goals are accentuated by the presence of a critical mass of peers who share a strong academic orientation. This interpretation suggests that the peer group itself can be a particularly valuable and positive educational resource when interacting with the motivational, intellectual, and normative resources that emanate, in large part, from the individual family.

Although it is reasonable to argue that the normative orientations of the school staff either reinforce or modify individual and collective student orientations, there is no systematic evidence either for or against such a proposition. It is likely that student peer groups create conditions within the classroom or school that affect the teacher's ability to use his own skills and normative resources efficiently. There is evidence in these studies to suggest that the teacher's preference for or experience in working with a particular type of student affects the kind of success he is likely to have. This supports a more rational matching of teacher and students (Thelen, 1967) than that used in most school systems, mainly as the result of teacher attrition, transfers, and arbitrary placement. There is consistent evidence in nearly all of the studies reviewed that the achievement levels of both blacks and whites are maximized when the average classroom and school contains a large proportion of middle-class whites. As we have seen, this may be due not only to the kinds of values held by these able middle-class students but also to the achievement standards they set as role models within the classroom.

In one of the most complex and methodologically adequate studies available on ability grouping (Goldberg, Passow, and Justman, 1966), mathematics achievement was highest in a variety of group settings, all of which had at least a few exceptionally bright students. A similar trend appears in the grouping literature on mathematics achievement. This, together with the studies documenting the relationship between friendship patterns and student outcomes, leaves little doubt that all three positive influence processes are operating within schools. These are generally more powerful than the comparative reference group process that appears in several studies of educational aspirations.

It is possible, of course, that these positive school effects are due not only to normative, role model, and interpersonal influence processes but, at least in part, to the unmeasured family variables to which Ribich and several critics of the *EEO* study point. The superior performance and aspirations of students in high SES or majority white schools may partially reflect the tendency of both black and white parents in the higher SES strata to provide their children with greater encouragement and support during out-of-school hours, to move into neighborhoods where both the school climate and available school resources are regarded as good or better than elsewhere, and to endure higher tax burdens in order to provide adequate funding for local schools. We return to the familiar issues of selection effects and differential family resources that account, in part, for the apparent link between school resources and student achievement.

Here, Hanushek's analysis provides some important evidence. Since he deals with year-by-year *gains* in achievement of students and the characteristics of their teachers, with SES controlled, many of these contaminating factors are appreciably reduced. What appears to benefit lower SES white students is the verbal ability and most recent educational experience of their teacher. This suggests that there may well be advantages to giving lower SES white students teachers with high verbal competence in order to compensate for the typically lower standard of formal and elaborated verbal usage in the home. According to Hanushek, higher SES students do not appear to benefit from this particular resource, although it provides a definite advantage for whites and most blacks in the Armor (1972) findings and in his own (1970) reanalysis of the *EEO* data. Recall, however, that the inferences drawn from the Armor (1972) data for urban blacks suggested that teacher ability might be an important resource for these students only after other more fundamental conditions were met. Among these were the teacher's ability to establish a rapport with his students and gain their respect, which is linked to several variables, such as his race, commitment, and attitude toward students.

Given all of the generalizations and qualifications stated thus far, two related questions remain unanswered: How does one explain the rather consistent associations between expenditure levels and student outcomes? And, in which directions should further research in this area move?

There are trends in the data that provide at least superficial answers to the first question. While the *EEO* findings and those from other studies show that achievement differences vary more consistently with variability in the numbers and characteristics of staff than in expenditures for particular facilities, Ribich shows that there are limits to the payoff of expenditures. Beyond a certain point, they do not account for increases in student achievement levels. This may be associated with threshold levels in the utility of teacher experience or formal training, but it is impossible to tell, since these two measures have been operationalized inadequately in nearly all the studies cited. Even with these two variables taken into account, salary levels still seem to have a positive association with formal achievement. Some of this, but certainly not all, may be the result of parents selecting "better" school systems. The rest may reflect the selection processes that school systems themselves exercise in hiring teachers. Since the typically measured formal qualifications of beginning teachers will vary only slightly, they will not reflect the real qualifications of a teacher on which hiring may be based. I am arguing, in effect, that more affluent school systems are able to hire teachers with the qualities as well as qualifications they desire. It is likely that some of these interpersonal and expertise variables are having a direct effect on student achievement but are reflected in these analyses only in higher salaries.

This illustrates one of the two major problems with which future research efforts must deal. There must be more precise development of the theoretical issues and models relevant to a given problem area, the use of appropriate research designs, and explicit operationalization of variables. The emphasis in these studies on familiar and easily quantifiable demographic, economic, and achievement variables precludes the clear specification of influence mechanisms and social process. The result is "research by proxy." Both the independent and dependent variables in many of these studies are little more than proxies for the variables that a more sensitive social scientist would want to tap in order to explain impacts rather than measure differences.

Future work should begin where this review has left off: with some sensitivity to the nature of the various influence processes that appear to be at work within the school and the creation of research designs that can document their operation. There must be more careful examination of actual social processes, including teaching styles, the mechanisms governing rewards and sanctions for academic effort within the school, and the structure of both classroom and extracurricular peer relationships. This implies the use of longitudinal and experimental designs, observation as a data gathering mechanism, and more explicit documentation of student exposure to and utilization of both human and material resources. The need to broaden our range of significant output variables beyond measures of cognitive achievement and college aspirations is self-evident. Merely replicating existing studies on different populations under different conditions without improving on the research design and the measurement of relevant variables is a mistake.

Many of these studies have provided a better understanding of "what seems to count" in education. A second problem for future research is to make far better use of existing data. There are at least three aspects to this problem. First, there are several conspicuous examples in the studies cited in which my analysis of reported data pointed up trends in the findings that were either missed entirely by the original authors or left only partially developed. More careful scrutiny and in-depth syntheses of existing findings are necessary.

Second, there are examples of authors analyzing data by means of highly sophisticated mathematical techniques that are not well understood even by reasonably expert researchers, let alone practitioners, policy makers, or the general public. Furthermore, results are communicated either in highly technical or obscure prose, which leaves both the substantive nature and methodological adequacy of the data in doubt, for even the informed reader. Not only are the reports of what has been done, what the data show, and what they mean inadequate, but the techniques themselves, particularly multiple regression analysis, are used injudiciously.

Among the important findings that emerged in this study of the literature were those that described interaction, threshold, accentuation, and contextual and curvilinear trends in the data. I discovered most of these in my examination or reanalysis of cross-tabular tables. Few emerged in the results of regression analyses, which (as they were used in nearly every case in these studies) described the results of linear additive relations in data that are clearly not describing strong linear additive relations in the real world. Both educational theory and educational policy will advance far more readily when research can specify the levels and conditions under which variables "make a difference," as opposed to knowing only which variables have strong linear associations with others. Unless research of this type either reverts back to detailed cross-tabular analyses or begins to use regression analysis to explore, in more imaginative ways, the kinds of interaction effects noted, it is bound to miss many important points in analyses of data.

Third, the large-scale studies reported here generally included a wealth of variables that could be combined and compared to answer a number of significant questions, but these questions have remained unexplored. Admittedly, there are serious methodological problems with impact studies, such as *EEO*, that can never be reconciled by merely analyzing the variables in different ways (Astin, 1970a,b; Mosteller and Moynihan, 1972), and researchers who hope to make significant contributions should avoid these pitfalls. This does not mean that the costly data in these studies should be abandoned. As surely as there are provocative findings hidden in the *EEO* data, there are many more waiting to be discovered by patient and imaginative data analysts. It is in these available but largely untapped data that many of the answers that I have sought unsuccessfully lie. Until they are tapped, the impact of school resources on students will remain a cloudy issue.

Acknowledgments

The author is deeply indebted to Charles E. Bidwell and David B. Nolle for their invaluable comments on earlier drafts of this chapter.

VIII Another Hour, Another Day: Quantity of Schooling, a Potent Path for Policy*

David E. Wiley
University of Chicago

Assessment of School Effects and Quantity of Schooling

In the last few years, we have been inundated with literature on a new mythology of schooling: From the report on *Equality of Educational Opportunity* (Coleman, Campbell, Hobson, McPartland, Mood, Weinfeld, and York, 1966) and the most recent reanalyses of its data (Mosteller and Moynihan, 1972) to Jencks' book, *Inequality* (Jencks, Smith, Acland, Bane, Cohen, Gintis, Heyns, and Michelson, 1972), we have been flooded with reports of the lack of effect of schooling. These reports have discouraged

* The American College Testing Program, through its research institute, provided the basic financial but also much intellectual support for the research. Additional financial support was provided by the National Science Foundation (Grant No. GS-35642). The author further thanks the Max-Planck-Institut für Bildungs-forschung, Berlin, for supplying facilities while the report was written.

The research reported herein was also supported, in part, by funds from the National Institute of Education, U.S. Department of Health, Education, and Welfare. The opinions expressed in this publication do not necessarily reflect the position, policy, or endorsement of the National Institute of Education (Contract No. NE-C-00-3-0102).

225

educational practitioners and have comforted and supported those who would reduce the resources allocated to education. However, the grounds for many of the investigators' conclusions are weak and those for the more popular policy interpretations even weaker. One has to consider the results of these analyses, but what is really needed is a more appropriate attitude toward assessing the effects of schooling. Rather than asking if there are any effects of schooling, we should be asking how much of an effect schooling has. If we regard the issue in this way, then we will be more successful in assessing these effects, and we will have a much clearer guide for educational policy.

To say that schooling has no effect is unwarranted. It is true that some middle-class children would learn to read even if they did not attend school and that school is not effective in teaching reading to some lower-class children. This does not mean, however, that children do not acquire appreciably better reading skills by attending school. It seems clear that some children, who learn to read, would not if they did not attend school and that some children, who would have learned to read, read much more capably because of their schooling.[1] The level of discussion, however, still has not risen above the question: Does schooling have any effect?

It is the degree of effect of schooling that is important for educational policy. If it were found, after a large concentration of resources in reading instruction, that only small gains in levels of competency were attained, then we might be dissatisfied with the return on our investment in this area. In this case, we would, perhaps, want to understand why there was such a small effect so that we could modify the conditions of our investment (i.e., change the curriculum), or we might wish to reduce our investment in this area, either to improve the yield of the system in another area, where we could use the same resources more valuably or to invest our resources in noneducational endeavours. In order to facilitate such educational decision making, we must be able to assess the extent of effect of a given amount of schooling. Under ordinary circumstances, the larger the effect of a given amount of schooling, the more we will value it. Our methods and our orientation must be directed toward assessing these impacts quantitatively, or our conclusions will be only tangentially useful for educational policy.

One distinct notion, which is also directly important in assessing the

---

[1] This example does not imply that achievement, especially in its most narrow sense, is all or the most important part of what schooling has to offer. Schooling occupies a major portion of the child's life in post-industrial societies and, as such, should have a major impact on the entire socialization process, including education in its broadest sense. Also, because of the major role it plays in childhood, attention must be given to its short-term effects and qualities as well as its long-term influences. For a more elegant exposition of these points, see Jackson (1973). This chapter is restricted to an assessment of the impact of schooling, using examples in the "achievement" category only, because of restrictions in the type and quality of data available.

impact of schooling, is the view of schooling itself, rather than its effect, as a quantitative rather than a qualitative phenomenon. We must not only begin to ask how much of an effect schooling has, we must also ask the more sophisticated question: What is the effect of a particular amount of schooling? A major mechanism for increments in resources allocated to a given instructional area is increasing the amount of instruction in that area.[2] If we wish to assess the impact of resources on outcomes useful for policy in a way, we must establish the relationship between the amount of schooling and achievement rather than attempting to answer the crude question of whether or not schooling has any effect. Husén (1972) has reviewed research findings with respect to the question: Does more schooling produce more achievement? Although he finds somewhat ambiguous results from prior studies, he concludes that an increase in the amount of schooling will not produce a proportionate increase in achievement. To us, his review does not seem to support his rather refined conclusion of nonproportionality, since the studies he reviews were neither originally designed nor reanalyzed to shed light on this issue. Our objective here is to detail our ideas about the ways in which school does affect achievement and to argue that this view dictates a drastic change in the ways in which data about schooling are collected and analyzed.

It is clear that if a child does not go to school at all, he will not directly benefit from schooling. If a child goes to school every day for a full school year, he will achieve his maximum benefit from that schooling, other circumstances being equal. If he attends school less than the full year but more than not at all, the benefits he derives from schooling should be intermediate. That is, the quantity of schooling should be a major determinant of school outcomes.

In addition, the effects of various components of schooling will probably vary with the child's exposure to them. If we assume that a teacher with a Master's degree is more effective in terms of achievement than one with a Bachelor's degree,[3] then, if a child does not go to school at all, that difference will not affect the child. If the child goes to school for the full year, that difference will have its maximum impact. If the child goes to school more than not at all and less than a full year, then that particular variable will have an intermediate impact.[4] The effects of various compo-

---

[2] A vital question, which is not addressed in this section, is concerned with the *measurement* of such a content area-specific quantity of instruction.

[3] The Master's versus Bachelor's degree dichotomy represents any of a number of alternative variables (e.g., library books, guidance counselors, field trips). Here the point applies to all of those aspects of school "quality" which investigators have used to "assess" the impact of schooling.

[4] Literally, of course, this difference cannot apply to a single child. The language is a shorthand used to describe the difference between two otherwise equivalent children.

nents of schooling should vary with the degree of exposure to them. If schooling has an influence on a child, it does so on a day-by-day basis, when he is present and subject to that influence, and cannot influence him when he is not there.

It seems, therefore, that Average Daily Attendance (ADA), the number of hours per day for which the school meets, and the number of days in the school year would be important characteristics of schools to assess. The average number of hours of schooling that a child in a given school receives may be calculated by multiplying the Average Daily Attendance by the number of hours in the school day by the number of days in the school year.[5] If schooling is quantified in this way, there are (see Table 8.10) variations of the order of 50% in the total number of hours of schooling per year; that is, typical pupils in some schools receive 50% more schooling than pupils in other schools. This indicates an enormous variation in exposure to schooling.

At a finer level of analysis, if one carries the concept of exposure to schooling even further, a deeper investigation of the amount of instruction in the school, that is, the amount of time that a pupil actually spends in a supervised educational experience, should result in a more valid measure of that concept. Carroll (1963) has, in fact, formulated a model of school learning in which the amount of time spent in learning plays the primary role. Extensions of that model would have been formulated by Wiley and Harnischfeger (1974) and an integrative conceptual framework has been developed more recently (Harnischfeger and Wiley, 1975). Work by Bloom (1971c) and his students have explored the implications of the time concept for modifying traditional methods of instruction.

If it is reasonable to believe that variations in exposure to schooling are as great as 50% and this factor is not taken into account, we might expect

---

[5] The maximum number of hours of schooling that a child in a given school may receive can be calculated by forming the product of the number of hours in the school day for the school in question and the number of days for which school met during the year. Each child in that school has a specific number of days of absence during the school year. The product, for a particular child, of the number of days for which he was present and the number of hours per day for which his school met, equals the total number of hours of schooling that the child received in the school year. The average of these figures, for all the children in the school, will yield the average number of hours of schooling in that school. The ratio of the hours of schooling received by a particular child to the maximum number of hours in that school defines his attendance rate since the hours per day in a particular school is constant. The average of these attendance rates is equal to the Average Daily Attendance (ADA) in that school. As a consequence, the average number of hours of schooling received in a school may be calculated by forming the product of the ADA and the maximum number of hours of schooling for that school. This is, of course, equal to the triple product of ADA, length of school day in hours, and length of school year in days for a particular school.

the effects of variables, such as teacher or school characteristics, to be obscured by the enormous variation in exposure. If we look at earlier studies from this perspective it is quite obvious that attendance was generally considered to be a student composition or background variable and, as such, was placed in the wrong category. One of the few exceptions to this generalization is a study by Douglas and Ross (1965). They investigated the effects of absence on primary school performance and found that effects depended on the child's social class level. Generally, absence had a larger detrimental effect on performance in lower-class children.

The first major influential study of the effect of schooling was the *Equality of Educational Opportunity* (Coleman et al., 1966) survey. The report based on this study set the major precedents for school effects analyses and also became the primary exemplar for subsequent criticism. It is interesting that although it has occasioned the greatest amount of controversy, the analysis of the relations between school characteristics and achievement occupies but a small proportion of the report.[6] The first component of the analysis was a study of the school-to-school variations in achievement. Pupil background factors had an important role in explaining this variation. However, it was also found that achievement varied more within schools than between schools.

Student-body characteristics were also used to explain school-to-school variation in achievement.[7] This category illustrates the principles used to allocate the attendance variable, which can be considered a measure of quantity of schooling. Another explanatory category was school facilities and curriculum.[8] When the percentages of variance explained by school characteristics and by school characteristics plus student-body characteristics (over and above pupil background) were examined, it was found that school characteristics alone accounted for a relatively small proportion of the variance but that a considerably larger proportion was explained by the combination of school *and* student-body characteristics. From the perspective of this chapter, these results hint that the intensity of schooling rather than the particular kind of schooling has a larger effect on student achievement. This conclusion contradicts some of the more general earlier interpretations of these data, which tend to identify the detected effects of school characteristics with the true effects of schooling. Furthermore,

---

[6] This section of the report runs for only 40 pages, including an appendix, out of 547 pages of text and tables.

[7] For the sixth grade, these measures were attendance, student mobility (number of transfers), proportion of pupils whose families own encyclopedias, and teachers' perception of student body quality.

[8] In this category for sixth grade were the following variables: per pupil expenditure on staff, volumes per student in library, and school location (city, suburb, town, country).

teacher variables were used to explain pupil achievement.[9] This category of variables did contribute to achievement, but only to a minor degree as compared to pupil background.

It is apparent that the focus of the *Equality of Educational Opportunity* report on the distribution of educational resources led to a dichotomy in categorization of school variables. The quantity measure with which we are concerned here, attendance (ADA), was categorized as a characteristic of the student-body composition, whereas the resource measures formed separate categories since these could be physically allocated to schools. It seems relatively clear that the original intent of the study—description of the distribution of resources among racial groups—was not conducive to a theoretically based analysis oriented toward the conceptualization of how school influences children's achievement. As a consequence, there was no effort to analyze or interpret the data with the objective of determining the impact of the quantity of schooling on pupil achievement. This original orientation also has conditioned the work of many subsequent investigators who have attempted to correct and modify the original analysis. In addition, the models and procedures used in the *Equality of Educational Opportunity* study and by most subsequent investigators also precluded an appropriate assessment of school effects, even when the "quantity" issue is ignored.

The method of analysis of the *Equality of Educational Opportunity* report was variance decomposition. In each of the several types of decomposition, the total variance of an outcome variable is partitioned into component parts, each allocated to a "source" of variation and representing the "importance" of that "source" in determining the outcome. In the particular type used in the report, the several classes of variables were ordered, and the percentage of variance accounted for by each succeeding group was ascertained. As explained earlier, the classes of variables used, in order, were pupil background, student-body, school facilities and curriculum, and teacher. Such a variance decomposition is dependent on the order of the variables. Because of the ordering, only for the last category can the increment in variance accounted for be attributed solely to that category. In this case, only the increment due to teacher variables may be interpreted as unique.

A means of avoiding the dependence of the decomposition on the order of the categories has been suggested, most recently, by Mood (1971). This method attempts to distinguish the unique and common contributions of variables, although it does not solve the basic problem of variance

---

[9] These variables consisted of: the average educational level of the teachers' families, the average years of experience in teaching, the localism of the teachers in the school, the average level of education of teachers themselves, the average score on vocabulary tests self-administered by the teachers, the teachers' preference for teaching middle-class white students, and the proportion of teachers in the school who were white.

decomposition. We will show that the difficulty lies in arriving at an unambiguous interpretation of the components. Since variables in different categories are correlated, the sum of the unique variance accounted for by each category does not equal the total variance. For example, if we consider pupil background and Average Daily Attendance (ADA) as two distinct categories (or variables) that are positively correlated, then the sum of the unique variance accounted for by pupil background and that accounted for by ADA will be less than the total variance of the variable being accounted for. Depending on the interrelations among the categories, the amount of variance accounted for by each category uniquely may sum to more or less than the total variance accounted for by the variables of all the categories combined.[10] As a consequence, the percentage of variance accounted

[10] The variance decomposition, as it is usually done, is as follows: Assume that two variables, x_1 and x_2, account, partially, for a third, y. Suppose $y = \alpha + \beta_1 x_1 + \beta_2 x_2 + \epsilon$. Then the proportion of variance accounted for by x_1, ignoring x_2, is $\rho^2_{y \cdot x_1}$. The proportion accounted for by x_2, ignoring x_1, is $\rho^2_{y \cdot x_2}$. The proportion accounted for by x_1 and x_2, together, is the squared multiple correlation, $\rho^2_{y \cdot x_1 x_2}$. The unique proportion accounted for by x_1 is the difference between the proportion jointly accounted for by x_1 and x_2 and that accounted for by x_2 without x_1: $\rho^2_{y \cdot x_1 x_2} - \rho^2_{y \cdot x_2}$. Similarly for x_2, the proportion is: $\rho^2_{y \cdot x_1 x_2} - \rho^2_{y \cdot x_1}$. The proportion commonly accounted for is the difference between the proportion which is jointly accounted and that which is uniquely accounted:

$$\rho^2_{y \cdot x_1 x_2} - (\rho^2_{y \cdot x_1 x_2} - \rho^2_{y \cdot x_2}) - (\rho^2_{y \cdot x_1 x_2} - \rho^2_{y \cdot x_1}) = \rho^2_{y \cdot x_2} + \rho^2_{y \cdot x_1} - \rho^2_{y \cdot x_1 x_2}.$$

To illustrate, suppose the two variables, x_1 and x_2, are correlated ρ. Also suppose that $y = x_1 + x_2$ (i.e., $\beta_1 = \beta_2 = 1$ and $\epsilon \equiv 0$) and that $\sigma^2_{x_1} = \sigma^2_{x_2} = 1$. Then the correlations between x_1 and x_2, on the one hand, and y, on the other, are both $(1 + \rho)/\sqrt{(2 + 2\rho)}$. The proportion of variance accounted for by each x, ignoring the other, is $[(1 + \rho)/\sqrt{(2 + 2\rho)}]^2 = (1 + \rho)^2/(2 + 2\rho)$. The proportion accounted for by both (multiple correlation), jointly, is one (since $\epsilon \equiv 0$), so the unique proportion for each is:

$$1 - \frac{(1 + \rho)^2}{2 + 2\rho} = \frac{2 + 2\rho - 1 - 2\rho - \rho^2}{2 + 2\rho} = \frac{1 - \rho^2}{2(1 + \rho)}$$

$$= \frac{(1 - \rho)(1 + \rho)}{2(1 + \rho)} = \frac{1 - \rho}{2}$$

Therefore, the common proportion is:

$$1 - \frac{1 - \rho}{2} - \frac{1 - \rho}{2} = \frac{2 - 1 + \rho - 1 + \rho}{2} = \frac{2\rho}{2} = \rho.$$

In this case, the total decomposition is:

unique due to x_1:	$(1 - \rho)/2$
unique due to x_2:	$(1 - \rho)/2$
common between x_1 and x_2:	ρ
Total:	1.00

for—either uniquely by a class of variables (pupil background *or* ADA) or jointly with overlapping parts of other categories of variables (pupil background *and* ADA)—is not an adequate index to use in assessing the impact of a variable or category.

The unique proportion of variance accounted for is also typically used as a basis for significance testing. The use of the proportion for this purpose, rather than as an index of "importance," is valid. The significance test, in this case, assesses hypotheses about the contribution of a particular category of variables to the outcome, when the others are held constant. If a particular category is highly related to another, then the unique proportion of variance accounted for may be relatively small and, as a consequence, the power of the test of significance based on it may be very low. In addition, the confidence intervals for the regression coefficients of the variables in this category will be very broad. This implies that the data do not determine the effects of these variables very precisely.

In summary, a variance decomposition, whether ordered as in Coleman *et al.* (1966) or symmetric as that proposed by Mood (1971), does not offer a reasonable method for assessing the importance of the contribution of variables or categories to outcomes. Some of these criticisms have been made previously by Bowles and Levin (1968b).

Some investigators who reanalyzed the Coleman *et al.* data (Armor, 1972; Cohen, Pettigrew, and Riley, 1972) have used standardized regression coefficients, instead of variance contributions, as indices of the influence of variables. Standardized coefficients suffer from serious defects as well. As

---

When $\rho = .50$ the decomposition is:

unique x_1:	$(1 - .5)/2 =$	.25
unique x_2:	$(1 - .5)/2 =$	.25
common:		.50
Total:		1.00

This set of numbers seems reasonable since it implies that 25% of the variance in the outcome is unique to each independent variable while 50% is shared variation in common. If we examine the decomposition when $\rho = -.50$ we get a different impression:

unique x_1:	$(1 - (-.5))/2 =$	.75
unique x_2:	$(1 - (-.5))/2 =$	.75
common:		−.50
Total:		1.00

The finding that −.50% of the variance in the outcome is shared in common by both independent variables is obviously nonsense.

Variance decomposition is typically only meaningful when the sources of variation are orthogonal to (uncorrelated with) one another (see Tukey, 1954).

the variance of an independent variable decreases, the standardized regression coefficient also decreases, even though the unstandardized regression coefficient (structural relation) remains unchanged. To be more concrete, if a unit increase in an independent variable, such as Number of Possessions in the Home, produces a 1.23 point increase in an outcome variable, such as Verbal Achievement, the unstandardized regression coefficient is equal to 1.23. In one of the data analyses reported below, this value was actually found. In the same analysis, the corresponding standardized regression coefficient for the possessions variable was .21, its standard deviation being 1.57. If we were to change the circumstances in such a way that the structural relation (unstandardized coefficient) was unchanged (i.e., the effect of increasing the number of possessions by one was still 1.23 verbal score points) but the standard deviation of the independent variable (possessions) was half as large (about .79), then the standardized regression coefficient would also be half as large (about .10). The effect of any change in the independent variable would be the same, while the standardized coefficient would be different. As a consequence, the *standardized* regression coefficient is a reasonable measure of variable importance for policy purposes only when the standard deviations of independent variables are proportionately related to the amount of societal effort necessary to change the value of the policy variable in question.

Another problem with previous data analyses has been the use of large numbers of correlated explanatory variables. For example, M. Smith (1972: 334–335, Table J) reports a reanalysis of the Coleman *et al.* data containing 30 explanatory variables for verbal achievement. The problem is especially acute in the analysis of school data. When variables defined at the level of the individual pupil are aggregated to the level of the school, their correlations tend to increase. As a result, with large numbers of such variables, effective analyses are hindered by excessive collinearity (high relations among independent variables). When the number of such collinear variables becomes very large, the effects of individual variables become very difficult to detect. This is due to the decrease in precision, which we referred to earlier, when we discussed the effects of correlations among the categories of independent variables. The problem is also aggravated by limitations in the effective sample size. Whenever variables are defined at the school level, as are many of those derived from the *Equality of Educational Opportunity* survey, the appropriate unit of analysis is the school and the number of independent observations (and consequently the degrees of freedom available) is limited by the number of schools.

The effects of individual variables also become difficult to interpret when there are many. For most kinds of conceptual or theoretical structures, the operational variables used in the analysis overlap the conceptual explanatory variables in such a way that also makes interpretation of individual regression coefficients difficult. For example, the child's report of the presence of an encyclopedia in his home probably reflects several more basic variables as well, such as parental use of the encyclopedia, encouragement of the child to use it, number of other reference works in the home. Given that these variables may be interpreted in and of themselves or may be considered to be functions of or partial definitions of the social status of the child's home, interpretation becomes difficult. In addition, since other variables used in the data analysis, such as child's report of mother's education, may reflect some of the same underlying variables, the interpretation of the results becomes doubly difficult.

A small number of conceptually well defined variables is needed to account for outcomes. To be useful for policy purposes, these variables should be meaningfully defined at the school level, and unstandardized regression analyses should be performed using them. When the number of such variables is small, interpretation is usually less ambiguous, and ordinary scientific processes of model revision are easier. Unreasonable results can be easily detected by inspecting coefficients against the background of prior expectations. Unexpected results should lead to revisions of the model and conceptual redefinition of variables, when this is necessary.

Because of the confusion surrounding school attendance in previous analyses, some further exposition of its role in the model for pupil achievement is necessary. Jencks (1972a) included Average Daily Attendance (ADA) in his category of regional and community characteristics and did not include it in his category of exposure to school.[11] Coleman *et al.*, as mentioned earlier, included it in their category of student-body characteristics. Both investigations did not place ADA in any category representing exposure to schooling and even ignored it as an important moderator of the effects of school characteristics. Attendance is clearly influenced by the child's background and by his home and the community in which he resides, but it is not a background variable; it is a mediating variable for outcomes. An appropriate causal model would have three parts. The first would be an explanatory submodel for pupil attendance. This model would contain explanatory variables, reflecting the pupil's home background and characteristics of the community, and, perhaps, allow for the possibility of an effect of the school itself.[12] A second component model would define exposure to schooling in terms of ADA and other characteristics of the amount of instruction. A third submodel would explain pupil achievement in terms of home background, community characteristics, and exposure to

---

[11] Variables included in this category were automatic promotion, hold back slow learners, transfer slow learners, percentage of students on split sessions, days in school year, and length of school day. By Jencks' method of analysis, he found no effects of variables in this category.

[12] Such an effect of school on attendance would imply the use of what economists call a simultaneous equation system. A preliminary exploration of the use of such a model in this context is reported in Footnote 22.

schooling. These three models together would constitute an explanatory system for achievement. The analysis that follows is an attempt to partially explicate such a system using data from the *Equality of Educational Opportunity* survey.

In summary, it seems that one of the reasons that investigators have not found very many or very large effects of schooling is that they have not taken into account the amount of schooling the child receives and have not tried to measure it in a systematic and integrated fashion.

A Conceptual and Analytic Model for the Analysis of the Effects of Quantity of Schooling

As was discussed in the previous section, the analysis of the impact of schooling in general and of school characteristics in particular has been obscured by both methodological and conceptual faults. The methodological shortcomings in these analyses are threefold: inadequate indices used to characterize the importance of independent variables; the problem of excessive numbers of variables and collinearity; and the lack of appropriate units of analysis in data structures that are defined at several hierarchical levels (e.g., schools, classrooms/teachers, pupils) together with the implications of these units for model construction and data analysis. We have already suggested a means of correcting the first two faults; the first part of this section will be devoted to a discussion of the third.

The major features of the solution of the problem of appropriate units of analysis can be discussed within the context of a hierarchical data structure containing only two levels. In what follows, the concrete counterparts of these levels will always be schools and pupils.

The typical data set used for the analysis of school effects contains variables defined at the level of the individual pupil, such as the various home background variables measured in the *Equality of Educational Opportunity* survey and the achievement criteria tested in that survey. This data set also includes variables defined solely at the level of the school, such as length of the school day and the highest degree held by the principal. The latter category of variables takes on the same value for every individual pupil in a particular school. In addition to these variables, which are naturally defined at the level of the school, there are other variables that may assume the same value for all individuals in a school by aggregating (usually averaging) individually defined characteristics for all individuals in a particular school.

One of the problems plaguing the literature in recent years has been the separation of the effects of these aggregated variables into parts reflecting their individual-level effects, on the one hand, and their effects via school climate and organization, on the other. This problem has been labeled "context effect." Some of the common practices in handling this problem have been criticized by Hauser (1970a). Hauser (1971) has also treated more general problems in the hierarchical analysis of school effects. The model presented here is related to Hauser's but is more detailed and refined.

One way of describing an appropriate method of analysis is in terms of the general notions of confounding and control. If we wish to assess the impact of one explanatory variable on an outcome and it is correlated with another variable, then, if we ignore the second, we will attribute to the first not only its effect but also a spurious effect that is due to both the correlation between it and the second and the effect of the second. If we utilize an appropriate method of analysis which takes into account the second variable (i.e., its effects) and its relation to the first, we may obtain an adjusted assessment of the effect of the first variable which is not confounded by the second.

In examining the basic problem of the assessment of school effects on achievement, for example, we may think of it as the problem of disentangling the effects of variables defined solely at the level of the school, such as length of the school day and highest degree held by the principal, from those defined at the level of the individual pupil, such as home background characteristics. (In the most general case, we may denote the value of the vector for the ith school by $\mathbf{z}_i$ and the value of the vector for the jth pupil in the ith school by $\mathbf{x}_{ij}$.) From this perspective, the problems of disentanglement may be seen as: (1) adjusting the *effects* of individual characteristics (denoted by β) on the outcome (denoted by y_{ij}) for those of the schools (denoted by γ) that the individuals attend and (2) adjusting the effects of school characteristics for those of the individuals. We may summarize the model implicit in this description by:

(1) $$y_{ij} = \gamma_0 + \gamma'\mathbf{z}_i + \theta_i + \beta'\mathbf{x}_{ij} + \epsilon_{ij},$$

where γ_0 is an additive constant and θ_i and ϵ_{ij} are errors or discrepancies defined at the school and individual levels, respectively. One means of obtaining the adjusted effect of one variable (e.g., home background) on another (e.g., achievement) is by adjusting each for the other variable and then relating the two adjusted variables.[13] Also, if we know the true effect of one variable or have a good estimate of it, we may calculate the adjusted

---

[13] This may be illustrated in the context of a simple linear model as follows: Assume,

$$y = \alpha + \beta_1 x_1 + \beta_2 x_2 + \epsilon,$$

then the regression coefficient of y on x_1, without x_2, is equal to

$$\beta_1 + \beta_2 \frac{\sigma_{x_1 x_2}}{\sigma_{x_1}^2}$$

since x_1 and x_2 are correlated.

effect of the other variable by relating a new variable, consisting of the criterion values minus the effect values of the first variable[14], to the other variable without adjustment. A common error, however, is to subtract the *unadjusted* effect value of the first variable from the criterion and then to estimate the effect of the second variable by relating it to the modified criterion. This procedure will not produce an appropriate adjustment, since subtracting the unadjusted effect value of the first variable does not remove all of its influence.

In the context of hierarchically defined school data, the key to finding appropriately adjusted estimates of the effects of individual-level variables

---

Thus, the adjusted y is equal to

$$y^* = y - \left(\beta_1 + \beta_2 \frac{\sigma_{x_1 x_2}}{\sigma_{x_1}^2} \right) x_1$$

$$= \alpha + \beta_1 x_1 + \beta_2 x_2 + \epsilon - \left(\beta_1 + \beta_2 \frac{\sigma_{x_1 x_2}}{\sigma_{x_1}^2} \right) x_1$$

$$= \alpha + \beta_2 \left(x_2 - \frac{\sigma_{x_1 x_2}}{\sigma_{x_1}^2} x_1 \right) + \epsilon.$$

The regression coefficient of x_2 on x_1 (ignoring y) is equal to

$$\frac{\sigma_{x_1 x_2}}{\sigma_{x_1}^2}.$$

The adjusted x_2 is equal to

$$x_2^* = x_2 - \frac{\sigma_{x_1 x_2}}{\sigma_{x_1}^2} x_1.$$

Consequently, the adjusted y may be written:

$$y^* = \alpha + \beta_2 x_2^* + \epsilon.$$

This implies that a linear regression relating the adjusted y (for x_1) to the adjusted x_2 (for x_1) will yield the correct (adjusted) coefficient for the effect of x_2 on y.

[14] Strictly speaking, we may only discuss the *effect* of a change in a variable and not the effect of a variable or one of its values. In the context of a *linear* model, the effect of a change of one unit in the value of the variable is always the same and is equal to the regression coefficient for that variable. As a consequence, in such a linear model we may talk about the effect of a change of one unit in the variable or, in shorthand, the effect of a variable. In general, when the model is nonlinear the effect of a change in a variable may depend on the value of the variable or even on the values of other variables (when there are interactions). In the text, when we discuss the "effect" of a variable, the reader should think in terms of a linear model. In this context, when we are discussing the general effect of a change in a variable, the effect is the regression coefficient of the variable. When we are discussing the adjustment of another variable, the effect *value* of a variable is the product of the regression coefficient and the value of the variable.

is to make sure that as many school based sources of variation as possible enter the adjustment. The simplest way to accomplish this is to adjust for all of them. We assume that if the model is completely specified at the school level (that is, all of the outcome-relevant school variables are measured) then $\text{cov}(\theta_i, \bar{x}_{i.}) = \mathbf{O}$, where $\bar{x}_{i.}$ is the mean of x_{ij} for the ith school. The basic stance implied by this model is that individual-level variables have direct impact on outcomes only at the level of the individual; their effects at the school level are mediated through other variables, whether measured or not, defined at the level of the school. The covariance condition given above would only be expected to hold if *all* the mediating variables, which convey the indirect effects of aggregate individual variables at the school level, are specified in the model. If all such variables are not specified and measured, then $\text{cov}(\theta_i^*, \bar{x}_{i.}) \neq \mathbf{O}$, where θ_i^* is the residual from the *measured* school variables. If this is the case, as it likely will be, direct fitting of the model will produce a biased estimate of β This source of bias may, however, be eliminated through analysis based on the variation within schools. This may be done by subtracting the relevant school means (school effect values) for the criterion variable and for each of the pupil-level explanatory variables from each of the individual values for these variables. An analysis using these adjusted (deviated) values will be effectively "controlled" or adjusted for all sources of variation among schools. This method of determining adjusted effects is an example of the application of the procedure, mentioned earlier, of adjusting both explanatory and criterion variable values. The covariance matrix of the adjusted (deviated) values is called the pooled within school covariance matrix. If this covariance matrix is computed for all individually defined variables and used as the basis for the regression of the outcome on the x_{ij} vectors, the resulting estimate of β, $\hat{\beta}$ will not be biased by specification errors at the school level.

Once the adjusted effects of the individual-level variables are determined, the average effect value for each school, aggregated over all the individual pupils, may be subtracted from the criterion mean for each school. Analyses, using the school as the unit with variables defined at the school level as explanatory and the modified criterion means as values to be explained, will produce estimates of the effects of the school variables adjusted for the effects of individually defined variables. That is, a school level analysis of

(2) $$\bar{y}_{i.} - \hat{\beta}'\bar{x}_{i.} = \gamma_0 + \gamma'\mathbf{z}_i + \phi_i,$$

where $\bar{y}_{i.}$ is the achievement mean for the ith school, will produce unbiased estimates of γ_0 and γ in the absence of specification error. If, however, as was our original concern, there is specification bias in the school-level model, this solution will not be adequate. The method of analysis may be refined in the following fashion. If we suppose that there is some specification bias at the level of school defined variables (perhaps some important variables are missing), then $\text{cov}(\theta_i, \bar{\mathbf{x}}_{i.}) \neq \mathbf{O}$ and $\text{cov}(\phi_i, \bar{\mathbf{x}}_{i.}) \neq 0$. We may remove some of the bias (in the estimates $\hat{\gamma}_0$ and $\hat{\gamma}$) by including the sum of the average effect values $(\hat{\beta}'\bar{\mathbf{x}}_{i.})$ of the individually defined variables as another variable in the school-level analysis—instead of just subtracting the sum from the school criterion mean. That is, we can fit the following model:

$$(3) \qquad\qquad \bar{y}_{i.} = \gamma_0 + \gamma'\mathbf{z}_i + \lambda(\hat{\beta}'\bar{\mathbf{x}}_{i.}) + \phi_i.$$

This (specifically the parameter λ) allows partial removal of some of the additional bias due to the omission of relevant school-level variables to the extent that the sum of these average effect values is correlated with the omitted variables.

In a situation where the number of schools is limited, this approach allows for the generation of a summary individual variable by using the great quantity of information available on variation and covariation among individuals within schools. At the same time, it saves the limited information on variation among schools for the assessment of school-level effects.

In summary, we have proposed a statistical model and method of data analysis for a data structure defined hierarchically (both at the level of the individual pupil and at the level of the school). In this approach, appropriate adjustments of the effects of variables defined at both levels of the hierarchy (e.g., length of school day at the school level and home background at the individual pupil level) can be readily and sensitively accomplished, without loss of important information at either level. The resulting economies are also helpful in solving the problem of excessive numbers of variables and their consequent collinearity, since all of the individual-level variables may be summarized into a single composite variable at the school level.

Effect of Quantity of Schooling: An Empirical Example

In the first section of this chapter we criticized the simplistic question: Does schooling have an effect? In its place, we substituted the question: How much of an effect does schooling have? Instead of attempting to establish the existence of schooling effects, we will analyze the relations between the quantity of schooling and quantitative measures of educational achievement. On the basis of the model outlined in the second section, we will give a concrete example of an analysis of the relationship between the amount of schooling and educational achievement. The data were obtained from the Detroit Metropolitan Area sixth-grade sample of the *Equality of Educational Opportunity* survey and had already been "laundered" to facilitate analyses.

Our model involves three categories of variables:

1. outcome variables,
2. variables defined at the school level,
3. explanatory variables defined at the level of the individual.

For the *outcome* category, we selected from the Coleman *et al.* survey the three variables that were most closely related to academic achievement: verbal ability, reading comprehension, and mathematics achievement. The *school* variables were chosen in order to derive an overall index of the quantity of schooling: Average Daily Attendance, number of hours in the school day, and number of days in the school year. As *individual*-level home background variables, we selected those most likely to be accurate indicators of the pupils' social background and home environment: the variables directly observable by the individual child. Indicators requiring inferences on the part of the child, such as parental education and occupation, are likely to be reported much less accurately than indicators which are observable to the child in his day-to-day environment. In their analysis of children's reports of father's occupation and parental education, Kerckhoff, Mason, and Poss (1973) find large reporting errors which are systematically related to actual parental status. This type of error has especially drastic consequences for regression analysis. The individual-level home background variables selected were the following: race, number of children in the child's family, and number of possessions in the child's home.

The selected variables were based on items and indices from the Coleman *et al.* (1966) survey. A detailed description of the variables follows.

1. *Outcome variables.* The verbal ability test was based on two sub-tests, a sentence completion and a synonym test, both of which were drawn from the Educational Testing Service's School and College Ability Test series. The test of reading comprehension was taken from the ETS Sequential Tests of Educational Progress (STEP) and required the pupils to answer questions identifying, interpreting, extracting and drawing inferences from passages of prose and poetry. The mathematics test was also selected from the STEP series. It consists of a series of verbally stated applied mathematics problems. All tests were scored with the number of correct responses.

2. *School variables.* Average Daily Attendance, defined as the average proportion of pupils attending a particular school during the school year in question, was obtained from the responses to the principal questionnaire.[15]

---

[15] The question is Number 42 on the principal questionnaire (Coleman *et al.*, 1966:662).
   42. About what is the average daily percentage of attendance in your school?
      (A) Over 98%
      (B) 97–98%
      (C) 95–96%
      (D) 93–94%

Number of hours in the school day was obtained from the principal questionnaire[16] and number of days in the school year from the superintendent questionnaire.[17] The total number of effective hours of schooling for an average child in a particular school was defined as a product of these three variables yielding a number in the metric of hours per year. It should be noted that the effective-hours-per-year variable is an exact composition of these three variables.

    3. *Individual explanatory variables.* The individual variables were obtained from the pupil questionnaire. The item on the pupil's race asked the pupil to choose one of five alternatives which he considered to best describe him.[18] The item on children asked for the number of children in the

---

    (E) 91–92%
    (F) 86–90%
    (G) 85% or lower
    These responses were coded: .99, .97, .95, .93, .91, .88, and .83, respectively. Missing data were coded .90.

[16] The question is Number 76 on the principal questionnaire (Coleman *et al.,* 1966:667).
    76. Approximately how long is the academic school day for pupils?
        (A) 4 hours or less
        (B) $4_{1/2}$ hours
        (C) 5 hours
        (D) $5_{1/2}$ hours
        (E) 6 hours
        (F) $6_{1/2}$ hours
        (G) 7 hours
        (H) $7_{1/2}$ hours
        (I) 8 hours or more
        These responses were coded: 4.0, 4.5, 5.0, 5.5, 6.0, 6.5, 7.0, 7.5, and 8.0, respectively. Missing data were coded as 5.5.
[17] The question is Number 34(A) on the superintendent questionnaire (Coleman *et al.,* 1966:700).
    34. Length of school term *1964–65*
        (A) The school year for *pupils:* How many *days* was school in session during the 1964–65 school year?
        (B) The school year for *classroom teachers:* How many *days,* including those when pupils were present, were teachers required to work?
    These responses were coded in exactly the same way as they were given.
[18] The question is Number 4 on the pupil questionnaire (Coleman *et al.,* 1966:628).
    4. Which one of the following best describes you?
        (A) Negro
        (B) White
        (C) American Indian
        (D) Oriental
        (E) Other
    These responses were coded: White—1, Negro—0. Individuals who responded in any other way or who did not respond at all were eliminated from the analyses of these data.

family.[19] The variable, possessions in the child's home, was measured by summing the number of yes-responses to nine items. The child was asked if his family has a television set, telephone, record player (including hi-fi or stereo), refrigerator, dictionary, encyclopedia, automobile, or vacuum cleaner, or if his family gets a newspaper every day.[20]

Figure 8.1, which graphically illustrates the conceptual model linking these variables, shows the nine basic variables in the three categories. If we pick a particular outcome variable and focus on the implications of the model for a school-level analysis, then we need to consider three variables, and they correspond to the categories in the diagram. These variables are an achievement outcome, the summary measure of quantity of schooling, and the aggregate pupil background composite. In a complete analysis of these data, we would attempt to explain the quantity of schooling that a child receives by means of our background measure and then explain achievement by both background and quantity of schooling. This complete model is reflected in the diagram by the arrows linking the categories. However, the determination of quantity of schooling by pupil background does not require explication to validly analyze the subsequent determination of achievement by background and schooling. We will concentrate on the analysis of achievement.In Section II, we described a model and two data analysis processes consistent with that model. The first process was a

[19] The question is Number 8 on the pupil questionnaire (Coleman *et al.*, 1966:628).
  8. How many children (under 18) are in your family? Count yourself.
    (A) 1—only me
    (B) 2
    (C) 3
    (D) 4
    (E) 5
    (F) 6
    (G) 7
    (H) 8
    (I) 9
    (J) 10 or more
    These responses were coded using the numbers given in the alternatives.
[20] The questions are Numbers 19 through 27 on the pupil questionnaire (Coleman *et al.*, 1966:629–630).
  19. Does your family have a television set?
    (A) Yes
    (B) No
  20. Does your family have a telephone?
    (A) Yes
    (B) No
  21. Does your family have a record player, hi-fi, or stereo?
    (A) Yes
    (B) No
  22. Does your family have a refrigerator?
    (A) Yes
    (B) No

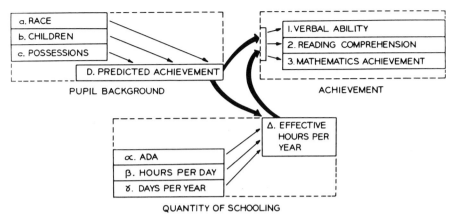

Figure 8.1 Basic model.

method of analysis that produced adjusted estimates of the effects of the individually defined variables. These estimates were to be computed from within-school regression analyses of the outcomes on the explanatory variables. This was actually accomplished by an analysis of variance and covariance. In addition to the adjustment of school-level effects, other parts of the variance and covariance analyses were used to characterize the extensiveness of the adjustments. The summary data set needed to perform the appropriate regression analysis is the pooled within-school covariance matrix. This within-school matrix is summarized in the form of the intercorrelation matrix of the individually defined variables together with their standard deviations in Table 8.1. The variance breakdown among and within schools for these six variables is given in the analyses of variance reported in Table 8.2.

---

23. Does your family have a dictionary?
    (A) Yes
    (B) No
24. Does your family have an encyclopedia?
    (A) Yes
    (B) No
25. Does your family have an automobile?
    (A) Yes
    (B) No
26. Does your family have a vacuum cleaner?
    (A) Yes
    (B) No
27. Does your family get a newspaper every day?
    (A) Yes
    (B) No
    The variable was coded as the total number of yes responses to the nine items. All other responses, including missing, did not contribute to the score.

TABLE 8.1

Within-School Standard Deviations and Correlations of Individual-Level Variables

	a	b	c	1	2	3	Standard Deviation
a. Race	1.000						0.302
b. Children	-0.061	1.000					2.195
c. Possessions	-0.008	-0.119	1.000				1.574
1. Verbal	0.135	-0.113	0.216	1.000			9.310
2. Reading	0.118	-0.082	0.165	0.765	1.000		6.751
3. Mathematics	0.173	-0.089	0.119	0.636	0.620	1.000	4.490

It is clear from that table that pupils are not randomly distributed among schools with respect to any of the background or achievement variables. Table 8.5 (Column 1), which reports the intraclass correlations (proportions of variance accounted for by schools) for each of these variables, shows that the largest degree of nonrandom allocation occurs for race (64% of the variance is among schools). The achievement variables and the possessions variable had between $11\frac{1}{2}$% and $15\frac{1}{2}$% of their variation among schools. The differences among schools were relatively small for the children variable

TABLE 8.2

Analyses of Variance for Individual-Level Variables

Source of Variation	Degree of Freedom	Mean Square	F-ratio
Among Schools	39		
a. Race		10.466	114.477
b. Children		22.813	4.736
c. Possessions		24.953	10.069
1. Verbal		883.355	10.192
2. Reading		423.976	9.304
3. Mathematics		256.406	12.719
Within Schools	2518		
a. Race		0.091	
b. Children		4.817	
c. Possessions		2.478	
1. Verbal		86.668	
2. Reading		45.571	
3. Mathematics		20.160	

TABLE 8.3

Results of the Within-School Regression Analyses for the Outcome Variables Using the Explanatory Variables

	Outcome Variable					
	1. Verbal		2. Reading		3. Mathematics	
Explanatory Variable	Coefficient	Standard Error	Coefficient	Standard Error	Coefficient	Standard Error
a. Race	4.053	0.593	2.591	0.436	2.526	0.289
b. Children	0.342	0.082	0.171	0.061	-0.134	0.040
c. Possessions	1.225	0.114	0.684	0.084	0.322	0.056
Squared Multiple Correlation (R^2)	0.072		0.045		0.049	
Standard Error of Estimate	8.976		6.602		4.382	

($5\frac{1}{2}\%$). These results are consistent with earlier analyses which found that by far the largest proportion of the variance was within rather than among schools.

One question to be asked, however, is: How much of the variation in the achievement scores among schools can be accounted for by the background variables, that is, how much of a difference in the among-school variation of achievement will adjustment for background make? In order to answer this question, we must examine the results of regressions of the achievement variables on the background variables within schools. The results of these regression analyses are presented in Table 8.3.

The percentages of variance explained—within school—are relatively small, ranging from $4\frac{1}{2}\%$ for reading to 7% for verbal ability. The results, however, in terms of the regression coefficients, are quite consistent from variable to variable and are rather precisely estimated. The difference between the races is 4 points on the verbal score and $2\frac{1}{2}$ on both reading comprehension and mathematics achievement. Each additional child in the family lowers the verbal score by about a third of a point and the reading and mathematics scores by .17 and .13 points, respectively. Each additional possession raises the verbal score by $1\frac{1}{4}$ points and the reading and mathematics scores by .7 and .3 points. The standard errors of these coefficients are uniformly small, relative to the sizes of the coefficients, indicating that none of the estimates are consistent with an hypothesis of no effect.

The results of the analyses of covariance, based on these regression analyses, are reported in Table 8.4. These results indicate that even after adjustment for the background variables, there is still nonrandom variation in the school achievement means for each of the outcome variables. When we turn to Table 8.5 again, however, we find that although there is nonrandom variation among schools after adjustment, it is much less than before adjustment. Table 8.5 (Column 2) displays the intraclass correlations (proportions of variance accounted for by schools) of the achievement variables after adjustment. These correlations are much smaller than the unadjusted ones. Column 3 displays the percentage change due to the adjustment. The largest adjustment occurs in the mathematics school means (82%), followed by verbal ability (75%) and reading (59%). Since all of the adjustments reduce the variance among schools by more than 50%, the adjustment obviously should have an important effect on the analysis of the school variation. Table 8.6 presents the correlations and standard deviations of the adjusted achievement variables within schools. The correlations and standard deviations are marginally smaller than before adjustment. These minimal adjustment effects were expected from the low values of the squared multiple correlations (Table 8.3). Note that there is no necessary relationship between the extent of adjustment for the within school versus among school variation. In this particular case, the adjustment was based on a within school analysis, and variation among schools had no influence. However, it made little difference within schools while having a quite large effect on the differences among schools.

TABLE 8.4

Analyses of Covariance for Outcome Variables, Adjusted for Explanatory Variables

Source of Variation	Degree of Freedom	Mean Square	F-ratio
Among Schools	39		
a. Verbal		246.183	3.056
b. Reading		182.880	4.195
c. Mathematics		51.857	2.701
Within Schools	2515		
1. Verbal		80.560	
2. Reading		43.591	
3. Mathematics		19.198	

The next stage in the analysis is to produce a school-level variable based on the adjusted effect values of the background variables. Since, in the analysis of covariance, the adjusted effects for the schools are equal to their unadjusted means minus the aggregated effect values, the aggregated effect values may be computed for each outcome variable by subtracting the adjusted from the unadjusted school means. Since the analysis of covariance subsumed the basic analysis, this method, which is an especially simple means of calculating the aggregate effects of the background variables, was used. Because of this method of calculation, the overall mean has been removed from each of the aggregated background variables. These variables, which are each in the metric of the corresponding achievement variable, will henceforce be labeled "predicted" (e.g., predicted verbal ability). The school means for verbal ability and predicted verbal ability (with the overall mean added back) are displayed in stem and leaf diagrams in Table 8.7.[21] The summary data for the predicted and

[21] The stem and leaf diagram (Tukey, 1970) is a method of displaying the data. It gives information about their distributional form as well as their actual values. In Table 8.7, the integer parts of the values are displayed between the parallel vertical lines, and the first decimal digits are displayed outside of those lines.

TABLE 8.5

Intraclass Correlations (Proportions of Variance Accounted for by Schools) of Individual-Level Variables and Outcome Variables, Adjusted for the Explanatory Variables, Together with Percent Change after Adjustment

Variables	(1) Unadjusted Intraclass Correlation	(2) Adjusted Intraclass Correlation	(3) Percent Change
Explanatory			
a. Race	0.640		
b. Children	0.055		
c. Possessions	0.124		
Outcome			
1. Verbal	0.126	0.031	75.2
2. Reading	0.116	0.048	58.9
3. Mathematics	0.155	0.028	82.0

unadjusted school achievement means are presented in Table 8.8, which shows their intercorrelations, means, and standard deviations together with those of other variables to be described later. Several things should be noted about this table. The intercorrelations of the school achievement means are much higher than the within school values. The predicted values, based on the background variables, are intercorrelated uniformly highly (from .98 to 1.00). Each of the predicted values has the same pattern of intercorrelation with the school achievement means, and these relatively high intercorrelations are consistent from variable to variable with the extent of the adjustment indicated by the percentage changes in the intraclass correlations (Table 8.5).

The summary characteristics of the quantity of schooling variables, discussed earlier, are also reported in Table 8.8. The distributions of three indices, days per year, hours per day, and Average Daily Attendance (ADA), are displayed in histograms in Table 8.9. The product of the three

TABLE 8.6

Correlations and Standard Deviations of Outcome Variables,
Adjusted for Explanatory Variables

	1	2	3	Standard Deviation
1. Verbal	1.000			8.976
2. Reading	0.753	1.000		6.602
3. Mathematics	0.619	0.604	1.000	4.382

components, which we have called "effective number of hours of school-ing," is displayed in a stem and leaf diagram in Table 8.10.

A parallel diagram shows the natural logarithms of those values. After inspecting the interrelations between these variables and the other vari-ables in the model, it became clear that uniformly more linear relations were obtained after logarithmic transformations than before these transfor-mations. This can be seen in rows 7 and 8 of the intercorrelation matrix of Table 8.8. The logarithm of "effective hours per year" is uniformly more highly correlated with all of the other variables than is the untransformed variable. The analyses, subsequently reported in this chapter, all use the natural logarithms of the quantity variables.

A regression analysis was performed employing two explanatory vari-ables for each of the three outcomes. The variables were the logarithm of the effective number of hours of schooling per year and the corresponding predicted value variable based on the three pupil background indices. The results of these analyses are given in Table 8.11. The Ln(effective hours per year) explanatory variable is related to each outcome. Typically, the ratio of the coefficient to its standard error is about three. The predicted outcome in each case has a coefficient (estimate of λ) significantly greater than one. This implies that, in fact, some of the specification error in the school-level model has been eliminated. The most encouraging finding, however, is the detectible impact of schooling on achievement.

The coefficients for Ln(effective hours per year) are 9.58, 9.57, and 4.08

TABLE 8.7

Stem and Leaf Diagrams for Aggregate Unadjusted and Predicted Achievement

	Average Achievement	Stem	Average Predicted Achievement	
Average	3	21		Average Predicted
Achievement	661	22		Achievement
	63	23		
	63	24		
Mean = 28.446	8871	25	67899	Mean = 28.445
Median = 28.62	41	26	12344556779	Median = 27.80
Standard Deviation	4110	27	3446	Standard Deviation
= 3.858	99851	28	018	= 2.196
Range = 14.60	5	29	148	Range = 6.49
	9884	30	23779	
	885210	31	01123679	
	0	32	1	
	8	33		
	81	34		
	93	35		

for verbal, reading, and mathematics, respectively. This implies that it would take an increase of 11% in the amount of schooling to augment the verbal and reading scores by one point, while it would require an increase of 28% to obtain the same result in mathematics. The discrepancy for mathematics achievement is not too surprising. Its standard deviation is only a little greater than two at the school level, while that of verbal ability is almost four. This discrepancy most likely reflects arbitrary differences in the measurement of these variables. What is surprising, however, is that the effect of schooling on reading comprehension is as large as that for verbal ability. The standard deviation for reading is only half a point higher than that for mathematics. If that value reflects the metric of the variable in

TABLE 8.8

Means, Standard Deviations, and Correlations of Aggregated Outcome Variables, Predicted Variables, and School-Level Explanatory Variables (N = 40 Schools)

	1'.	2'.	3'.	D1'.	D2'.	D3'.	Δ.	Δ'.	α'.	β'.	Y'.	Mean	Standard Deviation
1'. Verbal	1.000											28.446	3.859
2'. Reading	.919	1.000										19.228	2.585
3'. Mathematics	.896	.850	1.000									12.081	2.112
D1'. Predicted Verbal	.877	.782	.923	1.000								-.001	2.196
D2'. Predicted Reading	.865	.773	.922	.999	1.000							.000	1.342
D3'. Predicted Mathematics	.813	.732	.914	.978	.984	1.000						-.017	1.199
Δ. Effective Hours/Year	.387	.455	.345	.224	.218	.212	1.000					962.621	78.980
Δ'. Ln(Effective Hours/Year)	.403	.473	.360	.233	.227	.224	–	1.000				6.866	0.085
α'. Ln(Days/Year)	-.001	.001	.057	.101	.098	.151	–	.190	1.000			5.218	0.020
β'. Ln(ADA)	.219	.268	.170	.142	.125	.074	–	.299	.160	1.000		-0.085	0.030
Y'. Ln(Hours/Day)	.341	.395	.299	.166	.167	.170	–	.889	-.111	-.103	1.000	1.733	0.081

TABLE 8.9

Histograms for the Components of Quantity of Schooling

Days/Year

170	X
171	
172	
173	
174	
175	
176	
177	
178	
179	
180	XXXXXX
181	
182	XX
183	XX
184	XXXX
185	X
186	XXXXXXXXXXXXXXX
187	XXXXXX
188	X
189	
190	X
191	
192	X

Average Daily Attendance

83	X
84	
85	
86	
87	
88	XXXXX
89	
90	XX
91	XXXXXXXXXXX
92	
93	XXXXXXXXXXXXXX
94	
95	XXXXXX
96	
97	XX

Hours/Day

40	X
45	
50	X
55	XXXXXXXXXXXXXXXXXXXXXX
60	XXXXXXXXXXXXX
65	XXX

TABLE 8.10

Stem and Leaf Diagrams of Original and Ln-Transformed Values of Effective Numbers of Hours of Schooling per Year

Original Values[a]		Ln Original Values	
7	1	6.5	
7		6.5	6
8	2	6.6	
8	67	6.6	
9	02222333334444	6.7	1
9	5556667799	6.7	57
10	0012444	6.8	02222344444
10	668	6.8	5555666678899
11	1	6.9	112244
11	5	6.9	5779
		7.0	1
		7.0	5

[a]These values were divided by 10.

the same way that we assumed for the verbal and mathematics measurements, then this implies a much larger impact of schooling on reading than on verbal and mathematics achievement. A deeper assessment of the degree of impact of schooling on these variables will, however, be presented later; it involves comparisons to typical yearly increases in achievement.

The pattern of predictability of the outcome variables at the school level does not follow the pattern established in the within school regressions. The rank order of the variables, in terms of variance accounted for at the school level, is mathematics (86%), verbal (81%), and reading (69%). The mathematics and verbal variables have changed places in the rank ordering, and now those two variables are close and clearly higher than reading comprehension. In the within school analyses, verbal ability was discrepantly high.

An essential question concerning the analysis and the model on which it is based was raised earlier: Does schooling and the child's success within

TABLE 8.11

Results of Regression Analyses for Outcome Variables Using Ln(Effective Hours per Year) and Predicted Outcomes

| | Outcome Variables | | | | | |
| | 1. Verbal | | 2. Reading | | 3. Mathematics | |
Explanatory Variable	Coefficient	Standard Error	Coefficient	Standard Error	Coefficient	Standard Error
Constant	-37.34	----	-46.50	----	-15.93	----
Δ.Ln(Effective Hours/Year)	9.58	3.35	9.57	2.87	4.08	1.57
D. Predicted Outcome	1.46	0.13	1.35	0.18	1.55	0.11
Squared Multiple Correlation (R^2)	0.811		0.691		0.861	
Standard Error of Estimate	1.72		1.48		0.81	

the system influence attendance? This question must be answered with reference to a more complex model in which achievement influences attendance and vice versa. This "simultaneity" precludes the use of ordinary regression analysis as a method of estimating and testing the model. We have, however, attempted to explore the consequences of such an effect in order to discern possible biases that its exclusion from our model might have introduced. Fitting a model, which allows reciprocal influences, only slightly modifies the estimate of the effect of quantity of schooling. In the example that we analyzed extensively (verbal ability), the coefficient for Ln(effective number of hours per year) decreases from 9.58 to 8.85 after correction for the simultaneous determination of ADA and achievement.[22] This implies that the possibility that attendance may be

[22] In order to fit a simultaneous model for ADA and verbal ability, we must partially disaggregate the quantity-of-schooling variable into two parts: ADA and maximum number of hours of schooling per year. The school level variables used in this analysis are defined as follows:

1. z = predicted verbal ability
2. x_1 = ln(ADA)
3. x_2 = ln(maximum hours/year)
      = ln(hours/day) + ln(days/year)
4. x = $x_1 + x_2$ = ln(effective hours/year)
5. y = verbal ability

The model stated mathematically is:

(1) $$x_1 = \beta z + \lambda y + \theta$$
(2) $$x = x_1 + x_2$$
(3) $$y = \alpha x + \gamma z + \phi$$
$$= \alpha x_1 + \alpha x_2 + \gamma z + \phi,$$

which is simultaneous in y and x_1.
A path diagram illustrating the model is given in figure 8.2.

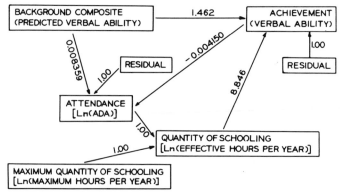

Figure 8.2 Path diagram for the simultaneous determination of ADA and verbal ability.

determined by achievement and vice versa does not affect the model substantially.

Another question left unanswered thus far concerns the simple product form of the aggregation of the three components of the quantity-of-schooling variable. The original effective-hours-per-year variable is the triple product of ADA, hours per day, and days per year. This implies that the logarithm of effective hours per year is the sum of the logarithms of ADA, hours per day, and days per year. Since the test of the simple product form involves comparing the adequacy of a model that uses the simple aggregate variable only with the adequacy of a model that uses each of the components of the aggregate as individual variables, the logarithmic transformation allows the specification of the latter model in a linear additive form rather than as a triple product. This greatly simplifies the estimation of the parameters in the disaggregated model and, thus, facilitates the comparison. Specifically, if those components are simply aggregable, then the regression coefficients for each of the three components should be equal to one another and to the coefficient for the aggregate variable.[23] We may test this hypothesis by performing a regression analysis using each of the three components as separate variables and comparing the result with the result of an analysis performed with the aggregate variable alone. The first analysis allows the coefficients for the three components to be different from one another, while the second analysis forces each of them to be equal to the coefficient for the aggregated variable. If the disaggregated analysis accounts for a larger proportion of the variance than the aggregated analysis, then only weighted versions of the variables can be consistently aggregated.

Table 8.12 summarizes the analyses of variance for testing this hypothesis. The sum of squares for the hypothesis of equality, for each outcome, is equal to the difference between the squared multiple correlations in the two analyses. The residual sum of squares is equal to one minus the squared multiple correlation from the disaggregated analysis, and it has as its

---

The estimates of the parameters obtained—any method of estimation will produce the same values since the model is just identified—are:

$$\hat{\beta} = .008359$$
$$\hat{\gamma} = 1.462$$
$$\hat{\alpha} = 8.846$$
$$\hat{\lambda} = -.004150.$$

[23] This is true because the aggregated model is:

$y = \alpha + \beta \ln(\text{effective hours per year}) + \gamma z + \epsilon$
$\quad = \alpha + \beta \ln[(\text{ADA})(\text{hours/day})(\text{days/year})] + \gamma z + \epsilon$
$\quad = \alpha + \beta [\ln(\text{ADA}) + \ln(\text{hours/day}) + \ln(\text{days/year})] + \gamma z + \epsilon$
$\quad = \alpha + \beta \ln(\text{ADA}) + \beta \ln(\text{hours/day}) + \beta \ln(\text{days/year}) + \gamma z + \epsilon$

This is just the disaggregated model for the logarithms of the components with coefficients all equal to β, which is the coefficient for effective hours per year in the aggregated model.

TABLE 8.12
Analyses of Variance for Testing the Hypothesis of Equality of Regression Coefficients for the
Logarithms of the Components of Effective Hours per Year of Schooling

Source of Variation	Sum of Squares	Degree of Freedom	Mean Square	F-ratio	Probability
1. Verbal					
Hypothesis	.019	2	.00950	1.955	$.10 < p < .25$
Residual	.170	35	.00486		
Total	.189	37			
2. Reading					
Hypothesis	.028	2	.01400	1.743	$.10 < p < .25$
Residual	.281	35	.00803		
Total	.309	37			
3. Mathematics					
Hypothesis	.017	2	.00850	2.436	$p \approx .10$
Residual	.122	35	.00349		
Total	.139	37			

degrees of freedom the number of observations (schools) minus the number of parameters fitted in that model (40 minus 1—for the constant term— minus 4—for the regression coefficients—equals 35). The degrees of freedom for the hypothesis equal the difference between the number of parameters fitted in the disaggregated model and the number fitted in the aggregated model (5 − 3 = 2).

The probability levels for the tests of the aggregability hypothesis for each of the outcome variables did not reach significance. These results are not cause for doubting our original hypothesis of the simple aggregability of our quantity variable. This simple aggregability implies that a change in the total effective number of hours of schooling will have the same effect regardless of whether the change is in ADA, hours per day, or days per year. If this were not true, then a 10% increase in the quantity of schooling would have had different consequences for achievement depending on the mode of change. In the extreme, these components certainly ought to have detectibly different effects: Increasing the length of the school day by 10%, if pupils have already a long school day, would probably not have as large an impact as increasing the length of a long school year by an equivalent amount. The simple aggregability only holds when the values of the variables are near those in our sample.

A key question in interpreting the results of the final analyses is: Do these estimated effects of the quantity of schooling tell us anything of practical importance for educational policy? In order to answer this, we must determine whether or not feasible manipulations of the quantity of schooling result in valuable increases in the amount of achievement. First, we must define these manipulations and determine the value of their consequences. It seems that changes in the number of days in the school year, in the number of hours in the school day, and in the Average Daily Attendance are reasonable and practical policy moves. In fact, at the moment, such changes are being made in many school districts to save money. However, this is being done without prior knowledge of the consequences.

In the state of Michigan, the minimum length of the school year required by law is 180 days. All of the schools in the sample (Table 8.9), except one, are at or above the minimum level, and two of the schools met for 190 days or more. A possible increase in the length of the school year for some Detroit schools, whose cost could be evaluated, would be from 180 to 190 days. If the number of hours per day and the ADA in those schools remained the same, this manipulation would result in a 5.5% increase in the quantity of schooling (190/180 = 1.0555).

The consequences of manipulations of the total amount of schooling are shown in Table 8.13. The aforementioned policy action and its consequences are displayed in the first row of the table. Column 1 gives the assumed initial value of the policy variable. Column 2 the goal value, and Column 3 the percentage change. Columns 4, 7, and 10 list the changes in the score points in verbal ability, reading comprehension, and mathematics

TABLE 8.13

The Predicted Effects of Various Policy Manipulations in Quantity of Schooling

Policy Variable	Δ. Quantity of Schooling			1. Verbal Ability			2. Reading Comprehension			3. Mathematics Achievement		
	(1) Assumed Initial Value	(2) Assumed Goal Value	(3) Percent Change	(1) Score Point Change	(2) Month-Equivalent Change	(3) Year-Percent Change	(1) Score Point Change	(2) Month-Equivalent Change	(3) Year-Percent Change	(1) Score Point Change	(2) Month-Equivalent Change	(3) Year-Percent Change
γ. Days/Year	180	190	5.55	.52	1.00	8.33	.52	1.97	16.42	.22	1.00	8.33
β. Hours/Day	5.0	5.5	10.00	.91	1.76	14.67	.91	3.44	28.67	.39	1.78	14.83
	5.5	6.0	9.09	.83	1.60	13.33	.83	3.13	26.08	.35	1.60	13.33
α. ADA	.88	.95	7.95	.73	1.41	11.75	.73	2.76	23.00	.31	1.42	11.83
Δ. Hours/Year	871[a]	1083[aa]	24.34	2.09	4.03	33.58	2.08	7.86	65.50	.89	4.07	33.92

[a] (180)(5.5)(.88) = 871

[aa] (190)(6.0)(.95) = 1083

achievement, respectively, that are expected on the basis of this assumed increase in quantity of schooling. This increase in the length of the school year is predicted to result in increases of .52, .52, and .22 score points for verbal ability, reading comprehension, and mathematics achievement.[24] Columns 5, 8, and 11 convert these score-point increases into grade-equivalent months.[25] These score-point increases correspond then to 1.00, 1.97, and 1.00 months. Columns 6, 9, and 12 express these grade-equivalent

---

[24] For example, the increase in verbal ability (.52), given in Column 4, was derived as follows: The predicted value based on the school-level regression of the number of verbal score points (y) for particular values of the quantity variable (x) and the predicted verbal outcome (z) is: $\hat{y} = \hat{\alpha} + \hat{\beta}lnx + \hat{\gamma}z$. ($\hat{\alpha}$, $\hat{\beta}$, and $\hat{\gamma}$ are, respectively, the estimates of the constant term and the regression coefficients for the quantity variable and the predicted outcome.) The difference between the predicted values for 190 and 180 days of schooling is:

$$\hat{y}_{190} - \hat{y}_{180} = \hat{\alpha} + \hat{\beta}ln[(ADA)(hours/day)(190)] + \hat{\gamma}z$$
$$- \hat{\alpha} - \hat{\beta}ln[(ADA)(hours/day)(180)] - \hat{\gamma}z$$
$$= \hat{\beta}ln(190) - \hat{\beta}ln(180) = \hat{\beta}ln(190/180)$$
$$= \hat{\beta}ln(1.0555) = (9.58)(.054) = .52 \text{ points.}$$

Because of the logarithmic transformation, the components for ADA and hours per day are additive and subtract out along with the other parts of the equation which remain constant when the difference is calculated.

[25] The grade-equivalence conversions were established as follows: In the *Equality of Educational Opportunity* report (Tables 3.121.1, 3.121.2, and 3.121.3: 274–75), the standard deviation and grade-equivalent gaps between various subpopulations are given for verbal, reading, and mathematics test scores. Their ratios yield estimates of the standard deviation–grade equivalence conversion for each achievement variable. The midmeans—defined as the average of the middle 50% of the observations—for each variable were used as estimates of the conversions (see Tukey, 1970). This was done because it is less sensitive than the mean to extreme values, caused here by the report's rounding process. The following estimates were obtained for the grade-equivalent of one standard deviation.

Verbal Ability:	1.60 years
Reading Comprehension:	2.25 years
Mathematics Achievement:	1.86 years

These values were then used to calculate the score point equivalents in grade units. The standard deviations, used for conversions, were those of the Detroit sample.

The verbal ability standard deviation, for example, is 9.96 score points. Consequently, 9.96 points is estimated to be equivalent to 1.60 years or 19.2 months [$=(1.60)(12)$]. If we divide this by 9.96, we obtain an equivalence of one score point to 1.93 months ($=19.2/9.96$). This value is close to Jencks' (1972a:112) equivalent of approximately two months to one score point. The results of applying this strategy to all three variables are as follows.

Verbal Ability:	1.93 months
Reading Comprehension:	3.78 months
Mathematics Achievement:	4.57 months

increases as percentages of a year (12 months). This conversion results in increases of 8.33, 16.42, and 8.33%.

We obtain somewhat larger effects if we change hours per day or ADA. An additional half hour in the school day (10% increase of a 5-hour day and 9% increase of a 5½-hour day) increases verbal ability and mathematics achievement by about 14% and reading comprehension by about 27%. Augmenting ADA from 88 to 95% improves these achievements about 12, 12, and 23%, respectively. If we simultaneously change days, hours (from 5 to 5½), and ADA, the consequent 24% increase in total effective hours of schooling results in 34, 34, and 66% gains in achievement.

Since we assume that a given percentage increase in schooling—Column 3—ought, on the average, to correspond to about the same percentage increase in achievement—Columns 6, 9, and 12—we are quite pleased with the predicted results of our policy actions: In every case, the gain in achievement exceeds the increase in schooling. Based on our estimates, Figure 8.3 displays in graphical form the expected percentage increase in each of the outcome variables for various percentages of increase in the quantity of schooling.

For verbal ability and mathematics achievement the ratios of the two percentage increases range from about 1.4 to 1.5, while for reading they range from 2.7 to 3.0. These results imply useful and important consequences of practicable manipulations of the amount of schooling for all outcomes. The benefits for reading comprehension even substantially exceed those for verbal ability and mathematics achievement.

We should also consider the precision of the computation of the expected consequences of policy manipulations. The coefficients from our analyses are not the real effects but only estimates of them. Therefore, the precision of the estimates must be considered in assessing the likely consequences of policy actions.

For example, the coefficient for quantity of schooling in the explanation of reading comprehension was 9.57, and its standard error was 2.87 (Table 8.11). If we establish a confidence interval for the coefficient—using the rough guide that 95% confidence may be placed in an interval bounded by the coefficient plus or minus twice its standard error—we obtain an interval indicating that the minimum effect of quantity of schooling on reading comprehension is 3.83 while the maximum is 15.31. These values can be used to predict the maximum and minimum changes in score points of a particular policy action in the same way that we calculated earlier the best single estimate of the change using the regression coefficient itself. If we do this for the policy action of increasing the total number of hours of schooling from 871 to 1083 (24% increase), we obtain a minimum score point increase in reading comprehension of .83 and a maximum of 3.34. This corresponds to a minimum increase of 3.15 grade-equivalent months and a maximum of 12.61 months, which are 26.3 and 100.5% of a grade-equivalent year, respectively. The minimum and maximum ratios of gain in achievement to increase in schooling are 1.08 and 4.13. These results are not only consistent with the inference of large effects of schooling, they imply them.

The purpose of presenting this example in such great detail was twofold. First, we wished to carry through, in a clearly understandable fashion, the application of what we think is the appropriate methodology for exploring the effects of schooling. Second, we wished to apply this methodology along a substantive path which will bring us to useful policy results in the assessment of school effects. We do not believe that our results have taken us to the end of that path, but we feel that these analyses lead in a new direction.

Our results should raise questions that are related to prior expectations about the effects of schooling: Is it reasonable to expect that a 24% increase in the quantity of schooling should result in a 65% gain in reading comprehension? Is this too large? If yes, why? Has the analysis been ineffective in controlling for pupil background? Is the quantity of schooling so stable over time that our analysis reflects the impact of more than one year? Is the Detroit sample atypical? These are the kinds of questions that need exploration if we are to produce a scientifically justifiable assessment of the effects of schooling.

Conclusions

A new mythology of schooling is snowing us. Based on a confusion between poor detective work and no clues, it tries to convince us of what is manifestly not true: Schooling has no effect. Instead of asking the inadequate question: Does schooling have an effect? We ask: What is the effect of a particular amount of schooling? The answer to the first question

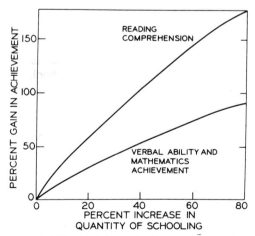

Figure 8.3 Percentage gain in grade-equivalent achievement for various percentages of increase in quantity of schooling.

must be "yes," regardless of the results of simplistic data analyses and their even more simplistic interpretations.

Our question would be a futile one if all pupils received the same amount of schooling. In fact, there are tremendous variations in the amounts of schooling pupils receive.

We view both schooling and its outcomes as quantitative phenomena. Consequently, our basic concerns are the measurement of: quantity of schooling, quantity of outcome, and the relationship between the two.

If our conceptualization of the effects of schooling is reasonable, why has this perspective never been taken before in the assessment of school effects? We have taken considerable space in an attempt to show that the most influential study of the effects of schooling, the Coleman *et al.* (1966) survey, from its original report to the most recent reanalyses of its data, has focused so intensely on issues of the allocation, to schools, of resources—such as, teacher training, textbooks, physics laboratories, and remedial instruction—that more general and basic sources of school effects, such as quantity of schooling, were neglected. All of these have mired in the swamps of inappropriate methodologies as well as the mudholes of conceptual misdirection.

As a path to dry land, we proposed unstandardized regression analysis, at the level of the school, with small numbers of conceptually well defined variables. These include, most importantly, a measure of the quantity of schooling.

To guide application, we have discussed in detail the logic of data analyses intended to assess the effects of schooling. The distinctive structure of these multi-level data requires special treatment and involves variables in at least three categories: outcome, school, and pupil. Outcome and pupil variables are defined for each individual, while school variables have the same values for all individuals in a particular school. Complete data sets may involve variables defined at many additional levels, such as state, school district, or teacher–classroom.

The problems inherent in data of this kind, especially those involving adjustment of variables in one category for those in another, have led to the formulation of a general statistical model. The elaboration of this model and a set of data analysis procedures consistent with it concretize our proposal for school-level unstandardized regression analysis. It also specifies a conceptually well-defined composite variable summarizing pupil-family-background variables.

Finally, we have detailed an empirical example of the application of the conceptual structure, statistical model, and analysis procedures to data from the Coleman *et al.* (1966) survey. Our intent was twofold: to illustrate our basic points in the most concrete fashion possible, and to provide a set of scientifically justifiable findings on the impact of schooling on achievement. We intended achievement to be only exemplary of the many effects of schooling. Some of the most important ones are very difficult to quantify. Our example was restricted because other data were not available.

We have concluded that

- our statistical model is useful for the generation of scientifically and policy useful analyses of schooling data;
- the quantity of schooling is an *important* determinant of achievement.

In addition, we have estimated the expected change in achievement for particular modifications in the quantity of schooling. We have also determined the effect of quantity of schooling in order to allow practicable policy actions with useful, predictable, and evaluatable implications.

Acknowledgments

The author wishes to thank Henry Levin for access to the data and for a critical comment, William Mason for his thoughtful and extensive criticisms, Richard Wolfe for insightful discussions concerning the statistical model, and especially Annegret Harnischfeger who participated in the statement of the thesis and the results so extensively that the main body of the paper grew from nine pages to its current length. Ward Keesling is a coinvestigator on this project and was of critical importance in the formulation of the structure of the analysis. Warm thanks to Angelika Neubauer for her assistance in typing the many drafts of this manuscript.

IX | A New Model of School Effectiveness[*]

Henry M. Levin
Stanford University

The effect of schools on the development of youngsters has been the subject of intensive study for at least 50 years. In most cases, the unit of analysis has been the classroom, where attempts are made to relate differences in environmental and instructional variables to differences in student performance. The usual approach has been to set up experimental and control groups, to apply the "treatment" to the experimental one, and to look for significant differences in outcomes between the two groups. Unfortunately, the extensive research utilizing this methodology has not come up with a reasonably consistent and reproducible set of findings on how differences in schools create differences in human development.

Certainly, one of the reasons for the inability of these experiments to provide useful conclusions is the assumption of ceteris paribus, that is, all other things being equal between control and experimental groups. The

* Reprinted from *Do Teachers Make a Difference?* A Report on Recent Research on Pupil Achievement. U.S. Department of Health, Education, and Welfare, Office of Education. U.S. Government Printing Office, Washington, D.C. 1970.

Research support has been provided by the Stanford Center for Research and Development in Teaching, and the editing of the data was done at the Brookings Institution. The Center for Educational Policy Research at Harvard supported some of the computational costs.

complexity of the world within which education takes place suggests, however, that observed similarities between control and experimental groups on one or two dimensions is not adequate for the ceteris paribus assumption. Many influences must be accounted for in seeking the determinants of scholastic achievement, attitude formation, and so on.

In the last decade, a number of studies have attempted to go beyond the standard type of educational experiment by using large-scale multivariate statistical models to account for many more variables than could be included in the typical control group–experimental group comparison. These studies have related the achievement of students to variables reflecting the student's race, socioeconomic status, teacher, and other school variables, as well as the characteristics of fellow students. The rather consistent set of findings emerging from these studies suggests that three measured factors are significantly related to student academic achievement: (1) race of student, (2) socioeconomic status of the student, and (3) characteristics of his teachers.[1]

Generally these studies have utilized survey data on student achievement, socioeconomic backgrounds, and school resources to explain variance in student achievement. Typically, their findings are based upon fitting a linear regression via the ordinary least-squares criterion for the following formulation.

$$A_{it} = f(B_{it}, S_{it}, O_{it})$$

A_{it} is the standardized achievement score of the ith student at time t; B_{it} represents a vector of family background characteristics at time t; S_{it} represents a vector of school resources, such as teacher characteristics, facilities, student environment created by peers, and so on at time t; and O_{it} represents community and other characteristics that might affect achievement. One might broadly conceive of them as attempts to estimate educational production functions. That is, studies of the educational production process are analogous to the econometric effort of estimating production processes in other industries.[2] While it is not the purpose of this study to review all of the properties of educational production functions and the problems encountered in estimating them, it is useful to briefly discuss a few of them.

Focus on a Single Output

Most studies of the educational production function have used standardized achievement scores as the output of the educational process. Yet,

---

[1] See the survey of these studies in Guthrie, Kleindorfer, Levin, and Stout (1971).

[2] For a survey of econometric work on production functions, see Walters (1963). The most comprehensive work on educational applications is Bowles (1970). The theory of production can be found in any basic text on econometrics; see, for example, Baumol (1963: Chapter 11).

schools are expected to produce many outcomes in addition to increasing academic achievement.[3] The acquisition of a variety of attitudes and skills, as well as many social externalities, are functions attributed to the schools (see Weisbrod, 1964). An empirical analysis of educational production that considers only one output ignores these others. Only if these other outcomes are produced in fixed proportion to the output under scrutiny, then no problem arises in focusing on a single output, such as standardized achievement.[4]

Ideally, the estimation of the educational production process should be based upon total educational output. That is, in some way, we would want to weight the outputs produced by some common factor (utilities, votes, social values) in order to obtain a total index of output. Multi-product firms that sell their outputs in the marketplace are able to obtain such a measure by using prices as weights to obtain a monetary value for total product. Unfortunately, we can neither measure all of the outputs that schools are supposed to produce nor do we possess a yardstick or *numéraire* with which to put them into an index of output.

This focus on achievement scores as the single measure of school output creates at least two problems in measuring the educational production process. First, the single focus on achievement limits the usefulness of educational production studies to providing insights for only one dimension of school output. The efficient ordering of inputs for producing achievement may be exceedingly inefficient for increasing student motivation, efficacy, imagination, and other desirable outcomes. This study will attempt to partly solve this problem by considering relationships among educational inputs and several outputs.

Second, estimates of the educational production process will underestimate the relationship between any single output and school resources as long as priorities for that output vary among schools. To take an extreme case, academic high schools tend to emphasize language skills much more heavily than do vocational high schools. Accordingly, equal resources devoted to both groups of schools, ceteris paribus, would likely have a greater impact on verbal achievement among the academic students than the vocational ones.

This relationship is further confounded if the priorities of schools vary according to the socioeconomic composition of their student bodies. Certainly, the middle-class schools are generally more academically oriented toward college preparation than are the lower-class schools, which seem to emphasize more heavily the general or job-oriented curriculums. In such a case, the socioeconomic background variables of the students act as a proxy for the emphasis on academic skills relative to other school goals, and their statistical importance in "producing" academic achievement

---

[3] For classifications of these, see Bloom (1956) and Krathwohl, Bloom, and Masia, 1964.

[4] There is no empirical verification of this assumption.

scores will be overstated while the impact of school resources will be understated.

Educational Production Theory and the Meaning of Production Data

Estimates of production functions in other industries are based upon the assumption that firms are maximizing output for any set of inputs; that is, firms are assumed to be technically efficient. Only under these conditions will estimates relating inputs to output reflect the most efficient way of producing that output.

This assumption presumes at least three general conditions: (1) The firm has knowledge of the relevant production set; (2) the firm has discretion over the way in which inputs are used; and (3) there is an effective incentive that spurs the firm to apply its knowledge of the production set and its ability to combine inputs into maximizing output for any set of physical inputs. Under these conditions, the observed production data depict the production frontier, the largest output attainable for each set of inputs. Whether these are valid presumptions for private firms may be open to question, but they are clearly inappropriate ones for the schools.[5] There is no basis for asserting that educational decision-makers know their relevant production sets or that they have a great deal of discretion over how their inputs are used. The present organization of school inputs tends to be based on sacrosanct traditions rather than management discretion. Finally, the incentives of the marketplace that spur firms to be technically (and allocatively) efficient—profits, sales, and so on—are conspicuously absent from the educational scene. In particular, there is no evidence that educational firms, such as schools and school districts, maximize standardized achievement. Thus, at best, the observations on inputs and outcomes represent average ones under the present state of operations, not maximum or technically efficient ones.

Moreover, the lack of knowledge on the relevant production set means that one cannot specify with reasonable accuracy the inputs germane to any particular output. Specification of the educational production model must depend more on intuition and hunch than on a body of well developed behavioral theory. That is, there is no validated theory of learning on human development that can be used as a guide in specifying inputs and the general functional relationships between inputs and outputs. In the absence of such a foundation, much of the early work in estimating educational production relations has necessarily been like a hunting expedition into the deep entangled forest of possible educational influences.

---

[5] For a discussion of their relevance to estimating production functions for industry, see Aigner and Chu (1968).

The problem with such an expedition is that we have been like hunters shooting at anything that moved since we have had no clear picture of the animals we wanted to collect.

A second and related problem is that even when we do know what kind of conceptual animal we wish to bag, we do not know how or where to capture it. Clearly, innate intelligence should be considered as an input when attempting to estimate the educational production function for achievement. Yet, like the mythical unicorn, much has been written about innate intelligence, but no one has ever seen one. That is, we have no way of measuring this important determinant of educational outcomes. Moreover, measures of teacher proficiency or other school inputs are not available. Rather, we must use conventional indicators, such as teacher experience, degree level, number of books in the library, and so on, in the hope of capturing some of the actual influences of which we are unaware or which we are unable to measure adequately.

Both not knowing how education is produced and not being able to measure many of the inputs results in a high probability of bias in the estimates of the production coefficients. The exclusion of variables that belong in the equation as well as the inclusion of erroneous variables all lead to such biases (Theil, 1957). Moreover, the fitting of such data to a linear function can also result in specification biases in a world that is characterized by nonlinearities. All of the empirical studies of the educational production process are prime candidates for such biases.

Data Refinement

Perhaps it is useful to divide data problems into two types: intransigent and remediable. In actuality, this dichotomy is a result of the state of the art. At a future time, intransigent difficulties may be alleviated by greater knowledge of the phenomenon or by better measurement techniques, such as our inability to measure innate abilities. As we noted earlier, the omission of such a variable is likely to introduce a bias in our estimates. In this case, it is important that we explore the biases of excluding such a measure in the specification of our production model, but we can do little beyond this.

On the other hand, data deficiencies arise that are partly or fully remediable. For example, a needed item is sufficiently measurable, but it was omitted from the survey on which the production estimates will be made. In this case, one can attempt to find a close proxy among the existing information source, or one can resurvey to obtain the missing item. The latter alternative is time consuming and costly, so the former course of action is often taken. Yet, the use of a proxy or surrogate piece of information is subject to the vagaries of interpretation, and its use may create more problems than it solves.[6] In many cases, it may be wise to acknowledge the omission and to speculate on the resulting bias rather than to use a questionable proxy.

In all too many instances, data problems are remediable, and, in those cases, the information should be refined to approximate more closely the concept to be represented. Most studies examining the educational production process have used school data for each student, whether or not the student had actually attended the school in the past. For example, the *Equality of Educational Opportunity* (EEO) survey was undertaken in September–October of the 1965–1966 school year. Clearly, the relevant school data for each child are those pertaining to the schools that he actually attended and, in many cases, the school that he was attending in 1965–1966 was different from the school or schools that he had previously attended. The high rate of residential mobility is translated into school mobility, and present school factors may be erroneous measures for actual school characteristics unless some data refinement is attempted (see Bowles and Levin, 1968b).

To the degree that the school factors used in the analysis are spurious ones, their estimated effect on achievement will be biased downward (see Hanushek and Kain, 1972). Unfortunately, this problem pervades the EEO work as well as its reanalysis, and the problem is more serious among the analyses for blacks and other minorities than for whites because of the higher mobility factor among the former groups. One way of correcting for this source of error is to include in the sample only those students who had received all of their education in the schools which they were currently attending. That is the approach taken in this study. Another possibility is obtaining historical data on all of the schools that the students attended. Given that much school mobility is among school districts and States, this task may be impractical.

Other remediable data problems are those resulting from missing observations of items for particular students. The EEO survey suffered particularly from this (see Bowles and Levin, 1968b). There are many ways of handling this problem, but ignoring it is clearly not one of them (see Elashoff and Elashoff, 1970). A final difficulty that characterizes the data sets used for measuring educational production is the interdependence among the so-called explanatory variables. In general, a child's home background and his school are highly correlated in that higher socioeco-

---

[6] As an illustration, Bowles (1970) uses the number of days that the school was in session as a proxy "to represent the general level of community interest in and support of education." Yet, such an indicator is more likely to be governed by state mandate than by community educational interests, educational support, and political processes. That is, each state requires a minimum session in order for the school district to qualify for aid. Accordingly, the main variance in the measure is accounted for among states. For the national sample used by Bowles, the mean for the "days-in-session" variable was 180 and the standard deviation was only 4.

nomic status children attend schools with greater resource endowments. This factor has prevented many studies from obtaining reliable estimates of the separate effects of school and background characteristics on achievement.[7] One way of circumventing this difficulty is to carry out the analysis for stratified subsamples of students with homogeneous socioeconomic backgrounds.[8]

Purpose of This Study

While we have noted some of the problems that arise in applying econometric analysis of production to the schools, this study will not claim heroically to having avoided such pitfalls. Rather, this effort addresses itself to moving toward estimating a model of the schools that more nearly mirrors what we know of the educational process. Indeed, we will proceed in the following way: First, we will posit a model of the schools and compare it with the more traditional formulation; second, we will discuss the data that will be used to estimate the structure of the model; third, we will review the estimation procedure and results; and, finally, we will discuss the implications.

Specification of the Model

Most studies of educational production have not attempted to specify in a systematic way the particular formulation of how schools affect achievement. Rather, they have taken a set of school and student background factors and related them statistically to achievement without discussing the underlying behavioral assumptions implied by their work. One exception has been an important study by Eric Hanushek that did posit a more concrete model of achievement (see Hanushek, 1968). The following formulation is based upon Hanushek's foundation.

Assume that we wish to examine the determinants of student achievement at a point in time. Clearly, that achievement level is related not only to the present influences that operate on the student, but also to past ones. That is, from the time a child is conceived, various environmental characteristics combine with his innate characteristics to mold his behavior. More specifically, a child's achievement performance is determined by the cumulative amounts of "capital" embodied in him by his family, his school, his community, and his peers, as well as his innate traits. The greater the amount and the quality of investment from each of these sources, the higher the student's achievement level will be. Thus, a

---

[7] This is discussed at length in Bowles and Levin (1968a,b).
[8] This is attempted in Kiesling (1967). See also Guthrie *et al.* (1971).

student's academic performance is viewed as a function of the amount of different kinds of capital embodied in him.

The general formulation of the capital embodiment model is as follows:

(1) $$A_{it} = g[F_{i(t)}, S_{i(t)}, P_{i(t)}, O_{i(t)}, I_{it}]$$

The i subscript refers to the ith student; the t subscript refers to time period t; and the t subscript in parentheses (t) refers to inputs cumulative to time period t. Thus:

A_{it} = a vector of educational outcomes for the ith student at time t.

$F_{i(t)}$ = a vector of individual and family background characteristics cumulative to time t.

$S_{i(t)}$ = a vector of school inputs relevant to the ith student cumulative to time t.

$P_{i(t)}$ = a vector of peer or fellow student characteristics cumulative to t.

$O_{i(t)}$ = a vector of other external influences (community, and so on) relevant to the ith student cumulative to t.

I_{it} = a vector of initial or innate endowment of the ith student at t.

It is assumed that g' is positive for all these arguments or that the marginal product of additional capital embodiment from any one of the five sources has a positive effect on student educational outcome.[9]

This formulation reflects the widely accepted concept that a child receives his educational investment from several sources in addition to the school. For example, the family provides a material, intellectual, and emotional environment that contributes to the child's performance level. Likewise, the school, peer groups, and community affect both learning and emotional behavior of students. Yet, in order to estimate these effects, one must take this general formulation and make it more specific.

Suppose we wish to follow the examples of other researchers by estimating a production function for achievement. Again, we can view a student's level of achievement on a verbal test, for example, as a function of his capital embodiment from several sources as well as his innate traits. In addition to these sources of capital embodiment, his educational achievement, at a point in time, is likely to be related to his educational attitudes and his parents' educational attitudes. More specifically, we might postulate that:

(2) $$A_{1_{it}} = g[F_{i(t)}, S_{i(t)}, P_{i(t)}, O_{i(t)}, I_{i(t)}, A_{2it}, A_{3it}, A_4]$$

[9] Following the capital embodiment approach more strictly, Dugan (1969) has calculated the monetary value of parents' educational investment in their offspring by calculating the opportunity cost or market value of such services. The values of father's educational investment, mother's educational investment, and school investment (all measured in dollars) seem to have high combined predictive value in explaining achievement levels.

where

$A_{1_{it}}$ = the achievement level of the ith student at t.
$F_{i(t)}$, $S_{i(t)}$, $P_{i(t)}$, and $O_{i(t)}$ are as previously defined.
$A_{2_{it}}$ = a measure of the student's sense of efficacy or fate control at t.
$A_{3_{it}}$ = a measure of educational motivation of the ith student at t.
$A_{4_{it}}$ = parents' educational expectations for the ith student at t.

Thus, we would expect student achievement to be higher the greater his sense of efficacy, his educational motivation, and his parents' expectations, ceteris paribus. By efficacy, we refer to the student's feeling that he has a measure of control over his destiny, that it does not depend strictly on chance. Educational motivation refers to the desire to succeed in an educational sense (for example, the desire to get good grades and to attain additional schooling). Parents' educational expectations might refer to how well the parents expect the child to perform by educational criteria.

These three variables, however, are of more than passing interest because *not only do they affect achievement levels, but they themselves are affected by achievement.* This raises the question of whether or not a single equation is adequate for estimating educational production, even when one is concerned with only a single measure of output, such as achievement. The single equation model tacitly assumes that each of the explanatory variables is determined outside of the system: They are exogenous. In other words, the explanatory variables influence the level of student achievement, but student achievement is assumed not to influence the so-called explanatory variables.

An illustration of this assumption and its lack of realism in the present instance is useful. Let us start off with a very simple model of achievement where student efficacy is considered to be the only factor affecting student achievement, all other factors being held constant. We can present this simple paradigm by drawing an arrow showing the assumed causal direction:

Student Achievement←Student Efficacy

This simple depiction suggests that student achievement increases with the level of efficacy. In process terms, students who believe that they have a measure of control over their achievement level are more likely to try to do well than students who believe that it all depends upon luck. It is probably also true that the higher the level of achievement, the higher the level of efficacy. Thus, by doing well, the student's sense of fate control is enhanced or reinforced because his efforts can really make a difference in his achievement. Thus, achievement stimulates efficacy, and efficacy stimulates achievement, as depicted below:

Student Achievement↔Student Efficacy

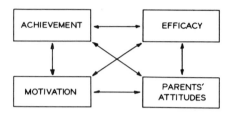

Figure 9.1 Simultaneously determined endogenous variables representing educational outcomes.

Moreover, the other attitudinal variables that influence school outputs, such as standardized achievement performance, are also influenced themselves by student achievement and by each other. For example, parents' educational expectations for a student will affect the student's performance level, but the student's performance level will also affect the parents' educational aspirations for him. Most parents will expect less from a child who has consistently low test scores and grades than one who has higher levels of both. The same is probably true of teacher expectations for pupil progress. In summary, many crucial variables in the educational process interact in such a way that prevents us from taking their levels as given in order to predict other factors. Rather, both explanatory variables and those to be explained are interdependent, and their values must be solved simultaneously in order to obtain unbiased estimates of their effects. That is, the relationship shown in Figure 9.1 exists in concept. In this particular system, everything depends upon everything else, so that complete simultaneity exists. Every one of the variables is linked by a double arrow to every other variable. In actuality, the simultaneity may be complete or partial, but, in either case, the ordinary least-squares solution of Equation 2 will lead to biased and inconsistent estimates.[10] Instead, we must estimate the full set of equations representing the simultaneous equations system.

The following formulation describes the simultaneous equation model:

(3) $\quad A_{1_{it}} = g_1 [F_{1_{i(t)}}, S_{1_{i(t)}}, P_{1_{i(t)}}, O_{1_{i(t)}}, I_{1_{it}}, A_{2_{it}}, A_{3_{it}}, A_{4_{it}}]$

(4) $\quad A_{2_{it}} = g_2 [F_{2_{i(t)}}, S_{2_{i(t)}}, P_{2_{i(t)}}, O_{2_{i(t)}}, I_{2_{it}}, A_{1_{it}}, A_{3_{it}}, A_{4_{it}}]$

(5) $\quad A_{3_{it}} = g_3 [F_{3_{i(t)}}, S_{3_{i(t)}}, P_{3_{i(t)}}, O_{3_{i(t)}}, I_{3_{it}}, A_{1_{it}}, A_{2_{it}}, A_{4_{it}}]$

(6) $\quad A_{4_{it}} = g_4 [F_{4_{i(t)}}, S_{4_{i(t)}}, P_{4_{i(t)}}, O_{4_{i(t)}}, I_{4_{it}}, A_{1_{it}}, A_{2_{it}}, A_{3_{it}}]$

In this system, there exists an equation for each of the endogenous variables. Two characteristics of the system are of immediate importance. First, the solution of the system depends upon its identifiability. In general,

[10] The residual term is likely to be correlated with $A_{2_{it}}$, $A_{3_{it}}$, and $A_{4_{it}}$, and the direct application of the ordinary least-squares estimator will not yield unbiased estimates of the structural parameters of Equation 2. See Johnston (1963:240–252).

proper identification requires that there be as many equations as endogenous variables and that all variables are not present in all relations.[11]

In this regard, it should be noted that the specification of each of the exogenous variables is unique in each relation. That is, it is reasonable to believe that different family factors, school factors, innate characteristics, and so on, affect achievement $(A_{1_{it}})$ than affect the other endogenous variables $A_{2_{it}}$, $A_{3_{it}}$, and $A_{4_{it}}$. Accordingly, $F_{1_{i(t)}}$ is considered to be a different vector of family influences than $F_{2_{i(t)}}$, $F_{3_{i(t)}}$, and $F_{4_{i(t)}}$.[12]

The potential uniqueness of $S_{i(t)}$ for each equation is also represented by the appropriate subscript as well as the uniqueness of the other vectors. It is particularly useful if we can distinguish between school characteristics that relate to achievement $(A_{1_{it}})$ and those that relate to student and parental attitudes.

A second characteristic of the system, represented by Equations 3, 4, 5, and 6, is that each of the endogenous variables represents an *output* of the educational process as well as an *input* into it. Just as schools are expected to increase achievement, they are also expected to contribute to such attitudes as efficacy and motivation. Thus, we can evaluate the system for each of several outcomes rather than restricting ourselves only to the analysis of student achievement.[13] The system of equations allows us to solve for student efficacy, student motivation, and parents' educational expectations as well as student achievement.

Estimating the Equations

The data used to estimate this system were derived from the *Equality of Educational Opportunity* survey on which the Coleman Report was based. The sample is composed of sixth-grade students in a large eastern city who had attended only the school in which they were enrolled at the time of the survey, 1965–1966.[14] Teacher characteristics are based upon averages for all of the teachers in each school who were teaching in grades three through five. These averages were intended to reflect the teacher characteristics that had influenced student behavior up to the time of the survey. Since family background characteristics and other educational influences

[11] A description of the identification problem is found in Johnston (1963:240–252). See also Fisher (1959).

[12] $F_{i(t)} = [f_{1_{i(t)}}, f_{2_{i(t)}}, \ldots, f_{n_{i(t)}}]$. That is, there are n elements in the $F_{i(t)}$ vector, but not all of them are germane to any particular equation.

[13] The parents' attitude variable might be considered to be an intermediate output in that its social value is more a function of its effectiveness in producing other outputs than it is its use as an end in itself. In a similar vein, the teachers' attitudes might be introduced into the model as an endogenous variable.

[14] These data were derived jointly with Stephan Michelson at The Brookings Institution from magnetic tapes provided by Alexander Mood.

were measured only at one point in time, it is tacitly assumed that these measures bear a constant relation to the stock of capital embodied in each child from these sources. Thus, the values of those inputs cumulative to time t bear a constant relation to the flow of inputs observed at time t.

While all of the equations specify innate traits as exogenous variables, we do not possess measures of I_{it}. Our statistical model does not include the I_{it} vectors, despite the fact that they belong in the system, a priori. It is important to speculate on the expected bias in the estimates of the other parameters, if the students' innate traits are not included in the equations. In general, those variables that are correlated with the omitted one will be biased upwards (see Theil, 1957).

It is probably reasonable to assume that innate traits have at least some component that is reflected in the vector of family background characteristics.[15] Even if one minimizes the possible genetic relationship between parental traits and the child's innate characteristics, there are other possible linkages. In particular, the child drawn from lower social origins is a more likely candidate for prenatal protein starvation, a factor which may limit his innate potential (see Scrimshaw, 1968). The result of the probable association between family background characteristics and student's innate traits is that the effect of the $F_{i(t)}$ vector on achievement (and perhaps on other outcomes) will be overstated. Family background characteristics will be biased upwards to the extent of their covariance with the missing variable, innate characteristics. In general, it is reasonable to conclude that all of the studies that have tried to explain the determinants of scholastic achievement have overstated the effects of family background by omitting measures of innate traits.

Some Results

What follows are some estimates of a simultaneous equation system similar to the one posited above. The particular sample in this analysis consists of almost 600 white students attending some 36 schools in Eastmet City. Particular variables were chosen to enter the relation partially on the basis of a priori judgment, partially on statistical tests of significance, and partially on the quality of the measures.

From over 100 items of information that we distilled from the original survey data, we chose those variables that might be expected, logically, to enter into each relation. As an example, the quality of library services, as represented by library books per student, might reasonably be expected to affect the student's achievement level; yet, one would be hard pressed to discern a direct relationship between student's and parents' attitudes and

[15] For contrasting views on the extent to which innate traits are genetically determined, with particular emphasis on "intelligence," see Hunt (1961) and Jensen (1969). See also Lesser and Stodolsky (1967).

library books. Accordingly, the library measure was specified only in the achievement equation. Likewise, information, such as teacher's salary, is reflected in the teacher characteristics that the salaries purchase.[16]

Some items that were entered showed statistical relationships that were so nearly random that they were eliminated from subsequent equations. Whether the lack of a statistical association was due to their poor measurement or their mis-specification cannot be determined a priori. What follows is a set of estimates that must be judged only for their heuristic values. That is, alternative specifications are equally plausible, and the grounds for specification biases are substantial.[17] Further refinement of the data and the specifications are undoubtedly necessary before firm policy conclusions can be drawn.

Table 9.1 shows the list of all variables included in the estimates, and tables 9.2, 9.3, 9.4, and 9.5 show estimates of the equations for verbal score, student's attitude, grade aspiration, and parents' attitude, respectively. The sample comprises 597 white students in the sixth grade of Eastmet City in the fall of 1965.

Before interpreting the results, it is important to note that the statistical model used here differs slightly from that presented in Equations 3, 4, 5, and 6 in that only the first three equations are estimated simultaneously; the fourth equation is estimated by ordinary least-squares, and it bears a recursive relation to the rest of the model. Figure 9.2 illustrates this property as well as the simultaneous relationships estimated among the other equations. The system is overidentified a priori because the endogenous variables are not common to each of the three simultaneous equations.

Two-stage least-squares was used for the three simultaneous equations. Each of the tables for the equations on verbal score, student's attitude, and grade aspiration show an ordinary least-squares estimate, a two-stage least-squares (simultaneous equations) estimate, and a reduced form. The latter is obtained by solving the simultaneous equations system via algebraic substitution (see Johnston, 1963:240–252).

Some Interpretations

The interpretations that follow are highly speculative. They are offered only as illustrations of the properties of the model. Further testing of the structure and improved data are necessary to confirm results reported here.

[16] For more information on this relationship, see Levin (1968). See also Levin (1970).

[17] Under certain conditions, the simultaneous equation estimates are subject to greater specification biases than the ordinary least-squares ones. See Summers (1965); see also Fisher (1966). Michelson has shown results for alternative specifications of the single model.

TABLE 9.1

List of Variables in Simultaneous Equations

Name of Variable	Measure of	Coding
Verbal Score	Student Performance	Raw Score

Student's Attitude	Efficacy	Index compiled from questions 33-40 in the Sixth Grade Student Questionnaire of the Equal Opportunity Survey. (e.g., I can do many things well.
		
		     Well
		     No
		     Not Sure
		 I sometimes feel I just can't learn.
		
		     Yes
		     No
		 The higher the value of the index, the greater the perceived efficacy of the student.)

Parents' Attitude	Educational Expectations of Parents	Index based upon three questions: (1) How good a student does your mother want you to be? (2) How good a student does your father want you to be? (3) Did anyone at home read to you when you were small, before you started school? (and how often?)
Grade Aspiration	Student Motivation	Grade level the student wishes to complete
Sex	Male-Female Differences	Male = 0 Female = 1
Age	Overage for Grade	Age 12 or over = 1 Less than 12 = 0

Possessions in Student's Home	Family Background (Socioeconomic Status)	Index of possessions:
		     television
		     telephone
		 Yes = 1 dictionary
		 No = 0 encyclopedia
		 for automobile
		 each; daily newspaper
		 index record player
		 is sum. refrigerator
		         vacuum cleaner

Family Size	Family Background	Number of people in home

280

TABLE 9.1 (continued)

Name of Variable	Measure of	Coding
Identity of Person Serving as Mother	Family Background	Real mother at home = 0 Real mother not living at home = 1 Surrogate mother = 2
Identity of Person Serving as Father	Family Background	Real father at home = 0 Real father not living at home = 1 Surrogate father = 2
Father's Education	Family Background	Number of years of school attained
Mother's Employment Status	Family Background	Has job = 1 No job = 0
Attended Kindergarten	Family Background	Yes = 1 No = 0
Teacher's Verbal Score	Teacher Quality	Raw score on vocabulary test
Teacher's Parents' Income	Teacher Socio-economic Status	Father's occupation scaled according to 1959 census income (1000's of dollars)
Teacher Experience	Teacher Quality	Number of years of full-time experience
Teacher's Undergraduate Institution	Teacher Quality	University or college = 3 Teacher institution = 1
Satisfaction with Present School	Teacher's Attitude	Satisfied = 3 Maybe prefers another school = 2 Prefers another school = 1
Percent of White Students	Student Body	Percentage estimated by teachers
Teacher Turnover	School	Proportion of teachers who left in previous year for reasons other than death or illness
Library Volumes Per Student	School Facilities	Number of volumes divided by school enrollment

NOTE: All data are taken from the Equal Opportunity Survey for Eastmet City. The survey instruments are found in James S. Coleman *et al, Equality of Educational Opportunity* (Washington, D.C.: U.S. Government Printing Office, 1966).

TABLE 9.2

Estimates of Verbal Score Equations for White Sixth Graders in Eastmet City (t Values in Parentheses)

	Ordinary Least Squares	Two Stage Least Squares	Reduced Form
Student's Attitude	0.641 (4.88)	2.649 (1.72)	
Grade Aspiration	0.921 (5.21)	0.591 (0.53)	
Parents' Attitude	0.605 (2.81)	0.873 (0.74)	
Sex	0.616 (1.06)	-0.571 (0.49)	0.817
Age	-6.099 (4.26)	-5.513 (2.78)	-6.010
Possessions	0.990 (3.84)	0.521 (1.05)	1.229
Family Size	-0.330 (2.14)	-0.036 (0.12)	-0.552
Identity of Mother	-----	-----	-0.433
Identity of Father	-----	-----	-0.327
Father's Education	0.243 (2.10)	0.026 (0.12)	0.273
Mother's Employment	-----	-----	-0.509
Attended Kindergarten	1.520 (1.73)	1.768 (1.32)	2.372
Teacher's Verbal Score	0.332 (1.61)	0.220 (0.84)	0.250
Teacher's Parents' Income	-----	-----	-0.118
Teacher Experience	0.751 (8.77)	0.694 (5.28)	0.787
Teacher Undergraduate Institution	6.547 (2.66)	5.833 (1.94)	6.525
Satisfaction with Present School	1.201 (0.90)	1.658 (0.86)	1.960

TABLE 9.2 (continued)

	Ordinary Least Squares	Two Stage Least Squares	Reduced Form
Percent of White Students	-----	-----	-0.047
Teacher Turnover	-0.054 (0.61)	0.044 (0.34)	-0.101
Library Volumes Per Student	0.562 (1.82)	0.498 (1.31)	0.565
Constant Term	-23.94	-29.75	-7.902
$\bar{R}^2$	.53	.34	

Accordingly, the interpretation of the findings is not an attempt to be exhaustive, as much as an effort to show how this approach might be used ultimately to examine various hypotheses.

Verbal Score

The variables entering the verbal score equation were selected as representative of the different vectors in Equation 3, with the obvious omission of innate traits. Such conventional teacher's characteristics as degree level showed no significant relation to student verbal score, although teacher's experience appears to be strongly related in this sample.

It is especially instructive to compare the ordinary least-squares estimates (which do not take the simultaneity into account) with the two-stage estimates (which do take it into account). Thus, we can note some of the biases in interpretation that might arise from the usual ordinary least-squares estimates. In particular, it appears that the direct effect of several family background characteristics on verbal achievement is overstated substantially in the single equation (OLS) estimate. For example, the coefficient for family size is only one-tenth as large in the TSLS estimate as the OLS one. This suggests that the large observed negative relationship between family size and achievement in the ordinary least-squares formulation should not be interpreted as a direct effect, but one that works through an intervening variable, student's attitude. The much larger coefficient for student's attitude in the TSLS estimate in combination with the large decline in the family size coefficient in the simultaneous equations formulation indicates that students from larger families probably have lower verbal scores because of their poorer attitudes, rather than because

TABLE 9.3

Estimates of Student Attitude Equations for White Sixth Graders in Eastmet City (t Values in Parentheses)

	Ordinary Least Squares	Two Stage Least Squares	Reduced Form
Verbal Score	0.061 (5.54)	0.052 (2.03)	
Parents' Attitude	0.112 (1.69)	0.042 (0.15)	
Sex	0.560 (3.15)	0.557 (3.08)	0.577
Age	0.241 (0.54)	0.135 (0.27)	-0.015
Possessions	0.107 (1.39)	0.143 (1.29)	0.174
Family Size	-0.108 (2.30)	-0.124 (2.05)	-0.138
Identity of Mother	-----	-----	-0.011
Identity of Father	-0.082 (1.30)	-.092 (1.36)	-0.100
Father's Education	0.070 (2.02)	0.081 (1.88)	0.088
Mother's Employment	-0.318 (1.58)	-0.307 (1.44)	-0.320
Attended Kindergarten	-----	-----	0.059
Teacher's Verbal Score	-----	-----	0.006
Teacher's Parents' Income	-----	-----	-0.003
Teacher Experience	-----	-----	0.163
Teacher Undergraduate Institution	-----	-----	0.020
Satisfaction with Present School	-0.163 (0.42)	-0.129 (0.33)	-0.089
Percent of White Students	-----	-----	-0.001

284

TABLE 9.3 (continued)

	Ordinary Least Square	Two Stage Least Square	Reduced Form
Teacher Turnover	-0.047 (2.70)	-0.048 (2.73)	-0.051
Library Volumes Per Student	5.132	5.330	5.132
$\bar{R}^2$	.19	.19	

of an inextricable link between family size and other background characteristics, on the one hand, and achievement, on the other. The existence of this phenomenon is also supported by the smaller cofficients in the TSLS estimate for socioeconomic factors, such as father's education and possessions.

The possible significance of these findings is that educational programs that focus on student attitudes may be able to compensate for "disadvantages" in socioeconomic background. Indeed, this tentative interpretaion argues against the simplistic observations of some social philosophers that educational programs cannot compensate for such background deficiencies as low socioeconomic status, since these background factors now appear to have much of their direct effects not on achievement, but on attitude and, *through* attitude, on achievement. Successful attempts to change student attitudes, therefore, might be used to offset "deleterious" background conditions.

In this vein, it is also interesting to note the reversal of sign for the sex variable between the OLS and TSLS estimates. In the OLS formulation, females show higher verbal scores than males, while in the TSLS they show

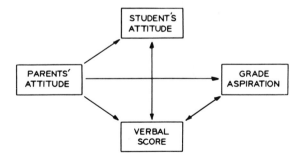

Figure 9.2 Partially simultaneous relationship among educational outcomes.

TABLE 9.4
Estimates of Grade Aspiration Equations for White Sixth Graders in Eastmet City (t Values in Parentheses)

	Ordinary Least Squares	Two Stage Least Squares	Reduced Form
Verbal Score	.0557 (6.75)	.0876 (4.18)	
Parents' Attitude	.0372 (0.75)	-0.391 (1.46)	
Sex	-0.111 (1.84)	-0.192 (1.30)	-0.077
Age	- 0.351 (1.05)	0.243 (0.63)	-0.772
Possessions	0.052 (0.87)	.074 (0.85)	0.092
Family Size	-0.057 (1.64)	-0.077 (1.62)	-0.079
Identity of Mother	-0.223 (2.35)	-0.310 (2.62)	-0.227
Identity of Father	-0.056 (1.11)	-0.560 (1.03)	-0.077
Father's Education	-----	-----	0.024
Mother's Employment	0.282 (1.89)	0.401 (2.34)	0.279
Attended Kindergarten	0.644 (3.20)	0.547 (2.47)	0.756
Teacher's Verbal Score	-----	-----	0.022
Teacher's Parents' Income	-0.0005 (0.38)	-0.176 (1.15)	-0.186
Teacher Experience	-----	-----	0.069
Teacher Undergraduate Institution	-0.460 (1.08)	-0.135 (0.28)	0.439
Satisfaction with Present School	0.785 (2.56)	0.693 (2.80)	0.866

286

TABLE 9.4 (continued)

	Ordinary Least Squares	Two Stage Least Squares	Reduced Form
Percent of White Students	-----	-----	0.021
Teacher Turnover	-----	-----	-0.005
Library Volumes Per Student	-----	-----	0.050
Constant Term	9.174	10.900	8.850
$\bar{R}^2$	.26	.15	

lower scores. Again, it appears that the higher verbal scores of females are more likely attributable to a higher sense of efficacy than to any direct sex-achievement effect. This is confirmed by the strong, positive coefficient for females in the student attitude equation in Table 9.3. It is also supported by the well established view that schools represent feminizing influences, receptive to girls and hostile to boys. Under such conditions, one would expect females to exhibit greater efficacy and, through efficacy, greater achievement (see Sexton, 1969). [18]

The reduced-form equation shows all of the system's influences on verbal score, whether directly through the verbal score equation or indirectly through students' attitudes, grade aspiration, or parents' attitudes. On balance, sex is positively related to verbal score. Those variables that affect attitudes and grade aspiration directly are shown to affect verbal score because attitudes and grade aspiration affect verbal score. Thus, while the identity of the mother showed no significant direct relation to verbal achievement, it does show a negative influence of a maternal substitute in the reduced form because of its direct negative relation to student grade aspiration. The same is true of father's identity, which shows a direct negative effect of a father surrogate on student's attitude and, thus, an indirect effect in the reduced form on verbal score.

Other Equations

Table 9.3 presents comparable equations for student's attitude and table 9.4 for grade aspiration. Because of the tentative nature of the findings at

[18] As we might expect, females show lower grade aspirations (see Table 9.4).

this stage, we will not detail all of these results. Rather, we will focus on a pattern that is of general interest. It appears that when the mother has a job, the child's grade aspiration is higher (Table 9.4), but his efficacy or attitude is lower (Table 9.3). Even in the reduced forms of these two equations, the differences in sign prevail, and, in the reduced form on verbal score (Table 9.2), a child whose mother works shows a lower test performance ostensibly because of the effect of his mother's employment on his own efficacy.

The findings in these tables are pregnant with suggestions, and it is interesting to speculate on their meaning. Yet we must caution against any final interpretation until improved measurement and replication of the model confirm the observed patterns. Accordingly, it is best to summarize now where this excursion has taken us.

TABLE 9.5

Estimate of Parent's Attitude Equation for White Sixth Graders in Eastmet City (t Values in Parentheses)

	Ordinary Least Squares
Sex	−0.110 (1.00)
Possessions	0.218 (4.84)
Family Size	−0.119 (4.14)
Identity of Mother	−0.309 (4.36)
Identity of Father	−0.018 (0.44)
Mother's Employment	0.198 (1.59)
Percent of White Students	−0.065 (2.11)
Teacher's Turnover	−0.009 (.89)
Constant Term	3.465
$\bar{R}^2$	.13

Summary

This chapter drew an analogy to the economist's concept of an educational production function. The problems of estimation have been emphasized. Despite these obstacles, the importance of knowing the production relationships in the educational sector has stimulated much recent research. This chapter presents an extension of this research by positing a simultaneous equations approach to viewing the educational process. It appears that the properties of a simultaneous equations system mirror the world more closely than the single equation approaches that are presently being used. Further developments in this direction are proceeding, and we hope that before long we can obtain a reasonably reliable set of estimates of school effectiveness with this technique.

Acknowledgments

The analysis in this chapter was drawn from a larger study which is being authored jointly with Stephan Michelson. In addition to Stephan Michelson, the author is indebted to Randall Weiss for his research assistance and for his thoughtful contributions. Emily Andrews assisted in the final preparation of this chapter.

X | Measuring Efficiency in Educational Production[*]

Henry M. Levin
Stanford University

The search for efficiency in public sector activities has been gaining substantial momentum in recent years. Rapid rises in the costs of public services, in conjunction with a widespread belief that their quality is deteriorating, has raised concerns in many quarters (Baumol, 1967). Economists have responded by attempting to explore the production of specific public goods, as well as their pricing (Hirsch, 1973: Chapter 12; Mushkin, 1972). In many cases, the analytic approaches have paralleled those used in the study of production in the private sector since the tools of production analysis have been largely forged and honed in that arena. In this chapter, we will explore some of the problems of understanding production in the public sector by reviewing the usual approach to estimating the production set in elementary and secondary education. We will suggest that the results that have been derived are likely to be misleading and that they may lead to decreased efficiency if they are adopted as a basis for public policy.

The elementary and secondary educational sector represents an interesting focus for studies that attempt to understand efficiency in the production

* Reprinted from *Public Finance Quarterly*, Jan. 1974, Vol. 2, No. 1. © 1974 Sage Publications, Inc. The paper is adapted from a work presented before the 1971 Meetings of the Psychometric Society (Levin, 1971).

of government services. It has represented a substantial portion of public activity (about $43 billion in 1971), and the per-pupil costs in constant dollars have risen very rapidly (about 6–7% per year between 1930 and 1970). Moreover, serious questions have been raised about the effectiveness of the educational system and the apparent inability of additional expenditures to improve educational outcomes (Averch, Carroll, Donaldson, Kiesling, and Pincus, 1972).

A large number of studies have been undertaken in the last few years to estimate the "educational production function" (Bowles, 1970; Bowles and Levin, 1968b; Burkhead *et al.*, 1967; Hanushek, 1972; Katzman, 1971; Kiesling, 1967; Levin, 1970; Michelson, 1970; Perl, 1973; Winkler, 1972). While they have relied upon very diverse sets of data and different measures of inputs, almost all have considered the appropriate measure of educational output to be pupil scores on standardized achievement tests. The general formulation of the production function that seems to underlie most of these studies is represented by Equation 1.

(1) $$A_{it} = g\,[F_{i(t)},\ S_{i(t)},\ P_{i(t)},\ O_{i(t)},\ I_{it}].$$

The i subscript refers to the ith student; (t) refers to an input that is cumulative to time t.

A_{it} = a vector of educational outcomes for the ith student at time t.
$F_{i(t)}$ = a vector of individual and family background characteristics cumulative to time t.
$S_{i(t)}$ = a vector of school inputs relevant to the ith student cumulative to t.
$P_{i(t)}$ = a vector of peer or fellow student characteristics cumulative to t.
$O_{i(t)}$ = a vector of other external influences (the community, for example) relevant to the ith student cumulative to t.
I_{it} = a vector of initial or innate endowments of the ith student at t.

Although only a few studies specify the general form of the educational production function as in Equation 1, most explorations seem to be based upon such a model.[1] In most of the applications, the A_{it} vector is reflected by one or more tests of standardized achievement for each pupil. $F_{i(t)}$ includes measures of family socioeconomic status and family structure. $P_{i(t)}$ attempts to capture the socioeconomic status of the student environment, and $O_{i(t)}$ represents a residual category of community and other educational influences. I_{it} is usually omitted for lack of a reliable measure, and the specification biases created by this omission have already been discussed (Levin, 1970:65–66). $S_{i(t)}$ includes school resources, such as the number and quality of teachers and other personnel, facilities, curriculum, and other inputs. It is essentially these school inputs that are of particular interest to economists in their quest for efficiency, for these resources represent the

---

[1] This formulation is based on Hanushek (1972). See his discussion of its components (1972: chapter 2).

ones that are purchased by the school budget and for which resource allocation decisions can be made.

The Efficient Production of Educational Achievement

Although the educational production function in Equation 1 is stated in a most general form, the efforts to measure it have concentrated principally on one school output: academic achievement. In general, the goals of these studies are to obtain the production set for student test scores and to assess the marginal product to price ratios for all of the inputs in order to recommend better ways of allocating school budgets. For the results of such studies to be valid, we must assume that the estimated production cofficients are unbiased. Yet, possible errors in the equations and in the variables must surely loom as a likely possibility in an area where we know so little about the psychological process of learning and socialization and where measurement is so difficult.

While there are numerous grounds for such errors and their resultant biases, one of the most important of these is the mis-specification of output. In short, schools are multi-product firms that are charged with producing many student outcomes in addition to increasing those qualities measured by cognitive achievement scores. The inculcation of attitudes and values has long been an important part of the school agenda. Based upon recent studies of earnings functions that use cognitive achievement scores among their independent variables, one cannot even argue that cognitive skills, as measured by test scores, are the most crucial determinant of earnings. To the contrary, it appears that variance in achievement scores explains only a relatively nominal portion of differences in success in the labor market (Griliches and Mason, 1972; Taubman and Wales, 1973).

A more insightful analysis of the relationship between educational production and labor market success seems to be reflected in the recent work of Bowles (1972b) and Gintis (1971, 1972). These studies suggest that the principal purpose of schools is to reproduce the social relations of production and that achievement scores are only one component of the productive hierarchy. "The school is a bureaucratic order with hierarchical authority rule-orientation, stratification of 'ability' (tracking) as well as by age role differentiation by sex (physical education, home economics, shop) and a system of external incentives (marks, promise of promotion, and threat of failure) much like pay and status in the sphere or work" (Bowles, 1973:352).

Even an examination of the incentive structures and the information available to school managers suggests that it is not likely that they are attempting to maximize cognitive achievement. Various studies have shown that school administrators have very little knowledge of how to improve achievement scores. They seem to lack substantial management discretion over their input mix; they do not operate under competitive forces that would force them to maximize student achievement, nor does the incentive or reward structure for personnel correspond to student achievement outcomes; and information feedback to school managers on the "value-added" to student test scores that is produced uniquely by school inputs is unavailable (Levin, 1971). These characteristics of schools are supported by the findings of Gintis (1971) that grades and other social rewards of schooling are more consistently correlated with the personality attributes of students than their cognitive achievement scores.

In order to estimate a production function for educational achievement, however, we must assume that all schools are operating on the production frontier for this output, so that the observed relations represent the maximum output that can be produced with the inputs that are being utilized. The fact that schools are producing other outputs besides cognitive achievement raises serious questions about this assumption, since it is reasonable to believe that the production of other outputs reduces the amount of cognitive learning that will be produced. In this case, it is obvious that statistical estimates among existing schools that consider only the achievement score outcomes of students will not give us estimates of the production frontier, since more achievement could be obtained by reducing the levels of all noncomplementary outputs to zero.

The obvious answer to estimating production functions in the multi-product case is to specify a system of equations that takes into account all of the outputs of schooling.[2] Unfortunately, our overall ignorance of the conceptual outputs of schools, of their measurement, and of their structural relationships to one another and to inputs limits our ability to include nonachievement outputs in the analysis. The result of these limitations is that almost every study that has attempted to estimate educational production functions has considered only educational achievement as an output.[3] In most cases, the obvious problems involved are either ignored, or the assumption is made that all other outputs are produced as perfect joint products in exact fixed proportion to achievement scores. There is no empirical substantiation for this assumption.

The situation is shown in Figure 10.1, which represents a hypothetical input–output space wherein S_1 and S_2 represent two different school inputs into the production of student achievement. (It is assumed here that other

[2] For a discussion of the problems in specifying the multi-product case in studies of production, see Pfouts (1961), Salter (1960), and Carlson (1956). Normally this problem is avoided in estimating production functions in the private sector, since the measure of output is valued in monetary terms. Thus, different market outputs can be weighted according to their prices in order to obtain a single monetary index of total market output. Of course, this procedure is based upon the normal assumptions of profit maximization. It does not account for nonmarket outputs.

[3] Exceptions to this are the multi-product estimations of Levin (1970) and Michelson (1970). Work in this area was also being carried out in 1973 by Otto Davis and his associates at Carnegie–Mellon University.

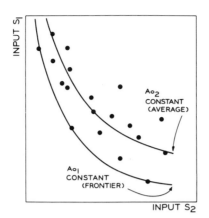

Figure 10.1 Frontier and average production isoquants for student achievement.

inputs are being held constant; of course, this example can be generalized algebraically for n inputs.) Each observation represents the combination of S_1 and S_2 that a particular school is using to produce a given amount of achievement output, Ao. That is, each school in the sample is using a different input mix even though the apparent output is the same.

Isoquant Ao_1 represents the production frontier defined as the locus of all observations that minimize the cominations of S_1 and S_2 required to produce constant product Ao. Presumably, these schools are producing only the socially minimal required levels of other school outputs.[4] Since Ao_1 is a mapping of the most efficient points for producing achievement A_o, it is the production frontier. All observations to the northeast of Ao_1 are of inefficient schools that are using higher input levels to produce the same achievement.[5] Now assume that we fit the observations statistically via

---

[4] In theory, schools on the frontier for student achievement are producing no other outputs. That is, the production of other outputs is assumed to detract from the production of student achievement. In fact, it is likely that there is a socially minimal level of other outputs (such as citizenship, work attitudes, and so on) that all schools produce. In this case, the schools that appear to be on the achievement frontier are on a "modified" frontier that assumes a socially minimal level of other outputs. That is, short of an experiment we are unable to obtain production data on schools that are producing only student achievement.

[5] Inefficiency is used here in a very narrow way. Specifically, it refers to the attainment of an increase in a particular output by reallocating existing resources from other outcomes. "Technical inefficiency" or "x-inefficiency" is just a misnomer for this condition. Under conditions of technical inefficiency, it appears that more output could be obtained with the same level of inputs, but, as we have shown elsewhere (Levin and Müller, 1973), the physical laws of production must surely behave according to the principles of conservation of mass and energy so that nothing is "lost" in the production process. One is always on the production frontier in that there is a mapping of outputs on inputs for any production process. When a

normal regression procedures. We obtain the statistical equivalent of Ao_2 for all schools (both efficient and inefficient ones). Of course, all points on Ao_2 are farther from the origin than those on Ao_1, showing that the average production relationship is a less efficient one than the frontier relationship.

Since virtually all estimates of educational productions have been based on the performance of both average and efficient schools rather than efficient ones only, the existing statistical studies of educational production are not production function studies in the frontier sense. Moreover, their results may suggest erroneous conclusions about which combination of inputs (program) maximizes achievement for a given budget constraint. For example, assume the two-input production function:

(2) $$A = h(S_1, S_2).$$

In equilibrium, we would wish to satisfy the conditions set out in Equation 3, where P_1 and P_2 represent the prices of S_1 and S_2 respectively.

(3) $$\frac{\partial A / \partial S_1}{P_1} = \frac{\partial A / \partial S_2}{P_2} \text{ or } \frac{h_1'}{P_1} = \frac{h_2'}{P_2}$$

Now consider two different values for h_1' and h_2'. At the frontier, $h_1' = \hat{h}_1'$, and, for the average of all schools, $h_1' = \overline{h}_1'$. The symbols for h_2' can be defined in the same way.

(4) $$\frac{\hat{h}_1'}{\hat{h}_2'} = \frac{\overline{h}_1'}{\overline{h}_2'} = \frac{P_1}{P_2}$$

Equation 4 reiterates the necessary conditions for a maximum, both for frontier estimates and for average estimates of the production function. In both cases, we wish to select the combination of inputs that equates the ratios of marginal products (first derivatives) to the ratios of prices.

Efficiency Implications of the Estimates

If we estimate only the average production function or only the frontier one, can the optimal ratio of inputs derived from one estimate also apply to

---

steel mill is producing less steel for a given set of inputs than another mill, it is producing more heat energy or worker leisure or other outputs. It just happens that the most valued or preferred output, from the perspective of the analyst, is steel rather than heat energy or worker leisure. Thus, so-called technical inefficiency can always be reduced to allocative or price inefficiency, since it is a function of values rather than energy losses in a physical sense. For further reference to the concept of technical efficiency or x-efficiency, see Farrell (1957) and Leibenstein (1966). In our view, their conception is erroneous for the aforementioned reasons and is outlined more systematically in Levin and Müller (1973).

the other? The answer to this question clearly depends on whether or not there are differences in the structural parameters associated with each input.

For example, it is possible that the inefficiencies of nonfrontier schools are neutral among inputs so that, at every level of input and for every combination of inputs, the ratios of the marginal products are identical for both frontier and average functions. That is, Equation 5 holds.

(5) $$\hat{h}_i{}' = \gamma \bar{h}_i{}' \qquad (i = 1,2)$$
$$\gamma \geq 1$$

This can be represented by Figure 10.2, where Ao_1 signifies the production isoquant for Ao for all efficient schools, and Ao_2 represents the same level of output for the entire set of schools, efficient and inefficient. B_1 B_2 and C_1 C_2 represent budget or isocost lines reflecting the various combinations of S_1 and S_2 obtainable for two given cost constraints, B and C, where $C > B$. The slope of the isocost lines is determined by the ratio of the prices, P_2/P_1. Thus, E and F represent equilibrium points that reflect Equation 4. That is, the combination of S_1 and S_2 that obtains Ao for budget constraint B is determined by the tangency of Ao_1 to B_1 B_2 at point E, for efficient or frontier schools, and of Ao_2 to C_1 C_2 at point F, for schools on the average.

It can be shown that the relative intensities of the two inputs will be identical for both groups of schools if a ray drawn from the origin intersects both points of tangency. O M satisfies that condition, so the same ratio of S_1/S_2 is optimal for both groups of schools. Whether we use the estimates of frontier schools or of all schools, the findings on the optimal combinations of S_1 and S_2 will be binding for both. In such a case, it does not matter which group we use to estimate the production function, although the absolute product will be higher for the set of schools at the frontier for any input level.

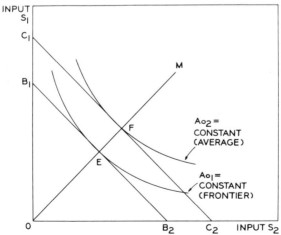

Figure 10.2 Technical inefficiency that is neutral between inputs.

On the other hand, there is a case in which Equation 5 does not hold. This can be shown in Figure 10.3, and it is also evident in Figure 10.1. Here, the relative inefficiency in the use of S_1 appears to be greater than that for S_2. For example, if S_1 represents physical school facilities and S_2 represents teachers, Figure 10.3 suggests that the organizational arrangements in inefficient schools are relatively more harmful to the productivity of the facilities than to that of the teachers. In this case, a ray drawn through the origin representing a constant ratio of inputs will not intersect both points of tangency. That is, the optimal ratio of S_1/S_2 for frontier schools will be different from that for inefficient schools. In this event, the results obtained for one group of schools (e.g., frontier ones) cannot be applied to another group (e.g., nonfrontier ones). Rather, each set of schools will have its own optimal combination of S_1/S_2, depending on its relative efficiency.

An Empirical Application

One major difficulty in demonstrating some of the empirical implications of the foregoing analysis is that the necessary relationships are much easier to obtain mathematically than they are statistically. The particular problems in deriving educational production functions have been described elsewhere, so they will not be detailed here (Bowles, 1970; Levin, 1970; Michelson, 1970). It is useful to note, however, that the statistical work in this area is subject to both errors in the equations and errors in the variables. In the former case, the proper specification of the model is still in the exploratory stage. The structure of the model, the specific variables to

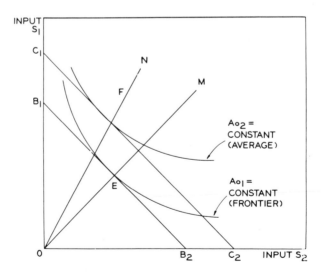

Figure 10.3 Technical inefficiency that is biased between inputs.

be included, and the relationship of the variables to one another have not been well established, and there are many gaps in our knowledge. Moreover, most of the operational variables used in the models are subject to varying degrees of measurement error.

Thus, no strict application of the findings to public policy is warranted. Rather, the empirical aspects are meant to suggest new directions and to provoke new thought on the process of evaluation. The results derived must surely be subject to replication and further analysis before they can be considered acceptable for policy consideration.

The data used in this analysis represent a subsample drawn from the *Equality of Educational Opportunity* survey, conducted by the United States Office of Education for the school year 1965–1966. Specifically, the subsample is composed of some 597 white sixth graders who had attended only the schools in which they were enrolled at the time of the survey (see Levin 1970, and Michelson, 1970 for details). Since the data were reanalyzed and recoded extensively for the purpose of estimating present relationships, they differ in important ways from the data used in other studies that have drawn information from the same survey. In the sample, 29 schools are represented, and the teacher characteristics identified are averages for each school for all teachers who were assigned to grades 3 through 5. These averages were intended to reflect the teacher characteristics that had influenced student behavior up to the time of the survey. Moreover, it was assumed that the observed measures of family background and other educational influences were related systematically to the cumulative impact of each of these variables.

The equation used to explore differences between frontier and average estimates is a linear equation based on Equation 1. Linearity not only violates our assumptions about the second derivative, but it also runs counter to our intuition about the real world. Nevertheless, the difficulties of estimating particular nonlinear functions and the risk of creating even greater specification biases in the coefficients by imposing another arbitrary functional form suggest that the linear equation might yield reasonable first approximations to the estimates that we seek. Following this procedure, of course, limits our comparison of the frontier and average estimates to the linear marginal products and price ratios.

The variables in the equation are shown in Table 10.1. These variables are taken from the reduced-form equation for verbal achievement derived from a four equation system encompassing three simultaneous equations and one that represents a recursive relationship. Once that system is estimated, one can solve for the reduced-form equation for any of the three endogenous variables. Since the estimation of that system is discussed elsewhere (Levin, 1970), this chapter is concerned only with the reduced form of the verbal equation. This equation was fitted to the entire sample of observations; thus, it represents the average production relationship for the sample of schools. Results are shown for this estimate in the right-hand column of Table 10.2.

TABLE 10.1
List of Variables

Variable	Item Measured	Coding
Verbal Score	Student Performance	Raw Score
Sex	Male-Female Differences	Male = 0 Female = 1
Age	Overage for Grade	Age 12 or over = 1 Less than 12 = 0
Possessions in Student's Home	Family Background (Socioeconomic Status)	Index of possessions: television Yes = 1 telephone No = 0 dictionary for each encyclopedia item; automobile index daily newspaper is sum. record player refrigerator vacuum cleaner
Family Size	Family Background	Number of people in home
Identity of Person Serving as Mother	Family Background	Real mother at home = 0 Real father not living at home = 1 Surrogate mother = 2
Identity of Person Serving as Father	Family Background	Real father at home = 0 Real father not living at home = 1 Surrogate father = 2
Father's Education	Family Background	Number of years of school attained
Mother's Employment Status	Family Background	Has job = 1 No job = 0
Attended Kindergarten	Family Background	Yes = 1 No = 0
Teacher's Verbal Score	Teacher Quality	Raw score on vocabulary test
Teacher's Parents' Income	Teacher Socio-economic Status	Father's occupation scaled according to 1959 census income (1000's of dollars)

TABLE 10.1 (continued)

Variable	Item Measured	Coding
Teacher experience	Teacher Quality	Number of years of full-time experience
Teacher's Undergraduate Institution	Teacher Quality	University or college = 3 Teacher institution = 1
Satisfaction With Present School	Teacher's Attitude	Satisfied = 3 Maybe prefers another school = 2 Prefers another school = 1
Percentage of White Students	Student Body	Percentage estimated by teachers
Teacher Turnover	School	Proportion of teachers who left in previous years for reasons other than death or illness
Library Volumes Per Student	School Facilities	Number of volumes divided by school enrollment

Obtaining Frontier Estimates

The same set of data and variables can be used to obtain estimates of the equation for only the most efficient observations. There are several ways of doing this; the method used here is the programming approach in input–output space suggested by Aigner and Chu (1968; the linear programming application draws upon the approach of Timmer, 1969). Since the individual observations are of students rather than schools, we wish to seek those students who show a particular outcome with the lowest application of resources.[6] Operationally, we wish to minimize Equation 6.

[6] The normal approach to estimating educational production functions is to use individual students as units of observation, rather than school averages. There are a variety of reasons for this, including the fact that there is a great deal more variance in standardized achievement scores within schools than among them and that collinearity increases markedly at the higher level of aggregation. In all cases, the school characteristics are aggregated to the classroom or multi-classroom level. Strictly speaking, the linear programming solution obtains coefficients for frontier

TABLE 10.2

Frontier and Average Production Relations for White Sixth Graders, Eastmet City

| | | Frontier Function | | | |
Variable	Run 1	Run 2 (-9)	Run 3 (-23)	Run 4 (-38)	Average Function
Personal Variables					
Sex	0.0	1.649	0.982	0.01956	0.817 (1.41)
Age	-7.714	-4.642	-4.769	-5.553	-6.010 (-4.49)
Family Size	-0.502	-0.500	-0.089	-0.770	-0.552 (-3.50)
Father's Identity	0.0	0.0	-0.283	-0.420	-0.327 (0.64)
Mother's Identity	-0.878	-1.342	-1.190	-1.202	-0.433 (-1.90)
Father's Education	0.509	0.179	0.0	0.103	0.273 (3.22)
Mother's Employment	-1.726	-2.293	-1.089	-0.951	-0.509 (-1.31)
Possessions	1.865	1.464	1.070	1.020	1.229 (5.201)
School Variables					
Kindergarten	0.0	2.866	1.920	2.106	2.372 (2.47)
Teacher's Verbal Ability	0.810	0.218	0.695	0.791	0.250 (1.70)
Teacher's Parents' Income	0.0	0.0	0.0	-0.0000	-0.118 (-0.64)
Undergraduate Institution	3.736	5.269	1.991	8.307	6.525 (2.09)
Teacher Experience	0.0	0.392	0.368	0.616	0.787 (4.93)

302

TABLE 10.2 (continued)

| | | Frontier Function | | | |
Variable	Run 1	Run 2 (-9)	Run 3 (-23)	Run 4 (-38)	Average Function
Teacher Satisfaction	3.630	7.078	4.666	3.608	1.960 (1.50)
Percent of White Students	0.0	-0.500	-0.264	-0.178	-0.047 (-.03)
Library Volumes Per Student	0.0	0.571	0.509	0.156	0.565 (1.53)
Teacher Turnover	0.0	0.0	0.0	-0.035	-0.101 (-1.27)
Constant	0.0	0.0	0.944	-4.051	-7.902 (.84)

$$(6) \qquad \sum_{i=0}^{n} \hat{a}_i \overline{X}_i$$

where $\hat{a}_i$ is the parameter for the ith input, $\overline{X}_i$ is the mean of input X_i, and $\overline{X}_o = 1$ in order to obtain a constant term. More specifically, the problem is to minimize Equation 6, which can be rewritten as 7 subject to the constraints of 8 where there are n inputs and m students.

$$(7) \qquad \text{Min. } \hat{a}_o + \hat{a}_1 \overline{X}_1 + \ldots + \hat{a}_n \overline{X}_n,$$

subject to:

$$(8) \qquad \hat{a}_o + \hat{a}_1 X_{11} + \ldots + \hat{a}_n X_{n1} \geq A_1$$

$$\hat{a}_o + \hat{a}_1 X_{im} + \ldots + \hat{a}_n X_{nm} \geq A_m$$
$$\hat{a}_i \geq 0$$

students rather than frontier firms. Since both average and frontier functions are obtained from samples of individuals, the approach is consistent. For a useful discussion of the choice of individual students as units of observation, see Michelson (1970:125–128).

Since this is essentially a linear programming problem, there will be as many "efficient" observations as there are inputs into the production function (assuming that no two observations are identical). Unfortunately, some of the observations will appear to be "efficient" when, in fact, they represent measurement errors. Thus, it is impossible to know a priori whether a particular observation is efficient or whether it is spurious. Therefore, extreme observations have been discarded in order to eliminate what might be spurious points. This is particularly important for the frontier estimates, since very few observations determine the structural coefficients.

Table 10.2 contrasts the frontier "estimates" with the estimates for the average function. Figures in parentheses beneath each coefficient for the average function signify the t-statistics of those coefficients. Each of the coefficients represents the first derivative or marginal product of the function.[7] Four linear programming runs were used to obtain frontier estimates. Run 1 eliminated no observations; run 2 discarded the 9 most "efficient" points; run 3 eliminated 23 observations; and run 4 discarded the 38 most extreme points (about 6% of the sample). We will compare the frontier function from run 4 and the average function and, at the same time, will examine two properties of the estimates: (1) the relative magnitudes of the coefficients, and (2) the implications for allocative or price efficiency.

Recall that in order for findings of optimal input intensities to yield the same relative applications of inputs for both average and frontier schools, the marginal products for both functions must bear a constant relation to each other as reflected in Equation 5. Table 10.3 shows the ratios of marginal products for the two sets of estimates for all of the school variables. According to this table, there is no systematic relationship between the two sets. At the frontier, inputs, such as the teacher's verbal facility and the proportion of white students to others, show marginal products that are more than three times their counterparts derived for the sample as a whole. On the other hand, variables, such as teacher turnover, teacher experience, and library volumes per student, show much smaller coefficients for the frontier function.

In summary, it appears that when student achievement is used as the criterion of educational output, so-called frontier schools are more efficient in the use of some inputs and less efficient in the use of others. Standard errors of the coefficients tend to be high relative to the differences in coefficients. Even so, the coefficient for teacher's verbal ability differs significantly in the two estimates, and other differences are on the margin of significance. This, in turn, suggests that the production isoquants for

---

[7] Since $a_i \geq 0$, those variables that showed negative coefficients for the average function represented problems for the programming estimates. The array for each such variable was multiplied by -1 for the programming estimates, and the signs were reversed in turn when reporting the results in Table 10.2. The author is indebted to Richard C. Carlson for computing the programming estimates (Carlson, 1970).

schools of different efficiencies, with regard to the production of student achievement, may be intersecting within the relevant ranges of factor substitution. This characteristic is probably attributable to differences in output mixes that are ignored in this type of analysis. Nevertheless, any optimal combination of inputs for any set of schools or any individual school, for the production of achievement, is likely to be less than optimal for any other set of schools or individual school pursuing a different combination of objectives. In other words, for any given array of prices $(P_1 P_2 \ldots, P_n)$, the optimal set of input proportions will vary from school to school depending upon its other priorities.

For purposes of generalizing about the optimal strategies for increasing student verbal scores, this is the worst of all possible worlds. That is, whereas we might be able to derive the optimal input structure for frontier schools or for schools on the average, as represented by equilibrium

TABLE 10.3

Ratio of Marginal Products at the Frontier to Marginal Products for the Entire Sample

School Variables	MP (frontier) —————— MP (average)
Kindergarten	.888
Teacher's Verbal Ability	3.164
Teacher's Parents' Income	.001 (.0005)
Undergraduate Institution	1.273
Teacher Experience	.783
Teacher Satisfaction	1.841
Percentage of White Students	3.787
Library Volumes Per Student	.276
Teacher Turnover	.347
Constant	.513

conditions stated in Equation 4, it is likely that the desirable combination of input intensities may differ between the two sets of schools (and may even differ significantly from school to school).

This is illustrated in Table 10.4, which shows the estimated ratios of prices for two inputs (teacher verbal score and teacher experience) as well as the two sets of marginal products for those inputs. The prices reflect the increments to annual teacher salaries for each of the teacher attributes; they were derived from an equation relating teacher attributes to earnings in the Eastmet teacher market (Levin, 1968, 1970). The marginal products associated with a unit change in the two inputs are taken from Table 10.2. In equilibrium, the ratios of the marginal products of the inputs should be equal to the ratios of their respective prices. For the average production estimates, these ratios are almost identical, so that allocative or price efficiency is implied even though the average estimates are assumed to be based on technically inefficient (nonfrontier) schools.

On the other hand, the frontier estimates show a ratio of marginal products four times as great as the price ratio for the two inputs. This suggests that the utilization of more verbally able teachers yields four times as much output per dollar as the utilization of additional teacher experience. If this is correct, the schools on the frontier could increase total output by reallocating their budgets in favor of teachers' verbal scores rather than their experience.

TABLE 10.4

Relative Prices and Marginal Products for Teacher Verbal Score and Teacher Experience

	(1) Teacher Verbal Score	(2) Teacher Experience	(3) Ratio of (1) to (2)
Price (salary increment)	$24.00	$79.00	0.303
Marginal Product at Frontier	0.791	0.616	1.284
Marginal Product on Average	0.250	0.787	0.317

Conclusions

The significant aspect of this analysis is that the combination of inputs that maximizes output for any set of prices differs between the two estimates. If these differences persist among schools of different apparent efficiencies in the production of achievement, the hope of obtaining general policy rules that can be applied across schools seems to be frustrated. That is, the lack of similarities among the production techniques used by different schools may mean that neither average nor frontier findings can be applied to any particular school. Indeed, in the extreme case, each individual school is on its own production function (which varies according to the outputs being pursued), and evaluation results for any group of schools will not be applicable to individual schools in the sample.

While measurement of educational production may be a useful exercise in itself, it is not clear that such studies can help us to improve the efficiency of the educational sector. In particular, our focus on a single and measurable output, student achievement, not only limits the analysis considerably, but it may allow for policy recommendations that would reduce the economic efficiency of the educational industry if they were adopted. Perhaps the only generalization that one can make from this pessimistic overview is that the analysis of production of public activities is fraught with difficulties that are unusually severe, given the present analytical state of the art. The implications of estimates of public sector production functions for improving social efficiency should probably be stated with far greater modesty than they have been in the past, for they may be totally misleading.

Acknowledgments

The author appreciates the comments of the two anonymous referees who provided constructive suggestions. He also wishes to thank both Pak Wai Liu and Kathy Diehl for assistance.

XI | High School Effects on Achievement[*]

Robert M. Hauser
William H. Sewell
The University of Wisconsin, Madison

Duane F. Alwin
Indiana University

For the past 15 years, sociologists have actively been working to identify, measure, and interpret the effects of schools on aspirations and achievements. Paradoxically, social science interest in school effectiveness gained in intensity and scope in the aftermath of the publication of *Equality of Educational Opportunity* (Coleman, Campbell, Hobson, McPartland, Mood, Weinfeld, and York, 1966). That massive study found that American public schools are remarkably homogeneous in resources and in educational outcomes, while there remain unacceptably large differentials among the achievements of major racial and socioeconomic groups. These broad conclusions appear to stand despite the challenges posed by systematic critical review and by further research (Mosteller and Moynihan, 1972; Jencks, Smith, Acland, Bane, Cohen, Gintis, Heyns, and Michelson, 1972; Averch, Carroll, Donaldson, Kiesling, and Pincus, 1972).

If schools do make a difference, the causative factors may be macro-social, as in variable length of temporal exposure to schooling (Wiley, Chapter 8 of this volume). Alternatively, the systematic variation in

* Prepared for the meetings of the American Sociological Association, Montreal, Quebec, August 1974. The research reported herein was supported by grants from the National Institutes of Health, U. S. Public Health Service (M-6275) and from the American College Testing Program.

309

schooling may be micro-social, perhaps involving the interpersonal contacts among students and teachers (Spaeth, Chapter 4 of this volume). In any event, it is abundantly clear that the observed differentiation of educational outcomes among American students has not been traced directly or in large measure to systematic variations in the social environment from school to school. The homogeneity of American schools may not be surprising when one takes into account the historic social pressures toward uniformity in teacher training, teaching methods, curricula, and school organization, as well as the differentiating forces of local custom, of social class, and of resource constraints.

Understandably, sociological investigations of school effects began with the hypothesis that global, normative features of the school or neighborhood environment would substantially affect educational outcomes and, thereby, the extent of social inequality (Wilson, 1959). The hypothesis was pursued with enthusiasm, although sociological researchers focused mainly on the possible effects of a secondary school's socioeconomic composition on college plans or aspirations (see Hauser, 1971, for a review of this literature). As Christopher Jencks et al. (1972:151–152) wrote:

> Research on the relationship between a high school's socio-economic composition and its students' college plans became a minor sociological industry during the 1960s. Most investigators found that students in predominantly middle-class high schools had higher aspirations than students in predominantly working-class high schools. These differences persisted even after various statistical adjustments had been made to take account of initial differences between the students entering middle-class and working-class schools. In recent years, however, sociologists have gathered better data and have become more sophisticated in their use of statistics. The best recent studies have concluded that the socio-economic composition of a high school has virtually no effect on students' aspirations.

However, a negative reading of the evidence of the 1960s is far from universal among sociologists, who have been remarkably reluctant to give up the school context hypothesis.

We suspect that many sociologists have held onto the school context hypothesis in the face of preponderantly negative evidence because it has singularly traditional sociological overtones and because it gives the discipline a unique offering in public discussions of schooling and social inequality. Thus, the finding of Sewell and Armer (1966a) that neighborhood socioeconomic contexts had little influence on college plans in Milwaukee was met with several critical replies (Turner, 1966; Michael, 1966; Boyle, 1966a), to which Sewell and Armer (1966b) responded in detail. Subsequently, there have been at least two secondary analyses of Sewell and Armer's published tables, each of which purports to reverse their conclusions. Spady (1970:17–19), in an exposition of simple multivariate analysis techniques, emphasized apparent interaction effects among sex, neighborhood SES, and college plans, which had been noted by Sewell and Armer, but not made explicit in their regression analysis. R. Smith (1972) noted that Kendall's tau-*b*, a symmetric ordinal measure of association, can be defined as a product-moment correlation, and, therefore, it may be used in a path analysis. From his ordinal path analysis of the Milwaukee data, Smith concluded (1972:199);

> Possibly, the small effect of neighborhood context reported by Sewell and Armer is a consequence of their ignoring a curvilinear relationship between neighborhood context and college plans, their assuming interval data, and their use of a linear multiple correlation model when in fact their data did not conform to the underlying assumptions.

However, using Sewell and Armer's categories for each independent variable (sex, mental ability, socioeconomic status, and neighborhood context), Smith's analysis increased the net contribution of neighborhood socioeconomic status only from 1.8% to 2.5% of the variance in college plans. Even after a post hoc regrouping of the data to increase the effect of neighborhood status, that variable explained less than 4% of the variance in college plans.

Suggestions that the evidence of schools' contextual effects was methodologically as well as empirically unsound were also received critically. Thus, Hauser's (1970a) parody of contextual analysis aroused both immediate and delayed criticism (Barton, 1970; Farkas, 1974), to which the author responded (Hauser, 1970c; 1974). In his critiques, Hauser argued that contextual analyses were frequently invalid because no real effort had been made to specify a viable model under the null hypothesis, for example, by including relevant covariates or by adjusting for measurement error in the covariates. If schools were explicitly selective with respect to the dependent achievement or aspiration variable, Hauser noted, no true contextual effects would exist, but neither could the specious effects be removed by statistical adjustment of the data. Hauser argued that aggregated school context variables typically were poor representations of the underlying social processes with which they were identified, and the importance of those processes was frequently understated in contextual analyses. Finally, confirming the work of Sewell and Armer, Hauser (1969, 1971) found only small effects of high schools on achievement and aspiration in Nashville, Tennessee.

While the flow of research on high school contexts has not abated, the sociological critics of contextual effects may have had some influence. Within the last few years sociological proponents of the school context hypothesis have suggested the possible importance of contextual variables other than the socioeconomic composition of student bodies, such as the average ability level of the students (Alexander and Eckland, 1973; Meyer, 1970) or educational climates (McDill and Rigsby, 1973). Furthermore, recent literature has emphasized the theoretical importance of the effects of school contexts, rather than their absolute size or direct implications for social policy.

Research Issues

Research on high school effects in the past decade has raised many questions whose answers are still tentative or incomplete. How large are the effects of high schools on aspirations and factors affecting them? Does a balance between normative and comparative social processes within schools tend to suppress the observable differences among schools (Meyer, 1970; Hauser, 1971; Nelson, 1972; Alexander and Eckland, 1973)? Do differences among high schools persist in adult life, that is, in educational or occupational careers (Folger, Astin, and Bayer, 1970; Alexander and Eckland, 1973)? Do the effects of schools interact with other variables in the process of socioeconomic achievement, such as sex and socioeconomic background? How large are the effects of the several dimensions of student body composition, and how can they best be interpreted?

In this paper, our purpose is to marshal new evidence on these questions by reanalyzing a sample of the Milwaukee data of Sewell and Armer (1966a) and by analyzing data from a statewide sample survey in Wisconsin (Sewell and Shah, 1967; Sewell, 1971). In our analyses, we use a more elaborate structural equation model of achievement than was used by Sewell and Armer or has been applied, thus far, in analyses of the statewide data (Sewell, Haller, and Ohlendorf, 1970), and we extend our analyses of high school effects to include post-secondary educational attainment. Our analysis consists of four parts. First, we undertake an exhaustive search for interaction effects of high schools on achievement in 20 Milwaukee high schools. Second, we give a detailed interpretation of the sources of aspiration and achievement within schools. Third, we estimate the additive effects of high schools on achievement in the statewide sample. Fourth, we examine the contextual effects of student-body composition on each variable in each equation of our model, and we look for consistency between these effects and other recent hypotheses and findings.

Samples

Our data are drawn from a panel study of Wisconsin youth who graduated from high school in the spring of 1957 and whose post-high school achievements were measured in a survey of their parents in 1964. The follow-up survey was carried out in a simple random sample of one-third of the 1957 graduates; a response rate of 87% was achieved. The Milwaukee County sample analyzed here includes the 903 persons for whom all relevant data were ascertained and who attended one of the 13 central city or 7 suburban Milwaukee high schools in 1957. This is a subsample of the Milwaukee data analyzed by Sewell and Armer (1966a). Our statewide data cover the schools in Milwaukee County and also 404 other schools in the State of Wisconsin, for a total of 424 schools. The statewide sample reported on here includes 7052 persons for whom all relevant data were ascertained. The present analysis excludes about 2000 persons for whom follow-up data were obtained, but with data missing on parents' income, rank in high school class, or occupational aspiration, and it excludes another 1300 persons for whom no response was obtained in the 1964 follow-up. From our analyses in other subsets of the Wisconsin sample (Sewell and Shah, 1967; Sewell et al., 1970; Hauser, 1972) and from detailed analyses of nonresponse bias (Sewell and Hauser, 1975:Chapter 2), we are confident that neither survey nor item nonresponse affects the validity of the analyses reported herein.

Variables

Five major groups of variables are included in our analysis: social background, high school characteristics, academic factors, social psychological factors, and educational attainment. Father's educational attainment (V) and mother's educational attainment (M) were reported by the student in a 1957 questionnaire and were coded in years of schooling completed, although they were originally reported as levels of educational certification. From studies of the reports of parents' education by youth of the same age, we believe these reports are reasonably accurate (Kerckhoff, Mason, and Poss, 1973; Borus and Nestel, 1973; Mason, Hauser, Kerckhoff, Poss, and Manton, Chapter 15 of this volume). Father's occupational status (X) was ascertained (with careful precautions to preserve anonymity) from the father's Wisconsin income tax return in 1957 or the closest year available and coded in the metric of Duncan's (1961) socioeconomic index (SEI) for occupations. In a few instances, occupations could not be ascertained from the tax returns, and reports from the 1957 student questionnaire were used. Parents' average income (I) for all available years, 1957–1960, was ascertained from Wisconsin income tax returns and coded in hundreds of dollars. These four socioeconomic background measures (V,M,X,I) are entered directly in our analyses of the statewide sample, but, in the smaller Milwaukee sample, we enter a socioeconomic index (B) constructed by giving roughly equal weight to the four background variables (Sewell et al., 1970).

Sex (S) is entered in our analysis as a dummy variable with men scored 1 and women 0. Throughout the present analyses, we have pooled the data for men and women, allowing sex to affect the mean levels of other variables, but not—with one exception—permitting sex to interact with other variables. That is, we assume that the relationships among socioeconomic background, academic and social psychological factors, and educational attainment are the same for men and women. Many investigators (including the present authors) have documented meaningful sex interactions in models of the achievement process. However, in our view, these interactions are not large enough to warrant the presentation of additional detail here. Fortunately, Nancy Carter (1972) has carried out an exhaustive analysis of the interactions of sex and marital status with variables in the achievement process in the statewide Wisconsin sample. While women obtained lower occupational returns to education than men, there was scant evidence that sex interacted with the determinants of educational attainment.

In much of the analysis, we treat the high school attended (H) as a categoric variable, either by entering dummy (0,1) variables in regression equations or equivalently by entering school averages on the dependent variable as regressors. In addition, where we wish to measure the impact of contextual variables, we introduce school averages as regressors. These procedures are consistent with the application of the analysis of covariance in studies of school effects as described by Hauser (1969, 1971) and Werts and Linn (1970).

Our model of achievement includes three academic factors, mental ability, rank in high school class, and completion of a college preparatory curriculum; the latter has not previously been used in analyses of the total Wisconsin sample (but see Alwin, 1974). Mental ability (Q) refers to the students' performance on the Henmon–Nelson Test of Mental Ability (Henmon and Nelson, 1954), ascertained from the State Testing Service of the Student Counseling Center of the University of Wisconsin. The tests were given during the students' junior year in high school. The scores are expressed in the metric of intelligence quotients, with a mean of 100 and a standard deviation of 15 in the standard population of Wisconsin high school juniors on which it was normed. Rank in high school class (G) was obtained from high school records, expressed as a percentile, and then transformed to produce an approximately normal distribution (i.e., a distribution similar to that of average high school grades). Completion of the college preparatory curriculum (C) is a dummy variable constructed from student reports of courses taken in high school. Students were given a high score if they had completed a pattern of courses that would qualify them for admission to the University of Wisconsin. Thus, the college preparatory variable, like high school rank, represents a cumulative outcome of the high school career, and it does not purport to represent, except indirectly, any decisions about curriculum placement earlier in the schooling process.

The educational and occupational aspirations of the students and their perceptions of the influence of significant others are the social psychological variables taken from the 1957 questionnaire. College plans (E) is a dummy variable which indicates whether or not the student planned to enroll in a degree granting college or university in the year following high school graduation. Occupational aspiration (J) is the Duncan SEI of the occupation category that the respondent said he eventually hoped to enter.

The three "significant other" variables are all based on the students' self-reported perceptions in 1957. Teachers' encouragement (*T*) and parental encouragement (*P*) are dummy variables which take on high values when the student reported that his teachers or parents wanted him to attend college. Friends' plans (*F*) is a dummy variable which has a high value when the student reported that most of his friends were planning to attend college. In the analysis of Milwaukee data, we sum the measures of teachers' and parents' encouragement and of friends' college plans to form a composite index of significant others' influence (*O*), even though this results in the loss of some interpretive detail (see Hauser, 1972, and the following analyses of the statewide data).

Educational attainment (*U*) was ascertained in the 1964 follow-up survey. It closely approximates the Census Bureau's concept of years of schooling completed. However, we gave up to a year's credit for vocational or technical education, and, in some instances, we credited students with a last year of regular schooling when we were not certain the year had been completed. In most cases, we were able to assign a normative number of school years completed that corresponded to the level of certification achieved (e.g., 16 years for college graduates with no further schooling).

A Model of Educational Attainment

Our analysis of the statewide and Milwaukee data is motivated and guided by a structural equation model of achievement derived from the work of many investigators over the past several years (see Blau and Duncan, 1967; Duncan, Featherman, and Duncan, 1972; Sewell, Haller, and Portes, 1969; Sewell *et al.*, 1970; Hauser 1969, 1971, 1972; Sewell and Hauser, Chapter 1 of this volume; and Heyns 1974). The linear, recursive model is shown in schematic form as a path diagram in Figure 11.1, where we have grouped certain variables for the sake of clarity. In the path diagram, the curved, two-headed arrows represent possible correlations which are not analyzed causally in the model, and the straight, single-

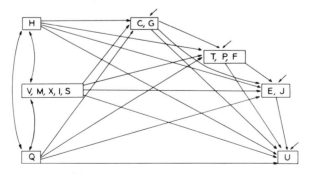

Figure 11.1 A path model for educational attainment. See text for explanation.

headed arrows represent possible lines of unidirectional causation (Duncan, 1966). The causal arrows with unlabeled origins represent random disturbances (error or unexplained variance). We offer no causal assumptions about relations among the variables within the boxes in the diagram. Thus, had we diagrammed the model in detail, we would have indicated the possibility of correlation among the disturbances of C and G, of T,P, and F, and of E and J.

The model states that socioeconomic background, sex, ability, and attendance at a particular high school are determined exogenously. That is, they are all causally prior to every other variable in the model, but no casual priority among them is postulated. The ordering of high school (H) relative to later variables in the model is, perhaps, the most dubious aspect of this specification, for if high schools are directly selective with respect to later variables in the model (Hauser, 1974), then the causal scheme should be modified to reflect this. It is, perhaps, fortunate that the controversy over contextual effects concerns the direct or net influence of schools, so the causal priority of H is not a critical matter.

The exogenous variables—socioeconomic background and sex, ability, and high school—directly affect high school rank (G) and curriculum (C). Following Heyns (1974), we posit·no causal ordering among G and C because both are cumulated outcomes of the high school experience. Grades and curriculum, along with the exogenous variables, are taken to affect perceptions of the expectations of significant others, and all of these variables, in turn, affect college plans and occupational aspirations. Finally, all of the preceding variables may influence the student's post-secondary schooling. The temporal and theoretical rationale for our causal ordering of the variables has been spelled out in greater detail elsewhere (Sewell et al., 1969; Sewell et al., 1970; Hauser, 1972). With the aforementioned exception, we think the ordering of the exogenous variables, grades and curriculum, the social psychological variables, and educational attainment is hard to dispute. One point of uncertainty is the causal ordering of the aspiration measures relative to the perceived expectations of significant others. There, we believe a reasonable case might be made for simultaneity bias. To a certain degree, students may perceive what others want them to do or are planning to do in terms of their own desires or plans.

Interaction Effects: The Milwaukee Sample

We began our analysis with an attempt to locate interaction effects of schools on the achievement process in Milwaukee. We wanted to see whether the relationships among variables in our model varied significantly from school to school. For several reasons, we chose to carry out our search for interaction effects in the Milwaukee sample, rather than in the statewide sample. We wanted to run global tests of nonadditivity, that is, without specifying the functional form of the interactions, but it was not computationally feasible to carry out such an analysis in a large number of schools. We wanted to look for interactions in a subset of the data where the number of sample cases per school would be large enough for us to identify statistical interactions where they were real. In the Milwaukee subsample there was an average of 45 cases per school, compared with about 17 per school in the statewide sample, which included many rural and small town schools. Furthermore, we had a special interest in looking for interaction effects in the Milwaukee sample, since the evidence of such effects in Sewell and Armer's (1966a) analysis was reemphasized by Spady (1970) and R. Smith (1972).

Finally, there is already substantial evidence that the relationships in our model do not vary markedly from place to place within Wisconsin (Sewell et al., 1970). Schoenberg (1972:23–25) has questioned this finding because Sewell, Haller, and Ohlendorf based their comparisons among city-size categories on standardized coefficients. He observed that Sewell, Haller, and Ohlendorf had overlooked a significant increase with city size in the regression of significant others' influence on socioeconomic status. However, we have examined the (unstandardized) regression coefficients in the Sewell, Haller, and Ohlendorf model in great detail, and the variation in slopes with city size is generally small and irregular. Indeed, Schoenberg apparently reported the one interaction out of 26 examined by Sewell, Haller, and Ohlendorf in which the slopes varied monotonically with size of place.

Table 11.1 summarizes our tests for interaction effects of schools in the Milwaukee data. The column headings refer to dependent achievement variables, and the row headings refer to predetermined variables or sets of predetermined variables on which the dependent variables have been regressed. The figures given in the table are either coefficients of determination (R^2) in a regression equation, or they are differences between coefficients of determination in a pair of regression equations which we compare in order to test an hypothesis (Cohen, 1968). Unless otherwise indicated, each of the coefficients of determination or differences between them is statistically significant beyond the $\alpha = .01$ level. However, the overall error rate in this part of our analysis is presumably larger than .01 because we are carrying out so many tests. The reported probability levels should not be taken too seriously because several of our dependent measures are dummy variables, and other statistical assumptions have probably also been violated. Given our large sample, however, we are reasonably confident of the robustness of our statistical procedures (Glass, Peckham, and Sanders, 1972).

There are enough variables and equations in our model to generate an enormous number of tests for interaction effects, even if we limit ourselves to first-order interactions of schools with other regressors in our model. To facilitate our analysis, we systematically looked at first-order interactions,

TABLE 11.1

*Coefficients of Determination and Increments in Coefficients of
Determination for Additive and Nonadditive Regression Models for
High School Effects: One-third Sample Respondents in the Milwaukee
County Public Schools (Twenty Schools) with Data Present (N = 903)*

Model		Dependent Variable					
		G	C	O	E	J	U
1.	H	.0129	.0973	.1497	.1303	.0857	.1514
2.	B,Q,S	.3761	.2441	.3348	.3206	.2187	.3362
3.	B,Q,S,H	.4428	.2955	.3742	.3479	.2491	.3680
	(3 vs. 2)	.0668	.0515	.0395	.0273	.0304	.0318
4.	B,Q,S,H,S×H	.4553	.3135	.3822	.3617	.2767	.3794
	(4 vs. 3)	.0125[a]	.0180[a]	.0080[a]	.0138[a]	.0276[a]	.0114[a]
5.	B,Q,S,H,Q×H	.4542	.3167	.3880	.3661	.2719	.3831
	(5 vs. 3)	.0113[a]	.0212[a]	.0138[a]	.0182[a]	.0227[a]	.0151[a]
6.	B,Q,S,H,B×H	.4549	.3149	.3845	.3621	.2717	.3807
	(6 vs. 3)	.0121[a]	.0194[a]	.0102[a]	.0142[a]	.0225[a]	.0128[a]
7.	B,Q,S,G			.3823	.3686	.2939	.4188
8.	B,Q,S,G,C			.4689	.4305	.3185	.4491
9.	B,Q,S,G,H			.4297	.4047	.3309	.4692
	(9 vs. 7)			.0474	.0361	.0370	.0503
10.	B,Q,S,G,C,H			.5064	.4590	.3511	.4909
	(10 vs. 8)			.0375	.0285	.0326	.0419
11.	B,Q,S,G,C,H,G×H			.5193	.4732	.3656	.5189
	(11 vs. 10)			.0129[a]	.0141[a]	.0145[a]	.0280
12.	B,Q,S,G,C,H,C×H			.5189	.4741	.3644	.5069
	(12 vs. 10)			.0126[a]	.0150[a]	.0133[a]	.0160[a]
13.	B,Q,S,G,C,O				.5104	.3598	.5077
14.	B,Q,S,G,C,O,H				.5249	.3836	.5351
	(14 vs. 13)				.0144[a]	.0238[a]	.0274
15.	B,Q,S,G,C,O,H,O×H				.5333	.3896	.5500
	(15 vs. 14)				.0084[a]	.0060[a]	.0149[a]
16.	B,Q,S,G,C,O,E,J						.5644
17.	B,Q,S,G,C,O,E,J,H						.5860
	(17 vs. 16)						.0217
18.	B,Q,S,G,C,O,E,J,H,E×H						.6027
	(18 vs. 17)						.0167[a]
19.	B,Q,S,G,C,O,E,J,H,J×H						.6021
	(19 vs. 17)						.0161[a]
20.	B,Q,S,G,C,O,E,J,H,G×H						.6084
	(20 vs. 17)						.0224

TABLE 11.1 (continued)

Variable abbreviations are as follows: B = family socioeconomic background, Q = academic ability, S = sex, G = rank in high school class, C = high school curriculum (college preparatory), O = significant other influence to attend college, E = college plans, J = occupational status aspirations, H = set of dummy variables representing high school attended by the respondent, SxH = variables representing sex by high school interactions, QxH = academic ability by high school interactions, BxH = family socioeconomic background by high school interactions, GxH = high school rank by high school interactions, CxH = high school curriculum by high school interactions, OxH = significant other influence by high school interactions, ExH = college plans by high school interactions, JxH = occupational aspirations by high school interactions.

ap < .01

one at a time, in the least complicated equation in which each regressor legitimately could appear, given our model. We adopted this strategy in the belief that interaction effects are more likely to appear in heterogeneous data (Kendall, 1951:189). Only in the one case where a significant first-order interaction appeared in the simplest (reduced-form) equation did we look to see if the interaction appeared in the full equation.

Line 3 of Table 11.1 gives the coefficients of determination in the set of reduced-form equations that we used to test for differences among schools in the effects of sex (S), mental ability (Q), and socioeconomic background (B) on subsequent variables. The coefficients of determination and increments to them in the equations with interaction effects are given in Lines 4, 5, and 6, respectively. For example, the regression of college plans (E) on background (B), ability (Q), sex (S), and high school (H) accounts for 34.79% of the variance in plans. When we allow the effect of sex (but of no other variable) on college plans to vary from school to school (Line 4), there is a statistically insignificant 1.38 percentage-point increase in the explained variance in the sample. When we allow the effect of ability (but of no other variable) on college plans to vary from school to school (Line 5), there is a statistically insignificant 1.82 percentage-point increase in the explained variance in the sample. Similarly, when we allow the effect of socioeconomic background (but of no other variable) on college plans to vary from school to school (Line 6), there is a statistically insignificant 1.42 percentage-point increase in the explained variance in the sample. We have chosen these interaction effects for close examination not merely by chance, but because the findings just reported speak directly and negatively to the suggestions that Sewell and Armer's (1966a) regression analyses were invalid because of contextual interactions in the Milwaukee data. Furthermore, we emphasize that the increments to explained variance, which are reported in Table 11.1, pertain to the sample, not the population. Estimates of the corresponding increments in the population would be smaller because every set of interaction effects uses 19 more degrees of freedom than the comparable additive model.

Not only are there no statistically significant interaction effects of schools with sex, socioeconomic status, or mental ability in the determination of college plans, but there are no statistically significant interaction effects of schools with sex, socioeconomic status, or mental ability in determining any of the six dependent variables in Table 11.1. Furthermore, there are no statistically significant interaction effects of schools with high school rank (G) in the determination of significant others' influence, college plans, or occupational aspirations, but there is statistically significant variation among schools in the regression of educational attainment (U) on high school rank (see Lines 10 and 11). We shall refer again to this shortly. There are no statistically significant interaction effects of schools with curriculum placement (C) in the determination of significant others' influence, college plans, occupational aspirations, or educational attainment (see Lines 10 and 12). There are no statistically significant interactions of schools with significant others' influence (O) in the determination of college plans, occupational aspirations, or educational attainment (see Lines 14 and 15). Finally, there are no statistically significant interactions of schools either with college plans (E) or occupational aspirations (J) in the determination of educational attainment (see Lines 17, 18, and 19).

We checked to see whether the interaction of schools with grades and educational attainment might disappear in the full equation. While the increment to explained variance in the sample was reduced from 2.80% to 2.24%, the interactions were still significant beyond the $\alpha = .01$ level (see Lines 17 and 20). In looking at the slope of educational attainment on grades in each school, however, we were not able to detect any systematic covariation of the slopes with composition of the student body. Obviously, this does not exhaust the possibility of interpreting the school-grade-education interactions, but we were not inclined to press the matter further. The increment to explained variance was small; 2.24% of more than 60% was explained by our model, and this was the only significant set of interactions among the many we investigated.

In summary, out of 31 tests for the statistical interaction of Milwaukee high schools with variables in the process of educational attainment, only one was nominally statistically significant. Beyond their implications for the controversy over Sewell and Armer's 1966 paper, we believe these results are substantively important in themselves. Furthermore, we think that our findings thus far amply justify the working assumption that school effects are additive in the statewide Wisconsin sample.

Table 11.1 also provides evidence of the additive effects of high schools, that is, the variance in achievement attributable to average differences among the schools. Line 1 summarizes the total variability in achievement variables among schools; the coefficients of determination reported there are also squares of the correlation ratios of the variables (Hauser, 1971:20).

Less than 10% of the variance in completion of a college preparatory curriculum (C) and of occupational aspirations (J) occurs among schools; 15% or less of the variance in significant others' influence (O), college plans (E), and educational attainment (U) occurs among the Milwaukee schools. As one would expect from the definition of the variable, virtually none of the variance in rank in high school class (G) occurs among schools. However, even if grade point averages, rather than ranks, were used to measure academic performance, we would have found little difference in grades among schools, simply because the average grade in any high school is a "C" (Hauser, 1971:47–51).

Line 2 of Table 11.1 gives coefficients of determination in the regressions of achievement variables on socioeconomic background (B), mental ability (Q), and sex (S). Clearly, these exogenous variables account for substantially more of the variability in achievement than does the high school attended by a student. For example, 13.03% of the variance in college plans and 15.14% of the variance in educational attainment occurs from school to school, but SES, ability, and sex account for 32.06% of the variance in college plans and 33.62% of the variance in post-secondary schooling. Line 3 of Table 11.1 adds the high schools to the regressions of achievement variables on SES, ability, and sex. As one would expect (Hauser, 1971:98–105), the variability between schools in rank in high school class increases when SES, ability, and sex are included in the equation. The reason is that average rank does not vary substantially from school to school, while the exogenous variables do vary from school to school and also affect grades within schools. Except in the case of rank in high school class, the schools contribute much less to the variability in achievement after SES, ability, and sex have been entered in the equation than before (compare Lines 2 and 3). Thus, schools add only 2.73%, net of SES, ability, and sex, to the explained variance in college plans, and they add only 3.18% to the explained variance in post-high school education, net of SES, ability, and sex. Note that schools have been treated as categories in this analysis, so the results in Table 11.1 take into account any possible curvilinearity in the influence of schools. Moreover, the exogenous variables (B, Q, and S) jointly add substantial increments to the explained variance when they are added to the equations in which the school variables are the only regressors (compare Lines 1 and 3). For example, those variables add more than 20% to the explained variance in both college plans and educational attainment, above and beyond the effects of high schools.

When the college preparatory curriculum (C) and rank in high school class (G) are added to the equations for subsequent achievement variables, the net effect of schools on significant others' influence (O) declines trivially, and its effect on college plans (E), occupational aspirations (J), and educational attainment (U) increases modestly (compare Lines 10, 8, and 3). The schools make a net contribution of three to four percentage points in the explained variance. Presumably, the increased school effects are attributable to the suppressor effect involving rank in high school class, the so-called "frog pond" phenomenon (Davis, 1966; Meyer, 1970; Nelson, 1972). When significant others' influence (O) is added to the equations for aspirations and attainment, the net effects of schools are reduced to statistically insignificant contributions of 1.44% and of 2.38% to college plans (E) and occupational aspirations (J), respectively (see Line 14), and the net effect of schools on educational attainment falls to 2.74%. When plans and aspirations are added to the final equation for post-secondary schooling (Line 17), the net contribution of high schools in the sample falls to 2.17%.

We believe these findings substantiate and extend those of Sewell and Armer (1966a). In the Milwaukee County sample, the gross differences among schools, including all aspects of the social and psychological composition of their student-bodies, account for at most 15% of the variance in post-high school education. After controlling for several relevant social and psychological variables, the high schools account for about 2% of the variance in educational attainment. Unless there is some unanticipated suppressor effect of schools, the latter figure may be taken as an upper bound estimate, because of the large number of degrees of freedom (19) used to represent schools and because some of our survey variables are, no doubt, subject to unreliability. We would emphasize that these results do not speak to the possible influence of school variables on achievement, but rather to their observed importance in a real population of schools and students.

Additive School Effects: The Statewide Sample

Here and in the next section of the chapter, we take up the measurement and interpretation of high school effects in the statewide Wisconsin sample. Table 11.2 gives descriptive statistics on the variables in our model of achievement and on their variation among the 424 Wisconsin high schools covered in the sample. The first two columns of the table give the arithmetic mean and the standard deviation of each of the variables. Clearly, there is wide variation in the social backgrounds and achievements of persons in the statewide sample, and there is no reason to suspect that the members of the sample are unrepresentative of high school graduates. The third column of the table gives the proportions of total variance in the variables in the model that occur among schools. These proportions are strictly comparable with entries in the first row of Table 11.1, but we have presented the proportions of variance between schools in the exogenous variables, as well as in the endogenous variables.

It may be of particular interest that approximately 27% of the variance in parents' income occurs among schools, and this appears to be significantly higher than the proportion for any other socioeconomic background variable. Beyond that, the measures of between-school variance present no surprises. There appears to be more variance among schools in friends'

TABLE 11.2

Descriptive Statistics for Achievement Variables: One-Third Sample Respondents in the State of Wisconsin with Data Present (N = 7052)

Variable	Grand Mean	Total Standard Deviation	Proportion of Total Variance Between Schools	Within School Standard Deviation	Between School Standard Deviation
S	.4860	.4998	.0924	.4761	.1522
V	10.02	3.087	.1656	2.820	1.257
M	10.44	2.980	.1429	2.759	1.128
X	31.04	22.36	.1927	20.09	9.824
I	59.16	32.90	.2673	28.17	17.02
Q	101.5	14.49	.1267	13.54	5.157
G	51.62	18.67	.0462	18.24	4.006
C	.6031	.4893	.1537	.4502	.1917
T	.4516	.4977	.0778	.4779	.1389
P	.5401	.4984	.1109	.4699	.1661
F	.3793	.4853	.1739	.4412	.2021
E	.3531	.4780	.1183	.4487	.1646
J	49.98	22.56	.1232	21.13	7.909
U	13.41	1.827	.1325	1.701	.6649

Variable abbreviations are as follows: S = sex, V = father's education, M = mother's education, X = father's occupational status, I = parental income, Q = academic ability, G = rank in high school class, C = college preparatory curriculum, T = teachers' encouragement, P = parents' encouragement, F = friends' college plans, E = college plans, J = occupational status aspirations, U = educational attainment.

college plans than in teachers' or parents' encouragement. Only 12–13% of the variance in college plans, occupational aspirations, and educational attainment occurs among schools in Wisconsin. Again, estimating these components of variance uses up more than 400 degrees of freedom, so an appropriate correction for loss of degrees of freedom would considerably reduce the proportions in Table 11.2.

In the last two columns of Table 11.2, we give within-school and between-school standard deviations of the variables in the sample (not adjusted for loss of degrees of freedom). These may give some readers a better notion of the variability among schools and among persons in the statewide sample. For example, the standard deviation of schoolwide averages of parents' income is $1700, but it is $2800 among students within schools. The standard deviation of the proportion of students planning to attend college is about one-sixth among schools, and it is almost one-half within schools. The standard deviation of post-secondary schooling is about two-thirds of a year in among schools, and it is about 1.7 years among individuals within schools. Of course, these within- and between-school standard deviations tell us nothing that is not already implicit in the sample standard deviations and proportions of variance between schools.

Within-School Models

Most of the variability in social background and achievement variables occurs within, rather than among high schools. For this reason, we thought it would be instructive and important to see how our model of achievement works within schools. Moreover, the within-school regressions are used, implicitly or explicitly, in estimating net or adjusted differences among schools. Following Hauser's (1971:Chapter 2) exposition, we estimated within-school regression equations, which are displayed in Table 11.3. Literally, the "within-school" variables were derived by deviating persons' values on each variable from the average of the variable in their school. This eliminated any possibility of confounding school effects with other aspects of the achievement process (without our having to specify any particular contextual variables). The first panel of Table 11.3 gives regression coefficients for variables in standard form, and the second panel gives the corresponding regression coefficients for variables in their original metrics. As an aid in interpretation of the table, both the standardized and corresponding metric coefficients are italicized whenever the standardized coefficient is larger than .1 in absolute value. Because of the large sample size, however, many smaller coefficients are statistically significant at conventional levels.

Within schools, the major influences on grades (G) are mental ability (Q) and sex (S), in that order. Women obtain grades that are about 10 points higher—more than half a standard deviation—on our scale than do men. Each one point increment in mental ability leads to a .8 point increase in grades on our scale. The effect of each socioeconomic background measure on grades within schools is quite small; for example, a full year more of mother's or father's education leads only to a .2 increase in grades on our scale. However, one should remember that there is a substantial splitting of effects among the four SES measures, and, jointly, they do have a significant effect on grades.

Indeed, from comparisons of the present within-school regressions with (unpublished) total regressions for men and women, we have observed that the within-school regressions of grades on socioeconomic background are steeper than the total regressions; the latter are virtually nil. Apparently,

TABLE 11.3

Within High School Regression Models: One-Third Sample Respondents in the State of Wisconsin with Data Present (N = 7052)

A. Regression coefficients in standard form

Predetermined Variable	Dependent Variable							
	G	C	T	P	F	E	J	U
S	-.2631	.1087	.0883	.1142	-.0149	.0918	-.0349	.1121
V	.0326	.0881	.0514	.0859	.0591	.0438	.0181	.0439
M	.0353	.0623	.0276	.0851	.0698	.0240	.0092	.0302
X	.0190	.0482	-.0109	.0681	.0561	.0325	.0257	.0133
I	.0252	.0554	.0414	.0724	.0656	.0572	.0376	.0443
Q	.5954	.3656	.0764	.0829	.0384	.0277	.0811	.0345
G			.3156	.1240	.1915	.1701	.2093	.2104
C			.1695	.2455	.1995	.0899	.0753	.0423
T						.1109	.0961	.0215
P						.2748	.1860	.1073
F						.1629	.1387	.1081
E								.3390
J								.0525
R^2	.4536	.2140	.2397	.2494	.1923	.4248	.3381	.5332

TABLE 11.3 (continued)

| | Dependent Variable | | | | | | | |
Predetermined Variable	G	C	T	P	F	E	J	U
B. Regression coefficients								
S	*-1008.*	*10.28*	*8.862*	*11.27*	*-1.381*	*8.654*	*-154.7*	*40.06*
V	21.08	1.406	.8715	1.432	.9242	.6968	13.52	2.649
M	23.31	1.017	.4780	1.449	1.116	.3908	7.032	1.865
X	1.725	.1081	-.0259	.1592	.1232	.0726	2.700	.1130
I	1.631	.0886	.0703	.1207	.1027	.0912	2.818	.2678
Q	*80.18*	1.215	.2695	.2876	.1251	.0918	12.66	.4339
G			*.8269*	.3196	.4632	.4184	24.24	1.963
C			17.99	25.63	19.55	8.960	353.4	16.00
T						*10.42*	424.9	7.643
P						*26.24*	836.4	*38.83*
F						*16.58*	664.3	41.69
E								*128.5*
J								.4226

NOTE: Effect measures are italicized when the standardized regression coefficients are greater than .10 in absolute value. All regression coefficients (unstandardized) are multiplied by 100 for ease of presentation.

Variable abbreviations are as follows: S = sex, V = father's education, M = mother's education, X = father's occupational status, I = parental income, Q = academic ability, G = rank in high school class C = college preparatory curriculum, T = teachers' encouragement, P = parents' encouragement, F = friends' college plans, E = college plans, J = occupational status aspirations, Π = educational attainment.

326

the lack of variability in average grades among schools suppresses the total regressions of grades on socioeconomic background. Thus, contrary to earlier findings in the Wisconsin data (Sewell et al., 1969, 1970; Hauser, 1972), there does appear to be some socioeconomic discrimination in the allocation of grades in school. Conceivably, the suppressor effect just noted accounts for the tendency of class discrimination in schools to be more obvious to those who do fieldwork than to survey analysts.

Curriculum placement depends primarily on ability, but to a lesser degree than do grades. A 10-point shift in mental ability (Q) leads to a 12 percentage-point shift in the probability of completing a college preparatory program (C). While boys obtain lower grades than girls, they have a likelihood 10 percentage points higher of completing a college preparatory program at any given level of socioeconomic background or ability. Thus, within schools, sex has opposite effects on these two academic variables, while the latter have generally similar effects on later aspirations and achievements. The opposing forces, thus generated, tend partly to compensate for one another, and, because of this, the specific advantages and disadvantages of boys and girls in school may easily be underestimated.

The direct effects of socioeconomic background (V,M,X,I) on curriculum placement (C) are somewhat larger than on grades (G), but less than on parental encouragement to attend college (P). The effects of socioeconomic background on curriculum are partly mediated by ability, as Heyns (1974) has observed, but it is our impression that the direct influence of SES is relatively greater in the Wisconsin sample. (However, with regard to the relative importance of socioeconomic and ability factors in determining grades and curriculum placement, our findings within schools generally agree with those of Heyns.) Thus, completion of a precollegiate program of study is an aspect of the scholastic differentiation—and, perhaps, labeling—of students, which is responsive to social factors of sex and socioeconomic background, aside from the possible influence of academic ability. Other things being equal, a youth whose parents are both college graduates is about 10 percentage points more likely to complete a college preparatory program than a youth whose parents are both high school graduates.

The variables with the largest direct effects on the three "significant other" variables (T,P,F) are the academic factors: grades and curriculum. However, socioeconomic background does have substantial direct effects on the perception of parental encouragement to attend college (P), and, in this respect, parents may be said to be more particularistic than friends or teachers. Grades (G) appear to be more important than curriculum (C) in their effect on teachers' encouragement (T), but the relative effects are reversed in the case of parents' encouragement (P). Thus, parents are perceived to be more responsive to the formal distinction between collegiate and noncollegiate programs, while teachers are perceived to respond more to performance than to the program followed by the student. All other things being equal, boys are almost 9 percentage points more likely than girls to perceive that their teachers want them to attend college, and boys are 11 percentage points more likely than girls to perceive that their parents want them to go to college. However, there is no difference between the sexes in the likelihood of perceiving that their friends will attend college.

The largest direct influences on college plans (E) and occupational aspirations (J) are grades (G) and the perceptions of significant others (T,P,F). A standard deviation shift in grades (G) gives rise to an 8 percentage-point shift in the likelihood that a student will plan to attend college and a 4.5 point shift in occupational status aspirations. Significant others have very large effects on college plans and occupational aspirations within schools. The chance of planning on college is increased 10.4 percentage points by the perception of teachers' encouragement, 26.2 percentage points by the perception of parents' encouragement, and 16.3 percentage points by the perception that most of one's friends will attend college. These same variables directly increase occupational aspirations on the Duncan SEI by 4.2 points, 8.4 points, and 6.6 points, respectively.

The effect of completing a college-preparatory program (C) on plans and aspirations is only slightly less than those just enumerated. Completion of a pre-college program directly increases the chance of planning on college by about 9 percentage points (and indirectly by almost another 12 percentage points). Completion of the pre-college program increases occupational aspiration directly by 3.5 points on the Duncan SEI (and indirectly by more than another 4 points). Furthermore, all other things being equal, boys are almost 9 percentage points more likely than girls to plan on college, but the occupational status aspirations of boys are actually lower than those of girls by a small margin. Even taking into account the splitting of effects among the socioeconomic background variables (V,M,X,I), their direct effects on plans and aspirations are quite small.

The largest direct influences on ultimate educational attainment are sex (S), grades (G), parental encouragement (P), friends' plans (F), and, largest of all, college plans (E). All other things being equal, persons who planned to attend college obtained 1.28 more years of post-secondary schooling than persons without college plans. Even after taking into account their indirect effects on schooling by way of college plans, the perception of parental encouragement and friends planning to attend college each led to about a .4 year increase in schooling. Furthermore, all other things being equal, a standard deviation shift in high school grades produced a .4 year shift in schooling, and boys completed about .4 more years of schooling than did girls.

An examination of the pattern of direct and indirect effects in our model of achievement provides further insights. Table 11.4 gives regression coefficients for standardized variables in various reduced-form and structural equations. We can identify direct and indirect effects conveniently by comparing coefficients in equations to which one or more intervening variables are successively added (Sewell and Hauser, 1975; Alwin and Hauser, 1975). We present only standardized regression coefficients in

TABLE 11.4

Coefficients of Variables in Standard Form, Reduced-Form and Structural Equations in Within-School Achievement Models: One-Third Sample Respondents in the State of Wisconsin with Data Present (N = 7052)

Dependent Variable	Predetermined Variables												
	S	V	M	X	I	Q	G	C	T	P	F	E	J
(1) G	-.263	.033	.035	.019	.025	.595							
(2) C	.109	.088	.062	.048	.055	.366							
(3) T	.024	.077	.049	.003	.059	.326							
(4) T	.088	.051	.028	-.011	.041	.076	.316	.170					
(5) P	.108	.112	.105	.082	.089	.246							
(6) P	.114	.086	.085	.068	.072	.083	.124	.246					
(7) F	-.044	.083	.089	.069	.082	.225							
(8) F	-.015	.059	.070	.056	.066	.038	.192	.200					
(9) E	.082	.110	.084	.074	.111	.302							
(10) E	.131	.083	.062	.059	.092	.065	.270	.209					
(11) E	.092	.044	.024	.032	.057	.028	.170	.090	.111	.275	.163		
(12) J	-.065	.071	.058	.058	.080	.342							
(13) J	-.007	.047	.037	.045	.064	.109	.289	.165					
(14) J	-.035	.018	.009	.026	.038	.081	.209	.075	.096	.186	.139		
(15) U	.093	.118	.094	.064	.113	.354							
(16) U	.168	.091	.070	.049	.095	.077	.358	.173					
(17) U	.141	.060	.039	.026	.066	.048	.279	.077	.064	.210	.171		
(18) U	.112	.044	.030	.013	.044	.034	.210	.042	.022	.107	.108	.339	.052

Variable abbreviations are as follows: H = high schools, S = sex, V = father's education, M = mother's education, X = father's occupational status, I = parental income, Q = academic ability, G = rank in high school class, C = college preparatory curriculum, T = teachers' encouragement, P = parents' encouragement, F = friends' college plans, E = college plans, J = occupational status aspirations, U = educational attainment.

Table 11.4, but the interpretations of direct and indirect effects are indifferent to standardization. For example, Lines 3 and 4 of Table 11.4 differ in the addition of grades (G) and curriculum (C) to the equation for teachers' encouragement. The coefficient of mental ability (Q) decreases from .326 in Line 3 to .076 in Line 4, so 77% of the effect of ability on teachers' encouragement is mediated by the academic variables, grades (G) and curriculum (C). The indirect effect, $.326 - .076 = .250$, may be decomposed as an indirect effect via grades, $.595 \times .316 = .188$, and another via curriculum, $.366 \times .170 = .062$. Thus, the model gives three components of the effect of mental ability on teachers' encouragement: 23% is a direct effect; 58% is mediated by grades; and the remaining 19% is mediated by curriculum placement. Bright youths perceive more encouragement from teachers mainly because they obtain high grades or complete a college-preparatory curriculum.

The total effects of socioeconomic background (V,M,X,I) on teachers' encouragement are small, and the direct effects are even smaller (compare Lines 3 and 4), but the direct effect of sex on teachers' encouragement is greater than its total effect (.088 versus .024). The indirect effect works to the disadvantage of boys ($.024 - .088 = -.064$). The tendency of girls to be encouraged more than boys because they obtain higher grades ($-.263 \times .316 = -.083$) is stronger than that of boys to receive more encouragement because they are more likely to be in a precollegiate curriculum.

In the case of parental encouragement to attend college (P), the direct effect of sex (S) is, again, larger than its total effect, but only by a small margin (.114 versus .108 in Lines 5 and 6). The tendency of girls to perceive more parental encouragement, because they obtain higher grades than boys ($-.263 \times .124 = -.033$), is greater than that of boys to perceive greater parental support, because they are more likely to have completed a college-preparatory course ($.109 \times .246 = .027$). Of course, both these indirect effects are small relative to the direct effect of sex, that is, the greater parental support for college attendance that is perceived by boys.

Each of the socioeconomic background variables (V,M,X,I) affects parental encouragement, net of sex and ability, and roughly 20% of these effects is mediated by grades (G) and curriculum (C). Of the substantial total effect of mental ability (Q) on parental encouragement, 8.5 percentage points per 10-point shift in ability, two-thirds is mediated by grades and curriculum. The indirect effects are mediated in roughly equal measure by grades and by curriculum.

Sex has rather small total, direct, and indirect effects on the perception of friends' plans to attend college (F). Roughly a quarter of the effect of socioeconomic background (V,M,X,I) on friends' plans is mediated by grades (C) and curriculum (Lines 7 and 8), but about five-sixths of the influence of ability on the perception of friends' plans is mediated by those two variables. Of the indirect effect of ability on friends' plans, about 60% is mediated by grades and 40% by curriculum.

The effect of mental ability (Q) on college plans (E) within schools is mediated mainly by grades (G) and curriculum (C) and, to a lesser degree, by the perceived influence of significant others. (Compare Lines 9, 10, and 11.) More than half (53%) of the effect of ability is attributable to the higher grades of brighter students, and another 25% is explained by the greater likelihood that a bright student will complete a college-preparatory course. Only 12% of the influence of ability is mediated by the influence of significant others (T,P,F) and only 9% of the effect of mental ability on college plans is direct.

Roughly 20% of the effect of socioeconomic background (V,M,X,I) on college plans is mediated by grades and curriculum, and almost another 40% is mediated by the influence of significant others (T,P,F). The total and direct effects of sex on college plans are of about the same size, but several conflicting components of the influence of sex must also be taken into account. Girls obtain a slight advantage because of their higher grades, but this is partly offset by the fact that girls are less likely to complete a college-preparatory curriculum and are less likely to perceive encouragement of teachers and of parents to attend college.

Of the effect of grades (G) on college plans, 37% is mediated by significant others, and the remaining 63% is direct. Of the effect of curriculum (C) on college plans, 43% is direct, and the majority is mediated via teachers, parents, and friends. The indirect effects of grades on college plans are mediated in roughly equal measure by the three significant others variables, but, in the case of curriculum choice, 57% of the indirect effect is mediated via perceptions of parental encouragement and only 16% via the perceived encouragement of teachers.

The interpretation of direct and indirect effects on occupational aspiration (J) parallels that of college plans. (Compare Lines 12, 13, and 14 of Table 11.4.) Within schools, mental ability (Q) has the largest total effect of any variable on occupational aspiration. Of the effect of ability on occupational aspirations, 68% is mediated by grades (G) and curriculum (C); 50% of the effect of ability is attributable to its effect on grades and consequent shifts in aspiration; and 18% is attributable to the effect of ability on curriculum and the impact of curriculum on aspirations. Only 8% of the influence of ability on occupational status aspirations may be traced to the direct effect of ability on perceptions of encouragement by significant others (T,P,F) and their effects on aspirations. Finally, 24% of the effect of mental ability on occupational status aspirations is unmediated by grades, curriculum placement, or significant others.

As with the preceding variables, the interpretation of each of the four socioeconomic background variables (V,M,X,I) is similar. Approximately 28% of the effect of background is mediated by grades and curriculum placement, 38% is mediated by significant others, and the remaining 34% is direct. The total and direct effects of sex (S) on occupational aspirations are small, and both give girls a slight advantage over boys. However, there are small compound paths that favor boys: an indirect effect from sex to grades and, thence, to aspirations, and also an indirect effect from sex to significant others and, thence, to occupational aspirations. Again, none of the effects involving sex is very large.

Only 28% of the influence of grades (G) on occupational status aspirations is mediated by perceptions of the encouragement or expectations of significant others (T,P,F); the remaining 72% is direct. However, 55% of the effect of curriculum (C) on occupational aspiration is mediated via teachers, parents, and friends. Again, the indirect effects of grades on occupational aspirations are mediated, to about the same degree, by the three significant others variables, but the indirect effects of curriculum choice are effected primarily by parental encouragement and, only to a small degree, by the teachers' encouragement to attend college.

The effect of mental ability (Q) on variation in post-secondary schooling (U) within high schools is almost entirely mediated by academic and social psychological factors. (See Lines 15–18 of Table 11.4.) Of the influence of ability on schooling, 78% is mediated by grades (G) and curriculum (C); of this 60% is explained by higher grades and their consequences and 18% by the effects of completing the college-preparatory curriculum. Of the influence of ability on schooling, 8% is attributable to the greater encouragement (T,P,F) perceived by brighter persons, regardless of sex, background, grades, or curriculum, and another 4% is explained by the influence of ability on plans and aspirations (E,J), irrespective of the values of other variables. Only 10% of the effect of ability is direct: Its effects are largely determined by social and psychological processes that are complete before a student finishes high school.

Unlike ability, the direct effects of socioeconomic background variables (V,M,X,I) persist in every stage of the achievement process; consequently, the indirect effects of socioeconomic background are also more evenly distributed throughout the stages of our model. Thus, 22% of the influence of SES on educational attainment is explained by its effects on grades and curriculum, 29% by its effects on the perceptions of significant others, and 15% by its influence on educational and occupational aspirations. Still, about a third of the effect of socioeconomic background on educational attainment is direct, even among students attending the same high school.

The effect of sex on educational attainment gives boys an advantage over girls at almost every stage of the process. Overall, boys obtain about a third of a year more of schooling than girls. Girls would have an advantage almost this large because their grades are so much higher than boys', but this advantage is offset by boys' perceptions of greater encouragement from significant others and by their higher aspirations. Moreover, the largest single component of the effect of sex on educational attainment is its direct influence, net of all preceding social, academic, and psychological factors, which gives boys .4 years more of schooling than girls.

The effect of grades (G) on educational attainment (U) is primarily direct (59%), but 22% of the effect of grades is mediated by perceptions of the expectations of significant others (T,P,F), and 19% by college plans (E) and occupational aspirations (*J*). With grades, as with other variables, college plans mediate the largest share of this indirect effect, because they have a much larger effect on schooling than occupational aspirations. The effects on schooling of the high school curriculum (*C*) are in marked contrast to those of grades. Not only is the effect of the curriculum only about half as strong as that of grades, but more than half of that effect (55%) is mediated by the perceived expectations of significant others (*T,P,F*), mainly encouragement from parents (*P*). Another 20% of the effect of the curriculum is mediated by college plans and occupational aspirations, and 24% of the effect is unmediated by other variables in our model.

The effects of perception of the expectations of significant others on educational attainment are each explained, to some extent, by the higher aspirations that they engender. Of the effect of perceived teachers' encouragement, 65% is mediated by college plans and educational aspirations. As has been noted elsewhere (Sewell, 1971; Hauser, 1972), neither the direct component nor the indirect component of this effect is very large. About half of the effect of perceived parental encouragement on postsecondary schooling is mediated by college plans and occupational aspirations, but there remains a significant lagged effect of perceived parental encouragement on schooling. Finally, the direct effect of perceived friends' college plans on ultimate educational attainment is about as large as that of parental encouragement, but the indirect effect is less. Thus, the effect of friends' plans on post-secondary educational attainment is primarily direct (63%); only 37% of this effect may be attributed to the higher aspirations of youths with friends who plan to attend college.

Before turning to the implications of these within-school analyses for the measurement and interpretation of high schools' effects in the Wisconsin sample, we think it will be useful to review certain of the findings of this section. Our analysis and interpretation are generally consistent with earlier reports on the process of status attainment among men or women in the Wisconsin sample (Hauser, 1972; Sewell, 1971; Sewell and Hauser, 1975; Sewell et al., 1969, 1970). However, the present analysis extends and modifies earlier reports in significant ways. As reported in the earlier analyses, the effect of sex on the process of educational attainment works overall to the disadvantage of women. However, our present analysis shows that this disadvantage would be even greater if there were not some processes working to the advantage of women; specifically, the higher grades that women earn are a significant counterbalancing force against the other advantages of men.

Also, we have found it necessary to qualify our earlier findings about the effect of socioeconomic background on grades in high school. In the total Wisconsin sample, the effect of socioeconomic background on grades is entirely due to its association with mental ability, but, having controlled for the lack of variability of rank in high school class from school to school in the present analysis, we have found small but significant effects of socioeconomic background on grades that persist even after the substantial influence of mental ability on grades has been controlled (see also Hauser, 1971:88–92).

Finally, the present analysis brings to light a substantial and important contrast in the way two academic variables—grades and curriculum choice—affect the process of educational attainment. Our finding is that completion of a college-preparatory curriculum functions, to some degree, as a particularistic aspect of school organization, whereas the function of grades in the process is more meritocratic. That is, the curriculum completed is absolutely and relatively more dependent on socioeconomic background and less dependent on mental ability than are grades in school. Furthermore, while the two variables have about the same impact on perceptions of friends' plans to attend college, grades have their largest effect on perceptions of teachers' encouragement to attend college, and the curriculum on perceptions of parental encouragement for college attendance. However, the importance of curriculum choice as a factor in the organization of the school, which functions to perpetuate social inequalities across generations, is mitigated by the fact that its effects on aspirations and on later schooling are less than those of high school grades. Indeed, the effect of the curriculum has been largely played out by the time a student leaves high school.

Net School Effects: The Statewide Sample

In Table 11.5, we present measures of the variability in educational outcomes among schools, before and after controlling the several causative factors in our model of achievement. The entries in the first row are proportions of variance that occur among schools, and the other entries are the squares of the standardized regression coefficients of adjusted school means, with the latter adjusted for effects of the causal variables indicated in the left-hand stub of the table (see Hauser, 1971:Chapter 2). Again, one should remember that the components of variance in Table 11.5 have not been corrected for loss of degrees of freedom, which means that our analysis overstates the variance attributable to schools. When this connection is made, the effect is substantial, because of the large number of schools (424) in the sample. For example, 11.83% of the sample variance in college plans occurs among schools, but the corrected percentage is 6.20%. Similarly, the observed and corrected percentages in the case of educational attainment are 13.25% and 7.71%, respectively.

As we would expect, the variability among high schools in grades (G) increases when we control sex, socioeconomic background, and mental ability (S,V,M,X,I,Q). Variability among schools in completion of a college-preparatory curriculum (C) and in teachers' encouragement (T) is scarcely affected by controlling the exogenous variables. Neither the accessibility of college-preparatory courses nor the prevalence of perceived encouragement from teachers to attend college is affected by the distribution of the

TABLE 11.5

Gross and Net Contributions of Schools to Variance in Achievement Variables: One-Third Sample Respondents in the State of Wisconsin with Data Present (N = 7052)

Predetermined Variables	Dependent Variable							
	G	C	T	P	F	E	J	U
1. None	.0462	.1537	.0778	.1109	.1739	.1183	.1232	.1325
2. S,V,M,X,I,Q	.0742	.1537	.0797	.0590	.1050	.0562	.0674	.0548
3. S,V,M,X,I,Q,G,C			.0679	.0568	.1063	.0561	.0656	.0578
4. S,V,M,X,I,Q,G,C,T,P,F						.0419	.0567	.0432
5. S,V,M,X,I,Q,G,T,P,F,E,J								.0357

Variable abbreviations are as follows: H = high schools, S = sex, V = father's education, M = mother's education, X = father's occupational status, I = parental income, Q = academic ability, G = rank in high school class, C = college preparatory curriculum, T = teachers' encouragement, P = parents' encouragement, F = friends' college plans, E = college plans, J = occupational status aspirations, U = educational attainment.

social and psychological characteristics which predispose students to terminate or continue their education after high school.

In the later achievement variables (P,F,E,J,U), controls for the exogenous variables reduce the between-school components of variance from 5 to 8 percentage points (Line 2). Controlling the exogenous variables, the sample variance in college plans among schools is reduced by 6.2 percentage points, from 11.8 to 5.6% of the total variance. Similarly, there is a marked reduction of 7.8 percentage points in the variance among schools in ultimate educational attainment. If variations among schools in average ability and socioeconomic levels have contextual effects that tend to suppress the true extent of interschool variability in aspirations or achievements (Nelson, 1972; Alexander and Eckland, 1973), these contextual effects are far less important in accounting for school-to-school variation in the educational achievements of students than are the characteristics of their student-bodies.

Controls for grades and the college curriculum scarcely affect the variability in educational outcomes among schools (Line 3), but there are further reductions in interschool variance when significant others' expectations (T,P,F) are controlled (Line 4). In the statewide sample, schools account directly for only 4.2% of the variance in college plans (E) and 5.7% of the variance in occupational status aspirations (J). Correcting for loss of degrees of freedom reduces these increments by more than two-thirds. Finally, when plans and aspirations, as well as the preceding variables, are controlled, the share of variance among schools in the sample is reduced to 3.6%, and the adjusted increment is less than 1 percentage point. Especially in the cases of college plans, occupational status aspirations, and ultimate educational attainments, the observed variations from school to school are virtually all accounted for by prior variables in our model of achievement.

Contextual Effects of Student-Body Composition

In our analyses of school effects in both the Milwaukee and statewide samples, we have, thus far, emphasized issues in the measurement of school-to-school variations in achievement and in parameters of our model of achievement. However, sociological analyses of school effects on aspirations and attainments appear to have been more concerned with so-called "contextual effects" of student-body composition. In contextual analysis, apparent effects of student-body composition, above and beyond those applicable in a demographic account of interschool variance, are given a sociologistic interpretation, usually in terms of normative climates, differential association, or relative deprivation. In our analysis of covariance, such effects will appear as differences of slope in the within-school and between-school regressions (Hauser, 1971:Chapter 2).

There are serious threats to the validity of contextual interpretations of heterogeneous slopes, which we have already reviewed. By estimating a fairly elaborate model of achievement in a large and representative sample of schools and students, we think it is fair to state that we have met some, but not all, of these threats. While we believe our survey data to be of high quality, we have made no reliability adjustments in our variables. Furthermore, our model is reasonably powerful and complete, given the limited content of our data. Still, there remain important questions about the interpretability of contextual effects in our data and, also, about the possible impact of unmeasured factors in respect to which schools are directly selective of students.

In spite of these problems and because of the completeness of our model, we thought it would be instructive to look for contextual effects in the statewide sample. Table 11.6 gives "contextual" regression coefficients in the reduced-form equations of our model, that is, the equations that express the systematic variation in each endogenous variable in terms of the exogenous variables. The upper panel gives the regression coefficients for variables in standard form, and the lower panel gives metric coefficients.

Only in the case of grades (G), is there a clearly interpretable pattern to the effects. As we expected from our operational definition of grades as rank in high school class, as from the lack of variability in nominal standards of achievement from school to school, the contextual effects of each variable are opposite in sign to corresponding coefficients in the within-school regressions. Beyond this, we believe that the effects in Table 11.6 defy interpretation. Of the remaining 42 coefficients, 14 are statistically significant at a nominal $\alpha = .01$ level. The coefficients are quite small and vary unsystematically in sign. It has been suggested by several authors (Wilson, 1959; Meyer, 1970; Nelson, 1972; and Alexander and Eckland, 1973), that high socioeconomic status contexts are conducive to aspiration and achievement. However, the coefficients of our socioeconomic background variables vary narrowly about zero, and, presumably, some of this fluctuation may be attributed to collinearity among the background variables. Their intercorrelations (between school means) vary from .54 to .85. How else can we explain why school levels of occupational status aspirations are inflated where fathers hold high-status jobs, but depressed where fathers are highly educated? Recently, several authors have suggested that aspiration levels are reduced when student-bodies are high in ability (Meyer, 1970; Nelson, 1972; Alexander and Eckland, 1973). Indeed, all of the contextual effects of mental ability are negative, but only 3 out of 8 are statistically significant, even in a sample of more than 7000 students in more than 400 schools. Except in the case of grades, none of these contextual effects involves a standardized coefficient as large as .05 in absolute value.

Our impression of a substantial homogeneity in slopes within and between schools is reinforced by the data in Table 11.7, where we give standardized contextual effects in the structural equations of our model. Again, the coefficients are generally small and statistically insignificant;

TABLE 11.6

Indirect (Contextual) Effects of Student Body Composition in Reduced-Form Equations of Achievement
Model: One-Third Sample Respondents in the State of Wisconsin with Data Present (N = 7052)

Predetermined Variable	Dependent Variables							
	G	C	T	P	F	E	J	U
Regression coefficients of standardized variables								
S	.041[a]	.001	.033[a]	.017	.038[a]	.015	.022	.031[a]
V	-.017	-.073[a]	-.055	-.032	.047	-.052[a]	-.098[a]	-.020
M	-.007	.011	.009	.061[a]	.072[a]	.067[a]	.037	.055[a]
X	-.038[a]	.112[a]	.003	.036	.034	.061	.124[a]	.065[a]
I	-.053[a]	.011	-.030[a]	-.040	-.013	-.024	.010	-.051
Q	-.115[a]	-.037[a]	-.044[a]	-.016	-.013	-.027	-.019	-.013
Regression Coefficients								
S	501.[a]	.33	10.7[a]	5.6	12.1[a]	4.7	328.[a]	37.7[a]
V	-25.3	-2.86[a]	-2.17	-1.25[a]	1.80	-1.99	-175.	-2.9
M	-12.0	.48	.39	2.70[a]	3.09[a]	2.84[a]	74.[a]	8.9[a]
X	-7.26	.557[a]	.01	.18	.17	.30	29.[a]	1.2[a]
I	-5.80[a]	.032	-.09	-.12	-.04	-.07	1.3	-.54
Q	-41.5[a]	-.348[a]	-.42[a]	-.15	-.12	-.25	-8.3	-.47

NOTE: Regression coefficients are multiplied by 100 for ease of presentation.

Variable abbreviations are as follows: S = sex, V = father's education, X = father's occupational status, I = parental income, Q = academic ability, G = rank in high school class, C = college preparatory curriculum, T = teachers' encouragement, P = parents' encouragement, F = friends' college plans, E = college plans, J = occupational status aspirations, U = educational attainment.

[a] Coefficients marked with an ([a]) are statistically significant at the α = .01 level.

338

TABLE 11.7

Indirect (Contextual) Effects of Student Body Composition on Achievement for Variables in Standard Form: One-Third Sample Respondents in the State of Wisconsin with Data Present (N = 7052)

Predetermined Variable	Dependent Variable							
	G	C	T	P	F	E	J	U
S	.041[a]	.001	.020	.015	.024	-.006	.004	.002
V	-.017	-.073[a]	-.039	-.015	.064[a]	-.040	-.082[a]	.005
M	-.007	.011	.011	.062[a]	.071[a]	.041[a]	.014	.013
X	-.038	.112[a]	.001	.026	.012	.050	.114[a]	.030
I	-.053[a]	.011	-.015	-.032	-.012	.001	.036	-.032
Q	-.115[a]	-.037[a]	.009	.015	.028	.016	.004	.036[a]
G			-.010	.002	-.030	-.010	.018	-.027[a]
C			-.023	-.037[a]	.008	-.026	-.001	-.003
T						.013	.010	.008
P						-.024	.005	.004
F						.020	-.009	.009
E								.008
J								-.009

[a] Coefficients marked with an ([a]) are statistically significant at the α = .01 level. Variable abbreviations are as follows: S = sex, V = father's education, M = mother's education, X = father's occupational status, I = parental income, Q = academic ability, G = rank in high school class, C = college preparatory curriculum, T = teachers' encouragement, P = parents' encouragement, F = friends' college plans, E = college plans, J = occupational status aspirations, U = educational attainment.

339

only 3 of the 71 coefficients, including the expected depressing effect of ability on grades, are as large as .1 in absolute value.

Given the possible flaws in our contextual analysis, we are impressed both by the lack of evidence of contextual effects in the Wisconsin data and by the failure of that evidence to substantiate other published hypotheses concerning sign and magnitude of contextual effects.

Summary

The goal of this chapter has been to produce new evidence of the extent and causes of differences among high schools in the aspirations and achievements of their students. Our analysis has been guided by a recursive structural equation model of achievement, which relates factors of sex, social background, and ability to academic and social psychological facets of high school experience and to subsequent educational attainments. We have analyzed samples of men and women in Milwaukee and throughout the State of Wisconsin who graduated from high school in 1957 and whose later attainments were ascertained in 1964.

Analyzing a subsample of the Milwaukee data of Sewell and Armer (1966a), we undertook an exhaustive search for first-order interactions of schools with processes of achievement in high school and in subsequent educational careers. In 31 statistical tests, we found only one interaction effect (schools by grades by educational attainment) at a nominal significance level of $\alpha = .01$. We looked also at additive effects of schools in Milwaukee, and we found (excepting grades) that school differences in aspiration and achievement variables were small and largely explained by factors of social composition. Both with regard to interaction effects and additive effects of schools, our findings tend to support the original conclusions of Sewell and Armer, rather than those of their critics. Moreover, it is important that these findings have been extended with equal force beyond aspirations to educational attainment.

Building upon the results of our Milwaukee analysis, we carried out an intensive analysis of variations in aspiration and achievement within and between 424 high schools throughout Wisconsin. In the State, as in Milwaukee, most of the variability in achievement variables and their causes occurred within, rather than between schools. Our analyses of within-school models of achievement were generally consistent with earlier analyses of the Wisconsin sample, with respect to matters such as the effects of ability and socioeconomic background and the importance of significant others and of aspirations, as intervening variables in the achievement process. However, our analysis has elaborated several significant differences between the sexes in the achievement process. Also, we found that academic performance—as measured by grades—works much differently in the achievement process than does curriculum placement. Grading functions more as a meritocratic social mechanism. Grades depend more on ability and less on background than does the curriculum. The effects of grades are larger and more persistent than those of the curriculum, and the effects of completing a college-preparatory curriculum are channeled, to a greater degree, through the perception of parental encouragement of college attendance. However, contrary to earlier findings in the total Wisconsin sample, our current analysis indicates that, within schools, socioeconomic background is a small but significant factor in the awarding of grades, even to students of equal mental ability.

Our findings on net school effects in the statewide sample closely paralleled those for the Milwaukee sample. The variables in our achievement model accounted for a large share of the variation in educational achievement among schools. With respect to college plans, occupational aspirations, and ultimate educational aspirations, it appears that high schools account for no more than 1 or 2% of the variance in the population, above and beyond the effects of individual social, psychological, and academic factors. Finally, we found minimal evidence of contextual effects of student-body composition in the statewide sample, and that evidence did not clearly support patterns of causation that had been proposed by several other sociologists.

We began with the observation that sociologists have been highly resistant to evidence that high school effects on aspiration and achievement are rather small and not systematically related to the social composition of student-bodies. We believe that the present analysis gives substantial new evidence in favor of this view, and that research on the schooling process could profitably be turned to issues other than the explanation of school-to-school variations in aspirations and achievement.

Acknowledgments

Computations were carried out by Peter J. Dickinson and James R. Kluegel using facilities of the Center for Demography and Ecology and the Madison Academic Computing Center. We benefited from discussions with J. Michael Armer at an early stage of this research.

XII Socioeconomic Background, Colleges, and Post-Collegiate Achievements*

Duane F. Alwin
Indiana University

Introduction

Over the past few decades, American higher education has been expanding in significant ways. This expansion has taken at least two forms. First, increasing proportions of high school graduates are obtaining some college experience, and some observers predict the eventual near universality of post-secondary education. In some areas, figures indicate that as many as 80% of high school graduates already enroll in post-secondary programs subsequent to their graduation (see Cross, 1971:11). Second, the diversity of institutions of higher education has increased, and, while there has been a homogenization of institutional goals in higher education, observers also point to increasing distinctions among centers of higher education (Newman, Cannon, Cavell, Cohen, Edgerton, Gibbons, Kremer, Rhodes, and Singleton, 1971). The present chapter is intended neither to document these

* The research reported here is part of a larger project concerned with the study of social and psychological factors related to achievement directed by William H. Sewell and Robert M. Hauser. Support for this research came from grant # M-6275 from the National Institute of Mental Health and grant # CRD-314 from the Social Security Administration. The author was supported by these grants and by American College Testing Program research funds.

trends nor investigate their sources in the history of American higher education, but rather to explore some of their possible implications for the system of socioeconomic stratification in the United States.[1]

In a system where secondary education is nearly universal (see Jencks, Smith, Acland, Bane, Cohen, Gintis, Heyns, and Michelson, 1972), and where the system of post-secondary education expands to meet the growing educational needs of the society, the distinctions among institutions of higher education may take on an added importance, particularly in the process of social stratification. Indeed, a number of social scientists have argued this point, and many have asserted that the quality of college attended has a sizeable impact on educational and socioeconomic achievements (see Astin, 1974: Clark, 1962; Collins, 1971; Milner, 1972; Wolfle, 1973). While the hypothesis of college effects is theoretically important, the empirical evidence brought forward as support for it is often inadequate.

The earliest sources of information on the question of college effects seemed to support the idea that "type of college" had an effect on educational and socioeconomic outcomes (see Babcock, 1941; Havemann and West, 1952; Knapp and Goodrich, 1952; Knapp and Greenbaum, 1953), but a careful examination of these sources indicates that they are inadequate on a variety of methodological grounds. These early sources do, however, recognize that processes of selection and recruitment operate in such a way as to make it difficult to ascertain the unique college effects that may operate to produce variation in achievements. It is recognized, for example, that certain colleges actively seek out the most academically able students or students with particular vocational interests. It is also obvious to most observers that colleges differ in the socioeconomic origins of their students (see Jencks and Riesman, 1968), as well as on a number of other family background factors (e.g., see Astin and Lee, 1972).

It is clear that, if we wish to assess the presence of institutional effects on educational and socioeconomic achievements in a certain population, we must be careful to adequately consider the general processes of selection and recruitment into colleges. A number of factors have been shown to be important in the selection–recruitment process: ability, academic performance, motivation, and socioeconomic and other background factors (see Wolfle, 1954; Jencks and Reisman, 1968; Wegner and Sewell, 1970). Control of these sources of variation, at least in part, has been important in assessing the effect of college differences on educational outcomes (Astin, 1968; Astin and Panos, 1969; Kamens, 1971; Spaeth and Greeley, 1970; Wegner and Sewell, 1970), occupational status attainment (Spaeth and Greeley, 1970), earnings (Hunt, 1963; Weisbrod and Karpoff, 1968; Reed and Miller, 1970; Daniere and Mechling, 1970; Solmon, 1973a; Wales, 1973), earnings within occupations (Kinloch and Perrucci, 1969; Laumann

---

[1] For an excellent review of the historical trends in higher education in the United States, see Jencks and Reisman, *The Academic Revolution* (1968).

and Rapoport, 1968), and other achievements within occupations (Ladinsky, 1963; Hargens and Hagstrom, 1967). A few other studies have been concerned with the relationship between undergraduate origins and later achievements but have not pursued the net effect attributable to college differences alone (Wright, 1964; Smigel, 1964; Perrucci, 1969; Folger, Astin, and Bayer, 1970; Sharp, 1970).[2]

There is little question that, in most sets of data, colleges differ in the achievements, both educational and socioeconomic, of their students and/or graduates. The important theoretical and empirical issue involves the extent to which these observed differences represent institutional effects involving differing socialization and/or certification processes *or* are artifactually due to differing college composition on various selection-recruitment factors. The aforementioned literature generally supports the hypothesis of *small* independent college "quality" effects on educational achievements and earnings, but essentially no effects on occupational status. Nevertheless, the issue of the "returns to college quality" is largely unsettled, owing to the diverse nature of published studies and the failure of these studies, in many cases, to adequately control variation in theoretically important selection–recruitment variables. Replication of such analyses of samples from known populations is badly needed.

A Theoretical Perspective

It is possible to interpret potential college effects within the framework of an explicit theoretical model, which views social stratification as the process by which an individual's socioeconomic background is expressed in his socioeconomic achievements (Blau and Duncan, 1967; Duncan, Featherman, and Duncan, 1972; Hauser, 1972; Sewell, Haller, and Ohlendorf, 1970; Sewell, Haller, and Portes, 1969; Sewell and Hauser, Chapter I of this volume). To the extent that an individual's social achievements depend on his social background, the stratification system is viewed as rigid, obstructing vertical social mobility, and, to the extent that they do not depend on social background, the system is viewed as open, facilitating mobility. The factors that are involved in the process, linking background to achievement, serve, therefore, to both obstruct and facilitate social mobility. The number of years of schooling completed has been described as a major mediator of the process of socioeconomic stratification (Blau and Duncan, 1967; Sewell *et al.*, 1969, 1970; Sewell and Hauser, Chapter I of this volume). The present research raises the issue of whether the effects of socioeconomic background might also be mediated by differences, such as quality differences, in the colleges attended. The question is twofold: (*1*) To

---

[2] For a more extensive review of the literature, see Alwin (1972), and, for a more thorough review of the selection–recruitment process, see Alwin, Hauser, and Sewell (1975).

what extent do institutional differences introduce variation in achievements that is independent of the influence of precollegiate experiences? (2) To what extent does choice of college represent a mechanism through which families pass on relative socioeconomic advantage to their offspring?

An additional source of variation in educational and socioeconomic achievements, part of which is unrelated to socioeconomic background, is academic ability. This is a major factor impinging on the stratification system and making it more open to vertical mobility. Differences in the colleges attended by individuals are also potential mediators of the effects of ability on later achievements. Likewise, the effects of variables that principally mediate the effects of both ability and socioeconomic background on later achievements (e.g., academic performance, aspirations, the influence of significant others; see Sewell and Hauser, Chapter 1 of this volume) can also be mediated by differences among colleges attended.

The theoretical model described thus far can be cast in terms of the familiar input–output model of school effects (see Werts, 1968), a variant of which appears in Figure 12.1. All of the factors which can be described as selection and/or recruitment factors for differential college attendance— academic ability, socioeconomic background, academic performance, motivational factors, and other background factors—are conveniently labeled as "inputs." Note that these inputs include the exogenous and intervening social psychological variables in the Duncan *et al.* (1972) and Sewell and Hauser (Chapter 1 of this volume) models of socioeconomic status attainment. For present purposes, it is unnecessary to order the input variables causally—they are *all* considered to be predetermined variables. The input variables are, by definition, causally prior to the "colleges" and can be thought of as factors that determine the specific college of attendance. There are a number of ways in which college differences can be characterized (see Alwin, 1972). For present purposes, it is convenient to view the "colleges" in Figure 12.1 as the specific colleges attended by a sample of college attenders. Finally, with regard to the model in Figure 12.1,

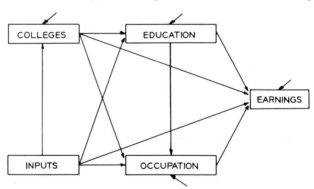

Figure 12.1 Input–output model for college effects on achievements.

educational achievement depends on both the inputs and the college attended; occupational status depends on the inputs, college attended, and educational achievement; and earnings depends on all of the preceding, including occupation.

Methods

The Population and Sample

The analysis reported here involves the assessment of college effects on educational achievement after high school, occupational status attainment 7 years after graduation from high school, and earnings 10 years after graduation. These effects are estimated for the male cohort of 1957 Wisconsin high school seniors with some college experience between 1957 and 1964, who were alive, not enrolled in any school, and not on active duty with the armed forces in 1964. The data used in this estimation come from a one-third probability sample of the cohort of 1957 Wisconsin high school graduates whose parents responded to a 1964 mail follow-up question-naire.[3] A total of 1198 men with college information available meet these eligibility criteria.

The Variables

The respondent's education (U) as of 1964 and his 1964 occupation (W) were obtained from a follow-up questionnaire. Education, although not reported as such, is scaled in years of schooling completed. Years of schooling is actually translated from statements of educational certification, so that, in a sense, it only approximates the number of years of schooling actually completed. Occupation in 1964 is coded into Duncan SEI scores representing occupational status (Duncan, 1961). Earnings for the year 1967 (Y) were ascertained from Social Security earnings records for persons in jobs covered by Federal withholdings.[4] Earnings is expressed as dollar units for present purposes. The means and standard deviations for these variables are presented in Table 12.1.

Several classes of variables are used to represent the criteria for selection and recruitment into different types of colleges: socioeconomic background, academic ability, academic performance in high school, aspirations, significant others' influence, and commitment to college. Socioeconomic background is measured by four variables: Mother's education (M)

---

[3] For a description of the several sources of these data, see Sewell and Hauser (1975).

[4] The care devoted to insuring confidentiality of this information is described in Sewell and Hauser (1975).

TABLE 12.1
Sample Means and Standard Deviations for Variables in the Analysis:
Eligible Subsample with Data Present

Variable	Mean	Standard Deviation	# of Cases
1. Respondent's education (U)	15.08	1.629	1198
2. Respondent's occupational prestige (W)	56.54	22.68	1198
3. Respondent's 1967 earnings (Y)	7916.	3626.	1119
4. Mother's education (M)	11.24	3.119	1198
5. Father's education (V)	11.14	3.225	1198
6. Parental income (I)	7531.	6564.	1087
7. Father's occupational prestige (X)	37.13	23.71	1198
8. Academic ability (Q)	107.7	13.11	1198
9. Academic performance (G)	104.5	12.91	1116
10. Occupational aspirations (J)	66.75	21.96	1168
11. Educational aspirations (E)	.7596	.4275	1198
12. High school curriculum (C)	.8765	.3292	1198
13. Willingness to borrow (B)	.6586	.4744	1198
14. Scholarship applications (S)	.2788	.4486	1198
15. Perceived value of college (A)	84.88	16.33	1198
16. Possible parental support (K)	1.978	.6168	1198
17. Consideration of college (D)	2.718	.5176	1198
18. Teacher encouragement (T)	2.682	.4852	1198
19. Parental encouragement (P)	3.879	.3438	1198
20. Friends' college plans (F)	.5885	.4923	1198

NOTE: The abbreviations for the variables are in parentheses
following the variable name.

and father's education (V) are coded in years of schooling completed.
Parental income (I) averaged over all available years for the period
1957–1960 is expressed in dollar units. In some instances in the following
analysis, the averaged father's income is used rather than parental income.
Father's occupation (X) is coded in the Duncan SEI scale.

The respondent's score on the Henmon–Nelson Test of Mental Ability
taken during his junior year in high school is used as a measure of academic
ability (Q). The scores are expressed in the metric of IQ scores with a mean
of 100 and a standard deviation of 15 (for the total one-third sample). The

respondent's academic performance (G) in high school is measured by a normalized percentile rank in high school class, so there is some control over interschool variation in the allocation of grades.

Occupational aspirations (J) is scored in Duncan SEI units for the occupation category that the respondent said he hoped to enter. Educational aspirations (E) is represented by a binary variable indicating whether or not the respondent planned to attend college. Several variables are included to tap the student's cognitive, financial, and academic commitment to attending college: The respondent's high school curriculum (college preparatory) (C), his willingness to borrow to finance his college education (B), and whether he had made applications for scholarships (S) are all treated as binary variables. The respondent's perceived value of college (A) is measured as a composite score based on several items. The respondent's perception of possible parental support (K) and his consideration of college attendance (D) are both measured as three-level ordinal variables and are treated as continuous in the present analysis. Three significant others' influence variables are included: Perception of teacher encouragement (T) and parental encouragement (P) to attend college are three-level ordinal variables treated as continuous, and the perception of friends' college plans (F) is expressed as a binary variable. The means and standard deviations of these variables are presented in Table 12.1. Table 12.2 presents the sample zero-order correlations among the aforementioned variables.

Colleges

The following analysis uses 12 categories of college in representing the variation in the types of college attended by the men in the sample. The first six of these categories—University of Wisconsin, Madison; University of Wisconsin, Milwaukee; University of Wisconsin Center System; Wisconsin State Universities; Wisconsin County Teachers colleges; and Marquette University—are simply single colleges or sets of quite homogenous colleges in the state of Wisconsin. The second set of categories—prestigious colleges and universities; liberal arts colleges, general; liberal arts colleges, Catholic; and universities—is based on a similarities analysis of 134 colleges and universities not included in the other categories.[5] The final two categories—technological colleges and institutes and other colleges—are based primarily on a priori considerations. The technological category includes engineering colleges, art schools, and military institutes. The final category is a residual category containing junior colleges, theological seminaries, business colleges, and foreign colleges.[6]

[5] See Alwin (1972).

[6] For the dependent variable years of schooling completed, college attended is defined as the first college attended by the respondent. For the variables occupational status and earnings, college attended is defined as the college graduated from or, if the respondent did not graduate, as the first college attended. Among those who

TABLE 12.2
Sample Correlations Among Selection/Recruitment and Outcome Variables in the Analysis: Eligible Subsample with Bivariate Subsample Data Present

Variable:	U	W	Y	M	V	I	X	Q	G	J	E	C	B	S	A	K	D	T	P	F
1. U	---																			
2. W	526	---																		
3. Y	157	232	---																	
4. M	146	092	078	---																
5. V	137	122	086	468	---															
6. I	094	106	157	216	332	---														
7. X	123	118	127	272	491	439	---													
8. Q	308	243	095	128	144	076	106	---												
9. G	420	296	121	043	007	-044	-037	524	---											
10. J	269	259	181	085	102	104	122	263	272	---										
11. E	268	210	104	116	083	126	133	201	244	619	---									
12. C	191	147	063	086	108	099	147	268	205	227	204	---								
13. B	139	069	048	020	012	022	006	119	128	151	135	110	---							
14. S	331	224	097	083	083	018	026	303	440	288	280	154	145	---						
15. A	149	138	064	047	044	036	080	153	186	326	341	260	156	129	---					
16. K	093	101	117	161	225	348	334	-010	-070	093	142	057	-034	-075	023	---				
17. D	232	173	059	106	113	131	102	174	222	426	569	217	193	296	330	133	---			
18. T	177	193	070	-002	-005	-002	002	192	312	209	235	089	152	197	218	-043	221	---		
19. P	141	151	104	135	137	098	136	162	096	248	285	200	064	127	291	149	277	215	---	
20. F	245	200	104	145	139	145	170	113	155	246	260	176	049	149	212	081	229	141	219	---

NOTE: Decimals and main diagonal are omitted. The smallest number of cases on which any correlation is based is 1,017, and most are based on the total 1,198.

Variable abbreviations are as follows: U = respondent's education, W = respondent's occupational status, Y = respondent's 1967 earnings, M = mother's education, V = father's education, I = parental income, X = father's occupational status, Q = academic ability, G = academic performance in high school, J = occupational aspirations, E = educational aspirations, C = high school curriculum, B = willingness to borrow, S = scholarship applications, A = perceived value of college, K = possible parental support, D = consideration of college, T = teachers' encouragement, P = parental encouragement, F = friends' college plans

Given the regional limitations placed on the colleges attended by the 1957 Wisconsin cohort of graduating seniors, one might argue that the external generality of the findings reported here is severely limited. Still, at the extremes one finds some representation of the eastern "elite" colleges in the category of prestigious colleges and universities and some representation of out-of-state junior colleges in the residual category. The liberal arts categories include both colleges within the state and out-of-state liberal arts colleges. The universities category is exclusively out-of-state universities. Thus, even though the amount of regional variation is not extensive, there appear to be grounds for generalizing about college effects in these data.

The Gross Effects of Colleges on Educational and Socioeconomic Achievements

The category means and deviations from the grand mean (referred to here as gross effects) are presented in Table 12.3. In addition, summary statistics indicating the proportion of variation in the outcomes that can be accounted for by differences between the categories (i.e., η^2) are presented in Table 12.3 as well. It is clear that most—well over 90%—of the variance in the outcome variables occurs *within* the college categories, while only about 8%, 6%, and 5% of the variance in education, occupational status, and earnings, respectively, occurs *between* categories. As a consequence, we cannot be as hopeful as others (cf. Astin, 1974) in making generalizations about the importance of differences in college quality for educational and socioeconomic achievements, at least insofar as these data permit such generalizations.[7]

Despite the general pessimism engendered by the numerical results, in Table 12.3, for the importance of college differences, it is possible to perceive some meaningful pattern in the category means. Consistent with earlier analysis (Wegner and Sewell, 1970), the prestigious colleges and universities (both within and outside the state of Wisconsin) and the liberal arts colleges appear to give their students an advantage in the attainment of years of higher education. In addition, the category of technological schools has a moderate positive gross effect on educational attainment. On

---

attend college, the latter definition is a very close approximation of the last college attended. The frequencies of college attendance for the twelve categories are as follows (first college, last college): University of Wisconsin, Madison (221, 231); University of Wisconsin, Milwaukee (124, 121); University of Wisconsin, Center System (71, 44); Wisconsin State Universities (361, 383); Wisconsin County Teachers colleges (21, 18); Marquette University (70, 74); prestigious colleges and universities (33, 31); liberal arts colleges, general (121, 120); liberal arts colleges, catholic (56, 45); universities (55, 61); technological colleges and institutes (38, 45); and other colleges (27, 25).

[7] These results are reported, in part, by Alwin (1974) and by Alwin *et al.* (1975).

TABLE 12.3
Educational Achievement, Occupational Status Attainment, and Earnings by Type of College Attended: Eligible Subsample with Data Present

	Category Means and Deviations from the Grand Mean					
	Education		Occupational Status		Earnings	
College Category	Mean	Dev.	Mean	Dev.	Mean	Dev.
University of Wisconsin, Madison	15.48	.40	63.3	6.7	8783	868
University of Wisconsin, Milwaukee	14.51	-.57	52.5	-4.0	7909	-7
University of Wisconsin, Center System	14.35	-.73	43.5	-13.0	7564	-352
Wisconsin State Universities	14.85	-.23	54.3	-2.3	7278	-638
Wisconsin County Teachers Colleges	14.38	-.70	50.3	-6.2	6088	-1828
Marquette University	15.61	.54	65.0	8.4	9627	1711
Prestigious Colleges and Universities	16.49	1.41	56.2	-.4	8246	330
Liberal Arts Colleges, General	15.35	.27	56.0	-.5	7313	-603
Liberal Arts Colleges, Catholic	15.36	.28	52.9	-3.6	7440	-476
Liberal Arts Colleges, Universities	14.93	-.15	58.1	1.6	8507	591
Technological Colleges and Institutes	15.50	.42	65.5	9.0	9190	1274
Other Colleges	14.81	-.26	46.3	-10.2	6573	-1343
Grand Mean	15.078		56.535		7916	
Standard Deviation	1.629		22.678		3626	
R^2	.0790		.0594		.0506	

the other hand, those students who first attend the University of Wisconsin at Milwaukee, one of the University of Wisconsin centers (two-year colleges), or one of the County Teachers Colleges in Wisconsin (two-year colleges) tend, on the average, to complete fewer years of schooling. Note that about 1.3 standard deviations separate the schools in the high and low categories.

In contrast to their gross effects on educational achievements, the categories of prestigious colleges and universities and liberal arts colleges do not have substantial positive effects on occupational status attainment. In general, the universities (University of Wisconsin, at Madison, Marquette University, and the schools in the university category) and the technological colleges have the largest positive effects on occupational status, while the two-year colleges (University of Wisconsin, Center, and some schools in the "other" category), and the Catholic liberal arts colleges have the largest negative effects. The results for 1967 earnings parallel those for occupational status to a large extent, with the universities and the technological schools having the largest positive gross effects and the two-year colleges, the Wisconsin State Universities, and the liberal arts colleges having negative effects. Less than one standard deviation separates the gross effects for earnings, and about 1.2 standard deviations separate the highest and lowest occupational status gross effects.

It is possible to entertain several hypotheses about the sources of these small gross effects. One possible interpretation of the positive effects of the prestigious and liberal arts colleges on educational achievement is that such schools are more likely to attract or select students who are certified by their high schools as more able to do college work or students who are more likely to be able to afford the costs of private schooling. One could argue that, since these factors—academic ability and parental wealth—also influence the attainment of further years of schooling, the relationship between college differences and education is spurious. Another possible interpretation involves the effect of the college experience itself. Such an interpretation might emphasize the "intellectual climate" of the college environment at the prestigious and liberal arts colleges (see Knapp and Greenbaum, 1953).

A possible interpretation of the positive gross effects of universities and technological schools on occupational status attainment and earnings is that these institutions are training grounds for highly specialized technical and/or professional occupations, such as law, dentistry, medicine, engineering, business. Therefore, controlling variation in occupational choice and educational attainment might reduce the apparent effect. Furthermore, one could argue that students attending large centers for mass education might obtain higher earnings by virtue of the fact that they are more likely to obtain jobs in large urban settings (earnings being generally higher in such areas). In contrast, one could argue that a particular characteristic of the larger universities (e.g., effectiveness of placement services) accounts for the differences in occupational status and earnings or that prospective employers respond to degrees from large universities in more positive ways (e.g., see Meyer, 1972).

Plausible interpretations for such gross effects can be easily generated. They are basically of two types: (1) those placing emphasis on selection and/or recruitment factors in differential college attendance and (2) those dealing with a unique college effect—differential socialization, certification, or both. The analysis reported in the following section is both an attempt to control variation in key selection–recruitment factors in assessing the unique college effects, and an attempt to discern the role of college differences in transmitting the effects of other variables on educational and socioeconomic achievements.

Educational and Socioeconomic Achievements—
the Net Effects of Colleges

Because the composition of colleges differs, to some extent, on a number of selection–recruitment factors, which also contribute to variation in the achievement process, we cannot seriously consider the gross college differences in achievement as indicative of the unique college effects. It is ultimately necessary to obtain estimates of the net effects of colleges, which we do in this section. We address two somewhat related questions: (1) *To what extent do institutional differences account for variation in educational and socioeconomic achievements, independent of precollegiate experiences?* (2) *To what extent do institutional differences provide a mechanism by which families pass on their relative socioeconomic advantage (or disadvantage) to their children, and to what extent are the effects of other precollegiate variables transmitted by college differences?* Clearly, our answer to the second question depends upon our answer to the first. If college differences have no unique impact on the achievement process, apart from selection–recruitment processes, they cannot act in an intervening capacity, transmitting the effects of precollegiate experiences on achievement outcomes. Conversely, if institutional differences contribute to variations in achievement, this may be one mechanism by which prior variables, namely selection–recruitment variables, operate in the achievement process.

The analytic strategy, by which we provide an answer to these questions, relies on the estimation of several multiple linear regression models. The regression equations estimated for these purposes are presented in Table 12.4. These provide the basis for most of the following discussion and are subsequently summarized and interpreted. The equations presented in Table 12.4 are for the three outcome variables, educational achievement (U), occupational status attainment (W), and earnings (Y). For each outcome variable, several regression equations are estimated, sequentially adding variables representing the selection–recruitment process. The first equation, in each case, contains the socioeconomic background variables

(V, M, X, and I) only; academic ability (Q) is added in the second equation, academic performance in high school (G) in the third, significant others' influence (T, P, and F) in the fourth, aspirations (E and J) in the fifth, and except in the case of earnings, the commitment to college variables (K, D, B, S, C, and A) in the sixth.[8] Finally, the last equation estimated for each outcome includes all the relevant selection–recruitment variables in the regression equation plus a set of dummy variables representing the college categories. Both metric and standard form coefficients are presented in Table 12.4. The rationale for the sequential presentation of coefficients is clarified when we discuss the extent to which colleges mediate the effects of prior variables on achievement.

Assuming that the pattern of effects of the selection–recruitment variables is similar for all categories of college used in the analysis (i.e., additivity of the effects of the college categories with respect to the selection–recruitment variables), we may apply a standard covariance adjustment procedure in estimating the net college effects. This adjustment takes the form:

$$\overline{Y}_i^* = \overline{Y}_i - \sum_{j}^{p} b_{YX_j}(\overline{X}_{ij} - \overline{X}_{.j}),$$

where $\overline{Y}_i^*$ is the adjusted mean for the ith college category; $\overline{Y}_i$ is the unadjusted mean for category i; b_{YX_j} is the pooled within-category partial regression coefficient (in metric form) for the regression of Y on a set of X_j ($j = 1$, p); $\overline{X}_{ij}$ is the ith category mean on X_j; and $\overline{X}_{.j}$ is the grand mean for variable X_j.

The question of the additivity of the effects of colleges is subject to empirical test, and an intensive examination of this issue was undertaken prior to the computation of the net college effects.[9] The results of this analysis (see Alwin, 1972) support the conclusion that for all outcome variables—education, occupational status, and earnings—*there is no discernible interaction of the college categories with the selection–recruitment variables included in the analysis*. Therefore, given no evidence to the contrary, we assume that the pattern of effects of the selection–recruitment variables is the same or similar over all categories of colleges. This allows

[8] In the earnings regressions, the commitment to college variables did not significantly increase the coefficient of determination over and above the variables already in the equation. Therefore, these results are not reported here, and these variables are not used to adjust the earnings means.

[9] Following a procedure described by Gujarati (1970), a set of variables can be created to represent potential nonadditivity. The null hypothesis of additivity can be examined statistically, by comparing the explained sums of squares for an equation containing nonadditivity with the explained sums of squares for the equation containing simply additivity. The results of this analysis are discussed in detail in Alwin (1972).

TABLE 12.4

Structural Coefficients for Multiple Regression Models Estimated for Educational Achievement, Occupational Status Attainment, and 1967 Earnings: Eligible Subsample with Bivariate Data Present

				Predetermined Variables					
		V	M	X	I^b	Q	G	T	P
A.	**Coefficients in standard form**								
1.	U	.053	.099^a	.057	.030				
2.	U	.028	.078^a	.046	.026	.287^a			
3.	U	.040	.072^a	.069^a	.046	.084^a	.377^a		
4.	U	.036	.058	.050	.033	.080^a	.345^a	.027	.035
5.	U	.040	.054	.042	.025	.069^a	.324^a	.012	.010
6.	U	.030	.049	.031	.007	.057	.278^a	.009	-.001
7.	U	.026	.036	.032	-.008	.058	.276^a	.009	.008
8.	W	.060	.038	.054	.054				
9.	W	.040	.021	.046	.051	.226^a			
10.	W	.048	.017	.062	.064	.090^a	.253^a		
11.	W	.045	.005	.044	.052	.080^a	.208^a	.085^a	.058
12.	W	.044	.005	.037	.047	.065	.189^a	.074^a	.037
13.	W	.039	.002	.023	.031	.062	.168^a	.078^a	.029
14.	W	.046	.007	.022	.040	.067	.157^a	.078^a	.032
15.	Y	-.004	.029	.034	.168^a				
16.	Y	-.010	.024	.032	.166^a	.075^a			
17.	Y	-.006	.022	.040	.168^a	.011	.119^a		
18.	Y	-.009	.015	.032	.164^a	.003	.106^a	.019	.059
19.	Y	-.013	.018	.028	.161^a	-.013	.092^a	.013	.048
20.	Y	-.006	.027	.011	.153^a	-.024	.064	.020	.044
B.	**Coefficients in metric form**								
1.	U	.027	.052^a	.004	.008				
2.	U	.014	.041^a	.003	.006	.036^a			
3.	U	.020	.037^a	.005^a	.011	.010^a	.048^a		
4.	U	.018	.030	.003	.008	.010^a	.044^a	.091	.164
5.	U	.020	.028	.003	.006	.009^a	.041^a	.041	.046
6.	U	.015	.026	.002	.002	.007	.035^a	.031	-.003
7.	U	.013	.019	.002	-.002	.007	.035^a	.030	.036
8.	W	.418	.276	.052	.187				
9.	W	.282	.153	.044	.176	.391^a			
10.	W	.338	.122	.059	.220	.156^a	.444^a		
11.	W	.316	.036	.042	.181	.138^a	.366^a	3.97^a	3.80
12.	W	.311	.038	.036	.161	.112	.332^a	3.43^a	2.46
13.	W	.274	.013	.022	.108	.107	.295^a	3.63^a	1.91
14.	W	.324	.049	.021	.139	.115	.276^a	3.65^a	2.11
15.	Y	-4.58	34.0	5.23	127.^{a}				
16.	Y	-11.8	27.6	4.86	126.^{a}	20.7^a			
17.	Y	-6.99	25.4	6.14	128.^{a}	3.03	33.5^a		
18.	Y	-10.4	17.3	4.85	124.^{a}	.836	29.8^a	141.	627.
19.	Y	-14.8	21.6	4.36	122.^{a}	-3.50	25.8^a	97.8	502.
20.	Y	-7.30	31.1	1.67	116.^{a}	-6.63	18.0	147.	465.

Variable abbreviations are as follows: U = respondent's education, W = respondent's occupational status, Y = respondent's 1967 earnings, M = Mother's education, V = father's education, X = father's occupational status, I = parental income, Q = academic ability, G = academic performance in high school, T = teachers' encouragement, P = parental encouragement, F = friends' college plans, E = educational aspirations, J = occupational aspirations, K = possible parental support, D = consideration of college,

Predetermined Variables

F	E	J	K	D	B	S	C	A	R^2
									.032
									.112
									.213
.145[a]									.237
.123[a]	.082[a]	.060							.250
.120[a]	.057	.042	.074[a]	.008	.055	.127[a]	.036	-.017	.270
.109[a]	.052	.052	.076[a]	.007	.048	.118[a]	.045	-.012	.293
									.023
									.073
									.118
.112[a]									.145
.092[a]	.006	.126[a]							.159
.091[a]	-.002	.119[a]	.072[a]	-.015	-.003	.068[a]	.019	.000	.166
.092[a]	-.005	.113[a]	.064[a]	-.019	-.008	.067	.023	-.000	.190
									.038
									.044
									.054
.037									.060
.024	-.062	.155[a]							.075
.026	-.056	.131[a]							.098

F	E	J	K	D	B	S	C	A	Constant
									14.00
									10.46
									8.07
.479[a]									7.58
.408[a]	.313[a]	.004							8.13
.396[a]	.217	.003	.194[a]	.026	.190	.462[a]	.177	-.002	8.70
.359[a]	.196	.004	.202[a]	.023	.165	.430[a]	.221	-.001	9.03
									45.43
									6.62
									-15.71
5.16[a]									-31.87
4.26[a]	.304	.130[a]							-26.79
4.20[a]	-.110	.123[a]	2.65[a]	-.674	-.153	3.45[a]	1.29	.000	-23.75
4.26[a]	-.264	.117[a]	2.37[a]	-.848	-.408	3.37	1.57	-.000	-26.97
									6508.
									4452.
									2766.
274.									620.
174.	-529.	25.6[a]							888.
187.	-474.	21.7[a]							1408.

B = willingness to borrow, S = scholarship applications, C = high school curriculum, A = perceived value of college.

[a] $p < .05$

[b] In the education and occupation regressions I is combined parents' average incomes; in the earnings regressions I is father's average income (see text). The metric coefficients for I in all cases are multiplied by one thousand for ease of presentation.

357

the use of the pooled within-category regression equations in adjusting the category means for differences in the composition of the categories in the precollegiate experiences of the students. The relevant regression equations for these adjustments appear in Table 12.4, in Line 7 for education, Line 14 for occupational status, and Line 20 for earnings, in the lower panel of metric coefficients.

The adjusted category means and the deviations of these means from the grand mean for all three outcomes are presented in Table 12.5. It is clear from these results that, compared with the gross deviations, the adjusted deviations represent a rather uniform reduction in the apparent effects. For example, for men attending the University of Wisconsin, Madison, the apparent effect on education is reduced from .4 to −.09 years, on occupational status from 6.7 to 1.8 SEI points, and on earnings from $868 to $533. Thus, when we control for the favorable advantage of men attending the University of Wisconsin, Madison on the input variables, the apparent effects of the school itself are reduced. At the other extreme, the negative deviations of the Wisconsin County Teachers Colleges are reduced when the achievement disadvantages of their students are considered. The apparent education effect is changed from −.70 to .22 years; the occupational status effect is changed from −6.2 to 5.1 SEI points; and the earnings effect from −$1828 to −$900. Taking the two examples discussed thus far, we should note that the adjusted means for the Wisconsin County Teachers Colleges on education and occupational status surpass those of the University of Wisconsin, Madison (note that this is the reverse of the unadjusted means), and the earnings gap between the two categories is substantially reduced by the adjustment.

In some cases, the effects are not diminished but, instead, are increased. For example, when the Catholic liberal arts colleges are equated with all other colleges on the input variables, which is the essence of the adjustment procedure, the apparent effect on education increases from .28 to .39 years. This results from the fact that the category's means on the input variables are generally lower than would be expected, given its mean achievement on education. Another example of this type of effect is the effect of the prestigious category on occupational status. Because the category's means on the input variables are generally much higher than would be expected on the basis of its mean occupational status, the negative net effect is increased. These occurrences are illustrated in a hypothetical example for a bivariate case shown in Figure 12.2. The figure depicts four groups (A, B, C, and D). The bivariate slope, b_{YX}, is the same in each group. The groups are different with respect to their means on variables X and Y. When the group means on Y for groups B and C are adjusted to the grand mean on X, $\bar{Y}^* = \bar{Y} - b_{YX}(\bar{X} - \bar{X}_.)$, the adjusted means "regress" toward the grand mean on Y. In some cases, depending upon the particular configuration of group means, the adjusted deviation from the grand mean can even change in sign. Most of the adjustments in Table 12.5 are typified by groups B and C in this illustration (except that the

Net College Category Differences on Educational Achievement, Occupational Status Attainment and Earnings: Eligible Subsample with Bivariate Subsample Data Present

Adjusted Category Means and Deviations from the Grand Mean

College Category	Education[a]		Occupational Status[a]		Earnings[b]	
	Mean	Dev.	Mean	Dev.	Mean	Dev.
University of Wisconsin, Madison	14.99	-.09	58.4	1.8	8449	533
University of Wisconsin, Milwaukee	14.54	-.54	53.8	-2.7	7974	58
University of Wisconsin, Center System	14.52	-.55	46.9	-9.6	7770	-146
Wisconsin State Universities	15.00	-.08	57.1	.6	7556	-360
Wisconsin County Teachers Colleges	15.29	.22	61.7	5.1	7016	-900
Marquette University	15.10	.02	60.8	4.3	9246	1330
Prestigious Colleges and Universities	15.48	.40	45.3	-11.3	7165	-751
Liberal Arts Colleges, General	15.19	.11	55.7	-.8	7251	-665
Liberal Arts Colleges, Catholic	15.47	.39	55.9	-.6	7544	-372
Universities	14.93	-.14	58.1	1.6	8459	543
Technological Colleges and Institutes	15.19	.12	63.4	6.8	8973	1057
Other Colleges	15.41	.33	52.7	-3.9	7104	-812
Grand mean	15.078		56.535		7916	
Standard deviation	1.629		22.678		3626	
Increment in R^2	.0227		.0242		.0239	

[a]Adjusted for differences on V, M, X, I, Q, G, T, P, F, E, J, K, D, B, S, C, and A.

[b]Adjusted for differences on V, M, X, I, Q, G, T, P, F, E, and J.

359

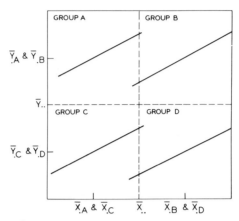

Figure 12.2 Illustration of covariance adjustment: four groups, bivariate case.

illustration involves a simple bivariate situation and our empirical model is a multivariate one). Group A of the illustration represents the case in which the category mean on Y is much higher than would be expected from the group mean on X. This represents the adjustment of the Catholic liberal arts category mean on education (see also the adjustment of the universities category mean on occupational status). Finally, group D of the illustration represents the case in which the category mean on X is much higher than would be expected on the basis of a rather low mean on Y. This type of occurrence is exemplified by the adjustment of the prestigious category mean on occupational status and by the adjustment of the general liberal arts category mean on earnings. In a number of cases, the adjusted means do not differ substantially from the unadjusted means. This stems from the fact that the category involved is very near the grand mean on the relevant input variables. This situation can be easily visualized with the aid of the coordinates in Figure 12.2.

We may assess the relative ability of the college categories to account for variation in achievements controlling for the selection–recruitment variables by examining the proportion of variance in the outcomes added by the dummy variables representing the college categories over and above that which can be explained by the selection–recruitment variables alone. These increments in explained variance are presented for each outcome in Table 12.5 on the last line of the table. The college categories add about 2.3% to the variance already explained in educational achievement by the input variables, about 2.4% to that already explained in occupational status attainment, and about 2.4% to that already explained in earnings.[10] In other

[10] There are alternative ways of partitioning the variance explained in these outcomes (see Werts and Linn, 1969; Duncan, 1970). No matter what method is used, there is little difference in the proportion that is allocated to the college categories (see Alwin, 1974).

words, through the adjustment procedures used here, we have reduced the between-college category variance in education from .0790 to .0227 (a reduction of about 71%), the between-category variance in occupational status from .0594 to .0242 (a reduction of about 59%), and the between-category variance in earnings from .0506 to .0239 (a 53% reduction). In general, by controlling for the between-category differences on selection–recruitment factors, we have reduced, by well over one-half, the variance in our achievement outcomes that can be explained by the college category differences.

Although the proportion of variance in the outcome variables uniquely attributable to unknown sources of difference between our college categories is small, it is a mistake to conclude that there are *no* college effects. It is evident from Table 12.5 that there are small net college category effects in these data which appear to be interpretable. Still, we should be aware that these net differences may be small relative to our ability to account for variation in the three achievements. Such is the case with educational and occupational status attainments in that, as indicated by the coefficients of determination in Lines 7 and 14 of Table 12.4, the ability of college differences to account for variance in these outcomes is small relative to the percentage of the total variance accounted for by both precollegiate and collegiate experiences, inasmuch as the collegiate experience is represented by the college attended. The coefficient of determination for educational attainment in Equation 7 of Table 12.4 is .293; about 7.7% of this is uniquely due to college category differences. Similarly, the coefficient of determination for occupational status attainment in Equation 14 is .190, of which about 12.7% is uniquely due to college differences. Obviously, college differences appear to be slightly more important with respect to explaining variance in occupational status. In contrast, in Equation 20, we note that the corresponding coefficient of determination for earnings is .098, of which about 24.4% is uniquely due to college differences. Therefore, relative to our overall ability to account for variation in these outcomes, college differences appear to be most important for earnings, less important for occupational status, and least important for education.

We have established that college differences appear to have small net effects on all three of our achievement outcomes, and it is now possible to question whether or not these effects operate in an intervening capacity, helping to transmit the effects of prior variables, particularly socioeconomic background. The choice of college may, through the effects of colleges on achievement, reflect the influence of social background and other precollegiate experiences, or the component of variation introduced in achievement by colleges may be unrelated to background and other inputs.

The regression equations in Table 12.4 have been arranged in a sequential manner for the purpose of obtaining the total effects of the selection-recruitment variables on each outcome variable. A causal ordering of groups of variables is assumed for these purposes. The causal sequence of variables is as follows: (1) socioeconomic background (V, M, X, and I), (2) academic ability (Q), (3) academic performance (G), (4) significant others' influence (T, P, and F), (5) aspirations (E and J), (6) commitment to college (K,D,B,S,C, and A), and (7) colleges. Following Duncan (1971), the total effect of one variable on another is the part of their total association which is neither due to their common causes, to correlation among their causes, nor to unanalyzed (predetermined) correlation. The total effect of a variable is, therefore, obtained from its regression coefficient in an equation that contains only variables occurring prior to it and/or contemporaneous with it in the causal sequence of variables. For example, the coefficients in Equation 1 are the total effects of the socioeconomic background variables on education given our model; the coefficient for academic ability in Equation 2 is the total effect of academic ability on education; the coefficient for academic performance in Equation 3 is the total effect of academic performance, and so on for all input variables.[11]

The total effects of the selection–recruitment variables in the model on education, occupational status, and earnings are summarized in the first columns of Tables 12.6, 12.7, and 12.8 respectively. The effects reported in these tables are in standard form. The total effects can be partitioned into those effects that are mediated by subsequent variables in the model and those effects that are unmediated by subsequent variables in the model. For our present purposes, it is important to consider two types of mediated effects, those effects mediated by other selection–recruitment variables and those mediated by colleges. In Tables 12.6, 12.7, and 12.8, we have partitioned the total effects into three parts: (1) the effect mediated by selection–recruitment variables, (2) the effect mediated by colleges, and (3) the unmediated effect. This decomposition of effects allows us to estimate the part of a given effect that is mediated by college differences. Given the mediated and unmediated effects as proportions of the total effect, any interpretation is invariant with regard to metric, so, for convenience, we deal solely with the standardized effects here.[12]

In Table 12.6, we find that mother's education (M), academic ability (Q), academic performance in high school (G), friends' college plans (F), educational aspirations (E), possible parental financial support (K), and scholarship applications (S) have significant effects on education net of prior and contemporaneous variables in the model. Of the effect of mother's education on son's education (.0994), about 51% (.0504) is mediated by other selection–recruitment variables, about 13% of it (.0127) is mediated by colleges, and about 34% of it (.0363) is unmediated by variables in the model. The other input variables mediating the effect of mother's education are principally academic ability (see Table 12.4), which accounts for about

[11] See Alwin and Hauser (1975) for a discussion of the decomposition of effects in path analysis.

[12] The reader interested in the metric coefficients should consult the lower panel of Table 12.4.

TABLE 12.6
Decomposition of Total Effects of Selection/Recruitment Factors on 1964 Educational Achievement
into Effects Mediated by other Selection/Recruitment Factors, Effects Mediated by Colleges, and
Unmediated Effects: Eligible Subsample with Bivariate Subsample Data Present

Predetermined Variable	Total Effect	Effect Mediated by Selection/Recruitment	Effect Mediated by Colleges	Unmediated Effect
V	.0530	----	----	.0256
M	.0994[a]	.0504	.0127	.0363
X	.0566	----	----	.0316
I	.0305	----	----	-.0084
Q	.2866[a]	.2279	-.0006	.0575[a]
G	.3767[a]	.0982	.0020	.2765[a]
T	.0270	----	----	.0090
P	.0346	----	----	.0075
F	.1447[a]	.0250	.0112	.1085[a]
E	.0822[a]	.0254	.0053	.0515
J	.0597	----	----	.0515
K	.0735[a]	----	-.0030	.0765[a]
D	.0082	----	----	.0072
B	.0552[a]	----	----	.0479
S	.1274[a]	----	.0111	.1183[a]
C	.0358	----	----	.0446
A	-.0171	----	----	-.0119

NOTE: The effects reported here are in standard form. Any interpretation given the mediated
and unmediated effects as proportions of the total effect are invariant with regard to metric.
Variable abbreviations are as follows: V = father's education, M = mother's education, X = father's
occupational status, I = parental income, Q = academic ability, G = academic performance in high
school, T = teachers' encouragement, P = parental encouragement, F = friends' college plans, E =
educational aspirations, J = occupational aspirations, K = possible parental support, D = consideration of college, B = willingness to borrow, S = scholarship applications, C = high school curriculum, A = perceived value of college.

[a] p < .05

21% (1.0 − .078/.099) of the total effect, and significant others' influence, which accounts for about 14% ((.072 − .058)/.099). The remaining part of the effect mediated by the input variables is due to minor indirect paths via high school grades (6%), aspirations (4%), and commitment to college (5%). Mother's education is, of course, just one of four variables used in the analysis to represent socioeconomic background, and, since the variables are intercorrelated at moderate levels of magnitude, their simultaneous presence in the same equation depresses their individual effects (see Gordon, 1968). One can argue, therefore, that the effects of the SES variables should be treated as a block, and the questions posed here should be answered in terms of the blocked SES effects. Using Heise's (1972) "sheaf" coefficient for *V, M, X,* and *I* taken as a block, the blocked effects of these SES variables are .1779 (this is computed on the basis of Equation 1 in Table 12.4).[13] The blocked unmediated effects of these variables are .0694 (using Equation 7), and the blocked effects, unmediated by selection–recruitment variables alone, are .0884 (using Equation 6). This leads to the conclusion that about 50% (.0884/.1779) of the effects of *V, M, X,* and *I* on education are mediated by selection–recruitment variables, about 11% ((.0896 − .0694)/.1779) by colleges, and about 39% (.0694/.1779) are unmediated by either inputs, colleges, or both.

The effect of academic ability (*Q*) on education is .2866. About 80% of this effect (.2279) is mediated by subsequent selection–recruitment variables, virtually none of it is mediated by college differences (−.0006), and about 20% (.0575) is unmediated by variables in the model. Almost all of the part mediated by other input variables (1.0 − .084/.287 = 70.7%) is indirect via academic performance in high school. The remaining indirect effects occur via the commitment to college variables (4%), aspirations (4%), and significant others' influence (1%).

The effect of high school academic performance (*G*) on education is .3767; 73% of this (.2765) is unmediated by variables in the model. Of the remainder (.1002), less than 1% of the total effect can be attributed to the operation of college differences as intervening variables, while about 26% (.098/.377) is mediated by other input variables. Of the 26% that is mediated by other input variables, about 12% is indirect via the commitment to college variables, about 8% is indirect via significant others' influence, and about 6% operates via aspirations.

The effect of friends' college plans (*F*) on education is .1447; 75% of this (.1085) is unmediated by variables in the model, 17% (.0250) is mediated by other selection–recruitment variables, and about 8% (.0112) is mediated by college differences. The part of the effect mediated by other input variables is principally transmitted by aspirations ((.145 − .123)/.145 = 15.2%). The remaining 2% operates via the commitment to college variables.

---

[13] The "sheaf" coefficient is actually the application of straightforward procedures of partitioning the coefficient of determination associated with a regression equation (see Heise, 1972 and Duncan, 1970).

The effect of educational aspirations (E) is .0822; 63% of this effect (.0515) is unmediated by other variables in the model, a slight amount, 6%, is mediated by colleges, and a modest amount, 30%, is mediated by the commitment to college variables. The effects of possible parental support (K) and scholarship applications (S) on education are .0735 and .1274, respectively. Virtually all of the effect of possible parental support is unmediated by college differences. Similarly, 93% of the effect of scholarship applications is unmediated by college differences.

In summary, with respect to effects on education, college differences mediate about 13% of the effect of mother's education (or 11% of the effects of SES variables), none of the effects of academic ability and academic performance, about 8% of the effect of friends' college plans, about 6% of the effect of educational aspirations, none of the effect of possible parental support, and about 7% of the effect of scholarship applications.

In Table 12.7, we find the following variables to have significant effects on occupational status net of prior and contemporaneous variables: academic ability (Q), high school grades (G), teachers' encouragement to attend college (T), friends' college plans (F), occupational aspirations (J), possible parental support (K), and scholarship applications (S).

Although the SES variables have no effects on occupational status, net of each other (see Equation 8), the blocked effects of these variables equal .1514, a moderate effect. This set of joint effects can be partitioned as follows: .0777 is mediated by the selection–recruitment variables, about 51% of the total blocked effect; −.0104 is mediated by college differences, a negative 7%; and .0878 consists of unmediated effects, 58% of the total SES effects.

The effect of academic ability (Q) on occupational status is .2259; of this, about 73% (.1640) is mediated by subsequent input variables, about 30% (.0666) is unmediated by variables in the model, and virtually nothing (−.0047) is attributable to the mediation of the effect by college differences. Of the effect mediated by other inputs, 60% is accounted for by the indirect effect via high school grades (1.0 − .090/.226 = 60.2%). The remaining 13%, represented by indirect effects transmitted by other input variables, includes effects via significant others' influence (4%), aspirations (7%), and commitment to college (1%).

The effect of academic performance (G) on occupational status is .2530; 62% of this (.1568) is unmediated by variables in the model, about 34% (.1854) is mediated by other input variables, and some 4% (.0108) is mediated by college differences. The effects of academic performance transmitted by other inputs is .0854. About one-half of it (or 18% of the total effect) is due to the indirect effects via significant others' influence, about one-fourth (or 8% of the total) is attributable to indirect effects via aspirations, and about one-fourth (8% of the total) to effects mediated by commitment to college.

Teachers' encouragement (T) has an effect of .0849 on occupational

TABLE 12.7
Decomposition of Total Effects of Selection/Recruitment Factors on 1964 Occupational Status Attainment into Effects Mediated by Other Selection/Recruitment Factors, Effects Mediated by Colleges, and Unmediated Effects: Eligible Subsample with Bivariate Subsample Data Present

Predetermined Variable	Total Effect	Effect Mediated by Selection/Recruitment	Effect Mediated by Colleges	Unmediated Effect
V	.0595	----	----	.0461
M	.0380	----	----	.0068
X	.0545	----	----	.0216
I	.0541	.1640	-.0047	.0666[a]
Q	.2259[a]	.0854	.0108	.1568[a]
G	.2530[a]	.0073	-.0005	.0781[a]
T	.0849[a]	----	----	.0320
P	.0575	.0209	----	.0924[a]
F	.1121[a]	----	-.0012	-.0050
E	.0057	----	.0061	.1129[a]
J	.1256[a]	.0066	.0076	.0644[a]
K	.0720[a]	----	----	.0193
D	-.0154	----	----	-.0085
B	-.0032	----	.0015	.0667
S	-.0682[a]	----	----	.0227
C	.0188	----	----	-.0002
A	.0003	----	----	----

NOTE: The effects reported here are in standard form. Any interpretation given the mediated and unmediated effects as proportions of the total effect are invariant with regard to metric. *Variable abbreviations are as follows:* V = father's education, M = mother's education, X = father's occupational status, I = parental income, Q = academic ability, G = academic performance in high school, T = teachers' encouragement, P = parental encouragement, F = friends' college plans, E = educational aspirations, J = occupational aspirations, K = possible parental support, D = consideration of college, B = willingness to borrow, S = scholarship applications, C = high school curriculum, A = perceived value of college.

[a] p < .05

status. Of this effect (.0781), 92% is unmediated by other variables in the system. The remaining 8% is due primarily to the intervening effects of aspirations and commitment to college. A second significant others variable, friends' college plans (F), also has an effect on occupational status, in the magnitude of .1121. Again, 82% of this effect (.0924) is unmediated by variables in the model. The effects mediated by other variables are primarily mediated by other inputs and not by college differences. In fact, 18% of the total effect is transmitted via aspirations, and college differences suppress about 1% of this effect.

Occupational aspirations (J) has an effect of .1256 on occupational attainment, which is largely unmediated by the intervening process (.1129/.1256 = 90%). Of the remaining 10%, about one-half is due to the indirect effect of aspirations via commitment to college (.0066), and about one-half is due to college differences (.0061).

The two remaining variables that affect occupational status are possible parental support (K) and scholarship applications (S), which have effects of .0720 and .0682, respectively. In both cases, most of the effects are unmediated by college differences, with about 89% (.0644/.0720) of the effect of possible parental support and about 98% (.0667/.0682) of the effect of scholarship applications being unmediated by subsequent variables in the model, namely college differences. Summarizing the discussion with respect to occupational status, it appears that very few of the effects of selection–recruitment variables are mediated by college differences. Their largest mediating roles are the transmission of about 4% of the effect of high school grades and some 7% (negative) of the effect of SES on occupational status.

The coefficients in Table 12.8 indicate that the selection–recruitment variables with a significant effect on earnings are as follows: father's income (I), academic ability (Q), academic performance (G, and occupational aspirations (J). The effect of father's income is .1675; 91% of this (.1531) is unmediated either by other input variables or college differences. Other input variables transmit about 4% of the effect (.0064), and college differences transmit about 5% of the effect (.0080), both of which are essentially trivial amounts. If we block the effects of all SES variables on earnings, we obtain very similar results. Here, the blocked total effects equal .1926; of this, 85% is unmediated (.1638) by intervening variables. Of the remaining 15% of the SES effects, 9% (.0168) is transmitted via other input variables and 6% (.0119) via college differences.

The effect of academic ability is .0749. This effect represents the operation of some suppressor effects in that an effect of .0875 is transmitted by other input variables, .0114 by college differences, and −.0240 directly. This suggests that within college categories, there is an overall positive effect of academic ability on earnings, but part of the effect is suppressed by unknown variables, represented by the unmediated portion of the effect. Using the absolute sum of the effects (.1229) as a base, the unmediated portion accounts for about 20% of the effect, colleges account

TABLE 12.8

Decomposition of Total Effects of Selection/Recruitment Factors on 1967 Earnings into Effects Mediated by Other Selection/Recruitment Factors, Effects Mediated by Colleges, and Unmediated Effects: Eligible Subsample with Bivariate Subsample Data Present

Predetermined Variable	Total Effect	Effect Mediated by Selection/Recruitment	Effect Mediated by Colleges	Unmediated Effect
V	-.0041	----	----	-.0065
M	.0292	----	----	.0268
X	.0342	----	----	.0109
I	.1675[a]	.0064	.0080	.1531[a]
Q	.0749[a]	.0875	.0114	-.0240
G	.1193[a]	.0274	.0278	.0641
T	.0189	----	----	.0196
P	.0594	----	----	.0441
F	.0371	----	----	.0255
E	-.0624[a]	----	----	-.0559[a]
J	.1551[a]	----	.0239	.1312[a]

NOTE: The effects reported here are in standard form. Any interpretation given the mediated and unmediated effects as proportions of the total effect are invariant with regard to metric.

Variable abbreviations are as follows: V = father's education, M = mother's education, X = father's occupational status, I = father's income, Q = academic ability, G = academic performance in high school, T = teachers' encouragement, P = parental encouragement, F = friends' college plans, E = educational aspirations, J = occupational aspirations.

[a] $p < .05$

for another 9%, and other input variables account for about 71%. Of the mediated effect, 52% is due to the indirect effects of academic ability via academic performance, about 7% operates via significant others' influence, about 13% operates via aspirations, and about 9% is transmitted by college differences.

The effect of high school academic performance (G) on earnings is .1193. Of this effect, 11% (.013) is transmitted by significant others' influence, 12% (.014) is transmitted by aspirations, 24% (.028) operates via college differences, and 54% (.064) is unmediated by variables in the model.

The only other selection–recruitment variable having a significant impact on earnings is occupational aspirations, which has an effect of .1551. Of this effect, 85% is unmediated by variables in the model, the remaining 15% of the effect (.0239) being transmitted via college differences.

In summary, college differences transmit about 5% of the effect of father's income on earnings (or about 6% of the blocked effects of SES variables), about 9% of the effect of academic ability, about 24% of the effect of high school grades, and about 15% of the effect of occupational aspirations on earnings. We should note that, of the outcome variables considered here, college differences appear to be most important in transmitting the effects of prior variables on early earnings.

Summary and Conclusions

The purpose of this chapter is twofold. First, we address the question of the presence of unique college effects on achievement outcomes for a population of male college attenders. The population studied is the male 1957 Wisconsin high school graduates followed up by Sewell and his associates in 1964 (see Sewell and Hauser, 1975), who were alive, who were neither in any school or college nor in the military in 1964, and who had received some post-secondary education (excepting vocational training) during the time interval. The achievements studied are years of schooling completed and occupational status attained 7 years after high school graduation and earnings 10 years after high school. Second, we attempt to assess the related question of the extent to which colleges operate in an intervening capacity, transmitting the effects of precollegiate experiences, particularly socioeconomic background, on later achievements for the population studied.

The empirical analysis undertaken to answer these questions is guided by a recursive structural equation model for achievements which includes both precollegiate and collegiate experiences. The precollegiate experiences of individuals are discussed in terms of processes by which colleges differentially select and recruit students, and they are also considered as part of a within-college achievement process. The collegiate experiences of individuals are not tapped directly but are represented here by the college attended. In this manner, interinstitutional differences in the outcomes of schooling are interpreted in terms of school-to-school differences in the experiences of students.

The empirical analysis begins with the observation that several categories of college differ with respect to the achievements of their students, but these gross differences in achievement represent a relatively small proportion of the total variance in the outcomes studied. Some 8% of the variance in years of schooling completed lies between our categories of college attended by the men in the sample, and some 6% and 5% of the variance in occupational status and earnings, respectively, lies between categories. We are cautioned by these results to be less than optimistic regarding the powerful role of college quality differences in the achievement process.

After considering some of the plausible interpretations of our initial results, we pursue an analysis that stresses the issue of differential selection and recruitment into colleges. Our analysis systematically considers an array of variables representing the selection–recruitment process by entering these variables into a set of equations for the achievement outcomes, and we undertake an adjustment for differing college composition on these variables. These results indicate that insofar as these data are concerned (1) the effects of colleges net of selection–recruitment processes are essentially additive, (2) the initial gross differences among our categories of college are substantially reduced when the selection–recruitment process is considered, and (3) the net college effects are not major mediators of the effects of precollegiate variables on achievements. In general, measured in terms of the net contributions of the colleges to explained variance in the outcomes, the college category differences are reduced by well over one-half. These findings prompt us to be even more cautious with regard to the importance of college quality differences in the achievement process. These observations are essentially consistent with comparable analyses of data for other populations reported in the literature (e.g., see Solmon, 1973a).

We opened this chapter with the observation that distinctions among institutions of higher education may be increasingly important in the achievement of young people in the United States. While this point of view has been widely advocated, the empirical support for it has to date been less than overwhelming. With the possible exception of the earnings outcome, we believe that the analyses presented here provide a firm basis for a somewhat more skeptical view of the importance of college differences, especially college quality, on educational and socioeconomic achievements.

While our skepticism of the importance of college effects on these outcomes is not unfounded, there remain small net college effects which require explanation. Several interpretations of these residual differences are possible. First, the residual effects may be spurious, due to the failure to adequately control selection and recruitment variables. Since our analysis has made a serious attempt to include the theoretically relevant sources of precollegiate variation in achievements, this is probably a weak interpretation of the results. Still, variables which have not been included here, due to the lack of data, may operate to produce the observed effects. For example, religion and ethnicity are known to have small observable effects on socioeconomic attainments (Duncan et al., 1972) and are important, in some cases, in the allocation of students to colleges (see Astin and Lee, 1972). Further research in other sets of data is needed to examine this interpretation.

A second possible interpretation of the net college effects involves the operation of processes of differential socialization and/or certification. While this interpretation is likely to be preferred by social scientists, the actual processes producing these results are not clear. Some authors (Meyer, 1972) have postulated a type of "charter" effect of colleges; this falls into the category of what we have referred to as certification effects. This type of interpretation posits the existence of norms in society governing the type of graduates various institutions are "chartered" to produce. As far as we can tell, this normative process has not been systematically studied to date, although the conceptual framework has been used to interpret the effects of variables, such as college size and prestige, on achievements (Kamens, 1971).

Another plausible interpretation that falls under the rubric of differential socialization and/or certification deals with the differing levels of competition in colleges and the differential allocation of grades by college within levels of ability. Our analyses here have not included a measure of academic performance in college, yet this appears to be an important determinant of dropping out of college (Astin, 1971; Kamens, 1971). Moreover, there is evidence of between-college variation in grades, net of ability, for college entrants (Drew and Astin, 1972) as well as college graduates (Davis, 1966). An explanation of this sort might be used in the interpretation of the small college effects on educational attainment and, indirectly, on socioeconomic attainments, inasmuch as education is a major determinant of both occupational status and earnings. In addition to this interpretation, one might speculate that the small college effects on occupational status occur by virtue of colleges' effects on education, and that the effects on earnings occur by virtue of their effects on both education and occupational status. If we examine this hypothesis for occupational status by considering the intervening educational attainment variable, we reduce the increment in the coefficient of determination which is associated with entering the college categories into the equation after the input variables from .0226 to .0187 (see Alwin, 1974). Finally, examining the hypothesis for the earnings outcome, that education and occupational status intervene to account for the observed college effects, we find that the increment in the coefficient of determination associated with colleges is reduced from .0239 to .0204 (see Alwin, Hauser, and Sewell, 1975). These results essentially fail to confirm the hypothesis that intervening achievements account for the effects, inasmuch as the total net effects are not removed. The issue must be pursued in other sets of data.

A final possible explanation for the present findings involves the issue of random measurement error in the selection–recruitment factors included in the analysis. Unreliability of measurement in these variables may result in biases in the within-category regression coefficients. Although biases may occur in either direction, the regression coefficients will most likely be attenuated, resulting in an overestimation of the variance in achievements attributable to college differences. It is not possible to investigate this issue here.

Whatever the interpretation of the residual effects of colleges on achievements that one favors, the overwhelming lesson to be learned from this type of analysis is that, with the possible exception of earnings (Alwin et al., 1975), the net college effects are rather small. Owing to the substantial interest among social scientists in studying the "environmental" and other impacts of colleges on their students (Feldman and Newcomb, 1969) and the parallel interest in studying "contextual" effects (see Hauser, 1970a), the type of results obtained here may go unattended. At the same time, it is important to emphasize the need for further study of these issues in other populations of interest, employing the type of analytic strategy used here, so that we may obtain a better grasp of the relative importance of college differences in the achievement process.

Acknowledgments

The author wishes to thank Professors William H. Sewell and Robert M. Hauser for their guidance in this research effort and for their generous comments on an earlier draft of this chapter.

XIII | Changes in Initial Differences among Major-Field Groups: An Exploration of the "Accentuation Effect" *

Kenneth A. Feldman
State University of New York, Stony Brook

John Weiler
University of California, Santa Barbara

The last 10 to 15 years have seen a sharp rise in the number of large-scale studies in which the *global* effects of different colleges on their students is researched (Alwin, 1974; Astin, 1972; Astin and Panos, 1969; Centra and Rock, 1971; Chickering and McCormick, 1973; Clark, Heist, McConnell, Trow, and Yonge, 1972; Gurin and Katz, 1966; McLeish, 1970; Nichols, 1967; Rock, Centra, and Linn, 1970; Rose, 1964; Skager, Holland, and Braskamp, 1966; Spaeth and Greeley, 1970). This increase in analyses of overall college settings should not be taken to imply that settings *within* colleges are unimportant in affecting student outcomes. Not only do subenvironments in a college generally differ from one another, but they also often differentially mediate any overall pressures from the more general college environment; for example, certain subsettings in college may reinforce the total college influence while others may contradict or even challenge it (see especially Astin, 1965; Becker, Geer, and Hughes, 1968; Brown, 1968; Feldman, 1969, 1972; Feldman and Newcomb, 1969; Finney, 1974; Frantz, 1969; Gamson, 1966, 1967; Gurin, 1971b; Hochbaum,

* This analysis was supported in part by grants from the State University of New York–Research Foundation (under the supervision of the Joint Awards Council–University Awards Committee) and the Research Institute of the American College Testing Program.

1968; Longino and Kart, 1973; Newcomb and Wilson, 1966; Newcomb, Koenig, Flacks, and Warwick, 1967; Sanford, 1962; Selvin, 1963; Siegel and Siegel, 1957; Suczek, 1972; Vreeland and Bidwell, 1965; Wallace, 1964, 1965, 1966, 1967; Williams and Reilley, 1972).

Among the many studies suggesting the significance of college subsettings is the research by Huntley (1965, 1967) on the change in students' values, as measured by the scales of the Allport–Vernon–Lindzey Study of Values. He found that students in different major fields at Union College were typically different in their values at entrance to and graduation from college. Moreover, students in the different academic majors evidenced differential change and stability of their values. On certain of the value scales, in fact, the changes for the various major fields were sufficiently counterbalancing in degree and direction that one might mistakenly conclude, from knowing only the overall average freshman and senior scores, that students typically changed very little in their values during college. While far from conclusive evidence, such differences in the changes of students in different college subsettings do suggest that subsettings may have varying impacts on the students in them.

Perhaps the most intriguing aspect of Huntley's study is his conclusion that the *initial differences* among the groups of students entering various curricula tended "to be accentuated or sharpened over the four years" (1965:381). In both of his research reports, he discusses accentuation in terms of *groups* of students entering the several academic majors, claiming that his data support "the contention that the groups have indeed moved farther apart" (Huntley, 1965:381). In the second of the two reports, he adds an interesting interpretation at an *individual* level of analysis: "It may be argued . . . that there is evidence for an accentuation of the student's central value(s) during the four years of college" (Huntley, 1967:48). Feldman and Newcomb (1969) incorporated both the group and individual levels of analysis in using the construct of "accentuation" as part of their integration of the research on the impacts of colleges on students. The term has since appeared in a number of other discussions and studies of higher education (Astin, 1970a; Athanasiou, 1969, 1971; Chickering, 1970; Clark *et al.*, 1972; Feldman, 1971, 1972; Franks, Falk, and Hinton, 1973; Gurin, 1971a; Newcomb, Brown, Kulik, Reimer, and Revelle, 1970, 1971; Moore, 1973; Stakenas, 1972; Thistlethwaite, 1968, 1972, 1973; Trent and Cohen, 1973; Walsh, 1973; Walsh, Vaudrin, and Hummel, 1972).

Considering only the empirical research dealing directly with the topic of accentuation, students have been studied as participants in different kinds of colleges (Chickering, 1970; Clark *et al.*, 1972; Feldman and Newcomb, 1969, Chapter 5) and as members of college subsettings, such as major fields (Feldman, 1972:230–232; Feldman and Newcomb, 1969, Chapter 6; Franks *et al.*, 1973; Thistlethwaite, 1968, 1972, 1973), clusters within an academic division (Athanasiou, 1969, 1971), and residential and living–learning arrangements (Feldman and Newcomb, 1969, Chapter 7; Moore, 1973; Newcomb *et al.*, 1970, 1971; Stakenas, 1972). The term "accentuation" does not have a uniform meaning across these studies, and, not unexpectedly, the research methods and analytic techniques used in these studies also differ. Yet each study does report some evidence of accentuation, although the nature, consistency, strength, and implications of this empirical support vary considerably. The purpose of this chapter is to clarify the conceptual and operational meanings of "accentuation" as a construct, as well as to present new data bearing on its existence as a phenomenon.

Accentuation: The Individual and the Group

At a group level of analysis, one use of accentuation has been to describe the phenomenon of increases in existing differences among groups or categories of persons. If, for example, the group characteristic under consideration is the average score of individuals on a given indicator, then accentuation refers to the increase in the initial differences among groups on these average scores. To qualify as accentuation in this context, the average scores must "pull apart" so that the relative positions of the group means remain either the same or similar. Thus, only the first two patterns of change, of the five patterns shown in Figure 13.1, demonstrate accentuation of group differences. (The means do not spread apart in Figures 13.1c or 13.1d; the means do pull apart in Figure 13.1e, but the pattern of differences among the groups is dissimilar at the two points in time.)

At an individual level of analysis, accentuation has been used to describe the phenomenon of an increase in emphasis of an already prominent characteristic of an individual. (see Feldman and Newcomb, 1969;55–58, 177–179). A central (important) value of an individual may increase in its

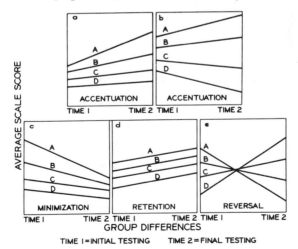

Figure 13.1 Hypothetical patterns of average changes of entrants to four different settings—A, B, C, D.

centrality, or an individual's initially favorable or unfavorable attitude may become even more favorable or more unfavorable. Likewise, a personality attribute that is particularly characteristic of an individual may increase in intensity. All of these examples have in common the fact that a prominently "high" (or prominently "low") attribute of the individual has become even higher (or lower).

An analysis of accentuation may consider both the group as a whole and the individuals within it (for example, see Feldman and Newcomb, 1969; Moore, 1973), but it need not necessarily do so. Thus, it is possible to study change in group differences without focusing on the change of any given individual's characteristics or even of subsets of individuals within each group (see Thistlethwaite, 1968, 1972, 1973: Huntley, 1965, 1967; Stakenas, 1972). Conversely, it is possible to explore the environmental, cultural, and social structural conditions under which individuals' prominent characteristics are likely to be further accentuated, without systematically examining the initial differences among groups of individuals and the change over time in these between-group differences (see Chickering, 1970; Clark *et al.*, 1972; Walsh *et al.*, 1972).

A third use of accentuation, which may be called the "accentuation of differences among individuals," is implicit in Feldman and Newcomb's analysis. Although they never use this particular phrase, they do explore the possible existence of a general "personality dynamic" or an "intrapersonal process," whereby persons already scoring high on some characteristics are the very ones who tend to make the greatest gains, as compared to persons who score lower on these characteristics (see especially Feldman and Newcomb, 1969:142–144, 177–179). This increasing dispersion ("pulling apart") of *individual differences* might occur among individuals regardless of the groups they are in, or it might occur only within certain groups and not others. In any case, such accentuation of differences among individuals may or may not underlie accentuation of differences among groups.[1]

More generally, accentuation of group differences does not presuppose one and only one pattern of change among individuals. Indeed, a variety of patterns of individual change could "produce" an accentuation of initial group differences. Six major patterns that might underlie an increase in the initial differences among groups of students entering different settings are

[1] It should be clear at this point that we have filled in three cells of a four-celled table. Either the group or the individual can be the primary focus of analysis; in either case, the focus can be on the increase of an already prominent characteristic (of either the individual or the group) or on the change in initial differences (among either individuals or groups). Thus, "accentuation of a group's (initially) prominent characteristics" must be analytically distinguished from "accentuation of an individual's (initially) prominent characteristics," "accentuation of (initial) differences among groups," and "accentuation of (initial) differences among individuals" (cf. Moore, 1973).

as follows.[2] For purposes of clarity, they are presented in simplified and exaggerated form. Models 1, 3, and 4 are built on the assumption of increasing heterogeneity of individuals within entrance groups, Models 5 and 6 on decreasing heterogeneity (increasing homogeneity), and Model 2 on neither.

Model 1: *No impact of settings, general accentuation of differences among individuals within and across entrance groups.* The higher the individual on a characteristic, the greater is his gain regardless of the setting entered. (Given differential distribution of individuals in the various entrance groups—by definition, initially high entrance groups have higher individuals and/or more of them—accentuation of initial group differences results.)

Model 2: *Differential impact of different settings, uniform change within each entrance group.* Every entrant to a setting undergoes the same degree of change, but the higher the entrance group, the greater is this uniform gain.

Model 3: *Differential impact of different settings, accentuation of differences among individuals within each entrance group.* For any given level of a characteristic, the higher the individual's entrance group, the greater is his (her) gain on this characteristic. Within each entrance group, the higher the individual, the *greater* is his (her) gain.

Model 4: *Differential impact of some settings, accentuation of differences among individuals within some settings.* (This is a less differentiated version of Model 3.) Prominently high individuals in certain (but not necessarily all) high entrance groups make greater gains than prominently high individuals in any of the other entrance groups. Within each of the (specified) high entrance groups, the higher the individual, the *greater* is his (her) gain.

Model 5: *Differential impact of different settings, minimization of differences among individuals within each entrance group.* For any given level of a characteristic, the higher the individual's entrance group, the

[2] The models vary with respect to which individuals in which entrance groups make what kinds of changes. In all six models, the individual is assumed to have entered one and only one of a specified range of settings. The models are based on the "scores" of persons on a given indicator of a given attribute, taken individually or aggregatively. Taken individually, the scores are properties of the individual; taken aggregatively (as averages), the scores are properties of groups. Throughout, we have used a short hand: For example, "initially high entrance group" refers to a group of individuals entering a setting who have an average score that is high relative to the average scores of other entering groups. We use the term "gain" in a relative sense to include both absolute increases in individual or aggregate scores (i.e., "positive" gains) and absolute decreases in individual or aggregate scores (i.e., "negative" gains). In relative terms, then, gains can be rank ordered from the largest increase (largest "positive" gain) to the largest decrease (largest "negative" gain).

greater is his (her) gain on this characteristic. Within each entrance group, the higher the individual, the *smaller* is his (her) gain.

Model 6: *Differential impact of some settings, minimization of differences among individuals within some settings.* (This is a less differentiated version of Model 5.) Prominently high individuals in certain (but not necessarily all) high entrance groups make greater gains than prominently high individuals in any of the other entrance groups. Within each of the (specified) high entrance groups, the higher the individual, the *smaller* is his (her) gain.

These models are based on presumed impact of the settings entered. If it is further assumed that the initial differences among the groups of entrants to the settings are due to selection—either individual self-selection (attraction of the setting to the individual), selection by those already in the settings (recruitment by the setting), or both—then each model, except the first, essentially posits a different type of interrelationship between selection into settings and the impacts of those settings.[3]

Measuring Accentuation of Initial Differences among Groups

Thus far, we have conceived accentuation of differences among groups to be the pulling apart of group means, resulting from various kinds of individual movement. Put in somewhat different terms, increases in between-group variation may be accompanied by a variety of patterns of change in within-group variation. Although an analysis of within-group variation (and changes therein) is obviously important in exploring the individual dynamics underlying accentuation of between-group differences, from research to date, it is not exactly clear what part within-group

---

[3] It is of interest that Feldman and Newcomb also propose that "processes of attracting and selecting students are interdependent with processes of impact" (1969:334). (Somewhat confusingly, they call this proposition the "principle of accentuation," thereby using the term accentuation to designate a principle, as well as to describe certain phenomena.) Because they focus on the change of prominently high individuals in high entrance groups (see 1969:333–336), their proposition is best represented by either Model 4 or 6. Which of these models pertain, if not both, cannot be clearly determined from their analysis. Since they do not speculate on the degree and direction of change of nonprominently high individuals in the high entrance groups, there is no firm basis for determining whether students become more heterogeneous (Model 4) or more homogeneous (Model 6) within these groups. Furthermore, Models 4 and 6, as we have presented them, seem to incorporate more cases than Feldman and Newcomb's analysis would include. Our models are based on "relative gains" (see footnote 2), while Feldmann and Newcomb presumably restrict their principle to absolute increases of prominently high individuals within (specified) high groups (see 1969:177–179, 328–329, 335); this matter is not without its ambiguities, however, for this restriction is *explicitly* relaxed at one point in their analysis (p. 334) and *implicitly* relaxed at another (pp. 143–144).

variation should play in the actual *measurement* of accentuation. A common way of establishing the existence of accentuation of initial group differences has been to correlate initial group scores with average group gain; a positive correlation indicates accentuation. This particular indicant is based on a statistical procedure that ignores initial within-group variation and any changes in such variation over time. In contrast, there are procedures based on analysis of variance and analysis of covariance which do take into account initial within-group variation as well as between-group variation, and changes in these over time.

In a very loose sense, these various procedures (details of which will be given later) may be seen as providing "alternative indicants" of accentuation of group differences (see Thistlethwaite, 1973). One must remember, however, that the various indicants are not strictly alternative, that is, not totally (or even highly) interchangeable (cf. Thistlethwaite, 1972). In general, indicants based on different statistical procedures implicitly impart somewhat different meanings to group "differences" and "accentuation" of these differences. Moreover, the different indicants vary in the ways in which they assume importance in the measurement process. For example, analyses of variance and covariance clearly play an important part in the search for accentuation of initial group differences, especially if one takes accentuation to mean that initially diverse groups become even more differentiated from one another over time. These procedures, however, cannot stand alone; in a sense, they only become relevant after it has been established that group means not only pull apart, but they do so in a way that totally or largely preserves the relative positions of these means (as in Figures 13.1a and 13.1b). Without this knowledge, one runs the risk of unearthing what might be called "false positives": For certain changes in between-group variation (as compared to the size of within-group change), indicants based only on variance analyses will misleadingly indicate accentuation of initial group differences for the pattern of mean changes shown in Figures 13.1c, 13.1d, and 13.1e.

Accentuation of (Initial) Group Differences:
Academic Majors

The research reported herein is concerned with changes in the initial differences among college students entering various fields of study. In part, we chose major fields as our focal subsetting because of the existing evidence that it is one of the more significant subsettings in college; the results of a relatively large body of research testify to the importance of major field as a generally important membership and reference group for students (among the many studies in this area, see Backman and Secord, 1968; Bereiter and Freedman, 1962; Elton and Rose, 1971; Farwell, Warren, and McConnell, 1962; Feldman, 1972:227–233; Feldman and Newcomb, 1969:227, 248–269 and Chapter 6; Holland and Nichols, 1964; Lehmann, 1965; Lehmann and Dressel, 1962; Nichols, 1964; Pace, 1964; Pierson, 1962;

Thistlethwaite, 1960, 1962; Vreeland and Bidwell, 1966; Walsh and Russel, 1969).

A significant element in students' choice of academic major is their assessment of the extent to which the perceived environment of the major field seems to be congruent with their self-conception and what they would like to become. Indeed, the relatively large turnover among major fields seems to be partially due to students leaving fields in which they feel incompatible and searching for new fields which seem to them to be more compatible. Students in different academic majors typically differ from one another in terms of their values, attitudes, and other personal attributes. Although these differences may merely reflect the selection of different types of students into different academic majors, some part of these differences possibly stem from the ongoing impacts of the various environments as well. Current evidence suggests that not only do students tend to interact more frequently with those who are in the same fields of study than with those who are not, but they also tend to select their close friends from their major fields. Moreover, students report that the course work and teachers of their major fields are influential—varying in degree, of course, with the individual student and the area of influence. In fact, for some students, the largest portion of their social and intellectual experiences in college revolve around their majors.

Another reason for our choice of academic major as the unit of analysis hinges on Feldman and Newcomb's report of rather consistent evidence for the existence of accentuation of initial differences among major-field groups. However, the support for this conclusion, based on a reanalysis of prior research, is ambiguous. A problematic feature of several of the longitudinal studies examined by Feldman and Newcomb (including Huntley's research) is that students were classified by the major field in which they were graduating or in which they had already established themselves (and presumably would graduate). Thus, these studies did not distinguish between those students who started and remained in a given curriculum (whom we shall call "primary recruits") and those students who switched from their original curriculum (the "secondary recruits"). Under these conditions, interpretation of results indicating accentuation of initial group differences is ambiguous because the following conceivable components cannot be separated: (1) attribute change of the primary recruits to the field, (2) attribute change of the secondary recruits before they entered their "new" field, (3) attribute change of the secondary recruits after they entered their "new" field, and (4) the mere switching of certain secondary recruits from one field to others without attribute change at any time. Moreover, the classification procedure used in these studies runs the risk of having artificially inflated the degree of the differences among students grouped by their actual major fields compared to the differences among the same groupings before the students had entered these fields: Because classification of students was made at a later time and then used to classify these same students at an earlier time, it is possible that the pattern of unreliability and measurement error works unduly in favor of finding accentuation in terms of so-called "regression in prediction from post-test scores to pre-test scores" (see Campbell and Stanley, 1963:180–181; also see discussions of "time-reversal analysis" in McNemar, 1940; Furby, 1973). Consequently, we were interested in determining whether accentuation of initial group differences could still be found for major-field groups after the reduction or elimination of these difficulties.

Methods

Subjects

The data for the present analysis come from a research project at the University of Michigan. Data collection included the administration of questionnaires and interviews to the students at the university during the period from the fall of 1962 through the spring of 1967. Random and purposive, longitudinal and cross-sectional samples were used in this project (see Gurin, 1971b:2–5, for elaboration and technical details). The primary analysis of this chapter began with the data for the 1271 students who were seniors during the spring semester of 1966 or 1967 and for whom 1962 or 1963 entrance data were available.[4]

Academic Majors

Included in the entrance questionnaire was a question asking if the respondent had "a major or academic field of interest in mind." For the purposes of our analysis, students have been classified as "primary recruits" to an academic major if their major as a senior was the same one they had in mind when entering the university. "Secondary recruits" to a major field are those students who had a different academic field in mind when entering the university from their actual major a few years later.

---

[4] These data were not available for some 153 senior students who were interviewed or given questionnaires in 1966 or 1967. As the sampling base for the entire project, virtually all freshmen entering the College of Literature, Science and the Arts in 1962 and 1963 (95% response rate) and selected freshmen entering other divisions at the same time were given a two–hour questionnaire battery during freshman orientation week ($N = 3890$). Some of the sampling procedures were designed to gain longitudinal information from these two entering cohorts of students as they progressed through college (at as many as three times after entrance). Other samples were not tied to students who had entered the university in 1962 or 1963; for these samples, students were interviewed or given questionnaires, regardless of whether or not they had taken the entrance questionnaire, or whether they had even entered the university in 1962 or 1963. We would like to thank Drs. Gerald Gurin and Theodore M. Newcomb, the directors of this research project, for making its data on students available to us.

Combining the secondary recruits with the primary recruits produces the "full" major-field groupings of our study (i.e., both those students who presumably always intended to major in the field *and* those who presumably changed their initial decision).

Males and females have been classified separately into fields of study. The categories used are the actual majors of students; they have not been combined to form larger clusters of related academic majors. "Full" major fields containing less than 15 male or 15 female respondents were dropped from our analysis, as were the relatively few respondents who did not name any major field of interest when entering the university. This reduced the total number of respondents in our primary analysis from 1271 to 826. The academic majors that have been retained for our analysis are listed below. For each, the number of students in the "full" sample is given, followed by the number of primary recruits alone. (Any particular analysis may have used somewhat fewer respondents than these totals, due to missing data on the measures of individual attributes.)

Males: Economics (64,8); English language and literature (59,11); Business Administration (45,18); Political Science (43, 10); Psychology (43, 8); History (41, 6); Mathematics (35, 21); Premedical Studies (28, 21); Chemistry (22, 10); Physics (15, 9)

Females: English language and literature (133, 45); Elementary Education (82, 22); Nursing (54, 44); Romance languages and literature (40, 18); History (38, 6); Psychology (31, 10); Political Science (31, 5); Mathematics (22, 20)

OPI Scales

Students entering the University of Michigan as freshmen in 1962 and 1963, as well as the seniors falling into the various samples of the Michigan research project during the spring of 1966 and 1967, were administered seven scales of the Omnibus Personality Inventory (OPI), Form C. Since several of the scales used in the project were somewhat shortened by a random deletion of items, the number of items in each scale are noted. This number also represents the maximum score that could be obtained by the subject, the lowest score being zero in each case. The items used and their exact wording can be found in Gurin, Newcomb, and Cope (1968) and Gurin (1971b). The description of each scale is the one presented in the OPI manual (Center for the Study of Higher Education, 1962):

Thinking Introversion (31): Persons scoring high on this measure are characterized by a liking for reflective thought, particularly of an abstract nature. They express interests in a variety of areas, such as literature, art, and philosophy. Their thinking tends to be less dominated by objective conditions and generally accepted ideas than that of thinking extroverts (low scorers). Extroverts show a preference for overt action and tend to evaluate ideas on the basis of their practical, immediate application.

Theoretical Orientation (30): This scale measures interest in science and in scientific activities, including a preference for using the scientific method in thinking. High scorers are generally logical, rational, and critical in their approach to problems.

Estheticism (23): The high scorers endorse statements indicating diverse interests in artistic matters and activities. The content of the statements in this scale extends beyond painting, sculpture, and music and includes interests in literature and dramatics.

Complexity (23): This measure reflects an experimental orientation rather than a fixed way of viewing and organizing phenomena. High scorers are tolerant of ambiguities and uncertainties, are fond of novel situations and ideas, and are frequently aware of subtle variations in the environment. Most persons high on this dimension prefer to deal with complexity, as opposed to simplicity, and are disposed to seek out and to enjoy diversity and ambiguity.

Autonomy (37): The characteristic measured is composed of nonauthoritarian thinking and a need for independence. High scorers are sufficiently independent of authority, as traditionally imposed through social institutions, that they oppose infringements on the rights of individuals. They are nonjudgmental, realistic, and intellectually liberal.

Impulse Expression (37): This scale assesses a general readiness to express impulses and to seek gratification either in conscious thought or in overt action. The high scorers value sensations, have an active imagination, and their thinking is often dominated by feelings and fantasies.

Religious Liberalism (29): The high scorers are skeptical of religious beliefs and practices and tend to reject most of them, especially those that are orthodox or fundamentalistic.

Self-Description Indices

The survey instruments of the Michigan research project contained an assessment of students' self-concepts in the form of 28 seven-point "scales" defined at each end by bi-polar adjectives—for example, strong/weak, conventional/unconventional. (The 28 items can be found in Gurin *et al.*, 1968; Gurin, 1971b.) Using the format commonly associated with the semantic differential, each student was asked to describe himself or herself "as a person" by indicating whether one or the other end of each scale was "extremely related," "quite closely related," or "only slightly related" to what he or she was like. Students were advised to check the middle point of the seven-position scales only when they "found it completely impossible" to check either side of the scale—that is, when both ends of a particular scale seemed "not at all relevant" to what they were like *or* if both ends of the scale seemed "equally relevant." Finally, students also received the following instructions: "Please do not be concerned with the way your answers would be judged by others. . . . You are describing yourself *to yourself*—not to other people."

To generate a smaller number of indices of self-description, we did a factor analysis of the 28 seven-point "scales" using an orthogonal (varimax) rotation. So as not to produce factors restricted to the respondents used in our particular analysis, the entrance factor analyses are based on self-description data from all students who answered the questionnaire during orientation week ($N = 3890$), and the senior factor analyses are based on the responses of all 1424 seniors who were part of one of the various samples of the Michigan research project. Separate factor analyses were performed for male and female students. In general, the factors for these two groups differed. Interestingly, all seven of the factors found for the female entrants were duplicated for the female seniors, while only one of the seven entrance factors found for males appeared as a factor for the male seniors.

Scores on the self-description indices of our study have been obtained by adding together the scores of the items loading highest on each factor (with equal weighting given to each item). Only those self-description indices based on factors that appeared for both entering freshmen and seniors are used in our analysis. The items that were used in constructing each index follow. For each index, the bi-polar adjectives are listed in order of their freshman factor weights. The asterisk by the adjective of each adjective pair indicates the "high" end of each bi-polar item, from which each of the names of the self-description indices (and the names of the underlying factors) have been derived. The range of possible scores for the self-description index based on the factor is given in parentheses. For women, the indices are ordered from high to low in terms of the eigen-values of each extracted factor.

MALES
Self-described Conventionality, Factor III (3–21): conventional(*)/unconventional, politically conservative(*)/politically liberal, religious(*)/agnostic

FEMALES
Self-described Social Extroversion, Factor I (6–42): social(*)/solitary, active(*)/quiet, happy go lucky(*)/serious, free(*)/constrained, rigid/spontaneous(*), closed/open(*)

Self-described Independence, Factor II (3–21): depend on others/others depend on me(*), rely on own opinions(*)/rely on others' opinions, strong(*)/weak

Self-described Self-esteem, Factor III (6–42): clever(*)/not clever, intellectual(*)/nonintellectual, artistic(*)/inartistic, competent(*)/not too competent, successful(*)/not too successful, handsome(*)/plain

Self-described Softness, Factor IV (5–35): soft(*)/hard, warm(*)/cold, sensitive(*)/insensitive, interested in others(*)/interested in self, masculine/feminine(*)

Self-described Spontaneousness, Factor V (2–14): practical/a dreamer(*), impulsive(*)/deliberate
Self-described Contentment, Factor VI (3–21): relaxed(*)/tense, anxious/confident(*), happy(*)/unhappy
Self-described Conventionality, Factor VII (3–21): religious(*)/agnostic, politically conservative(*)/liberal, conventional(*)/unconventional

Analyzing Changes in Initial Differences among Major-Field Groups

Respondents are compared upon entering the university (Wave 1) and near the end of their undergraduate career (Wave 2), in terms of their scores on the OPI scales and the self-description indices. For both waves, the statistical dependence of each of these variables (attributes) on major-field groups was determined by a one-way analysis of variance, and an Omega-square estimate of the proportion of variation in scores on the attribute scales accounted for by these groups was calculated. (The statistic, ω^2, is a proportional reduction in error measure indicating the strength of association: See Hays, 1963:381–384; Hays, 1973:484–488.) Assuming that group means spread out, accentuation of initial group differences is suggested by an increase over time in the percentage of variance associated with major-field groups, just as a minimization of these differences is suggested by a decrease in this percentage. For our purposes, an inference of either accentuation or minimization is only made if the differences among major-field groups are statistically significant for *both* waves. If the differences among groups are statistically significant for Wave 2 only, increase in the Omega-square estimate is interpreted as the "emergence" of group differences rather than as the accentuation of such differences. Likewise, if the initial group differences are statistically significant for Wave 1 only, decreases in the Omega-square estimate is termed "loss" rather than minimization of group differences.

As part of our analysis, we adjusted the mean differences among groups at Wave 2 on the basis of individuals' scores at Wave 1. This analysis of covariance (with initial score as the covariate) is an important complement to procedures based on a one-way analysis of variance. An advantage of an analysis of covariance is that it enables testing of the significance of the resulting *F*-ratio. Assuming that the one-way analysis of variance is statistically significant for both waves, if the *F*-ratio for the adjusted means (at Wave 2) does not reach statistical significance, then the differences among major-field groups, at this later time, may be attributed to the initial (Wave 1) differences among students as classified into the various groups. If, on the contrary, the *F*-ratio of the analysis of covariance is statistically significant, it may be inferred that the second-wave differences among groups amount to something more than mere retention of essentially the same differences that were initially present. By itself, however, a statistically significant *F*-ratio does not differentiate between accentuation and minimization of initial group differences. Therefore, the results of an analysis of covariance must be interpreted in light of the results of the one-way analysis of variance, as well as the pattern of mean changes that is found for the major-field groups.

To determine the pattern of mean change, we calculated a product-moment correlation between the initial mean score of the entrance groups and the mean gain score of these groups. A positive correlation, indicating that means have pulled apart, suggests accentuation of initial group differences (see Figures 13.1a and 13.1b); in this case, the correlation between initial (Wave 1) mean score and final (Wave 2) mean score will automatically be highly positive (indicating that the *relative* positions of the group means have changed little). A negative correlation between initial mean score of the entrance groups and the mean gain score suggests minimization of initial group differences (see Figure 13.1c) only under the condition that the correlation between initial and final mean scores is positive. If this correlation is negative, fields have "crossed each other" over time, producing a "reversal" of group means (Figure 13.1e).

For the purposes of the present analysis, a clear case of accentuation of initial group differences is indicated whenever (*a*) the correlation over major-field groups between mean initial level and mean gain is positive, (*b*) the Omega-square estimate of the proportion of variance accounted for by major-field classification increases between the two waves, accompanied by statistically significant one-way analysis of variance *F*-ratios for both waves, and (*c*) the *F*-ratio for adjusted major-field means (Wave 2) is also statistically significant. By the same token, minimization of initial group differences seems to us most clearly suggested by the following results: negative correlation between initial group score and group gain (but a positive correlation between initial and final group score); decrease in Omega-square estimates over time (with statistical significance of one-way analysis of variance *F*-ratios at both times); and a statistically significant *F*-ratio for the analysis of covariance.

Results

Changes in Initial Differences among Major-Field Groups (Males)

Table 13.1 presents data on both the initial differences among male primary recruits to various academic majors and the changes in these differences. The first two columns of this table present data for students entering the university (Wave 1): Column 1 lists the *F*-ratio results of one-way analysis of variance for each of the eight attributes under consideration for the males; Omega-square estimates of the proportion of variance in the scores accounted for by the major-field groups are given in

TABLE 13.1

Changes in Initial Differences Among Major-Field Groups on OPI Scales and Self-Description Indices, for Male Primary Recruits[a]

OPI Scales and Self-Description Indices	WAVE 1 F-ratio (ANOVA)	(1962, 1963) Omega-square estimate ($100 \times \omega^2$)	WAVE 2 F-ratio (ANOVA)	(1966, 1967) Omega-square estimate ($100 \times \omega^2$)	Correlation of mean initial score with mean final score	Correlation of mean initial score with mean gain score	Change in percent of variance associated with major-field groups	F-ratio (ANCOVA)
	(1)	(2)	(3)	(4)	(5)	(6)	(7)	(8)
Esteticism	7.112[d] (3.222[d])	31.3 (7.1)	5.580[d] (6.484[d])	25.4 (16.0)	.92[d]	-.00	-5.9	1.805
Thinking Introversion	5.177[d] 3.695	23.7 (8.6)	3.336[c] (3.647[d])	14.8 (8.4)	.74[b]	-.48	-8.9	0.789
Complexity	3.920[d] (2.702[c])	18.2 (5.6)	3.099[c] (2.977[c])	13.5 (6.3)	.81[c]	-.41	-4.7	1.432
Theoretical Orientation	2.966[c] (2.447)	12.9 (4.8)	4.426[d] (3.126[d])	20.6 (6.9)	.93[d]	.49	+7.7	1.815
Autonomy	2.634[c] (0.854)	11.0 (0.0)	4.994[d] (2.573[c])	23.2 (5.2)	.87[c]	.03	+12.2	2.334[b]
Impulse Expression	2.315[b] (1.575)	9.1 (1.9)	1.530 (1.852)	3.9 (2.8)	.85[c]	-.15	-5.2	0.747
Religious Liberalism	0.940 (2.861[c])	0.0 (6.1)	0.962[c] (2.257[b])	0.0 (4.2)	.76[b]	-.36	0.0	0.504
Self-described Conventionality	0.880 (2.026[b])	0.0 (3.3)	2.604[c] (4.252[d])	10.2 (9.6)	.97[d]	.81[c]	+10.2	1.658

[a] In columns 1 - 4, data for male secondary recruits are also given (in parentheses).

[b] p < .05

[c] p < .01

[d] p < .001

387

Column 2. The corresponding F-ratios and Omega-square estimates for the same students near the end of their undergraduate education (Wave 2) are given in Columns 3 and 4, respectively.[5] The attributes are ordered by the degree of initial association shown with the major-field categories (Column 2)—from estheticism and thinking introversion (for which major-field groups account for 31.3% and 23.7% of the variance in scores, respectively) to religious liberalism and self-described conventionality (for which the Omega-square measure of association is zero in both cases).

There is no strong evidence of accentuation of initial group differences among the six attributes that initially discriminated among the major-field groups. The results for the theoretical orientation scale of the OPI come the closest to providing such accentuation. The relative positions of mean scores remained about the same over time (as given in Column 5, the correlation between initial and final mean scores is .93). Both the positive correlation between initial group level and gain (.49, Column 6) and the increase in the percentage of variance associated with major-field groups (7.7%, Column 7) suggest accentuation of initial group differences. However, the F-ratio from the analysis of covariance (Column 8) is not statistically significant, although it is close ($p = .075$). With respect to minimization of initial group differences, by our definition, we found no evidence in Table 13.1 of this type of change for any of the attributes.

Of the six attributes that initially discriminated among the major-field groups, impulse expression no longer did at Wave 2; thus, the initial group differences with respect to this attribute were "lost." Of the two attributes on which major-field groups did not initially differ, religious liberalism still did not discriminate among the groups at Wave 2, but self-described conventionality did. The percentage variance in this self-description index increases to a statistically significant 10.2%, thus suggesting an "emergence" of group differences. The *adjusted* means in the covariance analysis for this variable are not significantly different from one another. This does not mean that the difference for the second-wave unadjusted means are not significant (statistically or otherwise), but that these differences rely on students' initial scores. We interpret these variance and covariance results as evidence of a certain kind of emergence of group differences. The difference among groups that emerged on self-described conventionality was "anticipated" by the earlier scores of students, although the initial difference among groups on this attribute was not sufficiently large to be statistically significant or even to produce a nonzero association on the

---

[5] Columns 1–4 of Table 13.1 also present the one-way analysis of variance results for the secondary recruits (males). The finding that, at Wave 1, in almost all cases, the secondary-recruit groups are less differentiated among themselves than are the primary-recruit groups is not particularly unexpected. Perhaps more surprising is the fact that this is also true at the second wave. These same results hold true for female students (see Columns 1–4 of Table 13.3).

Omega-square measure.[6] In short, the initially incipient pattern of group differences became "defined" over time. This particular interpretation is supported by (1) the positive correlation of .97 between the initial and final mean scores, and (2) the positive correlation of .81 between the initial mean score and mean gain of the groups.

The danger of mixing data for primary recruits with those for secondary recruits can be seen in the results shown in Table 13.2. The information given in this table parallels that presented in Table 13.1, but in Table 13.2, the two types of recruits are combined. If the data only for this "full" major-field sample were available, one would conclude that there are three rather clear-cut cases of accentuation of initial group differences (theoretical orientation, estheticism, and self-described conventionality) and one of minimization of initial group differences (complexity). Because of the conceptual and analytic ambiguities and the possible methodological artifacts involved in using "full" samples, however, as previously noted, this conclusion would be open to question. Indeed, as we have seen in Table 13.1, when data for primary recruits is disentangled from that for secondary recruits, there is at best only weak evidence for one instance of accentuation (theoretical orientation). Furthermore, the one instance of minimization of initial group differences found for the "full" sample is not confirmed by the data for primary recruits in Table 13.1.

Changes in Initial Differences
among Major-Field Groups (Females)

Table 13.3 presents data for the female primary recruits of our analysis. Once again, the attributes are ordered by the degree of initial differentiation among major-field groups. The largest Omega-square estimate is produced by thinking introversion (23.7%) and the smallest by self-described independence (1.1%). Of the 14 attributes analyzed for females, 10 show statistically significant differences among the entrance groups. Of these 10, religious liberalism and complexity are instances of accentuation of initial group differences. Perhaps estheticism can also be included, since all the conditions of our overall criterion are met, except for that for the analysis of covariance, where the F-ratio barely misses being statistically significant ($p = .056$). Although there are three instances of correlations between initial level of group scores and group gain being negative and of the percentage of variance associated with the major-field groups decreasing over time—self-described spontaneousness, self-described self-esteem, and self-described social extroversion—none of them show a statistically sig-

---

[6] In data not presented here, we found that the initial average scores of entering students ranged from a low of 9.75 for those entering in psychology to a high of 13.11 for entrants to business administration. However, the between sum of squares was only 124.1 (d.f. = 9) compared to the total sum of squares of 1833.2 (d.f. = 120).

TABLE 13.2

Changes in Initial Differences Among Major-Field Groups on OPI Scales and Self-Description Indices, for Male Primary and Secondary Recruits Combined

OPI Scales and Self-Description Indices	WAVE 1 (1962, 1963)		WAVE 2 (1966, 1967)		Correlation of mean initial score with mean final score	Correlation of mean initial score with mean gain score	Change in percent of variance associated with major-field groups	F-ratio (ANCOVA)
	F-ratio (ANOVA)	Omega-square estimate ($100 \times \omega^2$)	F-ratio (ANOVA)	Omega-square estimate ($100 \times \omega^2$)				
	(1)	(2)	(3)	(4)	(5)	(6)	(7)	(8)
Estheticism	7.471^c	13.5	11.014^c	19.5	$.95^c$	.60	+6.0	3.346^c
Thinking Introversion	6.476^c	11.7	6.299^c	11.4	$.92^c$	.13	-0.3	2.546^b
Complexity	5.302^b	9.4	4.669^c	8.2	$.81^b$	-.20	-1.2	2.629^b
Theoretical Orientation	5.058^c	9.0	7.703^c	14.0	$.93^c$	.50	+5.0	3.952^b
Autonomy	1.129	0.3	4.531^c	7.9	$.89^c$	.53	+7.6	3.119^b
Impulse Expression	3.414^c	5.5	3.375^c	5.4	$.78^b$	-.18	-0.1	2.121^a
Religious Liberalism	1.656	1.5	1.502	1.2	$.82^b$	-.57	-0.3	0.687
Self-described Conventionality	2.389^a	3.1	5.755^c	9.8	$.90^b$	.47	+6.7	3.910^c

[a] p < .05
[b] p < .01
[c] p < .001

TABLE 13.3

Changes in Initial Differences Among Major-Field Groups on OPI Scales and Self-Description Indices, for Female Primary Recruits[a]

OPI Scales and Self-Description Indices	WAVE 1 (1962, 1963) F-ratio (ANOVA)	(1962, 1963) Omega-square estimate $(100 \times \omega^2)$	WAVE 2 (1966, 1967) F-ratio (ANOVA)	(1966, 1967) Omega-square estimate $(100 \times \omega^2)$	Correlation of mean initial score with mean final score	Correlation of mean initial score with mean gain score	Change in percent of variance associated with major-field groups	F-ratio (ANCOVA)
	(1)	(2)	(3)	(4)	(5)	(6)	(7)	(8)
Thinking Introversion	8.375^d (5.135^d)	23.7 (10.3)	6.836^d (7.468^d)	19.2 (15.3)	$.97^d$	.32	-4.5	0.941
Autonomy	7.790^d (4.528^d)	22.6 (9.0)	7.795^d (4.467^d)	22.6 (11.1)	$.91^c$	-.19	0.0	1.596
Estheticism	7.732^d (2.672^b)	22.0 (4.2)	11.493^d (5.431^d)	30.6 (10.6)	$.96^d$	.36	+8.6	2.028
Religious Liberalism	6.149^d (2.512^b)	18.0 (4.1)	10.806^d (5.280^d)	29.5 (8.9)	$.96^d$	.56	+11.5	2.216^b
Complexity	5.503^d (1.921)	16.1 (2.5)	11.721^d (5.108^d)	31.4 (10.3)	$.93^d$	.54	+15.3	2.348^b
Self-described Spontaneousness	3.469^c (0.999)	9.0 (0.0)	3.093^c (1.581)	7.8 (1.5)	$.95^d$	-.14	-1.2	0.589
Self-described Self-esteem	3.158^c (4.497^c)	8.0 (8.7)	1.724 (1.604)	2.9 (1.6)	.68	-.36	-5.1	1.417

TABLE 13.3 (continued)

Self-described Conventionality	3.082[c] (2.141)	7.8 (2.9)	4.745[d] (6.063[d])	13.2 (11.7)	.86[c]	.06	**+5.4**	0.711
Self-described Social Extroversion	2.617[b] (0.775)	6.2 (0.0)	2.233[b] (1.133)	4.8 (0.3)	.77[b]	-.73[b]	-1.4	1.073
Self-described Softness	2.335[b] (1.376)	5.2 (1.0)	3.383[c] (2.671[b])	8.9 (4.3)	.89[c]	-.41	+3.7	0.613
Impulse Expression	2.133 (1.335)	4.6 (0.9)	4.952[d] (0.747)	14.4 (0.0)	.78[b]	.28	+9.8	1.280
Theoretical Orientation	1.966 (1.583)	4.0 (1.6)	5.109[d] (4.500[d])	14.5 (9.0)	.55	-.12	+10.5	2.228[b]
Self-described Contentment	1.422 (0.804)	1.7 (0.0)	1.854 (1.369)	3.3 (1.0)	.85[c]	-.24	+1.6	1.302
Self-described Independence	1.286 (1.640)	1.1 (1.6)	0.748 (0.852)	0.0 (0.0)	.80[b]	-1.00[d]	-1.1	0.441

[a] In columns 1 - 4, data for female secondary recruits is also given (in parentheses).
[b] $p < .05$
[c] $p < .01$
[d] $p < .001$

nificant analysis of covariance. The results for self-described self-esteem, the attribute having the largest decrease in Omega-square estimate (−5.1%), is a case in which initial group differences were lost altogether.

Of the four variables that did not show statistically significant initial differences among academic majors, self-described contentment and self-described independence also did not produce statistical significance nearly four years later. The data for the other two variables (impulse expression and theoretical orientation) offer evidence for the emergence of major-field differences; increases in Omega-square estimates for both attributes are large enough to produce statistically significant F-ratios for the one-way analysis of variance at Wave 2. Like self-described conventionality for males, impulse expression for females can be interpreted as an instance of emergence in which an initially incipient pattern of differences becomes delineated over time. In contrast, the emergence of group differences for theoretical orientation provides an instance in which the final pattern of group differences is not "anticipated" by either the initial group means or by students' initial scores: The correlation between initial and final mean scores on this OPI scale is only .55 (the lowest of all 22 cases shown in Tables 13.1 and 13.3, Column 5); mean gain is essentially unrelated to initial mean score ($r = -.12$), and the difference among the final mean scores of the groups is statistically significant, even when adjusted for initial scores ($p<.05$ for the analysis of covariance).

Turning to the "full" sample of female students (Table 13.4), the hazards of failing to disentangle the data of primary recruits from those of secondary recruits can again be noted. Of the six variables in Table 13.4 that seem to offer clear, strong evidence of accentuation of initial group differences, only religious liberalism, complexity, and (possibly) estheticism remain when data for the primary recruits alone are considered (Table 13.3); although accentuation "appears" for thinking introversion, self-described conventionality, and self-described softness in the "full" major-field sample, interpretation is problematic because of the mixture of the two kinds of recruits. Finally, paralleling the results in Table 13.3, there are no instances of minimization of initial differences in Table 13.4. It is not surprising that the results of the two tables agree in this instance, since the artifacts built into the "full" samples tend to exaggerate the frequency and strength of accentuation of initial group differences, not their minimization.

Residual Cases (Males and Females)

We have referred to various patterns of change in initial differences among groups (accentuation, minimization, reversal, and loss of initial group differences). We have also noted the continuation over time of a lack of differences among groups, as well as the emergence of group differences (where none initially existed). Of these six possible patterns, only four describe the results found for male and female primary recruits (Tables 13.1 and 13.3), since there was no evidence of either minimization or

TABLE 13.4

Changes in Initial Differences Among Major-Field Groups on OPI Scales and Self-Description Indices, for Female Primary and Secondary Recruits Combined

OPI Scales and Self-Description Indices	WAVE 1 (1962, 1963) F-ratio (ANOVA)	WAVE 1 (1962, 1963) Omega-square estimate $(100 \times \omega^2)$	WAVE 2 (1966, 1967) F-ratio (ANOVA)	WAVE 2 (1966, 1967) Omega-square estimate $(100 \times \omega^2)$	Correlation of mean initial score with mean final score	Correlation of mean initial score with mean gain score	Change in percent of variance associated with major-field groups	F-ratio (ANCOVA)
	(1)	(2)	(3)	(4)	(5)	(6)	(7)	(8)
Thinking Introversion	11.343[c]	15.0	13.006[c]	17.0	.97[c]	.60	+2.0	4.409[c]
Autonomy	8.521[c]	11.5	9.633[c]	12.9	.91[b]	-.30	+1.4	3.226[b]
Estheticism	7.954[c]	10.6	15.172[c]	19.4	.96[c]	.68	+8.8	4.810[c]
Religious Liberalism	7.623[c]	10.2	11.479[c]	15.3	.96[c]	.51	+5.1	3.672[c]
Complexity	5.605[c]	7.3	12.266[c]	16.2	.88[b]	.55	+8.9	6.164[c]
Self-described Spontaneousness	2.725[a]	2.7	3.785[b]	4.3	.91[b]	-.08	+1.6	1.564
Self-described Self-esteem	5.642[c]	7.1	2.805[a]	2.9	.65	-.71	-4.2	1.376
Self-described Conventionality	4.460[c]	5.3	9.006[c]	11.4	.95[c]	.69	+6.1	3.696[c]

Self-described Social Extroversion	1.943	1.5	2.190^a	1.9	.93^c	-.03	+0.4	0.771
Self-described Softness	2.443^a	2.4	5.335^c	6.6	.90^b	.50	+4.2	3.672^c
Impulse Expression	3.791^b	4.6	3.944^c	4.8	.79^a	+.00	+0.2	1.902
Theoretical Orientation	2.952^b	3.3	7.587^c	10.2	.88^b	.58	+6.9	5.803^c
Self-described Contentment	0.868	0.0	2.464^a	2.3	.67	.22	+2.3	2.757^b
Self-described Independence	2.176^a	1.9	1.088	0.1	.79^a	-.99^c	-1.8	0.594

^{a} p < .05

^{b} p < .01

^{c} p < .001

reversal of initial group differences, as we have defined these patterns. The 4 descriptive patterns that do apply to our results fit 12 of the 22 cases in Tables 13.1 and 13.3. The following are the remaining cases, which can be seen as falling into a residual category: estheticism, thinking introversion, complexity, autonomy (for males); and thinking introversion, autonomy, self-described spontaneousness, self-described conventionality, self-described social extroversion, self-described contentment (for females).

Of these 10 residual cases, autonomy for males is the most distinctive. Not only are the major-field groups differentiated from each other at the earlier and later times, but this is the only instance of the ten cases in which the analysis of covariance is statistically significant. Moreover, among the residual variables, this one shows the largest change in the Omega-square estimate (12.2%). Indeed, were it not for the fact that initial group score is unrelated to group gain (r = .03), the data for autonomy (males) would indicate accentuation of initial group differences. As it stands, the data do suggest increasing differentiation among major-field groups on this variable, but not full-fledged accentuation.

Like autonomy for males, the other nine attributes discriminate among major-field groups at both times. However, since the analysis of covariance is not statistically significant for any of these variables, the final major-field differences for each of them are not independent of earlier differences among students in terms of the particular attribute. In a very general sense, then, each of these cases is an instance in which the initial differences among groups has been "retained."

The phrase "retention of initial differences among groups" would refer to something less global if the following requirements were added: high similarity between the pattern of differences among group means at two points in time; little or no relation between initial level and mean gain of the groups; little or no change in the strength of the association between the groups and the attribute under consideration. Within this more restricted set of criteria, the data for autonomy (females) and self-described spontaneousness (females) provide the clearest indication of retention of initial group differences: The correlation between initial and final means score across major-field groups is .91 for autonomy and .95 for self-described spontaneousness; the correlations between initial and gain scores are only − .19 and − .14, respectively; and the change in the Omega-square estimate are 0.0% and − 1.2%, respectively.

With this stricter, and probably preferable, interpretation of "retention of initial group differences," the question arises whether some of the residual cases even fit the retention pattern at all. The set of results for males on the attribute of thinking introversion furnishes the clearest example. The negative correlation between initial position and gain on this attribute and the relatively large decrease of 8.9% in the Omega-square estimate suggest decreasing differentiation among major-field groups (although full-fledged minimization of initial group differences is not indicated). While the correlation between initial mean score and final mean score on thinking introversion is positive (.77), it is the lowest correlation between initial and final scores among the residual cases; moreover, the correlation is one of the lowest of all 22 cases in Tables 13.1 and 13.3. This result, too, suggests that the way in which major-field groups differ from one another on thinking introversion has altered somewhat over time.

Average Group Changes

Having broadly analyzed various patterns of change and stability in the initial differences among major-field groups, we return to a closer inspection of those attributes for which we found accentuation of initial group differences. One aspect of this focus is the average change in these attributes for *each* major-field group. Table 13.5 presents data for the female primary recruits on complexity (one of the two clearest cases of accentuation of initial group differences). As shown in Column 2 of this table, students entering English language and literature, Romance languages and literature, history, nursing, and psychology, typically increased in score on this variable during college. The average score of the female primary recruits to political science remained the same, while students entering either mathematics or elementary education typically decreased on this attribute. The positive—but less than perfect—association between the mean initial scores of these major-field groups and their mean change scores (as given in Table 13.3, Column 6) can be more specifically "traced through" in Columns 1 and 2 of Table 13.5. For example, English language and literature, which had the largest initial mean score on complexity, did make the largest increase in score. The entrance group with the second highest score (psychology) was one of the five fields in which the average score increased; however, this major-field group made the smallest increase of the five. The major-field group initially second lowest (political science) was the group that did not change, while the third lowest group (elementary education) was one of the two entrance groups that actually decreased in degree of complexity.

Table 13.6 presents data for female primary recruits on religious liberalism, the other relatively clear-cut instance of accentuation of initial group differences. Unlike complexity, the average change of religious liberalism is in the same direction for each major-field group (see Column 2); every entrance group increased in score on this attribute (with the overall average score across fields increasing from 11.80 to 15.58).[7] Again, the means of the major-field groups tended to pull apart over time, but not

---

[7] This "secular trend" across major-field groups was among the larger of those that we found. The largest such trends appeared for autonomy, for both men and women. Across major-field groups, the male students increased on the average from 22.31 to 27.89, and the female students increased from 19.64 to 24.45. For both males and females, this across-field trend was mirrored in the relatively large average increase of each and every major-field group in the analysis.

TABLE 13.5

Comparison of Female Primary Recruits in Different Major Fields at Two Points in Time on Complexity

Major-Field Setting	Initial mean score (1)	Change in mean score (2)	Initial standard deviation (3)	Change in standard deviation (4)	Correlation of initial score of individual with gain score of individual (5)	Correlation of initial score of individual with final score of individual (6)
English Language and Literature	15.36	+2.85	4.22	+0.49	-.34	.61
Psychology	14.60	+0.50	5.17	-0.26	-.48	.63
History	12.80	+0.80	5.68	-0.78	-.67	.30
Mathematics	11.85	-0.70	5.11	-0.60	-.62	.42
Romance Languages and Literature	11.35	+1.89	4.23	+0.89	.03	.88
Elementary Education	11.11	-0.89	3.69	-0.44	-.63	.40
Political Science	10.25	0.00	4.35	+1.56	.22	.85
Nursing	10.08	+0.55	3.89	+0.36	-.56	.26
Across Fields	12.41	+1.00	4.75	+0.75	-.29	.65

TABLE 13.6

Comparison of Female Primary Recruits in Different Major Fields at Two Points in Time on Religious Liberalism

Major-Field Setting	Initial mean score (1)	Change in mean score (2)	Initial standard deviation (3)	Change in standard deviation (4)	Correlation of initial score of individual with gain score of individual (5)	Correlation of initial score of individual with final score of individual (6)
Romance Languages and Literature	15.29	+3.42	4.36	+0.83	.06	.87
English Language and Literature	14.21	+5.00	5.53	−1.66	−.74	.46
History	13.80	+4.00	4.32	−1.46	−.76	.78
Psychology	12.50	+4.90	5.30	−0.17	−.31	.84
Elementary Education	11.56	+3.66	4.19	+0.90	−.17	.70
Mathematics	11.50	+2.60	6.50	−0.07	−.32	.81
Political Science	9.75	+2.00	7.23	+0.58	.05	.94
Nursing	7.73	+3.10	4.74	−0.10	−.40	.72
Across Fields	11.80	+3.78	5.78	+0.09	−.32	.77

perfectly (Columns 1 and 2). For example, the two largest increases were made by the groups initially second and fourth highest in score (English language and literature and psychology), while the two smallest increases were made by the two groups initially lowest in score (political science and nursing).

Within-Group Changes

In addition to examining average change of each major-field group, we also explored change in *initial differences among individuals within a major-field group* (in contrast to the analysis of change in *initial differences among the major-field groups* themselves). For those major-field groups showing a positive association between the initial and final attribute scores of individuals within them,[8] we use the phrase "accentuation of initial individual differences (within a group)," where the following is found: increase in the dispersion of scores among individuals in the major-field group (as indicated by an increase in standard deviation) *and* a positive association between the initial and gain score of the individuals. (We do not use this phrase for those cases in which initial scores of individuals within a major-field group become more dispersed over time, but the initial score is negatively associated with gain score.) "Minimization of initial individual differences (within a group)" refers to instances in which the association between initial and final score is positive, the association between initial and gain score is negative, and the dispersion of scores within the major-field group decreases.[9]

The distribution of these patterns among major-field groups can be noted for the female primary recruits on complexity and religious liberalism

[8] The direction of the correlation between primary recruits' initial and final scores was positive for 189 of the 192 correlations under consideration. The three exceptions, where this correlation was negative, all occurred for males: thinking introversion for political science; impulse expression for political science; and theoretical orientation for physics.

[9] Whenever there is unreliability of test (scale) scores and errors of measurement —or, more generally, any time a variable is less than perfectly correlated with itself across time—there is "a spurious negative element in the correlation of an initial score with gains on the same test," as Bereiter (1963:3) puts it (see also Bohrnstedt, 1969). From this, we assume that both the *number* of negative initial-score–gain-score correlations (across individuals within a major-field group) and the *degree* to which these correlations are negative are artificially inflated. It is possible that the import of this artifact (which is loosely called the "regression effect") is somewhat obviated by not relying exclusively on this correlation to designate patterns of change in initial individual differences, but it is not totally eliminated thereby. Although the meaning and existence of the patterns that are found in this part of our analysis are thus somewhat problematic, nevertheless, we feel it is useful to examine them briefly in at least an exploratory way.

(again referring to Tables 13.5 and 13.6). The dispersion of individual scores on complexity became greater over time for students entering political science, Romance languages and literature, nursing, and English language and literature (Column 4 of Table 13.5); by our criteria, the data (in Columns 4, 5, and 6) suggest accentuation of initial individual differences for only the first two of these four major-field groups (and note that the positive correlation between initial score and gain score is extremely small for Romance languages and literature). For psychology, history, mathematics, and elementary education, there is minimization of initial individual differences for this attribute. For religious liberalism (Table 13.6), there is a very weak indication of accentuation of initial individual differences for Romance languages and political science (the positive initial-score–gain-score correlation is very small for both). Elementary education is an instance of increasing dispersion of individual scores (but not accentuation of initial individual differences). Minimization of initial individual differences is indicated for the other five fields.

In tables not presented here, we also examined the pattern of change of initial individual differences for the two more tentative cases of accentuation of initial *group* differences that we reported earlier (estheticism for females and theoretical orientation for males). For the attribute of estheticism, minimization of initial individual differences is evident for the female primary recruits to the following three fields of study: English language and literature, political science, and history. The data for the other five fields show increasing dispersion of scores (but not accentuation of initial individual differences). With respect to theoretical orientation for the male primary recruits, we found one instance of accentuation of initial individual differences (for students entering chemistry), four instances of increasing dispersion of scores but not accentuation of initial individual differences (English language and literature, economics, mathematics, and business administration), and four instances of minimization of initial individual differences (premedical studies, political science, psychology, and history). The individual-level results for physics presented one of the extremely rare cases in which both the correlation between initial and final score and the correlation between initial and gain score were negative.

Within-Group and between-Group Changes

As we noted in our introductory comments, accentuation of initial *group* differences does not presuppose one and only one pattern of change among *individuals* in each of the groups under consideration. To demonstrate this point, we presented six of the conceivable models of individual change (within groups) that might underlie accentuation of initial group differences. Although the intent of our research was not to test these particular models against data (nor to fit models to empirical results), a brief and general comparison of these models with our results is useful. Models 1 and

2 are built, in part, on an assumption of accentuation of initial individual differences for every group in a particular analysis. For the major-field groups of our study, we did not find this to be true empirically for any of the four attributes under consideration (complexity, religious liberalism, and estheticism for females and theoretical orientation for males). Furthermore, none of these four attributes showed minimization of initial individual differences for every major-field group (an aspect of Model 5), nor did we find the uniformity of individual change within each group proposed in Model 2. Moreover, with one exception, a given pattern of change in initial individual differences did not tend to dominate the initially higher major-field groups (as suggested in Models 4 and 6). The results for estheticism furnish the one exception: For this attribute, the three cases of minimization of initial individual differences appeared for the first, third, and fourth initially highest major-field groups, thus fitting one part of Model 6.[10] Finally, in analyses not presented here, we found that female students with prominently high scores on complexity, religious liberalism, and estheticism, who were in the initially higher major-field groups, tended to make greater gains than female students with equally high scores who were in the initially lower major-field groups. Assuming that this particular result is not explainable in terms of the artifacts introduced by errors of measurement in the matching variable of initial score (see especially Rulon, 1941 and Astin, 1970a), it supports Models 3, 4, 5, and 6. This finding, however, was not duplicated for males for the one attribute under consideration (theoretical orientation).

---

[10] Not only did the pattern of change in initial individual differences vary from one major-field group to another for the four attributes under consideration, but the results at the individual and group level did not particularly mesh with each other. That is, the results of the group-level analysis (in this case, *accentuation* of initial group differences) was not obviously "foreshadowed" by the results of the individual-level analysis (or vice versa). For some of the other attributes in our analysis, we did find either one pattern of change in initial individual differences holding across all (or nearly all) major-field groups, or a distribution of patterns that more obviously "fit" the group pattern. As an example, for self-described conventionality (males), only chemistry and mathematics, out of the 10 major-field groups, did not show minimization of initial individual differences. This increased clustering of students' scores in 8 out of the 10 groups helps to "explain" the emergence of differences among *groups* that was found. Likewise, the "reason" for the loss of initial differences among groups for impulse expression (males) is clarified by the pattern of individual changes within groups. Minimization of initial individual differences occurred only for premedical studies. Standard deviations increased in the other nine fields—for political science, one of the rare instances in which both the correlation between initial and final score and the correlation between initial and gain score were negative, for economics and mathematics, as part of accentuation of initial differences, and for the other six groups, as increased dispersion of scores without such accentuation.

Discussion and Conclusion

For those students who remained in their intended major, we found accentuation of initial group differences for female students on the complexity and religious liberalism scales of the Omnibus Personality Inventory. Estheticism for females and theoretical orientation for males were near cases of accentuation; the results for these variables met all of the conditions necessary for accentuation of group differences except one (for both, $.05 < p < .10$ for the analysis of covariance). We found no instances of either minimization or reversal of initial group differences (as we have defined them). There were instances in which group differences emerged over time, just as there were instances in which initial group differences were lost. For some attributes, major-field groups were not different from one another, either when students entered the university or when they were leaving it. Finally, the remaining cases were put into a residual category, in which we distinguished clear-cut instances of retention of initial group differences from other possible patterns of change, such as increasing differentiation of major-field groups (but not accentuation of group differences) and decreasing differentiation of major-field groups (but not minimization of group differences).

It is of interest to compare our results with those presented by Thistlethwaite (1972, 1973), since among both the direct and indirect studies of accentuation of group differences, his is the most similar to ours in general format and in analytic techniques employed. The comparison can only be made with male students, since this was the sole group for which he collected data. Like Thistlethwaite, we have separated out primary recruits to major-field settings. Unlike his analysis, our study is based on data from one university rather than many universities. If students entering particular fields of study are not interchangeable across colleges, and if accentuation of group differences depends upon the distinctive influence of major fields within a given subsetting, then pooling data across similarly named major fields at different colleges would work against finding accentuation of initial differences among major-field groups. Also, unlike Thistlethwaite, we did not combine major fields into logical (but nevertheless somewhat arbitrary) categories—such as "social sciences," "physical sciences," "fine arts or humanities," and so forth—nor did we include a miscellaneous category in our analysis. We felt that, while having the advantage of increasing the number of respondents in a category, these sorts of combinations would have the disadvantage of increasing the diversity within groups[11] and creating less situationally concrete groupings. If so,

---

[11] In a preliminary and exploratory analysis of our data, we did find that Omega-square estimates of the strength of association between the attributes and major-field groups of our study were smaller for various combinations of major-field groups than for the "pure" groups.

this would also work against finding accentuation of initial group differences. For these various reasons, we anticipated finding more frequent and stronger indications of accentuation of initial group differences on our measures of individual attributes than Thistlethwaite did for his. (With respect to students' perceptions of their peers and teachers, Thistlethwaite did find a number of clear-cut cases of accentuation of initial differences among major-field groups, but only very few and weak instances of such accentuation were evident for students' own attitudinal characteristics). Despite the differences between the two studies, however, accentuation of initial group differences was no more evident in our analysis of male primary recruits than it was in Thistlethwaite's.

Our analysis turned up more and clearer cases of accentuation of group differences for female than for male students. Among the 10 attributes initially discriminating among major-field groups for the female primary recruits, there are two relatively strong cases of accentuation of group differences (complexity and religious liberalism) and one very near case (estheticism). The difference in results for males and females support our initial conviction of the importance of performing separate analyses. This conviction has been further strengthened by the results for our factor analysis of the self-description items included in our study: The seven factors found for entering females were duplicated for female seniors, but, except for one factor, the self-description factors for male students entering the university were different from those for males about to graduate.

Feldman and Newcomb (1969) found indications of accentuation of initial group differences in many different studies (some compared colleges and others compared one or another kind of setting within college). The number of cases is probably exaggerated in their reinterpretation and reanalysis of others' data, since there was no way to remove or adjust for artifacts that increased the likelihood of finding accentuation. More important than the possible exaggeration of the exact amount of evidence of accentuation of group differences in past studies is the possibility that such accentuation may be relatively widespread across studies of different groups and environmental settings, without necessarily being particularly pervasive in any given study. Indeed, in the present analysis, we did find a few instances of accentuation of initial differences among major-field groups, but it hardly was a pervasive tendency among the variables considered. It may well be that accentuation of initial group differences is unlikely to be the only or even the chief outcome in most studies. If this is so, then theoretical and research endeavors in this area should shift from a search for accentuation per se to a search for the conditions under which accentuation is more, rather than less, likely to occur.

There is an indirect suggestion in Feldman and Newcomb (1969:190–193) that accentuation of group differences is likely to be relatively pervasive in important settings within multiversities, the rationale being that subsettings in large, heterogeneous colleges are more likely to have distinctive impacts over and above any overall environmental effects than are the analogous settings within small, homogeneous colleges. Yet, in our analysis of data collected at the University of Michigan, we found only a few cases of accentuation for students entering various major fields, presumably an important set of subsettings in one of the nation's largest multiversities. As a conjecture on our part, we would argue that accentuation of group differences is likely to be more pervasive in those subsettings in large colleges and universities where students have more choice (than they do for major fields) of whether or not even to consider entering them, and where the subsettings themselves are more highly selective (than are major fields) as to which "applicants" can join. We have in mind settings such as informal friendship circles, certain extracurricular organizations, special educational programs, and the like. A somewhat overlapping prediction is that frequent and strong accentuation of initial group differences may also be more likely when environmental settings are extremely diverse and when the entrance groups themselves are highly differentiated from one another.

These propositions, based on the degree of selectivity of settings and the extremity of differences among these settings and the groups entering them, are consistent with the analyses and findings of Newcomb and his associates in their research on living-learning complexes (Newcomb *et al.*, 1970, 1971) and of Clark and his associates in their research on student changes in very different kinds of colleges (Clark *et al.*, 1972, see especially pp. 308–311). Also compatible with these hypotheses is the suggestion that, for any data set in general, accentuation of group differences is most likely to appear in those instances where initial differences among groups are the largest to begin with (Feldman, 1972:231). In this respect, we should call attention to the following, perhaps more than coincidental, finding for the female primary recruits of our analysis: The three attributes for which there was some indication of accentuation of group differences were among the five attributes that initially most strongly discriminated among the major-field groupings (out of some 14 attributes analyzed for the female students).

It has also been suggested that accentuation of group differences is most likely to occur for those attributes of individuals that become important elements in the socialization processes of the settings under consideration —that is, in effect, for those attributes that are relevant to the subsequent experiences of the individuals in the settings, upon which the impacts of the settings are relatively direct, focused, and intentional (see Athanasiou, 1971; Feldman, 1972:230–232; Feldman and Newcomb, 1969:178–179, 329; Newcomb *et al.*, 1970, 1971). Although this seems to be a sensible suggestion, we did not make predictions on these grounds for the attributes of our analysis. It might be possible to show, at this point, how accentuation for complexity (females), estheticism (females), and theoretical orientation (males) could be expected from the implications of this suggestion;

however, we feel that this suggestion is not particularly useful for explaining why religious liberalism showed accentuation for females or why certain of the other attributes in our analysis did not.

As part of our attempt to clarify the meaning of "accentuation of (initial) group differences," we have taken pains to separate this phenomenon from that of "emergence of group differences" and the pattern of change in our residual category that we have called "increasing differentiation." It is probably even more important to be clear about the exact conceptual and operational meaning of "minimization of (initial) group differences," since the term minimization has not fared well in the literature on accentuation. Usually, it is not mentioned at all. When not bypassed in this way, it is mentioned but not really defined (e.g., see Feldman, 1972:231; Feldman and Newcomb, 1969:180–182). The notion of minimization is also used as a somewhat amorphous contrast to accentuation of group differences—apparently including instances of what we have referred to as "loss of differences among groups" and (in the residual category) "decreasing differentiation," in addition to actual minimization of group differences as we have defined it (e.g., see Thistlethwaite, 1973). In this connection, we think it makes more sense to explicitly interpret and measure minimization of group differences as the strict opposite of accentuation of such differences, thus, clearly separating it from conceivably overlapping patterns.

The results of our analysis highlight the fact that accentuation of initial group differences is only one of many patterns of change and stability of initial differences among groups. It is true that such accentuation indicates a particularly interesting interdependence between selection into a setting and the impact of that setting (under the assumption, of course, that the underlying changes of individuals that produce accentuation of initial *group* differences across settings are due to one or more aspects of the settings' environments). At least by our definition, however, minimization of initial group differences can also describe an interesting relationship between initial selection into settings and their ongoing impacts. Moreover, the emergence of group differences may also be due to the influence of the environments of the settings that have been entered, although, in this case, the impact of the setting is not intertwined with selection, as it is for accentuation. It is even possible that, under certain conditions, the environmental settings are directly involved in the loss of initial group differences as well as the retention of such differences.

It is important to stress that data such as ours imply, but in no way definitively establish, the impact of particular settings on individuals. The pattern of individual change that underlies any change in initial differences among groups is not necessarily due to the influence of the particular settings the persons have entered. For example, a finding of accentuation of initial group differences could be totally due to the fact that various background factors (themselves initially associated with individuals' attributes) had influenced *both* individuals' choice of setting *and* their attribute change over time. Thus, it is important to control, in a systematic way, such background factors in determining the influence of social settings on individuals entering them. Moreover, even if the impact of the particular settings is established, there still remains the need to determine which of the many elements of the settings are producing which individual changes.

We might note, in conclusion, that it is not too early to begin taking stock of the analytic and empirical work on the so-called "accentuation phenomenon." Over the past few years, the phrase has gained a certain currency in the study of higher education, and various kinds of analyses have been undertaken in the area. The use of the idea of accentuation varies in these studies—from a framework informing the study from its outset to a more or less handy ad hoc interpretation apparently grafted on to the study at its completion. Accentuation has been studied in terms of both individuals and groups, and, even within each of these levels of analysis, the term has had different theoretical interpretations and empirical constructions. It is important that investigators clearly specify how they are using the term and at what analytic level(s). It is also important to be alert to the various artifacts that work for or against finding accentuation. When dealing with the more specific phenomenon of accentuation of initial *group* differences, it should be remembered that this is only one of several patterns of change and stability of initial differences among groups. Finally, when interest centers on the impacts of groups and social settings on individuals in them, a finding that initial differences among groups do actually accentuate is, at best, only a first step in the analysis.

Acknowledgment

Theodore M. Newcomb gave a draft of this chapter an especially careful reading, and we would like to thank him for his helpful comments.

Part 3 | METHODOLOGICAL ISSUES

Introductory Notes

In the past decade, there has been a dramatic increase both in the volume of research on processes of socioeconomic achievement and in the application of modern statistical methods in this research. These two developments have been complementary and almost coextensive. For example, the controversial finding of startlingly small effects of schools in the 1965 Equality of Educational Opportunity survey gave rise to a widespread and almost frantic search for statistical models and measures permitting statistical control and valid policy interpretation in the analysis of nonexperimental social data. Obversely, Otis Dudley Duncan's search for statistical methods for the analysis of social mobility led to the rapid diffusion of path analysis among sociologists, psychologists, political scientists, and educational researchers and also to the subsequent increased use of more powerful methods of structural equation modeling.

The historical melding of substantive and methodological issues is reflected in the contributions to this volume. Seldom were issues of research design and of the strength of empirical evidence forgotten in the discussions of the working group. Several of the earlier chapters treat important methodological issues or are exemplars of research method, and conversely the two chapters in this section are directly motivated by important substantive questions.

Chapter XIV, David Wiley's "Approximations to Ceteris Paribus," presents a lucid exposition of elementary but powerful methods of statistical control in studies of school effectiveness. He focuses on the problem of measuring institutional effects in the presence of confounding variables, when there are limited numbers of institutions or treatments to be compared. Wiley relies on the classic demographic techniques of direct and indirect standardization, and he skillfully illustrates the art of grouping data to maximize statistical control, when there are several interacting control variables and relatively few observations. A more extended and elaborate application of these methods is Wiley's other contribution to this volume, Chapter VIII, "Another Hour, Another Day."

Social scientists have become increasingly sensitive to the problems of reliability and validity when proxy reports of parental social status are used to measure or control the influence of social background on achievement variables. William Mason, Robert M. Hauser, Alan C. Kerckhoff, Sharon Sandomirsky Poss, and Kenneth Manton take up this issue in Chapter XV, "Models of Response Error in Student Reports of Parental Socioeconomic Characteristics." If Wiley has borrowed from the statistical repertory of demographers, Mason and his coauthors have drawn on recent developments in psychometrics, applying Karl Jöreskog's model for the analysis of covariance structures. They analyze a unique body of data from Fort Wayne, Indiana, in which schoolboys and their parents independently reported the socioeconomic characteristics of the parents, and, also, academic achievement and aspiration data were obtained. They construct and test several alternative specifications of response error, which vary in their assumptions with regard to the extent and sources of random and nonrandom reporting error in socioeconomic variables. By incorporating achievement and aspiration variables, as well as background measures, in their models, they are able to assess the distorting effects of response error on models of the achievement process and to measure the relationships between achievement variables and systematic response error. Furthermore, they compare patterns of response error across groups of black and white schoolboys at three grade levels. By grade 12 the proxy reports of black and white boys are about equal in quality and as good as those of their parents (which are not without error), but, at lower grades, the proxy reports are less valid, especially among blacks. Systematic variations in nonrandom response error across the grade levels are also noted.

While the chapters by Wiley and by Mason and his coauthors can stand on their merits, we think they are also important as exemplars of the interplay of substance and method, which is most fruitful in social research. Elaborate statistical models are not an end in themselves but only useful insofar as they encourage reasoned judgment about complex situations without removing the researcher too far from first-hand contact with the data.

XIV Approximations to Ceteris Paribus: Data Adjustment in Educational Research

David E. Wiley*
University of Chicago

Bias in Group Comparisons: An Example

A curriculum development group has recently been developing a new curriculum in general science for the elementary school. Controversy within the group arose over one aspect of this new curriculum: methods of teaching experimental inquiry in natural science in the fourth grade. Therefore, the staff developed two alternative approaches, which were based on the positions taken by its members. The basic difference between

* This chapter was written for a volume edited by Wolfgang Edelstein and Diether Hopf, entitled *Bedingungen des Bildungsprozesses: Psychologische und Pädagogische Forschung zum Lehren und Lernen in der Schule* (Klett Verlag, Stuttgart, 1973, pp. 458–488). The German title is "Auf dem Wege zum 'Ceteris Paribus': Datenkorrektur in der Bildungsforschung." It is one of a collection of papers resulting from the "Internationales Forschungsseminar über Lern- und Bildungsprozesse" (International Research Seminar on Learning and the Educational Process), held in Leoni am Starnberger See near Munich, Germany, in Summer 1971.

The chapter was written while the author was a Fellow at the Center for Advanced Study in the Behavioral Sciences, Stanford, California. He is ordinarily in the Department of Education and the Committee on Human Development, University of Chicago. The work reported here was partially supported by the American College Testing Program's Research Institute, Iowa City, Iowa, of which the author is a Research Associate.

the two approaches was that in one the children themselves were to carry out a planned set of experiments, while in the other the teacher was to demonstrate these experiments. One viewpoint was that, when the children carried out all of the steps of the experiments themselves, they would have to attend to all of the details of the procedure and would, therefore, learn much more about experimentation. The other view was that teacher demonstration would make for more efficient experiments and, therefore, more thorough coverage of the material.

Both methods were based on a new textbook especially designed for teaching young children basic scientific methods in the areas of physics, chemistry, geology, and biology. In each method, three hours per week were to be devoted to science instruction in grades two through four with one hour of that instruction devoted to the planned set of experiments. The instruction was to last for the whole school year. The teacher was given an explicit set of instructions for each experiment, was specially trained to perform the experiment and advise the children, and was given the opportunity to practice the experiment while the children were not present. In the demonstration version, the teacher was expected to devote that one hour per week to a careful and planned demonstration of the experiment.

The two methods were to be applied in elementary school settings, and an evaluation was to be made about which method was the most effective with ordinary elementary school pupils. The staff had developed an evaluation instrument for this purpose. The instrument consisted of multiple choice test items about a large sample of the experiments that were performed during the year and which were thought to be appropriate to the reading level of children in the fourth grade.

When I was asked to participate, the instruction had been completed and the data were already collected. A data analysis had been performed, and it was found that the average number of correctly answered items for those children who performed their own experiments was considerably more than for the children who observed the teacher demonstrating the experiment. The difference between these means was statistically significant and precisely estimated, since the sample size was rather large. Several of those involved in planning the evaluation study were willing to accept the idea that it was more effective for children to perform their own experiments than for the teacher to demonstrate them.

I was asked to evaluate the statistical adequacy of the study. After examining other data, it became clear that there were some major differences between the two groups other than the instructional treatments. Those classes in which the children performed their own experiments had, on the average, a smaller proportion of girls and a larger proportion of middle- and upper-class pupils than those classrooms in which the teachers performed the experiment. The major question became: Could the observed difference between the two instructional treatments be due to differences in achievement of these groups? In order to investigate this problem, we looked at the mean level of achievement by sex and social class in the sample of students who participated in the experiment. We found that the average number of items correct for girls and lower-class pupils was substantially less than that for the other groups. It seemed apparent that the differences observed between the two treatments might be attributed to differences in the achievement level of the various subgroups and to differences in their allocation to the treatments.

I was asked if there were more appropriate methods for conducting the study than had been used. My answer was that if the children (or classrooms) had been randomly assigned to the treatments, this would have resulted in an approximately equal proportion of girls and lower-class pupils in both groups, and the final comparison between the two groups would not have been biased by the unequal achievement of the various groups. Other characteristics, which were unequally distributed between the two groups, would also be approximately equally distributed after random assignment and would not bias the resulting comparison.

The above example is artificial, but it does illustrate some basic points about bias in making comparisons among naturally occurring groups. Of course, if it is possible, the most appropriate method of eliminating such bias is to randomly assign the instructional methods to individuals or classrooms. When random assignment methods are impossible or difficult because of financial, ethical, or other (e.g., organizational, structural) reasons, comparisons that minimize bias must still be attempted.

The goal of this paper is to describe some new methods which are available for adjusting data to reduce biasing effects of differences in the distributions of variables in groups that we wish to compare.

More generally, the problem of adjustment of data may be summarized in the following terms. We have a collection of units (pupils in the aforementioned example), which can be categorized into two or more groups (the instructional alternatives), and we wish to compare these groups with respect to some scaled response y (achievement). We can observe the characteristic y for each of the units within the groups. We may calculate a value for the typical level of response (mean achievement) in each of the two groups. There exists another variable, x (sex or social class), which influences the response y and whose distribution differs among groups. One question is: How do we infer the difference(s) in level of response (achievement) between the groups that would result if the distribution of x were identical in all groups? That is, we want to compare the groups with respect to y in a manner not biased by the differences in the distributions of x within them. These are called "standardization techniques" and have been in common use in demographic work for many years, although they have not been applied commonly in educational research. Here, the formulation of these techniques has been modified to be appropriate to quantitatively scaled responses rather than the dichotomous data typical of demographic research.

In many studies of educational phenomena, when adjustments of this type are performed, the typical methods have been covariance or regression adjustments.[1] The methods described in this chapter are related to these but are more flexible, easier for the investigator to understand and control, and do not require restrictive assumptions. We hope that these characteristics will encourage the use of adjustment techniques in reducing bias in the group comparisons that are the major focus of educational research.

Direct versus Indirect Standardization:
Some Methods of Adjustment for Bias;
Continuing with the Example

Continuing with our example, we have 200 pupils, 100 in pupil experimenting classrooms and 100 in demonstration classrooms. Information is available on three levels of social class, which I will call upper, middle, and lower, and sex, as earlier. This yields six subgroups for each type of classroom. Table 14.1 displays an artificially constructed data set of this kind. The 2 entries in each of the 12 cells are the achievement mean and the number of children on which that mean is based. The example was constructed so that there were 100 pupils in each of the instructional groups and also so that the number of pupils was unequally distributed over the sex, social class, and instructional groups. The table displays a slight difference in average level of achievement between girls and boys and a greater frequency of boys in the classrooms with pupil experiments than in the demonstration classrooms. This produces a small bias favoring pupil experimentation. Also, the social class groups are disproportionately represented in the two types of classrooms. In the pupil experimenting classrooms, we can see that there are more upper- and middle-class children, whereas more lower-class children attend classrooms with teacher demonstrations. Since these data show a positive relationship between social class and achievement, biases are produced which disfavor demonstration classrooms.

Bordering the table are the means and the total frequencies for each row and column. For each row, at the far right of the table, there is the average proportion of the children in each of the sex–social class subgroups. The numbers in Table 14.1 provide a basis for defining adjustment and two of its major varieties, indirect and direct standardization.

---

[1] The methods of analysis of covariance and multiple regression are discussed in several statistics textbooks, such as Snedecor and Cochran (1967), where the discussion is particularly lucid and very useful for practical research work. In the subsequent parts of the chapter, more technical material will be restricted to the footnotes.

TABLE 14.1

Summary Data for the Comparison of the Pupil Experimenting and Teacher Demonstration Groups

Control Variables		Experimenting		Demonstration		Total		
Sex	Social Class	Mean	Frequency	Mean	Frequency	Mean	Frequency	Proportion
Girls	Lower	35	10	33	25	33.57	35	0.175
	Middle	40	15	41	20	40.57	35	0.175
	Upper	45	20	46	10	45.33	30	0.150
Boys	Lower	39	10	38	20	38.33	30	0.150
	Middle	43	20	42	15	42.57	35	0.175
	Upper	47	25	46	10	46.71	35	0.175
Total		42.75	100	39.55	100	41.15	200	1.000

Direct Standardization

In direct standardization, adjusted mean levels are calculated from the means of the subgroups in each of the groups that one is interested in comparing. In our case, this amounted to an attempt to forecast what the means of the instructional groups would be if the distribution of pupils over the sex–social class subgroups were the same in each.[2]

In the pupil experimenting classrooms, there are 10% lower-class girls, whereas in the demonstration classrooms there are 25%. There are $17\frac{1}{2}$% $[=(10 + 25)/2]$ lower-class girls in the sample as a whole. If we choose the sample as a whole as a reference population (i.e., both instructional groups combined), then we would forecast what the mean level of achievement would be if both the pupil experimenting and demonstration classrooms contained (a reference percentage of) $17\frac{1}{2}$% lower-class girls. A directly standardized mean is produced by reweighting the means of the subgroups according to the proportion of children in those subgroups in the reference population (both instructional groups combined), rather than the proportion of children in those subgroups in the particular instructional group. If we do this for the pupil experimenting group, we perform the following computation: $(35)(.175) + (40)(.175) + (45)(.150) + (39)(.150) + (43)(.175) + (47)(.175) = 41.48$.

41.48 is the directly standardized achievement mean for children in pupil experimenting classrooms, and this is a simulation of the actual mean for this group, if the distribution of children, according to social class and sex, had been the same as in the sample as a whole. If we perform the same computation for the demonstration classrooms, we obtain: $(33)(.175) + (41)(.175) + (46)(.150) + (38)(.150) + (42)(.175) + (46)(.175) = 40.95$.

After these adjustments for the unequal distributions of sex and socio-economic background in the instructional groups, the means become 41.48 for the pupil experimenting classrooms and 40.95 for the demonstration classrooms, while the original means were 42.75 and 39.55 respectively. The original difference in the means was 3.20, whereas the difference between the directly standardized means is now only .53. By eliminating the bias due to sex and social class $(2.67 = 3.20 - .53)$ the difference between the two groups has shrunk by more than 80%.[3]

---

[2] A discussion of the method of direct standardization is given in Cochran (1968). An interesting exposition of the technique, together with indirect standardization and related topics, is presented in Moses (1969); this is a part of *The National Halothane Study* (Bunker, Forrest, Mosteller, and Vandan, 1969). This study applied the standardization techniques discussed here to the problem of assessing the effectiveness of various anesthetics in minimizing the mortality risk in surgical operations. This application of these techniques was a stimulus for their modification and their presentation to the educational research community for use in a different research context.

[3] Since the bias due to sex and social class has been estimated, we may inquire if the remaining difference can be attributed to chance or not. In order to answer this

We should note two important aspects of this process:

First, the reference population that produces the reference percentages does not have to be the average percentage of children in each of the categories. Any theoretically or practically relevant reference population can be used for generating a comparison. If we knew the distribution in a population, for example, in a country, corresponding to some age cohort of children over the six categories, we could use that distribution as a reference population for calculating these standardized values. In that case, the comparison would be appropriate to that reference population, even though the data being analyzed were not obtained from a random sample of that population. The choice of a reference population should be made carefully, if reasonable conclusions are to be drawn. The relevance of the population chosen to the objectives of the study should be carefully considered and made explicit. Usually, one should choose a reference group similar to the group under investigation.

When the differences between the two comparison groups differ for the various subpopulations, the results will depend on the reference population chosen. The reason is that the directly standardized difference between the comparison groups is a reweighted average of the differences for each subgroup; the weights for this averaging are the proportions in the reference population. In our example, the difference between the comparison groups for the upper-class girls was $45 - 46 = -1$, which received a weight of 0.150. The difference between the groups for upper-class boys was $47 - 46 = 1$, which received a weight of 0.175. If the subpopulation groups with smaller differences are given more weight, the resulting averaged difference will be smaller. This would occur in our example if there were a larger proportion of upper-class girls and a smaller proportion of upper-class boys in our reference population. If, however, the larger differences are given more weight by the reference proportions, then the resulting difference will be larger. In our example, this would require more upper-class boys and fewer upper-class girls in the reference population. When the differences between the comparison groups are the same for such subgroup, the choice of a particular reference population does not affect the result.

Another characteristic that should be noted about direct standardization is that, as a procedure, it applies to populations as well as to samples of data. The procedure defines the difference one calculates by specifying the

---

question, we must estimate the variance of the standardized difference. Since this difference (d) equals $\sum_{i=1}^{k} w_i(\bar{y}_{i1} - \bar{y}_{i2})$, where w_i is the reference population proportion in subgroup i, and $\bar{y}_{ij}$ is the mean of the ith subgroup in the ith comparison group (and n_{ij} the corresponding frequency), Var $(d) = \sum_{i=1}^{k} w_i^2[\text{Var }(\bar{y}_{i1}) + \text{Var }(\bar{y}_{i2})]$ $= \sigma^2 \sum_{i=1}^{k} w_i^2 n_i / n_{i1} n_{i2}$ if we assume equal variances in the groups. In the final formula, a dot ("."), in place of a subscript, denotes the sum over the index. If σ^2 is estimated by pooling the within-group variances and an estimate of Var(d) calculated, the square root of that estimate is an estimate of the standard error of d, and the ratio may be referred to the t-distribution for hypothesis testing and confidence interval generation (see Cochran, 1965).

method of standardization and reference proportions. In a sampling framework, then, we have both defined the population difference (by specifying the procedure) and estimated that difference in the sample.

A major weakness of the direct standardization procedure is that it is not applicable when one of the subgroups is nonexistent in a particular comparison group. This might happen, for example, in the case of lower-class boys in the pupil experimenting group. The sample size in that cell is 10. However, if there were not any pupils in the experimenting group, it would be impossible to use the method of direct standardization since we would not have a value that corresponds to the subclass mean of 39 for that cell. We would then be unable to combine this value with the others and produce a standardized value corresponding to 41.48. Consequently, if, in addition, the 20 corresponding individuals in demonstration classrooms were maintained, there would then be 10% ((0+20)/200 = 0.10) of the total sample in the subgroup of lower-class boys. However, we would not have a mean score value to multiply by this reference proportion of .10 when producing the directly standardized mean for the pupil experimenting classrooms.

Indirect Standardization

One method of avoiding this difficulty is to use the procedure of indirect standardization. In indirect standardization, instead of applying a set of reference proportions to the subgroup means for each group, we calculate the subgroup means for the whole group and then use the subgroup proportions in each comparison group to produce a predicted value for each subgroup. These predicted values are a forecast of the values that would result if there were no differences between the comparison groups except those biases generated by the unequal performances of the subgroups and the unequal distribution of subgroups in the comparison groups. These values, which estimate the biases in the original comparison group means, may then be used to adjust those means.

In the example, if we average the comparison groups for each subgroup, we obtain the mean achievement levels on the right of Table 14.1. For example, the mean achievement for lower-class girls is 33.57. This is produced by a weighted averaging of the 35 in the pupil experimenting classrooms and the 33 in the demonstration classrooms, using the frequencies in each of those cells as weights, so that ((10)(35) + (25)(33))/(10 + 25) = 33.57. If we average in this way for each of the six subgroups, we obtain the six averages displayed in the column labeled mean in Table 14.1. These, then, are the means that characterize the subgroups independent of the comparison groups. The averages were computed using weights corresponding to the cell frequencies in the sample at hand. This did not have to be the case; another set of weights could have been chosen, and a particular choice would define a reference population in the same fashion as in the direct standardization discussed earlier. The advantage, however, of allowing the cell frequencies to define the weights is a solution to the problem of empty cells. Using these six new means, we can predict the comparison group means as if these six characterize the subgroups in each comparison group, while the cell frequencies remain the same. We can find the value for the pupil experimenting group by multiplying the overall mean for each of the subgroups by the proportion of individuals in the corresponding cell for the pupil experimenting group: $(33.57)(.10) + (40.57)(.15) + (45.33)(.20) + (38.33)(.10) + (42.57)(.20) + (46.71)(.25) = 42.53$. Therefore, 42.53 is the predicted mean achievement for the pupil experimenting group, when the differences between the comparison groups are solely due to unequal distribution of the various subgroups. If we perform the same computation for the demonstration group, we obtain: $(33.57)(.25) + (40.57)(.20) + (45.33)(.10) + (38.33)(.20) + (42.57)(.15) + (46.71)(.10) = 39.76$.

We may compute the bias due to sex and social class in the original difference in the means of the comparison groups by calculating the difference between the predicted values: $42.53 - 39.76 = 2.77$.

If we wish to reconstitute numbers that would correspond to the indirectly standardized values, we may take the predicted values and subtract them from the original means for the pupil experimenting and demonstrational groups. When this is done, we find $42.75 - 42.53 = .22$ and $39.55 - 39.76 = -.21$. We then add the general overall mean to each of these differences and produce a value of $41.37 (= .22 + 41.15)$ for the pupil experimenting group and $40.94 (= -.21 + 41.15)$ for the demonstration group. These compare closely to the previously obtained directly standardized values of 41.48 for the pupil experimenting group and 40.95 for the demonstration group.

If we recall the differences between the original values for the two groups and compare them with the directly and indirectly standardized values, we can observe the amount of shrinkage in the difference between pupil experimenting and demonstration classroom achievement after standardization. The original difference was 3.20; the directly standardized difference was 0.53; and now the indirectly standardized difference is $41.37 - 40.94 = 0.43.$[4]

Both methods result in a reduction of over 80% of the original difference between the two groups. More than 80% of that difference was bias due to sex and social class differences in achievement, and less than 20% is attributable to other biases and to real differences between pupil experi-

---

[4] The variance of the indirectly standardized difference may be derived in a fashion similar to that for the directly standardized difference. The form of the difference can also be arranged so as to be written $d = \sum_{i=1}^{k} w_i(\bar{y}_{i1} - \bar{y}_{i2})$, so that the Var $(d) = \sigma^2 \sum_{i=1}^{k} w_i^2 n_i / n_{i1} n_{i2}$. Now, however, the weights, w_i, are the following: $w_i = ((n_{.1} + n_{.2})/n_{.1} n_{.2})(n_{i1} n_{i2}/n_{i.})$; the notation is defined in Footnote 3. For the original standardizing calculation, the weights used in producing the mean for subgroup i are n_{i1} and n_{i2}.

menting and demonstration classrooms. It should be clear, however, that we have only removed bias due to sex and social class and aspects of other variables that are associated with these characteristics. The selection of the most relevant factors for which to adjust depends on theoretical knowledge and insight into the phenomenon being studied. The factors selected should have strong relations with both the response variable and the variable or group difference under investigation. In practice, however, one can control only for measured variables. Bias due to nonmeasured variables remains in the adjusted difference. In order to infer that the remaining difference reflects true effects, the investigator must have substantive knowledge, empirical or theoretical, that the remaining bias is smaller than the adjusted difference.

The results of both sets of computations are summarized in Table 14.2. The method of direct standardization might be considered preferable if there are no empty cells, since the results are more directly interpretable. However, a more adequate decision about the choice of method might be based on the stability of the resulting adjustment.[5] In a particular application, it is not clear which method yields greater stability.

Grouping

Thus far, we have discussed the methods of direct and indirect standardization. Direct standardization is applicable only when there are no empty cells in the cross-classification being used for adjustment. In the case of empty cells, we learned how to apply the method of indirect standardization. Both procedures suffer from low precision when the cell sizes are small. However, this problem may be overcome by applying methods of "grouping" to the cross-classification, before implementing either method of standardization. Grouping is the collapsing of the cross-classification into a smaller number of cells. The basic criterion for grouping is that the cells should be grouped together according to the similarity of the values of their means.

A very simple procedure for grouping is to order the cells according to the sizes of the means and then group the adjacent cells. The new cells should be approximately equal in frequency and sufficiently large to assure stability of their means. This procedure is one of the simplest methods of grouping.[6] However, there are more precise procedures, some of

---

[5] The stabilities are inversely related to the variances defined in Footnotes 3 and 4.

[6] One problem with the simple method of grouping described in the text is the necessity of using the imprecise cell means as a basis for grouping. One solution to this problem would be to perform a least-squares analysis of the relations between the variables represented in the cross-classification and the response. An additive model will be sufficient to represent the data in many applications.

An additive model (in the context of our original example) assumes that the influence of sex and social class on an individual's achievement may be represented

TABLE 14.2

Summary Table for the Standardized Comparisons of the Pupil Experimenting and Teacher Demonstration Groups

| | Comparison Groups | | |
	Experimenting	Demonstration	Difference
Original Value	42.75	39.55	3.20
Directly Standardized			
Values	41.48	40.95	0.53[a]
Predictions	42.42	39.75	2.67[b]
Indirectly Standardized			
Values	41.37	40.94	0.43[a]
Predictions	42.53	39.76	2.77[b]

[a] These values are the adjusted differences.

[b] These values are the estimates of the bias due to sex and social class.

(Footnote 6 continued)

by the sum of a number, representing the effect of the individual's particular social class, and of another number, representing the impact of the individual's sex. There is no additional effect of the unique combination. The model implies that the average difference in achievement between the sexes is the same for each social class and that the difference between two social classes is the same for each sex.

Least squares is a method of determining these effects by finding the values that minimize the squares of the differences between the observed values and the predicted ones. (In this case, predicted values are the estimated means of the cells produced by summing the effects of sex and social class.) Least squares was devised by K. S. Gauss for the purpose of summarizing astronomical observations. (See Gauss [1809].) For a discussion of this particular additive model (which is usually called a two-way analysis of variance model) and of the least squares method, see Snedecor and Cochran (1967).

As an example, an additive model was fitted to the means for the six sex by social class subgroups. The basic data were the six cell means (averaged over the comparison groups) given at the right side of Table 14.1. The results are presented in Table 14.A. Bordering the table are the effects of the various levels of sex and social class together with the general mean. Inside the table are the simulated or "fitted" values for the cell means, when an additive model is assumed. The details of the method of calculation can be found in Snedecor and Cochran (1967).

When an additive model is not adequate, a reasonable extension of the strategy is to fit a more complex model without complete additivity. This becomes feasible when the number of variables in the cross-classification increases. It is then possible to assume that, while there is no unique effect of the combination of *all* variables in the cross-classification on the response, pairs, triples, or other small subsets do have

TABLE 14.A

Fitted Values Bordered by the Effects of Sex and Social Class and the General Mean for an Additive Model Fitted to the Summary Data for the Pupil Experimenting and Teacher Demonstration Comparison

| | Sex | | |
Social Class	Boys	Girls	Effects
Lower	37.66	34.96	-5.28
Middle	42.94	40.24	0.45
Upper	47.31	44.62	4.83
Effects	1.35	-1.35	41.14

which are based on prior statistical analysis and use more complex methods.[7]

On this basis, one could group together the six cells in the evaluation discussed earlier into, for example, three new and larger cells. In this case, these new cells would consist of the three social class groups, since the differences in achievement between boys and girls is small for each social class group. The grouping is probably not advisable in this context because the sample sizes for the original cells are reasonably large for this kind of data (achievement test scores) and the means are probably stable enough.

An Example of Indirect Standardization Based on the Coleman Survey

The example just presented was intended to aid the reader in comprehending the basic procedures involved in direct and indirect standardization and in understanding the rationale for those procedures. Therefore, the example was constructed in a simplified manner; certain common problems with data were not present so that the reader would not be distracted by those features of data analysis not directly related to the issues under consideration.

This section attempts to analyze a set of real survey data from empirical educational research in which some of the problems encountered are resolved by using the methods of adjustment. The goal of this approach is to increase the practical relevancy of the exposition by matching more closely the problems encountered in actual research.

The research methods used to generate the data in the following example are different from those described earlier. In the aforementioned example, a controversy over curriculum matters was resolved by setting up a quasi-experimental comparison; in the following example, educational problems

---

special effects. This will result in more summary numbers representing the data than in the additive model, but many fewer than would result from estimating each mean of each combination separately.

The critical factor in this process is the reciprocal relationship between bias and error in fitting statistical models. When we summarize the data with many summary numbers, we minimize the differences between the actual data and our simulation of it. When the data have a complex structure, we capture the complexity more adequately than when we summarize them with fewer numbers, but we do so at the cost of lower stability of our simulation. Low stability in this context means less precision in simulating a new set of data with the same structure. Since both aspects—adequate complexity and high stability—are important to the final result, careful consideration must be given to the data and to one's prior understanding of the phenomenon under investigation in arriving at a reasonable model. In the context of standardization, an excellent example of this process is given by Bishop and Mosteller (1969) for a qualitative response variable.

[7] A promising new grouping procedure called "smear-and-sweep" analysis has been recently developed (Gentleman, Gilbert, and Tukey, 1969) and has been applied in *The National Halothane Study* of anesthetics.

are investigated by means of an educational survey. The data set we have chosen is from the survey on *Equality of Educational Opportunity* (Coleman, Campbell, Hobson, McPartland, Mood, Weinfeld, and York, 1966). This survey, widely known as the Coleman survey, was originally intended to establish the extent of inequality in educational resource allocation in the United States. However, the main analyses of the data and subsequent scientific and policy interest have focused on questions concerning the relative impact of pupil background characteristics and educational resources on academic achievement. A major problem in these analyses has been the adjustment of the effects of the resource variables for differences in pupil backgrounds. The example that follows focuses on this problem.

The data collected in the survey contained the responses to a series of achievement instruments, pupil, teacher, and principal questionnaires, and teacher ability tests. The survey data were collected all over the United States. The data that are analyzed later derive only from the sixth grade in Detroit, since these data have been corrected for errors and were readily available. The analysis that I report here is based on 10 schools, which were selected as having the most equal distributions of black and white pupils in the Detroit sample. The percentage of white pupils in these schools varied from 15 to 85%.[8] A sample of 10 children was chosen from each of the 10 schools, which produced a sample of 100 children. The samples were taken so that the quantity of data was small enough for complete inclusion in the appendix to this chapter. In this way, the interested reader can check the computations and modify the analysis.

The response variable selected for analysis was achievement on the "verbal" test. The variables that form the bases for adjustments are the following:

1. the number of children residing in the child's home—based on the responses to an item in the pupil questionnaire;
2. the number of possessions in the child's home—based on nine questionnaire items concerning the presence of specific items (typical items were: television set, telephone, and other indicators of the affluence of the family);
3. the race of the child—which had three categories: black, white, and other.

The first goal of the analysis is to produce an indirectly standardized value for achievement for each school in the sample. The standardization is based on the three aforementioned variables: race, number of children in the home, and number of possessions. The data analysis illustrates the practical problems of determining the relationships between these vari-

---

[8] The samples from all of the remaining schools but one contained pupils of only one race.

ables and achievement and of producing reasonable subgroups by pooling the cells of the cross-classification based on these three variables. The new cells and the mean achievement in each are used to produce a comparison value (predicted achievement based on the distribution of the three variables) for each school. This value may be used to adjust the actual mean achievement of each school. These adjusted values may be related to other variables and are equalized for the variables, race, number of possessions, and number of children. At the end of the section, the relationship between the adjusted value and a school characteristic is explored to illustrate one of the uses of the adjusted values.

Exploratory Analysis

Tables 14.3, 14.4, and 14.5 summarize the relations among the three independent variables. Table 14.3 is a cross-tabulation of the number of children in the family and race. Table 14.4 is a similar cross-tabulation for the number of possessions in the home and race, and Table 14.5 shows the relative frequencies of various combinations of number of children and number of possessions.

We can see from the tables that each of these variables is systematically related to the others. The average number of children in the homes of black children is 5.00, while the average for whites is only 3.71. The average for children who report other than black or white is even higher than that for blacks (6.33). The black–white difference is also marked for the "number of possessions" variable, where the mean for blacks is 7.37, and for whites it is 8.09. The dispersion of this variable is rather large for the children who report "other" race. The cross-tabulation of number of possessions by number of children indicates that families with large numbers of children tend to have fewer possessions. For smaller numbers of children, the number of possessions is quite variable. We can somewhat clarify this issue by consulting Table 14.6, which presents a summary of the three-way cross-tabulation, eliminating the "other" racial groups. It is obvious here that the relationship between possessions and children is negative for whites. The relationship is similar for black families with between 3 and 10 children in the home. However, black families with only one or two children tend to have a smaller number of possessions than those with three or four children. An explanation for this is that the number of children is more strongly related to the age of parents in black families than in white families. This is so because black families tend to have more children. Therefore, black families with few children tend to be young. Because of this, they have had less opportunity to acquire possessions than white parents with the same numbers of children.

To illustrate the relationship between these variables and achievement, Figure 14.1 depicts the typical degree of achievement for black families for

TABLE 14.3

Crosstabulation of Number of Children in the Home by Race

| Number of Children | Race | | | Total |
	Black 1	White 2	Other 3	
1	2	6	0	8
2	7	5	0	12
3	9	8	0	17
4	8	12	2	22
5	4	4	1	9
6	6	3	2	11
7	3	2	1	6
8	1	2	0	3
9	5	0	1	6
10	4	0	2	6
Total	49	42	9	100

each number of children in the home.[9] The level was calculated for the black children who reported from two to ten children in their family. As the figure shows, for blacks there is little systematic relation between the two variables. Figure 14.2 relates the same information for whites. Here, we

[9] The values plotted in Figures 14.1, 14.2, and 14.3 are the medians of the achievement scores for the groups in question. The values plotted in Figure 14.4 and listed in Table 14.6 are the midmeans of the achievement scores for the groups. The midmean is a measure of central tendency devised by Tukey (1970) and is the mean of the observations between the 25th and 75th percentile points in the empirical

TABLE 14.4

Crosstabulation of Number of Possessions in the Home by Race

Number of Possessions	Race			Total
	Black	White	Other	
0	0	0	1	1
3	2	0	2	4
4	1	0	0	1
5	4	4	0	8
6	5	1	1	7
7	10	4	1	15
8	12	11	3	26
9	15	22	1	38
Total	49	42	9	100

note a systematic trend: As the number of children in the family increases, the achievement level diminishes. Reflecting on the findings shown in the three-way cross-tabulation, we might not be so confident of the accuracy of the simple relations depicted in these figures, as they do not take into account the number of possessions variable.

If we construct a similar figure for number of possessions, we find, after collapsing categories to achieve stable median values, a rather dramatic positive relationship between possessions and achievement level for blacks (Figure 14.3). A similar relationship exists for whites as well.

Because of this relationship and since a rather large difference also exists between blacks and whites in level of achievement in this sample, it

distribution of the scores. It is almost as adequate as the sample mean when the distribution of scores is Gaussian, and it is considerably more adequate when the distribution has long tails or if there are wild data values.

appears that each of these variables, race, number of possessions, and number of children in the home, is systematically related to achievement. Therefore, as background variables, they should produce useful adjustment variables for standardizing the achievement levels of the schools.

If we proceed in this manner, the next stage of exploration of the data is investigation of the relations of two or more variables to achievement simultaneously. This allows us to detect any lack of additivity in the data. If there are differences in the effects of one variable, depending on the levels of the others, then the eventual subgroupings that we establish for the standardization must be based on a thorough knowledge of these nonadditive relationships. However, as we mentioned in the second section, one problem in the generation of subgroupings is that the means of these subgroups become unstable as the sample sizes in each of them diminishes. For example, the cross-tabulation of race with number of possessions,

TABLE 14.5

Crosstabulation of Number of Children in the Home by Number of Possessions in the Home

Number of Children	Number of Possessions								
	0	3	4	5	6	7	8	9	Total
1	0	0	0	0	1	0	3	4	8
2	0	1	0	0	1	3	4	3	12
3	0	0	0	2	2	0	5	8	17
4	0	3	0	1	0	1	6	11	22
5	0	0	0	1	0	3	2	3	9
6	0	0	0	0	1	4	1	5	11
7	0	0	0	1	0	1	2	2	6
8	0	0	0	1	0	1	0	1	3
9	0	0	0	2	2	0	1	1	6
10	1	0	1	0	0	2	2	0	6
Total	1	4	1	8	7	15	26	38	100

TABLE 14.6

Collapsed Crosstabulation of Number of Children in the Home by Number of Possessions in the Home by Race

Number of Children	Black				White			
	Number of Possessions				Number of Possessions			
	3-7	8	9	Total	3-7	8	9	Total
1-2	5	3	1	9	1	4	6	11
3-4	4	4	9	17	3	7	10	20
5-6	5	2	3	10	3	0	4	7
7-8	2	1	1	4	2	0	2	4
9-10	6	2	1	9	0	0	0	0
Total	22	12	15	49	9	11	22	42

91

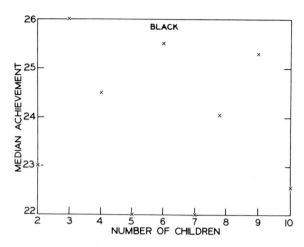

Figure 14.1 Median achievement for black children in families of varying size.

reported in Table 14.2, contains a number of empty cells. In that table, we also see that "other" race has a very low total frequency. In addition, the number of children, both black and white, who reported very few possessions, is small. As a consequence, to obtain reasonable sample sizes, we must group together the lower categories corresponding to small numbers of possessions. When we do this, a plot of a measure of the typical level of achievement for each of the resulting cells produces the graph that is presented in Figure 14.4. This figure displays the relationship between achievement and number of possessions for both blacks and whites, which, as we can observe, is positive for both groups. However, the white groups have higher achievement than the corresponding black groups. The achievement level for whites corresponding to nine possessions is slightly smaller than the level corresponding to eight possessions. This discrepancy from constant increase is rather small and may be a result of error.

As a result of a series of exploratory analyses similar to the ones just illustrated, we decided to group number of possessions into three categories: 3 to 7, 8, and 9, and to group the number of children in the home into two categories: 1 to 4 and 5 to 10. Because of the small number of children in the "other" racial group, we decided to eliminate it and to restrict the analysis to blacks and whites. In Table 14.7, the midmeans of the scores of individuals in the resulting groups are displayed. The cell frequencies are also given. One cell is empty; there were no white children with families having between 5 to 10 children in the home with 8 possessions. There are rather systematic differences among the cells. The lowest achievement occurs when there is a black child with 1 to 4 children in the home and 3 to 7 possessions. The level of achievement in that cell is 18.5, whereas the highest level of achievement is 41.2 for white children with 1 to 4 children in the home and whose families have 8 possessions.

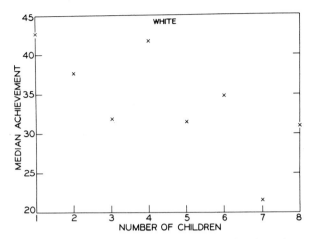

Figure 14.2 Median achievement for white children in families of varying size.

Having accomplished our goal of producing a small number of subgroups that systematically differ in achievement, we can now proceed to adjust the mean levels of achievement, in the 10 schools, using these subgroups.

Indirect Standardization

The value for a cell was assigned to each individual in that cell. These values constitute the column in the Appendix labeled Predicted Value. Then

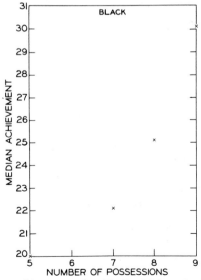

Figure 14.3 Median achievement for black children in families with varying numbers of possessions.

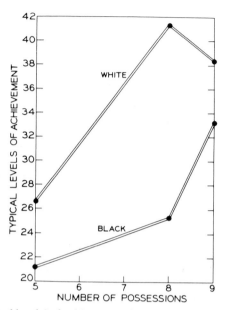

Figure 14.4 Typical levels[9] of achievement for black and white children in families with varying numbers of possessions.

the means of the actual achievement values and of the predicted achievement values for each child were averaged for each of the 10 schools. For example, in the second school, the average achievement was: (28 + 24 + 27 + 13 + 22 + 24 + 22 + 17 + 39 + 18)/10 = 23.40, while the average of the predicted values was: (22.00 + 22.00 + 24.00 + 22.00 + 22.00 + 30.25 + 20.00 + 20.00 + 30.25 + 20.00)/10 = 23.25. Note that, in the second school, the predicted values consist of four values of 22.00, two values of 30.25, three values of 20.00, and one value of 24.00. This is because all ten children fall into the four cells with these values. The 10 mean achievement values and the 10 corresponding mean predicted values (comparison values) for the 10 schools are displayed in Table 14.8. The children of "other" race were omitted from this analysis. A graph of the mean achievement values versus the comparison values for the 10 schools is given in Figure 14.5. This figure depicts the relationship between the mean achievement value for each school and the corresponding comparison value for each school. Figure 14.6 displays a graph of the adjusted values (the differences between the mean achievement and comparison values) versus the comparison values, which shows no systematic relationship.[10]

---

[10] If there is a systematic relationship between the comparison values and the adjusted values, a further adjustment can be made by performing a regression analysis relating the two and calculating the residuals from this regression. When this is accomplished, the resulting standardization is called superstandardization. The procedure was devised by Tukey (1969). It is particularly valuable when there is

TABLE 14.7
Achievement Midmeans[9] of Pooled Groups From Race by Possessions by Children Crosstabulation

		Possessions		
Race	Children	3-7	8	9
Black	1-4	20.00	25.33	30.25
		9	7	10
	5-10	22.00	24.00	37.00
		13	5	5
White	1-4	24.50	41.20	39.63
		4	11	16
	5-10	29.00	-----	31.50
		5		6

TABLE 14.8
Mean Achievement, Comparison Values and Typical Number of Hours of Instruction for the Ten Schools

School	Mean Achievement	Comparison Value	Adjusted Value	Hours of Instruction	Log Hours
1	28.00	30.29	-2.29	941.16	2.97
2	23.40	23.25	0.15	1004.40	3.00
3	20.22	23.81	-3.59	822.80	2.92
4	24.33	26.45	-2.12	930.93	2.97
5	29.74	28.69	1.05	1148.55	3.06
6	32.00	34.99	-2.99	920.70	2.96
7	36.80	37.11	-0.31	1060.20	3.03
8	28.78	28.93	-0.15	951.39	2.98
9	33.67	33.07	0.60	972.00	2.99
10	40.90	37.26	3.64	940.50	2.97

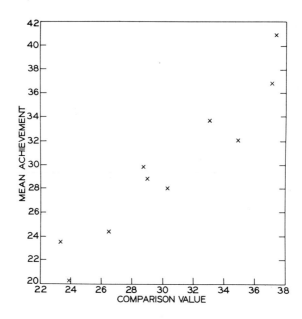

Figure 14.5 Mean achievement versus comparison values for 10 schools.

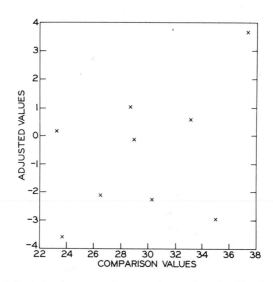

Figure 14.6 Adjusted values versus comparison values for 10 schools.

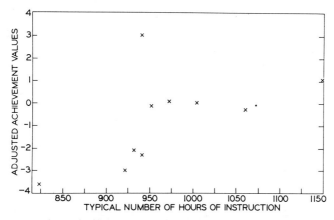

Figure 14.7 Adjusted achievement values versus the typical number of hours of instruction for 10 schools.

Since the adjusted values are available for each school, we can relate them to other characteristics of the schools to see if there are any systematic relationships, once the adjustment has been made for the variables: race, number of possessions, and number of children in home. The variable chosen to illustrate this possibility is the total number of hours of instruction that a typical child received in each of the schools. This was computed from the original data by multiplying the average daily attendance, the number of hours per day that the school was in session, and the total number of days per year that the school was open. This yields an estimate of the total number of hours of instruction that a typical child attending that school would receive in a 1-year period.

Figure 14.7 displays a plot of the adjusted achievement scores versus the typical total number of hours of instruction. There is a positive relation, but the fact that there are only 10 observations (schools) does not inspire much confidence in the relationship. The relationship appeared to be slightly nonlinear, and the distribution of the number of hours of instruction was skewed. Therefore, Figure 14.8 depicts a plot of the relationship when the number of hours of instruction is logarithmically transformed.

Discussion

The last graph illustrates one likely use of these procedures for the analysis of educational data. Most of the policy variables of interest in analyses of educational surveys are defined at the level of the school, and

error of measurement in the adjustment variables and will reduce the bias to a greater degree under these circumstances.

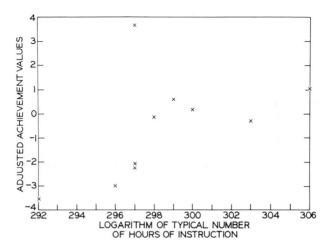

Figure 14.8 Adjusted achievement values versus the logarithm of the typical number of hours of instruction in 10 schools.

these school characteristics are amenable to changes resulting from educational policy decisions. Most appropriate data analyses of the impact of these school variables are conducted at the level of the school. This is necessary to produce a reasonable assessment of the precision of the estimated effects of these variables, since they are constant for individuals within a school. One problem that usually arises in these analyses is that there are many background characteristics of the pupils to be adjusted for. When these pupil characteristics are aggregated to the level of the school, there are many statistical analyses that are imprecise or impossible to perform when the number of variables approaches or exceeds the number of schools. The virtue of the procedure presented here is that these adjustments can be performed at the individual level, and then the comparison values can be aggregated to the school level. A school level analysis performed with the comparison value as a control variable should remove many of the influences of the individual background characteristics. The procedure will then accommodate more school level variables in the analysis and, thus, allow more complete analyses with high precision without increasing the size of the sample. Chapter VIII gives a more thorough presentation of the statistical basis for such analyses together with an extensive application.

In the first example, we saw how the methods of standardization presented could partially compensate for the unequal distributions of characteristics important to the outcome in instructional groups to be compared in the process of a curriculum evaluation. The procedures are structured to give the investigator more direct and flexible control over his adjustments than with standard methods of covariance or regression adjustment. Because of the straightforward nature of the procedures, it is easier to use them to make adjustments that are usually considered complicated: such as, taking nonadditive effects of the adjustment variables into account. This flexibility should allow more effective adjustments and inferences in evaluation studies and, thus, render these studies more effective tools in the improvement of our curricula.

Use of the methods of standardization should yield more information per unit cost in experimentation, curriculum, and in the analysis of educational surveys. They should be a considerable aid in increasing our understanding of the educational process.

Acknowledgment

The author would like to thank Annegret Harnischfeger for her critical advice, which greatly improved the chapter.

APPENDIX

Illustrative Achievement Data

Variable	Student										Total
	1	2	3	4	5	6	7	8	9	10	
School 1											
Race	3	3	3	3	2	2	2	2	2	2	
Children	10	10	7	4	5	4	4	3	2	2	
Possessions	7	0	8	3	5	9	7	5	9	7	
Achievement	22	11	34	6	29	29	23	29	32	26	28.00
Predicted Values	–	–	–	–	29.00	39.63	24.50	24.50	39.63	24.50	30.29
School 2											
Race	1	1	1	1	1	1	1	1	1	1	
Children	9	8	6	6	5	4	4	4	3	2	
Possessions	6	7	8	7	7	9	5	3	9	7	
Achievement	28	24	27	13	22	24	22	17	39	18	23.40
Predicted Values	22.00	22.00	24.00	22.00	22.00	30.25	20.00	20.00	30.25	20.00	23.25
School 3											
Race	3	1	1	1	1	1	1	1	1	1	
Children	9	10	9	9	7	7	6	3	3	1	
Possessions	8	7	5	5	8	7	9	8	5	6	
Achievement	21	17	25	14	13	22	37	16	19	19	20.22
Predicted Values	–	22.00	22.00	22.00	24.00	22.00	37.00	25.33	20.00	20.00	23.81
School 4											
Race	3	2	2	1	1	1	1	1	1	1	
Children	4	8	3	6	6	6	4	3	2	2	
Possessions	3	9	9	7	7	7	8	8	9	3	
Achievement	19	20	25	24	30	21	25	25	15	34	24.33
Predicted Values	–	31.50	39.63	22.00	22.00	22.00	25.33	25.33	30.25	20.00	26.45

APPENDIX (continued)

Variable					Student						
	1	2	3	4	5	6	7	8	9	10	Total
School 5											
Race	3	2	2	1	1	1	1	1	1	1	
Children	6	3	2	10	10	5	4	3	3	1	
Possessions	6	8	8	8	4	8	9	9	6	8	
Achievement	23	35	41	29	21	22	23	22	31	44	29.74
Predicted Values	-	41.20	41.20	24.00	22.00	24.00	30.25	30.25	20.00	25.33	28.69
School 6											
Race	2	2	2	2	2	2	2	2	2	2	
Children	6	6	5	5	4	4	4	3	2	1	
Possessions	9	9	7	7	8	8	8	9	8	8	
Achievement	28	35	14	34	38	31	40	21	37	42	32.00
Predicted Values	31.50	31.50	29.00	29.00	41.20	41.20	41.20	39.63	41.20	41.20	34.99
School 7											
Race	2	2	2	2	2	2	2	2	2	1	
Children	7	4	4	4	4	3	3	3	2	5	
Possessions	5	9	9	8	8	9	9	6	9	9	
Achievement	25	48	41	48	47	46	37	15	40	21	36.80
Predicted Values	29.00	39.63	39.63	41.20	41.20	39.63	39.63	24.50	39.63	37.00	37.11
School 8											
Race	3	1	1	1	1	1	1	1	1	1	
Children	6	10	5	4	4	3	3	2	2	2	
Possessions	9	8	9	9	9	9	9	8	6	7	
Achievement	9	24	27	39	30	39	35	27	15	23	28.78
Predicted Values	-	24.00	37.00	30.25	30.25	30.25	30.25	25.33	20.00	20.00	28.93

APPENDIX (continued)

						Student					
Variable	1	2	3	4	5	6	7	8	9	10	Total
School 9											
Race	3	2	2	2	1	1	1	1	1	1	
Children	5	5	4	1	9	9	7	4	3	2	
Possessions	8	9	9	9	9	6	9	9	8	8	
Achievement	21	43	46	35	39	16	37	32	26	25	33.67
Predicted Values	-	31.50	39.63	39.63	37.00	22.00	37.00	30.25	25.33	25.33	33.07
School 10											
Race	2	2	2	2	2	2	2	2	2	2	
Children	8	7	6	4	4	3	1	1	1	1	
Possessions	5	9	9	9	9	8	9	9	9	8	
Achievement	42	18	46	48	43	46	33	44	44	45	40.90
Predicted Values	29.00	31.50	31.50	39.63	39.63	41.20	39.63	39.63	39.63	41.20	37.26

XV | Models of Response Error in Student Reports of Parental Socioeconomic Characteristics[*]

William M. Mason
University of Michigan

Robert M. Hauser
University of Wisconsin

Alan C. Kerckhoff
Sharon Sandomirsky Poss
Kenneth Manton
Duke University

Introduction

This chapter investigates the structure of errors in children's and youths' reports of parental statuses and the implications of such errors in models of the achievement process (Haller and Portes, 1973). Our primary goals are to elucidate the error structure of children's reports of parental status and to take account of this structure in estimating the effects of family socioeconomic status on a number of variables in the early stages of the achievement process. Our work should be of general interest to students of the achievement process, since status origins are almost always ascertained from proxy reports of offspring. Also, there are reasons to suppose that the extent and pattern of reporting error varies by children's age and among social groups. As a secondary goal, we look for evidence of differences in the quality of proxy reports by children's grade in school and race.

Measurement errors in reports of parental social status may significantly

* This research was supported by grants from the American College Testing Program Research Institute, the Duke University Center for the Study of Aging and Human Development, and the National Institute of Mental Health (5T01-MH13112-02 and MH-06275).

affect interpretations of the achievement process. For example, random reporting errors in measured status origins will reduce the estimated joint effect of status origins on achievement (e.g., underestimate the extent to which occupational attainment depends on family background variables). Random errors in measured status origins will also increase estimated effects of achievement variables on one another (e.g., the effect of education on occupational status), because their mutual dependence on status origins will be underestimated. In addition, random errors will distort the relative effects of status origins on achievement (e.g., the effect on current income of mother's education will be too large, and that of father's occupation too small, or the converse). These biases will be accentuated or offset if measures of parental status are differentially unreliable or invalid and will be further compounded if their errors are positively intercorrelated (Bowles, 1972a). Finally, errors in reports of parental statuses may be correlated, positively or negatively, with later achievement variables, and this may counterbalance or compound the biases just enumerated. Unfortunately, it is reasonable to suspect that all these types of error affect proxy reports of parental status. Since the errors may be large or small, and their effects may be additive or offsetting, there is no way to assess the biases in naive (uncorrected) models of achievement processes without first investigating the separate and joint effects of each type of measurement error. Again, the analytic task is greater if error structures vary among population subgroups.

The possible importance of measurement error in status variables is increasingly recognized by students of the achievement process. Still, there are no definitive estimates of biases induced by measurement error in parameters of achievement process models. Few studies have attempted to estimate models of achievement that incorporate measurement errors, and their results cannot be taken as definitive. The major obstacle to progress in dealing with the effects of measurement errors in studies of the achievement process has been the lack of independent, alternative measures of relevant variables within a single data set. For example, Griliches and Mason (1972) attempt to derive unbiased estimates of the effects of error-free ability on earnings, but their model uses only one measure of ability and depends on a set of assumptions that are subject to criticism (Cardell and Hopkins, 1974). Using information from a variety of sources, Bowles (1972a), Bowles and Nelson (1974), and Jencks (1972b) estimate models that incorporate reliability adjustments of several correlations, but it is far from obvious that such wholesale adjustments are justified (Becker, 1972). Similarly, Treiman and Hauser (1970) and Kelley (1973a,b) have constructed achievement models with errors in parental status variables. However, the structure of those (random) errors was simply asserted, and validity estimates were deduced from the models without repeated measurement of the error-ridden variables. In sum, the effects of measurement error on models of the achievement process are not well understood. This fact motivates our analysis.

Many studies of the early stages of the achievement process collect data primarily from teenagers and younger children (e.g., Kerckhoff, 1974). Insofar as these studies obtain information from the youthful respondents about themselves without taking account of measurement errors, this represents nothing more than the usual state of affairs in many other areas of research besides the achievement process. But, when these studies collect information about other people from youthful respondents, measurement error problems are potentially greater. For example, it is common in these studies to ask children about their parents' social statuses, even though there are reasons for presuming that children are fallible informants of parental statuses. Among younger children especially, knowledge of the stratification system is not well developed (Weinstein, 1958; Simmons, 1962; Simmons and Rosenberg, 1971), and even older children are bound to have difficulty in assessing parental income (Kayser and Summers, 1973). Faced with questions about parental statuses that can be difficult to answer, children may respond by substituting information about one parent for the other, they may respond in terms of their own aspirations, or they may respond in other ways.

Coleman, Campbell, Hobson, McPartland, Mood, Weinfeld, and York (1966), Niemi (1974), Overlan (1968), Jencks, Smith, Acland, Bane, Cohen, Gintis, Heyns, and Michelson (1972), St. John (1970), Boruch and Creager (1972), Borus and Nestel (1973), Cohen and Orum (1972), Kayser and Summers (1973), and Kerckhoff, Mason and Poss (1973) have studied the extent to which children and youths' reports of parental statuses are accurate. Each of the data sets used in these studies is of modest dimensions, with respect both to sample size and the number of relevant variables measured. Each has been analyzed in different ways, none with an eye to direct translation into studies of the attainment process. The various data sets do not overlap much in the populations represented; hence, replication has been limited.

Few, if any, well substantiated conclusions have emerged from research on children's reporting errors, although there have been numerous suggestive findings. Perhaps the least questionable result is that older children report parental statuses more accurately than younger children, but the point at which older children's reports may be used interchangeably with parents' own reports is not yet known. We do not know for sure that younger black children are less accurate reporters of parental status than younger white children, although there is some evidence to support this conclusion. We are not yet certain about the relative accuracy of boys and girls, nor have we determined whether children's reporting errors are random, or at what age they become so.

Because interest in children's reporting errors has developed only recently, studies of the early stages of the achievement process have, thus far, been unable to take this kind of measurement error into account. Even if the measurement error studies noted earlier were not so recent, however, it would be difficult to use their results. Although they urge us to use caution inversely proportional to the ages of their youthful respondents, they give few practical instructions and typically do not provide enough information for application of their results in substantive analyses.

The simplest and most effective way to learn about measurement errors and to apply this knowledge in substantive analyses of the achievement process is to do both at once. This eliminates ambiguity about the implications of measurement errors for substantive analyses. It requires that models of the error generating process be developed prior to any analysis, a seemingly necessary step which has been taken only occasionally in this area of research. The outcome of this approach is that estimates of the parameters of the error generating structure are obtained simultaneously with estimates of the parameters in the achievement structure, and the models become inseparable. This allows methodological concerns to inform theoretical concerns maximally, and conversely. The strategy is a natural outgrowth of the approach taken by Siegel and Hodge (1968:51) and has been elaborated by others (e.g., Hauser and Goldberger, 1971; Werts, Jöreskog, and Linn, 1973), but not for the kind of measurement errors of interest in this chapter. Incidentally, our argument, that it is costly to divorce measurement error models from substantive models, applies equally to index construction, since construct indicators may also be viewed as fallible measures of underlying variables. Hauser (1972) illustrates the advantage of integrating index construction with substantive estimation problems.

This chapter takes up the problem of children's reporting errors where Kerckhoff et al. (1973) left it. They concluded with the observation that the study of children's reporting errors should be informed by a useful and valid conceptual and analytic model. This chapter attempts to provide that model. Our goals are to present the most helpful conceptual model, illustrate what we believe to be the most helpful analysis technique, reach new conclusions about measurement errors and the achievement process, and present these results in such a way that they can, under some circumstances, be incorporated directly into other analyses. The outline for the rest of this paper is as follows. Section II describes the sample and variables. Section III reviews the model and the findings of Kerckhoff et al. (1973) and presents the framework to be used in this chapter. Section IV gives the results of our analysis.

Data and Measurement

The data for this analysis were used by Kerckhoff et al. (1973); for details see the article and also Kerckhoff (1974). We have information from a 1969 sample of Fort Wayne school boys and their parents. Total sample size is about 500 families, distributed over sixth, ninth, and twelfth grade white and black youths and their parents.

At school, as participants in a study of the achievement process, the boys gave reports of their fathers' occupations and of their fathers' and mothers' years of schooling. The parents were subsequently interviewed at home, mothers independently from fathers and both parents independently from sons. As part of the interview, parents were asked how far they had gone in school, and fathers were asked for their current occupation. Each respondent's answers were coded independently from those of the other respondents, so these data have no consistency bias due to coding or to interaction between respondents during data collection.

The variables used in this analysis do not exhaust the list of those available to us. They are, however, among the most important for the study of status transmission, and we can fulfill the goals of this chapter by restricting our attention to them. Tables 15.1, 15.2, and 15.3 present the correlations, means, and standard deviations of the variables.[1] In models of the attainment process, certain of these variables are classified as endogenous, the others as predetermined. The endogenous variables are occupational expectations (OCEXP), occupational aspirations (OCASP), educational expectations (EDEXP), educational aspirations (EDASP), mental ability (IQ), and performance in school (GPA). The predetermined variables are father's report of his occupation (FAFOC), son's report of father's occupation (SOFOC), father's report of his education (FAFED), son's report of father's education (SOFED), mother's report of her education (MOMED), and son's report of mother's education (SOMED).

The education variables are coded by years of school aspired to, expected, or completed.[2] All of the occupation variables are coded in Duncan's (1961) socioeconomic index (SEI).[3] The mental ability scores are

---

[1] The correlations are "pair-wise present." That is, each correlation is based on the maximum number of nonmissing bivariate observations. The correlation matrices of Tables 15.1, 15.2, and 15.3 are positive definite. The standard deviations listed in these tables are based on the maximum number of nonmissing univariate observations. The Ns are approximately coincident with the smallest pair-wise present N in each matrix.

[2] The education questions vary only slightly in format. The father's education question in the student questionnaire is: "What was the highest grade in school your father completed? (If you are not sure, please give your best guess.)" The response categories are: "eighth grade or less," "ninth grade," "tenth grade," "eleventh grade" (these first 4 categories are combined and scored 10 in our analysis); "graduated from high school" (scored 12); "went to business or technical school after high school" (scored 13); "completed 1–3 years of college" (scored 14); "graduated from college" (scored 16); "went to graduate or professional school after college" (scored 18).

[3] The occupation questions have slightly different introductions but are otherwise identical. The introduction to the father's occupation question in the student questionnaire is: "What kind of job does your father have? (If he is retired or unemployed, write that on the first line, but also describe the last job he had.) *Print* your answer." No space is provided for an answer at this point; instead, two more specific questions are asked, with answer space following each: "What kind of work does he do? (for example, high school teacher, paint sprayer, repairs radio sets, grocery checker, civil engineer)" and "What kind of business or industry does he work in? (for example, city high school, auto assembly plant, radio service shop, retail supermarket, road construction)."

TABLE 15.1

Correlations, Means, and Standard Deviations: Twelfth Grade Youths by Race [a]

	Correlations [b]												Means	Standard Deviations
	OCEXP	OCASP	EDEXP	EDASP	IQ	GPA	FAFOC	SOFOC	FAFED	SOFED	MOMED	SOMED		
OCEXP	--	57	51	16	30	22	17	02	-08	-06	-03	-08	55.7	23.3
OCASP	53	--	37	39	50	35	26	20	23	11	-09	-21	59.2	24.8
EDEXP	66	29	--	73	24	32	24	15	11	06	17	25	14.2	1.8
EDASP	48	25	70	--	27	33	14	34	23	24	11	18	14.6	1.9
IQ	43	22	49	34	--	41	05	19	-09	-03	09	07	93.6	12.0
GPA	65	31	69	43	56	--	06	-01	02	-05	17	13	78.3	3.5
FAFOC	19	-06	40	27	22	30	--	74	25	20	14	-13	24.8	13.2
SOFOC	20	08	35	29	20	29	93	--	31	34	23	08	28.1	16.3
FAFED	28	05	48	35	32	36	72	71	--	81	20	05	11.3	2.2
SOFED	30	11	44	26	40	40	71	70	89	--	21	14	11.1	1.7
MOMED	29	10	31	18	38	28	28	35	36	45	--	83	10.7	1.4
SOMED	24	13	29	18	26	26	37	39	40	46	84	--	11.0	1.5
Means	57.4	59.4	14.8	14.7	110.9	82.5	47.4	45.9	12.8	12.7	12.0	12.2		
Std. Dev.	28.1	26.7	2.0	2.3	12.6	6.5	23.2	23.1	2.4	2.3	1.6	1.7		

NOTE: Item identifications are: OCEXP = son's occupational expectation, OCASP = son's occupational aspiration, EDEXP = son's educational expectation, EDASP = son's educational aspiration, IQ = son's IQ score, GPA = son's grade point average in school, FAFOC = father's report of his occupation, SOFOC = son's report of father's occupation, FAFED = father's report of his education, SOFED = son's report of father's education, MOMED = mother's report of her education, SOMED = son's report of mother's education.

[a] Entries above and to the right of the main diagonal are for blacks, for whom N = 30. Entries below and to the left of the main diagonal are for whites, for whom N = 80.

[b] Decimal points for the correlations are suppressed.

TABLE 15.2

Correlations, Means, and Standard Deviations: Ninth Grade Youths by Race[a]

	Correlations[b]												Means	Standard Deviations
	OCEXP	OCASP	EDEXP	EDASP	IQ	GPA	FAFOC	SOFOC	FAFED	SOFED	MOMED	SOMED		
OCEXP	--	60	29	32	09	22	20	12	13	04	-09	24	54.5	29.1
OCASP	72	--	33	39	13	32	38	07	08	13	11	22	50.6	26.7
EDEXP	61	45	--	64	06	18	19	09	17	17	-06	20	13.7	1.8
EDASP	58	54	76	--	05	10	19	07	21	23	-04	11	14.2	1.9
IQ	49	31	50	49	--	45	13	-14	03	-04	12	02	91.9	11.7
GPA	54	44	55	61	71	--	19	08	01	-03	-02	10	75.3	4.8
FAFOC	40	31	50	51	41	57	--	38	22	17	21	24	21.9	10.3
SOFOC	44	30	52	51	42	53	92	--	17	45	-07	19	26.0	20.1
FAFED	44	36	54	52	45	51	66	64	--	33	26	07	10.6	1.2
SOFED	49	39	56	55	41	57	63	67	82	--	25	35	11.1	1.5
MOMED	31	34	48	47	31	43	44	44	58	56	--	38	10.7	1.1
SOMED	29	29	48	47	30	42	44	47	56	61	90	--	11.3	1.7
Means	59.5	59.7	14.9	14.9	111.0	83.5	57.7	55.3	13.5	13.3	12.6	12.6		
Std. Dev.	27.2	25.9	2.1	2.2	12.9	6.2	24.2	24.7	2.9	2.7	2.1	2.0		

NOTE: Item identifications are: OCEXP = son's occupational expectation, OCASP = son's occupational aspiration, EDEXP = son's educational expectation, EDASP = son's educational aspiration, IQ = son's IQ score, GPA = son's grade point average in school, FAFOC = father's report of his occupation, SOFOC = son's report of father's occupation, FAFED = father's report of his education, SOFED = son's report of father's education, MOMED = mother's report of her education, SOMED = son's report of mother's education.

[a]Entries above and to the right of the main diagonal are for blacks, for whom N = 50. Entries below and to the left of the main diagonal are for whites, for whom N = 80.

[b]Decimal points for the correlations are suppressed.

449

TABLE 15.3
Correlations, Means, and Standard Deviations: Sixth Grade Boys by Race[a]

	OCEXP	OCASP	EDEXP	EDASP	IQ	GPA	FAFOC	SOFOC	FAFED	SOFED	MOMED	SOMED	Means	Standard Deviations
OCEXP	--	56	28	21	05	-04	22	-02	12	09	02	-01	54.0	24.7
OCASP	62	--	19	20	-01	14	25	02	20	13	02	-05	49.5	25.6
EDEXP	34	35	--	82	12	07	09	15	15	15	02	27	15.0	2.2
EDASP	28	24	72	--	02	10	03	17	14	09	05	27	15.0	2.1
IQ	35	26	35	33	--	77	30	13	33	-05	13	-12	87.8	11.6
GPA	29	29	42	40	72	--	05	03	12	-19	-02	-22	78.0	6.4
FAFOC	38	24	33	31	39	43	--	39	49	47	36	18	23.4	15.7
SOFOC	42	23	26	26	38	35	80	--	51	26	32	35	28.1	21.3
FAFED	35	21	46	46	50	53	62	60	--	35	15	09	10.8	1.2
SOFED	28	15	46	46	27	38	58	51	72	--	43	61	11.6	2.1
MOMED	38	30	44	42	50	41	63	52	71	51	--	40	10.8	1.2
SOMED	25	15	42	26	35	27	46	36	57	64	65	--	12.1	2.3
Means	55.1	56.1	15.2	15.4	106.0	81.7	50.6	49.4	12.6	13.2	12.0	12.6		
Std. Dev.	27.5	25.0	2.1	2.2	13.4	6.8	23.4	24.9	2.4	2.3	1.8	2.2		

NOTE: Item identifications are: OCEXP = son's occupational expectation, OCASP = son's occupational aspiration, EDEXP = son's educational expectations, EDASP = son's educational aspiration, IQ = son's IQ score, GPA = son's grade point average in school, FAFOC = father's report of his occupation, SOFOC = son's report of father's occupation, FAFED = father's report of his education, SOFED = son's report of father's education, MOMED = mother's report of her education, SOMED = son's report of mother's education.

[a]Entries above and to the right of the main diagonal are for blacks, for whom N = 50. Entries below and to the left of the main diagonal are for whites, for whom N = 80.

[b]Decimal points for the correlations are suppressed.

taken from school records, as are the academic performance scores, which are an average of grades during the previous two years in school in a metric ranging from zero (low) to 100 (high).

The variables we take to be subject to error are sons' and parents' reports of parental status. We have no information with which to assess the reliability of youthful aspirations and expectations nor are checks available on the accuracy of the IQ and GPA measures retrieved from school records.[4]

Because the education questions are closed ended, we assume that responses to them are coded with great accuracy. The occupation questions are open ended, however, and, especially when children provide little information, the matching of their responses to the detailed occupational titles for which SEI scores are available is subjective. We have been as meticulous as possible in coding occupations. Still, the parameters we estimate for the occupation variables are bounded by the reliability with which occupations are coded, as is the case in any study of the achievement process. An alternative to the use of a socioeconomic index would be to treat occupation as a nominal variable. Impressive methods are available for the study of classification errors with nominal variables (Murray, 1971; Goodman, 1974), but this strategy has its own problems. To follow it would require much grouping of occupational titles, because of our small sample sizes. Grouping has consequences for the study of measurement errors because it does not preserve all variations in the raw data and is again subjective, inasmuch as the choice of cutting points is neither unique nor self-evident. Moreover, the principal coding problem is that of assigning responses to occupation titles and not that of assigning numbers to coded responses, which can be done mechanically. Thus, treating occupation as a nominal variable does not eliminate the problem of coder reliability. In any case, the method we use here (Jöreskog, 1969) for scaled variables is at least as powerful as those for nominal variables and produces results that need no translation for use in parametric models of the achievement process.

Conceptual and Analytic Framework

Kerckhoff et al. (1973) examined the accuracy with which sixth-, ninth-, and twelfth-grade boys report their mother's and father's education and father's occupation. Working with parents' reports of their own status

[4] In the student questionnaire, educational and occupational expectations and aspirations were included in a section about the future, and father's occupation and education were elicited in succession, separated from mother's education by several pages. The expectation and aspiration questions were juxtaposed to clarify distinctions between them for the youthful respondents. Separating questions about mother from those about father probably increased the independence of responses about each parent. The measurement error implications in asking about father's occupation and education in succession are unclear.

characteristics and with sons' independent reports of these characteristics, the earlier paper assumed that the parents' reports were not subject to error, but that the sons' reports were. Although intended only for use in initial exploration, this model (hereafter, Model I) has some advantages. For example, it deals effectively with the question of upgrading. The equations for Model I are, for father's occupational status and father's and mother's education:

$$
\begin{aligned}
\text{SOFOC}_i &= \alpha_1 + \beta_1 \text{ FAFOC}_i + \epsilon_{i1} \\
\text{SOFED}_i &= \alpha_2 + \beta_2 \text{ FAFED}_i + \epsilon_{i2} \\
\text{SOMED}_i &= \alpha_3 + \beta_3 \text{ MOMED}_i + \epsilon_{i3}
\end{aligned}
\tag{1}
$$

where $i = 1, \ldots, n$ denotes the ith family, and, where for each equation, α, β, and ϵ are the population intercepts, slopes, and random disturbance terms, respectively. The basic results of Kerckhoff et al. (1973) were obtained by independent application of Model I to black and white boys and youths in the sixth, ninth, and twelfth grades.

Estimating Model I, using ordinary least squares regressions, sons' reports of parental status characteristics were found to be most inaccurate (smallest slopes and largest intercepts, largest standard errors of estimate and smallest correlations) among sixth graders, and more so for blacks than whites. Under the assumptions of Model I, the son–parent correlations are validity coefficients, but to apply them in adjustments of observed relationships in the achievement process would be premature, since the model is subject to criticism, and better models are available.

Model I ignores the possibility that sons' perceptions of other parental characteristics, other than the one present in a given regression, might affect the sons' reports. More generally, it ignores the possibility of nonzero covariances between the disturbances and the possibility that these nonzero covariances, should they exist, could be due to variables other than parental statuses. Perhaps most important, Model I assumes incorrectly that parents make no errors in their own reports, and that their reports are recorded without error.

As Siegel and Hodge (1968) have shown, and as common sense would lead one to expect, adult reports of their own status characteristics are subject to error. There is no reason to think that parents of sixth, ninth, or twelfth grade boys are an exception to this. We therefore discard Model I in favor of a model that allows for both the sons' and the parents' reports to be subject to error. In addition to giving a more realistic representation of the error generating process, the alternative model also allows evaluation of the seriousness of other objections to Model I. We now turn to our revised model.

Model

First, we will present the underlying assumptions of our model, and then we will describe its structure in detail. One part of the model is fixed; the other varies according to the hypotheses under consideration. The fixed part consists of a set of equations encompassing measurement error relationships in the achievement process. The part of the model which varies is the variance–covariance matrix of the disturbances of the equation system.

Assumptions   The following assumptions are basic. First, we assume that there is an underlying variable for each aspect of parental status that contains no erroneous values. For example, we assume there is a *true* father's education. This assumption is necessary to define measurement error. Second, we assume that youngsters' and parents' reports measure each true parental characteristic. That is, we assume that the children and adults queried made an attempt to respond with the information desired. Third, we assume that each observed status characteristic, whether reported by children or parents, is a linear function of the corresponding true variable. There is no reason to assume or allow for a more complicated functional relationship; this one makes estimation possible.

Fourth, we assume that the errors in children's and parent's reports do not covary with the true values of the characteristics measured. This is a reasonable assumption to make for parents, less so for children. With Model I, Kerckhoff *et al.* (1973) treated what is necessarily an assumption here as a question subject to empirical investigation. The only source of covariance between errors and true values for which there is a plausible theoretical rationale (see Kerckhoff *et al.*, 1973:228–230) is upgrading of children's reports relative to parents'. Kerckhoff *et al.* (1973) found little evidence of upgrading. Moreover, it is present only among sixth-grade children and only in their reports of mother's education (Kerckhoff *et al.*, 1973:237–238). This finding is consequential for the model under consideration here. If the errors in parents' reports of their own statuses do not covary with the true variables, as is reasonable to assume, it follows that evidence of upgrading, using Model I, is evidence of upgrading under the assumption that parents' reports contain random errors. The fourth assumption is, thus, counterfactual for sixth graders' reports of a single parental characteristic. Because it is necessary for the models we wish to estimate, and since it is valid in almost all instances, on balance, we believe the assumption to be tenable.

The fifth assumption is that the variances of the errors in the observed status reports are constant for all observations in any relationship we wish to estimate. Using Model I, Kerckhoff *et al.* (1973:239–240) examined the question of constant error variance by subdividing the already partitioned analytic subsamples and analyzing fluctuations in standard errors of estimate. They found no compelling evidence of heteroscedasticity, although the analysis was limited by small sample size. Since the models considered here are far more complex and are, nonetheless, based on the same data used by Kerckhoff *et al.* (1973), subdivision of the sample would be even less profitable than in the earlier model. Thus, the fifth assumption is not open to question, given the model used here and the size of the sample.

These five assumptions permit us to specify the model, to which we now turn. Before proceeding very far, we shall need to introduce a sixth assumption, whose purpose will be more clear in the context of the equations.

Structural Equations   Consider the equations:

$$
\begin{aligned}
(2) \quad \text{OCEXP} &= \lambda_{11}\text{TRFOC} + \lambda_{12}\text{TRFED} + \lambda_{13}\text{TRMED} + \psi_1 \\
\text{OCASP} &= \lambda_{21}\text{TRFOC} + \lambda_{22}\text{TRFED} + \lambda_{23}\text{TRMED} + \psi_2 \\
\text{EDEXP} &= \lambda_{31}\text{TRFOC} + \lambda_{32}\text{TRFED} + \lambda_{33}\text{TRMED} + \psi_3 \\
\text{EDASP} &= \lambda_{41}\text{TRFOC} + \lambda_{42}\text{TRFED} + \lambda_{43}\text{TRMED} + \psi_4 \\
\text{IQ} &= \lambda_{51}\text{TRFOC} + \lambda_{52}\text{TRFED} + \lambda_{53}\text{TRMED} + \psi_5 \\
\text{GPA} &= \lambda_{61}\text{TRFOC} + \lambda_{62}\text{TRFED} + \lambda_{63}\text{TRMED} + \psi_6 \\
\text{FAFOC} &= \lambda_{71}\text{TRFOC} \qquad\qquad\qquad\qquad\qquad\quad + \psi_7 \\
\text{SOFOC} &= \lambda_{81}\text{TRFOC} \qquad\qquad\qquad\qquad\qquad\quad + \psi_8 \\
\text{FAFED} &= \qquad\qquad\quad \lambda_{92}\text{TRFED} \qquad\qquad\qquad + \psi_9 \\
\text{SOFED} &= \qquad\qquad\quad \lambda_{10,2}\text{TRFED} \qquad\qquad\qquad + \psi_{10} \\
\text{MOMED} &= \qquad\qquad\qquad\qquad\qquad\quad \lambda_{11,3}\text{TRMED} + \psi_{11} \\
\text{SOMED} &= \qquad\qquad\qquad\qquad\qquad\quad \lambda_{12,3}\text{TRMED} + \psi_{12}
\end{aligned}
$$

In these equations, TRFOC is father's true occupational status, TRFED is father's true education, and TRMED is mother's true education. The λ_{ij} are structural coefficients relating the true variables to the observed status reports, and the ψ_i are stochastic disturbances. In the equations for the observed (measured) status reports of children and parents, but not in the other equations, we define the stochastic disturbances to be measurement errors.

In the first six of the equations just presented, the dependent variables are endogenous variables in the achievement process. Each of these dependent variables is treated as a function of the three true parental status characteristics and not as a function of any of the observed parental status measures. Inasmuch as the endogenous variables are functions of the true status characteristics and of no other variables, including other endogenous variables, the first six equations may be seen as reduced-form equations in a model of the early stages of the achievement process. Later, we consider the possibility of other relations between the endogenous variables and certain of the observed status variables.

The last six equations are for sons' and parents' reports of the various parental status characteristics and obviously satisfy the first three initial assumptions. Each status measure is an indicator of an assumed underlying status characteristic, and of only one such characteristic. All relations, including the first six, are linear.

Any reasonable model of the achievement process would allow individual status characteristics, even if unmeasured, to be correlated, and, therefore, we add this specification to Equations 2, so that the true status characteristics are correlated, just as the observed status characteristics are correlated. This brings us, finally, to the question of correlations among the stochastic disturbances.

Restrictions on the variance–covariance matrix for the disturbances of the endogenous variables. In the first six of Equations 2, the stochastic disturbances are not necessarily measurement errors, and we have, thus far, made no assumptions about them. At this point, we need a sixth assumption, namely, that the stochastic disturbances of the first six equations do not covary with the true status characteristics. This assumption is equivalent to the corresponding assumption in regression models. Criticism of the assumption, as applied to Equations 2, may be made in the usual way. That is, it is not difficult to mention omitted predetermined variables that are correlated with the included predetermined variables, for example, measures of income and wealth. Omission of these variables will bias the coefficients of the included variables and invalidate the assumption that the stochastic errors are independent of the included predetermined variables. This criticism is valid, but we do not consider more elaborate models because our data do not contain other predetermined variables.

Even if measured perfectly, the predetermined variables could not explain the relationships among the endogenous variables. For example, other factors held constant, greater ability leads to higher grades in school, and higher grades in school lead to higher educational aspirations, which may lead to higher occupational aspirations. Since we do not wish to estimate structural relationships among the endogenous variables, we allow instead for the possibility of correlations among the disturbances of the endogenous variables. That is, the disturbances of the first six of Equations 2 are allowed to covary.[5]

Restrictions on the variance–covariance matrix for the disturbances of the parental status reports. To complete the specification of the simplest model considered here, we assume that errors in the reports of one parental status characteristic do not covary with errors in the reports of another parental status characteristic, and that these errors do not covary with the stochastic disturbances of the equations for the endogenous variables in the achievement process. This formulation satisfies our most fundamental criticism of Model I, since it allows the parental reports, as well as the children's reports, to be given (and measured) with error, and it treats all reports as functions of true variables. Moreover, the model simultaneously embodies the structure of measurement errors and a reduced-form representation of the achievement process.

---

[5] The estimated values of these particular disturbance correlations are not central to the purposes of this chapter. Therefore, although we estimate them in order to avoid biases in other portions of our models, we neither present nor interpret them.

Equations 2 and subsequent specifications comprise a path model (hereafter, Model II), for which the following general algebraic structure holds:

$$(3) \qquad\qquad \Sigma = \Lambda\Phi\Lambda',$$

for which Figure 15.1 gives the graphic equivalent, and where Σ is, in this case, a 12×12 dispersion matrix whose entries are correlations involving sons' reports, parents' reports, and the six endogenous variables in the achievement process. The 12×15 coefficient matrix Λ has the form shown in Table 15.4. The coefficients in Λ are for the variables in precisely the order they are given in Equations 2. Because the stochastic disturbances are standardized, their coefficients are also included in Λ. Because some disturbances are allowed to be correlated, they are treated as unmeasured factors whose correlations appear in Φ (see Werts, Linn, and Jöreskog, 1971).

The 15×15 matrix Φ consists of correlations partitioned according to three classifications: true variables, disturbances of the endogenous variables, and disturbances of the parental status variables. Table 15.5 shows the partitions. Consistent with our specifications, $\Phi_{12} = \Phi'_{21}$ and $\Phi_{13} = \Phi'_{31}$ are composed entirely of zeroes, since the disturbances of Equations 2 are

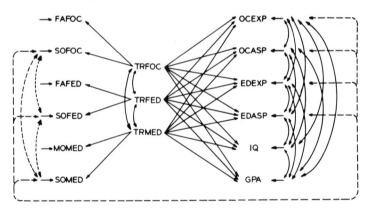

Figure 15.1 Composite schematic path diagram for Models II–V. Model II—solid lines; Model III—solid and dotted lines; Model IV—solid and broken lines; Model V—solid, dotted, and broken lines. Item identifications: OCEXP = son's occupational expectation; OCASP = son's occupational aspiration; EDEXP = son's educational expectation; EDASP = son's educational aspiration; IQ = son's IQ score; GPA = son's grade point average in school; FAFOC = father's report of his occupation; SOFOC = son's report of father's occupation; FAFED = father's report of his education; SOFED = son's report of father's education; MOMED = mother's report of her education; SOMED = son's report of mother's education; TRFOC = "true" father's occupation; TRFED = "true" father's education; TRMED = "true" mother's education.

TABLE 15.4
The Coefficient Matrix Λ^a

	TRFOC	TRFED	TRMED	Disturbances (Standardized ψ_i)
OCEXP:	λ_{11}	λ_{12}	λ_{13}	λ_{14}
OCASP:	λ_{21}	λ_{22}	λ_{23}	λ_{25}
EDEXP:	λ_{31}	λ_{32}	λ_{33}	λ_{36}
EDASP:	λ_{41}	λ_{42}	λ_{43}	λ_{47}
IQ:	λ_{51}	λ_{52}	λ_{53}	λ_{58}
GPA:	λ_{61}	λ_{62}	λ_{63}	λ_{69}
FAFOC:	λ_{71}	0	0	$\lambda_{7\ 10}$
SOFOC:	λ_{81}	0	0	$\lambda_{8\ 11}$
FAFED:	0	λ_{92}	0	$\lambda_{9\ 12}$
SOFED:	0	$\lambda_{10\ 2}$	0	$\lambda_{10\ 13}$
MOMED:	0	0	$\lambda_{11\ 3}$	$\lambda_{11\ 14}$
SOMED:	0	0	$\lambda_{12\ 3}$	$\lambda_{12\ 15}$

(Zeroes)

NOTE: Item identifications are: OCEXP = son's occupational expectation, OCASP = son's occupational aspiration, EDEXP = son's educational expectation, EDASP = son's educational aspiration, IQ = son's IQ score, GPA = son's grade point average in school, FAFOC = father's report of his occupation, SOFOC = son's report of father's occupation, FAFED = father's report of his education, SOFED = son's report of father's education, MOMED = mother's report of her education, SOMED = son's report of mother's education, TRFOC = "true" father's occupation, TRFED = "true" father's education, TRMED = "true" mother's education.

^{a}Zeroes indicate that a particular unmeasured variable is hypothesized to have no effect on the observed variable defining that row of Λ. These hypotheses are embodied as constraints in the estimation process.

457

TABLE 15.5

The Matrix Φ of Correlations Among and Between True Status Characteristics, Endogenous Disturbances and Status Indicator Disturbances: Composite for Models II-V [a]

	True Status			Disturbances of Endogenous Variables						Disturbances of Status Indicators					
	TRFOC	TRFED	TRMED	OCEXP	OCASP	EDEXP	EDASP	IQ	GPA	FAFOC	SOFOC	FAFED	SOFED	MOMED	SOMED
TRFOC	1	ϕ_{12}	ϕ_{13}	Zeroes						Zeroes					
TRFED		1	ϕ_{23}												
TRMED	ϕ_{11}		1												
OCEXP	ϕ_{21}			1	ϕ_{45}	ϕ_{46}	ϕ_{47}	ϕ_{48}	ϕ_{49}	0	$\phi_{4\,11}$	0	$\phi_{4\,13}$	0	$\phi_{4\,15}$
OCASP					1	ϕ_{56}	ϕ_{57}	ϕ_{58}	ϕ_{59}	0	$\phi_{5\,11}$	0	$\phi_{5\,13}$	0	$\phi_{5\,15}$
EDEXP				ϕ_{22}		1	ϕ_{67}	ϕ_{68}	ϕ_{69}	0	$\phi_{6\,11}$	0	$\phi_{6\,13}$	0	$\phi_{6\,15}$
EDASP							1	ϕ_{78}	ϕ_{79}	0	$\phi_{7\,11}$	0	$\phi_{7\,13}$	0	$\phi_{7\,15}$
IQ								1	ϕ_{89}	0	0	0	0	0	0
GPA									1	0	0	0	0	0	0
FAFOC	ϕ_{31}			ϕ_{32}						1	0	0	0	0	0
SOFOC											1	0	$\phi_{11\,13}$	0	$\phi_{11\,15}$
FAFED												1	0	0	0
SOFED										ϕ_{33}			1	0	$\phi_{13\,15}$
MOMED														1	0
SOMED															1

NOTE: For item identifications, see the note to Table 15.4.

[a] Subscripting of the ϕ entries (i.e., correlations) corresponds to their row and column positions in Φ. Entries below the main diagonal are the partition labels. Note that Φ_{11} is 3 × 3 and symmetric; $\Phi_{21} = \Phi'_{12}$ is 6 × 3; $\Phi_{31} = \Phi'_{13}$ is 6 × 3; Φ_{22} is 6 × 6 and symmetric; $\Phi_{32} = \Phi'_{23}$ is 6 × 6 but not symmetric; and Φ_{33} is 6 × 6 and symmetric. Model II constrains $\Phi_{32} = 0$ and $\Phi_{33} = I$ (identity matrix); model III constrains $\Phi_{32} = 0$ and $\Phi_{33} \neq I$; model IV constrains $\Phi_{32} \neq 0$ and $\Phi_{33} = I$; model V constrains $\Phi_{32} \neq 0$ and $\Phi_{33} \neq I$. Entries above the main diagonal indicate allowed correlations when $\Phi_{32} \neq 0$ or $\Phi_{33} \neq I$.

assumed uncorrelated with the true status variables. Also, Φ_{11} is a symmetric correlation matrix of the true status variables, and Φ_{22} is a symmetric correlation matrix of the disturbances of the endogenous variables. Because Model II specifies that errors in the reports of one parental status characteristic do not covary with the disturbances of the endogenous variables, Φ_{33} is a diagonal matrix of (standardized) disturbance variances of children's and parents' status reports, and $\Phi_{32} = \Phi'_{23}$ consists of zeroes.

Given our specification of the contents of Λ and Φ, Model II is overidentified and is estimable as a restricted factor model (Jöreskog, 1969, 1970, 1973) upon substitution into Equation 3 of a sample dispersion matrix of the observables.[6] The estimated coefficients of the first six structural equations, $\hat{\lambda}_{ij}$ ($i = 1, \ldots, 6$; $j = 1,2,3$), may be inspected to determine the effects of the underlying status characteristics on the endogenous variables. The estimated coefficients of the last six structural equations, $\hat{\lambda}_{ij}$ ($i = 7, \ldots, 12$; $j = 1,2,3$), may be inspected to determine the size of the coefficients of sons' reports in relation to parents'. Indeed, these particular coefficients are correlations and may be thought of as validity coefficients. Estimating Equation 3 separately for blacks and whites, by grade, enables us to examine how quickly children's reports approach the accuracy of parents', and to observe differences in accuracy between whites and blacks. This also parallels the strategy of Kerckhoff et al. (1973) and facilitates comparisons with the earlier work. We defer presentation of the analysis, however, until Model II is elaborated to account for additional criticisms of Model I.

Correlated measurement errors. Our initial criticism of Model I was that it does not allow for a son's perceptions of parental characteristics, other than the one he is nominally reporting, to affect his report. It may be that children guess at a particular status when they do not know it or think they do not know it. To aid in their guessing, they may use their knowledge of other parental statuses. For example, it may be that if a boy is not certain of his mother's education, he supplies a value close to his perception of his father's education. Since children's, especially younger children's, reports of parental status are imperfectly related to parental reports or true parental scores, and the various parental statuses are themselves imperfectly correlated, there is no a priori reason to rule out this possibility. It appears plausible and worth checking.

Figure 15.2 presents a causal diagram consistent with the process just described. It shows that each of the characteristics reported by sons is a

---

[6] Statistical inference, based on the application of the restricted factor model to our data, is probably unwarranted, because we use pair-wise present correlations, and because our variables do not appear to meet the distributional requirements of the maximum likelihood estimation procedure. We report the results of tests of fit, but do not rely exclusively on them to guide explorations or reach substantive conclusions (see Jöreskog, 1969:201).

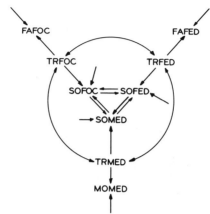

Figure 15.2 Schematic path diagram depicting the possibility that son's perception of a given parental status characteristic is also affected by his perception of other parental status characteristics. For clarity, the endogenous variables in the achievement process are excluded. Item identifications: FAFOC = father's report of his occupation; SOFOC = son's report of father's occupation; FAFED = father's report of his education; SOFED = son's report of father's education; MOMED = mother's report of her education; SOMED = son's report of mother's education; TRFOC = "true" father's occupation; TRFED = "true" father's education; TRMED = "true" mother's education.

function not only of the underlying status characteristic, but also of sons' perceptions of parents' other status characteristics. Although the model in Figure 15.2 appears to capture the hypothetical process we have suggested, it is not identified. However, if sons' reports for a given status dimension are partly based on their perceptions of another status dimension, reporting errors for the two dimensions will be correlated. Thus, we can deal with the identification problem by removing the simultaneity between sons' reports of parental status, positing instead that errors in sons' reports are correlated. This reduces the number of parameters to be estimated, and the new specification is overidentified. We shall call this revision Model III. Figure 15.1 includes a diagram of Model III, and Table 15.5 shows its nonzero correlations in Φ_{33}.

Since Model III can be estimated and is overidentified, we can test its fit. Correlations between errors set upper bounds on the degree of dependency between any two parental characteristics reported by sons which could be attributed to simultaneous relationships like those in Figure 15.2. Therefore, if it is unnecessary to posit correlated disturbances for sons' reports, we may dismiss the argument that sons base their reports on their perceptions of parental statuses other than the one about which they have been asked. If there are correlated disturbances, then the data are consistent with the original argument. There remains the problem of specifying an identifiable model incorporating the simultaneous relations depicted in Figure 15.2.

Correlations between measurement errors and the stochastic disturbances for the endogenous variables. Model I fails to take account not only of the possibility that sons' reports of parental status are a function of statuses other than the relevant one, but also that sons' reports depend on variables other than parental statuses. In particular, they might depend on youthful aspirations or expectations of occupational and educational attainment. This could happen if youngsters upgrade parental status to the level of their own high youthful aspirations, but it could also happen even if youngsters do not upgrade their parents' statuses from the true values. It could result from a desire for consistency between youngsters' aspirations and their parents' statuses. It is important to know if this pattern of error occurs. It would introduce a simultaneity bias into estimates of the effects of parental status in models of the achievement process that include aspirations as endogenous variables, if children's reports were used as proxies either for parents' own reports or for other independent measures of parental status. For example, if the dependent variable is son's occupational aspiration, and the independent variables are son's reports of parental statuses, estimated effects of parental statuses would be biased if sons' status reports were partly a function of their aspirations. Furthermore, children's aspirations and expectations may depend on their *perceptions* of their parents' statuses, apart from the influence of unperceived aspects of parental status.

Both of the processes just described imply biases in the coefficients of Models II and III. In particular, assuming these processes are real and substantial, omission of direct paths between aspirations and expectations and sons' reports of parental status is likely to bias estimates of the relationships between the underlying parental status characteristics and sons' reports of them. This suggests incorporating direct relationships between aspirations and expectations and sons' reports of parental status into the model. Positing simultaneous relationships in a fashion analogous to that shown in Figure 15.2 would again lead to underidentification, so, once again, we introduce the possibility of correlated errors, this time between aspirations or expectations and sons' reports of parental status. Our rationale is the same as in Model III: The absence of correlated errors would indicate that there was no feedback between sons' parental status reports and their aspirations and expectations. The presence of correlated errors would be consistent with such feedback. Figure 15.1 presents the extension graphically, and Table 15.5 shows the hypothesized nonzero correlations in Φ_{23}. We shall call this latest specification Model IV. Since Model IV can be estimated and is overidentified, we can again test the fit.

The different restrictions on Φ in Models III and IV may be included in the same structure without causing that structure to become underidentified. We call this combination Model V. Figure 15.1 includes a diagram of this model. The rationale for Model V is simply that there is no reason to suppose that the substantive processes that lead to the specification of Model III will occur only in the absence of the processes that lead to the specification of Model IV, or conversely. The point holds more generally: It is necessary to allow for models that are compounded from the processes just described. Model V is one such example, but there are others that may be obtained by various simplifications of Model V. In the context of a specific empirical analysis, there are clearly many possible models, and there is no mechanical technique for sifting through them to find the "best" one.

Finally, it is possible to specify variants of any model, thus far described or implied, by imposing equality restrictions among the nonzero coefficients in Λ and Φ. The substantive import of equality restrictions will be described in the context of the data analysis.

Review of Models   To summarize this part of the discussion, Models II–V all share these qualities: The endogenous variables are joint functions of the true parental status variables; their disturbances are allowed to be freely intercorrelated; the true status variables are allowed to be intercorrelated; the status reports are functions of *only* the particular true status variable they are presumed to measure.

Completing the list of specifications with the assumptions that the sons' and parents' reporting errors are random gives Model II. Alternatively, completing the list with the assumption that sons' reporting errors are correlated across status characteristics gives Model III. Completing the list with the assumption that some of the stochastic disturbances for the endogenous variables are correlated with sons' reporting errors gives Model IV. Combining the different specifications on Φ, in Models III and IV, into the same structure gives Model V. Alternative simplifications of Model V, obtained by reimposing zero restrictions on the nonzero elements of Φ, yield not only Models II–IV, but others too numerous to mention. Variants of Model V, or any of its simplifications, may be obtained by placing coefficient restrictions on parameters hypothesized to be nonzero.

Strategy and Hypotheses

The range of opportunities for analysis has now been presented, and next we consider the strategy to be employed. In general, we have proceeded by starting with the simplest model, which is Model II, and only progressing to Model III when Model II has been shown to provide a poor fit to the data. If Model III also does not fit the data, then we proceed to Model IV or V. If one of Models III–V fits the data, we attempt to simplify it where possible, in order to obtain a more parsimonious fit of the data. If none of these models fits, we try different strategies uniquely tailored to a particular data set.

As described earlier, we have data on boys in the sixth, ninth, and twelfth grades. Within each grade, we have all information separately for blacks and whites, which gives a total of six different data sets. In this section, we justify separate treatment of these data, rather than by grade, by race, or as a single data set. For additional justification, see Kerckhoff *et al.* (1973).

Grade (Age) Differences With respect to differences by grade, boys in higher grades are likely to be more accurate reporters of parental status than boys in lower grades. Of course, this and other age or grade differences in our sample may be attributable to patterns of school dropout or to intercohort change, but we think it reasonable to suppose that maturation is the predominant influence on between-grade differentials in the Fort Wayne sample (see Kerckhoff *et al.*, 1973:230, Footnote 10). In terms of the statistical model, the λ_{ij} for boys' reports should increase with grade. We presume greater knowledge among boys in higher grades, and there is no good reason to expect older boys to be less willing than younger boys to comply with requests for this information.

Since the pattern of nonresponse to the questions eliciting children's reports of parental status is not markedly related to children's grade in school, boys in lower grades, by virtue of less knowledge, and given the social pressure to respond to the items on the questionnaire, are more likely than boys in higher grades to base their status reports on their perceptions of other parental statuses. Furthermore, if such relationships occur for boys in all grades, they are likely to be stronger for younger boys. That is, relationships between reports of different parental statuses are most likely, in lower grades, to be stronger than can be accounted for by the relationships between underlying true statuses. Moreover, if this pattern occurs for all boys, it is likely to be strongest for boys in lower grades. In terms of the statistical model used here, this pattern is consistent with a nondiagonal Φ_{33}. We argue that the lower the grade, the more likely is Φ_{33} to be nondiagonal, and the larger its correlation.

Because of their greater awareness of and sensitivity to status distinctions, and because of their greater knowledge, boys in higher grades are more likely than boys in lower grades to have relationships between their reports of parental status and their educational and occupational aspirations and expectations, which cannot be accounted for by true parental status. Moreover, given widespread occurrence across grades, the pattern is likely to be strongest for boys in higher grades. We are likely to encounter this hypothesized outcome in our data if a substantial percentage of boys consciously or otherwise attempt to maintain consistency between their aspirations or expectations and the social status of their families. In terms of the statistical model used here, this process results in a nonzero disturbance correlation matrix (Φ_{23}) between measurement errors and the stochastic disturbances of certain of the endogenous variables, as specified earlier.

Race Differences St. John (1970) and Kerckhoff *et al.* (1973) found that black children appear to be less accurate reporters of parental status than white children but were not able to explain this difference. Borus and Nestel (1973) recorded wider discrepancies between sons and fathers in reports of father's education among blacks than among whites in a sample of men aged 14–24 and their fathers. Black–white differences in accuracy would seem to be a well-established finding, but models that assume parents' reports are the true scores (St. John, 1970; Kerckhoff *et al.*, 1973), or the absence of any model (Borus and Nestel, 1973), can be quite misleading on this matter. Siegel and Hodge (1968:37) observe lower reliabilities for adult nonwhites than for adult whites, for personal income and occupational status. There is no reason to expect the parents in this sample to be exceptions to this finding. This, in turn, suggests that previously observed differences in the accuracy of children's and youths' reports of parental status might be due to differential accuracy in white and black parents' reports of their own statuses. If this were true, then the problem would be to explain why black adults have lower reliabilities than white adults, and why black children's accuracy diverges from white children's as they grow up. However, this assumed pattern seems unrealistic, and we seek an alternative. It may be that black children are less accurate reporters of parental status than white children, and that they remain so as adults, although the difference in accuracy may narrow as the children mature. If so, then the problem is to explain why blacks of any age seem to be less accurate reporters of status, whether of their parents' status or their own status.

Whatever the reasons for the differential reporting accuracy of blacks and whites, the nature and extent of the differences between them in the parameters of the most appropriate measurement error model must first be known before an explanation is sought. Moreover, knowledge of these differences is fundamental if sensitive adjustments are to be made for measurement errors in models of the achievement process. Therefore, this analysis provides separate results for blacks and whites, and it does so in a way that makes it possible to examine estimates of the accuracy of parents' own reports as well as those of their children.

Results

This section summarizes the findings of our analyses of white and black twelfth-, ninth-, and sixth-grade youths and boys. The discussion treats each data set separately, first analyzing measurement errors and then the achievement process. It starts with twelfth-grade whites, alternates by race within grade, and finishes with sixth-grade blacks. For each group, we present the estimates of a specialization of one of Models II–V. For comparison, we also present tables in which the endogenous variables are regressed on sons' reports of parental status, and separately on parents' own reports of their status.

The data analyzed here are the correlation matrices presented in Tables 15.1, 15.2, and 15.3, except that the correlations used in the computations are carried to more significant digits. We do not use the standard deviations of the observed variables; hence, all our analyses are carried out in standardized form. Results in this form are useful for comparing coefficients across variables within equations, as well as across equations whose dependent variables have different metrics and do not require the selection of variances for unstandardized latent constructs (e.g., TRFOC). Unstandardized coefficients may be obtained from the results presented here, except in the case of models estimated with equality constraints on at least one pair of coefficients (Morrison, 1967:268; Werts et al., 1971; Wiley and Wiley, 1970), by applying the standard deviations given in Tables 15.1, 15.2, and 15.3 together with externally supplied standard deviations of the latent constructs.

Twelfth-Grade Whites

Measurement error structure. Tables 15.6 and 15.7 present the estimated structure coefficients and factor correlations for a specialization of Model IV, for white twelfth-grade youths.[7] In this application of Model IV, there is one correlation between the disturbances of sons' reports of their occupational aspirations and their reports of fathers' occupations that is not included in these tables. This model fits best in the sense that, for the class of models considered here, using only free parameters and constraining the rest of the coefficients to be zero, this model fits the data well using the fewest degrees of freedom. The likelihood ratio chi-square for this model, based on a comparison of the reproduced correlation matrix with the observed sample matrix, is 26.6, with 29 degrees of freedom, and it is significant at the $p = .54$ level, which indicates an excellent fit.[8]

White twelfth-grade youths appear to report parental statuses about as accurately as their parents do. Looking at the lower portion of Table 15.6, the coefficients for sons' reports are virtually identical to those for parents' reports, except for mother's education, and this difference is not great. A model in which filial and parental coefficients are constrained to be equal for each status characteristic fits the data as well as the model presented here. Indeed, constraining all indicators of parental status to be identical in quality, we obtain estimates which again fit the data well, though not as perfectly as the other models, which have more free parameters.

---

[7] The numbers in the R^2 column of Table 15.6 and subsequent similar tables are computed exactly as they would be in path equations with observed variables only (i.e., standardized multiple regression equations), under the assumption that the disturbance coefficients are coefficients of alienation. The approximate 95% confidence intervals for the disturbance coefficients may not be carried over to the R^2s. The restricted factor model confidence intervals are conservative, because the standard errors upon which they are based are uncorrected for the use of standardized data (Lawley and Maxwell, 1971:100–103).

[8] The comparison in this test is between our model and any model that uses all of the degrees of freedom. Such a model is more complex than ours, because it fits the data with more freely varying parameters. The results of the chi-square test indicate that the loss in fit to the data due to using our simpler model is more than offset by the gain in degrees of freedom.

TABLE 15.6

Estimated Coefficients of a Model Linking Observed Variables to Three Unmeasured Family Status Factors: White Twelfth Grade Youths

Dependent Variable	Coefficients (and Approximate 95% Confidence Intervals) of			R^2
	TRFOC	TRFED	TRMED	
OCEXP	-.12 ($\pm$.36)	.32 ($\pm$.38)	.19 ($\pm$.24)	.13
OCASP	-.34 ($\pm$.39)	.31 ($\pm$.41)	.10 ($\pm$.24)	.07
EDEXP	.04 ($\pm$.33)	.40 ($\pm$.36)	.12 ($\pm$.23)	.25
EDASP	.10 ($\pm$.36)	.21 ($\pm$.38)	.05 ($\pm$.25)	.11
IQ	-.23 ($\pm$.34)	.45 ($\pm$.37)	.25 ($\pm$.24)	.22
GPA	-.03 ($\pm$.35)	.37 ($\pm$.37)	.13 ($\pm$.24)	.18
FAFOC	.97 ($\pm$.16)			.94
SOFOC	.95 ($\pm$.17)			.91
FAFED		.93 ($\pm$.17)		.87
SOFED		.95 ($\pm$.17)		.91
MOMED			.96 ($\pm$.19)	.93
SOMED			.87 ($\pm$.20)	.76

NOTE: Item identifications are: OCEXP = son's occupational expectation, OCASP = son's occupational aspiration, EDEXP = son's educational expectation, EDASP = son's educational aspiration, IQ = son's IQ score, GPA = son's grade point average in school, FAFOC = father's report of his occupation, SOFOC = son's report of father's occupation, FAFED = father's report of his education, SOFED = son's report of father's education, MOMED = mother's report of her education, SOMED = son's report of mother's education, TRFOC = "true" father's occupation, TRFED = "true" father's education, TRMED = "true" mother's education.

The single disturbance correlation (.44 $\pm$ .30) is for son's report of father's occupation and son's occupational aspiration. The existence of this correlation does not contradict the finding that sons' reports are as accurate as those of their fathers. Rather, it indicates merely that a small

TABLE 15.7

Estimates of Correlations Among Three Unmeasured Family Status Factors: White Twelfth Grade Youths

	Variable[a]	
Variable	TRFOC	TRFED
TRFED	.78 (±.10)	
TRMED	.39 (±.20)	.47 (±.19)

NOTE: Item identifications are: TRFOC = father's occupation factor, TRFED = father's education factor, TRMED = mother's education factor.

[a]Numbers in parentheses are approximate 95% confidence intervals.

proportion of the error in sons' reports is nonrandom. We cannot explain this finding here. But, applying an earlier argument, it may be due both to a desire to equate the status of one's father with one's aspirations and to fallible perceptions of father's occupation. Sons aspire to higher-status occupations than those held by their fathers, but the averages for sons' and fathers' reports of father's occupational status are virtually identical. Thus, it is unlikely that these sons are upgrading fathers' statuses in order to make them consistent with their aspirations. Of course, it may be that neither sons' reports nor their stated aspirations affect each other; some third variable could affect both of them.

Table 15.7 presents the correlations among the unmeasured parental status variables. The correlation between father's education and occupational status is larger than either sample value, and it is large absolutely. The other correlations among unmeasured status characteristics are no larger than those observed for sons' reports. None of these differences is large.

Achievement process. The upper half of Table 15.6 presents the measurement model equations for the effects of the unmeasured parental status variables on aspirations, expectations, grades, and ability. Table 15.8

TABLE 15.8

Multiple Regressions of Achievement Variables on Parents' and Sons' Reports of Family Status Variables: White Twelfth Grade Youths

Dependent Variable	Standardized Regression Coefficients (and 95% Confidence Intervals) of			R^2	N
	Father's Occupation	Father's Education	Mother's Education		
		Parental Reports			
OCEXP	-.08 (±.31)	.26 (±.31)	.22 (±.23)	.12	80
OCASP	-.24 (±.33)	.18 (±.33)	.12 (±.24)	.04	80
EDEXP	.08 (±.29)	.37 (±.29)	.15 (±.21)	.25	80
EDASP	.03 (±.31)	.31 (±.31)	.06 (±.23)	.13	80
IQ	-.09 (±.30)	.27 (±.30)	.31 (±.22)	.18	80
GPA	.05 (±.31)	.26 (±.31)	.16 (±.23)	.15	80
		Sons' Reports			
OCEXP	-.04 (±.30)	.27 (±.31)	.13 (±.25)	.10	80
OCASP	-.02 (±.10)	.07 (±.33)	.10 (±.26)	.02	80
EDEXP	.07 (±.29)	.34 (±.29)	.11 (±.23)	.21	80
EDASP	.19 (±.31)	.10 (±.32)	.06 (±.25)	.09	80
IQ	-.17 (±.29)	.47 (±.30)	.11 (±.23)	.18	80
GPA	.01 (±.26)	.35 (±.30)	.10 (±.24)	.17	80

NOTE: Item identifications are: OCEXP = son's occupational expectation, OCASP = son's occupational aspiration, EDEXP = son's educational expectation, EDASP = son's educational aspiration, IQ = son's IQ score, GPA = son's grade point average in school.

presents the corresponding equations in observable regressions, the upper panel with parental reports as regressors, the lower panel with sons' reports as regressors. Since the sons' and parents' reports are apparently quite accurate we would expect few differences between the measurement model results and either set of regressions. The three sets of estimates are certainly not in perfect agreement, but the differences should be interpreted cautiously. Our sample is small, and there is collinearity among both observed regressors and unmeasured predetermined variables.

With regard to the fit of the equations, most of the R^2s for the measurement model are slightly larger than those for the parents' regressions, which, in turn, are slightly larger than those for the sons' regressions. That the measurement model fits the data better than the regressions do is, of course, to be expected, given that the measurement errors are primarily random. With regard to the parental status coefficients, those that are large in the measurement model are large in one or both sets of regressions. The converse does not hold, however, since a substantial or significant regression coefficient does not necessarily indicate that the corresponding coefficient in the measurement model will be substantial or significant. Thus, taking account of sons' and parents' reports jointly in the measurement model leads to conclusions not ascertainable by exclusive reliance on the regressions. The only exception to this observation is that, in both the regressions and the measurement model, father's occupational status has no effect on any of the endogenous variables.

In the measurement model, using the criterion that a coefficient must be greater than one-half its approximate 95% confidence interval, the notable coefficients are those in the equations for educational expectations and ability. With regard to the magnitudes of the coefficients, those for father's education are consistently largest, followed by those for mother's education, with the coefficients for father's occupational status typically negative or close to zero. By either criterion, father's education seems to be the most influential of the parental characteristics included here. Note, finally, that it is the education-related endogenous variables for which we obtain equations that fit best. This is consistent with the magnitudes of the parental education coefficients in comparison with those for father's occupational status.

To summarize, the model with unmeasured variables suggests that white twelfth-grade youths report father's and mother's education and father's occupation about as well as parents do, that most of the youths' measurement errors are random, and that using either the parents' reports or the sons' reports leads to slightly worse prediction of the endogenous variables in the achievement process, with some differences in which coefficients affect the endogenous variables. Since the measurement model is based, to some extent, on a weighting of the two sets of regressions, it is not surprising that, in general, there is no systematic downward or upward bias in the coefficients of the observed status reports, as compared with the coefficients of the unobserved status characteristics. However, sole reliance on the two sets of regressions, taken singly or together, will lead to conclusions not supported by the measurement model. Father's education is more important than mother's education in the measurement model, and father's occupational status apparently has no independent effect.

Twelfth-Grade Blacks

Measurement error structure.   Our sample of black twelfth-grade youths and their parents poses an analytic challenge. Estimating Model II, which does not allow for correlated measurement errors, leads to coefficients for FAFED, SOMED, and SOFOC that are equal to one. Moreover, this estimated structure poorly reproduces the sample correlations. This indicates that, for these data, the iteration procedure attempts to converge to solutions for these coefficients which are, in fact, greater than one. Such results are substantively implausible. Taken at face value, they state that sons' reports of fathers' occupation and mothers' education are more accurate than fathers' and mothers' reports and, indeed, that sons' reports are perfect. Although such values can occur, owing to sampling variability, they do not represent a stopping point for the analysis. It is unlikely that sons' reports of parental status are more accurate than those of their parents for any status characteristic, and it is unlikely that sons' reports of parental status are perfect. Moreover, it is curious that, in these data, fathers' reports of education are also estimated to be perfect.

In this situation, one option to explore is the possibility of the existence of correlated measurement errors and correlations between measurement errors and the stochastic disturbances of the endogenous variables. However, allowing for these disturbance correlations does not lead to substantively plausible solutions in these data. Indeed, we are unable to obtain any estimates whatsoever for Model V in these data. Thus, we exhausted the alternatives open to us with respect to estimating models that contain either free parameters or those specified to be zero on a priori grounds, and we still did not arrive at a satisfactory conclusion.

If the results thus far discussed for the black twelfth-grade sample have an empirical implication, it is that sons' reports are at least as accurate as parents'. This suggests specification of a model in which sons' and parents' coefficients are constrained to be equal, and in which correlated measurement errors are allowed, as well as correlations between the disturbances of the endogenous variables and the measurement errors. Estimating this variant of Model V leads to coefficients with admissible values that fit the data well by conventional standards ($p = .80$). Since most of the correlations involving the disturbances of the endogenous variables and the measurement errors are small, do not have substantively interpretable signs, and are less than one-half of their confidence intervals, we have reestimated this model, allowing only those correlated disturbances that are substantively and statistically significant. In this specialization of Model V, the fit to the data deteriorates but is still acceptable (chi-square = 40.0, degrees of freedom = 32, $p = .17$). Tables 15.9 and 15.10 present the estimated structure coefficients and factor correlations under this specification.

As the lower half of Table 15.9 shows, the correlations between the observed status reports and the underlying status characteristics are all

TABLE 15.9

Estimated Coefficients of a Model Linking Observed Variables to Three Unmeasured Family Status Factors: Black Twelfth Grade Youths

| Dependent Variable | Coefficients (and Approximate 95% Confidence Intervals) of | | | R^2 |
	TRFOC	TRFED	TRMED	
OCEXP	.17 (±.41)	-.13 (±.41)	-.05 (±.38)	.03
OCASP	.24 (±.39)	.15 (±.40)	-.22 (±.37)	.13
EDEXP	.34 (±.39)	.03 (±.39)	.07 (±.38)	.00
EDASP	.35 (±.38)	.22 (±.39)	-.05 (±.37)	.05
IQ	.18 (±.41)	-.15 (±.41)	.10 (±.38)	.04
GPA	.04 (±.41)	-.06 (±.41)	.17 (±.38)	.03
FAFOC	.89[a] (±.15)			.79
SOFOC	.89 (±.15)			.79
FAFED		.89 (±.15)		.79
SOFED		.89 (±.15)		.79
MOMED			.89 (±.15)	.79
SOMED			.89 (±.15)	.79

NOTE: Item identifications are: OCEXP = son's occupational expectation, OCASP = son's occupational aspiration, EDEXP = son's educational expectation, EDASP = son's educational aspiration, IQ = son's IQ score, GPA = son's grade point average in school, FAFOC = father's report of his occupation, SOFOC = son's report of father's occupation, FAFED = father's report of his education, SOFED = son's report of father's education, MOMED = mother's report of her education, SOMED = son's report of mother's education, TRFOC = "true" father's occupation, TRFED = "true" father's education, TRMED = "true" mother's education.

[a] Estimation procedure embodies the constraint that the coefficients for all observed parental status characteristics are equal.

equal to .89. This value is somewhat lower than an average of the corresponding values for families of white twelfth-grade youths but is still large. This result is consistent with the findings of other analyses that use other procedures (e.g., Borus and Nestel, 1973).

Table 15.10 gives the estimates of the correlations among the unmeasured status characteristics. Compared to the values for the families of white twelfth-grade youths, these correlations are low. This is not surprising, given the pervasive finding (e.g., Duncan, 1968b) that statuses are less crystallized for blacks than for whites.

There are disturbance correlations between son's report of mother's education and son's report of educational expectation (.48 ± .38), and between son's report of mother's education and educational aspiration (.54 ± .38). It is striking that these correlations involve education, and son's report of *mother's* education, rather than father's education. These results are compatible with speculations about the relatively more important roles imputed to black mothers, but we lack information internal to our own data sufficient to interpret these results beyond the general arguments advanced earlier about the meaning of correlated errors.

TABLE 15.10

Estimates of Correlations Among Three Unmeasured Family Status Factors: Black Twelfth Grade Youths

	Variable[a]	
Variable	TRFOC	TRFED
TRFED	.35 (±.36)	
TRMED	.10 (±.40)	.18 (±.39)

NOTE: Item identifications are: TRFOC = father's occupation factor, TRFED = father's education factor, TRMED = mother's education factor.

[a]Numbers in parentheses are approximate 95% confidence intervals.

Achievement process.   The upper half of Table 15.9 presents the measurement model equations for the effects of the unmeasured parental status variables on aspirations, expectations, grades, and ability. Table 15.11 presents the corresponding regressions, the upper panel with parental reports as regressors, the lower panel with sons' reports as regressors. No regression coefficient is greater than one-half its confidence interval, as is

TABLE 15.11

Multiple Regressions of Achievement Variables on Parents' and Sons' Reports of Family Status Variables: Black Twelfth Grade Youths

Dependent Variable	Standardized Regression Coefficients (and 95% Confidence Intervals) of			R^2	N
	Father's Occupation	Father's Education	Mother's Education		
	Parental Reports				
OCEXP	.21 ($\pm$.41)	-.13 ($\pm$.41)	-.03 ($\pm$.40)	.05	30
OCASP	.24 ($\pm$.39)	.20 ($\pm$.39)	-.16 ($\pm$.38)	.12	30
EDEXP	.21 ($\pm$.40)	.03 ($\pm$.40)	.14 ($\pm$.39)	.08	30
EDASP	.08 ($\pm$.40)	.20 ($\pm$.41)	.06 ($\pm$.40)	.06	30
IQ	.07 ($\pm$.41)	-.13 ($\pm$.41)	.11 ($\pm$.40)	.02	30
GPA	.05 ($\pm$.41)	-.03 ($\pm$.41)	.17 ($\pm$.40)	.03	30
	Sons' Reports				
OCEXP	.05 ($\pm$.42)	-.07 ($\pm$.43)	-.08 ($\pm$.40)	.01	30
OCASP	.19 ($\pm$.40)	.08 ($\pm$.41)	-.24 ($\pm$.38)	.10	30
EDEXP	.14 ($\pm$.41)	-.02 ($\pm$.41)	.24 ($\pm$.39)	.08	30
EDASP	.29 ($\pm$.39)	.12 ($\pm$.39)	.14 ($\pm$.37)	.15	30
IQ	.22 ($\pm$.41)	-.12 ($\pm$.42)	.07 ($\pm$.39)	.05	30
GPA	.00 ($\pm$.42)	-.07 ($\pm$.42)	.14 ($\pm$.40)	.02	30

NOTE: Item identifications are: OCEXP = son's occupational expectation, OCASP = son's occupational aspiration, EDEXP = son's educational expectation, EDASP = son's educational aspiration, IQ = son's IQ score, GPA = son's grade point average in school.

also the case in the measurement model (upper half of Table 15.9). In both the measurement model and in the regressions, the degree of fit is typically low. In both the measurement model and in the regressions, the coefficients for mother's and father's education are small, and many have negative signs, which are substantively implausible. In contrast, the coefficients for father's occupational status are consistently positive and typically the largest.

Comparing the measurement model results for twelfth-grade whites with those for twelfth-grade blacks, it is evident that the effects of status are different for the two groups. As we have already seen, it appears that, for whites, father's and mother's education have some effect on the endogenous variables used here, but father's occupational status does not, although interpretation must be guarded, because of the small sample size. Precisely the opposite is found for blacks, with father's occupational status appearing to be the only status variable whose coefficients are positive and, therefore, interpretable. In addition, however tenuous the linkages between parental status and sons' performance in school, ability, and occupational and educational aspirations and expectations, they are stronger for whites than for blacks. This finding is consistent with the lesser predictability of adult black males' attainment from their fathers' statuses, as compared to whites (Duncan, 1968b).

To summarize, black twelfth-grade youths appear to report parental statuses as accurately as their parents do. Of the parental status characteristics used here, only father's occupational status has consistently positive coefficients for the endogenous variables in the achievement process. These endogenous variables are largely independent of socioeconomic background.

Ninth-Grade Whites

Measurement error structure. Tables 15.12 and 15.13 present the estimates for Model II, for white ninth-grade youths. This model posits random errors in the parental status reports and fits the data well (chi-square = 25.5, degrees of freedom = 24, p = .38).

White ninth-grade youths appear to report parental statuses at least as accurately as their parents do. As may be seen in the lower portion of Table 15.12, the correlations between sons' reports and the unmeasured constructs are slightly larger than those for parents' reports. Constraining the parent and son coefficients to be equal for each status characteristic gives a virtually identical fit to the data, and the chi-square for testing the difference in fit between Model II and its constrained version strongly supports the conclusion of no difference. Further exploration to determine whether there are nonrandom reporting errors supports the conclusion that Model II is an appropriate stopping point for white ninth-grade youths. Finally, although the correlations between reports of father's education and the underlying construct are lower than the corresponding correlations for the other constructs, the differences are negligible, not statistically significant using the chi-square testing procedure, and demand no interpretation.

Table 15.13 gives the correlations between the unmeasured status characteristics. Given that the data fit a random measurement error model,

TABLE 15.12

Estimated Coefficients of a Model Linking Observed Variables to Three Unmeasured Family Status Factors: White Ninth Grade Youths

Dependent Variable	Coefficients (and Approximate 95% Confidence Intervals) of			R^2
	TRFOC	TRFED	TRMED	
OCEXP	.14 (±.32)	.44 (±.40)	-.06 (±.29)	.27
OCASP	.02 (±.34)	.35 (±.43)	.08 (±.30)	.18
EDEXP	.19 (±.29)	.34 (±.37)	.18 (±.26)	.40
EDASP	.21 (±.30)	.31 (±.37)	.18 (±.26)	.38
IQ	.19 (±.33)	.31 (±.41)	.01 (±.29)	.24
GPA	.29 (±.30)	.33 (±.37)	.09 (±.26)	.40
FAFOC	.95 (±.17)			.90
SOFOC	.96 (±.17)			.93
FAFED		.89 (±.18)		.80
SOFED		.92 (±.18)		.85
MOMED			.94 (±.18)	.87
SOMED			.96 (±.17)	.93

NOTE: Item identifications are: OCEXP = son's occupational expectation, OCASP = son's occupational aspiration, EDEXP = son's educational expectation, EDASP = son's educational aspiration, IQ = son's IQ score, GPA = son's grade point average in school, FAFOC = father's report of his occupation, SOFOC = son's report of father's occupation, FAFED = father's report of his education, SOFED = son's report of father's education, MOMED = mother's report of her education, SOMED = son's report of mother's education, TRFOC = "true" father's occupation, TRFED = "true" father's education, TRMED = "true" mother's education.

TABLE 15.13

Estimates of Correlations Among Three Unmeasured Family Status Factors: White Ninth Grade Youths

	Variable[a]	
Variable	TRFOC	TRFED
TRFED	.75 ($\pm$.12)	
TRMED	.50 ($\pm$.18)	.67 ($\pm$.14)

NOTE: Item identifications are: TRFOC = father's occupation factor, TRFED = father's education factor, TRMED = mother's education factor.

[a]Numbers in parentheses are approximate 95% confidence intervals.

these correlations must be larger than any of the corresponding sample correlations among observed variables. Bearing in mind that the standard errors of these correlations are large, comparison of these results with those for the twelfth-grade samples nonetheless suggests that the factor correlations observed here are of the same magnitude as those observed for families of white twelfth-grade youths (Table 15.7), but larger than those observed for families of black twelfth-grade youths (Table 15.10).

Achievement process. The upper half of Table 15.12 presents the measurement model equations for the effects of the unmeasured parental status variables on aspirations, expectations, grades, and ability. Table 15.14 presents the corresponding regressions, the upper panel with parental reports as regressors, the lower panel with sons' reports as regressors. The two sets of regressions yield different conclusions, although there are some similarities, inasmuch as father's occupational status and education are more likely than mother's education to affect the endogenous variables, and the fits of the two sets of regressions covary over equations. In the measurement model, the fits for the equations for the endogenous variables are larger than any seen thus far and, on the whole, are largest for the education-related variables and ability, as is also true for twelfth-grade

TABLE 15.14

Multiple Regressions of Achievement Variables on Parents' and Sons' Reports of Family Status Variables: White Ninth Grade Youths

Dependent Variable	Standardized Regression Coefficients (and 95% Confidence Intervals) of			R^2	N
	Father's Occupation	Father's Education	Mother's Education		
	Parental Reports				
OCEXP	.19 (±.27)	.26 (±.30)	.08 (±.25)	.22	80
OCASP	.11 (±.28)	.18 (±.31)	.19 (±.26)	.16	80
EDEXP	.23 (±.24)	.26 (±.27)	.23 (±.22)	.37	80
EDASP	.28 (±.25)	.21 (±.27)	.23 (±.23)	.35	80
IQ	.19 (±.27)	.29 (±.30)	.06 (±.25)	.23	80
GPA	.38 (±.24)	.16 (±.27)	.17 (±.22)	.38	80
	Sons' Reports				
OCEXP	.22 (±.27)	.37 (±.30)	-.04 (±.25)	.26	80
OCASP	.06 (±.28)	.31 (±.32)	.07 (±.27)	.16	80
EDEXP	.25 (±.24)	.27 (±.27)	.20 (±.23)	.38	80
EDASP	.24 (±.25)	.27 (±.28)	.30 (±.23)	.36	80
IQ	.26 (±.28)	.20 (±.31)	.06 (±.26)	.21	80
GPA	.27 (±.24)	.32 (±.27)	.10 (±.23)	.37	80

NOTE: Item identifications are: OCEXP = son's occupational expectation, OCASP = son's occupational aspiration, EDEXP = son's educational expectation, EDASP = son's educational aspiration, IQ = son's IQ score, GPA = son's grade point average in school.

whites. All of the coefficients are bounded by confidence intervals that include zero, but this precludes neither further description nor, ultimately, circumspect interpretation. The coefficients for father's education are consistently the largest, as has also been found for twelfth-grade whites, but the coefficients for father's occupational status are typically next largest, instead of mother's education. Whether this minor change in the average rank ordering of the coefficients from that found for twelfth-grade whites warrants interpretation is unclear.

To summarize, white ninth-grade youths are accurate reporters of parental status. The errors in their reports are random. Their expectations, aspirations, grades, and ability depend more heavily on parental status than has been found for twelfth graders. Father's occupational status and education are more likely than mother's education to contribute to variation in the endogenous variables, with father's education having the largest standardized coefficients.

Ninth-Grade Blacks

Measurement error structure. For ninth-grade blacks, estimation of Model V, or any simplification of it, leads to substantively implausible inferences. For example, allowing no correlated disturbances (Model II) results in sons' reports being estimated as the true parental status scores. Allowing correlated disturbances (Model V), we find that fathers' reports of occupational status are estimated to be true scores, that mother's report of her education is more accurate than son's report, and that son's report of father's education is quite inaccurate ($\hat{\lambda} = .6$) but is, nonetheless, estimated to be more accurate than father's report. However, allowing correlated disturbances, we do obtain a good fit to the sample correlations. By the goodness-of-fit criterion, in these data, Model V is distinctly preferable to any simpler model. Thus, the results of our preliminary analyses of measurement models for black ninth-grade youths indicate that, to obtain a satisfactory fit of the data, it is necessary to allow correlated disturbances, and that some variant of Model V is most appropriate. The initial investigations also indicate that, for at least two of the parental status characteristics, black ninth-grade youths provide reports far less accurate than those of their parents. Hypothesizing the contrary, and constraining the pair of coefficients for each status construct to be equal, gives an unsatisfactory fit of the data.

There is no good substantive reason to believe that fathers' reports of their education are any less accurate than their occupational reports, or less accurate than mothers' reports of their own education, despite the estimates of Model V. Indeed, the results already presented here for the families of twelfth-grade youths and white ninth-grade youths are consistent with the hypothesis that parents report the three status characteristics equally well. This suggests that we constrain the parental reports of the three status characteristics to be identically dependent on the underlying constructs or, in some way, use externally derived information. We prefer the expedient of fixing all of the coefficients for parental reports at .9. This value is based on a rounding of the results for the families of black twelfth-grade youths and is quite reasonable. Applying this constraint provides a good fit to the data for black ninth-grade youths. Moreover, many of the correlated disturbances are estimated to be small and have confidence intervals that include zero. When we eliminate these correlated disturbances from the specification and reestimate the constrained version of Model V, the fit of the model to the data deteriorates but is still satisfactory (chi-square = 19.8, degrees of freedom = 27, and p = .84). We present the estimates under this specification in Tables 15.15 and 15.16.

The coefficients in the lower half of Table 15.15 show black ninth-grade youths to be uniformly poor informants of their parents' status characteristics, with no validity coefficient as large as .4. In addition, the errors in sons' reports are nonrandom. There is a correlation between the errors of sons' reports of mother's and father's education (.29 ± .23) and between the errors of sons' reports of father's education and occupation (.39 ± .23), and there is a correlation between the errors in sons' reports of mother's education and the stochastic disturbance of son's occupational expectation (.25 ± .21). Table 15.16 presents the correlations among the unmeasured status characteristics. These values are small and of roughly the same magnitude as those for the families of black twelfth-grade youths.

Black ninth-grade youths' reports of parental statuses are, then, much less accurate than black twelfth-grade youths', and their errors are distinctly less random. It is unlikely that this is entirely the result of a change in extensiveness of knowledge about parental status between the ninth and twelfth grades. Such a change was not observed for the white youths in our sample, nor can the result be explained by respondents' lack of cooperation, since a review of data collection revealed nothing untoward about this group of students. The matter needs to be pursued with a larger sample.

Achievement process. The upper half of Table 15.15 presents the measurement model equations for the effects of the unmeasured parental status variables on aspirations, expectations, grades, and ability. Table 15.17 presents the corresponding regressions, the upper panel with parental reports as regressors, the lower panel with sons' reports as regressors. In the measurement model and in the regressions, the endogenous achievement variables are independent of parental status. The coefficients for father's and mother's education are frequently negative and, thus, not interpretable. The coefficients for father's occupational status are consistently positive in the measurement model and are typically larger than those for the other parental characteristics. None of the coefficients in the measurement model is significant at the 5% level, and only one of the regression coefficients is significant at that level. On the whole, the pattern observed for the coefficients in the measurement model is consistent with that for twelfth-grade blacks, as is the lack of predictive power for these equations.

To summarize, the measurement model estimates for black ninth-grade youths are not especially plausible. Nonetheless, they are substantively the most reasonable that we could obtain for this group. To enhance the substantive realism with which the data were fit, we fixed the parents'

TABLE 15.15

Estimated Coefficients of a Model Linking Observed Variables to Three Unmeasured Family Status Factors: Black Ninth Grade Youths

| Dependent Variable | Coefficients (and Approximate 95% Confidence Intervals) of | | | R^2 |
	TRFOC	TRFED	TRMED	
OCEXP	.19 (±.31)	.16 (±.32)	−.20 (±.32)	.11
OCASP	.41 (±.31)	−.02 (±.32)	.04 (±.32)	.17
EDEXP	.19 (±.32)	.20 (±.33)	−.17 (±.33)	.09
EDASP	.17 (±.32)	.26 (±.33)	−.17 (±.33)	.11
IQ	.11 (±.33)	−.03 (±.34)	.12 (±.34)	.03
GPA	.24 (±.32)	−.04 (±.34)	−.06 (±.33)	.05
FAFOC	.90[a]			.81
SOFOC	.39 (±.26)			.15
FAFED		.90		.81
SOFED		.36 (±.25)		.13
MOMED			.90	.81
SOMED			.34 (±.28)	.12

NOTE: Item identifications are: OCEXP = son's occupational expectation, OCASP = son's occupational aspiration, EDEXP = son's educational expectation, EDASP = son's educational aspiration, IQ = son's IQ score, GPA = son's grade point average in school, FAFOC = father's report of his occupation, SOFOC = son's report of father's occupation, FAFED = father's report of his education, SOFED = son's report of father's education, MOMED = mother's report of her education, SOMED = son's report of mother's education, TRFOC = "true" father's occupation, TRFED = "true" father's education, TRMED = "true" mother's education.

[a]Estimation procedure embodies the constraint that the coefficients for parents' reports of all three status characteristics are fixed at .9.

validity coefficients at .9. This did not produce estimates of uniformly low validities for sons' reports of parental statuses, since these estimates were low in the absence of constraints on the parental coefficients. Independently of those constraints, sons' reporting errors are nonrandom, and the

TABLE 15.16

Estimates of Correlations Among Three Unmeasured Family Status Factors: Black Ninth Grade Youths

	Variable[a]	
Variable	TRFOC	TRFED
TRFED	.28 (±.31)	
TRMED	.25 (±.32)	.34 (±.30)

NOTE: Item identifications are: TRFOC = father's occupation factor, TRFED = father's education factor, TRMED = mother's education factor.

[a]Numbers in parentheses are approximate 95% confidence intervals.

aspirations, expectations, grades, and abilities of black ninth-grade youths are independent of estimated true parental statuses.

Sixth-Grade Whites

Measurement error structure. Model II, which allows for no correlated disturbances, fits the data for the sixth-grade whites poorly. Exploration with more complex models yields the conclusion that a satisfactory fit to the data can be obtained by restricting Model III to a single correlation between disturbances, involving the errors of sons' reports of fathers' and mothers' education (chi-square = 30.1, degrees of freedom = 23, p = .15). The estimates of the structural coefficients and the factor correlations for this specialization of Model III are presented in Tables 15.18 and 15.19.

The lower portion of Table 15.18 gives the correlations between the observed status reports and the underlying status constructs. The coefficients for parents' reports are .9 or slightly higher. This is a little lower than was found for parents' reports of white ninth and twelfth graders. The boys' coefficients are lower than the parents', as is to be expected, although

TABLE 15.17

Multiple Regressions of Achievement Variables on Parents' and Sons' Reports of Family Status Variables: Black Ninth Grade Youths

Dependent Variable	Standardized Regression Coefficients (and 95% Confidence Intervals) of			R^2	N
	Father's Occupation	Father's Education	Mother's Education		
	Parental Reports				
OCEXP	.21 (±.30)	.13 (±.30)	-.17 (±.30)	.08	50
OCASP	.38 (±.29)	-.01 (±.29)	.03 (±.29)	.15	50
EDEXP	.18 (±.30)	.17 (±.30)	-.15 (±.30)	.07	50
EDASP	.17 (±.30)	.21 (±.30)	-.13 (±.30)	.08	50
IQ	.12 (±.30)	-.02 (±.31)	.10 (±.31)	.03	50
GPA	.20 (±.30)	-.01 (±.31)	-.07 (±.31)	.04	50
	Sons' Reports				
OCEXP	.12 (±.32)	-.11 (±.34)	.25 (±.31)	.07	50
OCASP	.01 (±.33)	.06 (±.34)	.20 (±.31)	.05	50
EDEXP	.01 (±.32)	.11 (±.34)	.16 (±.31)	.05	50
EDASP	-.04 (±.33)	.23 (±.34)	.04 (±.31)	.05	50
IQ	-.15 (±.33)	.01 (±.35)	.04 (±.32)	.02	50
GPA	.12 (±.33)	-.13 (±.34)	.12 (±.31)	.03	50

NOTE: Item identifications are: OCEXP = son's occupational expectation, OCASP = son's occupational aspiration, EDEXP = son's educational expectation, EDASP = son's educational aspiration, IQ = son's IQ score, GPA = son's grade point average in school.

the differences are not great. The difference in fit to the data produced by constraining the son and parent coefficients to be equal, separately for each status characteristic, is significant at the $p = .10$ level, which, given the small sample size, supports the conclusion that the boys' reports are less accurate than the parents'. Turning next to comparisons among the children's coefficients, it appears that white sixth-grade boys least accurately report mother's education and most accurately report father's occupation. Although these differences are not statistically significant, this pattern is nonetheless unsurprising since, within the family, father's occupation is more salient and more likely to be talked about than father's or mother's education.

TABLE 15.18
Estimated Coefficients of a Model Linking Observed Variables to Three Unmeasured Family Status Factors: White Sixth Grade Boys

Dependent Variable	Coefficients (and Approximate 95% Confidence Intervals) of			R^2
	TRFOC	TRFED	TRMED	
OCEXP	.30 (±.38)	.01 (±.49)	.18 (±.42)	.21
OCASP	.15 (±.40)	-.12 (±.52)	.29 (±.45)	.10
EDEXP	-.19 (±.39)	.49 (±.49)	.22 (±.41)	.30
EDASP	-.22 (±.38)	.68 (±.51)	.04 (±.41)	.31
IQ	.04 (±.36)	.15 (±.47)	.39 (±.41)	.31
GPA	.05 (±.36)	.58 (±.49)	-.07 (±.40)	.32
FAFOC	.93 (±.18)			.86
SOFOC	.86 (±.18)			.74
FAFED		.91 (±.18)		.83
SOFED		.79 (±.19)		.62
MOMED			.93 (±.18)	.86
SOMED			.75 (±.20)	.56

NOTE: Item identifications are: OCEXP = son's occupational expectation, OCASP = son's occupational aspiration, EDEXP = son's educational expectation, EDASP = son's educational aspiration, IQ = son's IQ score, GPA = son's grade point average in school, FAFOC = father's report of his occupation, SOFOC = son's report of father's occupation, FAFED = father's report of his education, SOFED = son's report of father's education, MOMED = mother's report of her education, SOMED = son's report of mother's education, TRFOC = "true" father's occupation, TRFED = "true" father's education, TRMED = "true" mother's education.

The disturbances of sons' reports of fathers' and mothers' education are correlated (.51 ± .19). Interpreting these disturbances as errors in sons' reports, we argued earlier that such correlated errors are likely to be consequences of lack of knowledge about a particular status characteristic, combined with an admittedly hypothesized children's willingness to hazard a guess on the basis of their perceptions of another status characteristic. Of the three white samples, we have found such a correlation only for the sixth-grade boys, which is consistent with and supports our interpretation of this correlation in terms of the children's lack of knowledge.

Finally, before turning to the achievement process coefficients, note that the estimated correlations for the "error-free" parental status characteristics (Table 15.19) do not differ materially from those for the families of ninth- and twelfth-grade whites.

Achievement process. The measurement model coefficients for the achievement process are presented in the upper half of Table 15.18, and the corresponding regression coefficients are presented in Table 15.20. As may corresponding coefficient in the regressions based on parents' reports. The

TABLE 15.19

Estimates of Correlations Among Three Unmeasured Family Status Factors: White Sixth Grade Boys

Variable	Variable[a]	
	TRFOC	TRFED
TRFED	.77 (±.13)	
TRMED	.69 (±.15)	.80 (±.12)

NOTE: Item identifications are: TRFOC = father's occupation factor, TRFED = father's education factor, TRMED = mother's education factor.

[a]Numbers in parentheses are approximate 95% confidence intervals.

be seen in Table 15.20, the regressions that use parents' reports of their statuses yield conclusions different from the regressions that use sons' reports, although there is some overlap. There is a significant regression coefficient for occupational expectations on father's occupation, for the regressions based on sons' reports, and a much smaller and insignificant

TABLE 15.20

Multiple Regressions of Achievement Variables on Parents' and Sons' Reports of Family Status Variables: White Sixth Grade Boys

Dependent Variable	Standardized Regression Coefficients (and 95% Confidence Intervals) of			R^2	N
	Father's Occupation	Father's Education	Mother's Education		
	Parental Reports				
OCEXP	.20 (±.28)	.10 (±.31)	.18 (±.31)	.18	80
OCASP	.10 (±.30)	-.03 (±.32)	.26 (±.33)	.09	80
EDEXP	-.01 (±.29)	.30 (±.30)	.23 (±.30)	.24	80
EDASP	-.02 (±.27)	.33 (±.30)	.20 (±.30)	.23	80
IQ	.04 (±.26)	.27 (±.29)	.28 (±.29)	.29	80
GPA	.16 (±.26)	.42 (±.29)	.01 (±.31)	.29	80
	Sons' Reports				
OCEXP	.38 (±.24)	.02 (±.29)	.10 (±.27)	.19	80
OCASP	.21 (±.26)	-.01 (±.36)	.08 (±.29)	.06	80
EDEXP	.03 (±.23)	.32 (±.28)	.21 (±.26)	.24	80
EDASP	.03 (±.24)	.47 (±.29)	-.06 (±.26)	.21	80
IQ	.31 (±.24)	.06 (±.29)	.27 (±.27)	.19	80
GPA	.21 (±.24)	.26 (±.29)	.03 (±.27)	.18	80

NOTE: Item identifications are: OCEXP = son's occupational expectation, OCASP = son's occupational aspiration, EDEXP = son's educational expectation, EDASP = son's educational aspiration, IQ = son's IQ score, GPA = son's grade point average in school.

contrast between these two regression coefficients suggests that, in the measurement model, there should be a correlation between the disturbances of sons' reports of father's occupation and the disturbances of sons' occupational aspirations. Allowing for this correlation in our initial exploration of the data, however, yielded a small, insignificant value (.20 ± .24), and that particular disturbance correlation has, thus, been constrained to be zero in the model of Tables 15.18 and 15.19. Further pursuit of the matter requires a larger sample.

Turning next to the measurement model coefficients (Table 15.18), the largest and most consistently positive coefficients are for father's education, then for mother's education; those for father's occupational status are most often negative and small. We observed the same pattern for white twelfth-grade youths, but not for white ninth-grade youths. Consistent with the pattern of regression coefficients observed here, the fit of the equations for the endogenous variables is impressive, except for occupational expectations and aspirations. This replicates the results observed for white youths in the ninth and twelfth grades. Although the explanation of these patterns is unclear, it must be sufficiently general to apply to both white twelfth-grade youths and white sixth-grade boys.

To summarize, white sixth-grade boys do not provide reports of parental statuses as accurate as those of white youths in higher grades. There is a single correlation between reporting errors in sons' reports of fathers' and mothers' education, and this correlation is substantively plausible. The schooling-related endogenous variables and ability are more dependent on parental status than are occupational aspirations and expectations, and this is consistent with the typically larger coefficients of father's and mother's education relative to those of father's occupation.

Sixth-Grade Blacks

Measurement error structure.   None of the Models II–V, nor any specialization or variant of these models discussed thus far, will fit the data for sixth-grade blacks. Extensive analysis of these data suggests that they cannot be fit by a model which assumes three factors for parental status characteristics, and that a single socioeconomic status factor will fit the data. This is substantively implausible and is, moreover, unprecedented in the analyses for the other subsamples we have studied. An additional difficulty with the estimates provided by Models II–V, and others as well, is that the coefficients for parents' reports are quite low and are not much larger than those for children's reports. This is also implausible. These data give the general impression that attempts to obtain substantively meaningful results in one portion of the model, by use of prior constraints on the coefficients in Λ and Φ, succeed for that part of the model but force anomalous estimates to appear in other parts of the model. In view of this conclusion, it seems appropriate to remove forcibly anomalies from those portions of the model dealing with the accuracy of parents' reports and the correlations among the status characteristics factors, by setting these coefficients to preassigned values rather than estimating them. The rationale for this strategy is that, whatever the source of the problems with these data, it is least likely to lie in the parental reports and most likely to lie in the boys' reports of parental characteristics. Thus, we assume reasonable values for the parents' validity coefficients and the correlations among the status characteristics and then consider the consequences of these assumptions for the rest of the model.

To estimate the model presented here, the coefficients linking parental reports to the parental status factors are set at .9, a value used in the estimation of the model for ninth-grade blacks and based on the results for twelfth-grade blacks. The values selected for the factor correlations (see Table 15.22) are derived from estimates obtained from various earlier attempts to model these data. The correlations are a little larger than those we have seen for the families of ninth- and twelfth-grade blacks, but their relative magnitudes are roughly the same. Correlations smaller than these will lead to a somewhat worse fit of the data but will not materially change the values of the remaining parameters. Upon supplying the various preassigned values to the model and carrying out the estimation procedure, we find two significant correlations among sons' reporting errors and two significant correlations between the errors in sons' reports and the disturbances of the endogenous variables. Upon reestimating this specially constrained version of Model V, we obtain the best fit to the data with the most plausible substantive results (chi-square = 38.0, degrees of freedom = 29, p = .12). Tables 15.21, 15.22, and 15.23 present the fixed and estimated coefficients of the final model.

The lower portion of Table 15.21 presents the coefficients linking sons' and parents' reports to the underlying status characteristics. The accuracy with which sons report parental statuses is far less than the presumed accuracy with which parents' report their own statuses, with sons' reports of mothers' education being reported least accurately. A similar result was found for the accuracy with which white sixth-grade boys report mother's education, although, for that group, the contrast in accuracy between reports for mother's education and the other status characteristics is much less accentuated. The reports of black sixth-grade boys are also at least as accurate as those of black ninth-grade youths. The data for whites suggest that considerable learning occurs between the sixth and ninth grades, and we would expect this to be true for blacks as well.. That our results for blacks are not consistent with this expectation strengthens our belief that the low accuracy indicated for black ninth-grade youths cannot all be due to sheer ignorance of parental statuses.

Table 15.23 presents the estimates of the disturbance correlations. All of these correlations involve sons' reports of mother's education. The existence of the correlated reporting errors is consistent with the hypothesis that younger children will rely on their perceptions of one status characteristic in responding to questionnaire items concerning another status

TABLE 15.21

Estimated Coefficients of a Model Linking Observed Variables to Three Unmeasured Family Status Factors: Black Sixth Grade Boys

Dependent Variable	Coefficients (and Approximate 95% Confidence Intervals) of			R^2
	TRFOC	TRFED	TRMED	
OCEXP	.26 (±.37)	-.01 (±.41)	-.08 (±.34)	.06
OCASP	.23 (±.37)	.11 (±.40)	-.11 (±.34)	.08
EDEXP	.03 (±.37)	.17 (±.40)	-.04 (±.34)	.03
EDASP	-.09 (±.37)	.20 (±.40)	.03 (±.35)	.01
IQ	.18 (±.37)	.22 (±.39)	.00 (±.33)	.14
GPA	.00 (±.38)	.14 (±.42)	-.07 (±.35)	.01
FAFOC	.90[a]			.81
SOFOC	.45 (±.26)			.20
FAFED		.90		.81
SOFED		.44 (±.23)		.19
MOMED			.90	.81
SOMED			.18 (±.23)	.03

NOTE: Item identifications are: OCEXP = son's occupational expectation, OCASP = son's occupational aspiration, EDEXP = son's educational expectation, EDASP = son's educational aspiration, IQ = son's IQ score, GPA = son's grade point average in school, FAFOC = father's report of his occupation, SOFOC = son's report of father's occupation, FAFED = father's report of his education, SOFED = son's report of father's education, MOMED = mother's report of her education, SOMED = son's report of mother's education, TRFOC = "true" father's occupation, TRFED = "true" father's education, TRMED = "true" mother's education.

[a] Estimation procedure embodies the constraint that the coefficients for parents' reports of all three status characteristics are fixed at .9.

characteristic. The correlated disturbances involving the errors in sons' reports of mothers' education and the disturbances for educational aspirations and expectations are also interpretable in terms of the process described earlier, involving a presumed desire for consistency between

TABLE 15.22

Preassigned Correlations Among Three Unmeasured Family Status Factors: Black Sixth Grade Boys

| Variable | Variable | |
	TRFOC	TRFED
TRFED	.53	
TRMED	.24	.41

NOTE: Item identifications are: TRFOC = father's occupation factor, TRFED = father's education factor, TRMED = mother's education factor.

aspirations and children's reports of parental statuses. In this connection, it is worth noting that the average for black sixth-grade boys' reports of mother's education is higher than the average for mothers' reports of their own education, and that the average levels of educational aspirations and expectations are much higher than this. It may well be that the greater a boy's educational aspiration and expectation, the more likely he is to upgrade his report of mother's educational attainment.

Achievement process. Table 15.21 presents the measurement model coefficients for the endogenous variables in the achievement process treated as functions of parental status factors. Table 15.24 presents the corresponding regressions for sons' and parents' reports of parental status characteristics. These achievement process results are similar to those we have seen for black ninth- and twelfth-grade youths. They show that occupational and educational aspirations and expectations are largely independent of parental status. In the measurement model and in the regressions, the coefficients are typically small, often negative, and never statistically significant. In the measurement model, the coefficients for father's occupational status and education are typically larger than the coefficients for mother's education and more often positive. Finally, of all the endogenous variables, only scholastic ability appears to be a function of parental status.

To summarize, using a highly constrained model we find that black sixth-grade boys apparently give highly inaccurate reports of parental

TABLE 15.23

Estimates of Disturbance Correlations in the Measurement Model: Black Sixth Grade Boys

Variable	Variable[a]
	SOMED
EDEXP	.22 (±.20)
EDASP	.24 (±.19)
SOFOC	.29 (±.20)
SOFED	.60 (±.17)

NOTE: Item identifications are: EDEXP = son's educational expectation, EDASP = son's educational aspiration, SOFOC = son's report of father's occupation, SOFED = son's report of father's education, SOMED = son's report of mother's education.

[a]Numbers in parentheses are approximate 95% confidence intervals.

status characteristics. To a greater extent than for any other group, the errors in their reports are correlated. Their occupational and educational aspirations and expectations and their scholastic ability and performance in school are largely independent of their parents' education and their fathers' occupational status.

Summary: Error Structures

Variation in the error structures of children's and youths' reports of parental status is not additive with respect to grade and race. Thus, we

TABLE 15.24

*Multiple Regressions of Achievement Variables on Parents' and
Sons' Reports of Family Status Variables: Black Sixth Grade Boys*

Dependent Variable	Standardized Regression Coefficients (and 95% Confidence Intervals) of			R^2	N
	Father's Occupation	Father's Education	Mother's Education		
	Parental Reports				
OCEXP	.24 ($\pm$.35)	.01 ($\pm$.32)	-.07 ($\pm$.31)	.05	50
OCASP	.23 ($\pm$.35)	.10 ($\pm$.33)	-.07 ($\pm$.31)	.07	50
EDEXP	.03 ($\pm$.36)	.14 ($\pm$.34)	-.01 ($\pm$.31)	.02	50
EDASP	-.07 ($\pm$.36)	.16 ($\pm$.34)	.05 ($\pm$.32)	.02	50
IQ	.17 ($\pm$.34)	.24 ($\pm$.32)	.03 ($\pm$.30)	.13	50
GPA	-.00 ($\pm$.36)	.13 ($\pm$.34)	-.04 ($\pm$.31)	.02	50
	Sons' Reports				
OCEXP	-.03 ($\pm$.32)	.15 ($\pm$.37)	-.09 ($\pm$.38)	.01	50
OCASP	.03 ($\pm$.31)	.20 ($\pm$.37)	-.22 ($\pm$.38)	.05	50
EDEXP	.06 ($\pm$.31)	-.03 ($\pm$.36)	.27 ($\pm$.37)	.08	50
EDASP	.09 ($\pm$.30)	-.12 ($\pm$.36)	.31 ($\pm$.37)	.09	50
IQ	.20 ($\pm$.31)	.02 ($\pm$.37)	-.20 ($\pm$.38)	.05	50
GPA	.13 ($\pm$.31)	-.09 ($\pm$.36)	-.21 ($\pm$.37)	.07	50

NOTE: Item identifications are: OCEXP = son's occupational expectation, OCASP = son's occupational aspiration, EDEXP = son's educational expectation, EDASP = son's educational aspiration, IQ = son's IQ score, GPA = son's grade point average in school.

begin this summary by pulling together our results between grades, separately for whites and blacks, and then for each grade, comparing the error structures of whites and blacks.

Variation over grades in the error structures for whites. Looking first at the (validity) coefficients linking sons' reports to the factorially defined "true" status characteristics, by the time they have reached ninth grade, white youths have become highly accurate informants of the parental status characteristics under consideration here. Between ninth and twelfth grade, there is no variation in the accuracy of their reports. Sixth-grade boys, however, are distinctly less accurate informants of parental statuses. The reporting errors of sixth-grade boys are, moreover, nonrandom; there is a positive correlation between the disturbances (errors) of their reports of mothers' and fathers' education. The reporting errors of ninth-grade youths are random. For twelfth-grade youths, there is a single correlation involving the disturbances (errors) of son's report of father's occupation and son's occupational aspiration. Although these exceptions to random reporting errors are hardly massive, their pattern is, nonetheless, wholly compatible with the hypotheses presented earlier, justifying analysis of these data separately by grade.

Variation over grade in the error structures for blacks. The (validity) coefficients linking sons' reports to the factorially defined "true" status characteristics indicate that only in the twelfth grade do black youths report parental status as accurately as their parents. There is no variation in accuracy between the ninth and sixth grades. The youths and boys in these grades provided reports markedly less accurate than those provided by the twelfth-grade youths. The ninth and sixth graders have correlated reporting errors; the twelfth graders do not. For all grades considered here, there are correlations between errors in reports of some parental status characteristics, mother's education in particular, and the disturbances of some of the endogenous variables. Contrary to our expectations, these correlations are more evident for the sixth and ninth graders than for the twelfth graders.

Comparisons between the error structures for whites and blacks. For each grade, the reports of whites are more accurate than those of blacks. The reporting errors of whites are more likely than those of blacks to be random. The gain by grade in reporting accuracy occurs more quickly for whites than for blacks. Ninth-grade whites report parental statuses as accurately as twelfth-grade whites, and as accurately as their parents. Although twelfth-grade blacks report parental statuses as accurately as their parents, ninth-grade blacks are no more accurate than sixth-grade blacks, and neither of these groups is as accurate as sixth-grade whites. Finally, our data suggest that black *parents* report their statuses less accurately than white parents. The point estimates of the validity coefficients for black parents were computed to be no greater than .9 (families of twelfth-grade blacks), which, with one exception, is less than the point estimates of the validity coefficients for white parents.

Summary: Achievement Process

The (reduced-form) effects for whites of parental status on the endogenous achievement process variables. All of the endogenous variables included in our analyses depend more on "true" parental status characteristics in the sixth and ninth grades than in the twelfth grade. Occupational expectations and aspirations are least dependent on family status, regardless of grade. Averaging coefficients over equations, for all grades, "true" father's education has the largest average effect on the endogenous variables. For twelfth and sixth graders, "true" mother's education has the second largest average effect on the endogenous variables, but, for ninth graders, "true" father's occupational status has the second largest average effect.

The (reduced-form) effects for blacks of parental status on the endogenous achievement process variables. For blacks, there is no systematic variation by grade in the extent to which the endogenous variables depend on "true" parental status. Occupational aspirations depend more on "true" parental status than do the other endogenous variables. Averaging coefficients over equations, for twelfth and ninth graders, "true" father's occupational status has the largest average effect on the endogenous variables. For sixth graders, "true" father's education has the largest average effect. The average effect for "true" mother's education is nil for all grades.

Comparisons between the (reduced-form) achievement process structures for whites and blacks. The endogenous variables analyzed here depend more heavily on parental status for whites than for blacks. For whites, the effects of father's education predominate over those of father's occupational status and mother's education. For blacks, however, the effects of father's occupational status predominate. Both a lower dependency, for blacks, of endogenous variables on parental status characteristics and white–black differences in the relative contributions of particular parental statuses (although not the same as those found here) have been encountered previously, with different data (Duncan, 1968b). In general, these results are consistent with the claim that the achievement process operates differently for whites and blacks (Porter, 1974).

Discussion

The results of our analysis of each grade–race data set, taken by itself, are suggestive rather than definitive, because each subsample is small. Our point estimates have large standard errors, and that hinders application of these estimates to other achievement process studies. Also, because of small samples, our dispersion matrices for blacks are recalcitrant. To obtain meaningful results from them requires more a priori restrictions than are ideal within the context of the basic model used here.

Taken as a whole, however, our results are more than suggestive. Upon scanning the various subsamples over grades and race, we do find some theoretically meaningful variation and consistency in error structures and in the relation of error structures to endogenous variables in the achievement process. Moreover, the primary goal of this analysis is not so much to secure precise numerical estimates, although that must ultimately be the goal, as to advance conceptualization of measurement errors and of their embodiment in models of the achievement process.

Studies of the early stages of the achievement process that base their family socioeconomic status measures on children's and youths' reports risk biasing their estimates of the effects of family status in several ways. First, the reports of youthful informants may be randomly erroneous. Second, errors in the reports of one status characteristic may covary with errors in the reports of another status characteristic. Third, errors in the reports of a status characteristic may covary with endogenous variables in the achievement process. We have found evidence of the existence of all of these kinds of errors, within a framework that allows us to take them into account.

It is often implicitly assumed that errors in regressors based on children's and youths' parental status reports are small and random and, consequently, that achievement model estimates obtained therefrom are only slightly less desirable than those based on error-free measures. The inference does not follow from the assumption, which in any case is dubious, given our results. Even if the status measures are randomly erroneous and of high and equal validity, failure to correct the regressions for measurement errors will result in (a) underestimates of the dependence of achievement variables on origins, (b) overestimates of the effects of achievement variables on one another, and (c) distortions of the effects of particular origin characteristics on achievement variables (some will be too large, others will be too small). These biases will be compounded or offset if the status measures are differentially valid. Clearly, the assumption of highly valid proxies with random errors provides no license to take the results of naive regressions at face value.

Finally, the traditional response to measurement errors, aside from ignoring them, has been to make reliability adjustments under the assumption of random errors. In only one data set that we examined was this assumption valid. In addition, although others before us have perceived that children's and youths' reporting errors might be nonrandom, the nature of possible deviations from randomness has been left largely unspecified. We have attempted to be explicit about the nature of nonrandom errors, starting from an awareness that measurement errors are embedded in a particular context and then translating substantive hypotheses into empirically testable consequences for statistical models. Not only is it unnecessary to treat measurement error problems separately from substantive problems, it is misleading to do so.

Acknowledgment

We are indebted to Arthur S. Goldberger for his comments at an early stage.

References

Adams, W. Academic Self-image as a Strong Determinant of College Entrance and Adult Prospects: Relative Deprivation Theory Applied to High School Curriculum Choice. *American Journal of Economics and Sociology*, 1970, **29,** 199–220.

Aigner, D. J., & Chu, S. F. On Estimating the Industry Production Function. *American Economic Review*, 1968, **58,** 826–839.

Alexander, K., & Eckland, B. K. Effects of Education on the Social Mobility of High School Sophomores Fifteen Years Later (1955–1970). Final Report, Project No. 10202 (OEG-4-71-0037), National Institute of Education, U.S. Department of Health, Education, and Welfare, Institute for Research in Social Science. Chapel Hill, North Carolina: University of North Carolina, 1973.

Alwin, D. F. College Effects on Educational and Socioeconomic Achievements. Unpublished doctoral dissertation, University of Wisconsin—Madison, 1972.

Alwin, D. F. College Effects on Educational and Occupational Attainments. *American Sociological Review*, 1974, **39,** 210–223.

Alwin, D. F., & Hauser, R. M. The Decomposition of Effects in Path Analysis. *American Sociological Review*, 1975, **40,** 37–47.

Alwin, D. F., Hauser, R. M., & Sewell, W. H. Colleges and Achievement. In W. H. Sewell and R. M. Hauser, *Education, occupation, and earnings: Achievement in the early career*. New York: Academic Press, 1975. Pp. 113–142.

American College Testing Program. Assessing Students on the Way to College: Technical Report for the ACT Assessment Program. Iowa City, Iowa: Author, 1973.

Angoff, W. H. (Ed.) *The college board admissions testing program.* A technical report on research and development activities relating to the Scholastic Aptitude Test and Achievement Tests. New York: College Entrance Board, 1971.

Armor, D. J. The Racial Composition of Schools and College Aspirations of Negro Students. In U.S. Commission on Civil Rights, *Racial isolation in the public schools.* Vol. 2. Washington, D.C.: U.S. Government Printing Office, 1967. Pp. 143–164.

Armor, D. J. School and Family Effects on Black and White Achievement: A Reexamination of the USOE Data. In F. Mosteller & D. P. Moynihan (Eds.), *On equality of educational opportunity.* New York: Vintage Books, 1972. Pp. 168–229.

Astin, A. W. Classroom Environment in Different Fields of Study. *Journal of Educational Psychology,* 1965, **56,** 275–282.

Astin, A. W. *The college environment.* Washington, D.C.: American Council on Education, 1968.

Astin, A. W. The Methodology of Research on College Impacts (I). *Sociology of Education,* 1970, **43,** 223–254. (a)

Astin, A. W. The Methodology of Research on College Impacts (II). *Sociology of Education,* 1970, **43,** 437–450. (b)

Astin, A. W. *Predicting academic performance in college.* New York: Free Press, 1971.

Astin, A. W. The Measured Effects of Higher Education. *Annals of the American Academy of Political and Social Science,* 1972, **404,** 1–20.

Astin, A. W. The Intermediate Effects of Inequality: Differences in Access and Utilization of Educational Resources. *American Educational Research Journal,* 1974, **11,** 155–159.

Astin, A. W., & Lee, C. B. T. *The invisible colleges.* The Carnegie Commission on Higher Education. New York: McGraw-Hill, 1972.

Astin, A. W., & Panos, R. J. *The educational and vocational development of college students.* Washington, D.C.: American Council on Education, 1969.

Athanasiou, R. B. Selection and Socialization: A Study of Engineering Student Attrition. Unpublished doctoral dissertation, University of Michigan, 1969.

Athanasiou, R. B. Selection and Socialization: A Study of Engineering Student Attrition. *Journal of Educational Psychology,* 1971, **62,** 157–166.

Atkinson, J. W. (Ed.) *Motives in fantasy, action, and society.* Princeton, New Jersey: Van Nostrand, 1958.

Atkinson, J. W. Strength of Motivation and Efficiency of Performance. In J. W. Atkinson and J. O. Raynor (Eds.), *Motivation and achievement.* Washington, D.C.: V. H. Winston and Sons, 1974. Pp. 193–218. (a)

Atkinson, J. W. Motivational Determinants of Intellective Performance and Cumulative Achievement. In J. W. Atkinson and J. O. Raynor (Eds.), *Motivation and achievement.* Washington, D.C.: V. H. Winston and Sons, 1974. Pp. 389–410. (b)

Atkinson, J. W., & Birch, D. *The dynamics of action.* New York: John Wiley and Sons, 1970.

Atkinson, J. W., & Feather, N. T. (Eds.) *A theory of achievement motivation.* New York: John Wiley and Sons, 1966.

Atkinson, J. W., & O'Connor, P. Effects of Ability Grouping in Schools Related to Individual Differences in Achievement-Related Motivation. Final Report, Office of Education Cooperative Research Program, Project 1283. Washington, D.C.: American Documentation Institute, Library of Congress, 1963.

Atkinson, J. W., & O'Connor, P. Neglected Factors in Studies of Achievement-Oriented Performance. Social Approval as an Incentive and Performance Decrement. In J. W. Atkinson and N. T. Feather (Eds.), *A theory of achievement motivation.* New York: John Wiley and Sons, 1966. Pp. 299–326.

Atkinson, J. W., & Raynor, J. O. (Eds.) *Motivation and achievement.* Washington, D.C.: V. H. Winston and Sons, 1974.

Averch, H. A., Carroll, S. J., Donaldson, T. S., Kiesling, H. J., & Pincus, J. *How effective is schooling? A critical review and synthesis of research findings.* Santa Monica, California: Rand Corporation, 1972.

Averch, H. A., & Kiesling, H. J. The Relationship of School and Environment to Student Performance: Some Simultaneous Models for the Project TALENT High Schools. Unpublished manuscript, Rand Corporation, 1970.

Babcock, F. L. *The U.S. college graduate.* New York: Macmillan, 1941.

Bachman, J. G. The Impact of Family Background and Intelligence on Tenth-Grade Boys. (*Youth in transition.* Vol. II.) Institute for Social Research. Ann Arbor, Michigan: University of Michigan, 1970.

Bachman, J. G., Kahn, R. L., Mednick, M. T., Davidson, T. N., & Johnston, L. D. Blueprint for a Longitudinal Study of Adolescent Boys. (*Youth in transition.* Vol. I.) Institute for Social Research. Ann Arbor, Michigan: University of Michigan, 1969.

Backman, C. W., & Secord, P. F. The Self and Role Selection. In C. Gordon and K. J. Gergen (Eds.), *The self in social interaction.* New York: John Wiley and Sons, 1968. Pp. 289–296.

Barton, A. H. Allen Barton Comments on Hauser's 'Context and Consex.' *American Journal of Sociology,* 1970, **76,** 514–517.

Baumol, W. J. *Economic theory and operations analysis.* Englewood Cliffs, New Jersey: Prentice-Hall, 1963.

Baumol, W. J. Macroeconomics of Unbalanced Growth: The Anatomy of Urban Crisis. *American Economic Review,* 1967, **52,** 415–426.

Becker, G. S. Comment. *Journal of Political Economy,* 1972, **80** (May/June, Part II), S252–S255.

Becker, H. S. The Career of the Chicago Public Schoolteacher. *American Journal of Sociology,* 1952, **57,** 470–477.

Becker, H. S., Geer, B., & Hughes, E. C. *Making the grade: The academic side of college life.* New York: John Wiley and Sons, 1968.

Bell, D. Notes on the Post-Industrial Society. *Public Interest,* 1967, **6,** 24–35; **7,** 102–118.

Bell, D. The Measurement of Knowledge and Technology. In E. B. Sheldon and W. E. Moore (Eds.), *Indicators of social change: Concepts and measurements.* New York: Russell Sage Foundation, 1968. Pp. 145–246.

Benedict, R. Continuities and Discontinuities in Cultural Conditioning. *Psychiatry,* 1938, **1,** 161–167.

Benson, C. S., Schmelzle, W. K., Gustafson, R. H., & Lange, R. A. State and Local Fiscal Relationships in Public Education in California. Report of the Senate Fact Finding Committee on Revenue and Taxation. Sacramento, California: State Senate, State of California, 1965.

Bereiter, C. Some Persisting Dilemmas in the Measurement of Change. In C. W. Harris (Ed.), *Problems of measuring change.* Madison, Wisconsin: University of Wisconsin Press, 1963. Pp. 3–20.

Bereiter, C., & Freedman, M. B. Fields of Study and the People in Them. In N.

Sanford (Ed.), *The American college: A psychological and social interpretation of the higher learning.* New York: John Wiley and Sons, 1962. Pp. 563–596.

Berg, I. *Education and jobs: The great training robbery.* New York: John Wiley and Sons, 1970.

Bernstein, B. Social Class and Linguistic Development: A Theory of Social Learning. In A. H. Halsey, J. Floud, and C. A. Anderson (Eds.), *Education, economy, and society: A reader in the sociology of education.* New York: Free Press, 1961. Pp. 288–314.

Bidwell, C. E. Schooling and Moral Socialization. *Interchange,* 1972, **3**, 3–22.

Bijou, S. W. Environment and Intelligence: A Behavioral Analysis. In R. Cancro (Ed.), *Intelligence: Genetic and environmental influences.* New York: Grune and Stratton, 1971. Pp. 221–239.

Birch, D. Measuring the Stream of Activity, MMPP 72–2, Michigan Mathematical Psychology Program. Ann Arbor, Michigan: University of Michigan, 1972.

Birch, D., Atkinson, J. W., & Bongort, K. Cognitive Control of Action. In B. Weiner (Ed.), *Cognitive views of human motivation.* New York: Academic Press, 1974. Pp. 71–84.

Bishop, Y. M. M., & Mosteller, F. Smoothed Contingency Table Analysis. In J. P. Bunker, W. H. Forrest, Jr., F. Mosteller, and L. D. Vandan (Eds.), *The national Halothane study: A study of the possible association between Halothane and anesthesia and postoperative hepatic necrosis.* Report of subcommittee on the National Halothane Study of the Committee on Anesthesia, National Academy of Sciences–National Research Council. Washington, D.C.: U.S. Government Printing Office, 1969.

Blalock, H. M., Jr. *Causal inferences in nonexperimental research.* Chapel Hill, North Carolina: University of North Carolina Press, 1964.

Blalock, H. M., Jr. *Causal models in the social sciences.* Chicago: Aldine-Atherton, 1971.

Blau, P. M. Structural Effects. *American Sociological Review,* 1960, **25**, 178–193.

Blau, P. M., & Duncan, O. D. *The American occupational structure.* New York: John Wiley and Sons, 1967.

Blishen, B. S. A Socioeconomic Index for Occupations in Canada. *Canadian Review of Sociology and Anthropology,* 1967, **4**, 41–53.

Block, J. H. Introduction. In J. H. Block (Ed.), *Mastery learning: Theory and practice.* New York: Holt, 1971. Pp. 2–12.

Bloom, B. S. (Ed.) *Taxonomy of educational objectives, Handbook 1: Cognitive domain.* New York: David McKay, 1956.

Bloom, B. S. *Stability and change in human characteristics.* New York: John Wiley and Sons, 1964.

Bloom, B. S. Affective Consequences of School Achievement. In J. H. Block (Ed.), *Mastery learning: Theory and practice.* New York: Holt, 1971. Pp. 13–28. (a)

Bloom, B. S. Mastery Learning. In J. H. Block (Ed.), *Mastery learning: Theory and practice.* New York: Holt, 1971. Pp. 47–63. (b)

Bloom, B. S. Learning for Mastery. In B. S. Bloom, J. T. Hastings, and G. Madaus (Eds.), *Handbook on formative and summative evaluation of student learning.* New York: McGraw-Hill, 1971. (c)

Bohrnstedt, G. W. Observations on the Measurement of Change. In E. F. Borgatta (Ed.), *Sociological methodology, 1969.* San Francisco: Jossey-Bass, 1969. Pp. 113–133.

Bohrnstedt, G. W., & Carter, T. M. Robustness in Regression Analysis. In H. L.

Costner (Ed.), *Sociological methodology, 1971.* San Francisco: Jossey-Bass, 1971. Pp. 118–146.

Boruch, R. F., & Creager, J. A. Measurement Error in Social and Education Research. ACE Research Reports, Vol. 7, No. 2. Washington, D.C.: Office of Research, American Council on Education, 1972.

Borus, M. E., & Nestel, G. Response Bias in Reports of Father's Education and Socioeconomic Status. *Journal of the American Statistical Association,* 1973, **68,** 816–820.

Bowles, S. Educational Production Functions. Final Report, OEC 1-7000451-2651, U.S. Office of Education, 1969 (February).

Bowles, S. Towards an Educational Production Function. In W. L. Hansen (Ed.), *Education, income, and human capital.* National Bureau of Economic Research. New York: Columbia University Press, 1970. Pp. 11–60.

Bowles, S. Schooling and Inequality from Generation to Generation. *Journal of Political Economy,* 1972, **80** (May/June, Part II), S219–S251. (a)

Bowles, S. Unequal Education and the Reproduction of the Social Division of Labor. In M. Carnoy (Ed.), *Schooling in a corporate society.* New York: David McKay, 1972. Pp. 36–66. (b)

Bowles, S. Understanding Unequal Economic Opportunity. *American Economic Review. Papers and Proceedings,* 1973, **63,** 346–356.

Bowles, S., & Gintis, H. I.Q. in the U.S. Class Structure. *Social Policy,* 1972–73, **3,** 65–96.

Bowles, S., & Levin, H. M. More on Multicollinearity and the Effectiveness of Schools. *Journal of Human Resources,* 1968, **3,** 393–400. (a)

Bowles, S., & Levin, H. M. The Determinants of Scholastic Achievement: An Appraisal of Some Recent Evidence. *Journal of Human Resources,* 1968, **3,** 3–24. (b)

Bowles, S., & Nelson, V. I. The 'Inheritance of IQ' and the Intergenerational Reproduction of Economic Inequality. *Review of Economics and Statistics,* 1974, **56,** 39–51.

Boyle, R. P. Neighborhood Context and College Plans (III). *American Sociological Review,* 1966, **31,** 706–707. (a)

Boyle, R. P. The Effect of the High School on Students' Aspirations. *American Journal of Sociology,* 1966, **71,** 628–639. (b)

Broadhurst, P. L. The Interaction of Task Difficulty and Motivation: The Yerkes–Dodson Law Revived. *Acta Psychologica,* 1959, **16,** 321–338.

Bronfenbrenner, U. The Changing American Child—A Speculative Analysis. *Journal of Social Issues,* 1961, **17,** 6–18.

Brown, R. D. Manipulation of the Environmental Press in a College Residence Hall. *Personnel and Guidance Journal,* 1968, **46,** 555–560.

Bunker, J. P., Forrest, W. H. Jr., Mosteller, F., & Vandan, L. D. (Eds.) *The national Halothane study: A study of the possible association between Halothane and anesthesia and postoperative hepatic necrosis.* Report of subcommittee on the National Halothane Study of the Committee on Anesthesia, National Academy of Sciences–National Research Council. Washington, D.C.: U.S. Government Printing Office, 1969.

Burkhead, J., Fox, T. G., & Holland, J. W. *Input and output in large city high schools.* Syracuse, New York: Syracuse University Press, 1967.

Burks, B. S. The Relative Influence of Nature and Nurture upon Mental Development: A Comparative Study of Foster Parent–Foster Child Resemblance and

True Parent–True Child Resemblance. In G. M. Whipple (Ed.), *Nature and nurture. Part I: Their influence on intelligence.* 27th Yearbook of the National Society for the Study of Education, Public School Publishing Co., 1928.

Campbell, D. T., & Stanley, J. C. Experimental and Quasi-Experimental Designs for Research on Teaching. In N. L. Gage (Ed.), *Handbook of research on teaching.* Chicago: Rand McNally, 1963. Pp. 171–246.

Campbell, E. Q., & Alexander, C. N. Structural Effects and Interpersonal Relations. *American Journal of Sociology,* 1965, **71,** 284–289.

Cardell, N. S., & Hopkins, M. M. The Influence of IQ on Income and on the Relationship between Education and Income. Manuscript, Department of Economics, Harvard University, 1974.

Carlson, R. C. Educational Efficiency and Effectiveness. Presented at the Stanford University Seminar in Economics of Education, 1970.

Carlson, S. *A study on the pure theory of production.* New York: Kelley & Millman, 1956.

Carroll, J. B. A Model of School Learning. *Teachers College Record,* 1963, **64,** 723–733.

Carter, N. D. The Effects of Sex and Marital Status on a Social–Psychological Model of Occupational Status Attainment. Unpublished master's thesis, University of Wisconsin—Madison, 1972.

Carter, T. M., Picou, J. S., Curry, E., & Tracy, G. Black–White Differences in Occupational Mobility: Some Preliminary Explanations. Paper presented at the annual meetings of the American Sociological Association, New Orleans, Louisiana, 1972.

Cattell, R. B. *Abilities: Their structure, growth, and action.* Boston: Houghton Mifflin, 1971.

Center for the Study of Higher Education, University of California. *Omnibus personality inventory: Research manual.* Berkeley, California: Author, 1962.

Centra, J. A., & Rock, D. College Environments and Student Achievement. *American Educational Research Journal,* 1971, **8,** 623–634.

Chickering, A. W. Civil Liberties and the Experience of College. *Journal of Higher Education,* 1970, **41,** 599–606.

Chickering, A. W., & McCormick, J. Personality Development and the College Experience. *Research in Higher Education,* 1973, **1,** 43–70.

Clark, B. *Educating the expert society.* San Francisco: Chandler, 1962.

Clark, B. R., Heist, P., McConnell, T. R., Trow, M. A., & Yonge, G. *Students and colleges: Interaction and change.* Center for Research and Development in Higher Education. Berkeley, California: University of California, 1972.

Cochran, W. G. The Planning of Observational Studies. *Journal of the Royal Statistical Society,* 1965, **128** (Ser. A), 234–266.

Cochran, W. G. The Effectiveness of Adjustment by Classification in Removing Bias in Observational Studies. *Biometrics,* 1968, **24,** 295–313.

Cohen, D. K., Pettigrew, T. F., & Riley, R. T. Race and the Outcomes of Schooling. In F. Mosteller, and D. P. Moynihan (Eds.), *On equality of educational opportunity.* New York: Vintage Books, 1972. Pp. 343–368.

Cohen, J. The Factorial Structure of the WISC at Ages 7–6, 10–6 and 13–6. *Journal of Consulting Psychology,* 1959, **23,** 285–299.

Cohen, J. Multiple Regression as a General Data-Analytic System. *Psychological Bulletin,* 1968, **70,** 426–443.

Cohen, R. S., & Orum, A. M. Parent–Child Consensus on Socioeconomic Data Obtained from Sample Surveys. *Public Opinion Quarterly*, 1972, **36**, 95–98.

Coleman, J. S. *The adolescent society.* Glencoe, Illinois: Free Press, 1961.

Coleman, J. S. *Introduction to mathematical sociology.* New York: Free Press, 1964.

Coleman, J. S., Campbell, E. Q., Hobson, C. J., McPartland, J., Mood, A. M., Weinfeld, F. D., & York, R. L. *Equality of educational opportunity.* 2 Vols. Office of Education, U.S. Department of Health, Education, and Welfare. Washington, D.C.: U.S. Government Printing Office, 1966.

Collins, R. Functional and Conflict Theories of Stratification. *American Sociological Review*, 1971, **36** (December), 1002–1019.

Crain, R. L. School Integration and Occupational Achievement of Negroes. *American Journal of Sociology*, 1970, **75**, 593–606.

Crain, R. L. School Integration and the Academic Achievement of Negroes. *Sociology of Education*, 1971, **44**, 1–26.

Cronbach, L. J. The Two Disciplines of Scientific Psychology. *American Psychology*, 1957, **12**, 671–684.

Cross, K. P. *Beyond the open door.* San Francisco: Jossey-Bass, 1971.

Cutright, P. Achievement, Mobility, and the Draft: Their Impact on the Earnings of Men. Staff Paper No. 14, U.S. Department of Health, Education, and Welfare. Washington, D.C.: Social Security Administration, Office of Research and Statistics, 1972.

Daniere, A., & Mechling, J. Direct Marginal Productivity of College Education in Relation to College Aptitude of Students and Production Costs of Institutions. *Journal of Human Resources*, 1970, **5**, 51–70.

Dave, R. H. The Identification and Measurement of Environmental Process Variables That Are Related to Educational Achievement. Unpublished doctoral dissertation, University of Chicago, 1963.

Davis, J. A. The Campus as a Frog Pond: An Application of the Theory of Relative Deprivation to Career Decisions of College Men. *American Journal of Sociology*, 1966, **72**, 17–31.

Davis, J. A., Spaeth, J. L., & Huson, C. A. A Technique for Analyzing the Effects of Group Composition. *American Sociological Review*, 1961, **26**, 215–226.

Davis, N. The Continuation of Education after Marriage among United States Women: 1970. Unpublished master's thesis, Department of Sociology, University of Wisconsin—Madison, 1973.

Douglas, J. W. B., & Ross, J. M. The Effects of Absence on Primary School Performance. *British Journal of Educational Psychology*, 1965, **35**, 28–40.

Dreeben, R. *On what is learned in school.* Reading, Massachusetts: Addison-Wesley, 1968.

Drew, D., & Astin, A. Undergraduate Aspirations: A Test of Several Theories. *American Journal of Sociology*, 1972, **77**, 1151–1164.

Dugan, D. The Impact of Parental and Educational Investments upon Student Achievement. Paper presented at 129th Annual Meeting of the American Statistical Association, New York City, 1969.

Duncan, B. Dropouts and the Unemployed. *Journal of Political Economy*, 1965, **53**, 121–134. (a)

Duncan, B. Family Factors and School Dropout: 1920–1960. Final Report, Cooperative Research Project No. 2258, U.S. Office of Education. Ann Arbor, Michigan: University of Michigan, 1965. (b)

Duncan, B. Early Work Experience of Graduates and Dropouts. *Demography*, 1967, **4**, 19–29.

Duncan, B. Trends in Output and Distribution of Schooling. In E. B. Sheldon and W. E. Moore (Eds.), *Indicators of social change: Concepts and measurements*. New York: Russell Sage Foundation, 1968. Pp. 601–674.

Duncan, O. D. A Socioeconomic Index for All Occupations. In A. J. Reiss, Jr., *Occupations and social status*. New York: Free Press of Glencoe, 1961. Pp. 109–138.

Duncan, O. D. Path Analysis: Sociological Examples. *American Journal of Sociology*, 1966, **72**, 1–16.

Duncan, O. D. Discrimination against Negroes. *Annals of the American Academy of Political and Social Science*, 1967, **371**, 85–103.

Duncan, O. D. Ability and Achievement. *Eugenics Quarterly*, 1968, **15**, 1–11. (a)

Duncan, O. D. Inheritance of Poverty or Inheritance of Race? In D. P. Moynihan (Ed.), *On understanding poverty*. New York: Basic Books, 1968. Pp. 85–110. (b)

Duncan, O. D. Contingencies in Constructing Causal Models. In E. F. Borgatta (Ed.), *Sociological methodology, 1969*. San Francisco: Jossey-Bass, 1969. Pp. 74–112.

Duncan, O. D. Partials, Partitions, and Paths. In E. F. Borgatta and G. W. Bohrnstedt (Eds.), *Sociological methodology, 1970*. San Francisco: Jossey-Bass, 1970. Pp. 38–47.

Duncan, O. D. Path Analysis: Sociological Examples (Addenda). In H. M. Blalock, Jr. (Ed.), *Causal models in the social sciences*. Chicago: Aldine-Atherton, 1971. Pp. 115–138.

Duncan, O. D., Featherman, D. L., & Duncan, B. *Socioeconomic background and achievement*. New York: Seminar Press, 1972.

Duncan, O. D., Haller, A. O., & Portes, A. Peer Influences on Aspirations: A Reinterpretation. *American Journal of Sociology*, 1968, **74**, 119–137.

Duncan, O. D., & Hodge, R. W. Education and Occupational Mobility: A Regression Analysis. *American Journal of Sociology*, 1963, **68**, 629–644.

Dyer, P. D. The Effects of Environmental Variables on the Achievement of Elementary School Children in Trinidad. Unpublished doctoral dissertation, University of Alberta, 1967.

Eckland, B. K. Social Class Structure and the Genetic Basis of Intelligence. In R. Cancro (Ed.), *Intelligence: Genetic and environmental influences*. New York: Grune and Stratton, 1971. Pp. 65–76.

Educational Testing Service. *Individuals and their options: Annual report '72*. Princeton, New Jersey: Author, 1973.

Educational Testing Service. 'Coming of Age' Brings COPA Consolidation. *ETS Examiner*, 1974, **4** (September 5), 1–2.

Elashoff, R. M., & Elashoff, J. Regression Analysis with Missing Data. In R. L. Bisco (Ed.), *Data bases, computers, and the social sciences*. New York: Wiley-Interscience, 1970. Pp. 198–207.

Ellis, R. A., & Lane, W. C. Structural Supports for Upward Mobility. *American Sociological Review*, 1963, **28**, 743–756.

Elton, C. F., & Rose, H. A. A Longitudinal Study of the Vocationally Undecided Male Student. *Journal of Vocational Behavior*, 1971, **1**, 85–92.

Erlenmeyer-Kimling, L., & Jarvik, L. F. Genetics and Intelligence: A Review. *Science*, 1963, **142**, 1477–1479.

Evans, G. T. *Transformation of factor matrices to achieve congruence*. Toronto, Ontario: The Ontario Institute for Studies in Education, Mimeograph, 1970.

Evers, M. Occupational Experience and Occupational Knowledge. Paper presented at the meetings of the American Sociological Association, New Orleans, Louisiana, 1972.

Eysenck, H. J. Personality and Experimental Psychology. *Bulletin of the British Psychological Society*, 1966, **19** (62), 1–28.

Farkas, G. Specification, Residuals, and Contextual Effects. *Sociological Methods and Research*, 1974, **2**, 333–363.

Farrar, D. E., & Glauber, R. R. Multicollinearity in Regression Analysis: The Problem Revisited. *Review of Economics and Statistics*, 1967, **49**, 92–107.

Farrell, M. The Measurement of Productive Efficiency. *Journal of the Royal Statistical Society*, 1957, **120** (3) (Ser. A), 253–281.

Farwell, E. D., Warren, J. R., & McConnell, T. R. Student Personality Characteristics Associated with Groups of Colleges and Fields of Study. *College and University*, 1962, **37**, 229–241.

Featherman, D. L. Residential Background and Socioeconomic Achievements in Metropolitan Stratification Systems. *Rural Sociology*, 1971, **36**, 107–124. (a)

Featherman, D. L. A Research Note: A Social Structural Model for the Socioeconomic Career. *American Journal of Sociology*, 1971, **77**, 293–304. (b)

Featherman, D. L. Achievement Orientations and Socioeconomic Career Attainments. *American Sociological Review*, 1972, **37**, 131–143.

Featherman, D. L. Comments on Models for the Socioeconomic Career. *American Sociological Review*, 1973, **38**, 785–790.

Featherman, D. L., & Hauser, R. M. Design for a Replicate Study of Social Mobility in the United States. In K. C. Land and S. Spilerman (Eds.), *Social indicator models*. New York: Russell Sage Foundation, 1975. Pp. 219–251.

Feld, S. C. Longitudinal Study of the Origins of Achievement Strivings. *Journal of Personality and Social Psychology*, 1967, **7**, 408–414.

Feldman, K. A. Studying the Impacts of Colleges on Students. *Sociology of Education*, 1969, **42**, 207–237.

Feldman, K. A. Using the Work of Others: Some Observations on Reviewing and Integrating. *Sociology of Education*, 1971, **44**, 86–102.

Feldman, K. A. (Ed.) *College and student: Selected readings in the social psychology of higher education*. Elmsford, New York: Pergamon Press, 1972.

Feldman, K. A., & Newcomb, T. M. *The impact of college on students*. San Francisco: Jossey-Bass, 1969.

Finney, H. C. Political Dimensions of College Impact on Civil-Libertarianism and the Integration of Political Perspective. *Sociology of Education*, 1974, **47**, 214–250.

Fisher, F. M. Generalization of the Rank and Order Conditions for Identifiability. *Econometrica*, 1959, **27**, 431–447.

Fisher, F. M. The Relative Sensitivity to Specification Error of Different *k*-Class Estimators. *Journal of the American Statistical Association*, 1966, **61** (314, Part I), 345–347.

Fisher, F. M. The Choice of Instrumental Variables in the Estimation of Economy-Wide Econometric Models. In H. M. Blalock, Jr. (Ed.), *Causal models in the social sciences*. Chicago: Aldine-Atherton, 1971. Pp. 245–272.

Flanagan, J. C., Davis, F. B., Dailey, J. T., Shaycoft, M. F., Orr, D. B., Goldberg, I., & Neyman, C. A., Jr. *The American high school student*. Project TALENT Office. Pittsburgh, Pennsylvania: University of Pittsburgh, 1964.

Folger, J. K., Astin, H. S., & Bayer, A. E. *Human resources and higher education:*

Staff report of the Commission on Human Resources and Advanced Education. New York: Russell Sage Foundation, 1970.

Franks, D. D., Falk, R. F., & Hinton, J. Differential Exposure to Courses in Two Majors and Differences in Students' Value Responses. *Sociology of Education,* 1973, **46,** 361–369.

Frantz, T. T. Student Subcultures. *Journal of College Student Personnel,* 1969, **10,** 16–20.

Fraser, E. *Home environment and the school.* London: University of London Press, 1959.

Friedlander, B. Z. Receptive Language Development in Infancy: Issues and Problems. *Merrill-Palmer Quarterly,* 1970, **16,** 7–51.

Furby, L. Interpreting Regression toward the Mean in Developmental Research. *Developmental Psychology,* 1973, **8,** 172–179.

Galbraith, J. K. *The new industrial state.* Boston: Houghton Mifflin, 1967.

Gamson, Z. F. Utilitarian and Normative Orientations toward Education. *Sociology of Education,* 1966, **39,** 46–73.

Gamson, Z. F. Performance and Personalism in Student–Faculty Relations. *Sociology of Education,* 1967, **40,** 279–301.

Gasson, R. M., Haller, A. O., & Sewell, W. H. *Attitudes and facilitation in the attainment of status.* Washington, D.C.: American Sociological Association, Rose Monograph Series, 1972.

Gauss, K. F. *Theoria motus corporum coelestium in sectionibus conicus solem ambientium.* Hamburg, Germany: Perthes and Besser, 1809.

Gentleman, W. M., Gilbert, J. P., & Tukey, J. W. The Smear-and-Sweep Analysis. In J. P. Bunker, W. H. Forrest, Jr., F. Mosteller, and L. D. Vandan (Eds.), *The national Halothane study: A study of the possible association between Halothane and anesthesia and postoperative hepatic necrosis.* Report of subcommittee on the National Halothane Study of the Committee on Anesthesia, National Academy of Sciences–National Research Council. Washington, D.C.: U.S. Government Printing Office, 1969.

Gintis, H. Education, Technology and the Characteristics of Worker Productivity. *American Economic Review,* 1971, **61,** 266–279.

Gintis, H. Toward a Political Economy of Education. *Harvard Educational Review,* 1972, **42,** 70–96.

Gjesme, J. Motive to Achieve Success and Motive to Avoid Failure in Relation to School Performance for Pupils of Different Ability Levels. *Scandinavian Journal of Educational Research,* 1971, **15,** 81–89.

Glass, G. V., Peckham, P. D., & Sanders, J. R. Consequences of Failure to Meet Assumptions Underlying the Fixed Effects Analyses of Variance and Covariance. *Review of Educational Research,* 1972, **42,** 237–288.

Goldberg, M. L., Passow, H. A., & Justman, J. *The effects of ability grouping.* New York: Teachers College Press, 1966.

Goldberger, A. S. Mysteries of the Meritocracy. Institute for Research on Poverty Discussion Paper 225–74. Madison, Wisconsin: University of Wisconsin—Madison, 1974. (a)

Goldberger, A. S. Professor Jensen, Meet Miss Burks. Institute for Research on Poverty. Madison, Wisconsin: University of Wisconsin—Madison, 1974. (b)

Goodman, L. A. The Analysis of Systems of Qualitative Variables When Some of the Variables Are Unobservable. Part I: A Modified Latent Structure Approach. *American Journal of Sociology,* 1974, **79,** 1179–1259.

Goodman, S. M. *The assessment of school quality.* Albany, New York: State Education Department of New York, 1959.

Gordon, C. W. *The social system of the high school.* Glencoe, Illinois: Free Press, 1957.

Gordon, R. A. Issues in Multiple Regression. *American Journal of Sociology,* 1968, **73,** 592–616.

Griliches, Z., & Mason, W. M. Education, Income, and Ability. *Journal of Political Economy,* 1972, **80** (May/June, Part II), S74–S103.

Guertin, W. H., Ladd, C. E., Frank, G. H., Rabin, A. I., & Heister, D. S. Research into the Wechsler Scales for Adults: 1960–1965. *Psychological Bulletin,* 1966, **66,** 385–409.

Gujarati, D. Use of Dummy Variables in Testing for Equality between Sets of Coefficients in Linear Regression: A Generalization. *American Statistician,* 1970, **24,** 18–22.

Gurin, G. The Impact of the College Experience. In S. B. Withey (Ed.), *A degree and what else? Correlates and consequences of a college education.* New York: McGraw-Hill, 1971. Pp. 25–54. (a)

Gurin, G. A Study of Students in a Multiversity. Office of Education, U.S. Department of Health, Education, and Welfare Project No. 5-0901. Survey Research Center, Institute for Social Research. Ann Arbor, Michigan: University of Michigan, 1971. (b)

Gurin, G., Newcomb, T. M., & Cope, R. G. Characteristics of Entering Freshmen Related to Attrition in the Literary College of a Large State University. Office of Education, U.S. Department of Health, Education, and Welfare Project No. 1938. Survey Research Center, Institute for Social Research. Ann Arbor, Michigan: University of Michigan, 1968.

Gurin, P., & Katz, D. Motivation and Aspiration in the Negro College. Office of Education, U.S. Department of Health, Education, and Welfare Project No. 5-0787. Survey Research Center, Institute for Social Research. Ann Arbor, Michigan: University of Michigan, 1966.

Guthrie, J. W., Kleindorfer, G., Levin, H. M., & Stout, R. T. *Schools and inequality.* Cambridge, Massachusetts: MIT Press, 1971.

Haller, A. O. Education and Occupational Achievement Process. In President's National Advisory Commission on Rural Poverty, *Rural poverty in the United States.* Washington, D.C.: U.S. Government Printing Office, 1968. Pp. 149–169.

Haller, A. O., & Miller, I. W. *The occupational aspiration scale.* Cambridge, Massachusetts: Schenkman Publishing, 1971.

Haller, A. O., & Portes, A. Status Attainment Processes. *Sociology of Education,* 1973, **46,** 51–91.

Haller, A. O., & Sewell, W. H. Occupational Choices of Wisconsin Farm Boys. *Rural Sociology,* 1967, **32,** 37–55.

Hanushek, E. The Education of Negroes and Whites. Unpublished doctoral dissertation, Massachusetts Institute of Technology, 1968.

Hanushek, E. The Production of Education, Teacher Quality, and Efficiency. In U.S. Department of Health, Education, and Welfare, *Do teachers make a difference?* Washington, D.C.: U.S. Government Printing Office, 1970. Pp. 79–99.

Hanushek, E. *Education and race.* Lexington, Massachusetts: D. C. Heath, 1972.

Hanushek, E. A., & Kain, J. F. On the Value of Equality of Educational Opportunity as a Guide to Public Policy. In F. Mosteller and D. P. Moynihan (Eds.), *On equality of educational opportunity.* New York: Vintage Books, 1972. Pp. 116–145.

Hargens, L. L., & Hagstrom, W. O. Sponsored and Contest Mobility of American Academic Scientists. *Sociology of Education,* 1967, **40,** 24–38.

Harman, H. H. *Modern factor analysis.* Chicago: University of Chicago Press, 1967.

Harnischfeger, A., & Wiley, D. E. Teaching–Learning Processes in Elementary School: A Synoptic View. *Studies of Educative Processes,* 1975. No. 9, University of Chicago. [Also in D. A. Erickson (Ed.), *Reading in educational research: Educational organization and administration.* American Educational Research Association, in preparation.]

Hauser, R. M. Schools and the Stratification Process. *American Journal of Sociology,* 1969, **74,** 587–611.

Hauser, R. M. Context and Consex: A Cautionary Tale. *American Journal of Sociology,* 1970, **75,** 645–664. (a)

Hauser, R. M. Educational Stratification in the United States. *Sociological Inquiry,* 1970, **40,** 102–129. (b)

Hauser, R. M. Hauser Replies. *American Journal of Sociology,* 1970, **76,** 517–520. (c)

Hauser, R. M. *Socioeconomic background and educational performance.* Washington, D.C.: American Sociological Association, Rose Monograph Series, 1971.

Hauser, R. M. Disaggregating a Social–Psychological Model of Educational Attainment. *Social Science Research,* 1972, **1,** 159–188.

Hauser, R. M. Contextual Analysis Revisited. *Sociological Methods and Research,* 1974, **2,** 365–375.

Hauser, R. M., & Goldberger, A. S. The Treatment of Unobservable Variables in Path Analysis. In H. L. Costner (Ed.), *Sociological methodology 1971.* San Francisco: Jossey-Bass, 1971. Pp. 81–117.

Hauser, R. M., Sewell, W. H., & Lutterman, K. G., Socioeconomic Background, Ability, and Achievement. In W. H. Sewell and R. M. Hauser, *Education, occupation and earnings: Achievement in the early career.* New York: Academic Press, 1975. Pp. 43–88.

Havemann, E., & West, P. S. *They went to college.* New York: Harcourt, 1952.

Hays, W. L. *Statistics for psychologists.* New York: Holt, 1963.

Hays, W. L. *Statistics for the social sciences.* 2nd ed. New York: Holt, 1973.

Hebb, D. O. *A textbook of psychology.* Philadelphia, Pennsylvania: W. B. Saunders, 1958.

Heckhausen, H. Intervening Cognitions in Motivation. In D. E. Berlyne and K. B. Madsen (Eds.), *Pleasure, reward, and preference: Their nature, determinants, and role in behavior.* New York: Academic Press, 1973. Pp. 217–242.

Heise, D. R. Employing Nominal Variables, Induced Variables, and Block Variables in Path Analysis. *Sociological Methods and Research,* 1972, **1,** 147–173.

Heise, D. R. (Ed.) *Personality: Biosocial bases.* Chicago: Rand McNally, 1973.

Henmon, V. A. C., & Nelson, M. J. *The Henmon–Nelson test of mental ability: Manual for administration.* Chicago: Houghton Mifflin, 1954.

Hess, R. D. The Transmission of Cognitive Strategies in Poor Families: The Socialization of Apathy and Underachievement. In V. L. Allen (Ed.), *Psychological factors in poverty.* Chicago: Markham, 1970. Pp. 73–92.

Hess, R. D., & Shipman, V. Early Experience and the Socialization of Cognitive Modes in Children. *Child Development,* 1965, **36,** 869–886.

Heyns, B. Social Selection and Stratification within Schools. *American Journal of Sociology,* 1974, **79,** 1434–1451.

Hirsch, W. Z. *Urban economic analysis.* New York: McGraw-Hill, 1973.

Hochbaum, J. Structure and Process in Higher Education. *College and University,* 1968, **43**, 190–202.

Hoffman, L. W., & Lippitt, R. The Measurement of Family Life Variables. In P. H. Mussen (Ed.), *Handbook of research methods in child development.* New York: John Wiley and Sons, 1960. Pp. 945–1013.

Holland, J. F., & Nichols, R. C. Explorations of a Theory of Vocational Choice: III. A Longitudinal Study of Change in Major Field of Study. *Personnel and Guidance Journal,* 1964, **43**, 235–242.

Horner, M. S. Femininity and successful achievement. In J. Bardwick *et al.* (Eds.), *Feminine personality and conflict.* Belmont, California: Brooks/Cole, 1970. Pp. 45–76.

Horner, M. S. The Measurement and Behavioral Implications of Fear of Success in Women. In J. W. Atkinson and J. O. Raynor (Eds.), *Motivation and achievement.* Washington, D.C.: V. H. Winston and Sons, 1974. Pp. 91–120.

Hoyt, D. P. The Relationship between College Grades and Adult Achievement: A Review of the Literature. ACT Research Report No. 7. Iowa City, Iowa: American College Testing Program, 1965.

Hunt, J. McV. *Intelligence and experience.* New York: Ronald Press, 1961.

Hunt, S. Income Determinants for College Graduates and the Return to Educational Investment. Unpublished doctoral dissertation, Yale University, 1963.

Huntley, C. W. Changes in Study of Values Scores during the Four Years of College. *Genetic Psychology Monographs,* 1965, **71**, 349–383.

Huntley, C. W. Changes in Values during the Four Years of College. *College Student Survey,* 1967, **1**, 43–48.

Huśen, T. Does More Time in School Make a Difference? *Saturday Review,* 1972 (April 29), 32–35.

Inkeles, A. The Modernization of Man. In M. Weiner (Ed.), *Modernization.* New York: Basic Books, 1966. Pp. 138–150. (a)

Inkeles, A. A Note on Social Structure and the Socialization of Competence. *Harvard Educational Review,* 1966, **36**, 265–283. (b)

Jackson, P. W. After Apple-Picking. *Harvard Educational Review,* 1973, **43**, 51–60.

Jencks, C. S. The Coleman Report and the Conventional Wisdom. In F. Mosteller and D. P. Moynihan (Eds.), *On equality of educational opportunity.* New York: Vintage Books, 1972. Pp. 69–115. (a)

Jencks, C. S. The Quality of the Data Collected by the Equality of Educational Opportunity Survey. In F. Mosteller and D. P. Moynihan (Eds.), *On equality of educational opportunity.* New York: Vintage Books, 1972. Pp. 437–512. (b)

Jencks, C. S., & Reisman, D. *The academic revolution.* New York: Doubleday, 1968.

Jencks, C. S., Smith, M., Acland, H., Bane, M. J., Cohen, D., Gintis, H., Heyns, B., & Michelson, S. *Inequality: A reassessment of the effect of family and schooling in America.* New York: Basic Books, 1972.

Jensen, A. R. How Much Can We Boost IQ and Scholastic Achievement? *Harvard Educational Review,* 1969, **39**, 1–123.

Jensen, A. R. *Educability and group differences.* New York: Harper and Row, 1973.

Johnson, D. R. School Impact on Educational Aspirations of U.S. Public High School Seniors: A Methodological and Causal Analysis. Unpublished doctoral dissertation, Vanderbilt University, 1972.

Johnston, J. *Econometric methods.* New York: McGraw-Hill, 1963.

Jöreskog, K. G. A General Approach to Confirmatory Maximum Likelihood Factor Analysis. *Psychometrika,* 1969, **34**, 183–202.

Jöreskog, K. G. A General Method for the Analysis of Covariance Structures. *Biometrika*, 1970, **57**, 239–251.

Jöreskog, K. G. A General Method for Estimating a Linear Structural Equation System. In A. S. Goldberger and O. D. Duncan (Eds.), *Structural equation models in the social sciences*. New York: Seminar Press, 1973. Pp. 85–112.

Jöreskog, K. G., Gruvaeus, G. T., & vanThillo, M. ACOVS—A General Computer Program for the Analysis of Covariance Structures. Research Bulletin 70–15. Princeton, New Jersey: Educational Testing Service, 1970.

Kagan, J., & Moss, H. A. *Birth to maturity: A study in psychological development*. New York: John Wiley and Sons, 1962.

Kahn, H., & Wiener, A. J. The Next Thirty-three Years: A Framework for Speculation. *Daedalus*, 1967, **96**, 705–732.

Kamens, D. H. The College "Charter" and College Size: Effects on Occupational Choice and College Attrition. *Sociology of Education*, 1971, **44**, 270–296.

Kamin, L. *The science and politics of IQ*. Potomac, Maryland: Erl Baum Associates, 1974.

Katz, I. Review of Evidence Relating to Effects of Desegregation on the Intellectual Performance of Negroes. *American Psychologist*, 1964, **19**, 381–399.

Katzman, M. T. Distribution and Production in a Big City Elementary School System. *Yale Economic Essays*, 1968, **8**, 201–256.

Katzman, M. T. *The political economy of urban schools*. Cambridge, Massachusetts: Harvard University Press, 1971.

Kayser, B. D., & Summers, G. F. The Adequacy of Student Reports of Parental SES Characteristics. *Sociological Methods and Research*, 1973, **1**, 303–315.

Kelley, J. Causal Chain Models for the Socioeconomic Career. *American Sociological Review*, 1973, **38**, 481–493. (a)

Kelley, J. History, Causal Chains, and Careers: A Reply. *American Sociological Review*, 1973, **38**, 791–796. (b)

Kemper, T. D. Reference Groups, Socialization, and Achievement. *American Sociological Review*, 1968, **33**, 31–45.

Kendall, M. G. *The advanced theory of statistics*. New York: Hafner, 1951.

Kerckhoff, A. C. *Ambition and attainment*. Washington, D.C.: American Sociological Association, Rose Monograph Series, 1974.

Kerckhoff, A. C., Mason, W. M., & Poss, S. S. On the Accuracy of Children's Reports of Family Social Status. *Sociology of Education*, 1973, **46**, 219–247.

Kiesling, H. J. Measuring a Local Government Service: A Study of School Districts in New York State. *Review of Economics and Statistics*, 1967, **49**, 356–367.

Kiesling, H. J. *The relationship of school inputs to public school performance in New York State*. Santa Monica, California: Rand Corporation, 1969.

Kinloch, G. C., & Perrucci, R. Social Origins, Academic Achievement, and Mobility Channels: Sponsored and Contest Mobility among College Graduates. *Social Forces*, 1969, **48**, 36–45.

Knapp, R. H., & Goodrich, H. B. *Origins of American scientists*. Chicago: University of Chicago Press, 1952.

Knapp, R. H., & Greenbaum, J. H. *The younger American scholar: His collegiate origins*. Chicago: University of Chicago Press, 1953.

Kohn, M. L. *Class and conformity: A study in values*. Homewood, Illinois: Dorsey Press, 1969.

Kohn, M. L., & Schooler, C. Occupational Experience and Psychological Functioning:

An Assessment of Reciprocal Effects. *American Sociological Review*, 1973, **38**, 97–118.

Krathwohl, D. R., Bloom, B. S., & Masia, B. B. *Taxonomy of educational objectives*. New York: David McKay, 1964.

Krauss, I. Sources of Educational Aspirations among Working-Class Youth. *American Sociological Review*, 1964, **29**, 867–889.

Ladinsky, J. Careers of Lawyers, Law Practice, and Legal Institutions. *American Sociological Review*, 1963, **28** (February), 47–54.

Laumann, E. O., & Rapoport, R. N. The Institutional Effect on Career Achievement of Technologists. *Human Relations*, 1968, **21**, 222–239.

Lawley, D. N., & Maxwell, A. E. *Factor analysis as a statistical method*. New York: American Elsevier, 1971.

Lazarsfeld, P. F. Interpretation of Statistical Relations as a Research Operation. In P. F. Lazarsfeld and M. Rosenberg (Eds.), *The language of social research*. New York: Free Press, 1955. Pp. 115–125.

Lehmann, I. J. Curricular Differences in Selected Cognitive and Affective Characteristics. *Journal of Educational Measurement*, 1965, **2**, 103–110.

Lehmann, I. J., & Dressel, P. L. Critical Thinking, Attitudes, and Values in Higher Education. U.S. Department of Health, Education, and Welfare Cooperative Research Project No. 590. East Lansing, Michigan: Michigan State University, 1962.

Leibenstein, H. Allocative Efficiency vs. X-efficiency. *American Economic Review*, 1966, **56**, 392–415.

Lens, W., & Atkinson, J. W. Academic Achievement in High School Related to 'Intelligence' and Motivation as Measured in 6th, 9th, and 12th Grade Boys. Unpublished manuscript, University of Michigan, 1973.

Lesser, G., & Stodolsky, S. S. Learning Patterns in the Disadvantaged. *Harvard Educational Review*, 1967, **37**, 546–593.

Levin, H. M. *Recruiting teachers*. Washington, D.C.: Brookings Institution, 1968.

Levin, H. M. A Cost-effectiveness Analysis of Teacher Selection. *Journal of Human Resources*, 1970, **5**, 24–33.

Levin, H. M. Frontier Functions: An Econometric Approach to the Evaluation of Educational Effectiveness. Stanford, California: Stanford Center for Research and Development in Teaching R. and D. Memo 80, 1971.

Levin, H. M., & Müller, J. The Meaning of Technical Efficiency. Unpublished manuscript, Stanford University, 1973.

Lewis, M., & Goldberg, S. Perceptual–Cognitive Development in Infancy: A Generalized Expectancy Model as a Function of Mother–Infant Interaction. *Merrill-Palmer Quarterly*, 1969, **15**, 81–100.

Li, J. B. *Statistical inference II*. Ann Arbor, Michigan: Edwards Brothers, 1964.

Linnan, R. J., & Airasian, P. W. Ethnic Comparisons of Environmental Process Predictors of Three Cognitive Abilities. American Educational Research Association Annual Meetings, Chicago, Illinois, 1974.

Little, J. K. *A statewide inquiry into decisions of youth about education beyond high school*. School of Education. Madison, Wisconsin: University of Wisconsin, 1958.

Longino, C. F., Jr., & Kart, C. S. The College Fraternity: An Assessment of Theory and Research. *Journal of College Student Personnel*, 1973, **14**, 118–125.

Mandler, G., & Sarason, S. B. A Study of Anxiety and Learning. *Journal of Abnormal and Social Psychology*, 1952, **47**, 166–173.

Marjoribanks, K. Environment, Social Class, and Mental Abilities. *Journal of Educational Psychology*, 1972, **63**, 103–109. (a)

Marjoribanks, K. Ethnic and Environmental Influences on Mental Abilities. *American Journal of Sociology*, 1972, **78**, 323–337. (b)

Mayeske, G., Wisler, C. E., Beaton, A. E., Weinfeld, F. D., Cohen, W. M., Okada, T., Proshek, J. M., & Tabler, K. A. *A study of our nation's schools.* Washington, D.C.: U.S. Office of Education, 1969.

McClelland, D. C. *Personality.* New York: William Sloane, 1951.

McClelland, D. C. The Importance of Early Learning in the Formation of Motives. In J. W. Atkinson (Ed.), *Motives in fantasy, action, and society.* Princeton, New Jersey: Van Nostrand, 1958. Pp. 437–452.

McClelland, D. C., Atkinson, J. W., Clark, R. A., & Lowell, E. L. *The achievement motive.* New York: Appleton, 1953. [Reissued, New York: Irvington Publishers (distributed by Halsted Press/Wiley), 1975.]

McDill, E. L., & Coleman, J. S. High School Social Status, College Plans, and Interest in Academic Achievement: A Panel Analysis. *American Sociological Review*, 1963, **28**, 905–918.

McDill, E. L., & Rigsby, L. C. *Structure and process in secondary schools: The academic impact of educational climates.* Baltimore, Maryland: Johns Hopkins Press, 1973.

McDill, E. L., Rigsby, L. C., & Meyers, E., Jr. Educational Climates of High Schools: Their Effects and Sources. *American Journal of Sociology*, 1969, **74**, 567–586.

McLeish, J. *Students' attitudes and college environments.* Cambridge, England: Cambridge Institute of Education, 1970.

McNemar, Q. A Critical Examination of the University of Iowa Studies of Environmental Influence upon the IQ. *Psychological Bulletin*, 1940, **18**, 47–55.

McPartland, J. The Relative Influence of School Desegregation and of Classroom Desegregation on the Academic Achievement of Ninth Grade Negro Students. *Journal of Social Issues*, 1969, **25**, 193–202.

McPartland, J., & York, R. Further Analysis of Equality of Educational Opportunity Survey. In U.S. Commission on Civil Rights, *Racial isolation in the public schools.* Vol. 2. Washington, D.C.: U.S. Government Printing Office, 1967. Pp. 35–142.

Meyer, J. W. High School Effects on College Intentions. *American Journal of Sociology*, 1970, **76**, 59–70.

Meyer, J. W. The Effects of the Institutionalization of Colleges in Society. In K. A. Feldman (Ed.), *College and student.* New York: Pergamon Press, 1972. Pp. 109–126.

Michael, J. A. High School Climates and Plans for Entering College. *Public Opinion Quarterly*, 1961, **25**, 585–595.

Michael, J. A. Communication on Neighborhood Context and College Plans (II). *American Sociological Review*, 1966, **31**, 702–706.

Michelson, S. The Association of Teacher Resourcefulness with Children's Characteristics. In U.S. Department of Health, Education, and Welfare, *Do teachers make a difference?* Washington, D.C.: U.S. Government Printing Office, 1970. Pp. 120–168.

Milner, E. A Study of the Relationship between Reading Readiness in Grade One School Children and Patterns of Parent–Child Interaction. *Child Development*, 1951, **22**, 95–112.

Milner, M., Jr. *The illusion of equality.* San Francisco: Jossey-Bass, 1972.

Mincer, J. *Schooling, experience, and earnings.* New York: National Bureau of Economic Research, 1974.

Mitchell, J. A. A Study of High School Environments and Their Impact on Students. Report of Project No. 5-8032. U.S. Office of Education, 1967.

Mollenkopf, W. G., & Melville, D. S. A Study of Secondary School Characteristics as Related to Test Scores. Research Bulletin 56-6. Educational Testing Service, 1956.

Mood, A. M. Partitioning Variance in Multiple Regression Analyses as a Tool for Developing Learning Models. *American Educational Research Journal,* 1971, **8,** 191–202.

Moore, W. E. The Accentuation Process: Some Preliminary Analyses. Unpublished manuscript, University of Michigan, 1973.

Morgan, J. N., Dickinson, K., Dickinson, J., Benus, J., and Duncan, G. *Five thousand American families—Patterns of economic progress.* Vol. 1. An Analysis of the First Five Years of the Panel Study of Income Dynamics. Survey Research Center, Institute for Social Research. Ann Arbor, Michigan: University of Michigan, 1974.

Morrison, D. F. *Multivariate statistical methods.* New York: McGraw-Hill, 1967.

Moses, L. E. Comparison of Crude and Standardized Death Rates. In J. P. Bunker, W. H. Forrest, Jr., F. Mosteller, and L. D. Vandan (Eds.), *The national Halothane study: A study of the possible association between Halothane and anesthesia and postoperative hepatic necrosis.* Report of subcommittee on the National Halothane Study of the Committee on Anesthesia, National Academy of Sciences–National Research Council. Washington, D.C.: U.S. Government Printing Office, 1969.

Mosteller, F., & Moynihan, D. P. (eds.) *On equality of educational opportunity.* New York: Vintage Books, 1972.

Mosychuk, H. Differential Home Environments and Mental Ability Patterns. Unpublished doctoral dissertation, University of Alberta, 1969.

Moulton, R. Motivational Implications of Individual Differences in Competence. In J. W. Atkinson and J. O. Raynor (Eds.), *Motivation and achievement.* Washington, D.C.: V. H. Winston and Sons, 1974. Pp. 77–82.

Moynihan, D. P. 'Peace'—Some Thoughts on the 1960's and 1970's. *The Public Interest,* 1973, **32,** 3–12.

Mueller, C. W. City Effects on Socioeconomic Achievements. Unpublished doctoral dissertation, University of Wisconsin, 1973.

Murray, J. R. Statistical Models for Qualitative Data with Classification Errors. Doctoral dissertation, University of Chicago, 1971.

Mushkin, S. (Ed.) *Public prices for public products.* Washington, D.C.: Urban Institute, 1972.

Nelson, J. I. High School Context and College Plans: The Impact of Social Structure on Aspirations. *American Sociological Review,* 1972, **37,** 143–148.

Newcomb, T. M., Brown, D. R., Kulik, J. A., Reimer, D. J., & Revelle, W. R. Self-selection and Change. In J. Gaff and associates (Eds.), *The cluster college.* San Francisco: Jossey-Bass, 1970. Pp. 137–160.

Newcomb, T. M., Brown, D. R., Kulik, J. A., Reimer, D. J., & Revelle, W. R. The University of Michigan's Residential College. In P. L. Dressel (Ed.), *The new colleges: Toward an appraisal.* Iowa City, Iowa: American College Testing Program, 1971. Pp. 99–141.

Newcomb, T. M., Koenig, K. E., Flacks, R., & Warwick, D. P. *Persistence and change: Bennington College and its students after twenty-five years.* New York: John Wiley and Sons, 1967.

Newcomb, T. M., & Wilson, E. K. (Eds.) *College peer groups: Problems and prospects for research.* Chicago: Aldine, 1966.

Newman, F., Cannon, W., Cavell, S., Cohen, A., Edgerton, R., Gibbons, J., Kramer, M., Rhodes, J., & Singleton, R. Report on Higher Education. Superintendent of Documents, Catalog No. HE 5.250:50065. Washington, D.C.: U.S. Department of Health, Education, and Welfare, 1971.

Nichols, R. C. Effects of Various College Characteristics on Student Aptitude Test Scores. *Journal of Educational Psychology,* 1964, **55,** 45–54.

Nichols, R. C. Personality Change and the College. *American Educational Research Journal,* 1967, **4,** 173–190.

Niemi, R. G. *How family members perceive each other; political and social attitudes in two generations.* New Haven, Connecticut: Yale University Press, 1974.

O'Connor, P., Atkinson, J. W., & Horner, M. S. Motivational Implications of Ability Grouping in Schools. In J. W. Atkinson and N. T. Feather (Eds.), *A theory of achievement motivation.* New York: John Wiley and Sons, 1966. Pp. 231–250.

O'Malley, P. M. Need Achievement and Test Anxiety in a Longitudinal Study of Adolescent Boys: Some Empirical Findings. Unpublished papers, directed to J. W. Atkinson, Ann Arbor, Michigan, University of Michigan, July 12, 1972, and August 27, 1973.

Ornstein, M. D. Entry Into the American Labor Force. Report No. 113, Center for Social Organization of Schools. Baltimore, Maryland: Johns Hopkins University, 1971.

Otto, L. B. Early Career Alienation and Socioeconomic Attainments of a Rural Population. Unpublished doctoral dissertation, University of Wisconsin—Madison, 1973.

Overlan, S. F. Out of the Mouths of Babes: The Accuracy of Students' Responses to Family and Educational Background Questionnaires. Manuscript, Graduate School of Education, Harvard University, 1968.

Pace, C. R. The Influence of Academic and Student Subcultures in College and University Environments. U.S. Department of Health, Education, and Welfare Cooperative Research Project No. 1083. Los Angeles: University of California—Los Angeles, 1964.

Parsons, T. The School Class as a Social System: Some of Its Functions in American Society. *Harvard Educational Review,* 1959, **29,** 297–318.

Perl, L. J. Family Background, Secondary School Expenditure, and Student Ability. *Journal of Human Resources,* 1973, **8,** 156–180.

Perrucci, C. C. Engineering and the Class Structure. In R. Perrucci and J. E. Gerstl (Eds.), *The engineers and the social system.* New York: John Wiley and Sons, 1969. Pp. 279–310.

Pfouts, R. W. The Theory of Cost and Production in the Multiproduct Firm. *Econometrica,* 1961, **29,** 650–658.

Pierson, R. R. Changes of Majors by University Students. *Personnel and Guidance Journal,* 1962, **70,** 458–461.

Porter, J. N. Race, Socialization and Mobility in Educational and Early Occupational Attainment. *American Sociological Review,* 1974, **39,** 303–316.

Portes, A., Haller, A. O., & Sewell, W. H. Professional–Executive vs. Farming as Unique Occupational Choices. *Rural Sociology,* 1968, **33,** 153–159.

Ramsøy, N. R. American High Schools at Midcentury. Unpublished manuscript, Columbia University, 1961.

Raynor, J. O. Future Orientation and Motivation of Immediate Activity: An Elaboration of the Theory of Achievement Motivation. *Psychological Review*, 1969, **76**, 606–610.

Raynor, J. O. Future Orientation in the Study of Achievement Motivation. In J. W. Atkinson and J. O. Raynor (Eds.), *Motivation and achievement*. Washington, D.C.: V. H. Winston and Sons, 1974. Pp. 121–154. (a)

Raynor, J. O. Motivation and Career Striving. In J. W. Atkinson and J. O. Raynor (Eds.), *Motivation and achievement*. Washington, D.C.: V. H. Winston and Sons, 1974. Pp. 369–388. (b)

Reed, R. H., & Miller, H. P. Some Determinants of Variation in Earnings for College Men. *Journal of Human Resources*, 1970, **5**, 177–190.

Rhodes, A. L., Reiss, A. J., Jr., & Duncan, O. D. Occupational Segregation in a Metropolitan School System. *American Journal of Sociology*, 1965, **70**, 682–694.

Ribich, T. I. *Education and poverty*. Washington, D.C.: Brookings Institution, 1968.

Rock, D. A., Centra, J. A., & Linn, R. L. Relationships between College Characteristics and Student Achievement. *American Educational Research Journal*, 1970, **7**, 109–121.

Rose, P. I. The Myth of Unanimity: Student Opinions on Critical Issues. *Sociology of Education*, 1964, **37**, 129–149.

Rosen, B. C., Crockett, H. J., Jr., & Nunn, C. Z. *Achievement in American society*. Cambridge, Massachusetts: Schenkman Publishing, 1969.

Rosen, B. C., & D'Andrade, R. The Psychosocial Origins of Achievement Motivation. *Sociometry*, 1959, **22**, 185–218.

Rulon, P. J. Problems of Regression. *Harvard Educational Review*, 1941, **11**, 213–223.

Ryder, N. B. Notes on the Concept of a Population. *American Journal of Sociology*, 1964, **69**, 447–463.

Ryder, N. B. The Cohort as a Concept in the Study of Social Change. *American Sociological Review*, 1965, **30**, 843–861.

St. John, N. The Validity of Children's Reports of Their Parents' Educational Level: A Methodological Note. *Sociology of Education*, 1970, **43**, 255–269.

St. John, N., & Smith, M. S. School Racial Composition, Achievement and Aspiration. Center for Educational Policy Research. Cambridge, Massachusetts: Harvard University, 1969.

Salter, W. E. G. *Productivity and technical change*. Cambridge, Massachusetts: Cambridge University Press, 1960.

Sanford, N. (Ed.) *The American college: A psychological and social interpretation of the higher learning*. New York: John Wiley and Sons, 1962.

Sawusch, J. R. Computer Simulation of the Influence of Ability and Motivation on Test Performance and Cumulative Achievement. Appendix B in J. W. Atkinson and J. O. Raynor (Eds.), *Motivation and achievement*. Washington, D.C.: V. H. Winston and Sons, 1974. Pp. 425–438.

Schoenberg, R. Strategies for Meaningful Comparison. In H. L. Costner (Ed.), *Sociological methodology, 1972*. San Francisco: Jossey-Bass, 1972. Pp. 1–35.

Schooler, C. Social Antecedents of Adult Psychological Functioning. *American Journal of Sociology*, 1972, **78**, 299–322.

Scrimshaw, N. S. Infant Malnutrition and Adult Learning. *Saturday Review*, 1968, **51** (March), 64–66.

Seltzer, R. A. Simulation of the Dynamics of Action. *Psychological Reports*, 1973, **32**, 859–872.

Seltzer, R. A., & Sawusch, J. R. Computer Program Written to Simulate the Dynamics of Action. Appendix A in J. W. Atkinson and J. O. Raynor (Eds.), *Motivation and achievement*. Washington, D.C.: V. W. Winston and Sons, 1974. Pp. 411–424.

Selvin, H. C. The Impact of University Experiences on Occupational Plans. *School Review*, 1963, **71**, 317–329.

Sewell, W. H. Community of Residence and College Plans. *American Sociological Review*, 1964, **29**, 24–38.

Sewell, W. H. Inequality of Opportunity for Higher Education. *American Sociological Review*, 1971, **36**, 793–809.

Sewell, W. H., & Armer, J. M. Neighborhood Context and College Plans. *American Sociological Review*, 1966, **31**, 159–168. (a)

Sewell, W. H., & Armer, J. M. Reply to Turner, Michael, and Boyle. *American Sociological Review*, 1966, **31**, 707–712. (b)

Sewell, W. H., & Haller, A. O. Educational and Occupational Perspectives of Farm and Rural Youth. In L. G. Burchinal (Ed.), *Rural youth in crisis: Facts, myths, and social change*. Washington, D.C.: U.S. Government Printing Office, 1965. Pp. 149–169.

Sewell, W. H., Haller, A. O., & Ohlendorf, G. W. The Educational and Early Occupational Status Attainment Process: Replication and Revision. *American Sociological Review*, 1970, **35**, 1014–1027.

Sewell, W. H., Haller, A. O., & Portes, A. The Educational and Early Occupational Attainment Process. *American Sociological Review*, 1969, **34**, 82–92.

Sewell, W. H., & Hauser, R. M. *Education, occupation, and earnings: Achievement in the early career*. New York: Academic Press, 1975.

Sewell, W. H., & Orenstein, A. M. Community of Residence and Occupational Choice. *American Journal of Sociology*, 1965, **70**, 551–563.

Sewell, W. H., & Shah, V. P. Socioeconomic Status, Intelligence, and the Attainment of Higher Education. *Sociology of Education*, 1967, **40**, 1–23.

Sewell, W. H., & Shah, V. P. Social Class, Parental Encouragement, and Educational Aspirations. *American Journal of Sociology*, 1968, **73**, 559–572. (a)

Sewell, W. H., & Shah, V. P. Parents' Education and Children's Educational Aspirations and Achievements. *American Sociological Review*, 1968, **33**, 191–209. (b)

Sexton, P. *Feminized male: Classrooms, white collars, and the decline of manliness*. New York: Random House, 1969.

Sharp, L. M. *Education and employment*. Baltimore, Maryland: Johns Hopkins Press, 1970.

Shulman, L. S. Reconstruction of Educational Research. *Review of Educational Research*, 1970, **40**, 371–396.

Siegel, A. E., & Siegel, S. Reference Groups, Membership Groups, and Attitude Change. *Journal of Abnormal and Social Psychology*, 1957, **55**, 360–364.

Siegel, P. M., & Hodge, R. W. A Causal Approach to the Study of Measurement Error. In H. M. Blalock, Jr., and A. B. Blalock (Eds.), *Methodology in social research*. New York: McGraw-Hill, 1968. Pp. 28–59.

Simmons, D. D. Children's Rankings of Occupational Prestige. *Personnel and Guidance Journal*, 1962, **41**, 332–336.

Simmons, R. G., & Rosenberg, M. Function of Children's Perceptions of the Stratification System. *American Sociological Review*, 1971, **36**, 235–249.

Skager, R., Holland, J. L., & Braskamp, L. A. Changes in Self-ratings and Life Goals among Students at Colleges with Different Characteristics. ACT Research Reports, No. 14. Iowa City, Iowa: American College Testing Program, 1966.

Smigel, E. O. Wall Street lawyer. New York: Free Press, 1964.

Smith, C. P. (Ed.) Achievement-related motives in children. New York: Russell Sage Foundation, 1969.

Smith, M. S. Equality of Educational Opportunity: The Basic Findings Reconsidered. In F. Mosteller and D. P. Moynihan (Eds.), On equality of educational opportunity. New York: Vintage Books, 1972. Pp. 230–342.

Smith, R. B. Neighborhood Context and College Plans: An Ordinal Path Analysis. Social Forces, 1972, 51, 199–217.

Snedecor, G., & Cochran, W. G. Statistical methods. 6th ed. Ames, Iowa: Iowa State University Press, 1967.

Solmon, L. C. The Definition and Impact of College Quality. In L. C. Solmon and P. J. Taubman (Eds.), Does college matter? New York: Academic Press, 1973. Pp. 77–102. (a)

Solmon, L. C. Schooling and Subsequent Success: Influence of Ability, Background, and Formal Education. In L. C. Solmon and P. J. Taubman (Eds.), Does college matter? New York: Academic Press, 1973. Pp. 13–34. (b)

Sorokin, P. A. Social mobility. New York: Harper and Brothers, 1927.

Spady, W. G. Simple Techniques for Multivariate Analysis. Interchange, 1970, 1, 3–20.

Spady, W. G. Mastery Learning: Its Sociological Implications. In J. H. Block (Ed.), Schools, society, and mastery learning. New York: Holt, 1974. Pp. 91–116.

Spaeth, J. L. Occupational Prestige Expectations among Male College Graduates. American Journal of Sociology, 1968, 73, 548–558.

Spaeth, J. L. Occupational Attainment among Male College Graduates. American Journal of Sociology, 1970, 75, 632–644.

Spaeth, J. L., & Greeley, A. M. Recent alumni and higher education: A survey of college graduates. New York: McGraw-Hill, 1970.

Stakenas, R. G. Student–Faculty Contact and Attitude Change: Results of an Experimental Program for College Freshmen. In K. A. Feldman (Ed.), College and student: Selected readings in the social psychology of higher education. Elmsford, New York: Pergamon Press, 1972. Pp. 463–471.

Stinchcombe, A. L. Creating efficient industrial administration. New York: Academic Press, 1973.

Suczek, R. F. The best laid plans: A study of student development in an experimental college program. San Francisco: Jossey-Bass, 1972.

Summers, R. A Capital Intensive Approach to the Small Sample Properties of Various Simultaneous Equations Estimators. Econometrica, 1965, 33, 1–47.

Suter, L., & Miller, H. Income Differences between Men and Career Women. American Journal of Sociology, 1973, 78, 962–974.

Tannenbaum, A. S., & Bachman, J. G. Structural versus Individual Effects. American Journal of Sociology, 1964, 69, 585–595.

Taubman, P. J., & Wales, T. J. Higher Education, Mental Ability, and Screening. Journal of Political Economy, 1973, 81, 28–55.

Theil, H. Specification Errors and the Estimation of Economic Relationships. Revue Internationale de Statistique, 1957, 25, 41–51.

Thelen, H. A. Classroom grouping for teachability. New York: John Wiley and Sons, 1967.

Thistlethwaite, D. L. College Press and Changes in Study Plans of Talented Students. *Journal of Educational Psychology,* 1960, **51,** 222–234.

Thistlethwaite, D. L. Fields of Study and Development of Motivation to Seek Advanced Training. *Journal of Educational Psychology,* 1962, **53,** 53–64.

Thistlethwaite, D. L. The Effects of College Environments on Students' Decisions to Attend Graduate School. U.S. Department of Health, Education, and Welfare Project No. 2993. Nashville, Tennessee: Vanderbilt University, 1968.

Thistlethwaite, D. L. *Effects of University subcultures on student attitudes.* Nashville, Tennessee: Vanderbilt University, 1972.

Thistlethwaite, D. L. Accentuation of Differences in Values and Exposures to Major Fields of Study. *Journal of Educational Psychology,* 1973, **65,** 279–293.

Thomas, J. A. Efficiency in Education: A Study of the Relationship between Selected Inputs and Mean Test Scores in a Sample of Senior High Schools. Unpublished doctoral dissertation, Stanford University, 1963.

Thorndike, R. L. *The concepts of over- and under-achievement.* New York: Columbia University, Bureau of Publications, Teachers College, 1963.

Timmer, C. P. On measuring technical efficiency. Unpublished doctoral dissertation, Harvard University, 1969.

Treiman, D. J., & Hauser, R. M. On the Intergenerational Transmission of Income: An Exercise in Theory Construction. Manuscript, Department of Sociology, University of Wisconsin—Madison, 1970.

Trent, J. W., & Cohen, A. M. Research on Teaching in Higher Education. In R. M. W. Travers (Ed.), *Second handbook of research on teaching.* Chicago: Rand McNally, 1973. Pp. 997–1071.

Tukey, J. W. Causation, Regression, and Path Analysis. In O. Kempthorne, T. A. Bancroft, T. W. Gowen, and J. L. Lush (Eds.), *Statistics and mathematics in biology.* Ames, Iowa: Iowa State College Press, 1954.

Tukey, J. W. A Further Inquiry into Institutional Differences by Means of Superstandardization (A Regression Adjustment beyond Standardization). In J. P. Bunker, W. H. Forrest, Jr., F. Mosteller, and L. D. Vandan (Eds.), *The national Halothane study: A study of the possible association between Halothane and anesthesia and postoperative hepatic necrosis.* Report of subcommittee on the National Halothane Study of the Committee on Anesthesia, National Academy of Sciences–National Research Council. Washington, D.C.: U.S. Government Printing Office, 1969.

Tukey, J. W. *Exploratory data analysis.* Limited preliminary edition. Reading, Massachusetts: Addison-Wesley, 1970.

Turner, R. H. *The social context of ambition.* San Francisco: Chandler, 1964.

Turner, R. H. Communication on Neighborhood Context and College Plans (I). *American Sociological Review,* 1966, **31,** 698–702.

U.S. Department of Health, Education, and Welfare. *Do teachers make a difference?* Office of Education. Washington, D.C.: U.S. Government Printing Office, 1970.

Vandenberg, S. G. What Do We Know Today about the Inheritance of Intelligence? In R. Cancro (Ed.), *Intelligence: Genetic and environmental influences.* New York: Grune and Stratton, 1971. Pp. 182–218.

Vernon, P. E. Ability Factors and Environmental Influences. *American Psychologist,* 1965, **20,** 723–733.

Veroff, J. Theoretical Background for Studying the Origins of Human Motivational Dispositions. *Merrill-Palmer Quarterly,* 1965, **11,** 3–18.

Veroff, J., Atkinson, J. W., Feld, S., & Gurin, G. The Use of Thematic Apperception to Assess Motivation in a Nationwide Interview Study. In J. W. Atkinson and J. O. Raynor (Eds.), *Motivation and achievement*. Washington, D.C.: V. H. Winston and Sons, 1974. Pp. 43–76.

Veroff, J., & Peele, S. Initial Effects of Desegregation on the Achievement Motivation of Negro Elementary School Children. *Journal of Social Issues*, 1969, **25**, 71–91.

Vreeland, R. S., & Bidwell, C. E. Organizational Effects on Student Attitudes: A Study of the Harvard Houses. *Sociology of Education*, 1965, **38**, 233–250.

Vreeland, R. S., & Bidwell, C. E. Classifying University Departments: An Approach to the Analysis of Their Effects upon Undergraduates' Values and Attitudes. *Sociology of Education*, 1966, **39**, 237–254.

Vroom, V. H. *Work and motivation*. New York: John Wiley and Sons, 1964.

Walberg, H. J., & Marjoribanks, K. Social Environment and Cognitive Development: Toward a Generalized Causal Analysis. In K. Marjoribanks (Ed.), *Environments for learning*. Windsor, Eng.: NFER Publishing, 1974. Pp. 259–273.

Wales, T. J. The Effect of College Quality on Earnings: Results from the NBER–Thorndike Data. *Journal of Human Resources*, 1973, **8**, 306–317.

Wallace, P. Complex Environments: Effects on Brain Development. *Science*, 1974, **185**, 1035–1037.

Wallace, W. L. Institutional and Life-Cycle Socialization of College Freshmen. *American Journal of Sociology*, 1964, **70**, 303–318.

Wallace, W. L. Peer Influences and Undergraduates' Aspirations for Graduate Study. *Sociology of Education*, 1965, **38**, 375–392.

Wallace, W. L. *Student culture: Social structure and continuity in a liberal arts college*. Chicago: Aldine, 1966.

Wallace, W. L. Faculty and Fraternities: Organizational Influences on Student Achievement. *Administrative Science Quarterly*, 1967, **11**, 643–670.

Waller, W. *The sociology of teaching*. New York: John Wiley and Sons, 1932.

Walsh, W. B. *Theories of person-environment: Implications for college students*. Iowa City, Iowa: American College Testing Program, 1973.

Walsh, W. B., & Russel, J. H. III. College Major Choice and Personal Adjustment. *Personnel and Guidance Journal*, 1969, **47**, 685–688.

Walsh, W. B., Vaudrin, D. M., & Hummel, R. A. The Accentuation Effect and Holland's Theory. *Journal of Vocational Behavior*, 1972, **2**, 77–85.

Walters, A. A. Production and Cost Functions: An Econometric Survey. *Econometrica*, 1963, **31**, 1–66.

Wechsler, D. *Wechsler Intelligence Scale for Children*. New York: Psychological Corporation, 1949.

Wechsler, D. *Wechsler Adult Intelligence Scale*. New York: Psychological Corporation, 1955.

Wechsler, D. *The measurement and appraisal of adult intelligence*. Baltimore, Maryland: Williams and Wilkins, 1958.

Wegner, E. L., & Sewell, W. H. Selection and Context as Factors Affecting the Probability of Graduation from College. *American Journal of Sociology*, 1970, **75**, 665–679.

Weiner, B. *Theories of motivation*. Chicago: Markham, 1972.

Weiner, B. *Achievement motivation and attribution theory*. Morristown, New Jersey: General Learning Press, 1974.

Weinstein, E. Children's Conceptions of Occupational Stratification. *Sociology and Social Research*, 1958, **42**, 278–284.

Weisbrod, B. A. *External benefits of public education, An economic analysis.* Industrial Relations Section, Department of Economics. Princeton, New Jersey: Princeton University, 1964.

Weisbrod, B. A., & Karpoff, P. Monetary Returns to College Education, Student Ability, and College Quality. *Review of Economics and Statistics,* 1968, **50,** 491–497.

Weiss, J. The Identification and Measurement of Home Environmental Factors Related to Achievement Motivation and Self Esteem. Unpublished doctoral dissertation, University of Chicago, 1969.

Werts, C. E. The Partitioning of Variance in School Effects Studies. *American Educational Research Journal,* 1968, **5,** 311–318.

Werts, C. E., Jöreskog, K. G., & Linn, R. L. Identification and Estimation in Path Analysis with Unmeasured Variables. *American Journal of Sociology,* 1973, **78,** 1469–1484.

Werts, C. E., & Linn, R. L. Analyzing School Effects: How to Use the Same Data to Support Different Hypotheses. *American Educational Research Journal,* 1969, **6,** 439–447.

Werts, C. E., & Linn, R. L. Path Analysis: Psychological Examples. *Psychological Bulletin,* 1970, **74,** 193–212.

Werts, C. E., & Linn, R. L., & Jöreskog, K. G. Estimating the Parameters of Path Models Involving Unmeasured Variables. In H. M. Blalock, Jr. (Ed.), *Causal models in the social sciences.* Chicago: Aldine-Atherton, 1971. Pp. 400–409.

White, R. W. Motivation Reconsidered: The Concept of Competence. *Psychological Review,* 1959, **66,** 297–333.

Whiteman, M., & Deutsch, M. Social Disadvantage as Related to Intellective and Language Development. In M. Deutsch, I. Katz, and A. R. Jensen (Eds.), *Social class, race, and psychological development.* New York: Holt, 1968. Pp. 86–114.

Wiley, D. E., & Harnischfeger, A. Explosion of a Myth: Quantity of Schooling and Exposure to Instruction, Major Educational Vehicles. *Studies of Educative Processes,* 1974, No. 8, University of Chicago. [Also: *Educational Researcher,* 1974, **3,** 7–12.]

Wiley, D. E., & Wiley, J. A. The Estimation of Measurement Error in Panel Data. *American Sociological Review,* 1970, **35,** 112–117.

Williams, D. E., & Reilley, R. R. The Impact of Residence Halls on Students. *Journal of College Student Personnel,* 1972, **13,** 402–410.

Williams, T. Cultural Deprivation and Intelligence: Extensions of the Basic Model. Unpublished doctoral dissertation, University of Toronto, 1973.

Williams, T. Competence Dimensions of Family Environments. American Educational Research Association Annual Meetings, Chicago, Illinois, 1974.

Willingham, W. W. Predicting Success in Graduate Education. *Science,* 1974, **183,** 273–278.

Wilson, A. B. Residential Segregation of Social Classes and Aspirations of High School Boys. *American Sociological Review,* 1959, **24,** 836–845.

Winer, B. J. *Statistical principles in experimental design.* 2nd ed. New York: McGraw-Hill, 1971.

Winkler, D. R. The Production of Human Capital: A Study of Minority Achievement. Unpublished doctoral dissertation, University of California—Berkeley, 1972.

Withey, S. B. *A degree and what else?* New York: McGraw-Hill, 1972.

Woelfel, J., & Haller, A. O. Significant Others, the Self-Reflective Act and the Attitude Formation Process. *American Sociological Review,* 1971, **36,** 74–86.

Wolf, R. M. The Identification and Measurement of Environmental Process Variables Related to Intelligence. Unpublished doctoral dissertation, University of Chicago, 1964.

Wolfle, D. L. *America's resources of specialized talent*. Report of the Commission on Human Resources and Advanced Training. New York: Harper and Brothers, 1954.

Wolfle, D. L. To What Extent Do Monetary Returns to Education Vary with Family Background, Mental Ability and School Quality? In L. C. Solmon and P. J. Taubman (Eds.), *Does college matter?* New York: Academic Press, 1973. Pp. 65–74.

Woodworth, R. W. *Dynamic psychology*. New York: Columbia University Press, 1918.

Wright, C. R. Success or Failure in Earning Graduate Degrees. *Sociology of Education*, 1964, **38**, 73–97.

Yerkes, R. M., & Dodson, J. D. The Relation of Strength of Stimulus to Rapidity of Habit Formation. *Journal of Comparative Neurology and Psychology*, 1908, **18**, 459–482.

Author Index

521

Subject Index